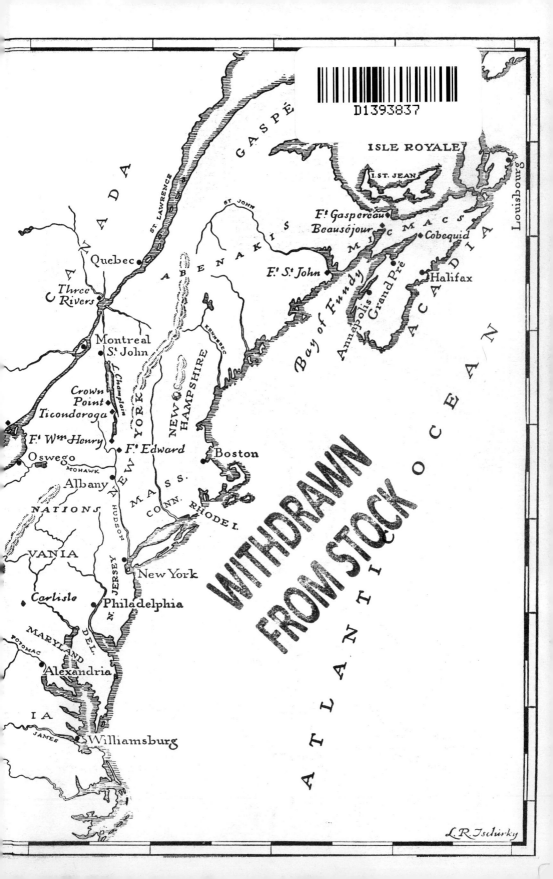

ISLE ROYALE

I. ST. JEAN

Louisbourg

GASPÉ

ST. LAWRENCE

ST. JOHN

Fᵗ Gaspereau

Beauséjour

M I C M A C S

Cobequid

ABENAKIS

Fᵗ Sᵗ John

Halifax

CANADA

Quebec

Bay of Fundy

Annapolis

Grand Pré

ACADIA

Three Rivers

Montreal

Sᵗ John

KENNEBEC

NEW HAMPSHIRE

L. Champlain

Crown Point

Ticonderoga

NEW YORK

Fᵗ Wᵐ Henry

Fᵗ Edward

Boston

Oswego

MOHAWK

MASS.

Albany

HUDSON

CONN.

RHODE I.

NATIONS

VANIA

JERSEY

New York

ATLANTIC OCEAN

Carlisle

Philadelphia

N.

DEL.

MARYLAND

POTOMAC

Alexandria

I A

JAMES

Williamsburg

L. R. Ischirky

Francis Parkman was born in Boston, Massachusetts, in 1823 and educated at Harvard. Over the following decades he would establish himself as one of the greatest 19th century American historians. Parkman's seven volume study, *France and England in North America*, of which the present volume is a condensation, is a landmark work in the field. A meticulous historian, Parkman was also a stylist, whose unacademic prose set him apart from all others in his own lifetime, and is admired today, more than a century later. He died in 1893.

Also by Francis Parkman

The California and Oregon Trail
The Jesuits in North America in the Seventeenth Century
History of the Conspiracy of Pontiac

John Tebbel, who is one-sixteenth Indian, the descendant of an historic Michigan family, worked for major newspapers and magazines until he became chairman of the Journalism Department at New York University, where he divided his time between teaching and writing. He is the author of forty books, including historical fiction, biographies of William Randolph Hearst and other media figures, and is the editor of Francis Parkman's *The Battle for North America*. He has contributed more than four hundred articles to magazines and newspapers. Retired but still writing, he lives in Durham, North Carolina.

Also by John Tebbel

HISTORY
The American Indian Wars (Phoenix Press) (*with Keith Jennison*)
George Washington's America

BIOGRAPHY
An American Dynasty
The Marshall Fields
George Horace Lorimer and The Saturday Evening Post
The Life and Good Times of William Randolph Hearst

NOVELS
The Conqueror
Touched with Fire
A Voice in the Streets

MEDICAL
The Magic of Balanced Living
Your Body: How to Keep it Healthy

TEXTBOOK
Makers of Modern Journalism (*with Kenneth N. Stewart*)

THE BATTLE
FOR NORTH AMERICA

Edited by
John Tebbel

from the works of
Francis Parkman

**PHOENIX
PRESS**

5 UPPER SAINT MARTIN'S LANE
LONDON
WC2H 9EA

A PHOENIX PRESS PAPERBACK

Originally published in seven volumes between 1865–1882
as *France and England in North America*
by Little, Brown & Co., Boston
This condensed version first published in 1948
by Doubleday & Co. Inc.
This paperback edition published in 2001
by Phoenix Press,
a division of The Orion Publishing Group Ltd,
Orion House, 5 Upper St Martin's Lane,
London WC2H 9EA

A CIP catalogue record for this book is available
from the British Library.

Printed and bound in Great Britain by
Clays Ltd, St Ives plc

ISBN 1 84212 416 1

Editor's Foreword

THE PURPOSE OF THIS VOLUME MAY BE STATED quite simply: It is to restore the principal work of Francis Parkman, *France and England in North America,* to its proper province, that of the general reader.

Parkman is described correctly as the greatest writer among American historians, surpassing his nineteenth-century Boston rivals, Jared Sparks, John Gorham Palfrey, George Bancroft, William Hickling Prescott and John Lothrop Motley. Of them all, only Parkman lives today. But in spite of the excellent scholarship done in his behalf during this century, and notwithstanding the fervent praise given him by the historians and students to whom he is familiar, he has long since joined the company of those writers who are greatly admired but little read.

That the average American reader should be deprived of so rich a part of his cultural heritage seems a loss as cruel as it is undeserved and unnecessary. That such a fate should befall Parkman, whose work was more widely read by the general public than any other historian of his time, is an irony not accounted for solely by the sharp change in reading habits during the past half century.

Is Parkman's nineteenth-century style too outdated for current reading? The most eminent critics do not think so. On the contrary, in reviewing Parkman's *Journals,* which were brought to light by Mason Wade and published in 1947, historians of the first rank were eloquent in their praise of Parkman's magnificent style—its unexampled exposition of historical fact in terms of vivid drama.

Is it, then, that Parkman has lost stature as a historian, as did some of his Boston contemporaries when later researchers began to sift romance from actuality? The reverse is true. Even though his field has been relatively neglected in comparison with other periods of American history, present-day scholars have found Parkman wrong in only a few minor particulars. If more accurate studies of certain episodes have been produced, as for example in Howard H. Peckham's *Pontiac and the Indian Uprising,* it is primarily because of the discovery of important new source material.

Nor can it be said that the century-long struggle between France and England for possession of the North American continent has less meaning for today's generations. Parkman complained, with reason, that the people of his own time understood very little of that conflict, and even thought of its most prominent aspect, the climactic Seven Years' War, as a piddling bush war between savages and raw militia, while the great issues between the French and English were decided on European battlefields. Today, however, it is better understood that the contest between feudal New France and the burgeoning democracy of the American colonies was in reality the crystallizing force which led to the precipitate action of the Revolution. If France had won, the birth of this nation might well have been long delayed. Moreover, the experience of the war had much to do with the military, political and moral ability of the colonies to overthrow British rule.

Granted these assumptions, it may at first be difficult to understand why most Americans who know Parkman at all know him for only two of his books, *The Conspiracy of Pontiac* and *The Oregon Trail,* neither of them part of his *magnum opus.* The latter, of course, is most widely read, chiefly by boys in the cowboy-and-Indian stage. No one can estimate how many Americans of the past fifty years got their first thrilling glimpse of the Great West in the pages of *The Oregon Trail.* As for *The Conspiracy of Pontiac,* it was Parkman's first historical book and contained all the faults he was able to overcome in his later writing. While it has its own considerable merits and is better than no reading of Parkman at all, it is, like the Western narrative, a youthful effort. America's best and most readable historian deserves a far greater availability than these two books provide.

France and England in North America, in seven parts and running to thirteen volumes in the collected edition, is Parkman's major work, upon which his enduring fame must rest. The sections of this tremendous story are so well knit that they may be referred to legitimately as a single book. It not only encompasses more than two centuries of events, from the beginnings of French colonization in North America to the downfall of New France on the Plains of Abraham, but it also (and this was one of Parkman's chief contributions to historical writing) relates that struggle for a continent to the developing course of events in Europe, so that the intimate connection between the two is plain.

The reason that this great work of Parkman's is so little read today is obvious. In his lifetime it was produced piecemeal and devoured in sections by the public. Since then it has been embalmed in collected editions, too expensive and far from plentiful enough for the general reader. If it is available at all, it is usually to be found in the libraries of large cities, and not always in these. The average small-town library does not possess a set.

The professional historians and the scholars have long since absorbed Parkman and passed on to refinements of his work. Thus *France and England in North America* has, for the past three or four decades, been read mostly by college students, who discover it more often at the insistence of a history professor than as a result of their own intellectual curiosity or of formal academic requirements.

This volume, then, is an attempt to remedy an unjustified lack and to bring Parkman within the province of the general reader by making his major work available in a condensed, one-volume edition. Such a project obviously has no scholarly or purely literary values, as in the case of the previously mentioned *Journals,* edited by Mr. Wade. Nor is it intended to "replace" Parkman. Rather, the editor hopes that it will inspire the reader to explore further and read the story in more detail, if he can find a collected edition.

The condensation offered herewith is not a rewrite of Parkman, in any sense. What I have done is to bring the narrative sections as closely together as possible, retaining a sufficient framework of background material to keep the story in proper perspective and to preserve the meaning of the whole work. I have modernized spelling and punctuation, eliminated archaic words and phrases, broken up long paragraphs, and divided the various large sections into convenient chapters for greater readability. The only words of mine in the book are phrases and clauses used in some places to link portions of the narrative.

The text used is that of the Frontenac Edition, which was the author's last revision. I have made two major omissions from this text. One is the initial volume of the first section, *Pioneers of France in the New World*. It deals with the early Spanish colonization of Florida, and the conflicts there and in Carolina between the Spaniards and their rival colonists, the French Huguenots. The period is from 1512 to 1583. While this is a fascinating story, for purposes of condensation it seemed more reasonable to begin with the second volume, starting with the first voyage of Jacques Cartier in 1534.

A two-volume section of the work titled *The Old Regime in Canada* is the second major omission. In this, Parkman stops the flow of his narrative to write, as Mr. Wade puts it, "a pioneer American essay in social history," in which he describes the feudal, Church-ridden, ruthlessly exploited condition of New France. Again, this is most interesting reading but not essential to the reader unless he is particularly concerned with historical detail, and so I have sacrificed it in the interests of condensation.

The major portions of the remaining ten volumes comprise the present book.

For those whose reading inspires them to further curiosity about the author, I can do no better than recommend Mason Wade's *Francis Parkman: Heroic Historian* (New York, 1942). As the foremost Parkman authority, Mr. Wade has given us the only modern and certainly the most reliable full-length biography of the historian. The *Journals* supplement this biography admirably.

John Tebbel

Contents

CONTENTS

PART FOUR: COUNT FRONTENAC

PART FIVE: A HALF CENTURY OF CONFLICT

PART SIX: MONTCALM AND WOLFE

CONTENTS

The French dominion is a memory of the past, and when we evoke its departed shades, they rise upon us from their graves in strange, romantic guise. Again their ghostly camp fires seem to burn, and the fitful light is cast around on lord and vassal and black-robed priest, mingled with wild forms of savage warriors, knit in close fellowship on the same stern errand.

A boundless vision grows upon us: an untamed continent; vast wastes of forest verdure; mountains silent in primeval sleep; river, lake and glimmering pool; wilderness oceans mingling with the sky. Such was the domain which France conquered for civilization. Plumed helmets gleamed in the shade of its forests, priestly vestments in its dens and fastnesses of ancient barbarism. Men steeped in antique learning, pale with the close breath of the cloister, here spent the noon and evening of their lives; ruled savage hordes with a mild, parental sway and stood serene before the direst shapes of death. Men of courtly nurture, heirs to the polish of a far-reaching ancestry, here, with their dauntless hardihood, put to shame the boldest sons of toil.

PART ONE

Pioneers of France in the New World

CHAPTER 1

~~~~~~

Early French Adventurers

THE ANCIENT TOWN OF ST. MALO—THRUST OUT LIKE a buttress into the sea, strange and grim of aspect, breathing war from its walls and battlements of ragged stone, a stronghold of privateers, the home of a race whose intractable and defiant independence neither time nor change has subdued—has been for centuries a nursery of hardy mariners. Among the earliest and most eminent on its list stands the name of Jacques Cartier. His portrait hangs in the town hall of St. Malo—bold, keen features bespeaking a spirit not apt to quail before the wrath of man or of the elements.

Sailing from St. Malo on the twentieth of April, 1534, Cartier steered for Newfoundland, passed through the straits of Belle Isle, entered the Gulf of Chaleurs, planted a cross at Gaspé and, never doubting that he was on the high road to Cathay, advanced up the St. Lawrence till he saw the shores of Anticosti. But autumnal storms were gathering. The voyagers took counsel together, turned their prows eastward and bore away for France, carrying there as a sample of the natural products of the New World two young Indians, lured into their clutches by an act of villainous treachery.

The voyage was a mere reconnaissance, but the spirit of discovery was awakened. A passage to India could be found, and a new France built up beyond the Atlantic. Mingled with such views of interest and ambition was another motive scarcely less potent. The heresy of Luther was convulsing Germany, and the deeper heresy of Calvin infecting France. Devout Catholics, kindling with redoubled zeal, burned

3

to requite the Church for her losses in the Old World by winning to her fold the infidels of the New. But in pursuing an end at once so pious and so politic, Francis I was setting at naught the Supreme Pontiff himself, since by the preposterous bull of Alexander VI all America had been given to the Spaniards.

In October 1534, Cartier received another commission, and in spite of secret but bitter opposition from jealous traders of St. Malo, he prepared for a second voyage. Three vessels, the largest not above a hundred and twenty tons, were placed at his disposal, and Claude de Pontbriand, Charles de la Pommeraye and other gentlemen of birth enrolled themselves for the adventure. On the sixteenth of May, 1535, officers and sailors assembled in the cathedral of St. Malo, where after confession and mass they received the parting blessing of the bishop. Three days later they set sail.

The dingy walls of the rude old seaport and the white rocks that line the neighboring shores of Brittany faded from their sight, and soon they were tossing in a furious tempest. The scattered ships escaped the danger and, reuniting at the Straits of Belle Isle, steered westward along the coast of Labrador till they reached a small bay opposite the island of Anticosti. Cartier called it the Bay of St. Lawrence—a name afterwards extended to the entire gulf and to the great river above.

To ascend this great river and tempt the hazards of its intricate navigation with no better pilots than the two young Indians kidnaped the year before was a venture of no light risk. But skill or fortune prevailed, and on the first of September the voyagers reached in safety the gorge of the gloomy Saguenay, with its towering cliffs and sullen depth of waters. Passing the Isle aux Coudres and the lofty promontory of Cape Tourmente, they came to anchor in a quiet channel between the northern shore and the margin of a richly wooded island, where the trees were so thickly hung with grapes that Cartier named it the Island of Bacchus.

Indians came swarming from the shores, paddled their canoes about the ships and clambered to the decks to gaze in bewilderment at the novel scene and listen to the story of their traveled countrymen, as marvelous in their ears as a visit to another planet. Cartier received them kindly, listened to the long harangue of the great chief

Donnacona, regaled him with bread and wine and, when relieved at length of his guests, set forth in a boat to explore the river above.

As he drew near the opening of the channel, the Hochelaga spread before him the broad expanse of its waters. A mighty promontory, rugged and bare, thrust its scarped front into the surging current. Here, clothed in the majesty of solitude, breathing the stern poetry of the wilderness, rose the cliffs now rich with heroic memories, where the fiery Count Frontenac cast defiance at his foes, where Wolfe, Montcalm and Montgomery fell. Then all was a nameless barbarism, and a cluster of wigwams held the site of the rock-built city of Quebec. Its name was Stadaconé, and it owned the sway of the royal Donnacona.

Cartier set out to visit this greasy potentate, ascended the river St. Charles (which he called the St. Croix), landed, crossed the meadows, climbed the rocks, threaded the forest and emerged upon a squalid hamlet of bark cabins.

Having satisfied their curiosity, he and his party were rowing for their ships when a friendly interruption met them at the mouth of the St. Charles. An old chief harangued them from the bank, men, boys and children screeched welcome from the meadow and a troop of hilarious squaws danced knee-deep in the water. The gift of a few strings of beads completed their delight and redoubled their agility. From the distance of a mile their shrill songs of jubilation still reached the ears of the receding Frenchmen.

The hamlet of Stadaconé, with its king Donnacona and its naked lords and princes, was not the metropolis of this forest state, since a town far greater—so the Indians averred—stood by the brink of the river, many days' journey above. It was called Hochelaga, and the great river itself, with a wide reach of adjacent country, had borrowed its name. There, with his two young Indians as guides, Cartier resolved to go, but misgivings seized the guides as the time drew near, while Donnacona and his tribesmen, jealous of the plan, set themselves to thwart it. The Breton captain turned a deaf ear to their discussions.

Cartier made ready to depart. First he caused the two larger vessels to be towed for safe harborage within the mouth of the St. Charles. With the smallest, a galleon of forty tons, and two open boats, carrying in all fifty sailors besides Pontbriand, La Pommeraye and other gentlemen, he set out for Hochelaga.

5

Slowly gliding on their way by walls of verdure brightened in the autumnal sun, they saw forests festooned with grapevines and waters alive with wildfowl; they heard the song of the blackbird, the thrush and, as they fondly thought, the nightingale. The galleon grounded. They left her and, advancing with the boats alone, on the second of October neared the goal of their hopes, the mysterious Hochelaga.

Just below, where later were seen the quays and storehouses of Montreal, a thousand Indians thronged the shore, wild with delight, dancing, singing, crowding about the strangers and showering into the boats their gifts of fish and maize. As it grew dark, fires lighted up the night, while far and near the French could see the excited savages leaping and rejoicing by the blaze.

At dawn of day, marshaled and accoutered, they marched for Hochelaga. An Indian path led them through the forest which covered the site of Montreal. The morning air was chill and sharp, the leaves were changing hue and beneath the oaks the ground was thickly strewn with acorns. They soon met an Indian chief with a party of tribesmen. Greeting them after the concise courtesy of the forest, he led them to a fire kindled by the side of the path for their comfort and refreshment, seated them on the ground and made them a long harangue, receiving in requital of his eloquence two hatchets, two knives and a crucifix, the last of which he was invited to kiss.

This done, they resumed their march and presently came upon open fields, covered far and near with the ripened maize, its leaves rustling and its yellow grains gleaming between the parting husks. Before them, wrapped in forests painted by the early frosts, rose the ridgy back of the Mountain of Montreal, and below, encompassed with its cornfields, lay the Indian town. Nothing was visible but its encircling palisades. These were of trunks of trees, set in a triple row. Within were galleries for the defenders, rude ladders to mount them and magazines of stones to throw down on the heads of assailants. It was a mode of fortification practiced by all the tribes speaking dialects of the Iroquois.

The voyagers entered the narrow portal. Within, they saw some fifty of those large oblong dwellings so familiar in after years to the eyes of the Jesuit apostles in Iroquois and Huron forests. They were about fifty yards in length and twelve or fifteen wide, framed of sapling poles closely covered with sheets of bark, and each containing several

6

fires and several families. In the midst of the town was an open area, or public square, a stone's throw in width. Here Cartier and his followers stopped, while the surrounding houses of bark disgorged their inmates —swarms of children, and young women and old, their infants in their arms. They crowded about the visitors, crying for delight, touching their beards, feeling their faces and holding up the screeching infants to be touched in turn. The marvelous visitors, strange in hue, strange in attire, with mustached lip and bearded chin, with arquebuse, halberd, helmet and cuirass, seemed rather demigods than men.

Due time having been allowed for this exuberance of feminine rapture, the warriors interposed, banished the women and children to a distance and squatted on the ground around the French, row within row of swarthy forms and eager faces, "as if," says Cartier, "we were going to act a play." Then appeared a troop of women, each bringing a mat, with which they carpeted the bare earth for the guests. The latter being seated, the chief of the nation was borne before them on a deerskin by a number of his tribesmen. He was a bedridden old savage, paralyzed and helpless, squalid as the rest in his attire, and distinguished only by a red fillet, inwrought with the dyed quills of the Canada porcupine, encircling his lank black hair. They placed him on the ground at Cartier's feet and made signs of welcome for him, while he pointed feebly to his powerless limbs and implored the healing touch from the hand of the French chief. Cartier complied and received in acknowledgment the red fillet of his grateful patient.

Then from surrounding dwellings appeared a woeful throng, the sick, the lame, the blind, the maimed, the decrepit, brought or led forth and placed on the earth before the perplexed commander, "as if," he says, "a god had come down to cure them." His skill in medicine being far behind the emergency, he pronounced over his petitioners a portion of the Gospel of St. John, made the sign of the cross and uttered a prayer, not for their bodies only but for their miserable souls. Next he read the Passion of the Saviour, to which, though comprehending not a word, his audience listened with grave attention.

Then came a distribution of presents. The squaws and children were recalled and, with the warriors, placed in separate groups. Knives and hatchets were given to the men and beads to the women, while pewter rings and images of the *Agnus Dei* were flung among the troop of children, and there ensued a vigorous scramble in the square of Hochelaga.

Now the French trumpeters pressed their trumpets to their lips and blew a blast that filled the air with warlike din and the hearts of the hearers with amazement and delight. Bidding their hosts farewell, the visitors formed their ranks and defiled through the gate once more, despite the efforts of a crowd of women, who with clamorous hospitality beset them with gifts of fish, beans, corn and other viands of uninviting aspect, which the Frenchmen courteously declined.

A troop of Indians followed and guided them to the top of the neighboring mountain. Cartier called it *Mont Royal,* Montreal; and hence the name of the busy city which now holds the site of the vanished Hochelaga.

The French re-embarked, bade farewell to Hochelaga, retraced their lonely course down the St. Lawrence and reached Stadaconé in safety. On the bank of the St. Charles their companions had built in their absence a fort of palisades, and the ships, hauled up the little stream, lay moored before it.

Here the self-exiled company were soon besieged by the rigors of the Canadian winter. The rocks, the shores, the pine trees, the solid floor of the frozen river, all alike were blanketed in snow beneath the keen cold rays of the dazzling sun. The drifts rose above the sides of their ships; masts, spars and cordage were thick with glittering incrustations and sparkling rows of icicles; a frosty armor, four inches thick, encased the bulwarks. Yet in the bitterest weather the neighboring Indians came daily to the fort, wading half naked, waist-deep through the snow. At length their friendship began to abate. Their visits grew less frequent and, during December, had wholly ceased when a calamity fell upon the French.

A malignant scurvy broke out among them. Man after man went down before the hideous disease, till twenty-five were dead and only three or four were left in health. The sound were too few to attend the sick, and the wretched sufferers lay in helpless despair, dreaming of the sun and the vines of France. The ground, hard as flint, defied their feeble efforts and, unable to bury their dead, they hid them in snowdrifts.

There was fear that the Indians, learning their misery, might finish the work that scurvy had begun. None of them, therefore, were allowed to approach the fort, and when a party of savages lingered within hearing, Cartier forced his invalid garrison to beat with sticks and stones against the walls, that their dangerous neighbors, deluded by the clatter, might think them engaged in hard labor.

These objects of their fear proved, however, the instruments of their salvation. Cartier, walking one day near the river, met an Indian who not long before had been prostrate, like many of his fellows, with the scurvy but who was now, to all appearance, in high health and spirits. What agency had wrought this marvelous recovery? According to the Indian, it was a certain evergreen, called by him *ameda,* a decoction of the leaves of which was sovereign against the disease. The experiment was tried. The sick men drank copiously of the healing draught—so copiously indeed that in six days they drank a tree as large as a French oak. Thus vigorously assailed, the distemper relaxed its hold, and health and hope began to revisit the hapless company.

When this winter of misery had worn away, and the ships were thawed from their icy fetters, Cartier prepared to return. He had made notable discoveries, but these were as nothing to the tales of wonder that had reached his ear—of a land of gold and rubies, of a nation white like the French, of men who lived without food and of others to whom Nature had granted but one leg.

Should he stake his credit on these marvels? It were better that they who had recounted them to him should, with their own lips, recount them also to the King, and to this end he resolved that Donnacona and his chiefs should go with him to court. He lured them therefore to the fort and led them into an ambuscade of sailors, who seized the astonished guests and hurried them on board the ships. Having accomplished this treachery, the voyagers proceeded to plant the emblem of Christianity. The cross was raised, the fleur-de-lis planted near it, and spreading their sails, they steered for home. It was the sixteenth of July, 1536, when Cartier again cast anchor under the walls of St. Malo.

The years rolled on, after this initial thrust into the upper reaches of the New World, and France, long tossed among the surges of civil commotion, plunged at last into a gulf of fratricidal war. Blazing hamlets, sacked cities, fields steaming with slaughter, profaned altars and ravished maidens marked the track of the tornado. There was little room for schemes of foreign enterprise. Yet far aloof from siege and battle, the fishermen of the western ports still plied their craft on the Banks of Newfoundland. Humanity, morality, decency might be forgotten, but codfish must still be had for the use of the faithful in Lent and on fast days. Still the wandering Eskimo saw the Norman and Breton sails hovering around some lonely headland, or anchored in fleets in the harbor of St. John. And still, through salt spray and driving mist, the fishermen dragged up the riches of the sea.

But if the wilderness of ocean had its treasures, so too had the wilderness of woods. It needed only a few knives, beads and trinkets and the Indians would throng to the shore, burdened with the spoils of their winter hunting. Fishermen threw up their old vocation for the more lucrative trade in bearskins and beaver skins. They built rude huts along the shores of Anticosti, where at that day the bison, it is said, could be seen wallowing in the sands. They outraged the Indians; they quarreled with each other; and this infancy of the Canadian fur trade showed rich promise of the disorders which marked its riper growth. Others, meanwhile, were ranging the gulf in search of walrus tusks, and the year after the Battle of Ivry, St. Malo sent out a fleet of small craft in quest of this new prize.

But soon a power was in the field against which all St. Malo might clamor in vain. A Catholic nobleman of Brittany, the Marquis de la Roche, bargained with the King to colonize New France. On his part, he was to receive a monopoly of the trade and a profusion of worthless titles and empty privileges. He was declared Lieutenant General of Canada, Hochelaga, Newfoundland, Labrador and the countries adjacent, with sovereign power within his vast and ill-defined domain. He could levy troops, declare war and peace, make laws, punish or pardon at will, build cities, forts and castles and grant out lands in fiefs, seigniories, counties, viscounties and baronies.

Thus was effete and cumbrous feudalism to make a lodgment in the New World. It was a scheme of high-sounding promise but, in performance, less than contemptible. La Roche ransacked the prisons and, gathering a gang of thieves and desperadoes, embarked them in a small vessel and set sail to plant Christianity and civilization in the

West. Suns rose and set and the wretched bark, deep freighted with brutality and vice, held on her course. She was so small that the convicts, leaning over her side, could wash their hands in the water. At length on the gray horizon they descried a long gray line of ridgy sand. It was Sable Island, off the coast of Nova Scotia. A wreck lay stranded on the beach, and the surf broke ominously over the long submerged arms of sand, stretched far out into the sea on the right hand and on the left.

Here La Roche landed the convicts, forty in number, while with his more trusty followers he sailed to explore the neighboring coasts and choose a site for the capital of his new dominion, to which in due time he proposed to remove the prisoners. But suddenly a tempest from the west assailed him. The frail vessel was forced to run before the gale. Howling on her track, the storm drove her off the coast and chased her back towards France.

Meanwhile the convicts watched in suspense for the returning sail. Days passed, weeks passed, and still they strained their eyes in vain across the waste of ocean. La Roche had left them to their fate. Rueful and desperate, they wandered among the sand hills, through the stunted whortleberry bushes, the rank sand grass and the tangled cranberry vines which filled the hollows. Not a tree was to be seen, but they built huts of the fragments of the wreck. For food they caught fish in the surrounding sea and hunted the cattle which ran wild about the island. They killed seals, trapped black foxes and clothed themselves in their skins.

Their native instincts clung to them in their exile. As if not content with inevitable miseries, they quarreled and murdered one another. Season after season dragged on. Five years elapsed, and of the forty only twelve were left alive. Sand, sea and sky—there was little else around them. To break the dead monotony, the walrus would sometimes rear his half-human face and glistening sides on the reefs and sand bars. At length, on the far verge of the watery desert, they descried a sail. She stood on towards the island; a boat's crew landed on the beach, and the exiles were once more among their countrymen.

Meanwhile a new era had dawned on France. Exhausted with thirty years of conflict, she had sunk at last to a repose, uneasy and disturbed, yet the harbinger of recovery. Art, industry and commerce, so long crushed and overborne, were stirring into renewed life, and a crowd of adventurous men, nurtured in war and incapable of repose, must seek employment for their restless energies in fields of peaceful enterprise.

Two small, quaint vessels, not larger than the fishing craft of Gloucester and Marblehead—one was of twelve, the other of fifteen tons—held their way across the Atlantic, passed the tempestuous headlands of Newfoundland and the St. Lawrence and, with adventurous knight-errantry, glided deep into the heart of the Canadian wilderness. On board one of them was the Breton merchant, Pontgravé, and with him a man of spirit widely different, a Catholic of good family— Samuel de Champlain, born in 1567 at the small seaport of Brouage on the Bay of Biscay. His father was a captain in the royal navy, where he himself seems also to have served, though during the war he had fought for the King in Brittany, under the banners of D'Aumont, St. Luc and Brissac. His purse was small, his merit great, and Henry IV out of his own slender revenues had given him a pension to maintain him near his person.

Like specks on the broad bosom of the waters, the two pygmy vessels held their course up the lonely St. Lawrence. They passed abandoned Tadoussac, the channel of Orleans and the gleaming cataract of Montmorenci; the tenantless rock of Quebec, the wide Lake of St. Peter and its crowded archipelago, till now the mountain reared before them its rounded shoulder above the forest-plain of Montreal. All was solitude. Hochelaga had vanished. Of the savage population that Cartier had found here, sixty-eight years before, no trace remained. In its place were a few wandering Algonquins, of different tongue and lineage. In a skiff, with a few Indians, Champlain essayed to pass the rapids of St. Louis. Oars, paddles and poles alike proved vain against the foaming surges and he was forced to return. On the deck of his vessel the Indians drew rude plans of the river above, with its chain of rapids, its lakes and cataracts, and the baffled explorer turned his prow homeward, the objects of his mission accomplished but his own adventurous curiosity unsated.

Soon afterward the gentleman Pierre du Guast, Sieur de Monts, gentleman in ordinary of the King's chamber and governor of Pons, petitioned the King for leave to colonize La Cadie, or Acadie, a region defined as extending from the fortieth to the forty-sixth degree of north latitude, or from Philadelphia to beyond Montreal. The King's minister Sully, as he himself tells us, opposed the plan on the ground that the colonization of this northern wilderness would never repay the outlay, but De Monts gained his point. He was made Lieutenant General in Acadia, with viceregal powers, and withered Feudalism, with her antique forms and tinseled follies, was again to seek a new home among the rocks and pine trees of Nova Scotia.

A clause in the De Monts commission empowered him to impress idlers and vagabonds as material for his colony—an ominous provision of which he largely availed himself. His company was strangely incongruous. The best and the meanest of France were crowded together in his two ships. Here were thieves and ruffians dragged on board by force, and here were many volunteers of condition and character, including Baron de Poutrincourt and the indefatigable Champlain. Here, too, were Catholic priests and Huguenot ministers, for though De Monts was a Calvinist, the Church as usual displayed her banner in the van of the enterprise, and he was forced to promise that he would cause the Indians to be instructed in the dogmas of Rome.

De Monts, with one of his vessels, sailed from Havre de Grace on the seventh of April, 1604. Pontgravé, with stores for the colony, was to follow in a few days.

Scarcely were they at sea when ministers and priests fell first to discussion, then to quarreling, then to blows. "I have seen our *curé* and the minister," says Champlain, "fall to with their fists on questions of faith. I cannot say which had the more pluck, or which hit the harder; but I know that the minister sometimes complained to the Sieur de Monts that he had been beaten. This was their way of settling points of controversy. I leave you to judge if it was a pleasant thing to see."

De Monts, who had been to the St. Lawrence and had learned to dread its rigorous winters, steered for a more southern and, as he flattered himself, a milder region. The first land seen was Cap la Hêve, on the southern coast of Nova Scotia. Four days later they entered a small bay, where to their surprise they saw a vessel lying at anchor. Here was a piece of good luck. The stranger was a fur trader, pursuing her traffic in defiance, or more probably in ignorance, of De Monts's monopoly. The latter, as empowered by his patent, made a prize of ship and cargo, consoling the commander, one Rossignol, by giving his name to the scene of his misfortune. It is now called Liverpool Harbor.

In an adjacent harbor, called by them Port Mouton because a sheep leaped overboard there, they waited nearly a month for Pontgravé's storeship. At length, to their great relief, she appeared, laden with the spoils of four Basque fur traders captured at Canseau. The supplies delivered, Pontgravé sailed for Tadoussac to trade with the Indians, while De Monts, followed by his prize, proceeded on his voyage.

He doubled Cape Sable and entered St. Mary's Bay, where he lay two weeks, sending boats' crews to explore the adjacent coasts. A party one day went on shore to stroll through the forest. Among them was Nicolas Aubry, a priest from Paris, who, tiring of the scholastic haunts of the Rue de la Sorbonne and the Rue d'Enfer, had persisted despite the remonstrance of his friends in joining the expedition. Thirsty from a long walk under the sun of June through the tangled and rock-encumbered woods, he stopped to drink at a brook, laying his sword beside him on the grass. Rejoining his companions, he found that he had forgotten the weapon and, turning back in search of it, more skilled in the devious windings of the Quartier Latin than in the intricacies of the Canadian forest, he soon lost his way.

His comrades, alarmed, waited for a time and then ranged the woods, shouting his name to the echoing solitudes. Trumpets were sounded and cannon fired from the ships, but the priest did not appear. All now looked askance on a certain Huguenot, with whom Aubry had often quarreled on questions of faith, and who was now accused of having killed him. In vain he denied the charge. Aubry was given up for dead, and the ship sailed from St. Mary's Bay while the wretched priest roamed to and fro, famished and despairing; or, couched on the rocky soil in the troubled sleep of exhaustion, dreamed perhaps as the wind swept moaning through the pines that he heard once more the organ roll through the columned arches of Ste. Geneviève.

The voyagers proceeded to explore the Bay of Fundy, which De Monts called La Baye Françoise. Their first notable discovery was that of Annapolis Harbor. A small inlet invited them. They entered and suddenly the narrow strait dilated into a broad and tranquil basin, compassed by sunny hills, wrapped in woodland verdure and alive with waterfalls. Poutrincourt was delighted with the scene. The fancy seized him of removing there from France with his family, and to this end he asked a grant of the place from De Monts, who by his patent had nearly half the continent in his gift. The grant was made, and Poutrincourt called his new domain Port Royal.

Then they sailed round the head of the Bay of Fundy, coasted its northern shore, visited and named the river St. John and anchored at last in Passamaquoddy Bay.

The untiring Champlain, exploring, surveying, sounding, had made charts of all the principal roads and harbors, and now, pursuing his research, he entered a river which he calls La Rivière des Etechemins, from the name of the tribe of whom the present Passamaquoddy Indians are descendants. Near its mouth he found an islet, fenced round with rocks and shoals, and called it St. Croix, a name now borne by the river itself. With singular infelicity, this spot was chosen as the site of a new colony. It commanded the river and was well fitted for defense; these were its only merits. Yet cannon were landed on it, a battery was planted on a detached rock at one end and a fort begun on a rising ground at the other.

At St. Mary's Bay the voyagers thought they had found traces of iron and silver, and Champdoré, the pilot, was now sent back to pursue the search. As he and his men lay at anchor fishing, not far from land, one of them heard a strange sound, like a weak human voice, and looking towards the shore, they saw a small black object in motion, apparently a hat waving on the end of a stick. Rowing in haste to the spot, they found the priest Aubry. For sixteen days he had wandered in the woods, sustaining life on berries and wild fruits. Haggard and emaciated, he was carried back to St. Croix, where he was greeted as a man risen from the grave.

There was little leisure at St. Croix. Soldiers, sailors and artisans betook themselves to their task. Before the winter closed in, the northern end of the island was covered with buildings, surrounding a square, where a solitary tree had been left standing. On the right was a spacious house, well built and surmounted by one of those enormous roofs characteristic of the time. This was the lodging of De Monts. Behind it, and near the water, was a long covered gallery for labor or amusement in foul weather. Champlain and the Sieur d'Orville, aided by the servants of the latter, built a house for themselves nearly opposite that of De Monts, and the remainder of the square was occupied by storehouses, a magazine, workshops, lodgings for gentlemen and artisans and a barrack for the Swiss soldiers, the whole enclosed with a palisade. Adjacent there was an attempt at a garden, under the auspices of Champlain, but nothing would grow in the sandy soil. There was a cemetery, too, and a small rustic chapel on a projecting point of rock.

Their labors over, Poutrincourt set sail for France, proposing to return and take possession of his domain of Port Royal. Seventy-nine men remained at St. Croix. Here was De Monts, feudal lord of half a continent by virtue of two potent syllables, "Henri," scrawled on parchment by the rugged hand of the Béarnais. Here were gentlemen of birth and breeding: Champlain, D'Orville, Beaumont, Sourin, La Motte, Boulay and Fougeray. Here also were the pugnacious *curé* and his fellow priests, with the Huguenot ministers, objects of their unceasing ire. The rest were laborers, artisans and soldiers, all in the pay of the company and some of them forced into service.

Poutrincourt's receding sails vanished between the water and the sky. The exiles were left to the solitude. From the Spanish settlements in Florida northward to the Pole there was no domestic hearth, no lodgment of civilized men, save one weak band of Frenchmen, clinging as it were for life to the fringe of the vast and savage continent.

The gray and sullen autumn sank upon the waste, and the bleak wind howled down the St. Croix and swept the forest bare. Then the whirling snow powdered the vast sweep of desolate woodland and shrouded in white the gloomy green of pine-clad mountains. Ice in sheets or broken masses swept by their island with the ebbing and flowing tide, often debarring all access to the main and cutting off their supplies of wood and water. A belt of cedars hedged the island, but De Monts had ordered them to be spared that the north wind might spend something of its force with whistling through their shaggy

16

boughs. Cider and wine froze in the casks and were served out by the pound. As they crowded round their half-fed fires, shivering in the icy currents that pierced their rude tenements, many sank into a desperate apathy.

Soon the scurvy broke out and raged with a fearful malignity. Of the seventy-nine, thirty-five died before spring and many more were brought to the verge of death. In vain they sought that marvelous tree which had relieved the followers of Cartier. Their little cemetery was peopled with nearly half their number, and the rest, bloated and disfigured with the relentless malady, thought more of escaping from their woes than of building up a transatlantic empire. Yet among them there was one, at least, who amid languor and defection held to his purpose with indomitable tenacity. Where Champlain was present, there was no room for despair.

Spring came at last, and with the breaking up of the ice, the melting of the snow and the clamors of the returning wildfowl, the spirits and the health of the woebegone company began to revive. But anxiety and suspense succeeded misery. Where was the succor from France? Were they abandoned to their fate like the wretched exiles of La Roche? In a happy hour, they saw an approaching sail. Pontgravé, with forty men, cast anchor before their island on the sixteenth of June, and they hailed him as the condemned hails the messenger with his pardon.

Weary of St. Croix, De Monts resolved to seek out a more auspicious site on which to rear the capital of his wilderness dominion. During the preceding September, Champlain had ranged the westward coast in a pinnace, visited and named the island of Mount Desert and entered the mouth of the river Penobscot, called by him the Pemetigoet, or Pentegoet, and previously known to fur traders and fishermen as the Norembega, a name which it shared with all the adjacent region. Now, embarking a second time in a bark of fifteen tons, with De Monts, several gentlemen, twenty sailors and an Indian with his squaw, he set forth on the eighteenth of June on a second voyage of discovery.

They coasted the strangely indented shores of Maine, with its reefs and surf-washed islands, rocky headlands and deep enbosomed bays, passed Mount Desert and the Penobscot, explored the mouths of the Kennebec, crossed Casco Bay and descried the distant peaks of the White Mountains. The ninth of July brought them to Saco Bay.

They were now within the limits of a group of tribes who were called by the French the Armouchiquois and who included those whom the English afterwards called the Massachusetts. They differed in habits as well as in language from the Etechemins and Micmacs of Acadia, for they were tillers of the soil and around their wigwams were fields of maize, beans, pumpkins, squashes, tobacco and the so-called Jerusalem artichoke. Near Prout's Neck more than eighty of them ran down to the shore to meet the strangers, dancing and yelping to show their joy. They had a fort of palisades on a rising ground by the Saco, for they were at deadly war with their neighbors toward the east.

On the twelfth the French resumed their voyage and, like some adventurous party of pleasure, held their course by the beaches of York and Wells, Portsmouth Harbor, the Isles of Shoals, Rye Beach and Hampton Beach, till on the fifteenth they descried the dim outline of Cape Ann. Champlain called it Cap aux Isles, from the three adjacent islands, and in a subsequent voyage he gave the name of Beauport to the neighboring harbor of Gloucester. Steering southward and westward, they entered Massachusetts Bay, gave the name of Rivière du Guast to a river flowing into it, probably the Charles, passed the islands of Boston Harbor, which Champlain describes as covered with trees, and were met on the way by great numbers of canoes filled with astonished Indians.

On Sunday, the seventeenth, they passed Point Allerton and Nantasket Beach, coasted the shores of Cohasset, Scituate and Marshfield and anchored for the night near Brant Point. On the morning of the eighteenth a head wind forced them to take shelter in Port St. Louis, which they called the Harbor of Plymouth, where the Pilgrims made their memorable landing fifteen years later. Indian wigwams and garden patches lined the shore. A troop of the inhabitants came down to the beach and danced, while others who had been fishing approached in their canoes, came on board the vessel and showed Champlain their fishhooks, consisting of barbed bones lashed at an acute angle to slips of wood.

From Plymouth the party circled round the bay, doubled Cape Cod, called by Champlain Cap Blanc because of its glistening white sands, and steered southward to Nausett Harbor, which they named Port Mallebarre, for its shoals and sand bars. Here their prosperity

18

deserted them. A party of sailors went behind the sandbanks to find fresh water at a spring, when an Indian snatched a kettle from one of them, and its pursuing owner fell, pierced with arrows by the robber's comrades. The French in the vessel opened fire. Champlain's arquebuse burst and was near killing him, while the Indians, swift as deer, quickly gained the woods. Several of the tribe chanced to be on board the vessel but flung themselves with such alacrity into the water that only one was caught. They bound him hand and foot but later humanely set him at liberty.

At Nausett Harbor provisions began to fail, and steering for St. Croix, the voyagers reached that ill-starred island on the third of August. De Monts had found no spot to his liking. He now thought of that inland harbor of Port Royal which he had granted to Poutrincourt, and there he resolved to remove. Stores, utensils, even portions of the buildings were placed on board the vessels, carried across the Bay of Fundy and landed at the chosen spot. It was on the north side of the basin opposite Goat Island, and a little below the mouth of the river Annapolis, called by the French the Equille, and afterwards the Dauphin. The axmen began their task. The dense forest was cleared away and the buildings of the infant colony soon rose in its place.

But while De Monts and his company were struggling against despair at St. Croix, the enemies of his monopoly were busy at Paris, and by a ship from France he was warned that prompt measures were needed to thwart their machinations. Therefore he set sail, leaving Pontgravé to command at Port Royal, while Champlain, Champdoré and others, undaunted by·the past, volunteered for a second winter in the wilderness.

As for De Monts, his return home was heralded by evil reports of a pitiless climate, disease, misery and death. The outlay had been great, the returns small, and when he reached Paris he found his friends cold, his enemies active and keen. Poutrincourt, however, was still full of zeal. Though his private affairs urgently called for his presence in France, he resolved, at no small sacrifice, to go in person to Acadia. He had, moreover, a friend who proved an invaluable ally. This was Marc Lescarbot, *"avocat en Parlement,"* who had been roughly handled by fortune and was in the mood for such a venture, being desirous, as he tells us, "to fly from a corrupt world" in which he had just lost a lawsuit.

Lescarbot was no common man. Not that his abundant gift for versemaking was likely to avail much in the woods of New France, nor yet his classic lore, dashed with a little harmless pedantry, born not of the man but of the times. But his zeal, his good sense, the vigor of his understanding and the breadth of his views were as conspicuous as his quick wit and his lively fancy. He professed himself a Catholic, but his Catholicity sat lightly on him.

De Monts and Poutrincourt bestirred themselves to find a priest, since the foes of the enterprise had been loud in lamentation that the spiritual welfare of the Indians had been slighted. But it was Holy Week. All the priests were, or professed to be, busy with exercises and confessions and not one could be found to undertake the mission of Acadia. They were more successful in engaging mechanics and laborers for the voyage. These were paid a portion of their wages in advance and were sent in a body to Rochelle, consigned to two merchants of that port, members of the company. De Monts and Poutrincourt went there by post. Lescarbot soon followed, and no sooner reached Rochelle than he penned and printed his *Adieu à la France,* a poem which gained for him some credit.

More serious matters awaited him, however, than this dalliance with the muse. Their ship, bearing the inauspicious name of the *Jonas,* lay anchored in the stream, her cargo on board, when a sudden gale blew her adrift. She struck on a pier, then grounded on the flats, bilged, careened and settled in the mud. Her captain, who was ashore with Poutrincourt, Lescarbot and others, hastened aboard and the pumps were set in motion, while all Rochelle came to gaze from the ramparts with faces of condolence but at heart well pleased with the disaster.

The ship and her cargo were saved, but she had to be emptied, repaired and reladen. Thus a month was lost. At length, on the thirteenth of May, 1606, the disorderly crew were all brought on board and the *Jonas* put to sea. Poutrincourt and Lescarbot had charge of the expedition, De Monts remaining in France.

Lescarbot describes his emotions at finding himself on an element so deficient in solidity, with only a two-inch plank between him and death. Off the Azores they spoke a supposed pirate. For the rest, they beguiled the voyage by harpooning porpoises, dancing on deck in calm weather and fishing for cod on the Grand Bank. They were two months on their way and feverish with eagerness to reach land; they listened hourly for the welcome cry. But they were involved in impenetrable fogs.

Suddenly the mists parted, the sun shone forth and streamed fair and bright over the fresh hills and forests of the New World, in near view before them. Black rocks lay between, lashed by the snow-white breakers.

"Thus," writes Lescarbot, "doth a man sometimes seek the land as one doth his beloved, who sometimes repulseth her sweetheart very rudely. Finally, upon Saturday, the fifteenth of July, about two o'clock in the afternoon, the sky began to salute us as it were with cannon shots, shedding tears, as being sorry to have kept us so long in pain . . . but, whilst we followed on our course, there came from the land odors incomparable for sweetness, brought with a warm wind so abundantly that all the Orient ports could not produce greater abundance. We did stretch out our hands as it were to take them, so palpable were they, which I have admired a thousand times since."

It was noon on the twenty-seventh when the *Jonas* passed the rocky gateway of Port Royal Basin, and Lescarbot gazed with delight and wonder on the calm expanse of sunny waters, with its amphitheater of woody hills, wherein he saw the future asylum of distressed merit and impoverished industry. Slowly, before a favoring breeze, they held their course towards the head of the harbor, which narrowed as they advanced, but all was solitude—no moving sail, no sign of human presence.

At length, on their left, nestling in deep forests, they saw the wooden walls and roofs of the infant colony. Then appeared a birch canoe, cautiously coming towards them, guided by an old Indian. Then a Frenchman, arquebuse in hand, came down to the shore, and then from the wooden bastion sprang the smoke of a saluting shot. The ship replied. The trumpets lent their voices to the din and the forests and the hills gave back unwonted echoes. The voyagers landed and found the colony of Port Royal dwindled to two solitary Frenchmen.

They soon told their story. The preceding winter had been one of

21

much suffering, though by no means the counterpart of the woeful experience of St. Croix. But when the spring had passed, the summer far advanced, and still no tidings of De Monts had come, Pontgravé grew deeply anxious. To maintain themselves without supplies and succor was impossible. He caused two small vessels to be built and set out in search of some of the French vessels on the fishing stations. This was but twelve days before the arrival of the ship *Jonas*. Two men had bravely offered themselves to stay behind and guard the buildings, guns and munitions, and an old Indian chief named Membertou, a fast friend of the French and still a redoubted warrior though reputed to number more than a hundred years, proved to be a stanch ally.

When the ship approached, the two guardians were at dinner in their room at the fort. Membertou, always on the watch, saw the advancing sail and, shouting from the gate, roused them from their repast. In doubt who the newcomers might be, one ran to the shore with his gun while the other repaired to the platform where four cannon were mounted, in the valorous resolve to show fight should the strangers prove to be enemies. Happily this redundancy of mettle proved needless. He saw the white flag fluttering at the masthead and joyfully fired his pieces as a salute.

The voyagers landed and eagerly surveyed their new home. Some wandered through the buildings; some visited the cluster of Indian wigwams hard by; some roamed in the forest and over the meadows that bordered the neighboring river. The deserted fort now swarmed with life, and the better to celebrate their prosperous arrival, Poutrincourt placed a hogshead of wine in the courtyard at the discretion of his followers, whose hilarity, in consequence, became exuberant. Nor was it diminished when Pontgravé's vessels were seen entering the harbor. A boat sent by Poutrincourt, more than a week before, to explore the coasts had met them near Cape Sable, and they joyfully returned to Port Royal.

Pontgravé, however, soon sailed for France in the *Jonas,* hoping on his way to seize certain contraband fur traders reported to be at Canseau and Cape Breton.

Most bountiful provision had been made for the temporal wants of the colonists, and Lescarbot is profuse in praise of the liberality of

De Monts and two merchants of Rochelle, who had freighted the ship *Jonas*. Of wine, in particular, the supply was so generous that every man in Port Royal was served with three pints daily.

The principal persons of the colony sat, fifteen in number, at Poutrincourt's table, which by an ingenious device of Champlain was always well furnished. He formed the fifteen into a new order, christened "L'Ordre de Bon-Temps." Each was Grand Master in turn, holding office for one day. It was his function to cater for the company, and as it became a point of honor to fill the post with credit, the prospective Grand Master was usually busy for several days before coming to his dignity in hunting, fishing or bartering provisions with the Indians. Thus did Poutrincourt's table groan beneath all the luxuries of the winter forest—flesh of moose, caribou and deer, beaver, otter and hare, bears and wildcats; with ducks, geese, grouse and plover; sturgeon, too, and trout and fish innumerable, speared through the ice of the Equille or drawn from the depths of the neighboring bay.

Nor did this bounteous repast lack a solemn and befitting ceremonial. When the hour had struck—after the manner of our fathers, they dined at noon—the Grand Master entered the hall, a napkin on his shoulder, his staff of office in his hand and the collar of the Order, valued by Lescarbot at four crowns, about his neck. The brotherhood followed, each bearing a dish. The invited guests were Indian chiefs, of whom old Membertou was daily present, seated at table with the French, who took pleasure in this redskin companionship. Those of humbler degree, warriors, squaws and children, sat on the floor or crouched together in the corners of the hall, eagerly waiting their portion of biscuit or of bread, a novel and much-coveted luxury. Being always treated with kindness, they became fond of the French, who often followed them on their moose hunts and shared their winter bivouacs.

At the evening meal there was less of form and circumstance. When the winter night closed in, when the flame crackled and the sparks streamed up the wide-throated chimney, and the founders of New France with their tawny allies were gathered around the blaze, then the Grand Master resigned the collar and the staff to the successor of his honors and, with jovial courtesy, pledged him in a cup of wine. Thus these ingenious Frenchmen beguiled the winter of their exile.

Good spirits and good cheer saved them in great measure from the scurvy. Towards the end of winter severe cold set in, but only four men died. The snow thawed at last, and as patches of the black and oozy soil began to appear they saw the grain of their last autumn's sowing already piercing the mold. The forced inaction of the winter was over. The carpenters built a water mill on the stream now called Allen's River. Others enclosed fields and laid out gardens. With scoop nets and baskets others caught the herrings and alewives as they ran up the innumerable rivulets. The leaders of the colony set a contagious example of activity. Poutrincourt forgot the prejudices of his noble birth and went himself into the woods to gather turpentine from the pines, which he converted into tar by a process of his own invention. Lescarbot, eager to test the qualities of the soil, was again, hoe in hand, at work all day in his garden.

On a morning late in spring, as the French were at breakfast, the ever-watchful Membertou came in with news of an approaching sail. They hastened to the shore, but the vision of the centenarian chief put them all to shame. They could see nothing. At length their doubts were resolved. A small vessel stood on towards them and anchored before the fort. She was commanded by one Chevalier, a young man from St. Malo, and was freighted with disastrous tidings. De Monts's monopoly was rescinded. The life of the enterprise was stopped, and the establishment at Port Royal could no longer be supported, for its expense was great, the body of the colony being laborers in the pay of the company.

Choice there was none, and Port Royal must be abandoned. Built on a false basis, sustained only by the fleeting favor of a government, the generous enterprise had come to naught. Yet Poutrincourt, who by virtue of his grant from De Monts owned the place, bravely resolved that, come what might, he would see the adventure to an end, even should it involve emigration with his family to the wilderness. Meanwhile he began the dreary task of abandonment, sending boatloads of men and stores to Canseau, where lay the ship *Jonas,* eking out her diminished profits by fishing for cod.

With a heavy heart Lescarbot bade farewell to the dwellings, the cornfields, the gardens and all the dawning prosperity of Port Royal and sailed for Canseau in a small vessel on the thirtieth of July.

Poutrincourt and Champlain remained behind, for the former was resolved to learn before his departure the results of his agricultural labors.

At Canseau, a harbor near the strait now bearing the name, the ship *Jonas* still lay, her hold well stored with fish. There, on the twenty-seventh of August, Lescarbot was rejoined by Poutrincourt and Champlain, who had come from Port Royal in an open boat. For a few days they amused themselves with gathering raspberries on the islands. Then they spread their sails for France and, early in October 1607, anchored in the harbor of St. Malo.

At home again, they found that the Jesuits were strong in the French court. One of their number, the famous Father Coton, was confessor to Henry IV and, on matters of this world as of the next, was ever whispering at the facile ear of the renegade King. New France offered a fresh field of action to the indefatigable Society of Jesus, and Coton urged upon the royal convert that, for the saving of souls, some of its members should be attached to the proposed enterprise in the New World.

The King, profoundly indifferent in matters of religion, saw no evil in a proposal which at least promised to place the Atlantic between him and some of those busy friends whom at heart he deeply mistrusted. Other influences, too, seconded the confessor. Devout ladies of the court, and the Queen herself, supplying the lack of virtue with an overflowing piety, burned with a holy zeal for snatching the tribes of the West from the bondage of Satan. Therefore it was insisted that any new colony should combine the spiritual with the temporal character—or, in other words, that Poutrincourt should take Jesuits back with him. Pierre Biard, professor of theology at Lyons, was named for the mission and repaired in haste to Bordeaux, the port of embarkation, where he found no vessel and no sign of preparation. There, in wrath and discomfiture, he remained for a whole year.

Poutrincourt owned the barony of St. Just in Champagne, inherited a few years before from his mother. From that point, early in February 1610, he set out in a boat loaded to the gunwales with provisions, furniture, goods and munitions for Port Royal, descended the rivers Aube and Seine and reached Dieppe safely with his charge. Here his

25

ship was awaiting him, and on the twenty-sixth of February he set sail, giving the slip to the indignant Jesuit at Bordeaux.

The tedium of a long passage was unpleasantly broken by a mutiny among the crew. It was suppressed, however, and Poutrincourt entered at length the familiar basin of Port Royal. The buildings were still standing, whole and sound save a partial falling in of the roofs. Even furniture was found untouched in the deserted chambers. The centenarian Membertou was still alive, his leathern, wrinkled visage beaming with welcome.

Poutrincourt set himself without delay to the task of Christianizing New France, in an access of zeal which his desire of proving that Jesuit aid was superfluous may be supposed largely to have reinforced. He had a priest with him, one La Flèche, whom he urged to the pious work. No time was lost. Membertou first was catechized, confessed his sins and renounced the Devil, whom we are told he had faithfully served during a hundred and ten years. His squaws, his children, his grandchildren and his entire clan were next won over.

It was in June, the day of St. John the Baptist, when the naked proselytes, twenty-one in number, were gathered on the shore at Port Royal. Here was the priest in the vestments of his office; here were gentlemen in gay attire, soldiers, laborers, lackeys, all the infant colony. The converts kneeled. The sacred rite was finished, *Te Deum* was sung and the roar of cannon proclaimed this triumph over the powers of darkness. Membertou was named Henri, after the King; his principal squaw Marie, after the Queen. One of his sons received the name of the Pope, another that of the Dauphin. His daughter was called Marguerite, after the divorced Marguerite de Valois, and in like manner the rest of the squalid company exchanged their barbaric appellatives for the names of princes, nobles and ladies of rank.

The fame of this *chef-d'œuvre* of Christian piety, as Lescarbot gravely calls it, spread far and wide through the forest, whose denizens —partly out of a notion that the rite would bring good luck, partly to please the French and partly to share in the good cheer with which the apostolic efforts of Father La Flèche had been sagaciously seconded—came flocking to enroll themselves under the banners of the Faith. Their zeal ran high. They would take no refusal. Membertou was for war on all who would not turn Christian. A living skeleton was

26

seen crawling from hut to hut in search of the priest and his saving waters, while another neophyte, at the point of death, asked anxiously whether in the realms of bliss to which he was bound pies were to be had comparable to those with which the French had regaled him.

A formal register of baptisms was drawn up to be carried to France in the returning ship, of which Poutrincourt's son, Biencourt, a spirited youth of eighteen, was to take charge. He sailed in July, his father keeping him company as far as Port la Hêve.

CHAPTER 2

The Jesuits

THERE IS AN ANCIENT STREET IN PARIS, THE RUE DE
la Ferronnerie, where a great thoroughfare contracts to a narrow
pass. Tall buildings overshadow it, packed from pavement to tiles
with human life, and from the dingy front of one of them the sculptured
head of a man looks down on the throng that ceaselessly defiles beneath.

On the fourteenth of May, 1610, a ponderous coach, studded with
fleurs-de-lis and rich with gilding, rolled along this street. In it was a
small man, well advanced in life, whose profile once seen could not be
forgotten—a hooked nose, a protruding chin, a brow full of wrinkles,
grizzled hair, a short grizzled beard and stiff gray mustaches, bristling
like a cat's. One would have thought him some whiskered satyr, grim
from the rack of tumultuous years, but his alert, upright carriage
bespoke unshaken vigor and his clear eye was full of buoyant life.

Following on the footway strode a tall, strong and somewhat corpu-
lent man, with sinister deep-set eyes and a red beard, his arm and shoulder covered with his cloak. In the throat of the thoroughfare, where the
sculptured image of Henry IV still guards the spot, a collision of two
carts stopped the coach. Ravaillac, the assassin, quickened his pace.
In an instant he was at the door. With his cloak dropped from his
shoulders and a long knife in his hand, he set his foot upon a guard-
stone, thrust his head and shoulders into the coach and with frantic
force stabbed thrice at the King's heart. A broken exclamation, a
gasping convulsion—and then the grim visage drooped on the bleeding

28

breast. Henry breathed his last, and the hope of Europe died with him.

The omens were sinister for Old France and for New. Marie de Médicis, coarse scion of a bad stock, false wife and faithless queen, paramour of an intriguing foreigner, tool of the Jesuits and of Spain, was Regent in the minority of her imbecile son. The Huguenots drooped, the national party collapsed, the vigorous hand of Sully was felt no more, and the treasure gathered for a vast and beneficent enterprise became the instrument of despotism and the prey of corruption. Under such dark auspices young Biencourt entered the thronged chambers of the Louvre.

He gained audience of the Queen and displayed his list of baptisms, while the ever-present Jesuits did not fail to seize him by the button, assuring him not only that the late King had deeply at heart the establishment of their Society in Acadia but that to this end he had made them a grant of two thousand livres a year.

Biencourt saw it vain to resist. Biard must go with him in the returning ship and also another Jesuit, Enemond Masse. The two fathers repaired to Dieppe, wafted on the wind of court favor, which they never doubted would bear them to their journey's end.

Not so, however. Poutrincourt and his associates, in the dearth of their own resources, had bargained with two Huguenot merchants of Dieppe, Du Jardin and Du Quesne, to equip and load the vessel, in consideration of their becoming partners in the expected profits. Their indignation was extreme when they saw the intended passengers. They declared that they would not aid in building up a colony for the profit of the King of Spain, nor risk their money in a venture where Jesuits were allowed to intermeddle. They closed with a flat refusal to receive them on board, unless, they added with patriotic sarcasm, the Queen would direct them to transport the whole order beyond the seas. Biard and Masse insisted, on which the merchants demanded reimbursement for their outlay, as they would have no further concern in the business.

Biard, in the name of the "Province of France of the Order of Jesus," bought out the interest of the two merchants for thirty-eight hundred livres, thus constituting the Jesuits equal partners in business with their enemies. Nor was this all. Out of the ample proceeds of the subscription, he lent to the needy associates a further sum of seven hundred and thirty-seven livres and advanced twelve hundred and

29

twenty-five more to complete the outfit of the ship. Well pleased, the triumphant priests now embarked, and friend and foe set sail together on the twenty-sixth of January, 1611.

The voyage was one of inordinate length—beset, too, with icebergs larger and taller, according to the Jesuit voyagers, than the Church of Notre Dame. But on the day of Pentecost their ship, *The Grace of God,* anchored before Port Royal.

Then first were seen in the wilderness of New France the close black cap, the close black robe of the Jesuit father, and the features seamed with study and thought and discipline. Then first did this mighty Proteus, this many-colored Society of Jesus, enter upon that rude field of toil and woe, where in after years the devoted zeal of its apostles was to lend dignity to their order and do honor to humanity.

When the voyagers landed they found at Port Royal a band of half-famished men, eagerly expecting their succor. The voyage of four months had, however, nearly exhausted their own very moderate stock of provisions, and the mutual congratulations of the old colonists and the new were dampened by a vision of starvation. A friction, too, speedily declared itself between the spiritual and the temporal powers. Pontgravé's son, then trading on the coast, had exasperated the Indians by an outrage on one of their women and, dreading the wrath of Poutrincourt, had fled to the woods. Biard saw fit to take his part, remonstrated for him with vehemence, gained his pardon, received his confession and absolved him. The Jesuit says that he was treated with great consideration by Poutrincourt and he should be forever beholden to him. The latter, however, chafed at Biard's interference.

"Father," he said, "I know my duty, and I beg you will leave me to do it. I, with my sword, have hopes of paradise, as well as you with your breviary. Show me my path to heaven. I will show you yours on earth."

Poutrincourt soon set sail for France, leaving his son Biencourt in charge. This hardy young sailor, of ability and character beyond his years, had on his visit to court received the post of vice-admiral in the seas of New France, and in this capacity had a certain authority over the trading vessels of St. Malo and Rochelle, several of which were upon the coast. To compel the recognition of this authority, and also to purchase provisions, he set out along with Biard in a boat filled with armed followers. His first collision was with young Pontgravé, who with a few men had built a trading hut on the St. John, where he proposed to winter. Meeting with resistance, Biencourt took the whole party prisoners, in spite of the remonstrances of Biard.

Next, proceeding along the coast, he levied tribute on four or five traders wintering at St. Croix and, continuing his course to the Kennebec, found the Indians of that region greatly enraged at the conduct of certain English adventurers, who three or four years before had, as they said, set dogs upon them and otherwise maltreated them. These were the colonists under Popham and Gilbert, who in 1607 and 1608 made an abortive attempt to settle near the mouth of the river. Nothing now was left of them but their deserted fort. The neighboring Indians were Abenakis, one of the tribes included by the French under the general name of Armouchiquois. Their disposition was doubtful, and it needed all the coolness of young Biencourt to avoid a fatal collision.

Biard did not like the Indians, whom he describes as "lazy, gluttonous, irreligious, treacherous, cruel and licentious." He makes an exception in favor of Membertou, whom he calls "the greatest, most renowned and most redoubted savage that ever lived in the memory of man," and especially commends him for contenting himself with but one wife, hardly a superlative merit in a centenarian. Biard taught him to say the Lord's Prayer, though at the petition "Give us this day our daily bread," the chief remonstrated, saying, "If I ask for nothing but bread, I shall get no fish or moosemeat."

His protracted career was now drawing to a close, and being brought to the settlement in a dying state, he was placed in Biard's bed and attended by the two Jesuits. He was as remarkable in person as in character, for he was bearded like a Frenchman. Though alone among La Flèche's converts the Faith seemed to have left some impression upon him, he insisted on being buried with his heathen forefathers, but was persuaded to forego a wish fatal to his salvation and slept at last in consecrated ground.

Biard's greatest difficulty was with the Micmac language. Young Biencourt was his best interpreter and on common occasions served him well. But the moment that religion was in question he was, as it were, stricken dumb—the reason being that the language was totally without abstract terms. Biard resolutely set himself to the study of it,

31

a hard and thorny path, on which he made small progress and often went astray. Seated, pencil in hand, before some Indian squatting on the floor, whom with the bribe of a moldy biscuit he had lured into the hut, he plied him with questions which the savage often neither would nor could answer. What was the Indian word for Faith, Hope, Charity, Sacrament, Baptism, Eucharist, Trinity, Incarnation? The perplexed savage, willing to amuse himself and impelled, as Biard thinks, by the Devil, gave him scurrilous and unseemly phrases as the equivalent of things holy. Studiously incorporated into the father's Indian catechism, these phrases produced on his pupils an effect the reverse of that intended.

The dark months wore slowly on. A band of half-famished men gathered about the huge fires of their barnlike hall, moody, sullen and quarrelsome. Discord was here in the black robe of the Jesuit and the brown capote of the rival trader. The position of the wretched little colony may well provoke reflection. Here lay the shaggy continent, from Florida to the Pole, outstretched in savage slumber along the sea, the stern domain of Nature. On the banks of the James River was a nest of woebegone Englishmen, a handful of Dutch fur traders at the mouth of the Hudson and a few shivering Frenchmen among the snow-drifts of Acadia, while deep within the wild monotony of desolation, on the icy verge of the great northern river, the hand of Champlain upheld the fleur-de-lis on the rock of Quebec.

These were the advance guard, the forlorn hope of civilization, messengers of promise to a desert continent. Yet, unconscious of their high function, not content with inevitable woes, they were rent by petty jealousies and miserable feuds, while each of these detached fragments of rival nationalities, scarcely able to maintain its own wretched existence on a few square miles, begrudged to the others the smallest share in a domain which all the nations of Europe could hardly have sufficed to fill.

One evening, as the forlorn tenants of Port Royal sat together disconsolate, Biard was seized with a spirit of prophecy. He called upon Biencourt to serve out the little of wine that remained—a proposal which met with high favor from the company present, though apparently with none from the youthful vice-admiral. The wine was ordered, however, and as an unwonted cheer ran round the circle the Jesuit announced that an inward voice told him how, within a month, they should see a ship from France. In truth, they saw one within a week. On the twenty-third of January, 1612, arrived a small vessel laden with a moderate store of provisions and abundant seeds of future strife.

This was the expected succor sent by Poutrincourt. A series of ruinous voyages had exhausted his resources, but he had staked all on the success of the colony, had even brought his family to Acadia, and he would not leave them and his companions to perish. In his discouragement, he had abandoned his plan of liberal colonization and now thought of nothing but beaver skins. He wished to make a trading post; the Jesuits wished to make a mission.

When the vessel anchored before Port Royal, Biencourt, with disgust and anger, saw another Jesuit landed at the pier. This was Gilbert du Thet, a lay brother, versed in affairs of this world, who had come out as representative and administrator of Madame de Guercheville, the Jesuits' powerful friend in the French court. Poutrincourt also had his agent on board, and without the loss of a day, the two began to quarrel. A truce ensued, then a smothered feud, pervading the whole colony and ending in a notable explosion. The Jesuits, chafing under the sway of Biencourt, had withdrawn without ceremony and betaken themselves to the vessel, intending to sail for France.

Biencourt, exasperated at such a breach of discipline and fearing their representations at court, ordered them to return, adding that since the Queen had commended them to his especial care he could not in conscience lose sight of them. The indignant fathers excommunicated him. On this, the sagamore Louis, son of the grisly convert Membertou, begged leave to kill them, but Biencourt would not countenance this summary mode of relieving his embarrassment. Again, in the King's name, he ordered the clerical mutineers to return to the fort. Biard declared that he would not, threatened to excommunicate any who should lay hand on him and called the vice-admiral a robber. His wrath, however, soon cooled. He yielded to necessity and came quietly ashore, where for the next three months neither he nor his colleagues would say mass or perform any office of religion.

At length a change came over him. He made advances of peace, prayed that the past might be forgotten, said mass again and closed with a petition that Brother du Thet might be allowed to go to France in a trading vessel then on the coast. His petition being granted, he wrote to Poutrincourt a letter overflowing with praises of his son, and charged with this missive, Du Thet set sail.

Scarcely had the good Brother arrived in France when Madame de Guercheville and her Jesuit friends, strong in court favor and in the charity of wealthy penitents, prepared to take possession of the empire beyond the seas, having involved Poutrincourt in a network of litigation and even succeeding in getting him thrown into jail for a time.

While the unfortunate man, liberated but ill of mind and heart, was setting himself to the forlorn task of sending relief to his son and his comrades, the *Mayflower* of the Jesuits sailed from Honfleur for the shores of New England, on the twelfth of March, 1613. Their ship was the *Jonas,* formerly in the service of De Monts, a small craft bearing forty-eight sailors and colonists, including two Jesuits, Father Quentin and Brother du Thet. She carried horses, too, and goats, and was abundantly stored with all things needful by the pious munificence of her patrons. A courtier named La Saussaye was chief of the colony, Captain Charles Fleury commanded the ship, and as she winged her way across the Atlantic, benedictions hovered over her from lordly halls and perfumed chambers.

On the sixteenth of May, La Saussaye touched at La Hêve, where he heard mass, planted a cross and displayed the scutcheon of Madame de Guercheville. Passing on to Port Royal, he found Biard, Masse, their servant boy, and apothecary and one man beside. Biencourt and his followers were scattered about the woods and shores, digging the tuberous roots called groundnuts, catching alewives in the brooks, and by similar expedients sustaining their miserable existence.

Taking the two Jesuits on board, the voyagers steered for the Penobscot. A fog rose upon the sea. They sailed to and fro, groping their way in blindness, straining their eyes through the mist and trembling each instant lest they should descry the black outline of some deadly reef and the ghostly death dance of the breakers. But Heaven heard their prayers. At night they could see the stars. The sun rose resplendent on a laughing sea, and his morning beams streamed fair and full on the wild heights of the island of Mount Desert. They entered a bay that stretched inland between ironbound shores and gave it the name of St. Sauveur. It is now called Frenchman's Bay.

They saw a coast line of weather-beaten crags set thick with spruce and fir, the surf-washed cliffs of Great Head and Schooner Head, the rocky front of Newport Mountain, patched with ragged woods, the arid domes of Dry Mountain and Green Mountain, the round bristly backs of the Porcupine Islands and the waving outline of the Gouldsborough Hills.

La Saussaye cast anchor not far from Schooner Head, and here he lay till evening. There was peace in the wilderness and peace on the sea, but none in the missionary bark, pioneer of Christianity and civilization. A rabble of angry sailors clamored on her deck, ready to mutiny over the terms of their engagement. Should the time of their stay be reckoned from their landing at La Hêve or from their anchoring at Mount Desert? Fleury, the naval commander, took their part. Sailor, courtier and priest gave tongue together in vociferous debate. Poutrincourt was far away, a ruined man, and the intractable vice-admiral had ceased from troubling, yet the omens of the pious enterprise were no less dark and sinister. The company, however, went ashore, raised a cross and heard mass.

At a distance in the woods they saw the signal smoke of Indians, whom Biard lost no time in visiting. Some of them were from a village on the shore, three leagues westward. They urged the French to go with them to their wigwams. The astute savages had learned already how to deal with a Jesuit.

"Our great chief, Asticou, is there. He wishes for baptism. He is very sick. He will die unbaptized. He will burn in hell, and it will be all your fault."

This was enough. Biard embarked in a canoe and they paddled him to the spot, where he found the great chief Asticou in his wigwam, with a heavy cold in the head. Disappointed of his charitable purpose, the priest consoled himself with observing the beauties of the neighboring shore, which seemed to him better fitted than St. Sauveur for the intended settlement. It was a gentle slope, descending to the water, covered with tall grass and backed by rocky hills. It looked southeast upon a harbor where a fleet might ride at anchor, sheltered from the gales by a cluster of islands.

The ship was brought to the spot, and the colonists disembarked. First they planted a cross; then they began their labors, and with their labors their quarrels. La Saussaye, zealous for agriculture, wished to break ground and raise crops immediately. The rest opposed him, wishing first to be housed and fortified. Fleury demanded that the ship should be unladen, and La Saussaye would not consent. Debate ran high, when suddenly all was harmony and the disputants were friends once more in the pacification of a common danger.

Far out at sea, beyond the islands that sheltered their harbor, they saw an approaching sail, and as she drew near, straining their anxious eyes, they could descry the red flags that streamed from her masthead and her stern, then the black muzzles of her cannon—they counted seven on a side—and then the throng of men upon her decks. The wind was brisk and fair; all her sails were set. She came on, writes a spectator, more swiftly than an arrow.

This was the ship of one Samuel Argall, a man of ability and force— one of those compounds of craft and daring in which the age was fruitful. For the rest, he was unscrupulous and grasping. In the spring of 1613 he had achieved a characteristic exploit: the abduction of Pocahontas, that most interesting of young squaws. Sailing up the Potomac, he lured her on board his ship and then carried off the benefactress of the colony a prisoner to Jamestown. Here a young man of family, Rolfe, became enamored of her, married her with more than ordinary ceremony and thus secured a firm alliance between her tribesmen and the English.

Meanwhile, Argall had set forth on another enterprise. With a ship of one hundred and thirty tons, carrying fourteen guns and sixty men, he sailed in May for islands off the coast of Maine to fish, as he says, for cod. He had a more important errand, however. Sir Thomas Dale, governor of Virginia, had commissioned him to expel the French from any settlement they might have made within the limits of King James's patents.

Thick fogs involved him, and when the weather cleared he found himself not far from the Bay of Penobscot. Canoes came out from shore. The Indians climbed the ship's side and, as they gained the deck, greeted the astonished English with an odd pantomime of bows and flourishes, which their hosts thought could have been learned from none but Frenchmen. By signs, too, and by often repeating the word *Norman* (by which they always designated the French), they betrayed

36

the presence of the latter. Argall questioned them as well as his total ignorance of their language would permit, and learned by signs the position and numbers of the colonists. Clearly they were no match for him. Assuring the Indians that the Normans were his friends and that he longed to see them, he retained one of the visitors as a guide, dismissed the rest with presents and shaped his course for Mount Desert.

Now the wild heights rose in view; now the English could see the masts of a small ship anchored in the sound; and now, as they rounded the islands, four white tents were visible on the grassy slope between the water and the woods. They were a gift from the Queen to Madame de Guercheville and her missionaries. Argall's men prepared for fight, while their Indian guide, amazed, broke into a howl of lamentation.

On shore all was confusion. Bailleul, the pilot, went to reconnoiter and ended by hiding among the islands. La Saussaye lost presence of mind and did nothing for defense. La Motte, his lieutenant, with Captain Fleury, an ensign, a sergeant, the Jesuit Du Thet and a few of the bravest men hastened on board the vessel but had no time to cast loose her cables. Argall bore down on them, with a furious din of drums and trumpets, showed his broadside and replied to their hail with a volley of cannon and musket shot.

"Fire! Fire!" screamed Fleury. But there was no gunner to obey, till Du Thet seized and applied the match. "The cannon made as much noise as the enemy's," writes Biard, but as the inexperienced artillerist forgot to aim the piece, no other result ensued. Another storm of musketry, and Brother Gilbert du Thet rolled helpless on the deck.

The French ship was mute. The English plied her for a time with shot, then lowered a boat and boarded. Under the awnings which covered her, dead and wounded men lay strewn about her deck, and among them the brave lay brother, smothering in his blood. He had his wish, for on leaving France he had prayed with uplifted hands that he might not return but perish in that holy enterprise. Like the Order of which he was a humble member, he was a compound of qualities in appearance contradictory. La Motte, sword in hand, showed fight to the last, and won the esteem of his captors.

The English landed without meeting any show of resistance and ranged at will among the tents, the piles of baggage and stores and the buildings and defenses newly begun. Argall asked for the commander, but La Saussaye had fled to the woods. The crafty Englishman seized his chests, caused the locks to be picked, searched till he found the royal letters and commissions, withdrew them, replaced everything else as he had found it and again closed the lids.

In the morning La Saussaye, between the English and starvation, preferred the former and issued from his hiding place. Argall received him with studious courtesy. That country, he said, belonged to his master, King James. Doubtless they had authority from their own sovereign for thus encroaching upon it, and for his part, he was prepared to yield all respect to the commissions of the King of France, that the peace between the two nations might not be disturbed. Therefore he prayed that the commissions might be shown to him.

La Saussaye opened his chests. The royal signature was nowhere to be found. At this Argall's courtesy changed to wrath. He denounced the Frenchmen as robbers and pirates who deserved the gallows, removed their property on board his ship and spent the afternoon in dividing it among his followers. The disconsolate French remained on the scene of their woes, where the greedy sailors as they came ashore would snatch from them now a cloak, now a hat and now a doublet, till the unfortunate colonists were left half naked. In other respects the English treated their captives well—except two of them, whom they flogged. Argall, whom Biard, after recounting his knavery, calls "a gentleman of noble courage," having gained his point, returned to his former courtesy.

But how to dispose of the prisoners? Fifteen of them, including La Saussaye and the Jesuit Masse, were turned adrift in an open boat, at the mercy of the wilderness and the sea. Nearly all were landsmen, but while their unpracticed hands were struggling with the oars, they were joined among the islands by the fugitive pilot and his boat's crew. Worn and half starved, the united bands made their perilous way eastward, stopping from time to time to hear mass, make a procession or catch codfish. Thus sustained in the spirit and in the flesh, cheered too by the Indians, who proved fast friends in need, they crossed the Bay of Fundy, doubled Cape Sable and followed the southern coast of Nova Scotia, till they happily fell in with two French trading vessels, which bore them in safety to St. Malo.

Meanwhile, Father Biard, with his fourteen companions in misfortune, were prisoners on board Argall's ship and the prize, headed for Virginia. Throughout the voyage the prisoners were soothed with flattering tales of the benignity of Governor Dale, of his love for the French and his respect for the memory of Henry IV, to whom, they were told, he was much beholden for countenance and favor.

On their landing at Jamestown, this consoling picture was reversed. The governor fumed and blustered, talked of halter and gallows and declared that he would hang them all. In vain Argall remonstrated, urging that he had pledged his word for their lives. Dale, outraged by their invasion of British territory, was deaf to all appeals till Argall, driven to extremity, displayed the stolen commissions and proclaimed his stratagem, of which the French themselves had to that moment been ignorant. As they were accredited by their government, their lives at least were safe. Yet the wrath of Sir Thomas Dale still burned high. He summoned his council and they resolved promptly to wipe off all stain of French intrusion from shores which King James claimed as his own.

Their action was utterly unauthorized; the two kingdoms were at peace. But Argall's ship, the captured ship of La Saussaye and another smaller vessel were at once equipped and dispatched on an errand of havoc. Argall commanded, and Biard, with Quentin and several others of the prisoners, were embarked with him. They shaped their course first for Mount Desert. Here they landed, leveled La Saussaye's unfinished defenses, cut down the French cross and planted one of their own in its place. Next they sought out the island of St. Croix, seized a quantity of salt and razed to the ground all that remained of the dilapidated buildings of De Monts.

They crossed the Bay of Fundy to Port Royal, guided by an Indian chief, says Biard—an improbable assertion, since the natives of these coasts hated the English as much as they loved the French, and now well knew the designs of the former. The unfortunate settlement was tenantless. Biencourt, with some of his men, was on a visit to neighboring bands of Indians, while the rest were reaping in the fields on the river, two leagues above the fort. Succor from Poutrincourt had arrived during the summer. The magazines were by no means empty, and there were cattle, horses and hogs in adjacent fields and enclosures. Exulting at their good fortune, Argall's men butchered or carried off the animals, ransacked the buildings, plundered them even to the locks and bolts of the doors and then laid the whole in ashes.

Having demolished Port Royal, the marauders went in boats up the river to the fields where the reapers were at work. These fled and took refuge behind the ridge of a hill, from which they gazed helplessly on the destruction of their harvest. Biard approached them and, according to the declaration of Poutrincourt made and attested before the Admiralty of Guienne, tried to persuade them to desert his son, Biencourt, and take service with Argall. The reply of one of the men gave little encouragement for further parlay:

"Begone, or I will split your head with this hatchet."

The English had scarcely re-embarked when Biencourt arrived with his followers and beheld the scene of destruction. Hopelessly outnumbered, he tried to lure Argall and some of his officers into an ambuscade, but they would not be entrapped. Biencourt now asked for an interview. The word of honor was mutually given, and the two chiefs met in a meadow not far from the demolished dwellings. An anonymous English writer says that Biencourt offered to transfer his allegiance to King James, on condition of being permitted to remain at Port Royal and carry on the fur trade under a guaranty of English protection, but that Argall would not listen to his overtures. The interview proved a stormy one.

His work done and, as he thought, the French settlements of Acadia effectually blotted out, Argall set sail for Virginia on the thirteenth of November. Scarcely was he at sea when a storm scattered the vessels. Of the smallest of the three nothing was ever heard. Argall, severely buffeted, reached his port in safety, having first, it is said, compelled the Dutch at Manhattan to acknowledge for a time the sovereignty of King James.

The captured ship of La Saussaye, with Biard and his colleague Quentin on board, was forced to yield to the fury of the western gales and bear away for the Azores. To Biard the change of destination was not unwelcome. He stood in fear of the truculent governor of Virginia, and his tempest-rocked slumbers were haunted with unpleasant visions of a rope's end. It seems that some of the French at Port Royal, disappointed in their hope of hanging him, had commended him to Sir Thomas Dale as a proper subject for the gallows, drawing up a paper, signed by six of them, containing allegations of a nature well fitted to kindle the wrath of that vehement official.

The vessel was commanded by Turnel, Argall's lieutenant, apparently an officer of merit, a scholar and linguist. He had treated his prisoner with great kindness, because, says the latter, "he esteemed and loved him for his naïve simplicity and ingenuous candor." But of late, thinking his kindness misplaced, he had changed it for extreme coldness, preferring, in the words of Biard himself, "to think that the Jesuit had lied, rather than so many who accused him."

Water ran low, provisions began to fail, and they eked out their meager supply by butchering the horses taken at Port Royal. At length they came within sight of Fayal, when a new terror seized the minds of the two Jesuits. Might not the Englishmen fear that their prisoners would denounce them to the fervent Catholics of that island as pirates and sacrilegious kidnapers of priests? From such hazard the escape was obvious. What more simple than to drop the priests into the sea?

In truth, the English had no little dread of the results of conference between the Jesuits and the Portuguese authorities of Fayal, but the conscience or humanity of Turnel revolted at the expedient which awakened such apprehension in the troubled mind of Biard. He contented himself with requiring that the two priests should remain hidden while the ship lay off the port. Biard does not say that he enforced the demand either by threats or by the imposition of oaths. He and his companion, however, rigidly complied with it, lying close in the hold or under the boats while suspicious officials searched the ship.

Once more at sea, Turnel shaped his course for home, having with some difficulty gained a supply of water and provisions at Fayal. All was now harmony between him and his prisoners. When he reached Pembroke, in Wales, the appearance of the vessel—a French craft in English hands—again drew upon him the suspicion of piracy. The Jesuits, dangerous witnesses among the Catholics of Fayal, could at the worst do little harm with the vice-admiral at Pembroke. To him, therefore, he led the prisoners in the sable garb of their Order, now much the worse for wear, and commended them as persons without reproach, "wherein," adds the modest father, "he spoke the truth."

The result of their evidence was that Turnel was henceforth treated not as a pirate but, according to his deserts, as an honorable gentleman. This interview led to a meeting with certain dignitaries of the Anglican Church, who, much interested in an encounter with Jesuits in their robes, were filled, says Biard, with wonder and admiration at what they were told of their conduct.

Biard was sent to Dover and thence to Calais, returning, perhaps, to the tranquil honors of his chair of theology at Lyons. La Saussaye, La Motte, Fleury and other prisoners were at various times sent from Virginia to England, and ultimately to France. Madame de Guercheville, her pious designs crushed in the bud, seems to have gained no further satisfaction than the restoration of the vessel. The French ambassador complained of the outrage, but answer was postponed, and in the troubled state of France the matter appears to have been dropped.

In spite of these reverses, the French kept hold on Acadia. Biencourt rebuilt Port Royal, partially at least, while winter after winter the smoke of fur traders' huts curled into the still, sharp air of these frosty wilds, till at length, with happier auspices, plans of settlement were resumed.

Thus, in an obscure stroke of lawless violence, began the strife of France and England, Protestantism and Rome, which for a century and a half shook the struggling communities of North America and closed at last in the memorable triumph on the Plains of Abraham.

CHAPTER 3

~~~~~~

Champlain at Quebec

C HAMPLAIN WAS IN PARIS, BUT HIS UNQUIET
thoughts turned westward. He was enamored of the New World,
whose rugged charms had seized his fancy and his heart. As explorers
of Arctic seas have pined in their repose for polar ice and snow, so
did his restless thoughts revert to the fog-wrapped coasts, the piny
odors of forests, the noise of waters, the sharp and piercing sunlight
so dear to his remembrance. He longed to unveil the mystery of that
boundless wilderness and plant the Catholic faith and the power of
France amid its ancient barbarism.

Five years before, he had explored the St. Lawrence as far as the
rapids above Montreal. On its banks, as he thought, was the true
site for a settlement—a fortified post from which the waters of the
vast interior might be traced back towards their sources and a western
route discovered to China and Japan. For the fur trade, too, the innumerable streams that descended to the great river might all be
closed against foreign intrusion by a single fort at some commanding
point and made tributary to a rich and permanent commerce while
countless savage tribes, in the bondage of Satan, might by the same
avenues be reached and redeemed.

De Monts embraced his views and, fitting out two ships, gave command of one to the elder Pontgravé, of the other to Champlain. The
former was to trade with the Indians and bring back the cargo of
furs which, it was hoped, would meet the expense of the voyage. To
Champlain fell the harder task of settlement and exploration.

43

Pontgravé, laden with goods for the Indian trade of Tadoussac, sailed from Honfleur on the fifth of April, 1608. Champlain, with men, arms and stores for the colony, followed eight days later. On the fifteenth of May he was on the Grand Bank; on the thirtieth he passed Gaspé, and on the third of June neared Tadoussac. No living thing was to be seen. He anchored, lowered a boat and rowed into the port, round the rocky point at the southeast, then called La Pointe de Tous les Diables, from the fury of its winds and currents. There was life enough within, and more than he cared to find. In the still anchorage under the cliffs lay Pontgravé's vessel, and at her side another ship, which proved to be a Basque fur trader.

Pontgravé, arriving a few days before, had found himself anticipated by the Basques, who were busied in a brisk trade with bands of Indians cabined along the borders of the cove. He displayed the royal letters and commanded a cessation of the prohibited traffic, but the Basques proved refractory, declared that they would trade in spite of the King, fired on Pontgravé with cannon and musketry, wounded him and two of his men and killed a third. They then boarded his vessel and carried away all his cannon, small arms and ammunition, saying that they would restore them when they had finished their trade and were ready to return home.

Champlain found his comrade on shore, in a disabled condition. The Basques, though still strong enough to make fight, were alarmed for the consequences of their conduct and anxious to come to terms. A peace, therefore, was signed on board their vessel. All differences were referred to the judgment of the French courts, harmony was restored and the choleric strangers betook themselves to catching whales.

Peace being established with the Basques, and the wounded Pontgravé busied, as far as might be, in transferring to the hold of his ship the rich lading of the Indian canoes, Champlain spread his sails and again held his course up the St. Lawrence. Far to the south, in sun and shadow, slumbered the woody mountains from which fell the countless springs of the St. John, behind tenantless shores.

Above the point of the Island of Orleans a constriction of the vast channel narrows it to less than a mile, with the green heights of Point Levi on one side and on the other the cliffs of Quebec. Here a small stream, the St. Charles, enters the St. Lawrence, and in the angle between them rises the promontory, on two sides a natural fortress. Between the cliffs and the river lay a strand covered with walnuts and other trees. From this strand, by a rough passage gullied downward from the place where Prescott Gate now guards the way, one might climb the heights to the broken plateau above. By a gradual ascent the rock sloped upward to its highest summit, Cape Diamond, looking down on the St. Lawrence from a height of three hundred and fifty feet. Here the citadel now stands. Then the fierce sun fell on the bald, baking rock, with its crisped mosses and parched lichens.

On the strand between the water and the cliffs Champlain's ax-men fell to their work. They were pioneers of an advancing host —advancing, it is true, with feeble and uncertain progress—of priests, soldiers, peasants, feudal scutcheons, royal insignia. Not the Middle Age, but engendered of it by the stronger life of modern centralization, sharply stamped with a parental likeness, heir to parental weakness and parental force.

In a few weeks a pile of wooden buildings rose on the brink of the St. Lawrence, on or near the site of the market place of the Lower Town of Quebec. A strong wooden wall, surmounted by a gallery loopholed for musketry, enclosed three buildings, containing quarters for himself and his men, together with a courtyard from one side of which rose a tall dovecot, like a belfry. A moat surrounded the whole, and two or three small cannon were planted on salient platforms towards the river. There was a large storehouse near at hand, and a part of the adjacent ground was laid out as a garden.

In this garden Champlain was one morning directing his laborers when Têtu, his pilot, approached him with an anxious countenance and muttered a request to speak with him in private. Champlain assenting, they withdrew to the neighboring woods, where the pilot unburdened himself of his secret. One Antoine Natel, a locksmith, smitten by conscience or fear, had revealed to him a conspiracy to murder his commander and deliver Quebec into the hands of the Basques and Spaniards then at Tadoussac. Another locksmith named Duval was author of the plot and, with the aid of three accomplices, had befooled or frightened nearly all the company into taking part in it. Each was assured that he should make his fortune, and all were mutually pledged to poniard the first betrayer of the secret. The critical point of their enterprise was the killing of Champlain. Some were for strangling him, some for raising a false alarm in the night and shooting him as he came out from his quarters.

Having heard the pilot's story, Champlain remained in the woods and asked his informant to find Antoine Natel and bring him to the spot. Natel soon appeared, trembling with excitement and fear, and a close examination left no doubt of the truth of his statement. A small vessel, built by Pontgravé at Tadoussac, had lately arrived and orders were now given that it should anchor close at hand. On board was a young man in whom confidence could be placed. Champlain sent him two bottles of wine, with a direction to tell the four ringleaders that they had been given him by his Basque friends at Tadoussac and to invite them to share the good cheer. They came aboard in the evening and were seized and secured.

It was ten o'clock and most of the men on shore were asleep. They were wakened suddenly and told of the discovery of the plot and the arrest of the ringleaders. Pardon was then promised them, and they were dismissed again to their beds, greatly relieved, for they had lived in trepidation, each fearing the other. Duval's body, swinging from a gibbet, gave wholesome warning to those he had seduced, and his head was displayed on a pike, from the highest roof of the buildings, food for birds and a lesson to sedition.

On the eighteenth of September, Pontgravé set sail for home, leaving Champlain with twenty-eight men to hold Quebec through the winter. Three weeks later and shores and hills glowed with gay prognostics of approaching desolation—the yellow and scarlet of the maples, the deep purple of the ash, the garnet hue of young oaks, the crimson of the tupelo at the water's edge and the golden plumage of birch saplings in the fissures of the cliff. It was a short-lived beauty. The forest dropped its festal robes. Shriveled and faded, they rustled to the earth. The crystal air and laughing sun of October passed away, and November sank upon the shivering waste, chill and somber as the tomb.

A roving band of Montagnais had built their huts near the buildings and were busying themselves with their autumn eel fishery, on which they greatly relied to sustain their miserable lives through the winter. Their slimy harvest being gathered and duly smoked and dried, they gave it for safekeeping to Champlain and set out to hunt beavers. It was deep in the winter before they came back, reclaimed their eels, built their birch cabins and disposed themselves for a life of ease, until famine or their enemies should put an end to their enjoyments.

These were by no means without alloy. While, gorged with food, they lay dozing on piles of branches in their smoky huts, where through the crevices of the thin birch bark streamed in a cold capable at times of congealing mercury, their slumbers were beset with nightmare visions of Iroquois forays, scalpings, butcherings and burnings. As dreams were their oracles, the camp was wild with fright. They sent out no scouts and placed no guard, but with each repetition of these nocturnal terrors they came flocking in a body to beg admission within the fort. The women and children were allowed to enter the yard and remain during the night, while anxious fathers and jealous husbands shivered in the darkness without.

On one occasion a group of wretched beings was seen on the farther bank of the St. Lawrence, like wild animals driven by famine to the borders of the settler's clearing. The river was full of drifting ice, and there was no crossing without risk of life. The Indians, in their desperation, made the attempt. Midway their canoes were ground to atoms among the tossing masses. Agile as wildcats, they all leaped upon a huge raft of ice, the squaws carrying their children on their shoulders, a feat at which Champlain marveled when he saw their starved and emaciated condition. Here they began a wail of despair, when happily the pressure of other masses thrust the sheet of ice against the northern shore. They landed and soon made their appearance at the fort, worn to skeletons and horrible to look upon. The French gave them food, which they devoured with a frenzied avidity and, unappeased, fell upon a dead dog left on the snow by Champlain for two months past as a bait for foxes. They broke this carrion into fragments and thawed and devoured it, to the disgust of the spectators, who tried vainly to prevent them.

This was but a severe access of the periodical famine which during winter was a normal condition of the Algonquin tribes of Acadia and the Lower St. Lawrence, who unlike the cognate tribes of New

47

England never tilled the soil or made any reasonable provision against the time of need.

One would gladly know how the founders of Quebec spent the long hours of their first winter, but on this point the only man among them, perhaps, who could write has not thought it necessary to enlarge. He himself beguiled his leisure with trapping foxes, or hanging a dead dog from a tree and watching the hungry martens in their efforts to reach it. Towards the close of winter all found abundant employment in nursing themselves or their neighbors, for the inevitable scurvy broke out with virulence. At the middle of May only eight men of the twenty-eight were alive, and of these half were suffering from disease.

This wintry purgatory wore away. The icy stalactites that hung from the cliffs fell crashing to the earth; the clamor of wild geese was heard; the bluebirds appeared in the naked woods; the water willows were covered with their soft caterpillarlike blossoms; the twigs of the swamp maple were flushed with ruddy bloom; the ash hung out its black tufts; the shadbush seemed a wreath of snow; the white stars of the bloodrot gleamed among dank, fallen leaves; and in the young grass of the wet meadows the marsh marigolds shone like spots of gold.

Great was the joy of Champlain when, on the fifth of June, he saw a sailboat rounding the Point of Orleans, betokening that the spring had brought with it the longed-for succors. A son-in-law of Pontgravé, named Marais, was on board and he reported that Pontgravé was then at Tadoussac, where he had lately arrived. Champlain hastened there, to take counsel with his comrade. His constitution or his courage had defied the scurvy. They met, and it was determined between them that while Pontgravé remained in charge of Quebec, Champlain should enter at once on his long-meditated explorations, by which, like La Salle seventy years later, he had good hope of finding a way to China.

But there was a lion in the path. The Indian tribes, to whom peace was unknown, infested with their scalping parties the streams and pathways of the forest and increased tenfold its inseparable risks. The after career of Champlain gives abundant proof that he was more than indifferent to all such chances. Yet now an expedient for evading them offered itself, so consonant with his instincts that he was glad to accept it.

During the last autumn a young chief from the banks of the then unknown Ottawa had been at Quebec and, amazed at what he saw, he had begged Champlain to join him in the spring against his enemies. These enemies were a formidable race of savages—the Iroquois, or Five Confederate Nations, who dwelt in fortified villages within limits now embraced by the state of New York, and who were a terror to all the surrounding forests. They were deadly foes of their kindred the Hurons, who dwelt on the lake which bears their name, and were allies of Algonquin bands on the Ottawa. All alike were tillers of the soil, living at ease when compared with the famished Algonquins of the Lower St. Lawrence.

By joining these Hurons and Algonquins against their Iroquois enemies, Champlain might make himself the indispensable ally and leader of the tribes of Canada and at the same time fight his way to discovery in regions which otherwise were barred against him.

But the middle of June came and passed, and the expected warriors from the upper country did not come. This delay seems to have given Champlain little concern, for without waiting longer he set out with no better allies than a band of Montagnais. As he moved up the St. Lawrence, however, he saw thickly clustered in the bordering forest the lodges of an Indian camp and, landing, found his Huron and Algonquin allies. Few of them had ever seen a white man and they surrounded the steel-clad strangers in speechless wonder.

Champlain asked for their chief, and the staring throng moved with him towards a lodge where sat not one chief but two, for each band had its own. There were feasting, smoking and speeches. The needful ceremonies over, all descended together to Quebec, for the strangers were bent on seeing those wonders of architecture the fame of which had pierced the recesses of their forests.

Arriving, they feasted their eyes and glutted their appetites, yelped consternation at the sharp explosions of the arquebuse and the roar of the cannon, pitched their camps and bedecked themselves for their war dance. In the still night their fire glared against the black and jagged cliff, and the fierce red light fell on tawny limbs convulsed with frenzied gestures and ferocious stampings; on contorted visages, hideous with paint; on brandished weapons, stone war clubs, stone hatchets and stone-pointed lances, while the drum kept up its hollow boom and the air was split with mingled yells.

The war feast followed, and then all embarked together. Champlain was in a small shallop, carrying besides himself eleven men of Pontgravé's party, including his son-in-law Marais and the pilot La Routte. They were armed with the arquebuse—a matchlock or firelock somewhat like the later carbine, and from its shortness not ill suited for use in the forest. On the twenty-eighth of June they spread their sails and held their course against the current, while around them the river was alive with canoes and hundreds of naked arms plied the paddle with a steady, measured sweep.

They crossed the Lake of St. Peter, threaded the devious channels among its many islands and reached at last the mouth of the Rivière des Iroquois, since called the Richelieu, or the St. John. Here, probably on the site of the town of Sorel, the leisurely warriors encamped for two days, hunted, fished and took their ease, regaling their allies with venison and wildfowl. They quarreled, too; three fourths of their number seceded, took to their canoes in dudgeon and paddled towards their homes, while the rest pursued their course up the broad and placid stream.

Walls of verdure stretched on left and right. Now aloft in the lonely air rose the cliffs of Belœil, and now before them, framed in circling forests, the Basin of Chambly spread its tranquil mirror, glittering in the sun.

The shallop outsailed the canoes. Champlain, leaving his allies behind, crossed the basin and tried to pursue its course, but as he listened in the stillness, the unwelcome noise of rapids reached his ear, and by glimpses through the dark foliage of the Islets of St. John, he could see the gleam of snowy foam and the flash of hurrying waters. Leaving the boat by the shore in charge of four men, he went with Marais, La Routte and five others to explore the wild before him. They pushed their way through the damps and shadows of the wood, through thickets and tangled vines, over mossy rocks and moldering logs. Still the hoarse surging of the rapids followed them. Parting the screen of foliage, they looked out upon the river and saw it thick set with rocks where, plunging over ledges, gurgling under drift logs, darting along clefts and boiling in chasms, the angry waters filled the solitude with monotonous ravings.

Champlain retraced his steps. He had learned the value of an Indian's word. His allies had promised him that his boat could pass unobstructed throughout the whole journey. "It afflicted me," he says, "and troubled me exceedingly to be obliged to return without having seen so great a lake, full of fair islands and bordered with the fine countries which they had described to me."

When he reached the boat he found the whole savage crew gathered at the spot. He mildly rebuked their bad faith but added that though they had deceived him, he would fulfill his pledge. To that end he directed Marais, with the boat and the greater part of the men, to return to Quebec, while he, with two who offered to follow him, should proceed in the Indian canoes.

The warriors lifted their canoes from the water and bore them on their shoulders half a league through the forest to the smoother stream above. Here the chiefs made a muster of their forces, counting twenty-four canoes and sixty warriors. All embarked again and advanced once more by marsh, meadow, forest and scattered islands.

Late in the day they landed and drew up their canoes, ranging them closely side by side. Some stripped sheets of bark to cover their camp sheds; others gathered wood, the forest being full of dead, dry trees; others felled the living trees for a barricade. They seem to have had steel axes, obtained by barter from the French, for in less than two hours they had made a strong defensive work in the form of a half circle, open on the river side, where their canoes lay on the strand, and large enough to enclose all their huts and sheds. Some of their number had gone forward as scouts and, returning, reported no signs of an enemy. This was the extent of their precaution, for they placed no guard but in full security stretched themselves to sleep.

They had not forgotten, however, to consult their oracle in the woods. The medicine man pitched his magic lodge, formed of a small stack of poles planted in a circle and brought together at the tops like stacked muskets. Over these he placed the filthy deerskins which served him for a robe and, creeping in at a narrow opening, hid himself from view. Crouched in a ball upon the earth, he invoked the

51

spirits in mumbling inarticulate tones, while his naked auditory, squatted on the ground like apes, listened in wonder and awe.

Suddenly the lodge moved, rocking with violence to and fro—by the power of the spirits, as the Indians thought, while Champlain could plainly see the tawny fist of the medicine man shaking the poles. They begged him to keep a watchful eye on the peak of the lodge, from which fire and smoke would presently issue, but with the best efforts of his vision, he discovered none.

Meanwhile the medicine man was seized with such convulsions that, when his divination was over, his naked body streamed with perspiration. In loud, clear tones, and in an unknown tongue, he invoked the spirit, who was understood to be present in the form of a stone and whose feeble and squeaking accents were heard at intervals, like the wail of a young puppy.

In this manner they consulted the spirit—as Champlain thinks, the Devil—at all their camps. His replies, for the most part, seem to have given them great content, yet they took other measures, of which the military advantages were less questionable. The principal chief gathered bundles of sticks and, without wasting his breath, stuck them in the earth in a certain order, calling each by the name of some warrior, a few taller than the rest representing the subordinate chiefs. Thus was indicated the position which each was to hold in the expected battle. All gathered round and attentively studied the sticks, ranged like a child's wooden soldiers or the pieces on a chessboard. Then, with no further instruction, they formed their ranks, broke them and re-formed them again and again with excellent alacrity and skill.

The canoes advanced, the river widening as they went. Great islands appeared, leagues in extent—Isle à la Motte, Long Island, Grande Isle. Channels where ships might float and broad reaches of water stretched between them, and Champlain entered the lake which preserves his name to posterity. Cumberland Head was passed, and from the opening of the great channel between Grande Isle and the main he could look forth on the wilderness sea. Edged with woods, the tranquil flood spread southward beyond the sight. Far on the left rose the forest ridges of the Green Mountains, and on the right the Adirondacks.

The progress of the party was becoming dangerous. They changed their mode of advance and moved only in the night. All day they lay close in the depth of the forest, sleeping, lounging, smoking tobacco of their own raising and beguiling the hours, no doubt, with the shallow banter and obscene jesting with which knots of Indians were wont to amuse their leisure. At twilight they embarked again, paddling their cautious way till the eastern sky began to redden. Their goal was the rocky promontory where Fort Ticonderoga was long afterward built. From this they would pass the outlet of Lake George and launch their canoes again on that Como of the wilderness whose waters, limpid as a fountainhead, stretched far southward between their flanking mountains. Landing at the future site of Fort William Henry, they would carry their canoes through the forest to the river Hudson and, descending it, attack perhaps some outlying town of the Mohawks.

On the morning of the twenty-ninth of July, after paddling all night, they hid as usual in the forest on the western shore, apparently between Crown Point and Ticonderoga. The warriors stretched themselves to their slumbers, and Champlain, after walking till nine or ten o'clock through the surrounding woods, returned to take his repose on a pile of spruce boughs.

Sleeping, he dreamed a dream wherein he beheld the Iroquois drowning in the lake, and trying to rescue them, he was told by his Algonquin friends that they were good for nothing and had better be left to their fate. For some time past he had been beset every morning by his superstitious allies, eager to learn about his dreams, and to this moment his unbroken slumbers had failed to furnish the desired prognostics. The announcement of this auspicious vision filled the crowd with joy, and at nightfall they embarked, flushed with anticipated victories.

It was ten o'clock in the evening when, near a projecting point of land which was probably Ticonderoga, they descried dark objects in motion on the lake before them. These were a flotilla of Iroquois canoes, heavier and slower than theirs, for they were made of oak bark. Each party saw the other, and mingled war cries pealed over the darkened water. The Iroquois, who were near the shore, having no stomach for an aquatic battle, landed and made the night hideous with their clamors while they began to barricade themselves. Champlain could see them in the woods, laboring like beavers, hacking down trees with iron axes taken from the Canadian tribes in war and with stone hatchets of their own making. The allies remained on the lake, a bowshot from the hostile barricade, their canoes made fast together by poles lashed across.

All night they danced with as much vigor as the frailty of their vessels would permit, their throats making amends for the enforced restraint of their limbs. It was agreed on both sides that the fight should be deferred till daybreak. Meanwhile a commerce of abuse, sarcasm, menace and boasting gave unceasing exercise to the lungs and fancy of the combatants—"much," says Champlain, "like the besiegers and besieged in a beleaguered town."

As day approached he and his two followers put on the light armor of the time. Champlain wore the doublet and long hose then in vogue. Over the doublet he buckled on a breastplate and probably a backpiece, while his thighs were protected by cuisses of steel and his head by a plumed casque. Across his shoulder hung the strap of his bandoleer, or ammunition box; at his side was his sword, and in his hand his arquebuse. Such was the equipment of this ancient Indian fighter, whose exploits date eleven years before the landing of the Puritans at Plymouth and sixty-six years before King Philip's War.

Each of the three Frenchmen was in a separate canoe, and as it grew light they kept themselves hidden, either by lying at the bottom or covering themselves with an Indian robe. The canoes approached the shore, and all landed without opposition at some distance from the Iroquois, whom they presently could see filing out of their barricade—tall, strong men, some two hundred in number, the boldest and fiercest warriors of North America. They advanced through the forest with a steadiness which excited the admiration of Champlain. Among them could be seen three chiefs, made conspicuous by their tall plumes. Some bore shields of wood and hide, and some were covered with a kind of armor made of rough twigs interlaced with a vegetable fiber supposed by Champlain to be cotton.

The allies, growing anxious, called with loud cries for their champion and opened their ranks that he might pass to the front. He did so and, advancing before his red companions in arms, stood revealed

54

to the gaze of the Iroquois, who, beholding the warlike apparition in their path, stared in mute amazement.

"I looked at them," says Champlain, "and they looked at me. When I saw them getting ready to shoot their arrows at us, I leveled my arquebuse, which I had loaded with four balls, and aimed straight at one of the three chiefs. The shot brought down two, and wounded another. On this, our Indians set up such a yelling that one could not have heard a thunderclap, and all the while the arrows flew thick on both sides. The Iroquois were greatly astonished and frightened to see two of their men killed so quickly, in spite of their arrow-proof armor. As I was reloading, one of my companions fired a shot from the woods, which so increased their astonishment that, seeing their chiefs dead, they abandoned the field and fled into the depth of the forest."

The allies dashed after them. Some of the Iroquois were killed, and more were taken. Camp, canoes, provisions, all were abandoned, and many weapons flung down in the panic flight. The victory was complete.

At night the victors led out one of the prisoners, told him that he was to die by fire and ordered him to sing his death song if he dared. Then they began the torture and presently scalped their victim alive, when Champlain, sickening at the sight, begged leave to shoot him. They refused, and he turned away in anger and disgust, on which they called him back and told him to do as he pleased. He turned again, and a shot from his arquebuse put the wretch out of misery.

The scene filled him with horror. But a few months later, on the Place de la Grève at Paris, he might have witnessed tortures equally revolting and equally vindictive, inflicted on the regicide Ravaillac by the sentence of grave and learned judges.

The allies made a prompt retreat from the scene of their triumph. Three or four days brought them to the mouth of the Richelieu. Here they separated. The Hurons and Algonquins made for the Ottawa, their homeward route, each with a share of prisoners for future torments. At parting, they invited Champlain to visit their towns and aid them again in their wars, an invitation which this paladin of the woods failed not to accept.

The companions now remaining to him were the Montagnais. In

their camp on the Richelieu, one of them dreamed that a war party of Iroquois was close upon them. In a torrent of rain they left their huts, paddled in dismay to the islands above the Lake of St. Peter and hid themselves all night in the rushes. In the morning they took heart, emerged from their hiding places, descended to Quebec and went to Tadoussac, where Champlain accompanied them. Here the squaws, stark naked, swam out to the canoes to receive the heads of the dead Iroquois and, hanging them from their necks, danced in triumph along the shore. One of the heads and a pair of arms were then bestowed on Champlain—touching memorials of gratitude which, however, he was by no means to keep for himself, but to present to the King.

Thus did New France rush into collision with the redoubted warriors of the Five Nations. Here was the beginning, and in some measure doubtless the cause, of a long suite of murderous conflicts, bearing havoc and flame to generations yet unborn.

CHAPTER 4

~~~~~~

War, Trade and Discovery

THERE IS AN ISLAND IN THE ST. LAWRENCE NEAR the mouth of the Richelieu. On the nineteenth of June, 1610, it was swarming with busy and clamorous savages—Champlain's Montagnais allies, cutting down the trees and clearing the ground for dance and a feast. They were hourly expecting the Algonquin warriors and were eager to welcome them with befitting honors.

But suddenly, far out on the river, they saw an advancing canoe. Now on this side, now on that, the flashing paddles urged it forward as if death were on its track, and as it drew near, the Indians on board cried out that the Algonquins were in the forest, a league distant, engaged with a hundred warriors of the Iroquois, who, outnumbered, were fighting savagely within a barricade of trees.

The air was split with shrill outcries. The Montagnais snatched their weapons—shields, bows, arrows, war clubs, sword blades made fast to poles—and ran headlong to their canoes, impeding each other in their haste, screeching to Champlain to follow and invoking with no less vehemence the aid of certain fur traders, just arrived in four boats from below. As it was not their cue to fight, the traders lent the Indians a deaf ear, on which, in disgust and scorn, they paddled off, calling to the recusants that they were women, fit for nothing but to make war on beaver skins.

Champlain and four of his men were in the canoes. They shot across the intervening water, and as their prows grated on the pebbles each warrior flung down his paddle, snatched his weapons and ran

57

into the woods. The five Frenchmen followed, striving vainly to keep pace with the naked, light-limbed rabble bounding like shadows through the forest.

They quickly disappeared. Even their shrill cries grew faint, till Champlain and his men, discomforted and vexed, found themselves deserted in the midst of a swamp. The day was sultry, the forest air heavy, close and filled with hosts of mosquitoes "so thick," says the chief sufferer, "that we could scarcely draw breath, and it was wonderful how cruelly they persecuted us."

Through black mud, spongy moss, water knee-deep, over fallen trees, among slimy logs and entangling roots, tripped by vines, lashed by recoiling boughs, panting under their steel headpieces and heavy corselets, the Frenchmen struggled on, bewildered and indignant. At length they descried two Indians running in the distance and shouted to them in desperation that, if they wanted their aid, they must guide them to the enemy.

At length they could hear the yells of the combatants. There was light in the forest before them and they issued into a partial clearing made by the Iroquois axmen near the river. Champlain saw their barricade. Trees were piled into a circular breastwork, trunks, boughs and matted foliage forming a strong defense within which the Iroquois stood savagely at bay. Around them flocked the allies, half hidden in the edges of the forest, like hounds around a wild boar, eager, clamorous, yet afraid to rush in. They had attacked and had met a bloody rebuff. All their hope was now in the French; and when they saw them a yell arose from hundreds of throats that outdid the wilderness voices whence its tones were borrowed—the whoop of the horned owl, the scream of the cougar, the howl of starved wolves on a winter night.

A fierce response pealed from the desperate band within, and amid a storm of arrows from both sides the Frenchmen threw themselves into the fray, firing at random through the fence of trunks, boughs and drooping leaves with which the Iroquois had encircled themselves.

Champlain felt a stone-headed arrow splitting his ear and tearing through the muscles of his neck. He drew it out and, the moment after, did a similar office for one of his men. But the Iroquois had not recovered from their first terror of the arquebuse, and when the mysterious and terrible assailants, clad in steel and armed with thunderbolts, ran up to the barricade, thrust their pieces through the openings and shot death among the crowd within, they could not control their fright but with every report threw themselves flat on the ground. Animated with unwonted valor, the allies, covered by their large shields, began to drag out the felled trees of the barricade, while others under Champlain's direction gathered at the edge of the forest, preparing to close the affair with a final rush.

New actors soon appeared on the scene. These were a boat's crew of the fur traders under a young man of St. Malo, one Des Prairies, who, when he heard the firing, could not resist the impulse to join the fight. On seeing them, Champlain checked the assault, in order, as he says, that the newcomers might have their share in the sport. The traders opened fire, with great zest and no less execution, while the Iroquois, now wild with terror, leaped and writhed to dodge the shot which tore through their frail armor of twigs. Champlain gave the signal. The crowd ran to the barricade, dragged down the boughs or clambered over them and bore themselves, in their own words, "so well and manfully" that, though scratched and torn by the sharp points, they quickly forced an entrance. The French ceased their fire and, followed by a smaller body of Indians, scaled the barricade on the farther side.

Now, amid howlings, shouts and screeches, the work was finished. Some of the Iroquois were cut down as they stood, hewing with their war clubs and foaming like slaughtered tigers. Some climbed the barrier and were killed by the furious crowd without, and some were drowned in the river, while fifteen, the only survivors, were made prisoners.

"By the grace of God," writes Champlain, "behold the battle won!" Drunk with ferocious ecstasy, the conquerors scalped the dead and gathered fagots for the living, while some of the fur traders, too late to bear part in the fight, robbed the carcasses of their blood-bedrenched robes of beaver skin amid the derision of the surrounding Indians.

That night the torture fires blazed along the shore. Champlain saved one prisoner from their clutches, but nothing could save the rest. One body was quartered and eaten. "As for the rest of the prisoners," says Champlain, "they were kept to be put to death by the women and girls, who in this respect are no less inhuman than the men, and, indeed, much more so; for by their subtlety they invent more cruel tortures, and take pleasure in it."

Next day a large band of Hurons appeared at the rendezvous, greatly vexed that they had come too late. The shores were thickly studded with Indian huts and the woods were full of them. Here were warriors of three designations, including many subordinate tribes, and representing three grades of savage society—the Hurons, the Algonquins of the Ottawa and the Montagnais, afterwards styled by a Franciscan friar (than whom few men knew them better) the nobles, the burghers and the peasantry and paupers of the forest. Many of them, from the remote interior, had never before seen a white man, and wrapped like statues in their robes, they stood gazing on the French with a fixed stare of wild and wondering eyes.

Judged by the standard of Indian war, a heavy blow had been struck on the common enemy. Here were hundreds of assembled warriors, yet none thought of following up their success. Elated with unexpected fortune, they danced and sang, then loaded their canoes, hung their scalps on poles, broke up their camps and set out triumphant for their homes.

Champlain had fought their battles and now might claim, on their part, guidance and escort to the distant interior. Why he did not do so is scarcely apparent. There were cares, it seems, connected with the very life of his puny colony which demanded his return to France. Nor were his anxieties lessened by the arrival of a ship from his native town of Brouage, with tidings of the King's assassination. Here was a deathblow to all that had remained of De Monts's credit at court, while that unfortunate nobleman, like his old associate Poutrincourt, was moving with swift strides toward financial ruin. With the revocation of his monopoly, fur traders had swarmed to the St. Lawrence. Tadoussac was full of them, and for that year the trade was spoiled. Far from aiding to support a burdensome enterprise of colonization, it was in itself an occasion of heavy loss.

Champlain bade farewell to his garden at Quebec, where maize, wheat, rye and barley, with vegetables of all kinds and a small vineyard of native grapes—for he was a zealous horticulturist—held forth a promise which he was not to see fulfilled. He left one Du Parc in command, with sixteen men, and, sailing on the eighth of August, arrived at Honfleur with no worse accident than that of running over a sleeping whale near the Grand Bank.

But Champlain was not long in France before he made preparations to return, this time with new representatives of the Church. These were members of the Récollets, a reformed branch of the Order sometimes known as Franciscans of the Strict Observance. Four of their number had been named for a mission to New France—Denis Jamay, Jean Dolbeau, Joseph le Caron and the lay brother Pacifique du Plessis. "They packed their church ornaments," says Champlain, "and we, our luggage." All alike confessed their sins and, embarking at Honfleur, reached Quebec at the end of May, 1615.

Great was the perplexity of the Indians as the apostolic mendicants landed beneath the rock. Their garb was a form of that common to the brotherhood of St. Francis, consisting of a rude garment of coarse gray cloth, girt at the waist with the knotted cord of the Order and furnished with a peaked hood, to be drawn over the head. Their naked feet were shod with wooden sandals more than an inch thick.

Their first care was to choose a site for their convent, near the fortified dwellings and storehouses built by Champlain. This done, they made an altar and celebrated the first mass ever said in Canada. Dolbeau was the officiating priest. All New France kneeled on the bare earth around him, and cannon from the ship and the ramparts hailed the mystic rite. Then, in imitation of the Apostles, they took counsel together and assigned to each his province in the vast field of their mission—to Le Caron the Hurons, and to Dolbeau the Montagnais, while Jamay and Du Plessis were to remain for the present near Quebec.

The Indians were more eager for temporal than for spiritual succor and beset Champlain with clamors for aid against the Iroquois. He and Pontgravé were of one mind. The aid demanded must be given, and that from no motive of the hour but in pursuance of a deliberate policy. It was evident that the innumerable tribes of New France, otherwise divided, were united in a common fear and hate of these formidable bands, who in the strength of their fivefold league spread havoc and desolation through all the surrounding wilds.

It was the aim of Champlain, as of his successors, to persuade the threatened and endangered hordes to live at peace with each other, and to form against the common foe a virtual league of which the French colony would be the heart and the head and which would continually widen with the widening area of discovery. With French soldiers to fight their battles, French priests to baptize them and French traders to supply their increasing wants, their dependence would be complete. They would become assured tributaries to the growth of New France. It was a triple alliance of soldier, priest and trader. The soldier might be a roving knight and the priest a martyr and a saint, but both alike were subserving the interests of that commerce which formed the only solid basis of the colony. The scheme of English colonization made no account of the Indian tribes. In the scheme of French colonization, they were all in all.

In one point the plan was fatally defective, since it involved the deadly enmity of a race whose character and whose power were as yet but ill understood. The Iroquois were the fiercest, boldest, most politic and most ambitious savages to whom the American forest has ever given birth.

The chiefs and warriors met in council—Algonquins of the Ottawa and Hurons from the borders of the great Fresh-Water Sea. Champlain promised to join them with all the men at his command, while they, on their part, were to muster without delay twenty-five hundred warriors for an inroad into the country of the Iroquois. He descended at once to Quebec for needful preparation, but when after a short delay he returned to Montreal, he found to his chagrin a solitude. The wild concourse had vanished. Nothing remained but the skeleton poles of their huts, the smoke of their fires and the refuse of their encampments. Impatient at the delay, they had set out for their villages, and with them had gone Father Joseph le Caron.

Twelve Frenchmen, well armed, had attended him. Summer was at its height, and as the good father's canoe stole along the bosom of the glassy river and he gazed about him on the tawny multitude whose fragile craft covered the water like swarms of gliding insects, he thought, perhaps, of his whitewashed cell in the convent of Brouage, of his book, his table, his rosary and all the narrow routine of that familiar life from which he had awakened to contrasts so startling. That his progress up the Ottawa was far from being an excursion of pleasure is attested by his letters, fragments of which have come down to us.

"It would be hard to tell you," he writes to a friend, "how tired I was with paddling all day, with all my strength, among the Indians; wading the rivers a hundred times and more, through the mud and over the sharp rocks that cut my feet; carrying the canoe and luggage through the woods to avoid the rapids and frightful cataracts; and half starved all the while, for we had nothing to eat but a little *sagamite,* a sort of porridge of water and pounded maize, of which they gave us a very small allowance every morning and night. . . ."

While Le Caron made his way towards the scene of his apostleship through such tribulations, Champlain was following on his track. With two canoes, ten Indians, his interpreter Etienne Brulé and another Frenchman, he pushed up the Ottawa till he reached the Algonquin villages which had formed the term of his former journeying. He passed the two lakes of the Allumettes, and now, for twenty miles, the river stretched before him straight as the bee can fly, deep, narrow and black between its mountain shores. He passed the rapids of the Joachims and the Caribou, the Rocher Capitaine and the Deux Rivières, and reached at length the tributary waters of the Mattawan. He turned to the left, ascended this little stream forty miles or more and, crossing a portage track, well trodden, reached the margin of Lake Nipissing.

The canoes were launched again and glided by leafy shores and verdant islands till at length appeared signs of human life and clusters of bark lodges, half hidden in the vastness of the woods. It was the village of an Algonquin band called the Nipissings, a race so beset with spirits, infested by demons and abounding in magicians that the Jesuits afterwards stigmatized them as "the Sorcerers." In this questionable company Champlain spent two days, feasting on fish, deer and bears. Then, descending to the outlet of the lake, he steered his canoes westward down the current of French River.

Days passed and no sign of man enlivened the rocky desolation.

Hunger was pressing them hard, for the ten gluttonous Indians had devoured already nearly all their provision for the voyage, and they were forced to subsist on the blueberries and wild raspberries that grew abundantly in the meager soil, when suddenly they encountered a troop of three hundred savages, whom, from their strange and startling mode of wearing their hair, Champlain named the *Cheveux Relevés*. "Not one of our courtiers," he says, "takes so much pains in dressing his locks." Here, however, their care of the toilet ended, for though tattooed on various parts of the body, painted and armed with bows, arrows and shields of bison hide, they wore no clothing whatever. Savage as was their aspect, they were busied in the pacific task of gathering blueberries for their winter store. Their demeanor was friendly, and from them the voyager learned that the great lake of the Hurons was close at hand.

Now, far along the western sky, was traced the watery line of that inland ocean, and first of white men except the Friar Le Caron, Champlain beheld the "Mer Douce," the Fresh-Water Sea of the Hurons. Before him, too far for sight, lay the spirit-haunted Manitoulins, and southward spread the vast bosom of the Georgian Bay. For more than a hundred miles his course was along its eastern shores, among islets countless as the sea sands—an archipelago of rocks worn for ages by the wash of waves. He crossed Byng Inlet, Franklin Inlet, Parry Sound and the wider bay of Matchedash, and seems to have landed at the inlet now called Thunder Bay, at the entrance of the Bay of Matchedash and a little west of the Harbor of Penetanguishine.

An Indian trail led inland, through woods and thickets, across broad meadows, over brooks and along the skirts of green acclivities. To the eye of Champlain, accustomed to the desolation he had left behind, it seemed a land of beauty and abundance. He reached at last a broad opening in the forest, with fields of maize, pumpkins ripening in the sun, patches of sunflowers, from the seeds of which the Indians made hair oil, and in the midst the Huron town of Otouacha. In all essential points it resembled that which Cartier, eighty years before, had seen at Montreal—the same triple palisade of crossed and intersecting trunks, and the same long lodges of bark, each containing several families. Here, within an area of thirty or forty miles, was the seat of one of the most remarkable savage communities on the continent.

In Champlain the Hurons saw the champion who was to lead them to victory. There was bountiful feasting in his honor in the great lodge at Otouacha. Other welcome, too, was tendered, of which the Hurons were ever liberal, but which, with all courtesy, was declined by the virtuous Champlain.

Next he went to Carmaron, a league distant, and then to Touaguainchain and Tequenonquihaye, till at length he reached Carhagouha, with its triple palisade thirty-five feet high. Here he found Le Caron. The Indians, eager to do him honor, were building for him a bark lodge in the neighboring forest, fashioned like their own but much smaller. In it the friar made an altar, garnished with those indispensable decorations which he had brought with him through all the vicissitudes of his painful journeying. There, night and day, came a curious multitude to listen to his annunciation of the new doctrine. It was a joyful hour when he saw Champlain approach his hermitage, and the two men embraced like brothers long sundered.

The twelfth of August was a day evermore marked with white in the friar's calendar. Arrayed in priestly vestments, he stood before his simple altar, behind him his little band of Christians—the twelve Frenchmen who had attended him and the two who had followed Champlain. Here stood their devout and valiant chief, and at his side that pioneer of pioneers, Etienne Brulé, the interpreter. The Host was raised aloft; the worshipers kneeled.

Then their rough voices joined in the hymn of praise, *Te deum laudamus,* and a volley of their guns proclaimed the triumph of the faith to the *okies,* the *manitous* and all the brood of anomalous devils who had reigned with undisputed sway in these wild realms of darkness. The brave friar, a true soldier of the Church, had led her forlorn hope into the fastnesses of Hell. Now, with contented heart, he might depart in peace, for he had said the first mass in the country of the Hurons.

CHAPTER 5

Champlain's Last Battle

AFTER LONG MONTHS OF EXPLORATION, AND BAT-
tles on behalf of his Indian allies, a change began in the life
of Champlain. His forest rovings were over. To struggle with savages
and the elements was more congenial with his nature than to nurse
a puny colony into growth and strength, yet to this later task he
gave himself with the same strong devotion.

His difficulties were great. Quebec was half trading factory, half
mission. Its permanent inmates did not exceed fifty or sixty persons
—fur traders, friars and two or three wretched families who had no
inducement and little wish to labor. The fort is facetiously represented
as having two old women for garrison and a brace of hens for sentinels.
All was discord and disorder. Champlain was the nominal commander, but the actual authority was with the merchants, who held
nearly everybody in their pay except the friars. Each was jealous of
the other, but all were united in a common jealousy of Champlain.
The few families whom they brought over were forbidden to trade
with the Indians and compelled to sell the fruits of their labor to the
agents of the company at a low, fixed price, receiving goods in return
at an inordinate valuation.

Some of the merchants were of Rouen, some of St. Malo. Some
were Catholics, some were Huguenots. Hence uneasy bickerings. All
exercise of the Reformed religion, on land or water, was prohibited
within the limits of New France, but the Huguenots set the prohibition
at naught, roaring their heretical psalmody with such vigor from

66

their ships in the river that the unhallowed strains polluted the ears of the Indians on shore. The merchants of Rochelle, who had refused to join the company, carried on a bold illicit traffic along the borders of the St. Lawrence, endangering the colony by selling firearms to the Indians, eluding pursuit or, if hard pressed, showing fight. This was a source of perpetual irritation to the incensed monopolists.

The colony could not increase. The company of merchants, though pledged to promote its growth, did what they could to prevent it. They were fur traders, and the interests of the fur trader are always opposed to those of settlement and population. They feared, too, and with reason, that their monopoly might be suddenly revoked, like that of De Monts, and they thought only of making profit from it while it lasted. They had no permanent stake in the country, nor had the men in their employ, who formed nearly all the scanty population of Canada. Few, if any, of these had brought wives to the colony, and none of them thought of cultivating the soil. They formed a floating population, kept from starving by yearly supplies from France.

Champlain, in his singularly trying position, displayed a mingled zeal and fortitude. He went every year to France, laboring for the interests of the colony. To throw open the trade to all competitors was a measure beyond the wisdom of the times, and he hoped only to bind and regulate the monopoly so as to make it subserve the generous purpose to which he had given himself.

Champlain had succeeded in binding the company of merchants with new and more stringent engagements, and in the vain belief that these might not be wholly broken, he began to conceive fresh hopes for the colony. In this faith he embarked with his wife for Quebec in the spring of 1620, and as the boat drew near the landing the cannon welcomed her to the rock of her banishment. The buildings were falling to ruin; rain entered on all sides. The courtyard, says Champlain, was as squalid and dilapidated as a grange pillaged by soldiers.

Madame de Champlain was still very young. If the Ursuline tradition is to be trusted, the Indians, amazed at her beauty and touched by her gentleness, would have worshiped her as a divinity. Her husband had married her at the age of twelve, when to his horror he presently discovered that she was infected with the heresies of her father, a disguised Huguenot. He addressed himself at once to her conversion, and his pious efforts were something more than successful.

During the four years which she passed in Canada her zeal, it is true, was chiefly exercised in admonishing Indian squaws and catechizing their children, but on her return to France nothing would content her but to become a nun. Champlain refused, but as she was childless he at length consented to a virtual though not formal separation. After his death she gained her wish, became an Ursuline nun, founded a convent of that order at Meaux and died with a reputation almost saintly.

At Quebec, meanwhile, matter grew from bad to worse. The few emigrants, with no inducement to labor, fell into a lazy apathy, lounging about the trading houses, gaming, drinking when drink could be had or roving into the woods on vagabond hunting excursions. The Indians could not be trusted. In the year 1617 they had murdered two men near the end of the Island of Orleans. Frightened at what they had done, and incited perhaps by other causes, the Montagnais and their kindred bands mustered at Three Rivers to the number of eight hundred, resolved to destroy the French. The secret was betrayed and the childish multitude, naked and famishing, became suppliants to their intended victims for the means of life. The French, themselves at the point of starvation, could give little or nothing. An enemy far more formidable awaited them, and now were seen the fruits of Champlain's intermeddling in Indian wars.

In the summer of 1622 the Iroquois descended upon the settlement. A strong party of their warriors hovered about Quebec but, still fearful of the arquebuse, forbore to attack it and assailed the Récollet convent on the St. Charles. The prudent friars had fortified themselves. While some prayed in the chapel, the rest with their Indian converts manned the walls. The Iroquois respected their palisades and demilunes and withdrew after burning two Huron prisoners.

The Viceroy Montmorency, yielding at length to reiterated complaints, suppressed the company of St. Malo and Rouen and conferred the trade of New France, burdened with similar conditions destined to be similarly broken, on two Huguenots, William and Emery de Caen.

The change was a signal for fresh disorders. The enraged monopolists refused to yield. The rival traders filled Quebec with their quarrels, and Champlain, seeing his authority set at naught, was forced to occupy his newly built fort with a band of armed followers. The evil rose to such a pitch that he joined with the Récollets and the better disposed among the colonists in sending one of the friars to lay their grievances before the King. The dispute was compromised by a temporary union of the two companies, together with a variety of *arrêts* and regulations, suited, it was thought, to restore tranquillity.

The Récollets had labored with an unflagging devotion at spiritual labors while the traders fought among themselves. The six friars of their Order—for this was the number which the Calvinist Caen had bound himself to support—had established five distinct missions, extending from Acadia to the borders of Lake Huron, but the field was too vast for their powers. Ostensibly by a spontaneous movement of their own, but in reality, it is probable, under influences brought to bear on them from without, the Récollets applied for the assistance of the Jesuits, who, strong in resources as in energy, would not be compelled to rest on the reluctant support of Huguenots.

Three of their brotherhood—Charles Lalemant, Enemond Masse and Jean de Brébeuf—accordingly embarked, and fourteen years after Biard and Masse had landed in Acadia, Canada beheld for the first time those whose names stand so prominent in her annals—the mysterious followers of Loyola.

Their reception was most inauspicious. Champlain was absent. Caen would not lodge them in the fort; the traders would not admit them to their houses. Nothing seemed left for them but to return as they came, when a boat bearing several Récollets approached the ship to proffer them the hospitalities of the convent on the St. Charles. They accepted and became guests of the charitable friars, who nevertheless entertained a lurking jealousy of these formidable co-workers.

The viceroy had been deeply scandalized by the contumacious heresy of Emery de Caen, who not only assembled his Huguenot sailors at prayers but forced Catholics to join them. He was ordered thenceforth to prohibit his crews from all praying and psalm-singing on the river St. Lawrence. The crews revolted and a compromise was made. It was agreed that for the present they might pray but not sing. "A bad bargain," says the pious Champlain, "but we made the best of it we could." Caen, enraged at the viceroy's reproofs, lost no opportunity to vent his spleen against the Jesuits, whom he cordially hated.

Eighteen years had passed since the founding of Quebec, and still the colony could scarcely be said to exist but in the founder's brain. Those who should have been its support were engrossed by trade or propagandism. Champlain might look back on fruitless toils, hopes deferred, a life spent seemingly in vain. The population of Quebec had risen to a hundred and five persons, men, women and children. Of these, one or two families only had learned to support themselves from the products of the soil. All withered under the monopoly of the Caens. Champlain had long desired to rebuild the fort, which was weak and ruinous, but the merchants would not grant the men and means which, by their charter, they were bound to furnish. At length, however, his urgency in part prevailed and the work began to advance.

The great champion of absolutism, Richelieu, was now supreme in France. His thin frame, pale cheek and calm, cold eye concealed an inexorable will and a mind of vast capacity, armed with all the resources of boldness and of craft. Under his potent agency the royal power, in the weak hands of Louis XIII, waxed and strengthened daily, triumphing over the factions of the court, the turbulence of the Huguenots, the ambitious independence of the nobles and all the elements of anarchy which, since the death of Henry IV, had risen into fresh life. With no friends and a thousand enemies, disliked and feared by the pitiful King whom he served, making his tool by turns of every party and of every principle, he advanced by countless crooked paths toward his object—the greatness of France under a concentrated and undivided authority.

In the midst of more urgent cares, he addressed himself to fostering the commercial and naval power. Montmorency then held the ancient charge of Admiral of France. Richelieu bought it, suppressed it and in its stead constituted himself Grand Master and Superintendent of Navigation and Commerce.

In this new capacity, the mismanaged affairs of New France were not long concealed from him and he applied a prompt and powerful remedy. The privileges of the Caens were annulled. A company was formed, to consist of a hundred associates and to be called the Company of New France. Richelieu himself was the head, and the Maréchal Deffiat and other men of rank, besides many merchants and burghers of condition, were members. The whole of New France, from Florida to the Arctic Circle and from Newfoundland to the sources of the St. Lawrence and its tributary waters, was conferred on them forever, with the attributes of sovereign power. A perpetual monopoly of the fur trade was granted them, with a monopoly of all other commerce within the limits of their government for fifteen years. The trade of the colony was declared free, for the same period, from all duties and imposts. Nobles, officers and ecclesiastics, members of the Company, might engage in commercial pursuits without derogating from the privileges of their order, and in evidence of his good will, the King gave them two ships of war, armed and equipped.

On their part, the Company were bound to convey to New France during the next year, 1628, two or three hundred men of all trades, and before the year 1643 to increase the number to four thousand persons of both sexes; to lodge and support them for three years and, when this time had expired, to give them cleared lands for their maintenance. Every settler must be a Frenchman and a Catholic, and for every new settlement at least three ecclesiastics must be provided. Thus was New France to be forever free from the taint of heresy. The stain of her infancy was to be wiped away. Against the foreigner and the Huguenot the door was closed and barred.

A trading company was now feudal proprietor of all domains in North America within the claim of France. The King heaped favors on the new corporation. Twelve of the bourgeois members were ennobled, while artisans and even manufacturers were tempted, by extraordinary privileges, to emigrate to the New World. The associates, of whom Champlain was one, entered upon their functions with a capital of three hundred thousand livres.

The first care of the new Company was to succor Quebec, whose inmates were on the verge of starvation. Four armed vessels, with a fleet of transports commanded by Roquemont, one of the associates, sailed from Dieppe with colonists and supplies in April 1628, but nearly at the same time another squadron, destined also for Quebec, was sailing from an English port.

War had at length broken out in France. The Huguenot revolt had come to a head. Rochelle was in arms against the King, and Richelieu, with his royal ward, was beleaguering it with the whole strength of the kingdom. Charles I of England, urged by the heated passions of Buckingham, had declared himself for the rebels and sent a fleet to their aid. At home, Charles detested the followers of Calvin as dangerous to the authority of a rival. In France, Richelieu crushed Protestantism as a curb to the house of Bourbon; in Germany, he nursed and strengthened it as a curb to the house of Austria.

The attempts of Sir William Alexander to colonize Acadia had of late turned attention in England towards the New World, and at the breaking out of the war an expedition was set on foot under the auspices of that singular personage to seize on the French possessions in North America.

Meanwhile the famished tenants of Quebec were eagerly waiting the expected succor. Daily they gazed beyond Point Levi and along the channels of Orleans, in the vain hope of seeing the approaching sails. At length, on the ninth of July, two men, worn with struggling through forests and over torrents, crossed the St. Charles and mounted the rock. They were from Cape Tourmente, where Champlain had some time before established an outpost, and they brought news that, according to the report of Indians, six large vessels lay in the harbor of Tadoussac. The friar Le Caron was at Quebec, and with a brother Récollet he went in a canoe to gain further intelligence. As the missionary scouts were paddling along the borders of the Island of Orleans they met two canoes advancing in hot haste, manned by Indians who with shouts and gestures warned them to turn back.

The friars, however, waited till the canoes came up, when they saw a man lying disabled at the bottom of one of them, his mustaches burned by the flash of the musket which had wounded him. He proved to be Foucher, who commanded at Cape Tourmente. On that morning twenty men had landed at that post from a small fishing vessel. Being to all appearance French, they were hospitably received, but no sooner had they entered the houses than they began to pillage and burn all before them, killing the cattle, wounding the commandant and making several prisoners.

The character of the fleet at Tadoussac was now sufficiently clear.

72

Quebec was incapable of defense. Only fifty pounds of gunpowder were left in the magazine, and the fort, owing to the neglect and ill will of the Caens, was so wretchedly constructed that a few days before two towers of the main building had fallen. Champlain, however, assigned to each man his post and waited the result.

On the next afternoon a boat was seen issuing from behind the Point of Orleans and hovering hesitatingly about the mouth of the St. Charles. On being challenged, the men on board proved to be Basque fishermen, lately captured by the English and now sent by Admiral David Kirke, commander of the invading expedition, as unwilling messengers to Champlain. Climbing the steep pathway to the fort, they delivered their letter—a summons, couched in terms of great courtesy, to surrender Quebec. There was no hope but in courage. A bold front must supply the lack of batteries and ramparts, and Champlain dismissed the Basques with a reply in which, with equal courtesy, he expressed his determination to hold his position to the last.

All now stood on watch, hourly expecting the enemy, when instead of the hostile squadron a small boat crept into sight and one Desdames, with ten Frenchmen, landed at the storehouses. He brought stirring news. The French commander, Roquemont, had dispatched him to tell Champlain that the ships of the Hundred Associates were ascending the St. Lawrence with reinforcements and supplies of all kinds. But on his way Desdames had seen an ominous sight: the English squadron standing under full sail out of Tadoussac and steering downwards as if to intercept the advancing succor. He had only escaped them by dragging his boat up the beach and hiding it, and scarcely were they out of sight when the booming of cannon told him that the fight was begun.

Racked with suspense, the starving tenants of Quebec waited the result. But they waited in vain. No white sail moved athwart the green solitudes of Orleans. Neither friend nor foe appeared, and it was not till long afterward that Indians brought them the tidings that Roquemont's crowded transports had been overpowered and all the supplies destined to relieve their miseries sunk in the St. Lawrence or seized by the victorious English. Kirke, however, deceived by the bold attitude of Champlain, had been too discreet to attack Quebec, and after his victory employed himself in cruising for French vessels along the borders of the gulf.

Meanwhile the suffering at Quebec increased daily. Somewhat less than a hundred men, women and children were cooped up in the fort, subsisting on a meager pittance of pease and Indian corn. The garden of the Heberts, the only thrifty settlers, was ransacked for every root or seed that could afford nourishment. Months wore on, and in the spring the distress had risen to such a pitch that Champlain had well nigh resolved to leave to the women, children and sick the little food that remained and with the able-bodied men invade the Iroquois, seize one of their villages, fortify himself in it and sustain his followers on the buried stores of maize with which the strongholds of these provident savages were always furnished.

Seven ounces of pounded pease were now the daily food of each, and at the end of May even this failed. Men, women and children betook themselves to the woods, gathering acorns and grubbing up roots. Those of the plant called Solomon's-seal were most in request. Some of these food-searching inhabitants joined the Hurons or the Algonquins. Some wandered towards the Abenakis of Maine, and some descended in a boat to Gaspé, trusting to meet a French fishing vessel. There was scarcely one who would not have hailed the English as deliverers. But the English had sailed home with their booty, and the season was so late that there was little prospect of their return. Forgotten alike by friends and foes, Quebec was on the verge of extinction.

On the morning of the nineteenth of July an Indian renowned as a fisher of eels, who had built his hut on the St. Charles, hard by the new dwelling of the Jesuits, came with his usual imperturbability of visage to Champlain. He had just discovered three ships sailing up the south channel of Orleans. Champlain was alone. All his followers were absent, fishing or searching for roots. At about ten o'clock his servant appeared with four small bags of roots and the tidings that he had seen the three ships a league off, behind Point Levi.

As man after man hastened in, Champlain ordered the starved and ragged band, sixteen in all, to their posts. With hungry eyes they watched the English vessels anchoring in the basin below and a boat with a white flag moving towards the shore. A young officer landed with a summons to surrender.

The terms of capitulation were at length settled. The French were to be conveyed to their own country, and each soldier was allowed to take with him his clothes and in addition a coat of beaver skin. At this some murmuring arose, several of those who had gone to the Hurons having lately returned with peltry of no small value. Their complaints were vain, and on the twentieth of July, amid the roar of cannon from the ships, Lewis Kirke, one of the admiral's two brothers, landed at the head of his soldiers and planted the cross of St. George where the followers of Wolfe again planted it a hundred and thirty years later.

After inspecting the worthless fort, he repaired to the houses of the Récollets and Jesuits on the St. Charles. He treated the former with great courtesy, but displayed against the latter a violent aversion, expressing his regret that he could not have begun his operations by battering their houses about their ears. The inhabitants had no cause to complain of him. He urged the widow and family of the settler Hebert—the patriarch, as he has been styled, of New France—to remain and enjoy the fruits of their industry under English allegiance, and as beggary in France was the alternative, his offer was accepted.

Champlain, bereft of his command, grew restless and begged to be sent to Tadoussac, where the admiral, David Kirke, lay with his main squadron, having sent his brothers Lewis and Thomas to seize Quebec. Accordingly, Champlain with the Jesuits, embarking with Thomas Kirke, descended the river. Off Mal Bay a strange sail was seen. As she approached she proved to be a French ship. In fact, she was on her way to Quebec with supplies, which if sent earlier would have saved the place. She had passed the admiral's squadron in a fog, but here her good fortune ceased. Thomas Kirke bore down on her and the cannonade began. The fight was hot and doubtful, but at length the French struck and Kirke sailed into Tadoussac with his prize. Here lay his brother, the admiral, with five armed ships.

The admiral's voyages to Canada were private ventures, and though he had captured nineteen fishing vessels, besides Roquemont's eighteen transports and other prizes, the result had not answered his hopes.

His mood, therefore, was far from benign, especially as he feared that, owing to a declaration of peace between England and France, he would be forced to disgorge a part of his booty. Yet, excepting the Jesuits, he treated his captives with courtesy and often amused himself with shooting larks on shore in company with Champlain.

The Huguenots, however, of whom there were many in his ships, showed an exceeding bitterness against the Catholics. Chief among them was one Captain Michel, who had instigated and conducted the enterprise, the merchant admiral being but an indifferent seaman. Michel, whose skill was great, held a high command and the title of rear admiral. He was a man of sensitive temperament, easily piqued on the point of honor. His morbid and irritable nerves were wrought to a pitch of frenzy by the reproaches of treachery and perfidy with which the French prisoners assailed him, while on the other hand he was in a state of continual rage at the fancied neglect and contumely of his English associates. He raved against Kirke, who, as he declared, treated him with an insupportable arrogance. "I have left my country," he exclaimed, "for the service of foreigners, and they give me nothing but ingratitude and scorn." His fevered mind, acting on his diseased body, often excited him to transports of fury in which he cursed indiscriminately the people of St. Malo, against whom he had a grudge, and the Jesuits, whom he detested. On one occasion Kirke was conversing with some of the latter.

"Gentlemen," he said, "your business in Canada was to enjoy what belonged to Monsieur de Caen, whom you dispossessed."

"Pardon me, sir," answered Brébeuf, "we came purely for the glory of God and exposed ourselves to every kind of danger to convert the Indians."

Here Michel broke in: "Ay, ay, convert the Indians! You mean, convert the beaver!"

"That is false," retorted Brébeuf.

Michel raised his fist, exclaiming, "But for the respect I owe the general, I would strike you for giving me the lie."

Brébeuf, a man of powerful frame and vehement passions, nevertheless regained his practiced self-command and replied: "You must excuse me. I did not mean to give you the lie. I should be very sorry to do so. The words I used are those we use in the schools when a

76

doubtful question is advanced, and they mean no offense. Therefore I ask you to pardon me."

Despite the apology, Michel's frenzied brain harped on the presumed insult and he raved about it without ceasing.

"Bon Dieu!" said Champlain, "you swear well for a Reformer!"

"I know it," returned Michel. "I should be content if I had but struck that Jesuit who gave me the lie before my general."

At length one of his transports of rage ended in a lethargy from which he never awoke. His funeral was conducted with a pomp suited to his rank, and amid discharges of cannon whose dreary roar was echoed from the yawning gulf of the Saguenay, his body was borne to its rest under the rocks of Tadoussac. Good Catholics and good Frenchmen saw in his fate the immediate finger of Providence. "I do not doubt that his soul is in perdition," remarks Champlain.

Having finished their carousings, which were profuse, and their trade with the Indians, which was not lucrative, the English steered down the St. Lawrence. Kirke feared greatly a meeting with Razilly, a naval officer of distinction who was to have sailed from France with a strong force to succor Quebec, but peace having been proclaimed, the expedition had been limited to two ships under Captain Daniel. Thus Kirke, willfully ignoring the treaty of peace, was left to pursue his depredations unmolested. Daniel, though too weak to cope with him, nonetheless achieved a signal exploit.

On the island of Cape Breton, near the site of Louisbourg, he found an English fort, built two months before under the auspices doubtless of Sir William Alexander. Daniel, regarding it as a bold encroachment on French territory, stormed it at the head of his pikemen, entered sword in hand and took it with all its defenders.

Meanwhile, Kirke with his prisoners was crossing the Atlantic. His squadron at length reached Plymouth, whence Champlain set out for London. Here he had an interview with the French ambassador, who at his instance gained from the King a promise that, in pursuance of the terms of the treaty concluded in the previous April, New France should be restored to the French Crown.

Yet Champlain, who had obtained it, was not given the honor of making the restoration a reality. That was accomplished by Emery de Caen, who anchored before Quebec on Monday the fifth of July,

1632. He had been commissioned by the French Crown to reclaim the place from the English; to hold for one year a monopoly of the fur trade, as an indemnity for his losses in the war; and, when this time had expired, to give place to the Hundred Associates of New France.

When de Caen arrived, Thomas Kirke, obedient to an order from the King of England, struck his flag, embarked his followers and abandoned the scene of his conquest. Caen landed with the Jesuits, Paul le Jeune and Anne de la Nouë. They climbed the steep stairway which led up to the rock, and as they reached the top the dilapidated fort lay on their left, while farther on was the stone cottage of the Heberts, surrounded with its vegetable gardens—the only thrifty spot amid a scene of neglect.

But few Indians could be seen. True to their native instincts, they had at first left the defeated French and welcomed the conquerors. Their English partialities, however, were short-lived. Their intrusion into houses and storerooms, the stench of their tobacco and their importunate begging, though before borne patiently, were rewarded by the newcomers with oaths and sometimes with blows. The Indians soon shunned Quebec, seldom approaching it except when drawn by necessity or a craving for brandy. This was not now the case, and several Algonquin families, maddened with drink, were howling, screeching and fighting within their bark lodges. The women were frenzied like the men. It was dangerous to approach the place unarmed.

In the following spring, 1633, on the twenty-third of May, Champlain, commissioned anew by Richelieu, resumed command at Quebec in behalf of the Company. Father le Jeune, Superior of the mission, was wakened from his morning sleep by the boom of the saluting cannon. Before he could sally forth, the convent door was darkened by the stately form of his brother Jesuit, Brébeuf, newly arrived, and the Indians who stood by uttered ejaculations of astonishment at the raptures of their greeting. The father hastened to the fort and arrived in time to see a file of musketeers and pikemen mounting the pathway of the cliff below and the heretic Caen resigning the keys of the citadel into the Catholic hands of Champlain.

In his youth Champlain had fought on the side of that more liberal and national form of Romanism of which the Jesuits were the most

emphatic antagonists. Now, as Le Jeune tells us with evident content-
ment, he chose him, the Jesuit, as director of his conscience. In truth,
there were none but Jesuits to confess and absolve him, for the
Récollets, prevented from returning to the missions they had founded,
were seen no more in Canada, and the followers of Loyola were sole
masters of the field.

A stranger visiting the fort of Quebec would have been astonished
at its air of conventual decorum. Black-robed Jesuits and scarfed
officers mingled at Champlain's table. There was little conversation,
but in its place, histories and the lives of saints were read aloud, as in
a monastic refectory. Prayers, masses and confessions followed one
another with an edifying regularity, and the bell of the adjacent chapel,
built by Champlain, rang morning, noon and night. Godless soldiers
caught the infection and whipped themselves in penance for their
sins. Debauched artisans outdid each other in the fury of their contri-
tion. Quebec was become a mission.

Indians gathered there as of old, not from the baneful lure of
brandy, for the traffic in it was no longer tolerated, but from the less
pernicious attractions of gifts, kind words and politic blandishments.
To the vital principle of propagandism both the commercial and the
military character were subordinated, or, to speak more justly, trade,
policy and military power leaned on the missions as their main support, the grand instrument of their extension. The missions were to
explore the interior; the missions were to win over the savage hordes
at once to Heaven and to France. Peaceful, benign, beneficent were
the weapons of this conquest. France aimed to subdue not by the
sword but by the cross; not to overwhelm and crush the nations she
invaded, but to convert, civilize and embrace them among her children.

Two years passed. The mission of the Hurons was established, and
here the indomitable Brébeuf, with a band worthy of him, toiled
amid miseries and perils as fearful as ever shook the constancy of
man, while Champlain at Quebec, in a life uneventful yet harrassing
and laborious, was busied in the round of cares which his post involved.

Christmas Day, 1635, was a dark day in the annals of New France.
In a chamber of the fort, breathless and cold, lay the hardy frame
which war, the wilderness and the sea had buffeted so long in vain.

After two and a half months of illness, Champlain, stricken with paralysis at the age of sixty-eight, was dead. His last cares were for his colony and the succor of its suffering families. Jesuits, officers, soldiers, traders and the few settlers of Quebec followed his remains to the church. Le Jeune pronounced his eulogy and the feeble community built a tomb to his honor.

The colony could ill spare him. For twenty-seven years he had labored hard and ceaselessly for its welfare, sacrificing fortune, repose and domestic peace to a cause embraced with enthusiasm and pursued with intrepid persistency. His character belonged partly to the past, partly to the present. The *preux chevalier,* the crusader, the romance-loving explorer, the curious, knowledge-seeking traveler, the practical navigator, all claimed their share in him.

His views, though far beyond those of the mean spirits around him, belonged to his age and his creed. He was less statesman than soldier. He leaned to the most direct and boldest policy, and one of his last acts was to petition Richelieu for men and munitions for repressing that standing menace to the colony, the Iroquois. His dauntless courage was matched by an unwearied patience, proved by lifelong vexations and not wholly subdued even by the saintly follies of his wife.

He is charged with credulity, from which few of his age were free, and which in all ages has been the foible of earnest and generous natures, too ardent to criticize and too honorable to doubt the honor of others. Perhaps the heretic might have liked him more if the Jesuit had liked him less.

The adventurous explorer of Lake Huron, the bold invader of the Iroquois, befitted indifferently the monastic sobrieties of the fort of Quebec and his somber environment of priests. Yet Champlain was no formalist, nor was his an empty zeal. A soldier from his youth, in an age of unbridled license, his life had answered to his maxims, and when a generation had passed after his visit to the Hurons, their elders remembered with astonishment the continence of the great French war chief.

With the life of this faithful soldier closes the opening period of New France.

PART TWO

The Jesuits
in North America

CHAPTER 1

The Advance Guard

OPPOSITE QUEBEC LIES THE TONGUE OF LAND called Point Levi. In the summer of 1634 one who stood on its margin and looked northward across the St. Lawrence would have seen, at the distance of a mile or more, a range of lofty cliffs, rising on the left into the bold heights of Cape Diamond and on the right sinking abruptly to the bed of the tributary river St. Charles. Beneath these cliffs, at the brink of the St. Lawrence, he would have descried a cluster of warehouses, sheds and wooden tenements. Immediately above, along the verge of the precipice, he could have traced the outlines of a fortified work, with a flagstaff and a few small cannon to command the river; while at the only point where Nature had made the heights accessible, a zigzag path connected the warehouses and the fort.

Now, embarked in the canoe of some Montagnais Indian, let the observer cross the St. Lawrence, land at the pier and, passing the cluster of buildings, climb the pathway up the cliff. Pausing for rest and breath, he might see, ascending and descending, the tenants of this outpost of the wilderness—a soldier of the fort, or an officer in slouched hat and plume; a factor of the fur company, owner and sovereign lord of all Canada; a party of Indians; a trader from the upper country, one of the precursors of that hardy race of *coureurs de bois,* destined to form a conspicuous and striking feature of the Canadian population. Next, perhaps, would appear a figure widely different. The close black cassock, the rosary hanging from the waist and the wide black hat looped up at the sides proclaimed the Jesuit, Father Le Jeune, Superior of the Residence of Quebec.

Of the six Jesuits who gathered with the good father in the refectory for evening meals, one was conspicuous among the rest—a tall, strong man, with features that seemed carved by Nature for a soldier but which the mental habits of years had stamped with the visible impress of the priesthood. This was Jean de Brébeuf, descendant of a noble family of Normandy, and one of the ablest and most devoted zealots whose names stand on the missionary rolls of his Order. His companions were Masse, Daniel, Davost and De Nouë.

The fathers, in their intervals of leisure, worked with the eight or ten workmen employed by the mission, spade in hand. For the rest they were busied in preaching, singing vespers, saying mass and hearing confessions at the fort of Quebec, catechizing a few Indians and striving to master the enormous difficulties of the Huron and Algonquin languages.

Well might Father Le Jeune write to his Superior, "The harvest is plentiful, and the laborers few." These men aimed at the conversion of a continent. From their hovel on the St. Charles they surveyed a field of labor whose vastness might tire the wings of thought itself, a scene repellent and appalling, darkened with omens of peril and woe. They were an advance guard of the great army of Loyola, strong in a discipline that controlled not alone the body and the will, but the intellect, the heart, the soul and the inmost consciousness.

Their life was incredibly hard. The year before, winter had closed in with a severity rare even in Canada. The St. Lawrence and the St. Charles were hard frozen; rivers, forests and rocks were mantled alike in dazzling sheets of snow. The humble mission house of Notre Dame des Anges was half buried in the drifts, which, heaped up in front where a path had been dug through them, rose two feet above the low eaves. The priests, sitting at night before the blazing logs of their wide-throated chimney, heard the trees in the neighboring forest cracking with frost, with a sound like the report of a pistol. Le Jeune's ink froze and his fingers were benumbed as he toiled at his declensions and conjugations or translated the *Pater Noster* into blundering Algonquin. The water in the cask beside the fire froze nightly, and the ice was broken every morning with hatchets. The blankets of the priests were fringed with the icicles of their congealed breath, and the frost lay in a thick coating on the lozenge-shaped glass of their cells.

On two points Le Jeune had gained convictions: first, that little progress could be made in converting the wandering hordes of Algonquins till they could be settled in fixed abodes; and secondly, that their scanty numbers, their geographical position and their slight influence in the politics of the wilderness offered no flattering promise that their conversion would be fruitful in further triumphs of the Faith. It was to another quarter that the Jesuits looked most earnestly. By the vast lakes of the West dwelt numerous stationary populations, and particularly the Hurons, on the lake which bears their name. Here was a hopeful basis of indefinite conquests, for with the Hurons won over, the Faith would spread in wider and wider circles, embracing one by one the kindred tribes—the Tobacco Nation, the Neutrals, the Eries and the Andastes. In His own time, God might lead into His fold even the potent and ferocious Iroquois.

The way was pathless and long, by rock and torrent and the gloom of savage forests. The goal was more dreary yet. Toil, hardship, famine, filth, sickness, solitude, insult, all that is most revolting to men nurtured among arts and letters, all that is most terrifying to monastic credulity—such were the promise and the reality of the Huron mission. In the eyes of the Jesuits the Huron country was the innermost stronghold of Satan, his castle and his donjon-keep. All the weapons of his malice were prepared against the bold invader who should assail him in this, the heart of his ancient domain. Far from shrinking, however, the priest's zeal rose to tenfold ardor. He signed the cross, invoked St. Ignatius, St. Francis Xavier or St. Francis Borgia, kissed his reliquary, said nine masses to the Virgin and stood prompt to battle with all the hosts of Hell.

In July 1633, a Huron Indian well known to the French had come to Quebec with the tidings that the annual canoe fleet of his countrymen was descending the St. Lawrence. On the twenty-eighth the river was alive with them. A hundred and forty canoes, with six or seven hundred savages, landed at the warehouses beneath the fortified rock of Quebec and set up their huts and camp sheds on the strand now covered by the lower town. The greater number brought furs and tobacco for the trade; others came as sight-seers; others to gamble and others to steal, accomplishments in which the Hurons were proficient. Their gambling skill was exercised chiefly against each other, and their thieving talents against those of other nations.

On the second day of the encampment a long file of chiefs and warriors mounted the pathway to the fort: tall, well-molded figures, robed in the skins of the beaver and the bear, each wild visage glowing with paint and glistening with the oil which the Hurons extracted from the seeds of the sunflower. The lank black hair of one streamed loose upon his shoulders. That of another was close shaven, except for an upright ridge, which, bristling like the crest of a dragoon's helmet, crossed the crown from the forehead to the neck, while that of a third hung long and flowing from one side but on the other was cut short. Sixty chiefs and principal men, with a crowd of younger warriors, formed their council circle in the fort, those of each village grouped together, and all seated on the ground with a gravity of bearing sufficiently curious to those who had seen the same men in the domestic circle of their lodge fires. Here, too, were the Jesuits, robed in black, anxious and intent. Here was Champlain, who surveyed the throng and recognized among the elder warriors not a few of those who, eighteen years before, had been his companions in arms on his hapless foray against the Iroquois.

Their harangues of compliment being made and answered, and the inevitable presents given and received, Champlain introduced to the silent conclave the three missionaries, Brébeuf, Daniel and Davost. To their lot had fallen the honors, dangers and woes of the Huron mission. "These are our fathers," Champlain said. "We love them more than we love ourselves. The whole French nation honors them. They do not go among you for your furs. They have left their friends and their country to show you the way to heaven. If you love the French, as you say you love them, then love and honor these our fathers."

Two chiefs rose to reply, and each lavished all his rhetoric in praises of Champlain and of the French. Brébeuf rose next and spoke in broken Huron, while the assembly brought repeated ejaculations of applause from the bottom of their throats. Then they surrounded him and vied with each other for the honor of carrying him in their canoes. In short, the mission was accepted and the chiefs of the different villages disputed among themselves the privilege of receiving and entertaining the three priests.

The eve of departure came. The priests packed their baggage and Champlain paid their passage, or in other words made presents to the Indians who were to carry them in their canoes. They lodged that night in the storehouse of the fur company, around which the Hurons were encamped. Le Jeune and De Noüe stayed with them to bid them farewell in the morning. At eleven at night they were aroused by a loud voice in the Indian camp and saw Le Borgne, the one-eyed chief of Allumette Island, walking round among the huts, haranguing as he went. Brébeuf, listening, caught the import of his words.

"We have begged the French captain to spare the life of the Algonquin of the Petite Nation whom he keeps in prison, but he will not listen to us. The prisoner will die. Then his people will revenge him. They will try to kill the three black robes whom you are about to carry to your country. If you do not defend them, the French will be angry, and charge you with their death. But if you do, then the Algonquins will make war on you, and the river will be closed. If the French captain will not let the prisoner go, then leave the three black robes where they are, for if you take them with you, they will bring you to trouble."

Such was the substance of Le Borgne's harangue. The anxious priests hastened up to the fort, gained admittance and roused Champlain from his slumbers. He sent his interpreter with a message to the Hurons that he wished to speak to them before their departure, and accordingly in the morning an Indian crier proclaimed through their camp that none should embark till the next day. Champlain convoked the chiefs and tried persuasion, promises and threats, but Le Borgne had been busy among them with his intrigues, and now he declared in the council that unless the prisoner were released the missionaries would be murdered on their way and war would ensue.

The politic savage had two objects in view. On the one hand, he wished to interrupt the direct intercourse between the French and the Hurons; and on the other, he thought to gain credit and influence with the nation of the prisoner by effecting his release. His first point was won. Champlain would not give up the prisoner, who was charged with slaying one of his men, knowing those with whom he was dealing too well to take a course which would have proclaimed the killing of a Frenchman a venial offense. The Hurons thereupon refused to carry the missionaries to their country, coupling the refusal with many regrets and many protestations of love, no doubt partly sincere, for the Jesuits had contrived to gain no little favor in their eyes. The council broke up, the Hurons embarked and the priests returned to their convent.

Here, under the guidance of Brébeuf, they employed themselves amid their other avocations in studying the Huron tongue. A year passed, and again the Indian traders descended from their villages. In the meanwhile grievous calamities had befallen the nation. They had suffered deplorable reverses at the hands of the Iroquois, while a pestilence, similar to that which a few years before had swept off the native populations of New England, had begun its ravages among them. They appeared at Three Rivers—this year the place of trade— in small numbers and in a miserable state of dejection and alarm. Du Plessis Bochart, commander of the French fleet, called them to a council, harangued them, feasted them and made them presents, but they refused to take the Jesuits. In private, however, some of them were won over; then again refused; then, at the eleventh hour, a second time consented. On the eve of embarkation they once more wavered. All was confusion, doubt and uncertainty, when Brébeuf bethought him of a vow to St. Joseph. The vow was made. At once, he says, the Indians became tractable. The fathers embarked and, amid salvos of cannon from the ships, set forth for the wild scene of their apostleship.

They reckoned the distance at nine hundred miles, but distance was the least repellent feature of this most arduous journey. Barefoot, lest their shoes should injure the frail vessel, each crouched in his canoe, toiling with unpracticed hands to propel it. Before him, week after week, he saw the same lank, unkempt hair, the same tawny shoulders and long, naked arms ceaselessly plying the paddle. The canoes were soon separated, and for more than a month the Frenchmen rarely or never met. Brébeuf spoke a little Huron and could converse with his escort, but Daniel and Davost were doomed to a silence unbroken save by the occasional unintelligible complaints and menaces of the Indians, of whom many were sick with the epidemic, and all were terrified, desponding and sullen. Their only food was a pittance of Indian corn, crushed between two stones and mixed with water. The toil was extreme. Brébeuf counted thirty-five portages, where the canoes were lifted from the water and carried on the shoulders of the voyagers around rapids or cataracts. More than fifty times besides they were forced to wade in the raging current, pushing up their empty barks or dragging them with ropes.

Brébeuf tried to do his part, but the boulders and sharp rocks wounded his naked feet and compelled him to desist. He and his companions bore their share of the baggage across the portages, sometimes a distance of several miles. Four trips, at the least, were required to convey the whole. The way was through the dense forest, encumbered with rocks and logs, tangled with roots and underbrush, damp with perpetual shade and redolent of decayed leaves and moldering wood. The Indians themselves were often spent with fatigue. Brébeuf, a man of iron frame and a nature unconquerably resolute, doubted if his strength would sustain him to the journey's end. He complains that he had no moment to read his breviary, except by the moonlight or the fire, when stretched out to sleep on a bare rock by some savage cataract of the Ottawa, or in a damp nook of the adjacent forest.

Descending French River and following the lonely shores of the great Georgian Bay, the canoe which carried Brébeuf at length neared its destination, thirty days after leaving Three Rivers. Before him, stretched in savage slumber, lay the forest shore of the Hurons. Having landed, the Indians threw the missionary's baggage on the ground, leaving him to his own resources, and without heeding his remonstrances set forth for their respective villages some twenty miles distant. Thus abandoned, the priest kneeled, not to implore succor in his perplexity but to offer thanks to the Providence which had shielded him thus far. Then, rising, he pondered as to what course he should take.

He knew the spot well. It was on the borders of the small inlet called Thunder Bay. In the neighboring Huron town of Toanché he had lived three years, preaching and baptizing, but Toanché had now ceased to exist. Here Etienne Brulé, Champlain's adventurous interpreter, had recently been murdered by the inhabitants, who in excitement and alarm, dreading the consequences of their deed, had deserted the spot and built a few miles distant a new town called Ihonatiria. Brébeuf hid his baggage in the woods, including the vessels for the mass, more precious than all the rest, and began his search for this new abode. He passed the burned remains of Toanché, saw the charred poles that had formed the frame of his little chapel of bark and found, as he thought, the spot where Brulé had fallen. Evening was near and, in bewilderment and anxiety, he was following a gloomy forest path when he issued upon a wild clearing and saw before him the bark roofs of Ihonatiria.

A crowd ran out to meet him. "Echom has come again! Echom has come again!" they cried, recognizing in the distance the stately figure, robed in black, that advanced from the border of the forest.

They led him to the town and the whole population swarmed about him. After a short rest he set out with a number of young Indians in quest of his baggage, returning with it at one o'clock in the morning. There was a certain Awandoay in the village, noted as one of the richest and most hospitable of the Hurons, a distinction not easily won where hospitality was universal. His house was large and amply stored with beans and corns, and though his prosperity had excited the jealousy of the villagers, he had recovered their good will by his generosity. With him Brébeuf made his abode, anxiously waiting, week after week, the arrival of his companions.

One by one they appeared—Daniel, weary and worn; Davost, half dead with famine and fatigue; and their French attendants, each with his tale of hardship and indignity. At length all were assembled under the roof of the hospitable Indian and once more the Huron mission was begun.

By the ancient Huron custom, when a man or a family wanted a house the whole village joined in building one. In the present case not Ihonatiria only but the neighboring town of Wenrio also took part in the work, though not without the expectation of such gifts as the priests had to bestow. Before October the task was finished. The house was constructed after the Huron model. It was thirty-six feet long and about twenty feet wide, framed with strong sapling poles planted in the earth to form the sides, with the ends bent into an arch for the roof—the whole lashed firmly together, braced with cross poles and closely covered with overlapping sheets of bark.

The structure was strictly Indian outside, but the priests with the aid of their tools made innovations inside which were the astonishment of all the country. They divided their dwelling by transverse partitions into three apartments, each with its wooden door, a wondrous novelty in the eyes of their visitors. The first served as a hall, an anteroom and a place of storage for corn, beans and dried fish. The second—the largest of the three—was at once kitchen, workshop, dining room, drawing room, schoolroom and bedchamber. The third was the chapel. Here they made their altar, and here were their images, pictures and sacred vessels. Their fire was on the ground, in the middle of the second apartment, the smoke escaping by a hole in the roof. At the sides were placed two wide platforms, after the Huron fashion, four feet from the earthen floor. On these were chests in which they kept their clothing and vestments, and beneath them they slept, reclining on sheets of bark and covered with skins and the garments they wore by day. Rude stools, a hand mill, a large Indian mortar of wood for crushing corn and a clock completed the furniture of the room.

There was no lack of visitors, for the house of the black robes contained marvels the fame of which was noised abroad to the uttermost confines of the Huron nation. Chief among them was the clock. The guests would sit in expectant silence by the hour, squatted on the ground, waiting to hear it strike. They thought it was alive and asked what it ate. As the last stroke sounded, one of the Frenchmen would cry "Stop!"—and to the admiration of the company, the obedient clock was silent. The mill was another wonder and they were never tired of turning it. Besides these there were a prism and a magnet, also a magnifying glass, wherein a flea was transformed into a frightful monster, and a multiplying lens which showed them the same object eleven times repeated.

"All this," says Brébeuf, "serves to gain their affection and make them more docile in respect to the admirable and incomprehensible mysteries of our Faith; for the opinion they have of our genius and capacity makes them believe whatever we tell them."

"What does the Captain say?" was the frequent question, for by this title of honor they designated the clock.

"When he strikes twelve times," the fathers replied, "he says, 'Hang

91

on the kettle,' and when he strikes four times, he says, 'Get up and go home.' "

Both interpretations were well remembered. At noon visitors were never wanting to share the fathers' sagamité, but at the stroke of four all rose and departed, leaving the missionaries for a time in peace.

At every opportunity the priests gathered together the children of the village at their house. On these occasions Brébeuf, for greater solemnity, put on a surplice and the close, angular cap worn by Jesuits in their convents. First he chanted the *Pater Noster,* translated by Father Daniel into Huron rhymes, the children chanting in their turn. Next he taught them the sign of the cross, made them repeat the *Ave,* the *Credo* and the Commandments, questioned them as to past instructions, gave them briefly a few new ones and dismissed them with a present of two or three beads, raisins or prunes. A great emulation was kindled among this small fry of heathendom. The priests, with amusement and delight, saw them gathered in groups about the village, vying with each other in making the sign of the cross or in repeating the rhymes they had learned.

Notwithstanding all their exhortations, the Jesuits for the present baptized but few Hurons. Indeed, during the first year or more they baptized no adults except those apparently at the point of death, for with excellent reason they feared backsliding and recantation. They found especial pleasure in the baptism of dying infants, rescuing them from the flames of perdition and changing them, to borrow Le Jeune's phrase, "from little Indians into little angels."

The fathers' slumbers were brief and broken. Winter was the season of Huron festivity, and as they lay stretched on their hard couch, suffocating with smoke and tormented by an inevitable multitude of fleas, the thumping of the drum resounded all night long from a neighboring house, mingled with the sound of the tortoise-shell rattle, the stamping of moccasined feet and the cadence of voices keeping time with the dancers. Again, some ambitious villager woud give a feast and invite all the warriors of the neighboring towns, or else some grand wager of gambling, with its attendant drumming, singing and outcries, filled the night with discord.

The approach of summer brought with it a comparative peace. Many of the villagers dispersed, some to their fishing, some to expeditions of trade and some to distant lodges by their detached cornfields. The priests availed themselves of the respite to engage in those exercises of private devotion which the rule of St. Ignatius enjoins. About mid-summer, however, their quiet was suddenly broken. The crops were withering under a severe drought, a calamity which the sandy nature of the soil made doubly serious. The sorcerers put forth their utmost power and from the tops of the houses yelled incessant invocations to the spirits. All was in vain. The pitiless sky was cloudless. There was thunder in the east and thunder in the west, but over Ihonatiria all was serene.

A renowned rain maker, seeing his reputation tottering under his repeated failures, bethought him of accusing the Jesuits and gave out that the red color of the cross which stood before their house scared the bird of thunder and caused him to fly another way. A clamor arose. The popular ire turned against the priests and the obnoxious cross was condemned to be hewn down. Aghast at the threatened sacrilege, they attempted to reason away the storm, assuring the crowd that the lightning was not a bird but certain hot and fiery exhalations, which, being imprisoned, darted this way and that, trying to escape. As this philosophy failed to convince the hearers, the missionaries changed their line of defense.

"You say that the red color of the cross frightens the bird of thunder. Then paint the cross white, and see if the thunder will come."

This was accordingly done, but the clouds still kept aloof. The Jesuits followed up their advantage.

"Your spirits cannot help you, and your sorcerers have deceived you with lies. Now ask the aid of Him who made the world, and perhaps He will listen to your prayers." And they added that if the Indians would renounce their sins and obey the true God, they would make a procession daily to implore His favor towards them.

There was no want of promises. The processions were begun, as were also nine masses to St. Joseph, and as heavy rains occurred soon after, the Indians conceived a high idea of the efficacy of the French "medicine."

In spite of the hostility of the sorcerers and the transient commotion raised by the red cross, the Jesuits had gained the confidence and good will of the Huron population. Their patience, their kindness, their

93

intrepidity, their manifest disinterestedness, the blamelessness of their lives and the tact which, in the utmost fervors of their zeal, never failed them, had won the hearts of these wayward savages. Chiefs of distant villages came to urge that they would make their abode with them. As yet the results of the mission had been faint and few, but the priests toiled on courageously, high in hope that an abundant harvest of souls would one day reward their labors.

CHAPTER 2

Persecution

THE TOWN OF OSSOSSANÉ, OR ROCHELLE, STOOD ON the borders of Lake Huron, at the skirts of a gloomy wilderness of pine. To this place in May 1637 repaired Father Pierre Pijart, who had joined his brother Jesuits in 1635 to found one of the largest of the Huron towns, the new mission of the Immaculate Conception. The Indians had promised Brébeuf to build a house for the black robes, and Pijart found the work in progress. There were at this time about fifty dwellings in the town, each containing eight or ten families. A quadrangular fort had now been completed by the Indians, under the instruction of the priests.

The new mission house was about seventy feet in length. No sooner had the savage workmen secured the bark covering on its top and sides than the priests took possession and began their preparations for a notable ceremony.

At the farther end they made an altar and hung such decorations as they had on the rough walls of bark throughout half the length of the structure. This formed their chapel. On the altar was a crucifix, with vessels and ornaments of shining metal, while above hung several pictures, among them a painting of Christ and another of the Virgin, both life size. There was also a representation of the Last Judgment, wherein dragons and serpents might be seen feasting on the entrails of the wicked, while demons scourged them into the flames of Hell. The entrance was adorned with a quantity of tinsel, together with green boughs skillfully disposed.

Never before were such splendors seen in the land of the Hurons. Crowds gathered from afar and gazed in awe and admiration at the marvels of the sanctuary. A woman came from a distant town to behold it and, tremulous between curiosity and fear, thrust her head into the mysterious recess, declaring that she would see it though the look should cost her life.

· A great event had called forth all this preparation. Of the many baptisms achieved by the fathers in the course of their indefatigable ministry, the subjects had all been infants or adults at the point of death. But at length a Huron, in full health and manhood, respected and influential in his tribe, had been won over to the Faith and was now to be baptized with solemn ceremonial in the chapel thus gorgeously adorned.

It was a strange scene. Indians were there in throngs and the house was closely packed: warriors, old and young, glistening in grease and sunflower oil, with uncouth locks a trifle less coarse than a horse's mane and faces perhaps smeared with paint in honor of the occasion; wenches in gay attire; hags muffled in filthy discarded deerskins, their leathery visages corrugated with age and malice and their hard, glittering eyes riveted on the spectacle before them. The priests, no longer in their daily garb of black but radiant in their surplices, the genuflections, the tinkling of the bell, the swinging of the censer, the sweet odors so unlike the fumes of the smoky lodge fires, the mysterious elevation of the Host (for a mass followed the baptism) and the agitation of the neophyte, whose Indian imperturbability fairly deserted him—all these combined to produce on the minds of the savage beholders an impression that seemed to promise a rich harvest for the Faith. To the Jesuits it was a day of triumph and of hope. The ice had been broken; the wedge had entered; light had dawned at last on the long night of heathendom.

But there was one feature of the situation which in their rejoicing they overlooked. The Devil had taken alarm. He had borne with reasonable composure the loss of individual souls snatched from him by former baptisms, but here was a convert whose example and influence threatened to shake his Huron empire to its very foundation. In fury and fear, he rose to the conflict and put forth all his malice and all his hellish ingenuity. Such, at least, is the explanation given by the Jesuits of the scenes that followed.

The mysterious strangers, garbed in black, who of late years had made their abode among them from motives past finding out, marvelous in knowledge, careless of life, had awakened in the breasts of the Hurons mingled emotions of wonder, perplexity, fear, respect and awe. From the first they had held them answerable for the changes of the weather, commending them when the crops were abundant and upbraiding them in times of scarcity. They thought them mighty magicians, masters of life and death, and they came to them for spells, sometimes to destroy their enemies and sometimes to kill grass-hoppers. And now it was whispered abroad that it was they who had bewitched the nation and caused the dreaded smallpox which at that time was threatening to exterminate it.

The slander spread fast and far. Their friends looked at them askance; their enemies clamored for their lives. Some said that they concealed in their houses a corpse, which infected the country—a per-verted notion derived from some half-instructed neophyte concerning the body of Christ in the Eucharist. Others ascribed the evil to a ser-pent, others to a spotted frog, others to a demon which the priests were supposed to carry in the barrel of a gun. Others again gave out that they had pricked an infant to death with awls in the forest, in order to kill the Huron children by magic.

The picture of the Last Judgment became an object of the utmost terror. It was regarded as a charm. The dragons and serpents were supposed to be the demons of the pest, and the sinners whom they were so busily devouring to represent its victims. On the top of a spruce tree, near their house at Ihonatiria, the priests had fastened a small streamer to show the direction of the wind. This, too, was taken for a charm, throwing off disease and death to all quarters. The clock, once an object of harmless wonder, now excited the wildest alarm, and the Jesuits were forced to stop it since, when it struck, it was supposed to sound the signal of death. At sunset one would have seen knots of Indians, their faces dark with dejection and terror, listening to the measured sounds which issued from within the neighboring house of the mission, where with bolted doors the priests were singing litanies, mistaken for incantations by the awe-struck savages.

97

Had the objects of Huron alarm been Indians, their term of life would have been very short. The blow of a hatchet, stealthily struck in the dusky entrance of a lodge, would have promptly avenged the victims of their sorcery and delivered the country from peril. But the priests inspired a strange awe. Nocturnal councils were held. The death of the fathers was decreed, and as they walked their rounds, whispering groups of children gazed after them as men doomed to die. They were reviled and upbraided. The Indian boys threw sticks at them as they passed and then ran behind the houses. When they entered one of these pestiferous dens, this impish crew clambered on the roof to pelt them with snowballs through the smoke holes. The old squaw who crouched by the fire scowled on them with mingled anger and fear and cried out, "Begone! there are no sick ones here." The invalids wrapped their heads in their blankets, and when the priests accosted some dejected warrior the savage looked gloomily on the ground and answered not a word.

Yet nothing could divert the Jesuits from their ceaseless quest of dying subjects for baptism, and above all of dying children. They penetrated every house in turn. When, through the thin walls of bark, they heard the wail of a sick infant, no menace and no insult could repel them from the threshold. They pushed boldly in, asked to buy some trifle, spoke of late news of Iroquois forays—of anything, in short, except the pestilence and the sick child. Then they conversed for a while till suspicion was partially lulled to sleep and, pretending to observe the sufferer for the first time, approached it, felt its pulse and asked of its health.

Now, while apparently fanning the heated brow, the dexterous visitor touched it with a corner of his handkerchief, which he had previously dipped in water, murmured the baptismal words with motionless lips and snatched another soul from the fangs of the "Infernal Wolf," as they often called the Devil. Thus, with the patience of saints, the courage of heroes and an intent truly charitable, did the fathers put forth a nimble-fingered adroitness that would have done credit to the profession of which the function is less to dispense the treasures of another world than to grasp those which pertain to this.

The Huron chiefs were summoned to a great council to discuss the state of the nation. The crisis demanded all their wisdom, for while

98

the continued ravages of disease threatened them with annihilation, the Iroquois scalping parties infested the outskirts of their towns and murdered them in their fields and forests. The assembly met in August 1637, and the Jesuits, knowing their deep stake in its deliberations, failed not to be present with a liberal gift of wampum, to show their sympathy in the public calamities. In private they sought to gain the good will of the deputies, one by one. But though they were successful in some cases, the result on the whole was far from hopeful.

In the intervals of the council Brébeuf discoursed to the crowd of chiefs on the wonders of the visible heavens—the sun, the moon, the stars and the planets. They were inclined to believe what he told them, for he had lately, to their great amazement, accurately predicted an eclipse. From the fires above he passed to the fires beneath, till the listeners stood aghast at his hideous pictures of the flames of perdition. This was the only species of Christian instruction which produced any perceptible effect on this unpromising auditory.

The council opened on the evening of the fourth of August, with all the usual ceremonies, and the night was spent in discussing questions of treaties and alliances, with a deliberation and good sense which the Jesuits could not help admiring. A few days after, the assembly took up the more exciting question of the epidemic and its causes. Deputies from three of the four Huron nations were present, each deputation sitting apart. The Jesuits were seated with the Nation of the Bear, in whose towns their missions were established. Like all important councils, the session was held at night. The light of the fires flickered aloft into the smoky vault and among the soot-begrimed rafters of the great council house and cast an uncertain gleam on the wild and dejected throng that filled the platforms and the floor.

A grisly old chief named Ontitarac, withered with age and stone-blind but renowned in past years for eloquence and counsel, opened the debate in a loud though tremulous voice. First he saluted each of the three nations present, then each of the chiefs in turn, congratulated them that all were there assembled to deliberate on a subject of the last importance to the public welfare and exhorted them to give it a mature and calm consideration. Next rose the chief whose office it was to preside over the Feast of the Dead. He painted in dismal colors the

99

woeful condition of the country and ended with charging it all upon the sorceries of the Jesuits. Another old chief followed him.

"My brothers," he said, "you know well that I am a war chief and very rarely speak except in councils of war, but I am compelled to speak now, since nearly all the other chiefs are dead and I must utter what is in my heart before I follow them to the grave. Only two of my family are left alive, and perhaps even these will not long escape the fury of the pest. I have seen other diseases ravaging the country, but nothing that could compare with this. In two or three moons we saw their end, but now we have suffered for a year or more, and yet the evil does not abate. And, what is worst of all, we have not yet discovered its source."

Then, with words of studied moderation, alternating with bursts of angry invective, he proceeded to accuse the Jesuits of causing, by their sorceries, the unparalleled calamities that afflicted them, and in support of his charge he adduced a prodigious mass of evidence. When he had spent his eloquence, Brébeuf rose to reply and in a few words exposed the absurdity of his statements, whereupon another accuser brought a new array of charges. A clamor soon arose from the whole assembly, and they called upon Brébeuf with one voice to give up a certain charmed cloth which was the cause of their miseries. In vain the missionary protested that he had no such cloth. The clamor increased.

"If you will not believe me," said Brébeuf, "go to our house; search everywhere; and if you are not sure which is the charm, take all our clothing and all our cloth and throw them into the lake."

"Sorcerers always talk in that way," was the reply.

"Then what will you have me say?" demanded Brébeuf.

"Tell us the cause of the pest."

Brébeuf replied to the best of his power, mingling his explanations with instructions in Christian doctrine and exhortations to embrace the Faith. He was continually interrupted, and the old chief Ontitarac still called upon him to produce the charmed cloth.

Thus the debate continued till after midnight, when several of the assembly, seeing no prospect of a termination, fell asleep and others went away. One old chief, as he passed out, said to Brébeuf, "If some young man should split your head, we should have nothing to say."

100

The priest still continued to harangue the diminished conclave on the necessity of obeying God and the danger of offending Him, when the chief of Ossossané called out impatiently, "What sort of men are these? They are always saying the same thing and repeating the same words a hundred times. They are never done with telling us about their *Oki,* and what he demands and what he forbids, and Paradise and Hell."

"Here was the end of this miserable council," writes Le Mercier. The Fathers had escaped for the time, but they were still in deadly peril. They had taken pains to secure friends in private and there were those who were attached to their interests, yet none dared openly take their part. The few converts they had lately made came to them in secret and warned them that their death was determined upon. Their house was set on fire. In public every face was averted from them and a new council was called to pronounce the decree of death. They appeared before it with a front of such unflinching assurance that their judges, Indian-like, postponed the sentence. Yet it seemed impossible that they should much longer escape. Brébeuf, therefore, wrote a letter of farewell to his Superior, Le Jeune, at Quebec and confided it to some converts whom he could trust, to be carried by them to its destination.

The imperiled Jesuits now took a singular but certainly a very wise step. They gave one of those farewell feasts—*festins d'adieu*—which Huron custom enjoined on those about to die, whether in the course of Nature or by public execution. Being interpreted, it was a declaration that the priests knew their danger and did not shrink from it. It might have the effect of changing overawed friends into open advocates, and even of awakening a certain sympathy in the breasts of an assembly on whom a bold bearing could rarely fail of influence.

The house was packed with feasters, and Brébeuf addressed them as usual on his unfailing themes of God, Paradise and Hell. The throng listened in gloomy silence. When he had emptied his bowl each one rose and departed, leaving his entertainers in utter doubt as to his feelings and intentions. From this time forth, however, the clouds that overhung the fathers became less dark and threatening. Voices were heard in their defense and looks were less constantly averted. They ascribed the change to the intercession of St. Joseph, to whom they had vowed a nine days' devotion. By whatever cause produced, the lapse of a week wrought a hopeful improvement in their prospects, and when they went out of doors in the morning it was no longer with the expectation of having a hatchet struck into their brains as they crossed the threshold.

The persecution of the Jesuits as sorcerers continued, in an intermittent form, for years; and several of them escaped very narrowly. But in all the copious records of this dark period not a line gives occasion to suspect that one of this loyal band flinched or hesitated. The iron Brébeuf, the gentle Garnier, the all-enduring Jogues, the enthusiastic Chaumonot, Lalemant, Le Mercier, Chatelain, Daniel, Pijart, Ragueneau, Du Peron, Poncet, Le Moyne—one and all bore themselves with a tranquil boldness which amazed the Indians and enforced their respect.

It had been the first purpose of the Jesuits to form permanent missions in each of the principal Huron towns, but before the close of the year 1639 the difficulties and risks of this scheme had become fully apparent. They resolved, therefore, to establish one central station to be a base of operations and a focus from which the light of the Faith should radiate through all the wilderness around. It was to serve at once as residence, fort, magazine, hospital and convent. From it the priests would set forth on missionary expeditions far and near, and there they might retire, as to an asylum, in times of sickness or extreme peril. Here the neophytes could be gathered together, safe from perverting influences, and here in time a Christian settlement, Hurons mingled with Frenchmen, might spring up and thrive under the shadow of the cross.

The site of the new station was admirably chosen. The little river Wye flows from the southward into the Matchedash Bay of Lake Huron and at about a mile from its mouth passes through a small lake. The Jesuits chose the right bank of the Wye, where it issues from this lake, gained permission to build from the Indians (though not without difficulty) and began their labors with an abundant energy and a very deficient supply of workmen and tools. The new establishment was called Ste. Marie. The house at Teanaustayé and the house and chapel at Ossossané were abandoned, and all was concentrated at this spot. On one hand, it had a short water communication with

Lake Huron, and on the other, its central position gave the readiest access to every part of the Huron territory.

During the summer before, the priests had made a survey of their field of action, visited all the Huron towns and christened each of them with the name of a saint. This heavy draft on the calendar was followed by another, for the designation of the nine towns of the neighboring and kindred people of the Tobacco Nation. The Huron towns were portioned into four districts, while those of the Tobacco Nation formed a fifth, and each district was assigned to the charge of two or more priests. They began their missionary excursions in November and December, for the Indians were now gathered in their settlements, and journeyed on foot through the denuded forests in mud and snow, bearing on their backs the vessels and utensils necessary for the service of the altar.

The new and perilous mission of the Tobacco Nation fell to Garnier and Jogues. They were well chosen, and yet neither of them was robust by nature, in body or mind, though Jogues was noted for personal activity. The Tobacco Nation lay at the distance of a two days' journey from the Huron towns, among the mountains at the head of Nottawassaga Bay. The two missionaries tried to find a guide at Ossossané, but none would go with them and they set forth on their wild and unknown pilgrimage alone.

The forests were full of snow and the soft, moist flakes were still falling thickly, obscuring the air, beplastering the gray trunks, weighing to the earth the boughs of spruce and pine and hiding every footprint of the narrow path. The fathers missed their way and toiled on till night, at every step shaking down from the burdened branches a shower of fleecy white on their black cassocks. Night overtook them in a spruce swamp. Here they made a fire with great difficulty, cut the evergreen boughs, piled them for a bed and lay down. The storm presently ceased, and "praised be God," writes one of the travelers, "we passed a very good night."

In the morning they breakfasted on a morsel of corn bread and, resuming their journey, fell in with a small party of Indians, whom they followed all day without food. At eight in the evening they reached the first Tobacco town—a miserable cluster of bark cabins, hidden among forests and half buried in snowdrifts, where the savage children, seeing the two black apparitions, screamed that Famine and the Pest were coming. Their evil fame had gone before them. They were unwelcome guests. Nevertheless, shivering and famished as they were in the cold and darkness, they boldly pushed their way into one of these dens of barbarism.

It was precisely like a Huron house. Five or six fires blazed on the earthen floor and around them were huddled twice that number of families, sitting, crouching, standing or flat on the ground. Old and young, women and men, children and dogs, mingled pell-mell. The scene would have been a strange one by daylight; it was doubly strange by the flicker and glare of the lodge fires. Scowling brows, sidelong looks of distrust and fear, the screams of scared children, the scolding of squaws, the growling of wolfish dogs—this was the greeting of the strangers.

The chief man of the household treated them at first with the decencies of Indian hospitality, but when he saw them kneeling in the litter and ashes at their devotions, his suppressed fears found vent and he began a loud harangue addressed half to them and half to the Indians: "Now, what are these *okies* doing? They are making charms to kill us, and destroy all that the pest has spared in this house. I heard that they were sorcerers, and now, when it is too late, I believe it."

In other Tobacco towns their reception was much the same, but at the largest, called by them St. Peter and St. Paul, they fared worse. They reached it on a winter afternoon. Every door of its capacious bark houses was closed against them and they heard the squaws within calling on the young men to go out and split their heads, while children screamed abuse at the black-robed sorcerers. As night approached they left the town. A band of young men followed them, hatchet in hand, to put them to death. Darkness, the forest and the mountain favored them, and eluding their pursuers, they escaped. Thus began the mission of the Tobacco Nation.

In the following November a yet more distant and perilous mission was begun. Brébeuf and Chaumonot set out for the Neutral Nation. This fierce people occupied that part of Canada which lies immediately north of Lake Erie, while a wing of their territory extended across the Niagara into western New York. In their athletic propor-

104

tions, the ferocity of their manners and the extravagance of their superstitions, no American tribe has ever exceeded them. They carried to a preposterous excess the Indian notion that insanity is endowed with a mysterious and superhuman power. Their country was full of pretended maniacs, who to propitiate their guardian spirits, or *okies,* and acquire the mystic virtue which pertained to madness, raved stark naked through the villages, scattering the brands of the lodge fires and upsetting everything in their way.

The two priests left Ste. Marie on the second of November, found a Huron guide at St. Joseph and, after a dreary march of five days through the forest, reached the first Neutral town. Advancing, they visited in turn eighteen others, and their progress was a storm of maledictions. Brébeuf especially was accounted the most pestilent of sorcerers. The Hurons, restrained by a superstitious awe and unwilling to kill the priests lest they should embroil themselves with the French at Quebec, conceived that their object might be safely gained by stirring up the Neutrals to become their executioners. To that end they sent two emissaries to the Neutral towns, who called the chiefs and young warriors to a council, denounced the Jesuits as destroyers of the human race and made their auditors a gift of nine French hatchets on condition that they would put them to death.

It was then that Brébeuf, fully conscious of the danger, half starved and half frozen, driven with revilings from every door, struck and spit upon by pretended maniacs, beheld in a vision a great cross which moved onward through the air, above the wintry forests that stretched towards the land of the Iroquois.

"Late at night," write Chaumonot, "our host came back from the council, where the two Huron emissaries had made their gift of hatchets to have us killed. He wakened us to say that three times we had been on the point of death; for the young men had offered three times to strike the blow, and three times the old men had dissuaded them . . ."

They had escaped for the time, but the Indians agreed among themselves that thenceforth no one should give them shelter. At night, pierced with cold and faint with hunger, they found every door closed against them. They stood and watched, saw an Indian issue from a house, and by a quick movement pushed through the half-open door

into this abode of smoke and filth. The inmates, aghast at their boldness, stared in silence. Then a messenger ran out to carry the tidings
and an angry crowd collected.

"Go out and leave our country," said an old chief, "or we will
put you into the kettle and make a feast of you."

"I have had enough of the dark-colored flesh of our enemies," said
a young brave. "I wish to know the taste of white meat, and I will
eat yours."

A warrior rushed in like a madman, drew his bow and aimed the
arrow at Chaumonot. "I looked at him fixedly," writes the Jesuit,
"and commended myself in full confidence to St. Michael. Without
doubt, this great archangel saved us; for almost immediately the fury
of the warrior was appeased, and the rest of our enemies soon began
to listen to the explanation we gave them of our visit to their country."

The mission was barren of any fruit other than hardship and danger,
and after a stay of four months the two priests resolved to return. On
the way they met a genuine act of kindness. A heavy snowstorm
arresting their progress, a Neutral woman took them into her lodge,
entertained them for two weeks with her best fare, persuaded her
father and relatives to befriend them and aided them to make a vo-
cabulary of the dialect. Bidding their generous hostess farewell, they
journeyed northward through the melting snows of spring and reached
Ste. Marie in safety.

The Jesuits had borne all that the human frame seems capable of
bearing. They had escaped as by miracle from torture and death. Did
their zeal flag or their courage fail? A fervor intense and unquenchable
urged them on to more distant and more deadly ventures. They
burned to do, to suffer and to die; and now, from out a living martyrdom, they turned their heroic gaze towards a horizon dark with perils
yet more appalling and saw in hope the day when they should bear the
cross into the bloodstained dens of the Iroquois.

CHAPTER 3

~~~~~~

New Life at Quebec

A T QUEBEC, MEANWHILE, CHAMPLAIN'S DEATH HAD left the colony without a governor. Who should succeed him, and would the successor be equally zealous for the Faith and friendly to the mission? These doubts agitated the mind of Father Le Jeune, but they were happily set at rest on a morning in June 1636 when he saw a ship anchoring in the basin below and, hastening with his brethren to the landing place, was met there by Charles Hualt de Montmagny, a Knight of Malta, followed by a train of officers and gentlemen.

As they all climbed the rock together, Montmagny saw a crucifix planted by the path. He instantly fell on his knees before it, and nobles, soldiers, sailors and priests imitated his example. The Jesuits sang *Te Deum* at the church, and the cannon roared from the adjacent fort.

A considerable reinforcement had come out with Montmagny, and among the rest several men of birth and substance with their families and dependents. "It was a sight to thank God for," exclaims Father Le Jeune, "to behold these delicate young ladies and these tender infants issuing from their wooden prison, like day from the shades of night." The father, it will be remembered, had for some years past seen nothing but squaws, with papooses swathed like mummies and strapped to a board.

He was even more pleased with the contents of a huge packet of letters that was placed in his hands, bearing the signatures of nuns, priests, soldiers, courtiers and princesses. A great interest in the mission had been kindled in France. Le Jeune's printed *Relations* had been read with avidity, and his Jesuit brethren, who as teachers, preachers and confessors had spread themselves through the nation, had successfully fanned the rising flame. The Father Superior finds no words for his joy. "Heaven," he exclaims, "is the conductor of this enterprise! Nature's arms are not long enough to touch so many hearts."

He reads how, in a single convent, thirteen nuns have devoted themselves by a vow to the work of converting the Indian women and children; how, in the church of Montmartre, a nun lies prostrate day and night before the altar, praying for the mission; how "the Carmelites are all on fire, the Ursulines full of zeal, the sisters of the Visitation have no words to speak their ardor"; how some person unknown but blessed of Heaven means to found a school for Huron children; how the Duchesse d'Aiguillon has sent out six workmen to build a hospital for the Indians; how in every house of the Jesuits young priests turn eager eyes toward Canada; and how on the voyage thither the devils raised a tempest, endeavoring in vain fury to drown the invaders of their American domain.

Great was Le Jeune's delight at the exalted rank of some of those who gave their patronage to the mission, and again and again his satisfaction flows from his pen in mysterious allusions to these eminent persons. In his eyes, the vicious imbecile who sat on the throne of France was the anointed champion of the Faith, and the cruel and ambitious priest who ruled king and nation alike was the chosen instrument of Heaven. Church and State, linked in alliance close and potential, played faithfully into each other's hands, and that enthusiasm in which the Jesuit saw the direct inspiration of God was fostered by all the prestige of royalty and all the patronage of power. And as often happens where the interests of a hierarchy are identified with the interests of a ruling class, religion was become a fashion, as graceful and as comforting as the courtier's embroidered mantle or the court lady's robe of fur.

Such, we may well believe, was the complexion of the enthusiasm which animated some of Le Jeune's noble and princely correspondents. But there were deeper fervors, glowing in the still depths of convent cells and kindling the breasts of their inmates with quenchless long-ings. It was to the combustible hearts of female recluses that the torch was most busily applied, and here accordingly blazed forth a prodi-gious and amazing flame. "If all had their pious will," writes Le Jeune, "Quebec would soon be flooded with nuns."

Both Montmagny and De Lisle were half churchmen, for both were Knights of Malta. More and more the powers spiritual engrossed the colony. As nearly as might be, the sword itself was in priestly hands. The Jesuits were all in all. Authority, absolute and without appeal, was vested in a council composed of the governor, Le Jeune and the syndic, an official supposed to represent the interests of the inhabit-ants. There was no tribunal of justice, and the governor pronounced summarily on all complaints. The church adjoined the fort, and before it was planted a stake bearing a placard with a prohibition against blasphemy, drunkenness or neglect of mass and other religious rites. To the stake was also attached a chain and iron collar. Hard by was a wooden horse, where a culprit was now and then mounted by way of example and warning. In a community so absolutely priest-governed, overt offenses were, however, rare. Except on the annual arrival of the ships from France, when the rock swarmed with godless sailors, Quebec was a model of decorum, and wore, as its chroniclers tell us, an aspect unspeakably edifying.

The country around Quebec was still an unbroken wilderness, with the exception of a small clearing made by the Sieur Giffard on his seigniory of Beauport, another made by Monsieur de Puiseaux be-tween Quebec and Sillery, and possibly one or two feeble attempts in other quarters. The total population did not exceed two hundred, including women and children. Of this number, by far the greater part were agents of the fur company known as the Hundred Associ-ates, and men in their employ. Some of these had brought over their families. The remaining inhabitants were priests, nuns and a very few colonists.

There was no real motive for emigration. No persecution expelled the colonist from his home, for none but good Catholics were tolerated in New France. The settler could not trade with the Indians, except on condition of selling again to the Company at a fixed price. He might hunt, but he could not fish; and he was forced to beg or buy food for years before he could obtain it from that rude soil in sufficient quantity for the wants of his family. The Company imported provisions every year for those in its employ, and of these supplies a portion was needed for the relief of starving settlers.

Aside from the fur trade of the Company, the whole life of the colony was in missions, convents, religious schools and hospitals. Here on the rock of Quebec were the appendages, useful and otherwise, of an old-established civilization. While as yet there were no inhabitants and no immediate hope of any, there were institutions for the care of children, the sick and the decrepit. All these were supported by a charity in most cases precarious. The Jesuits relied chiefly on the Company, who by the terms of their patent were obliged to maintain religious worship.

Quebec wore an aspect half military, half monastic. At sunrise and sunset a squad of soldiers in the pay of the Company paraded in the fort, and as in Champlain's time, the bells of the church rang morning, noon and night. Confessions, masses and penances were punctiliously observed. From the governor to the meanest laborer, the Jesuit watched and guided all. The social atmosphere of New England itself was not more suffocating. By day and by night, at home, at church or at his daily work, the colonist lived under the eyes of busy and overzealous priests. At times the denizens of Quebec grew restless. In 1639 deputies were covertly sent to beg relief in France and "to represent the hell in which the consciences of the colony were kept by the union of the temporal and spiritual authority in the same hands."

The very amusements of this pious community were acts of religion. Thus on the fete day of St. Joseph, the patron of New France, there was a show of fireworks to do him honor. On the anniversary of the Dauphin's birth there was a dramatic performance, in which an unbeliever, speaking Algonquin for the profit of the Indians present, was hunted into Hell by fiends. Religious processions were frequent.

Methods of conversion at Quebec were much the same as those practiced among the Hurons. The principal appeal was to fear. "You do good to your friends," said Le Jeune to an Algonquin chief, "and you burn your enemies. God does the same." And he painted Hell to the startled neophyte as a place where, when he was hungry, he would get nothing to eat but frogs and snakes and, when thirsty, nothing to drink but flames.

Pictures were found invaluable. "These holy representations," pursues the Father Superior, "are half the instruction that can be given to the Indians. I wanted some pictures of Hell and souls in perdition, and a few were sent us on paper, but they are too confused. The devils and the men are so mixed up that one can make out nothing without particular attention. If three, four or five devils were painted tormenting a soul with different punishments—one applying fire, another serpents, another tearing him with pincers and another holding him fast with a chain—this would have a good effect, especially if everything were made distinct, and misery, rage and desperation appeared plainly in his face."

The preparation of the convert for baptism was often very slight. A dying Algonquin, who, though meager as a skeleton, had thrown himself with a last effort of expiring ferocity on an Iroquois prisoner and torn off his ear with his teeth was baptized almost immediately. It was not very easy to make an Indian comprehend the nature of baptism. An Iroquois at Montreal, hearing a missionary speaking of the water which cleansed the soul from sin, said that he was well acquainted with it, as the Dutch had once given him so much that they were forced to tie him, hand and foot, to prevent him from doing mischief.

And still more spiritual forces arrived at Quebec. On the fourth of May, 1639, Madame de la Peltrie, an ardently pious and wealthy widow bent on establishing a convent; two equally ardent Ursuline nuns, Marie de l'Incarnation and Marie de St. Bernard; and another Ursuline embarked at Dieppe for Canada. In the ship were also three young hospital nuns, sent out to found at Quebec a Hôtel-Dieu, endowed by the famous niece of Richelieu, the Duchesse d'Aiguillon. Here, too, were the Jesuits Chaumonot and Poncet, on the way to their mission, together with Father Vimont, who was to succeed Le Jeune in his post of Superior.

To the nuns, pale from their cloistered seclusion, there was a strange and startling novelty in this new world of life and action— the ship, the sailors, the shouts of command, the flapping of sails, the salt wind and the boisterous sea. The voyage was long and

111

tedious. Sometimes they lay in their berths, seasick and woebegone; sometimes they sang in choir on deck or heard mass in the cabin. Once, on a misty morning, a wild cry of alarm startled crew and passengers alike. A huge iceberg was drifting close upon them. The peril was extreme. Madame de la Peltrie clung to Marie de l'Incarnation, who stood perfectly calm and gathered her gown about her feet that she might drown with decency. It is scarcely necessary to say that they were saved by a vow to the Virgin and St. Joseph. Vimont offered it in behalf of all the company, and the ship glided into the open sea unharmed.

They arrived at Tadoussac on the fifteenth of July. The nuns ascended to Quebec in a small craft deeply laden with salted codfish, on which, uncooked, they subsisted until the first of August, when they reached their destination. Cannon roared welcome from the fort and batteries; all labor ceased; the storehouses were closed; and the zealous Montmagny, with a train of priests and soldiers, met the newcomers at the landing. All the nuns fell prostrate and kissed the sacred soil of Canada. They heard mass at the church, dined at the fort and presently set forth to visit the new settlement of Sillery, four miles above Quebec.

Noel Brulart de Sillery, a Knight of Malta, who had once filled the highest offices under the Queen Marie de Médicis, had severed his connection with his Order, renounced the world and become a priest. He devoted his vast revenues—for a dispensation of the Pope had freed him from his vow of poverty—to the founding of religious establishments. Among other endowments, he had placed an ample fund in the hands of the Jesuits for the formation of a settlement of Christian Indians at the spot which still bears his name. On the strand of Sillery, between the river and the woody heights behind, were clustered the small log cabins of a number of Algonquin converts, together with a church, a mission house and an infirmary, the whole surrounded by a palisade. It was to this place that the six nuns were now conducted by the Jesuits. The scene delighted and edified them, and in the transports of their zeal, they seized and kissed every female Indian child on whom they could lay hands, "without minding," says Father Le Jeune, "whether they were dirty or not." "Love and charity," he adds, "triumphed over every human consideration."

112

The nuns of the Hôtel-Dieu soon after took up their abode at Sillery, whence they removed to a house built for them at Quebec by their foundress, the Duchesse d'Aiguillon. The Ursulines, in the absence of better quarters, were lodged at first in a small wooden tenement under the rock of Quebec, at the brink of the river. Here they were soon beset with such a host of children that the floor of their wretched tenement was covered with beds and their toil had no respite. Then came the smallpox, carrying death and terror among the neighboring Indians. These thronged to Quebec in misery and desperation, begging succor from the French. The labors both of the Ursulines and of the hospital nuns were prodigious. In the infected air of their miserable hovels, where sick and dying savages covered the floor and were packed one above another in berths, amid all that is most distressing and most revolting, with little food and less sleep, these women passed the rough beginning of their new life. Several of them fell ill. But the excess of the evil at length brought relief, for so many of the Indians died in these pesthouses that the survivors shunned them in horror.

It was three years later before the Ursulines and their pupils took possession of a massive convent of stone. Money had failed before the work was done, and the interior was as unfinished as a barn. Beside the cloister stood a large ash tree. Beneath its shade, says the convent tradition, Marie de l'Incarnation and her nuns instructed the Indian children in the truths of salvation. But it might seem rash to affirm that their teachings were always either wise or useful, since Father Vimont tells us approvingly that they reared their pupils in so chaste a horror of the other sex that a little girl whom a man had playfully taken by the hand ran crying to a bowl of water to wash off the unhallowed influence.

CHAPTER 4

The Birth of Montreal

AT LA FLÈCHE, IN ANJOU, DWELT ONE JÉRÔME LE Royer de la Dauversière, receiver of taxes. His portrait shows us a round *bourgeois* face, somewhat heavy perhaps, decorated with a slight mustache and redeemed by bright and earnest eyes. On his head he wears a black skullcap, and over his ample shoulders spreads a stiff white collar of wide expanse and studious plainness. Though he belonged to the *noblesse,* his look is that of a grave burgher, of good renown and sage deportment. Dauversière was, however, an enthusiastic devotee of mystical tendencies, who whipped himself with a scourge of small chains till his shoulders were one wound, wore a belt with more than twelve hundred sharp points and invented for himself other torments which filled his confessor with admiration.

One day, while at his devotions, he heard an inward voice commanding him to become the founder of a new Order of hospital nuns. He was further ordered to establish, on the island called Montreal in Canada, a hospital or Hôtel-Dieu to be conducted by these nuns. But Montreal was a wilderness and the hospital would have no patients. Therefore, in order to supply them, the island must first be colonized. Dauversière was greatly perplexed. On the one hand, the voice of Heaven must be obeyed; on the other, he had a wife, six children and a very moderate fortune.

Again, there was at Paris a young priest about twenty-eight years of age: Jean Jacques Olier, afterwards widely known as founder of the Seminary of St. Sulpice. Judged by his engraved portrait, his

114

countenance, though marked both with energy and intellect, was anything but prepossessing. Every lineament proclaims the priest. Yet the Abbé Olier has high titles to esteem. He signalized his piety, it is true, by the most disgusting exploits of self-mortification, but at the same time he was strenuous in his efforts to reform the people and the clergy. So zealous was he for good morals that he drew upon himself the imputation of a leaning to the heresy of the Jansenists, a suspicion strengthened by his opposition to certain priests who, to secure the faithful in their allegiance, justified them in lives of licentiousness. Yet Olier's Catholicity was past attainment, and in his horror of Jansenists he yielded to the Jesuits alone.

He was praying in the ancient church of St. Germain des Prés, when, like Dauversière, he thought he heard a voice from Heaven, saying that he was destined to be a light to the Gentiles. It is recorded as a mystic coincidence attending this miracle that the choir was at that very time chanting the words *Lumen ad revelationem Gentium*, and it seems to have occurred neither to Olier nor to his biographer that, falling on the ear of the rapt worshiper, they might have unconsciously suggested the supposed revelation.

But there was a further miracle. An inward voice told Olier that he was to form a society of priests and establish them on the island called Montreal in Canada, for the propagation of the True Faith. While both he and Dauversière were totally ignorant of Canadian geography, it is asserted that they suddenly found themselves in possession, they knew not how, of the most exact details concerning Montreal, its size, shape, situation, soil, climate and productions.

Dauversière pondered the revelation he had received, and the more he pondered the more he was convinced that it came from God. He therefore set out for Paris, to find some means of accomplishing the task assigned him. Here, as he prayed before an image of the Virgin in the Church of Notre-Dame, he fell into an ecstasy and beheld a vision.

From Paris he went to the neighboring château of Meudon, which overlooks the valley of the Seine, not far from St. Cloud. Entering the gallery of the old castle, he saw a priest approaching him. It was Olier. We are told that neither of these men had ever seen or heard of the other, and yet, says the pious historian, "impelled by a kind of inspiration, they knew each other at once, even to the depths of their hearts; saluted each other by name, as we read of St. Paul, the Hermit, and St. Anthony, and of St. Dominic and St. Francis; and ran to embrace each other, like two friends who had met after a long separation."

"Monsieur," exclaimed Olier, "I know your design, and I go to commend it to God, at the holy altar."

And he went at once to say mass in the chapel. Dauversière received the communion at his hands, and then they walked for three hours in the park, discussing their plans. They were of one mind, in respect both to objects and means. When they parted, Olier gave Dauversière a hundred louis, saying, "This is to begin the work of God."

They proposed to found at Montreal three religious communities— three being the mystic number—one of secular priests to direct the colonists and convert the Indians, one of nuns to nurse the sick and one of nuns to teach the Faith to the children, white and red. To borrow their own phrases, they would plant the banner of Christ in an abode of desolation and a haunt of demons. To this end a band of priests and women were to invade the wilderness and take post between the fangs of the Iroquois. But first they must make a colony, and to do so must raise money. Olier had pious and wealthy penitents; Dauversière had a friend, the Baron de Fancamp, devout as himself and far richer. Anxious for his soul and satisfied that the enterprise was an inspiration of God, he was eager to bear part in it. Olier soon found three others, and the six together formed the germ of the Society of Notre-Dame de Montreal. Among them they raised the sum of seventy-five thousand livres.

The feeble settlement at Quebec was at this time in danger of utter ruin, for the Iroquois, enraged at the attacks made on them by Champlain, had begun a fearful course of retaliation and the very existence of the colony trembled in the balance.

But if Quebec was exposed to their ferocious inroads, Montreal was incomparably more so. A settlement here would be a perilous outpost, a hand thrust into the jaws of the tiger. It would provoke attack and lie almost in the path of the war parties. The associates could gain nothing by the fur trade, for they would not be allowed to share in it. On the other hand, danger apart, the place was an excellent one for a mission, for here met two great rivers: the St. Lawrence, with its countless tributaries, flowed in from the west, while the Ottawa descended from the north; Montreal, embraced by their uniting waters, was the key to a vast inland navigation. There the Indians would naturally resort, and thus the missionaries could make their way into the heart of a boundless heathendom. None of the ordinary motives of colonization had part in this design. It owed its conception and its birth to religious zeal alone.

Their title assured, they matured their plan. First they would send out forty men to take possession of Montreal, intrench themselves and raise crops. Then they would build a house for the priests and two convents for the nuns. Meanwhile, Olier was toiling at Vaugirard, on the outskirts of Paris, to inaugurate the seminary of priests, and Dauversière at La Flèche to form the community of hospital nuns.

The Associates needed a soldier-governor to take charge of their forty men, and directed as they supposed by Providence, they found one wholly to their mind. This was Paul de Chomedey, Sieur de Maisonneuve, a devout and valiant gentleman, who in long service among the heretics of Holland had kept his faith intact and had held himself resolutely aloof from the license that surrounded him. He loved his profession of arms and wished to consecrate his sword to the Church.

Past all comparison, he is the manliest figure that appears in this group of zealots. The piety of the design, the miracles that inspired it, the adventure and the peril all combined to charm him and he eagerly embraced the enterprise. His father opposed his purpose, but he met him with a text of St. Mark: "There is no man that hath left house, or brethren, or sisters, or father . . . for my sake . . . but he shall receive an hundred-fold." At this the elder Maisonneuve, deceived by his own worldliness, imagined that the plan covered some hidden speculation from which enormous profits were expected and therefore withdrew his opposition.

There was imperative need of more money, and Dauversière, under judicious guidance, was active in obtaining it. This miserable victim of illusions had a squat, uncourtly figure and was not proficient in the graces either of manners or of speech; hence his success in commending his objects to persons of rank and wealth is set down as one of the many miracles which attended the birth of Montreal.

But zeal and earnestness are in themselves a power, and the ground had been well marked out and plowed for him in advance. That attractive though intricate subject of study, the female mind, has always engaged the attention of priests, more especially in countries where, as in France, women exert a strong social and political influence. The art of kindling the flames of zeal and the more difficult art of directing and controlling them have been themes of diligent and profound reflection. Accordingly we find that a large proportion of the money raised for this enterprise was contributed by devout ladies. Many of them became members of the Association of Montreal, which was eventually increased to about forty-five persons, chosen for their devotion and their wealth.

Olier and his associates had resolved, though not from any collapse of zeal, to postpone the establishment of the seminary and the college until after a settlement should be formed. The hospital, however, they thought might be begun at once, for blood and blows would be the assured portion of the first settlers. At least a discreet woman ought to embark with the first colonists as their nurse and housekeeper. Scarcely was the need recognized when it was supplied.

Mademoiselle Jeanne Mance was born of an honorable family of Nogent-le-Roi, and in 1640 was thirty-four years of age. These Canadian heroines began their religious experiences early. Of Marie de l'Incarnation we read that at the age of seven Christ appeared to her in a vision, and the biographer of Mademoiselle Mance assures us, with admiring gravity, that at the same tender age she bound herself to God by a vow of perpetual chastity. This singular infant in due time became a woman, of a delicate constitution and manners graceful yet dignified. Though an earnest devotee, she felt no vocation for the cloister, yet while still "in the world" she led the life of a nun. The Jesuit *Relations* and the example of Madame de la Peltrie, of whom she had heard, inoculated her with the Canadian enthusiasm, then so prevalent.

Under the pretense of visiting relatives, she made a journey to Paris to take counsel of certain priests. Of one thing she was assured: the Divine will called her to Canada, but to what end she neither knew nor asked to know, for she abandoned herself as an atom to be borne to unknown destinies on the breath of God. At Paris, Father St. Jure, a Jesuit, assured her that her vocation to Canada was, past doubt, a call from Heaven, while Father Rapin, a Récollet, spread abroad the fame of her virtues and introduced her to many ladies of rank, wealth and zeal. Then, well supplied with money for any pious work to which she might be summoned, she journeyed to Rochelle, whence ships were to sail for New France.

Thus far she had been kept in ignorance of the plan with regard to Montreal, but now Father La Place, a Jesuit, revealed it to her. On the day after her arrival at Rochelle, as she entered the Church of the Jesuits, she met Dauversière coming out.

"Then," says her biographer, "these two persons, who had never seen nor heard of each other, were enlightened supernaturally, whereby their most hidden thoughts were mutually made known, as had happened already with M. Olier and this same M. de la Dauversière."

A long conversation ensued between them, and the delights of this interview were never effaced from the mind of Mademoiselle Mance. "She used to speak of it like a seraph," writes one of her nuns, "and far better than many a learned doctor could have done."

She had found her destiny. The ocean, the wilderness, the solitude, the Iroquois—nothing daunted her. She would go to Montreal with Maisonneuve and his forty men. Yet when the vessel was about to sail, a new and sharp misgiving seized her. How could she, a woman not yet bereft of youth or charms, live alone in the forest among a troop of soldiers? Her scruples were relieved by two of the men, who at the last moment refused to embark without their wives, and by a young woman who, impelled by enthusiasm, escaped from her friends and took passage in spite of them in one of the vessels.

All was ready; the ships set sail. But Olier, Dauversière and Fancamp remained at home, as did also the other Associates, with the exception of Maisonneuve and Mademoiselle Mance. In the following February an impressive scene took place in the Church of Notre Dame at Paris. The Associates, at this time numbering about forty-five, with Olier at their head, assembled before the altar of the Virgin and by a solemn ceremonial consecrated Montreal to the Holy Family.

119

Henceforth it was to be called Villemarie de Montreal—a sacred town reared to the honor and under the patronage of Christ, St. Joseph and the Virgin, to be typified by three persons on earth, founders respectively of the three destined communities: Olier, Dauversière and a maiden of Troyes, Marguerite Bourgeoys. The seminary was to be consecrated to Christ, the Hôtel-Dieu to St. Joseph and the college to the Virgin.

Maisonneuve, with his forty men and four women, reached Quebec too late to ascend to Montreal that season. They encountered distrust, jealousy and opposition. The agents of the Company of the Hundred Associates looked on them askance, and the governor of Quebec, Montmagny, saw a rival governor in Maisonneuve. Every means was used to persuade the adventurers to abandon their project and settle at Quebec. Montmagny called a council of the principal persons of his colony, who gave it as their opinion that the newcomers had better exchange Montreal for the Island of Orleans, where they would be in a position to give and receive succor, while by persisting in their first design they would expose themselves to destruction and be of use to nobody. Maisonneuve, who was present, expressed his surprise that they should assume to direct his affairs.

"I have not come here," he said, "to deliberate, but to act. It is my duty and my honor to found a colony at Montreal, and I would go if every tree were an Iroquois!"

At Quebec there was little ability and no inclination to shelter the new colonists for the winter, and they would have fared ill but for the generosity of Monsieur Puiseaux, who lived not far distant at a place called St. Michel. This devout and most hospitable person made room for them all in his rough but capacious dwelling.

There Maisonneuve employed his men in building boats to ascend to Montreal and in various other labors for the future colony. Thus the winter wore away, but as celestial minds are not exempt from ire, Montmagny and Maisonneuve fell into a quarrel.

The twenty-fifth of January was Maisonneuve's birthday, and as he was greatly beloved by his followers, they resolved to celebrate the occasion. Accordingly, an hour and a half before daylight, they made a general discharge of their muskets and cannon. The sound reached Quebec, two or three miles distant, startling the governor from his morning slumbers. His indignation was redoubled when he heard it again at night, for Maisonneuve, pleased at the attachment of his men, had feasted them and warmed their hearts with a distribution of wine. Montmagny, jealous of his authority, resented these demonstrations as an infraction of it, affirming that they had no right to fire their pieces without his consent. Arresting the principal offender, one Jean Gory, he put him in irons.

On being released a few days after, Gory's companions welcomed him with great rejoicing and Maisonneuve gave them all a feast. He himself came in during the festivity, drank the health of the company, shook hands with the late prisoner, placed him at the head of the table and addressed him as follows:

"Jean Gory, you have been put in irons for me; you had the pain, and I the affront. For that, I add ten crowns to your wages." Then, turning to the others: "My boys," he said, "though Jean Gory has been misused, you must not lose heart for that, but drink, all of you, to the health of the man in irons. When we are once in Montreal, we shall be our own masters and can fire our cannon when we please."

Montmagny was wroth when this was reported to him, and on the ground that what had passed was "contrary to the service of the King and the authority of the Governor," he summoned Gory and six others before him and put them separately under oath. Their evidence failed to establish a case against their commander, but thenceforth there was great coldness between the powers of Quebec and Montreal.

Early in May, Maisonneuve and his followers embarked. They had gained an unexpected recruit during the winter in the person of Madame de la Peltrie. The piety, the novelty and the romance of their enterprise all had their charms for this fair enthusiast, and an irresistible impulse—imputed by a slandering historian to the levity of her sex—urged her to share their fortunes. Her zeal was more admired by the Montrealists whom she joined than by the Ursulines whom she abandoned. She carried off all the furniture she had lent them and left them in the utmost destitution. Nor did she remain quiet after reaching Montreal, but was presently seized with a longing to visit the Hurons and preach the Faith in person to those benighted heathen. It needed all the eloquence of a Jesuit, lately returned from

121

that most arduous mission, to convince her that the attempt would be as useless as rash.

It was the eighth of May when Maisonneuve and his followers embarked at St. Michel, and as the boats, deep-laden with men, arms and stores, moved slowly on their way, the forest, with leaves just opening in the warmth of spring, lay on their right hand and on their left in a flattering semblance of tranquillity and peace. But behind woody islets, in tangled thickets and damp ravines and in the shade and stillness of the columned woods lurked everywhere a danger and a terror.

On the seventeenth of May, 1642, Maisonneuve's little flotilla—a pinnace, a flat-bottomed craft moved by sails, and two rowboats—approached Montreal, and all on board raised in unison a hymn of praise. Montmagny was with them to deliver the island in behalf of the Company of the Hundred Associates to Maisonneuve, representative of the Associates of Montreal. And here, too, was Father Vimont, Superior of the missions, for the Jesuits had been prudently invited to accept the spiritual charge of the young colony.

On the following day they glided along the green and solitary shores now thronged with the life of a busy city and landed on the spot which Champlain thirty-one years before had chosen as the fit site of a settlement. It was a tongue or triangle of land formed by the junction of a rivulet with the St. Lawrence and known afterwards as Point Callière. The rivulet was bordered by a meadow and beyond rose the forest with its vanguard of scattered trees. Early spring flowers were blooming in the young grass and birds of varied plumage flitted among the boughs.

Maisonneuve sprang ashore and fell on his knees. His followers imitated his example. All joined their voices in enthusiastic songs of thanksgiving. Tents, baggage, arms and stores were landed. An altar was raised on a pleasant spot near at hand, and Mademoiselle Mance, with Madame de la Peltrie, aided by her servant, Charlotte Barré, decorated it with a taste which was the admiration of the beholders. Now all the company gathered before the shrine. Here stood Vimont, in the rich vestments of his office. Here were the two ladies, with their servant; Montmagny, no very willing spectator; and Maisonneuve, a warlike figure, erect and tall, his men clustering around him—soldiers, sailors, artisans and laborers—all alike soldiers at need. They kneeled in reverent silence as the Host was raised aloft, and when the rite was over the priest turned and addressed them:

"You are a grain of mustard seed, that shall rise and grow till its branches overshadow the earth. You are few, but your work is the work of God. His smile is on you, and your children shall fill the land."

The afternoon waned; the sun sank behind the western forest and twilight came on. Fireflies were twinkling over the darkened meadow. They caught them, tied them with threads into shining festoons and hung them before the altar where the Host remained exposed. Then they pitched their tents, lighted their bivouac fires, stationed their guards and lay down to rest. Such was the birth night of Montreal.

In the morning they all fell to their work—Maisonneuve hewing down the first tree—and labored with such good will that their tents were soon enclosed with a strong palisade and their altar covered by a provisional chapel, built in the Huron mode of bark. Soon afterward their canvas habitations were supplanted by solid structures of wood, and the feeble germ of a future city began to take root.

The Iroquois had not yet found them out, nor did they discover them till they had had ample time to fortify themselves. Meanwhile, on a Sunday, they would stroll at their leisure over the adjacent meadow and in the shade of the bordering forest, where, as the old chronicler tells us, the grass was gay with wildflowers and the branches with the flutter and song of many strange birds.

The summer passed prosperously, but with the winter their faith was put to a rude test. In December there was a rise of the St. Lawrence, threatening to sweep away in a night the results of all their labor. They fell to their prayers and Maisonneuve planted a wooden cross in face of the advancing deluge, first making a vow that, should the peril be averted, he would bear another cross on his shoulders up the neighboring mountain and place it on the summit. The vow seemed in vain. The flood still rose, filled the fort ditch, swept the foot of the palisade and threatened to sap the magazine. But here it stopped and presently began to recede, till at length it had withdrawn within its lawful channel, and Villemarie was safe.

Now it remained to fulfill the promise from which such happy results had proceeded. Maisonneuve set his men at work to clear a path through the forest to the top of the mountain. A large cross was made and solemnly blessed by the priest. Then, on the sixth of January, the Jesuit Du Peron led the way, followed in procession by Madame de la Peltrie and the artisans and soldiers, to the destined spot. The commandant, who with all the ceremonies of the Church had been declared First Soldier of the Cross, walked behind the rest, bearing on his shoulder a cross so heavy that it needed his utmost strength to climb the steep and rugged path. They planted it on the highest crest, and all knelt in adoration before it. Du Peron said mass, and Madame de la Peltrie, always romantic and always devout, received the sacrament on the mountaintop, a spectacle to the virgin world outstretched below. Sundry relics of saints had been set in the wood of the cross, which remained an object of pilgrimage to the pious colonists of Villemarie.

The French hoped to form an agricultural settlement of Indians in the neighborhood of Villemarie, and they spared no exertion to this end, giving them tools and aiding them to till the fields. They might have succeeded but for that pest of the wilderness, the Iroquois, who hovered about them, harassed them with petty attacks and again and again drove the Algonquins in terror from their camps.

Some time had elapsed before the Iroquois discovered Villemarie, but at length ten fugitive Algonquins, chased by a party of them, made for the friendly settlement as a safe asylum and thus their astonished pursuers became aware of its existence. They reconnoitered the place and went back to their towns with the news. From that time forth the colonists had no peace; no more excursions for fishing and hunting; no more Sunday strolls in woods and meadows. The men went armed to their work and returned at the sound of a bell, marching in a compact body, prepared for an attack.

At Villemarie it was usually dangerous to pass beyond the ditch of the fort or the palisades of the hospital. Sometimes a solitary warrior would lie hidden for days, without sleep and almost without food, behind a log in the forest or in a dense thicket, watching like a lynx for some rash straggler. Sometimes parties of a hundred or more made ambuscades near by and sent a few of their number to lure out the soldiers by a petty attack and a flight. The danger was much diminished, however, when the colonists received from France a number of dogs, which proved most efficient sentinels and scouts.

Of the instinct of these animals, the writers of the time speak with astonishment. Chief among them was a bitch named Pilot, who every morning made the rounds of the forests and fields about the fort, followed by a troop of her offspring. If one of them lagged behind, she bit him to remind him of his duty, and if any skulked and ran home, she punished them severely in the same manner on her return. When she discovered the Iroquois, which she was sure to do by the scent if any were near, she barked furiously and ran at once straight to the fort, followed by the rest. The Jesuit chronicler adds that while this was her duty, "her natural inclination was for hunting squirrels."

On the morning of the thirtieth of March, Pilot was heard barking with unusual fury in the forest eastward from the fort, and in a few moments they saw her running over the clearing where the snow was still deep, followed by her brood, all giving tongue together. The excited Frenchmen flocked about their commander.

"Monsieur, our enemies are in the woods; shall we go look for them?"

Maisonneuve, habitually composed and calm, answered sharply: "Yes, you shall see the enemy. Get yourselves ready at once, and take care that you are as brave as you profess to be. I shall lead you myself."

All was bustle in the fort. Guns were loaded, pouches filled and snowshoes tied on by those who had them and knew how to use them. There were not enough, however, and many were forced to go without. When all was ready, Maisonneuve sallied forth at the head of thirty men, leaving the remainder to hold the fort.

They crossed the snowy clearing and entered the forest, where all was silent as the grave. They pushed on, wading through the deep snow with the countless pitfalls hidden beneath it, when suddenly they were greeted with the screeches of eighty Iroquois, who sprang up from their lurking places and showered bullets and arrows upon the advancing French. The emergency called for woodcraft, not chivalry, and Maisonneuve ordered his men to take shelter, like their assailants, behind trees. They stood their ground resolutely for a long time, but the Iroquois pressed them close. Three of their number were killed,

125

others were wounded and their ammunition began to fail. Their only alternatives were destruction or retreat, and to retreat was not easy.

The order was given. Though steady at first, the men soon became confused and overeager to escape the galling fire which the Iroquois sent after them. Maisonneuve directed them towards a sledge track which had been used in dragging timber for building the hospital and where the snow was firm beneath the foot. He himself remained to the last, encouraging his followers and aiding the wounded to escape.

The French, as they struggled through the snow, faced about from time to time and fired back to check the pursuit, but no sooner had they reached the sledge track than they gave way to their terror and ran in a body for the fort. Those within, seeing this confused rush of men from the distance, mistook them for the enemy. An overzealous soldier touched the match to a cannon which had been pointed to rake the sledge track. Had not the piece missed fire, from dampness of the priming, he would have done more execution at one shot than the Iroquois in all the fight of that morning.

Maisonneuve was left alone, retreating backwards down the track and holding his pursuers in check with a pistol in each hand. They might easily have shot him but, recognizing him as the commander of the French, they were bent on taking him alive. Their chief coveted this honor for himself and his followers held aloof to give him the opportunity. He pressed close upon Maisonneuve, who snapped a pistol at him, which missed fire. The Iroquois, who had ducked to avoid the shot, rose erect and sprang forward to seize him, when Maisonneuve, with his remaining pistol, shot him dead.

Then ensued a curious spectacle, not infrequent in Indian battles. The Iroquois seemed to forget their enemy in their anxiety to secure and carry off the body of their chief, and the French commander continued his retreat unmolested till he was safe under the cannon of the fort. From that day he was a hero in the eyes of his men.

Quebec and Montreal are happy in their founders. Samuel de Champlain and Chomedey de Maisonneuve are among the names that shine with a fair and honest luster on the infancy of nations.

CHAPTER 5

Isaac Jogues: A Heroic Saga

THE WATERS OF THE ST. LAWRENCE ROLLED
through a virgin wilderness. In the vastness of the lonely wood-
lands, civilized man found a precarious harborage at only three
points—at Quebec, Montreal and Three Rivers. Here and in the scattered missions was the whole of New France, a population of some
three hundred souls in all. And now, over these miserable settlements,
rose a war cloud of frightful portent.

It was thirty-two years since Champlain had first attacked the
Iroquois. They had nursed their wrath for more than a generation,
and at length their hour was come. The Dutch traders at Fort Orange,
now Albany, had supplied them with firearms. The Mohawks, the
most easterly of the Iroquois nations, had among their seven or eight
hundred warriors no less than three hundred armed with arquebuses.
They were masters of the thunderbolts which, in the hands of Champlain, had struck terror into their hearts.

In the early morning of the second of August, 1642, twelve Huron
canoes were moving slowly along the northern shore of the expansion
of the St. Lawrence known as the Lake of St. Peter. There were on
board about forty persons, including four Frenchmen, one of them
being the Jesuit, Isaac Jogues. Early in the summer of that year
Jogues had descended to Three Rivers and Quebec with the Huron
traders, to procure necessary supplies. He had accomplished his task
and was on his way back to the mission. With him were a few Huron
converts, and among them a noted Christian chief, Eustache Ahatsis-

127

tari. Others of the party were in course of instruction for baptism, but the greater part were heathen whose canoes were deeply laden with the proceeds of their bargains with the French fur traders.

Jogues sat in one of the leading canoes. Born at Orleans in 1607, he was thirty-five years of age. His oval face and the delicate mold of his features indicated a modest, thoughtful and refined nature. He was constitutionally timid, with a sensitive conscience and great religious susceptibilities. He was a finished scholar and might have gained a literary reputation, but he had chosen another career, one for which he seemed ill fitted. Physically, however, he was well matched with his work. Though his frame was slight, he was so active that none of the Indians could surpass him in running.

With him were two young men, René Goupil and Guillaume Couture, *donnés* of the mission—that is to say, laymen who, from a religious motive and without pay, had attached themselves to the service of the Jesuits.

The twelve canoes had reached the western end of the Lake of St. Peter, where it is filled with innumerable islands. The forest was close on their right; they kept near the shore to avoid the current, and the shallow water before them was covered with a dense growth of tall bulrushes. Suddenly the silence was frightfully broken. The war whoop rose from among the rushes, mingled with the reports of guns and the whistling of bullets, and several Iroquois canoes filled with warriors pushed out from their concealment and bore down upon Jogues and his companions. The Hurons in the rear were seized with a shameful panic. They leaped ashore, left canoes, baggage and weapons and fled into the woods. The French and the Christian Hurons made fight for a time, but when they saw another fleet of canoes approaching from the opposite shores or islands, they lost heart and those escaped who could.

Goupil was seized amid triumphant yells, as were also several of the Huron converts. Jogues sprang into the bulrushes and might have escaped, but when he saw Goupil and the neophytes in the clutches of the Iroquois he had no heart to abandon them but came out from his hiding place and gave himself up to the astonished victors. A few of them had remained to guard the prisoners; the rest were chasing the fugitives. Jogues mastered his agony and began to baptize those of the captive converts who needed baptism.

Couture had eluded pursuit, but when he thought of Jogues and of what perhaps awaited him, he resolved to share his fate and, turning, retraced his steps. As he approached, five Iroquois ran forward to meet him. One of them snapped his gun at his breast, but it missed fire. In his confusion and excitement, Couture fired his own piece and laid the savage dead. The remaining four sprang upon him, stripped off all his clothing, tore away his fingernails with their teeth, gnawed his fingers with the fury of famished dogs and thrust a sword through one of his hands. Jogues broke from his guards and, rushing to his friend, threw his arms about his neck. The Iroquois dragged him away, beat him with their fists and war clubs till he was senseless and, when he revived, lacerated his fingers with their teeth, as they had done those of Couture. Then they turned upon Goupil and treated him with the same ferocity. The Huron prisoners were left for the present unharmed. More of them were brought in every moment, till at length the number of captives amounted in all to twenty-two, while three Hurons had been killed in the fight and pursuit.

The Iroquois, about seventy in number, now embarked with their prey, but not until they had knocked on the head an old Huron whom Jogues with his mangled hands had just baptized and who refused to leave the place. Then, under a burning sun, they crossed to the spot on which the town of Sorel now stands, at the mouth of the river Richelieu, where they encamped.

Their course was southward, up the river Richelieu and Lake Champlain, then by way of Lake George to the Mohawk towns. The pain and fever of their wounds and the clouds of mosquitoes which they could not drive off left the prisoners no peace by day nor sleep by night. On the eighth day they learned that a large Iroquois war party on its way to Canada was near at hand, and they soon approached its camp, on a small island near the southern end of Lake Champlain.

The warriors, two hundred in number, saluted their victorious countrymen with volleys from their guns. Then, armed with clubs and thorny sticks, they ranged themselves in two lines between which the captives were compelled to pass up the side of a rocky hill. On the way they were beaten with such fury that Jogues, who was last in the line, fell powerless, drenched in blood and half dead. As the chief man among the French captives, he fared the worst. His hands were again mangled and fire applied to his body, while the Huron chief Eustache was subjected to tortures even more atrocious. At night, when the exhausted sufferers tried to rest, the young warriors came to lacerate their wounds and pull out their hair and beards.

In the morning they resumed their journey. And now the lake narrowed to the semblance of a tranquil river. Before them was a woody mountain, close on their right a rocky promontory, and between these flowed a stream, the outlet of Lake George. On those rocks, more than a hundred years after, rose the ramparts of Ticonderoga. They landed, shouldered their canoes and baggage, took their way through the woods, passed the spot where the fierce Highlanders and the dauntless regiments of England breasted in vain the storm of lead and fire, and soon reached the shore where Abercrombie landed and Lord Howe fell. First of white men, Jogues and his companions gazed on the romantic lake that bears the name, not of its gentle discoverer, but of the dull Hanoverian king.

Again the canoes were launched, and the wild flotilla glided on its way, now in the shadow of the heights, now on the broad expanse, now among the devious channels of the narrows, beset with woody islets, where the hot air was redolent of the pine, the spruce and the cedar. At length they neared that tragic shore where, in the following century, New England rustics baffled the soldiers of Dieskau, where Montcalm planted his batteries, where the red cross waved so long amid the smoke and where at length the summer night was hideous with carnage and an honored name was stained with a memory of blood.

The Iroquois landed at or near the future site of Fort William Henry, left their canoes and with their prisoners began their march for the nearest Mohawk town. Each bore his share of the plunder. Even Jogues, though his lacerated hands were in a frightful condition and his body covered with bruises, was forced to stagger on with the rest under a heavy load. He and his fellow prisoners, and indeed the whole party, were half starved, subsisting chiefly on wild berries. They crossed the upper Hudson and in thirteen days after leaving the St.

Lawrence neared the wretched goal of their pilgrimage—a palisaded town, standing on a hill by the banks of the river Mohawk.

The whoops of the victors announced their approach and the savage hive sent forth its swarms. They thronged the side of the hill, the old and the young, each with a stick or slender iron rod, bought from the Dutchmen on the Hudson. They ranged themselves in a double line, reaching upward to the entrance of the town, and through this "narrow road of Paradise," as Jogues calls it, the captives were led in single file—Couture in front, after him a halfscore of Hurons, then Goupil, then the remaining Hurons and at last Jogues. As they passed they were saluted with yells, screeches and a tempest of blows. One, heavier than the others, knocked Jogues's breath from his body and stretched him on the ground. But it was death to lie there, and regaining his feet, he staggered on with the rest. When they reached the town the blows ceased and they were all placed on a scaffold, or high platform, in the middle of the place. The three Frenchmen had fared the worst and were frightfully disfigured. Goupil, especially, was streaming with blood and livid with bruises from head to foot.

They were allowed a few minutes to recover their breath, undisturbed except by the hootings and gibes of the mob below. Then a chief called out, "Come, let us caress these Frenchmen!" The crowd, knives in hand, began to mount the scaffold.

They ordered a Christian Algonquin woman, a prisoner among them, to cut off Jogues's left thumb, which she did, and a thumb of Goupil was also severed, a clamshell being used as the instrument in order to increase the pain. It is needless to specify further the tortures to which they were subjected, all designed to cause the greatest possible suffering without endangering life. At night they were removed from the scaffold and placed in one of the houses, each stretched on his back, with his limbs extended and his ankles and wrists bound fast to stakes driven into the earthen floor. The children now profited by the examples of their parents and amused themselves by placing live coals and red-hot ashes on the naked bodies of the prisoners, who, bound fast and covered with wounds and bruises which made every movement a torture, were sometimes unable to shake them off.

131

In the morning they were again placed on the scaffold, where during this and the two following days they remained exposed to the taunts of the crowd. Then they were led in triumph to the second Mohawk town, and afterwards to the third, suffering at each a repetition of cruelties, the details of which would be as monotonous as revolting.

In a house in the town of Teonontogen, Jogues was hung by the wrists between two of the upright poles which supported the structure in such a manner that his feet could not touch the ground. Thus he remained for some fifteen minutes, in extreme torture, until, as he was on the point of swooning, an Indian with an impulse of pity cut the cords and released him. While they were in this town four fresh Huron prisoners, just taken, were brought in and placed on the scaffold with the rest. Jogues, in the midst of his pain and exhaustion, took the opportunity to convert them. An ear of green corn was thrown to him for food and he discovered a few raindrops clinging to the husks. With these he baptized two of the Hurons. The remaining two received baptism soon after from a brook which the prisoners crossed on the way to another town.

Couture, though he had incensed the Indians by killing one of their warriors, had gained their admiration by his bravery, and after torturing him most savagely they adopted him into one of their families in place of a dead relative. Thenceforth he was comparatively safe.

Jogues and Goupil were less fortunate. Three of the Hurons had been burned to death, and they expected to share their fate. A council was held to pronounce their doom, but dissensions arose and no result was reached. They were led back to the first village, where they remained, racked with suspense and half dead with exhaustion. Jogues, however, lost no opportunity to baptize dying infants, while Goupil taught children to make the sign of the cross.

On one occasion he made the sign on the forehead of a child, grandson of an Indian in whose lodge they lived. The superstition of the old savage was aroused. Some Dutchmen had told him that the sign of the cross came from the Devil and would cause mischief. He thought that Goupil was bewitching the child and, resolving to rid himself of so dangerous a guest, applied for aid to two young braves. Jogues and Goupil, clad in their squalid garb of tattered skins, were soon after walking together in the forest that adjoined the town, consoling themselves with prayer and mutually exhorting each other to suffer patiently for the sake of Christ and the Virgin, when, as they were returning, reciting their rosaries, they met the two young Indians and read in their sullen visages an augury of ill.

The Indians joined them and accompanied them to the entrance of the town, where one of the two, suddenly drawing a hatchet from beneath his blanket, struck it into the head of Goupil, who fell murmuring the name of Christ. Jogues dropped on his knees and, bowing his head in prayer, awaited the blow, when the murderer ordered him to get up and go home. He obeyed, but not until he had given absolution to his still breathing friend, and presently saw the lifeless body dragged through the town amid hootings and rejoicings.

Jogues passed a night of anguish and desolation, and in the morning, reckless of life, set forth in search of Goupil's remains. "Where are you going so fast?" demanded the old Indian, his master. "Do you not see those fierce young braves, who are watching to kill you?" Jogues persisted, and the old man asked another Indian to go with him as a protector.

The corpse had been flung into a neighboring ravine, at the bottom of which ran a torrent. Here, with the Indian's help, Jogues found Goupil's body, stripped naked and gnawed by dogs. He dragged it into the water and covered it with stones to save it from further mutilation, resolving to return alone on the following day and secretly bury it. But with the night there came a storm. In the gray of morning Jogues descended to the brink of the stream and found it a rolling, turbid flood, and the body was nowhere to be seen. Had the Indians or the torrent borne it away? Jogues waded into the cold current. It was the first of October. He sounded it with his feet and with his stick; he searched the rocks, the thicket, the forest. But all in vain. Crouched by the pitiless stream, he mingled his tears with its waters and, in a voice broken with groans, chanted the service of the dead.

The Indians and not the flood had robbed him of the remains of his friend. Early in the spring, when the snows were melting in the woods, he was told by Mohawk children that the body was lying where it had been flung, in a lonely spot lower down the stream. He went to seek it and found the scattered bones, stripped by the foxes and the birds. Tenderly gathering them up, he hid them in a hollow tree, hoping that a day might come when he could give them a Christian burial in consecrated ground.

After the murder of Goupil, Jogues's life hung by a hair. He lived in hourly expectation of the tomahawk and would have welcomed it as a boon. By signs and words he was warned that his hour was near, but as he never shunned his fate, it fled from him and each day, with renewed astonishment, he found himself still among the living.

Late in the autumn a party of the Indians set forth on their yearly deer hunt and Jogues was ordered to go with them. Shivering and half famished, he followed them through the chill November forest and shared their wild bivouac in the depths of the wintry desolation. The game they took was devoted to Areskoui, their god, and eaten in his honor. Jogues would not taste the meat offered to a demon and thus he starved in the midst of plenty.

At night, when the kettle was slung and the savage crew made merry around their fire, he crouched in a corner of the hut, gnawed by hunger and pierced to the bone with cold. They thought his presence unpropitious to their hunting, and the women especially hated him. His demeanor at once astonished and incensed his masters. He brought them firewood, like a squaw; he did their bidding without a murmur and patiently bore their abuse. But when they mocked at his God and laughed at his devotions, their slave assumed an air and tone of authority and sternly rebuked them.

He would sometimes escape from "this Babylon," as he calls the hut, and wander in the forest, telling his beads and repeating passages of Scripture. In a remote and lonely spot he cut the bark in the form of a cross from the trunk of a great tree and he made his prayers—a living martyr, half clad in shaggy furs, kneeling on the snow among the icicled rocks and beneath the gloomy pines, bowing in adoration before the emblem of the faith in which was his only consolation and his only hope.

The Indians at last grew tired of him and sent him back to the village. Here he remained till the middle of March, baptizing infants and trying to convert adults. He told them of the sun, moon, planets and stars. They listened with interest, but when from astronomy he passed to theology he spent his breath in vain. In March the old man with whom he lived set forth for his spring fishing, taking with him his squaw and several children. Jogues also was of the party.

They repaired to a lake, perhaps Lake Saratoga, four days distant. Here they subsisted for some time on frogs, the entrails of fish and other garbage. Jogues passed his days in the forest, repeating his prayers and carving the name of Jesus on trees as a terror to the demons of the wilderness. A messenger at length arrived from the town, and on the following day, under the pretense that signs of an enemy had been seen, the party broke up their camp and returned home in hot haste.

The messenger had brought tidings that a war party, which had gone out against the French, had been defeated and destroyed and that the whole population were clamoring to appease their grief by torturing Jogues to death. This was the true cause of the sudden and mysterious return. But when they reached the town other tidings had arrived. The missing warriors were safe and on their way home in triumph with a large number of prisoners. Again Jogues's life was spared, but he was forced to witness the torture and butchery of the converts and allies of the French. Existence became unendurable to him and he longed to die. War parties were continually going out. Should they be defeated and cut off, he would pay the forfeit at the stake, and if they came back, as they usually did, with booty and prisoners, he was doomed to see his countrymen and their Indian friends mangled, burned and devoured.

Jogues had shown no disposition to escape, and great liberty was therefore allowed him. He went from town to town, giving absolution to the Christian captives and converting and baptizing the heathen. On one occasion he baptized a woman in the midst of the fire, under pretense of lifting a cup of water to her parched lips. There was no lack of objects for his zeal. A single war party returned from the Huron country with nearly a hundred prisoners, who were distributed among the Iroquois towns and the greater part burned. Of the children of the Mohawks and their neighbors, he had baptized about seventy before August. He began to regard his captivity as a providential interposition for the saving of souls.

At the end of July he went with a party of Indians to a fishing place on the Hudson, about twenty miles below Fort Orange. While here, he learned that another war party had lately returned with prisoners, two of whom had been burned to death at Osseruenon. Hearing this, his conscience smote him that he had not remained in the town to give the sufferers absolution or baptism, and he begged leave of the old woman who had him in charge to return at the first opportunity. A canoe soon after went up the river with some of the Iroquois and he was allowed to go in it. When they reached Rensselaerswyck the Indians landed to trade with the Dutch and took Jogues with them.

The center of this rude little settlement was Fort Orange, a miserable structure of logs standing on a spot now within the limits of the city of Albany. It contained several houses and other buildings and behind it was a small church, recently erected and serving as the abode of the pastor, Dominie Megapolensis. Some twenty-five or thirty houses, roughly built of boards and roofed with thatch, were scattered at intervals on or near the borders of the Hudson, above and below the fort. Their inhabitants, about a hundred in number, were for the most part rude Dutch farmers, tenants of Van Rensselaer, the patroon or lord of the manor. They raised wheat, of which they made beer, and oats, with which they fed their numerous horses. They traded, too, with the Indians, who profited greatly by the competition among them, receiving guns, knives, axes, kettles, cloth and beads at moderate rates in exchange for their furs. The Dutch were on excellent terms with their red neighbors, met them in the forest without the least fear and sometimes intermarried with them. They had known of Jogues's captivity and, to their great honor, had made efforts for his release, offering for that purpose goods to a considerable value, but without effect.

At Fort Orange, Jogues heard startling news. The Indians of the village where he lived were, he was told, enraged against him and determined to burn him. About the first of July a war party had set out for Canada and one of the warriors had offered to Jogues to be the bearer of a letter from him to the French commander at Three Rivers, thinking probably to gain some advantage under cover of a parley. Jogues knew that the French would be on their guard, and he felt it his duty to lose no opportunity of informing them as to the state of affairs among the Iroquois. A Dutchman gave him a piece of paper and he wrote a letter, in a jargon of Latin, French and Huron,

136

warning his countrymen to be on their guard, as war parties were constantly going out and they could hope for no respite from attack until late in the autumn.

When the Iroquois reached the mouth of the river Richelieu, where a small fort had been built by the French the preceding summer, the messenger asked for a parley and gave Jogues's letter to the commander of the post, who, after reading it, turned his cannon on the savages. They fled in dismay, leaving behind them their baggage and some of their guns. Returning home in a fury, they charged Jogues with having caused their discomfiture. Jogues had expected this result and was prepared to meet it, but several of the principal Dutch settlers, and among them Van Curler, who had made the previous attempt to rescue him by barter, urged that his death was certain if he returned to the Indian town and advised him to make his escape.

In the Hudson opposite the settlement lay a small Dutch vessel nearly ready to sail. Van Curler offered him a passage in her to Bordeaux or Rochelle, representing that the opportunity was too good to be lost and making light of the prisoner's objection that a connivance in his escape on the part of the Dutch would excite the resentment of the Indians against him. Jogues thanked him warmly but, to his amazement, asked for a night to consider the matter and take counsel of God in prayer.

He spent the night in great agitation, tossed by doubt and full of anxiety lest his self-love should beguile him from his duty. Was it not possible that the Indians might spare his life and that, by a timely drop of water, he might still rescue souls from torturing devils and eternal fires of perdition? On the other hand, would he not, by remaining to meet a fate almost inevitable, incur the guilt of suicide? And even should he escape torture and death, could he hope that the Indians would again permit him to instruct and baptize their prisoners? Of his French companions, one, Goupil, was dead, while Couture had urged Jogues to flight, saying that he would then follow his example, but that as long as the father remained a prisoner, he, Couture, would share his fate.

Before morning Jogues had made his decision. God, he thought, would be better pleased should he embrace the opportunity given him. He went to find his Dutch friends and, with a profusion of thanks, accepted their offer. They told him that a boat should be left for him on the shore and that he must watch his time and escape in it to the vessel, where he would be safe.

He and his Indian masters were lodged together in a large building like a barn, belonging to a Dutch farmer. It was a hundred feet long and had no partition of any kind. At one end the farmer kept his cattle; at the other he slept with his wife, a Mohawk squaw, and his children, while his Indian guests lay on the floor in the middle. As he is described as one of the principal persons of the colony, it is clear that the civilization of Rensselaerswyck was not high.

In the evening Jogues went out to reconnoiter, in such a manner as not to excite the suspicion of the Indians. There was a fence around the house, and as he was passing it a large dog belonging to the farmer flew at him and bit him very severely in the leg. The Dutchman, hearing the noise, came out with a light, led Jogues back into the building and bandaged his wound. He seemed to have some suspicion of the prisoner's design; and fearful perhaps that his escape might exasperate the Indians, he made fast the door in such a manner that it could not readily be opened. Jogues now lay down among the Indians, who were stretched around him, rolled in their blankets. He was fevered with excitement, and the agitation of his mind, joined to the pain of his wound, kept him awake all night.

About dawn, while the Indians were still asleep, a laborer in the employ of the farmer came in with a lantern, and Jogues, who spoke no Dutch, gave him to understand by signs that he needed his help and guidance. The man was disposed to aid him, silently led the way out, quieted the dogs and showed him the path to the river. It was more than half a mile distant and the way was rough and broken. Jogues was greatly exhausted. His wounded limb gave him such pain that he walked with the utmost difficulty. When he reached the shore the day was breaking and he found, to his dismay, that the ebb of the tide had left the boat high and dry. He shouted to the vessel, but no one heard him. His desperation gave him strength, and by working the boat to and fro, he pushed it at length, little by little, into the water, entered it and rowed to the vessel. The Dutch sailors received him kindly and hid him in the bottom of the hold, placing a large box over the hatchway.

He remained two days, half stifled, in this foul lurking place, while the Indians, furious at his escape, ransacked the settlement in vain to find him. They came off to the vessel and so terrified the officers that Jogues was sent on shore at night and led to the fort. Here he was hidden in the garret of a house occupied by a miserly old man, to whose charge he was consigned. Food was sent to him, but as his host appropriated the larger part to himself, Jogues was nearly starved. There was a compartment of his garret separated from the rest by a partition of boards. Here the old Dutchman, who carried on a trade with the Mohawks like many others of the settlers, kept a quantity of goods for that purpose and here he often brought his customers. The boards of the partition had shrunk, leaving wide crevices, and Jogues could plainly see the Indians as they passed between him and the light. They, on their part, might as easily have seen him if he had not, when he heard them entering the house, hidden himself behind some barrels in the corner where he would sometimes remain crouched for hours in a constrained and painful posture, half suffocated with heat and afraid to move a limb.

His wounded leg began to show dangerous symptoms, but he was relieved by the care of a Dutch surgeon of the fort. The minister, Megapolensis, also visited him and did all in his power for the comfort of his Catholic brother, with whom he seems to have been well pleased and whom he calls "a very learned scholar."

When Jogues had remained for six weeks in this hiding place, his Dutch friends succeeded in satisfying his Indian masters by the payment of a large ransom. A vessel from Manhattan soon after brought up an order from the director-general, Kieft, that he should be sent to them. Accordingly he was placed in a small vessel which carried him down the Hudson. The Dutch on board treated him with great kindness, and to do him honor, they named after him one of the islands in the river. At Manhattan he found a dilapidated fort garrisoned by sixty soldiers and containing a stone church and the director-general's house, together with storehouses and barracks. Near it were ranges of small houses, occupied chiefly by mechanics and laborers, while the dwellings of the remaining colonists, numbering in all four or five hundred, were scattered here and there on the island and the neighboring shores.

139

The settlers were of different sects and nations, but chiefly Dutch Calvinists. Kieft told his guest that eighteen different languages were spoken at Manhattan. The colonists were in the midst of a bloody Indian war, brought on by their own besotted cruelty, and while Jogues was at the fort some forty of the Dutchmen were killed on the neighboring farms and many barns and houses burned.

The director-general, with a humanity that was far from usual with him, exchanged Jogues's squalid and savage dress for a suit of Dutch cloth and gave him passage in a small vessel which was then about to sail. The voyage was rough and tedious and the passenger slept on deck or on a coil of ropes, suffering greatly from cold and often drenched by the waves that broke over the vessel's side.

At length she reached Falmouth, on the southern coast of England, where all the crew went ashore for a carouse, leaving Jogues alone on board. A boat presently came alongside with a gang of desperadoes, who boarded her and rifled her of everything valuable, threatened Jogues with a pistol and robbed him of his hat and coat. He obtained some assistance from the crew of a French ship in the harbor and, on the day before Christmas, took passage in a small coal vessel for the neighboring coast of Brittany.

In the following afternoon he was set on shore a little to the north of Brest, and seeing a peasant's cottage not far off, he approached it and asked the way to the nearest church. The peasant and his wife, as the narrative gravely tells us, mistook him, by reason of his modest deportment, for some poor but pious Irishman and asked him to share their supper after finishing his devotions, an invitation which Jogues, half famished as he was, gladly accepted. He reached the church in time for the early mass, and with an unutterable joy knelt before the altar and renewed the communion of which he had been deprived so long.

When he returned to the cottage the attention of his hosts was at once attracted to his mutilated and distorted hands. They asked with amazement how he could have received such injuries, and when they heard the story of his tortures their surprise and veneration knew no bounds. Two young girls, their daughters, begged him to accept all they had to give, a handful of sous, while the peasant made known the character of his new guest to his neighbors. A trader from Rennes brought a horse to the door and offered the use of it to Jogues, to carry him to the Jesuit college in that town. He gratefully accepted it and, on the morning of the fifth of January, 1644, reached his destination.

He dismounted and knocked at the door of the college. The porter opened it and saw a man wearing on his head an old woolen nightcap and in an attire little better than that of a beggar. Jogues asked to see the rector, but the porter answered coldly that the rector was busied in the sacristy. Jogues begged him to say that a man was at the door with news from Canada. The missions of Canada were at this time an object of primal interest to the Jesuits, and above all to the Jesuits of France. A letter from Jogues, written during his captivity, had already reached France, as had also the Jesuit *Relation* of 1643, which contained a long account of his capture, and he had no doubt been an engrossing theme of conversation in every house of the French Jesuits.

The father rector was putting on his vestments to say mass, but when he heard that a poor man from Canada had asked for him at the door he postponed the service and went to meet him. Jogues, without discovering himself, gave him a letter from the Dutch director-general attesting his character. The rector, without reading it, began to question him as to the affairs of Canada and at length asked him if he knew Father Jogues.

"I knew him very well," was the reply.

"The Iroquois have taken him," pursued the rector. "Is he dead? Have they murdered him?"

"No," answered Jogues, "he is alive and at liberty, and I am he." And he fell on his knees to ask his Superior's blessing.

That night was a night of jubilation and thanksgiving in the college of Rennes.

Jogues became a center of curiosity and reverence. He was summoned to Paris. The Queen, Anne of Austria, wished to see him, and when the persecuted slave of the Mohawks was conducted into her presence she kissed his mutilated hands while the ladies of the court thronged around to do him homage. We are told, and no doubt with truth, that these honors were unwelcome to the modest and single-hearted missionary, who thought only of returning to his work of converting the Indians. A priest with any deformity of body is debarred from saying mass. The teeth and knives of the Iroquois had inflicted an injury worse than the torturers imagined, for they had robbed Jogues of the privilege which was the chief consolation of his life, but the Pope, by a special dispensation, restored it to him, and with the opening spring he sailed again for Canada. There his last trial awaited him.

By 1645 an impressive but uneasy peace had been concluded between the Mohawks, the Algonquins, the Hurons and the French, but an agent of acknowledged weight was needed to hold the Mohawks to their faith, and Jogues was chosen for the task because no white man, Couture excepted, knew their language and their character so well. His errand was half political, half religious. Not only was he to be the bearer of gifts, wampum belts and messages from the governor, but he was also to found a new mission, christened in advance with a prophetic name—the Mission of the Martyrs.

For two years Jogues had been at Montreal, and it was here that he received the order of his Superior to proceed to the Mohawk towns. At first nature asserted itself and he recoiled involuntarily at the thought of the horrors of which his scarred body and his mutilated hands were a living memento. It was a transient weakness, and he prepared to depart with more than willingness, giving thanks to Heaven that he had been found worthy to suffer and to die for the saving of souls and the greater glory of God.

He felt a presentiment that his death was near and wrote to a friend, "I shall go and shall not return." An Algonquin convert gave him sage advice. "Say nothing about the Faith at first, for there is nothing so repulsive, in the beginning, as our doctrine, which seems to destroy everything that men hold dear, and as your long cassock preaches as well as your lips, you had better put on a short coat." Jogues therefore exchanged the uniform of Loyola for a civilian's doublet and hose, "for," observes his Superior, "one should be all things to all men, that he may gain them all to Jesus Christ."

Jogues left Three Rivers about the middle of May, 1646, with the Sieur Bourdon, engineer to the governor, two Algonquins with gifts to confirm the peace and four Mohawks as guides and escort. He passed the Richelieu and Lake Champlain, well-remembered scenes of former miseries, and reached the foot of Lake George on the eve of Corpus Christi. Hence he called the lake "Lac St. Sacrement," and this name it preserved until a century after, when an ambitious Irishman, in compliment to the sovereign from whom he sought advancement, gave it the name it bears.

From Lake George they crossed on foot to the Hudson, where, being greatly fatigued by their heavy loads of gifts, they borrowed canoes at an Iroquois fishing station and descended to Fort Orange. Here Jogues met the Dutch friends to whom he owed his life, and who now kindly welcomed and entertained him. After a few days he left them and ascended the river Mohawk to the first Mohawk town. Crowds gathered from the neighboring towns to gaze on the man whom they had known as a scorned and abused slave, and who now appeared among them as the ambassador of a power which hitherto, indeed, they had despised, but which in their present mood they were willing to propitiate.

There was a council in one of the lodges. While his crowded auditory smoked their pipes, Jogues stood in the midst and harangued them. He offered in due form the gifts of the governor, with the wampum belts and their messages of peace, while at every pause his words were echoed by a unanimous grunt of applause from the attentive concourse. Peace speeches were made in return, and all was harmony. When, however, the Algonquin deputies stood before the council, they and their gifts were coldly received. The old hate, maintained by traditions of mutual atrocity, burned fiercely under a thin semblance of peace, and though no outbreak took place, the prospect of the future was very ominous.

The business of the embassy was scarcely finished when the Mohawks counseled Jogues and his companions to go home with all dispatch, saying that if they waited longer, they might meet on the way warriors of the four upper nations, who would inevitably kill the two Algonquin deputies, if not the French also. Jogues, therefore, set out on his return, but not until, despite the advice of the Indian convert, he had made the round of the houses, confessed and instructed a few Christian prisoners still remaining here and baptized several dying Mohawks. Then he and his party crossed through the forest to the southern extremity of Lake George, made bark canoes and descended to Fort Richelieu, where they arrived on the twenty-seventh of June.

His political errand was accomplished. Now, should he return to the Mohawks, or should the Mission of the Martyrs be for a time abandoned? Lalemant, who had succeeded Vimont as Superior of the missions, held a council at Quebec with three other Jesuits, of whom Jogues was one, and it was determined that, unless some new contingency should arise, he should remain for the winter at Montreal.

This was in July. Soon after, the plan was changed for reasons which do not appear and Jogues received orders to repair to his dangerous post. He set out on the twenty-fourth of August, accompanied by a young Frenchman named Lalande and three or four Hurons. On the way they met Indians who warned them of a change of feeling in the Mohawk towns, and the Hurons, alarmed, refused to go farther. Jogues, naturally perhaps the most timid man of the party, had no thought of drawing back and pursued his journey with his young companion, who, like other *donnés* of the missions, was scarcely behind the Jesuits themselves in devoted enthusiasm.

The reported change of feeling had indeed taken place and the occasion of it was characteristic. On his previous visit to the Mohawks, Jogues, meaning to return, had left in their charge a small chest or box. From the first they were distrustful, suspecting that it contained some secret mischief. He therefore opened it and showed them the contents, which were a few personal necessaries, and having thus reassured them, as he thought, locked the box and left it in their keeping.

The Huron prisoners in the town attempted to make favor with their Iroquois enemies by abusing their French friends, declaring them to be sorcerers who had bewitched, by their charms and mummeries, the whole Huron nation and caused drought, famine, pestilence and a host of insupportable miseries. Thereupon the suspicions of the Mohawks against the box revived with double force and they were convinced that famine, the pest or some malignant spirit was shut up in it, waiting the moment to issue forth and destroy them.

There was sickness in the town and caterpillars were eating their corn; this was ascribed to the sorceries of the Jesuit. Still they were divided in opinion. Some stood firm for the French; others were furious against them. Among the Mohawks three clans or families were predominant, if indeed they did not compose the entire nation—the clans of the Bear, the Tortoise and the Wolf. Though, by the nature of their constitution, it was scarcely possible that these clans should come to blows, so intimately were they bound together by ties of blood, yet they were often divided on points of interest or policy, and on this occasion the Bear raged against the French and howled for war, while the Tortoise and the Wolf still clung to the treaty.

Among savages with no government except the intermittent one of councils, the party of action and violence must always prevail. The Bear chiefs sang their war songs and, followed by the young men of their own clan and by such others as they had infected with their frenzy, set forth in two bands on the warpath.

The warriors of one of these bands were making their way through the forests between the Mohawk and Lake George when they met Jogues and Lalande. They seized them, stripped them and led them in triumph to their town. Here a savage crowd surrounded them, beating them with sticks and with their fists.

One of them cut thin strips of flesh from the back and arms of Jogues, saying as he did so, "Let us see if this white flesh is the flesh of an *oki*."

"I am a man like yourselves," replied Jogues, "but I do not fear death or torture. I do not know why you would kill me. I come here to confirm the peace and show you the way to heaven, and you treat me like a dog."

"You shall die tomorrow," cried the rabble. "Take courage, we shall not burn you. We shall strike you both with a hatchet and place your heads on the palisade, that your brothers may see you when we take them prisoners."

The clans of the Wolf and the Tortoise still raised their voices in behalf of the captive Frenchmen, but the fury of the minority swept all before it.

In the evening—it was the eighteenth of October—Jogues, smarting with his wounds and bruises, was sitting in one of the lodges when an Indian entered and asked him to a feast. To refuse would have been an offense. He arose and followed the savage, who led him to the lodge of the Bear chief. Jogues bent his head to enter when another Indian, standing concealed within at the side of the doorway, struck at him with a hatchet.

An Iroquois, called by the French Le Berger, who seems to have followed in order to defend him, bravely held out his arm to ward off the blow, but the hatchet cut through it and sank into the missionary's brain. He fell at the feet of his murderer, who at once finished the work by hacking off his head. Lalande was left in suspense all night, and in the morning was killed in a similar manner. The bodies of the two Frenchmen were then thrown into the Mohawk and their heads displayed on the points of the palisade which enclosed the town.

Thus died Isaac Jogues, one of the purest examples of Roman Catholic virtue which this Western continent has seen.

CHAPTER 6

~~~~~~

A Doomed Nation

IT WAS A STRANGE AND MISERABLE SPECTACLE TO behold the savages of this continent at the time when the knell of their common ruin had already sounded. Civilization had gained a foothold on their borders. The long and gloomy reign of barbarism was drawing near its close and their united efforts could scarcely have availed to sustain it. Yet in this crisis of their destiny these doomed tribes were tearing each other's throats in a wolfish fury, joined to an intelligence that served little purpose but mutual destruction.

How the quarrel began between the Iroquois and their Huron kindred no man can tell and it is not worth while to conjecture. At this time the ruling passion of the savage Confederates was the annihilation of this rival people and of their Algonquin allies—if the understanding between the Hurons and these incoherent hordes can be called an alliance. United they far outnumbered the Iroquois. Indeed, the Hurons alone were not much inferior in force, for by the largest estimates the strength of the five Iroquois nations must now have been considerably less than three thousand warriors.

The true superiority of the Iroquois was a moral one. They were in one of those transports of pride, self-confidence and rage for ascendancy which in a savage people marks an era of conquest. With all the defections of their organization, it was far better than that of their neighbors. There were bickerings, jealousies, plottings and counter-plottings, separate wars and separate treaties among the five members of the league; yet nothing could sunder them. The bonds that united them were like cords of India rubber: they would stretch and the parts would be seemingly disjoined, only to return to their old union with the recoil. Such was the elastic strength of those relations of clanship which were the life of the league.

The first meeting of white men with the Hurons found them at blows with the Iroquois, and from that time forward the war raged with increasing fury. Small scalping parties infested the Huron forests, killing squaws in the cornfields or entering villages at midnight to tomahawk their sleeping inhabitants. Often, too, invasions were made in force. Sometimes towns were set upon and burned and sometimes there were deadly conflicts in the depths of the forests and the passes of the hills.

The invaders were not always successful. A bloody rebuff and a sharp retaliation now and then requited them. Thus, in 1638, a war party of a hundred Iroquois met in the forest a band of three hundred Huron and Algonquin warriors. They might have retreated, and the greater number were for doing so, but Ononkwaya, an Oneida chief, refused.

"Look!" he said, "the sky is clear; the Sun beholds us. If there were clouds to hide our shame from his sight, we might fly. But as it is, we must fight while we can."

They stood their ground for a time but were soon overborne. Four or five escaped; the rest were surrounded and killed or taken. That year Fortune smiled on the Hurons. They took, in all, more than a hundred prisoners, who were distributed among their various towns to be burned. These scenes, with them, occurred always in the night, and it was held to be of the last importance that the torture should be protracted from sunset till dawn.

The too valiant Chief Ononkwaya was among the victims. Even in death he took his revenge, for it was thought an augury of disaster to the victors if no cry of pain could be extorted from the sufferer, and on the present occasion he displayed an unflinching courage, rare even among Indians warriors. His execution took place at the town of Teanaustayé, called St. Joseph by the Jesuits. The fathers could not save his life, but what was more to the purpose, they baptized him.

On the scaffold where he was burned he wrought himself into a fury which seemed to render him insensible to pain. Thinking him nearly

148

spent, his tormentors scalped him, when to their amazement, he leaped up, snatched the brands that had been the instruments of his torture, drove the screeching crowd from the scaffold and held them all at bay while they pelted him from below with sticks, stones and showers of live coals. At length he made a false step and fell to the ground, where they seized him and threw him into the fire. He instantly leaped out, covered with blood, cinders and ashes, and rushed upon them with a blazing brand in each hand. The crowd gave way before him and he ran towards the town, as if to set it on fire. They threw a pole across his way, which tripped him and flung him headlong to the earth. Then they all fell upon him, cut off his hands and feet and again threw him into the fire. He rolled himself out and crawled forward on his elbows and knees, glaring upon them with such unutterable ferocity that they recoiled once more, till, seeing that he was helpless, they threw themselves upon him and cut off his head.

But despite petty triumphs, the Hurons felt themselves on the verge of ruin. Pestilence and war had wasted them away and left but a skeleton of their former strength. In their distress, they cast about them for succor and, remembering an ancient friendship with a kindred nation, the Andastes, they sent an embassy to ask of them aid in war, or intervention to obtain peace. This powerful people dwelt on the river Susquehanna. The way was long, even in a direct line, but the Iroquois lay between and a wide circuit was necessary to avoid them.

A Christian chief, whom the Jesuits had named Charles, together with four Christian and four heathen Hurons bearing wampum belts and gifts from the council, departed on this embassy on the thirteenth of April, 1647, and reached the great town of the Andastes early in June. It contained, as the Jesuits were told, no less than thirteen hundred warriors. The council assembled and the chief ambassador addressed them:

"We come from the Land of Souls, where all is gloom, dismay and desolation. Our fields are covered with blood; our houses are filled only with the dead; and we ourselves have but life enough to beg our friends to take pity on a people who are drawing near their end."

Then he presented the wampum belts and other gifts, saying that they were the voice of a dying country. The Andastes, who had a mortal quarrel with the Mohawks and who had before promised to

149

aid the Hurons in case of need, returned a favorable answer, but were disposed to try the virtue of diplomacy rather than the tomahawk. After a series of councils they determined to send ambassadors, not to their old enemies the Mohawks, but to the Onondagas, Oneidas and Cayugas, who were geographically the central nations of the Iroquois league, while the Mohawks and the Senecas were respectively at its eastern and western extremities. By inducing the three central nations—and, if possible, the Senecas also—to conclude a treaty with the Hurons, these last would be enabled to concentrate their force against the Mohawks, whom the Andastes would attack at the same time unless they humbled themselves and made peace. This scheme, it will be seen, was based on the assumption that the dreaded league of the Iroquois was far from being a unit in action or counsel.

Charles, with some of his colleagues, now set out for home to report the result of their mission, but the Senecas were lying in wait for them and they were forced to make a wide sweep through the Alleghenies, western Pennsylvania and apparently Ohio to avoid these vigilant foes. It was October before they reached the Huron towns and meanwhile hopes of peace had arisen from another quarter.

Early in the spring a band of Onondagas had made an inroad but were roughly handled by the Hurons, who killed several of them, captured others and put the rest to flight. The prisoners were burned, with the exception of one who committed suicide to escape the torture and one other, the chief man of the party, whose name was Annenrais. Some of the Hurons were dissatisfied at the mercy shown him and gave out that they would kill him, at which the chiefs, who never placed themselves in open opposition to the popular will, secretly fitted him out, made him presents and aided him to escape at night, with an understanding that he should use his influence at Onondaga in favor of peace. After crossing Lake Ontario, he met nearly all the Onondaga warriors on the march to avenge his supposed death, for he was a man of high account. They greeted him as one risen from the grave, and on his part he persuaded them to renounce their warlike purpose and return home. On their arrival, the chiefs and old men were called to council and the matter was debated with the usual deliberation.

About this time the ambassador of the Andastes appeared with his wampum belts. Both this nation and the Onondagas had secret motives which were perfectly in accordance. The Andastes hated the Mohawks as enemies and the Onondagas were jealous of them as confederates, for since they had armed themselves with Dutch guns, their arrogance and boastings had given umbrage to their brethren of the league and a peace with the Hurons would leave the latter free to turn their undivided strength against the Mohawks and curb their insolence.

The Oneidas and the Cayugas were of one mind with the Onondagas. Three nations of the league, to satisfy their spite against a fourth, would strike hands with the common enemy of all. It was resolved to send an embassy to the Hurons.

Yet it may be that, after all, the Onondagas had but half a mind for peace. At least they were unfortunate in their choice of an ambassador. He was by birth a Huron who, having been captured when a boy, adopted and naturalized, had become more an Iroquois than the Iroquois themselves, and scarcely one of the fierce confederates had shed so much Huron blood. When he reached the town of St. Ignace, which he did about midsummer, and delivered his messages and wampum belts, there was a great division of opinion among the Hurons. The Bear Nation—the member of their confederacy which was farthest from the Iroquois and least exposed to danger—was for rejecting overtures made by so offensive an agency. But those of the Hurons who had suffered most were eager for peace at any price, and after solemn deliberation it was resolved to send an embassy in return.

At its head was placed a Christian chief named Jean Baptiste Atironta, and on the first of August he and four others departed for Onondaga, carrying a profusion of presents and accompanied by the apostate envoy of the Iroquois. As the ambassadors had to hunt on the way for subsistence, besides making canoes to cross Lake Ontario, it was twenty days before they reached their destination. When they arrived there was great jubilation and for a full month nothing but councils. Having thus sifted the matter to the bottom, the Onondagas determined at last to send another embassy with Jean Baptiste on his return, and with them fifteen Huron prisoners as an earnest of their good intentions, retaining on their part one of Baptiste's colleagues as a hostage.

This time they chose for their envoy a chief of their own nation named Scandawati, a man of renown sixty years of age, joining with him two colleagues. The old Onondaga entered on his mission with a troubled mind. His anxiety was not so much for his life as for his honor and dignity, for while the Oneidas and the Cayugas were acting in concurrence with the Onondagas, the Senecas had refused any part in the embassy and still breathed nothing but war. Would they, or still more the Mohawks, so far forget the consideration due to one whose name had been great in the councils of the League as to assault the Hurons while he was among them in the character of an ambassador of his nation, whereby his honor would be compromised and his life endangered?

His mind brooded on this idea and he told one of his colleagues that if such a slight were put upon him, he should die of mortification.

"I am not a dead dog," he said, "to be despised and forgotten. I am worthy that all men should turn their eyes on me while I am among enemies, and do nothing that may involve me in danger."

What with hunting, fishing, canoe-making and bad weather, the progress of the august travelers was so slow that they did not reach the Huron towns till the twenty-third of October. Scandawati presented seven large belts of wampum, each composed of three or four thousand beads, which the Jesuits call the pearls and diamonds of the country. He delivered, too, the fifteen captives and promised a hundred more on the final conclusion of peace. The three Onondagas remained as surety for the good faith of those who sent them until the beginning of January, when the Hurons on their part sent six ambassadors to conclude the treaty, one of the Onondagas accompanying them.

Soon there came dire tidings. The prophetic heart of the old chief had not deceived him. The Senecas and Mohawks, disregarding negotiations in which they had no part and resolved to bring them to an end, were invading the country in force. It might be thought that the Hurons would take their revenge on the Onondaga envoys, now hostages among them, but they did not do so, for the character of an ambassador was, for the most part, held in respect.

One morning, however, Scandawati had disappeared. They were full of excitement, for they thought that he had escaped to the enemy. They ranged the woods in search of him and at length found him in a thicket near the town. He lay dead on a bed of spruce boughs which he had made, his throat deeply gashed with a knife. He had died by his own hand, a victim of mortified pride.

Meanwhile the Mission had thriven beyond hope in these days of woe and terror. The Hurons, in their time of trouble, had become tractable. They humbled themselves and, in their desolation and despair, came for succor to the priests. There was a harvest of converts, not only exceeding in numbers that of all former years but giving in many cases undeniable proofs of sincerity and fervor. In some towns the Christians outnumbered the heathen and in nearly all they formed a strong party.

The mission of La Conception, or Ossossané, was the most successful. Here there were now a church and one or more resident Jesuits, as also at St. Joseph, St. Ignace, St. Michel and St. Jean Baptiste, for we have seen that the Huron towns were christened with names of saints. Each church had its bell, which was sometimes hung in a neighboring tree. Every morning it rang its summons to mass, and issuing from their dwellings of bark, the converts gathered within the sacred precinct, where the bare rude walls, fresh from the ax and saw, contrasted with the sheen of tinsel and gilding and the hues of gay draperies and gaudy pictures. At evening they met again in prayers, and on Sunday, masses, confession, catechism, sermons and repeating the rosary consumed the whole day.

Undeniably the Faith was making progress, yet it is not to be supposed that its path was a smooth one. The old opposition and the old calumnies were still alive and active.

"It is *la prière* that kills us. Your books and your strings of beads have bewitched the country. Before you came, we were happy and prosperous. You are magicians. Your charms kill our corn and bring sickness and the Iroquois. Echon [Brébeuf] is a traitor among us, in league with our enemies." Such discourse was rife, openly and secretly.

Among the slanders devised by the heathen party against the teachers of the obnoxious doctrine was one which found wide credence, even among the converts, and produced a great effect. They gave out that a baptized Huron girl, who had lately died and was buried in the cemetery at Ste. Marie, had returned to life and given a deplorable account of the heaven of the French. No sooner had she entered—such was the story—than they seized her, chained her to a stake and tormented her all day with inconceivable cruelty. They did the same to all the other converted Hurons, for this was the recreation of the French, and especially of the Jesuits, in their celestial abode. They baptized Indians with no other object than that they might have them to torment in heaven, to which end they were willing to meet hardships and dangers in this life, just as a war party invades the enemy's country at great risk that it may bring home prisoners to burn. After her painful experience, an unknown friend secretly showed the girl a path down to the earth, and she hastened there to warn her countrymen against the wiles of the missionaries.

But the mission survived the agitation produced by this tale and its influence was strengthened by the victory. The future would have been full of hope but for the portentous cloud of war that rose, black and wrathful, from where lay the dens of the Iroquois.

In the summer of 1647 the Hurons dared not go down to the French settlements, but in the following year they took heart and resolved at all risks to make the attempt, for the kettles, hatchets and knives of the traders had become necessaries of life. Two hundred and fifty of their best warriors therefore embarked, under five valiant chiefs.

They made the voyage in safety, approached Three Rivers on the seventeenth of July and, running their canoes ashore among the bul-rushes, began to grease their hair, paint their faces and otherwise adorn themselves that they might appear after a befitting fashion at the fort. While they were thus engaged, the alarm was sounded. Some of their warriors had discovered a large body of Iroquois, who for several days had been lurking in the forest, unknown to the French garrison, watching their opportunity to strike a blow. The Hurons snatched their arms and, half greased and painted, ran to meet them. The Iroquois received them with a volley. They fell flat to avoid the shot, then leaped up with a furious yell and sent back a shower of arrows and bullets. The Iroquois, who were outnumbered, gave way and fled, excepting a few who for a time made fight with their knives. The Hurons pursued. Many prisoners were taken and many dead left on the field. The rout of the enemy was complete, and when their trade was ended the Hurons returned home in triumph, decorated with the laurels and the scalps of victory. As it proved, it would have been well had they remained there to defend their families and firesides.

The oft-mentioned town of Teanaustayé, or St. Joseph, lay on the southeastern frontier of the Huron country, near the foot of a range of forest-covered hills and about fifteen miles from Ste. Marie, the center and base of the Huron missions. It had been the chief town of the nation, and its population, by the Indian standard, was still large, for it had four hundred families and at least two thousand inhabitants. It was well fortified with palisades, after the Huron manner, and was esteemed the chief bulwark of the country. Here countless Iroquois had been burned and devoured. Its people had been truculent and intractable heathen, but many of them had surrendered to the Faith, and for four years past Father Daniel had preached among them with excellent results.

On the morning of the fourth of July, when the forest around basked lazily in the early sun, you might have mounted the rising ground on which the town stood and passed unchallenged through the opening in the palisade. Within, you would have seen the crowded dwellings of bark, shaped like the arched coverings of huge baggage wagons and decorated with the totems or armorial devices of their owners, daubed on the outside with paint. Here some squalid wolfish dog lay sleeping in the sun, a group of Huron girls chatted together in the shade, old squaws pounded corn in large wooden mortars, idle youths gambled with cherry stones on a wooden platter and naked infants crawled in the dust.

Scarcely a warrior was to be seen. Some were absent in quest of game or of Iroquois scalps, and some had gone with the trading party to the French settlements. You followed the foul passageways among the houses and at length came to the church. It was full to the door. Daniel had just finished the mass and his flock still knelt at their devotions. It was only the day before that he had returned to them, warmed with new fervor, from his meditations in retreat at Ste. Marie.

Suddenly an uproar of voices, shrill with terror, burst upon the languid silence of the town. "The Iroquois! the Iroquois!" A crowd of hostile warriors had issued from the forest and were rushing across the clearing, towards the opening in the palisade. Daniel ran out of the church and hurried to the point of danger. Some snatched weapons; some rushed to and fro in the madness of a blind panic. The priest rallied the defenders, promised heaven to those who died for their homes and their faith, then hastened from house to house, calling on unbelievers to repent and receive baptism, to snatch them from the hell that yawned to engulf them.

They crowded around him, imploring to be saved, and immersing his handkerchief in a bowl of water, he shook it over them and baptized them by aspersion. They pursued him as he ran again to the church, where he found a throng of women, children and old men gathered as in a sanctuary. Some cried for baptism, some held out their children to receive it, some begged for absolution and some wailed in terror and despair. "Brothers," he exclaimed again and again, as he shook the baptismal drops from his handkerchief, "brothers, today we shall be in heaven!"

The fierce yell of the war whoop now rose close at hand. The palisade was forced and the enemy was in the town. The air quivered with the infernal din.

"Fly!" screamed the priest, driving his flock before him. "I will stay here. We shall meet again in heaven."

Many of them escaped through an opening in the palisade opposite to that by which the Iroquois had entered, but Daniel would not follow, for there still might be souls to rescue from perdition. The hour had come for which he had long prepared himself. In a moment he saw the Iroquois and came forth from the church to meet them. When they saw him in turn, radiant in the vestments of his office, confronting them with a look kindled with the inspiration of martyrdom, they stopped and stared in amazement. Recovering themselves, they bent their bows and showered him with a volley of arrows that tore through his robes and his flesh. A gunshot followed. The ball pierced his heart and he fell dead, gasping the name of Jesus.

They rushed upon him with yells of triumph, stripped him naked, gashed and hacked his lifeless body and, scooping his blood in their hands, bathed their faces in it to make them brave. The town was in a blaze. When the flames reached the church, they flung the priest into it and both were consumed together.

Teanaustayé was a heap of ashes and the victors took up their

156

march with a train of nearly seven hundred prisoners, many of whom they killed on the way. Many more had been slain in the town and the neighboring forest, where the pursuers hunted them down and where women, crouching for refuge among thickets, were betrayed by the cries and wailing of their infants.

The triumph of the Iroquois did not end here, for a neighboring fortified town included within the circle of Daniel's mission shared the fate of Teanaustayé. Never had the Huron nation received such a blow.

Dreary winter months passed after the catastrophe of St. Joseph, and around Ste. Marie the forests were gray and bare. In the cornfields the oozy, half-thawed soil, studded with the sodden stalks of the last autumn's harvest, showed itself in patches through the melting snow.

At nine o'clock on the morning of the sixteenth of March the priests saw a heavy smoke rising over the naked forest towards the southeast, about three miles distant. They looked at each other in dismay. "The Iroquois! They are burning St. Louis!" Flames mingled with the smoke, and as they stood gazing, two Christian Hurons came, breathless and aghast, from the burning town. Their worst fear was realized. The Iroquois were there, but where were the priests of the mission, Brébeuf and Lalemant?

Late in the autumn a thousand Iroquois, chiefly Senecas and Mohawks, had taken the warpath for the Hurons. They had been all winter in the forests, hunting for subsistence and moving at their leisure towards their prey. The destruction of the two towns of the mission of St. Joseph had left a wide gap, and in the middle of March they entered the heart of the Huron country, undiscovered.

Common vigilance and common sense would have averted the calamities that followed, but the Hurons were like a doomed people, stupefied, sunk in dejection, fearing everything yet taking no measures for defense. They could easily have met the invaders with double their force, but the besotted warriors lay idle in their towns or hunted at leisure in distant forests. Nor could the Jesuits, by counsel or exhortation, rouse them to face the danger.

Before daylight of the sixteenth the invaders approached St. Ignace, which with St. Louis and three other towns formed the mission of the same name. They reconnoitered the place in the darkness. It was defended on three sides by a deep ravine and further strengthened by palisades fifteen or sixteen feet high, planted under the direction of the Jesuits. On the fourth side it was protected by palisades alone, and these were left, as usual, unguarded. This was not from a sense of security, for the greater part of the population had abandoned the town, thinking it too much exposed to the enemy, and there remained only about four hundred, chiefly women, children and old men, whose infatuated defenders were absent hunting or on futile scalping parties against the Iroquois.

It was just before dawn when a yell as of a legion of devils startled the wretched inhabitants from their sleep, and the Iroquois, bursting in upon them, cut them down with knives and hatchets, killing many and reserving the rest for a worse fate. They had entered by the weakest side. On the other sides there was no exit, and only three Hurons escaped. The whole was the work of a few minutes. The Iroquois left a guard to hold the town and secure the retreat of the main body in case of a reverse, then smearing their faces with blood, after their ghastly custom, they rushed in the dim light of the early dawn towards St. Louis, about a league distant.

The three fugitives had fled, half naked, through the forest for the same point, which they reached about sunrise, yelling the alarm. The number of inhabitants here was less, at this time, than seven hundred, and of these all who had strength to escape, excepting about eighty warriors, made in wild terror for a place of safety. Many of the old, sick and decrepit were left perforce in the lodges. The warriors, ignorant of the strength of the assailants, sang their war songs and resolved to hold the place to the last. It had not the natural strength of St. Ignace but, like it, was surrounded by palisades.

Here were the two Jesuits, Brébeuf and Lalemant. Brébeuf's converts entreated him to escape with them, but the Norman zealot, bold scion of a warlike stock, had no thought of flight. His post was, in the teeth of danger, to cheer on those who fought and open heaven to those who fell. His colleague, slight of frame and frail of constitution, trembled despite himself, but deep enthusiasm mastered the weakness of Nature and he, too, refused to fly.

Scarcely had the sun risen and scarcely were the fugitives gone when

158

the Iroquois rushed to the assault like a troop of tigers. Yell echoed yell and shot answered shot. The Hurons, brought to bay, fought with the utmost desperation, and with arrows, stones and the few guns they had, killed thirty of their assailants and wounded many more.

Twice the Iroquois recoiled, and twice renewed the attack with unabated ferocity. They swarmed at the foot of the palisades and hacked at them with their hatchets till they had cut them through at several different points. For a time there was a deadly fight at these breaches. Here were the two priests, promising heaven to those who died for their faith—one giving baptism and the other absolution. At length the Iroquois broke in and captured all the surviving defenders, the Jesuits among the rest. They set the town on fire, and the helpless wretches who had remained, unable to fly, were consumed in their burning dwellings. Next they fell upon Brébeuf and Lalemant, stripped them, bound them fast and led them with the other prisoners back to St. Ignace, where all turned out to wreak their fury on the two priests, beating them savagely with sticks and clubs as they drove them into the town. At present there was no time for further torture, for there was work at hand.

The victors divided themselves into several bands, to burn the neighboring villages and hunt their flying inhabitants. In the flush of their triumph, they meditated a bolder enterprise, and in the afternoon their chiefs sent small parties to reconnoiter Ste. Marie, with a view to attacking it the next day.

Meanwhile the fugitives of St. Louis, joined by other bands as terrified and as helpless as they, were struggling through the soft snow which clogged the forests towards Lake Huron, where the treacherous ice of spring was still unmelted. One fear expelled another. They ventured upon it and pushed forward all that day and all the following night, shivering and famished, to find refuge in the towns of the Tobacco Nation. Here, when they arrived, they spread a universal panic.

Ragueneau, Bressani and their companions waited in suspense at Ste. Marie. On the one hand, they trembled for Brébeuf and Lalemant; on the other, they looked hourly for an attack. When at evening they saw the Iroquois scouts prowling along the edge of the bordering forest, their fears were confirmed. They had with them about forty

159

Frenchmen, well armed, but their palisades and wooden buildings were not fireproof and they had learned from fugitives the number and ferocity of the invaders. They stood guard all night, praying to the saints, and above all to their great patron St. Joseph, whose festival was close at hand.

In the morning they were somewhat relieved by the arrival of about three hundred Huron warriors, chiefly converts from La Conception and Ste. Madeleine, tolerably well armed and full of fight. They were expecting others to join them, and meanwhile, dividing into several bands, they took post by the passes of the neighboring forest, hoping to waylay parties of the enemy.

Their expectation was fulfilled, for at this time two hundred of the Iroquois were making their way from St. Ignace, in advance of the main body, to begin the attack on Ste. Marie. They fell in with a band of Hurons, set upon them, killed many, drove the rest to headlong flight and, as they plunged in terror through the snow, chased them within sight of Ste. Marie. The other Hurons, hearing the yells and firing, ran to the rescue and attacked so fiercely that the Iroquois in turn were routed and ran for shelter to St. Louis, followed closely by the victors. The houses of the town had been burned, but the palisade around them was still standing, though breached and broken. The Iroquois rushed in, but the Hurons were at their heels. Many of the fugitives were captured, the rest killed or put to utter rout, and the triumphant Hurons remained masters of the place.

The Iroquois who escaped fled to St. Ignace. Here, or on the way, they found the main body of the invaders. When they heard of the disaster, the whole swarm, beside themselves with rage, turned towards St. Louis to take their revenge. Now ensued one of the most furious Indian battles on record. The Hurons within the palisade did not much exceed a hundred and fifty, for many had been killed or disabled and many, perhaps, had straggled away. Most of their enemies had guns, while they had but few. Their weapons were bows and arrows, war clubs, hatchets and knives, and of these they made good use, sallying repeatedly, fighting like devils and driving back their assailants again and again.

There are times when the Indian warrior forgets his cautious maxims and throws himself into battle with a mad and reckless feroc-

160

ity. The desperation of one party and the fierce courage of both kept
up the fight after the day had closed, and the scout from Ste. Marie,
as he bent listening under the gloom of the pines, heard far into the
night the howl of battle rising from the darkened forest. The principal
chief of the Iroquois was severely wounded and nearly a hundred of
their warriors were killed on the spot. When at length their numbers
and persistent fury prevailed, their only prize was some twenty Huron
warriors, spent with fatigue and faint with loss of blood. The rest lay
dead around the shattered palisades which they had so valiantly defended. Fatuity, not cowardice, was the ruin of the Huron nation.

The lamps burned all night at Ste. Marie, and its defenders stood
watching till daylight, musket in hand. The Jesuits prayed without
ceasing, and St. Joseph was besieged with invocations.

"Those of us who were priests," writes Ragueneau, "each made a
vow to say a mass in his honor every month, for the space of a year;
and all the rest bound themselves by vows to divers penances." The
expected onslaught did not take place. Not an Iroquois appeared.
Their victory had been bought too dear and they had no stomach for
more fighting. All the next day, the eighteenth, a stillness like the dead
lull of a tempest followed the turmoil of yesterday—as if, says the
Father Superior, "the country were waiting, palsied with fright, for
some new disaster."

On the following day—the journalist fails not to mention that it
was the festival of St. Joseph—Indians came in with tidings that a
panic had seized the Iroquois camp, that the chiefs could not control
it and that the whole body of invaders was retreating in disorder,
possessed with a vague terror that the Hurons were upon them in
force. They had found time, however, for an act of atrocious cruelty.
They planted stakes in the bark houses of St. Ignace and bound to
them those of their prisoners whom they meant to sacrifice—male and
female, from old age to infancy, husbands, mothers and children, side
by side. Then, as they retreated, they set the town on fire and laughed
with savage glee at the shrieks of anguish that rose from the blazing
dwellings.

They loaded the rest of their prisoners with their baggage and
plunder and drove them through the forest southward, braining with
their hatchets any who gave out on the march. An old woman, who

had escaped out of the midst of the flames of St. Ignace, made her way to St. Michel, a large town not far from the desolate site of St. Joseph. Here she found about seven hundred Huron warriors, hastily mustered. She set them on the track of the retreating Iroquois and they took up the chase, but evidently with no great eagerness to overtake their dangerous enemy, well armed as he was with Dutch guns, while they had little besides their bows and arrows.

They found, as they advanced, the dead bodies of prisoners tomahawked on the march, and others bound fast to trees and half burned by the fagots piled hastily around them. The Iroquois pushed forward with such headlong speed that the pursuers could not, or would not, overtake them. After two days they gave over the attempt.

On the morning of the twentieth the Jesuits at Ste. Marie received full confirmation of the reported retreat of the invaders, and one of them, with seven armed Frenchmen, set out for the scene of havoc. They passed St. Louis, where the bloody ground was strewn thick with corpses, and two or three miles farther on reached St. Ignace. Here they saw a spectacle of horror, for among the ashes of the burned town were scattered in profusion the half-consumed bodies of those who had perished in the flames. Apart from the rest, they saw a sight that banished all else from their thoughts, for they had found what they had come to seek—the scorched and mangled bodies of Brébeuf and Lalemant.

They had learned their fate already from Huron prisoners, many of whom had made their escape in the panic and confusion of the Iroquois retreat. They described what they had seen, and the condition in which the bodies were found confirmed their story.

On the afternoon of the sixteenth—the day when the two priests were captured—Brébeuf was led apart and bound to a stake. He seemed more concerned for his captive converts than for himself and addressed them in a loud voice, exhorting them to suffer patiently and promising heaven as their reward.

The Iroquois, incensed, scorched him from head to foot to silence him, whereupon, in the tone of a master, he threatened them with everlasting flames for persecuting the worshipers of God. As he continued to speak, with voice and countenance unchanged, they cut away his lower lip and thrust a red-hot iron down his throat. He

162

still held his tall form erect and defiant, with no sign or sound of pain, and they tried another means to overcome him.

They led out Lalemant, that Brébeuf might see him tortured. They had tied strips of bark, smeared with pitch, about his naked body. When he saw the condition of his Superior he could not hide his agitation and called out to him with a broken voice in the words of St. Paul: "We are made a spectacle unto the world, and to angels, and to men." Then he threw himself at Brébeuf's feet, upon which the Iroquois seized him, made him fast to a stake and set fire to the bark that enveloped him. As the flames rose he threw his arms upward with a shriek of supplication to Heaven.

Next they hung around Brébeuf's neck a collar made of hatchets heated red-hot, but the indomitable priest stood like a rock. A Huron in the crowd, who had been a convert of the mission but was now an Iroquois by adoption, called out with the malice of a renegade to pour hot water on their heads, since they had poured so much cold water on those of others. The kettle was accordingly slung and the water boiled and poured slowly on the heads of the two missionaries.

"We baptize you," they cried, "that you may be happy in heaven, for nobody can be saved without a good baptism."

Brébeuf would not flinch, and in a rage, they cut strips of flesh from his limbs and devoured them before his eyes. Other renegade Hurons called out to him, "You told us that the more one suffers on earth, the happier he is in heaven. We wish to make you happy; we torment you because we love you, and you ought to thank us for it."

After a succession of other revolting tortures, they scalped him. Seeing him nearly dead, they laid open his breast and came in a crowd to drink the blood of so valiant an enemy, thinking to imbibe with it some portion of his courage. A chief then tore out his heart and devoured it.

Thus died Jean de Brébeuf, the founder of the Huron mission, its truest hero and its greatest martyr.

CHAPTER 7

~~~~~~

End of a Mission

ALL WAS OVER WITH THE HURONS. THE DEATH KNELL of their nation had struck. Without a leader, without organization, without union, crazed with fright and paralyzed with misery, they yielded to their doom without a blow. Their only thought was flight.

Within two weeks after the disasters of St. Ignace and St. Louis fifteen Huron towns were abandoned and the greater number burned, lest they should give shelter to the Iroquois. The last year's harvest had been scanty. The fugitives had no food and they left behind them the fields in which was their only hope of obtaining it. In bands, large or small, some roamed northward and eastward through the half-thawed wilderness. Some hid themselves on the rocks or islands of Lake Huron; some sought an asylum among the Tobacco Nation; a few joined the Neutrals on the north of Lake Erie. The Hurons, as a nation, ceased to exist.

Hitherto Ste. Marie had been covered by large fortified towns which lay between it and the Iroquois, but these were all destroyed—some by the enemy and some by their own people—and the Jesuits were left alone to bear the brunt of the next attack. There was, moreover, no reason for their remaining. Ste. Marie had been built as a basis for the missions, but its occupation was gone. The flock had fled from the shepherds and its existence had no longer an object. If the priests stayed to be butchered, they would perish not as martyrs but as fools.

164

The necessity was as clear as it was bitter. All their toil must come to nothing. Ste. Marie must be abandoned.

Several of the priests set out to follow and console the scattered bands of fugitive Hurons. One embarked in a canoe and coasted the dreary shores of Lake Huron northward among the wild labyrinth of rocks and islets, where his scared flock had fled for refuge. Another betook himself to the forest with a band of half-famished proselytes and shared their miserable rovings through the thickets and among the mountains. Those who remained took counsel together at Ste. Marie. Whither should they go, and where should be the new seat of the mission?

They chose Grand Manitoulin Island, called by them Isle Ste. Marie, and by the Hurons *Ekaentoton*. It lay near the northern shores of Lake Huron and by its position would give a ready access to numberless Algonquin tribes along the borders of all these inland seas. Moreover, it would bring the priests and their flock nearer to the French settlements by the route of the Ottawa, whenever the Iroquois should cease to infest that river. The fishing, too, was good and some of the priests who knew the island well made a favorable report of the soil.

There they had resolved to transplant the mission when twelve Huron chiefs arrived and asked for an interview with the Father Superior and his fellow Jesuits. The conference lasted three hours. The deputies declared that many of the scattered Hurons had determined to reunite and form a settlement on a neighboring island of the lake, called by the Jesuits Isle St. Joseph. They needed the aid of the fathers, they declared. Without them they were helpless, but with them they could hold their ground and repel the attacks of the Iroquois. They urged their plea in language which Ragueneau describes as pathetic and eloquent, and to confirm their words they gave him ten large collars of wampum, saying that these were the voices of their wives and children. They gained their point. The Jesuits abandoned their former plan and promised to join the Hurons on Isle St. Joseph.

They had built a boat, or small vessel, and in this they embarked such of their stores as it would hold. The greater part were placed on a large raft made for the purpose, like one of the rafts of timber which every summer float down the St. Lawrence and the Ottawa. Here was their stock of corn—in part the produce of their own fields and in part bought from the Hurons in former years of plenty—pictures, vestments, sacred vessels and images, weapons, ammunition, tools, goods for barter with the Indians, cattle, swine and poultry.

Ste. Marie was stripped of everything that could be moved. Then, lest it should harbor the Iroquois, they set it on fire and saw consumed in an hour the results of nine or ten years of toil. It was near sunset, on the fourteenth of June. The houseless band descended to the mouth of the Wye, went on board their raft, pushed it from the shore and, with sweeps and oars, urged it on its way all night. The lake was calm and the weather fair, but it crept so slowly over the water that several days elapsed before they reached their destination, about twenty miles distant.

Near the entrance of Matchedash Bay lie the three islands now known as Faith, Hope and Charity. Of these, Charity or Christian Island, called *Ahoendoé* by the Hurons and St. Joseph by the Jesuits, is by far the largest. It is six or eight miles wide, and when the Hurons sought refuge there it was densely covered with the primeval forest.

The priests landed with their men—some forty soldiers, laborers and others—and found about three hundred Huron families bivouacked in the woods. Here were wigwams and sheds of bark, and smoky kettles slung over fires, each on its tripod of poles, while around lay groups of famished wretches, with dark, haggard visages and uncombed hair, in every posture of despondency and woe. They had not been wholly idle, for they had made some rough clearings and planted a little corn. The arrival of the Jesuits gave them new hope, and weakened as they were with famine, they set themselves to the task of hewing and burning down the forest, making bark houses and planting palisades. The priests, on their part, chose a favorable spot and began to clear the ground and mark out the lines of a fort.

Their men (the greater part serving without pay) labored with admirable spirit and before winter had built a square, bastioned fort of solid masonry, with a deep ditch and walls about twelve feet high. Within were a small chapel, houses for lodging and a well. Detached redoubts were also built near at hand, where French musketeers could aid in defending the adjacent Huron village. Though the island was called St. Joseph, the fort, like that on the Wye, received the name of Ste. Marie. Jesuit devotion scattered these names broadcast over all the field of their labors.

The island, thanks to the vigilance of the French, escaped attack throughout the summer, but Iroquois scalping parties ranged the neighboring shores, killing stragglers and keeping the Hurons in perpetual alarm. As winter drew near, great numbers who, trembling and by stealth, had gathered a miserable subsistence among the northern forests and islands rejoined their countrymen at Joseph, until six or eight thousand expatriated wretches were gathered here under the protection of the French fort.

They were housed in a hundred or more bark dwellings, each containing eight or ten families. Here were widows without children and children without parents, for famine and the Iroquois had proved more deadly enemies than the pestilence which a few years before had wasted their towns. Of this multitude but few had strength enough to labor, scarcely any had made provision for the winter, and numbers were already perishing from want, dragging themselves from house to house like living skeletons.

The priests had spared no effort to meet the demands upon their charity. They sent men during the autumn to buy smoked fish from the northern Algonquins and employed Indians to gather acorns in the woods. Of this miserable food they succeeded in collecting five or six hundred bushels. To diminish its bitterness, the Indians boiled it with ashes, or the priests served it out to them pounded and mixed with corn.

As winter advanced the Huron houses became a frightful spectacle. Their inmates were dying by scores daily. The priests and their men buried the bodies and the Indians dug them from the earth or the snow and fed on them, sometimes in secret and sometimes openly. Notwithstanding their superstitious feasts on the bodies of their enemies, their repugnance and horror were extreme at the thought of devouring those of relatives and friends. An epidemic presently appeared to aid the work of famine. Before spring about half of their number were dead.

Meanwhile, though the cold was intense and the snow several feet deep, not an hour was free from the danger of the Iroquois, and from

167

sunset to daybreak, under the cold moon or in the driving snowstorm, the French sentries walked their rounds along the ramparts.

The priests rose before dawn and spent the time till sunrise in their private devotions. Then the bell of their chapel rang and the Indians came in crowds at the call, for misery had softened their hearts and nearly all on the island were now Christian. There was a mass, followed by a prayer and a few words of exhortation, then the hearers dispersed to make room for others. Thus the little chapel was filled ten or twelve times, until all had had their turn.

Meanwhile other priests were hearing confessions and giving advice and encouragement in private, according to the needs of each applicant. This lasted till nine o'clock, when all the Indians returned to their village and the priests presently followed to give what assistance they could. Their cassocks were worn out and they were dressed chiefly in skins. They visited the Indian houses and gave to those whose necessities were most urgent small scraps of hide, severally stamped with a particular mark and entitling the recipients, on presenting them at the fort, to a few acorns, a small quantity of boiled maize or a fragment of smoked fish, according to the stamp on the leather ticket of each. Two hours before sunset the bell of the chapel rang again and the religious exercises of the morning were repeated.

Thus this miserable winter wore away.

As spring approached, the starving multitude on Isle St. Joseph grew reckless with hunger. Along the main shore, in spots where the sun lay warm, the spring fisheries had already begun and the melting snow was uncovering the acorns in the woods. There was danger everywhere, for bands of Iroquois were again on the track of their prey. The miserable Hurons, gnawed with inexorable famine, stood in the dilemma of a deadly peril and an assured death.

They chose the former and early in March began to leave their island and cross to the mainland to gather what sustenance they could. The ice was still thick but the advancing season had softened it, and as a body of them were crossing, it broke under their feet. Some were drowned, while others dragged themselves out, drenched and pierced with cold, to die miserably on the frozen lake before they could reach a shelter. Other parties, more fortunate, gained the shore safely and began their fishing, divided into companies of from eight or ten to a hundred persons.

But the Iroquois were in wait for them. A large band of warriors had already made their way through ice and snow from their towns in central New York. They surprised the Huron fishermen, surrounded them and cut them in pieces without resistance, tracking out the various parties of their victims and hunting down fugitives with such persistency and skill that, of all who had gone over to the main, the Jesuits knew of but one who escaped.

The Jesuits at St. Joseph knew not what course to take. The doom of their flock seemed inevitable. When dismay and despondency were at their height, two of the principal Huron chiefs came to the fort and asked an interview with Ragueneau and his companions. They told them that the Indians had held a council the night before and resolved to abandon the island. Some would disperse in the most remote and inaccessible forests; others would take refuge in a distant spot, apparently the Grand Manitoulin Island; others would try to reach the Andastes; and others would seek safety in adoption and incorporation with the Iroquois themselves.

"Take courage, brother," continued one of the chiefs, addressing Ragueneau. "You can save us, if you will but resolve on a bold step. Choose a place where you can gather us together, and prevent this dispersion of our people. Turn your eyes towards Quebec and transport there what is left of this ruined country. Do not wait till war and famine have destroyed us to the last man. We are in your hands. Death has taken from you more than ten thousand of us. If you wait longer, not one will remain alive, and then you will be sorry that you did not save those whom you might have snatched from danger and who showed you the means of doing so. If you do as we wish, we will form a church under the protection of the fort at Quebec. Our faith will not be extinguished. The examples of the French and the Algonquins will encourage us in our duty, and their charity will relieve some of our misery. At least we shall sometimes find a morsel of bread for our children, who so long have had nothing but bitter roots and acorns to keep them alive."

The Jesuits were deeply moved. They consulted together again and again, and prayed in turn during forty hours without ceasing, that their minds might be enlightened. At length they resolved to grant the petition of the two chiefs and save the poor remnant of the

169

Hurons by leading them to an asylum where there was at least a hope of safety. Their resolution once taken, they pushed their preparations with all speed, lest the Iroquois might learn their purpose and lie in wait to cut them off. Canoes were made ready, and on the tenth of June they began the voyage with all their French followers and about three hundred Hurons. The Huron mission was abandoned.

"It was not without tears," writes the Father Superior, "that we left the country of our hopes and our hearts, where our brethren had gloriously shed their blood."

The fleet of canoes held its melancholy way along the shores where two years before had been the seat of one of the chief savage communities of the continent, and where now all was a waste of death and desolation. Then they steered northward along the eastern coast of the Georgian Bay, with its countless rocky islets. Everywhere they saw the traces of the Iroquois. When they reached Lake Nipissing they found it deserted, nothing remaining of the Algonquins who dwelt on its shore except the ashes of their burnt wigwams. A little farther on there was a fort built of trees, where the Iroquois who made this desolation had spent the winter. A league or two below there was another similar fort. The river Ottawa was a solitude. The Algonquins of Allumette Island and the shores adjacent had all been killed or driven away, never again to return.

As the voyagers descended the river they had a serious alarm. Their scouts came in and reported that they had found fresh footprints of men in the forest. These proved, however, to be the tracks of friends. In the preceding autumn Bressani had gone down to the French settlements with about twenty Hurons, and was now returning with them and twice their number of armed Frenchmen for the defense of the mission. His scouts had also been alarmed by discovering the footprints of Ragueneau's Indians, and for some time the two parties stood on their guard, each taking the other for an enemy. When at length they discovered their mistake, they met with embraces and rejoicing. Bressani and his Frenchmen had come too late. All was over with the Hurons and the Huron mission. As it was useless to go farther, they joined Ragueneau's party and retraced their course for the settlements.

A day or two before, they had had a sharp taste of the mettle of the enemy. Ten Iroquois warriors had spent the winter in a little fort of felled trees on the borders of the Ottawa, hunting for subsistence and waiting to waylay some passing canoe of Hurons, Algonquins or Frenchmen. Bressani's party outnumbered them six to one, but they resolved that it should not pass without a token of their presence. Late on a dark night the French and Hurons lay encamped in the forest, sleeping about their fires. They had set guards, but these, it seems, were drowsy or negligent, for the ten Iroquois, watching their time, approached with the stealth of lynxes and glided like shadows into the midst of the camp, where by the dull glow of the smoldering fires they could distinguish the recumbent figures of their victims.

Suddenly they screeched the war whoop and struck like lightning with their hatchets among the sleepers. Seven were killed before the rest could spring to their weapons. Bressani leaped up and received on the instant three arrow wounds in the head. The Iroquois were surrounded and a desperate fight ensued in the dark. Six of them were killed on the spot and two made prisoners, while the remaining two, breaking through the crowd, bounded out of the camp and escaped in the forest.

The united parties soon after reached Montreal, but the Hurons refused to remain in a spot so exposed to the Iroquois. Accordingly, they all descended the St. Lawrence and at length, on the twenty-eighth of July, reached Quebec. Here the Ursulines, the hospital nuns and the inhabitants taxed their resources to the utmost to provide food and shelter for the exiled Hurons. Their good will exceeded their power, for food was scarce at Quebec and the Jesuits themselves had to bear the chief burden of keeping the sufferers alive.

But if famine was an evil, the Iroquois were a far greater one, for while the western nations of their confederacy were engrossed with the destruction of the Hurons, the Mohawks kept up incessant attacks on the Algonquins and the French. A party of Christian Indians, chiefly from Sillery, planned a stroke of retaliation and set out for the Mohawk country, marching cautiously and sending forward scouts to scour the forest.

One of these, a Huron, suddenly fell in with a large Iroquois war party and, seeing that he could not escape, formed on the instant a villainous plan to save himself. He ran towards the enemy, crying out

171

that he had long been looking for them and was delighted to see them; that his nation, the Hurons, had come to an end; and that henceforth his country was the country of the Iroquois, where so many of his kinsmen and friends had been adopted. He had come, he declared, with no other thought than that of joining them and turning Iroquois, as they had done.

The Iroquois demanded if he had come alone. He answered, "No," and said that in order to accomplish his purpose he had joined an Algonquin war party who were in the woods not far off. The Iroquois, in great delight, demanded to be shown where they were. This Judas, as the Jesuits call him, at once complied and the Algonquins were surprised by a sudden onset and routed with severe loss. The treacherous Huron was well treated by the Iroquois, who adopted him into their nation.

Not long after, he came to Canada and with a view, as it was thought, to some further treachery, rejoined the French. A sharp cross-questioning put him to confusion and he presently confessed his guilt. He was sentenced to death and the sentence was executed by one of his own countrymen, who split his head with a hatchet.

In the course of the summer the French at Three Rivers became aware that a band of Iroquois was prowling in the neighborhood and sixty men went out to meet them. Far from retreating, the Iroquois, who were about twenty-five in number, got out of their canoes and took post waist-deep in mud and water among the tall rushes at the margin of the river. Here they fought stubbornly and kept all the Frenchmen at bay. At length, finding themselves hard pressed, they entered their canoes again and paddled off.

The French rowed after them and soon became separated in the chase, whereupon the Iroquois turned and made desperate fight with the foremost, retreating again as soon as the others came up. This they repeated several times and then made their escape after killing a number of the best French soldiers. Their leader in this affair was a famous half-breed known as the Flemish Bastard, who is styled by Ragueneau "an abomination of sin, and a monster produced between heretic Dutch father and a pagan mother."

In the forests far north of Three Rivers dwelt the tribe called the *Atticamegues,* or "Nation of the White Fish." From their remote position and the difficult nature of the intervening country, they thought themselves safe, but a band of Iroquois, marching on snowshoes a distance of twenty days' journey northward from the St. Lawrence, fell upon one of their camps in the winter and made a general butchery of the inmates. The tribe, however, still held its ground for a time and, being all good Catholics, gave its missionary, Father Buteux, an urgent invitation to visit them in their own country. Buteux, who had long been stationed at Three Rivers, was in ill-health and for years had rarely been free from some form of bodily suffering. Nevertheless, he acceded to their request and, before the opening of spring, made a remarkable journey on snowshoes into the depths of this frozen wilderness.

In the year following he repeated the undertaking. With him were a large party of Atticamegues and several Frenchmen. Game was exceedingly scarce and they were forced by hunger to separate. A Huron convert and a Frenchman named Fontarabie remained with the missionary.

The snows had melted and all the streams were swollen. The three travelers, in a small birch canoe, pushed their way up a turbulent river, where falls and rapids were so numerous that many times daily they were forced to carry their bark vessel and their baggage through forests and thickets and over rocks and precipices. On the tenth of May they made two such portages, and soon after, reaching a third fall, again lifted their canoe from the water. They toiled through the naked forest, among the wet, black trees, over tangled roots, green, spongy mosses, moldering leaves and rotten, prostrate trunks, while the cataract foamed amidst the rocks hard by.

The Indian led the way with the canoe on his head, while Buteux and the other Frenchman followed with the baggage. Suddenly they were set upon by a troop of Iroquois who had crouched behind thickets, rocks and fallen trees to waylay them. The Huron was captured before he had time to fly. Buteux and the Frenchman tried to escape but were instantly shot down, the Jesuit receiving two balls in the breast. The Iroquois rushed upon them, mangled their bodies with tomahawks and swords, stripped them and then flung them into the torrent.

This wilderness tragedy was repeated time and time again, on various scales, until the destroyers had finished their deadly labors.

It was well for the European colonies, above all for those of England, that the wisdom of the Iroquois was but the wisdom of savages. Their sagacity is past denying; it showed itself in many ways. But it was not equal to a comprehension of their own situation and that of their race. Could they have read their destiny and curbed their mad ambition, they might have leagued with themselves four great communities of kindred lineage to resist the encroachments of civilization and oppose a barrier of fire to the spread of the young colonies of the East. But their organization and their intelligence were merely the instruments of a blind frenzy, which impelled them to destroy those whom they might have made their allies in a common cause.

They had an organization with which the ideas and habits of several generations were interwoven, and they had also sagacious leaders for peace and war. They discussed all questions of policy with the coolest deliberation, and knew how to turn to profit even imperfections in their plan of government which seemed to promise only weakness and discord. They carried all before them because they were animated throughout, as one man, by the same audacious pride and insatiable rage for conquest. Like other Indians, they waged war on a plan altogether democratic—that is, each man fought or not, as he saw fit, and they owed their unity and vigor of action to the homicidal frenzy that urged them all alike.

Their bloody triumphs were complete in 1675. They had "made a solitude and called it peace." All the surrounding nations of their own lineage were conquered and broken up, while neighboring Algonquin tribes were suffered to exist only on condition of paying a yearly tribute of wampum. The confederacy remained a wedge thrust between the growing colonies of France and England.

But what was the state of the conquerors? Their triumphs had cost them dear. As early as the year 1660, a writer evidently well-informed reports that their entire force had been reduced to twenty-two hundred warriors, while of these not more than twelve hundred were of the true Iroquois stock. The rest was a medley of adopted prisoners— Hurons, Neutrals, Eries and Indians of various Algonquin tribes. Still their aggressive spirit was unsubdued. These incorrigible warriors pushed their murderous raids to Hudson's Bay, Lake Superior, the Mississippi and the Tennessee. They were the tyrants of all the intervening wilderness and they remained for more than half a century a terror and scourge to the afflicted colonists of New France.

With the fall of the Hurons fell the best hope of the Canadian mission. They and the stable and populous communities around them had been the rude material from which the Jesuit would have formed his Christian empire in the wilderness. But one by one these kindred peoples were uprooted and swept away; while the neighboring Algonquins, to whom they had been a bulwark, were involved with them in a common ruin.

The land of promise was turned to a solitude and a desolation. There was still work at hand, it is true: vast regions to explore and countless heathens to snatch from perdition. But these for the most part were remote and scattered hordes from whose conversion it was vain to look for the same solid and decisive results.

In a measure the occupation of the Jesuits was gone. Some of them went home, "well resolved," writes the Father Superior, "to return to the combat at the first sound of the trumpet," while of those who remained, about twenty in number, several soon fell victims to famine, hardship and the Iroquois. A few years more and Canada ceased to be a mission. Political and commercial interests gradually became ascendant and the story of Jesuit propagandism was interwoven with her civil and military annals.

The cause of the failure of the Jesuits is obvious. The guns and tomahawks of the Iroquois were the ruin of their hopes. Could they have curbed or converted those ferocious bands, it is little less than certain that their dream would have become a reality. Savages tamed— not civilized, for that was scarcely possible—would have been distributed in communities through the valleys of the Great Lakes and the Mississippi, ruled by priests in the interest of Catholicity and of France. Their habits of agriculture would have been developed and their instincts of mutual slaughter repressed. The swift decline of the Indian population would have been arrested and it would have been made, through the fur trade, a source of prosperity to New France.

Unmolested by Indian enemies and fed by a rich commerce, she would have put forth a vigorous growth. True to her far-reaching and adventurous genius, she would have occupied the West with traders, settlers and garrisons, and cut up the virgin wilderness into fiefs while as yet the colonies of England were but a weak and broken line along the shore of the Atlantic. When at last the great conflict came, England and Liberty would have been confronted, not by a depleted antagonist still feeble from the exhaustion of a starved and persecuted infancy, but by an athletic champion of the principles of Richelieu and of Loyola.

Liberty may thank the Iroquois that, by their insensate fury, the plans of her adversary were ruined and a peril and a woe averted from her future. They ruined the trade which was the lifeblood of New France; they stopped the current of her arteries and made all her early years a misery and a terror.

Not that they changed her destinies. The contest on this continent between Liberty and Absolutism was never doubtful, but the triumph of one would have been dearly bought and the downfall of the other incomplete. Populations formed in the ideas and habits of a feudal monarchy and controlled by a hierarchy profoundly hostile to freedom of thought would have remained a hindrance and a stumbling block in the way of that majestic experiment of which America is the field.

PART THREE

La Salle and the Discovery of the Great West

~~~~~~

First Voyage

AMONG THE BURGHERS OF ROUEN WAS THE OLD and rich family of the Caveliers. Though citizens and not nobles, some of their connections held high diplomatic posts and honorable employments at Court. They were destined to find a better claim to distinction. In 1643 was born at Rouen Robert Cavelier, better known by the designation of La Salle. His full name was Réné-Robert Cavelier, Sieur de la Salle, La Salle being the name of an estate near Rouen belonging to the Caveliers.

His father Jean and his uncle Henri were wealthy merchants, living more like nobles than like burghers, and the boy received an education answering to the marked traits of intellect and character which he soon began to display. He showed an inclination for the exact sciences, and especially for mathematics, in which he was most proficient. At an early age, it is said, he became connected with the Jesuits.

But Nature had shaped him for other uses than to teach a class of boys on the benches of a Jesuit school. Nor, on his part, was he likely to please his directors. Self-controlled and self-contained as he was, he was far too intractable a subject to serve their turn. A youth whose calm exterior hid an inexhaustible fund of pride; whose inflexible purposes, nursed in secret, the confessional and the "manifestations of conscience" could hardly drag to the light; whose strong personality would not yield to the shaping hand; and who, by a necessity of his nature, could obey no initiative but his own—such a man was not after the model that Loyola had commended to his followers.

La Salle left the Jesuits, parting with them, it is said, on good terms and with a reputation of excellent acquirements and unimpeachable morals. This last is very credible. The cravings of a deep ambition, the hunger of an insatiable intellect, the intense longing for action and achievement subdued in him all other passions. In his faults the love of pleasure had no part.

He had an elder brother in Canada, the Abbé Jean Cavelier, a priest of St. Sulpice. Apparently it was this that shaped his destinies. His connection with the Jesuits had deprived him, under the French law, of the inheritance of his father, who had died not long before. An allowance was made to him of three or four hundred livres a year, the capital of which was paid over to him. With this pittance he sailed for Canada to seek his fortune in the spring of 1666.

The priests of the Seminary of St. Sulpice, now the feudal lords of Montreal, were granting out their lands on very easy terms to settlers. They wished to extend a thin line of settlements along the front of their island to form a sort of outpost from which an alarm could be given on any descent of the Iroquois. La Salle was the man for such a purpose. Had the priests understood him—which they evidently did not, for some of them suspected him of levity, the last foible with which he could be charged—they would have seen in him a young man in whom the fire of youth glowed not the less ardently for the veil of reserve that covered it; who would shrink from no danger but would not court it in bravado; and who would cling with an invincible tenacity of grip to any purpose which he might espouse.

There is good reason to think that he had come to Canada with purposes already conceived, and that he was ready to avail himself of any steppingstone which might help to realize them. Queylus, Superior of the seminary, made him a generous offer and he accepted it. This was the gratuitous grant of a large tract of land at the place now called La Chine, above the great rapids of the same name and eight or nine miles from Montreal. On one hand, the place was greatly exposed to attack, and on the other, it was favorably situated for the fur trade. La Salle and his successors became its feudal proprietors, on the sole condition of delivering to the seminary on every change of ownership a medal of fine silver weighing one mark. He entered on the

180

improvement of his new domain with what means he could command and began to grant out his land to such settlers as would join him.

That La Salle came to Canada with objects distinctly in view is probable from the fact that he at once began to study the Indian languages, with such success that he is said to have mastered the Iroquois and seven or eight other languages and dialects within two or three years. From the shore of his seigniory he could gaze westward over the broad breast of the Lake of St. Louis, bounded by the dim forests of Chateauguay and Beauharnois, but his thoughts flew far beyond, across the wild and lonely world that stretched towards the sunset. Like Champlain and all the early explorers, he dreamed of a passage to the South Sea and a new road for commerce to the riches of China and Japan.

Indians often came to his secluded settlement and on occasion he was visited by a band of the Seneca Iroquois, not long before the scourge of the colony but now, by virtue of a new treaty, wearing the semblance of friendship. The visitors spent the winter with him and told him of a river called the Ohio, rising in their country and flowing into the sea, but at such a distance that its mouth could be reached only after a journey of eight or nine months. [The Iroquois always called the Mississippi the Ohio, while the Algonquins gave the river its present name.]

In accordance with geographical views then prevalent, La Salle conceived that this great river must needs flow into the "Vermilion Sea," that is, the Gulf of California. If so, it would give him what he sought, a western passage to China, while in any case the populous Indian tribes said to inhabit its banks might be made a source of great commercial profit.

La Salle's imagination took fire. His resolution was soon formed and he descended the St. Lawrence to Quebec, to gain the countenance of the governor for his intended exploration. Few men were more skilled than he in the art of clear and plausible statement. Both Governor Courcelle and the intendant, Jean Talon, were readily won over to his plan, for which, however, they seem to have given him no more substantial aid than that of the governor's letters patent authorizing the enterprise. The cost was to be his own and he had no money, having spent it all on his seigniory. He therefore proposed that the Seminary, which had given it to him, should buy it back again, with such improvements as he had made.

Queylus, the Superior, was favorably disposed towards him, consented, and bought the greater part from him, while La Salle sold the remainder, including the clearings, to one Jean Milot, an ironmonger, for twenty-eight hundred livres. With this he bought four canoes, with the necessary supplies, and hired fourteen men.

Meanwhile the seminary itself was preparing a similar enterprise. The Jesuits at this time not only held an ascendancy over the other ecclesiastics in Canada, but exercised an inordinate influence on the civil government. The seminary priests of Montreal were jealous of these powerful rivals and eager to emulate their zeal in the saving of souls and the conquering of new domains for the Faith.

Under this impulse they had, three years before, established a mission at Quinté, on the north shore of Lake Ontario, in charge of two of their number, one of whom was the Abbé Fénelon, elder brother of the celebrated Archbishop of Cambray. Another of them, Dollier de Casson, had spent the winter in a hunting camp of the Nipissings, where an Indian prisoner captured in the Northwest told him of populous tribes of that quarter living in heathenish darkness. The seminary priests resolved to essay their conversion, and an expedition to be directed by Dollier was fitted out to this end.

Dollier was not ill suited to the purpose. He had been a soldier in his youth and had fought valiantly as an officer of cavalry under Turenne. He was a man of great courage; of a tall, commanding person; and of uncommon bodily strength, which he had notably proved in the campaign of Courcelle against the Iroquois, three years before.

While Dollier was at Quebec to procure the necessary outfit, he was urged by Courcellé to modify his plans so far as to act in concert with La Salle in exploring the mystery of the great unknown river of the West. Dollier and his brother priests consented. One of them, Galinée, was joined with him as a colleague because he was skilled in surveying and could make a map of their route. Three canoes were procured and seven hired men completed the party. It was determined that La Salle's expedition and that of the seminary should be combined in one—an arrangement ill suited to the character of the young explorer, who was unfit for any enterprise of which he was not the undisputed chief.

La Chine was the starting point, and the combined parties, in all twenty-four men with seven canoes, embarked on the Lake of St. Louis. With them were two other canoes, bearing the party of Senecas who had wintered at La Salle's settlement and who were now to act as guides.

Father Galinée recounts the journey. He was no woodsman: the river, the forests, the rapids were all new to him and he dilates on them with the minuteness of a novice. Above all, he admired the Indian birch canoes. "If God," he says, "grants me the grace of returning to France, I shall try to carry one with me."

Then he describes the bivouac: "Your lodging is as extraordinary as your vessels, for after paddling or carrying the canoes all day, you find mother earth ready to receive your wearied body. If the weather is fair, you make a fire and lie down to sleep without further trouble, but if it rains, you must peel bark from the trees and make a shed by laying it on a frame of sticks. As for your food, it is enough to make you burn all the cookery books that ever were written, for in the woods of Canada one finds means to live well without bread, wine, salt, pepper or spice. The ordinary food is Indian corn, or Turkey wheat as they call it in France, which is crushed between two stones and boiled, seasoning it with meat or fish, when you can get them. This sort of life seemed so strange to us that we all felt the effects of it, and before we were a hundred leagues from Montreal, not one of us was free from some malady or other. At last, after all our misery, on the second of August we discovered Lake Ontario, like a great sea with no land beyond it."

After an uneasy month's delay in a Seneca village, where they tried vainly to procure guides, the party coasted the south shore of the lake, passed the mouth of the Niagara, where they heard the distant roar of the cataract, and on the twenty-fourth of September reached Otinawatawa, which was a few miles north of the present city of Hamilton. The inhabitants proved friendly and La Salle received the welcome present of a Shawanoe prisoner, who told them that the Ohio could be reached in six weeks and that he would guide them to it. Delighted at this good fortune, they were about to set out when they heard, to their astonishment, of the arrival of two other Frenchmen at a neighboring village.

One of the strangers was destined to hold a conspicuous place in the history of western discovery. This was Louis Joliet, a young man of about the age of La Salle. Like him, he had studied for the priesthood, but the world and the wilderness had conquered his early inclinations and changed him to an active and adventurous fur trader. Talon had sent him to discover and explore the copper mines of Lake Superior. He had failed in the attempt and was now returning. His Indian guide, afraid of passing the Niagara portage lest he should meet enemies, had led him from Lake Erie by way of Grand River, towards the head of Lake Ontario. Thus it was that he met La Salle and the Sulpitians.

This meeting caused a change of plan. Joliet showed the priests a map which he had made of such parts of the Upper Lakes as he had visited and gave them a copy of it, telling them at the same time of the Potawatomis and other tribes of that region in grievous need of spiritual succor. The result was a determination on their part to follow the route which he suggested, notwithstanding the remonstrances of La Salle, who in vain reminded them that the Jesuits had preoccupied the field and would regard them as intruders. They resolved that the Potawatomis should no longer sit in darkness. As for the Mississippi, it could be reached, as they conceived, with less risk by this northern route than by that of the south.

La Salle was of a different mind. His goal was the Ohio, and not the northern lakes. A few days before, while hunting, he had been attacked by a fever, sarcastically ascribed by Galinée to his having seen three large rattlesnakes crawling up a rock. He now told his two colleagues that he was in no condition to go forward and should be forced to part with them. There can be no doubt that he used his illness as a pretext for escaping from their company without ungraciousness and following his own path in his own way.

On the last day of September the priests made an altar, supported by the paddles of the canoes laid on forked sticks. Dollier said mass. La Salle and his followers received the sacrament, as did also those of his late colleagues, and thus they parted, the Sulpitians and their party descending the Grand River towards Lake Erie, while La Salle, as they supposed, began his return to Montreal.

After leaving the priests, La Salle went to Onondaga, where we are left to infer that he succeeded better in getting a guide than he had before among the Senecas. Thence he made his way to a point six or seven leagues distant from Lake Erie, where he reached a branch of the Ohio and, descending it, followed the river as far as the rapids at Louisville—or, as has been maintained, beyond its confluence with the Mississippi. His men now refused to go farther and abandoned him, escaping to the English and the Dutch. He retraced his steps alone.

It appears, according to one memoir, that the indefatigable explorer embarked the following year on Lake Erie, ascended the Detroit to Lake Huron, coasted the unknown shores of Michigan, passed the Straits of Michilimackinac and, leaving Green Bay behind him, entered what is described as an incomparably larger bay, but which was evidently the southern portion of Lake Michigan. Then he crossed to a river flowing westward—evidently the Illinois—and followed it until it was joined by another river flowing from the northwest to the southeast. By this, only the Mississippi can be meant. He is reported to have said that he descended it to the thirty-sixth degree of latitude, where he stopped, assured that it discharged itself not into the Gulf of California but into the Gulf of Mexico, and resolved to follow it there at a future day, when he was better provided with men and supplies.

La Salle discovered the Ohio, and in all probability the Illinois. But that he discovered the Mississippi has not been proved, nor in the light of the evidence we have is it likely.

CHAPTER 2

The Discovery of the Mississippi

J EAN TALON, INTENDANT OF CANADA, WAS FULL OF
projects for the good of the colony. On the one hand, he set
himself to the development of its industries, and on the other, to the
extension of its domain. He meant to occupy the interior of the continent, control the rivers, which were its only highways, and hold it for
France against every other nation. On the east, England was to be
hemmed within a narrow strip of seaboard, while on the south, Talon
aimed at securing a port on the Gulf of Mexico, to keep the Spaniards
in check and dispute with them the possession of the vast regions
which they claimed as their own. But the interior of the continent
was still an unknown world. It behooved him to explore it, and to
that end he availed himself of Jesuits, officers, fur traders and enterprising schemers like La Salle.

Talon was resolved to find the Mississippi, the most interesting
object of search and seemingly the most attainable in the wild and
vague domain which he claimed for the King. The Indians had described it; the Jesuits were eager to discover it; and La Salle, if he
had not reached it, had explored two several avenues by which it
might be approached.

Looking about him for a fit agent of the enterprise, Talon chose
Louis Joliet, who had returned from Lake Superior. But the intendant
was not to see the fulfillment of his design. His busy and useful career
in Canada was drawing to an end. A misunderstanding had arisen
between him and the governor, Courcelle. Both were faithful servants

of the King, but the relations between the two chiefs of the colony were of a nature necessarily so critical that a conflict of authority was scarcely to be avoided. Each thought his functions encroached upon and both asked for recall. Another governor succeeded, one who was to stamp his mark, broad, bold and ineffaceable, on the most memorable page of French-American history: Louis de Buade, Count of Palluau and Frontenac.

If Talon had remained in the colony, Frontenac would infallibly have quarreled with him, but he was too clear-sighted not to approve his plans for the discovery and occupation of the interior. Before sailing for France, Talon recommended Joliet as a suitable agent for the discovery of the Mississippi and the governor accepted his counsel.

Louis Joliet was the son of a wagonmaker in the service of the Company of the Hundred Associates, then owners of Canada. He was born at Quebec in 1645 and was educated by the Jesuits. When still very young, he resolved to be a priest. He received the tonsure and the minor orders at the age of seventeen. Four years after, he is mentioned with especial honor for the part he bore in the disputes in philosophy, at which the dignitaries of the colony were present and in which the intendant himself took part. Not long after, he renounced his clerical vocation and turned fur trader.

In what we know of Joliet there is nothing that reveals any salient or distinctive trait of character, any special breadth of view or boldness of design. He appears to have been simply a merchant, intelligent, well educated, courageous, hardy and enterprising. Though he had renounced the priesthood, he retained his partiality for the Jesuits and it is more than probable that their influence had aided not a little to determine Talon's choice. One of their number, Jacques Marquette, was chosen to accompany him.

Joliet passed up the lakes to Michilimackinac and found his destined companion at Point St. Ignace, on the north side of the strait, where in his palisaded mission house and chapel he had labored for two years past to instruct the Huron refugees from St. Esprit and a band of Ottawas who had joined them.

Marquette was born in 1637 of an old and honorable family at Laon, in the north of France, and was now thirty-five years of age. When about seventeen, he had joined the Jesuits, evidently from motives purely religious, and in 1666 he was sent to the missions of Canada. At first he was destined to the station of Tadoussac, and to prepare himself for it he studied the Montagnais language under Gabriel Druilletes. But his destination was changed and he was sent to the Upper Lakes in 1668, where he had since remained. His talents as a linguist must have been great, for within a few years he learned to speak with ease six Indian languages. The traits of his character are unmistakable. He was of the brotherhood of the early Canadian missionaries, and the true counterpart of Granier or Jogues.

The outfit of the travelers was very simple. They provided themselves with two birch canoes and a supply of smoked meat and Indian corn, embarked with five men and began their voyage on the seventeenth of May. They had obtained all possible information from the Indians, and had made, by means of it, a species of map of their intended route.

Their course was westward, and plying their paddles, they passed the Straits of Michilimackinac and coasted the northern shores of Lake Michigan, landing at evening to build their campfire at the edge of the forest and draw up their canoes on the strand.

They soon reached the river Menomonie (now spelled Menominee) and ascended it to the village of the Menomonies, or Wild-rice Indians. When they told them the object of their voyage, these Indians were filled with astonishment and used their best ingenuity to dissuade them. The banks of the Mississippi, they said, were inhabited by ferocious tribes who put every stranger to death, tomahawking all newcomers without cause or provocation. They added that there was a demon in a certain part of the river whose roar could be heard at a great distance and who would engulf them in the abyss where he dwelt; that its waters were full of frightful monsters who would devour them and their canoe; and, finally, that the heat was so great that they would perish inevitably. Marquette ignored their counsel, gave them a few words of instruction in the mysteries of the Faith, taught them a prayer and bade them farewell.

The travelers next reached the mission at the head of Green Bay, entered Fox River, with difficulty and labor dragged their canoes up the long and tumultuous rapids, crossed Lake Winnebago and followed the quiet windings of the river beyond, where they glided through an endless growth of wild rice and scared the innumerable birds that fed upon it. On either hand rolled the prairie, dotted with groves and trees, browsing elk and deer.

On the seventh of June they reached the great town of the Miamis and Mascoutins and called the chiefs and elders to a council. Joliet told them that the governor of Canada had sent him to discover new countries and that God had sent his companion to teach the true faith to the inhabitants, and he prayed for guides to show them the way to the waters of the Wisconsin.

The council readily consented, and on the tenth of June the Frenchmen embarked again with two Indians to conduct them. All the town came down to the shore to see their departure. Here were the Miamis, with long locks of hair dangling over each ear, after a fashion which Marquette thought very becoming; and here, too, the Mascoutins and the Kickapoos, whom he describes as mere boors in comparison with their Miami townsmen. All stared alike at the seven adventurers, marveling that men could be found to risk an enterprise so hazardous.

The river twisted among lakes and marshes choked with wild rice, and but for their guides, they could scarcely have followed the perplexed and narrow channel. It brought them at last to the portage, where after carrying their canoes a mile and a half over the prairie and through the marsh, they launched them on the Wisconsin, bade farewell to the waters that flowed to the St. Lawrence and committed themselves to the current that was to bear them they knew not where —perhaps to the Gulf of Mexico, perhaps to the South Sea or the Gulf of California.

They glided calmly down the tranquil stream, by islands choked with trees and matted with entangling grapevines; by forests, groves and prairies, the parks and pleasure grounds of a prodigal Nature; by thickets and marshes and broad bare sand bars; under the shadowing trees, between whose tops looked down from afar the bold brow of some woody bluff. At night the bivouac—the canoes inverted on the bank, the flickering fire, the meal of bison flesh or venison, the evening pipes and slumber beneath the stars. When they embarked again in the morning, the mist hung on the river like a bridal veil, then melted before the sun till the glassy water and the languid woods basked breathless in the sultry glare.

On the seventeenth of June they saw on their right the broad meadows, bounded in the distance by rugged hills, where later stood the town and fort of Prairie du Chien. Before them a wide and rapid current coursed athwart their way, by the foot of lofty heights wrapped thick in forests. They had found what they sought, and "with a joy," writes Marquette, "which I cannot express," they steered their canoes on the eddies of the Mississippi.

Turning southward, they paddled down the stream through a solitude unrelieved by the faintest trace of man. A large fish, apparently one of the huge catfish of the Mississippi, blundered against Marquette's canoe with a force which seems to have startled him, and once as they drew in their net they caught a "spadefish" whose eccentric appearance greatly astonished them. At length the buffalo began to appear, grazing in herds on the great prairies which then bordered the river. Marquette describes the fierce and stupid look of the old bulls as they stared at the intruders through the tangled mane which nearly blinded them.

They advanced with extreme caution, landed at night and made a fire to cook their evening meal, then extinguished it, embarked again, paddled some way farther and anchored in the stream, keeping a man on the watch till morning. They had journeyed more than a fortnight without meeting a human being, when on the twenty-fifth they discovered footprints of men in the mud of the western bank and a well-trodden path that led to the adjacent prairie. Joliet and Marquette resolved to follow it and, leaving the canoes in charge of their men, they set out on their hazardous adventure.

The day was fair and they walked two leagues in silence, following the path through the forest and across the sunny prairie till they discovered an Indian village on the banks of a river and two others on a hill half a league distant. Now, with beating hearts, they invoked the aid of Heaven and, again advancing, came so near without being seen that they could hear the voices of the Indians among the wigwams. Then they stood forth in full view and shouted to attract attention.

There was great commotion in the village. The inmates swarmed out of their huts and four of their chief men presently came forward to meet the strangers, advancing very deliberately and holding up toward the sun two calumets, or peace pipes, decorated with feathers.

They stopped abruptly before the two Frenchmen and stood gazing at them without speaking a word. Marquette was much relieved on seeing that they wore French cloth, from which he judged that they must be friends and allies. He broke the silence and asked them who they were, whereupon they answered that they were Illinois and offered the pipe, which having been duly smoked, they all went together to the village.

Here the chief received the travelers after a singular fashion, meant to do them honor. He stood stark naked at the door of a large wigwam, holding up both hands as if to shield his eyes. "Frenchmen, how bright the sun shines when you come to visit us! All our village awaits you, and you shall enter our wigwams in peace." So saying, he led them into his own, which was crowded to suffocation with savages, staring at their guests in silence.

Having smoked with the chiefs and old men, they were invited to visit the great chief of all the Illinois at one of the villages they had seen in the distance, and there they proceeded, followed by a throng of warriors, squaws and children. On arriving, they were forced to smoke again and listen to a speech of welcome from the great chief, who delivered it standing between two old men, naked like himself.

His lodge was crowded with the dignitaries of the tribe, whom Marquette addressed in Algonquin, announcing himself as a messenger sent by the God who had made them and whom it behooves them to recognize and obey. He added a few words touching the power and glory of Count Frontenac and concluded by asking information concerning the Mississippi and the tribes along its banks, whom he was on his way to visit. The chief replied with a speech of compliment, assuring his guests that their presence added flavor to his tobacco, made the river more calm, the sky more serene and the earth more beautiful. In conclusion, he gave them a young slave and a calumet, begging them at the same time to abandon their purpose of descending the Mississippi.

A feast of four courses now followed. First a wooden bowl full of a porridge of Indian meal boiled with grease was set before the guests, and the master of ceremonies fed them in turn, like infants, with a large spoon. Then appeared a platter of fish, and the same functionary, carefully removing the bones with his fingers and blowing on the morsels to cool them, placed them in the mouths of the two French-men. A large dog, killed and cooked for the occasion, was next placed before them but, failing to tempt their fastidious appetites, was sup-planted by a dish of fat buffalo meat, which concluded the entertain-ment. The crowd having dispersed, buffalo robes were spread on the ground and Marquette and Joliet spent the night on the scene of the late festivity. In the morning the chief, with some six hundred of his tribesmen, escorted them to their canoes and bade them, after their stolid fashion, a friendly farewell.

Again they were on their way, slowly drifting down the great river. They passed the mouth of the Illinois and glided beneath that line of rocks on the eastern side, cut into fantastic forms by the elements and marked as "The Ruined Castles" on some of the early French maps.

Suddenly they were aroused by a real danger. A torrent of yellow mud rushed furiously athwart the calm blue current of the Mississippi, boiling and surging and sweeping in its course logs, branches and uprooted trees. They had reached the mouth of the Missouri, where that savage river, descending from its mad career through a vast un-known of barbarism, poured its turbid floods into the bosom of its gentler sister. Their light canoes whirled on the miry vortex like dry leaves on an angry brook. "I never," writes Marquette, "saw anything more terrific," but they escaped with their fright and held their way down the turbulent and swollen current of the now united rivers.

They passed the lonely forest that covered the site of the destined city of St. Louis, and a few days later saw on their left the mouth of the stream to which the Iroquois had given the well-merited name of Ohio, or the "Beautiful River." Soon they began to see the marshy shores buried in a dense growth of the cane, with its tall straight stems and feathery light green foliage. The sun glowed through the hazy air with a languid stifling heat, and by day and night mosquitoes in myriads left them no peace.

They floated slowly down the current, crouched in the shade of the sails which they had spread as awnings, when suddenly they saw Indians on the east bank. The surprise was mutual and each party was as much frightened as the other. Marquette hastened to display the calumet which the Illinois had given him by way of passport, and the Indians, recognizing the pacific symbol, replied with an invitation to land. Evidently they were in communication with Europeans, for they were armed with guns, knives and hatchets, wore garments of cloth and carried their gunpowder in small bottles of thick glass. They feasted the Frenchmen with buffalo meat, bear's oil and white plums, and gave them a variety of doubtful information, including the agreeable but delusive assurance that they would reach the mouth of the river in ten days. It was, in fact, more than a thousand miles distant.

Resuming their course, they floated again down the interminable monotony of river, marsh and forest. Day after day passed on in solitude, and they had paddled some three hundred miles since their meeting with the Indians, when, as they neared the mouth of the Arkansas, they saw a cluster of wigwams on the west bank. Their inmates were all astir, yelling the war whoop, snatching their weapons and running to the shore to meet the strangers, who on their part called for succor to the Virgin.

In truth, they had need of her aid, for several large wooden canoes filled with savages were putting out from the shore above and below them to cut off their retreat, while a swarm of headlong young warriors waded into the water to attack them. The current proved too strong, and failing to reach the canoes of the Frenchmen, one of them threw his war club, which flew over the heads of the startled travelers.

Meanwhile, Marquette had not ceased to hold up his calumet, to which the excited crowd gave no heed but strung their bows and notched their arrows for immediate action. At length the elders of the village arrived, saw the peace pipe, restrained the ardor of the youth and urged the Frenchmen to come ashore. Marquette and his companions complied, trembling, and found a better reception than they had reason to expect. One of the Indians spoke a little Illinois and served as interpreter. A friendly conference was followed by a feast of sagamité and fish, and the travelers, not without sore misgivings, spent the night in the lodges of their entertainers.

Early in the morning they embarked again and proceeded to a village of the Arkansas tribe, about eight leagues below. Notice of their coming was sent before them by their late hosts and as they drew near they were met by a canoe, in the prow of which stood a naked personage, holding a calumet, singing and making gestures of friendship.

On reaching the village, which was on the east side opposite the mouth of the river Arkansas, they were conducted to a sort of scaffold before the lodge of the war chief. The space beneath had been prepared for their reception, the ground being neatly covered with rush mats. On these they were seated. The warriors sat around them in a semicircle, then the elders of the tribe, and then the promiscuous crowd of villagers, standing and staring over the heads of the more dignified members of the assembly. All the men were naked, but to compensate for the lack of clothing they wore strings of beads in their noses and ears. The women were clothed in shabby skins and wore their hair clumped in a mass behind each ear.

By good luck there was a young Indian in the village who had an excellent knowledge of Illinois, and through him Marquette endeavored to explain the mysteries of Christianity and to gain information concerning the river below. To this end he gave his auditors the presents indispensable on such occasions, but received very little in return. They told him that the Mississippi was infested by hostile Indians, armed with guns procured from white men, and that they, the Arkansas, stood in such fear of them that they dared not hunt the buffalo but were forced to live on Indian corn, of which they raised three crops a year.

All day there was feasting without respite, after the merciless practice of Indian hospitality, but at night some of their entertainers proposed to kill and plunder them, a scheme which was defeated by the vigilance of the chief, who visited their quarters and danced the calumet dance to reassure his guests.

The travelers now held counsel as to what course they should take. They had gone far enough, as they thought, to establish one important point—that the Mississippi discharged its waters not into the Atlantic or sea of Virginia, nor into the Gulf of California or Vermilion Sea, but into the Gulf of Mexico. They thought themselves nearer to its mouth than they actually were, the distance being still about seven hundred miles, and they feared that if they went farther they might be killed by Indians or captured by Spaniards, whereby the results of their discovery would be lost. Therefore they resolved to return to Canada and report what they had seen.

They left the Arkansas village and began their homeward voyage on the seventeenth of July. It was no easy task to urge their way upward, in the heat of midsummer, against the current of the dark and gloomy stream, toiling all day under the parching sun and sleeping at night in the exhalations of the unwholesome shore, or in the narrow confines of their birchen vessels, anchored on the river.

Marquette was attacked with dysentery. Languid and well-nigh spent, he invoked his celestial mistress as day after day and week after week they won their slow way northward. At length they reached the Illinois and, entering its mouth, followed its course, charmed as they went with its placid waters, its shady forests and its rich plains, grazed by the bison and the deer. They stopped at a spot soon to be made famous in the annals of western discovery. This was a village of the Illinois, then called "Kaskaskia," a name afterwards transferred to another locality. A chief, with a band of young warriors, offered to guide them to the Lake of the Illinois, that is to say, Lake Michigan.

There they repaired and, coasting its shores, reached Green Bay at the end of September, after an absence of about four months during which they had paddled their canoes somewhat more than two thousand five hundred miles.

CHAPTER 3

La Salle and Frontenac

L A SALLE AT LA CHINE DREAMED OF A WESTERN
passage to China and nursed vague schemes of western discovery. When his earlier journeyings revealed to him the valley of the
Ohio and the fertile plains of Illinois, his imagination took wing over
the boundless prairies and forests drained by the great river of the
West. His ambition had found its field. He would leave barren
and frozen Canada behind, and lead France and civilization into the
valley of the Mississippi. Neither the English nor the Jesuits should
conquer that rich domain: the one must rest content with the country
east of the Alleghenies, and the other with the forests, savages and
beaver skins of the northern lakes. It was for him to call into light the
latent riches of the great West.

But the way to his land of promise was rough and long. It lay
through Canada, filled with hostile traders and hostile priests, and
barred by ice for half the year. The difficulty was soon solved. La
Salle became convinced that the Mississippi flowed into the Gulf of
Mexico. By a fortified post at its mouth, he could guard it against
both English and Spaniards and secure for the trade of the interior an
access and an outlet under his own control, and open at every season.
Of this trade, the hides of the buffalo would at first form the staple,
and along with furs would reward the enterprise till other resources
should be developed.

Such were the vast projects that unfolded themselves in the mind
of La Salle. Canada must needs be, at the outset, his base of action,

and without the support of its authorities he could do nothing. This support he found. From the moment Count Frontenac assumed the government of the colony, he seems to have looked with favor on the young discoverer. There were points of likeness between the two men. Both were ardent, bold and enterprising. The irascible and fiery pride of the noble found its match in the reserved and seemingly cold pride of the ambitious burgher. Each could comprehend the other, and they had, moreover, strong prejudices and dislikes in common. An understanding, not to say an alliance, soon grew up between them.

Frontenac had come to Canada a ruined man. He was ostentatious, lavish, and in no way disposed to let slip an opportunity of mending his fortune. He presently thought that he had found a plan by which he could serve both the colony and himself. His predecessor, Courcelle, had urged upon the King the expediency of building a fort on Lake Ontario in order to hold the Iroquois in check and intercept the trade which the tribes of the Upper Lakes had begun to carry on with the Dutch and English of New York. Thus a stream of wealth would be turned into Canada which would otherwise enrich her enemies.

Here, to all appearance, was a great public good, and from the military point of view it was so in fact, but it was clear that the trade thus secured might be made to profit, not the colony at large but those alone who had control of the fort, which would then become the instrument of a monopoly. This the governor understood and without doubt he meant that the projected establishment should pay him tribute. How far he and La Salle were acting in concurrence at this time it is not easy to say, but Frontenac often took counsel of the explorer, who on his part saw in the design a possible first step towards the accomplishment of his own far-reaching schemes.

Such of the Canadian merchants as were not in the governor's confidence looked on his plan with extreme distrust. Frontenac, therefore, thought it expedient "to make use," as he expresses it, "of address." He gave out merely that he intended to make a tour through the upper parts of the colony with an armed force in order to inspire the Indians with respect and secure a solid peace.

He had neither troops, money, munitions, nor means of transportation, yet there was no time to lose, for should he delay the execution of his plan, it might be countermanded by the King. His only resource, therefore, was in a prompt and hardy exertion of the royal authority, and he issued an order requiring the inhabitants of Quebec, Montreal, Three Rivers and other settlements to furnish him, at their own cost, as soon as the spring sowing should be over, with a certain number of armed men, besides the requisite canoes. At the same time he invited the officers settled in the country to join the expedition—an invitation which, anxious as they were to gain his good graces, few of them cared to decline.

Regardless of murmurs and discontent, he pushed his preparation vigorously, and on the third of June left Quebec with his guard, his staff, a part of the garrison of the Castle of St. Louis and a number of volunteers. He had already sent to La Salle, who was then at Montreal, directing him to repair to Onondaga, the political center of the Iroquois, and invite their sachems to meet the governor in council at the Bay of Quinté on the north of Lake Ontario. La Salle had set out on his mission, but first sent Frontenac a map which convinced him that the best site for his proposed fort was the mouth of the Cataraqui, where Kingston now stands. Another messenger was accordingly dispatched to change the rendezvous to this point.

Meanwhile the governor proceeded at his leisure towards Montreal, stopping by the way to visit the officers settled along the bank, who, eager to pay their homage to the newly risen sun, received him with a hospitality which under the roof of a log hut was sometimes graced by the polished courtesies of the salon and the boudoir.

Reaching Montreal, which he had never seen before, he gazed, we may suppose, with some interest at the long row of humble dwellings which lined the bank, the massive buildings of the seminary, and the spire of the church predominant over all.

Having sent men, canoes and baggage by land to La Salle's old settlement of La Chine, Frontenac himself followed on the twenty-eighth of June. Including Indians from the missions, he now had with him about four hundred men and a hundred and twenty canoes, besides two large flatboats which he caused to be painted in red and blue with strange devices, intended to dazzle the Iroquois by a display of unwonted splendor.

Now their hard task began. Shouldering canoes through the forest, dragging the flatboats along the shore, working like beavers—some-

times in water to the knees, sometimes to the armpits, their feet cut
by the sharp stones, and they themselves well nigh swept down by
the furious current—they fought their way upward against the chain
of mighty rapids that break the navigation of the St. Lawrence. The
Indians were of the greatest service. Frontenac, like La Salle, showed
from the first a special faculty of managing them, for his keen, in-
cisive spirit was exactly to their liking and they worked for him as
they would have worked for no man else.

As they approached the Long Saut, rain fell in torrents. The
governor, without his cloak and drenched to the skin, directed in
person the amphibious toil of his followers. Once, it is said, he lay
awake all night in his anxiety lest the biscuit should be wet, which
would have ruined the expedition. No such mischance took place, and
at length the last rapid was passed and smooth water awaited them to
their journey's end. Soon they reached the Thousand Islands and
their light flotilla glided in long file among those watery labyrinths,
by rocky islets where some lonely pine towered like a mast against the
sky; by sun-scorched crags, where the brown lichens crisped in the
parching glare; by deep dells, shady and cool, rich in rank ferns and
spongy dark green mosses; by still coves, where the water lilies lay
like snowflakes on their broad, flat leaves—till at length they neared
their goal and the glistening bosom of Lake Ontario opened on
their sight.

Frontenac, to impose respect on the Iroquois, now set his canoes
in order of battle. Four divisions formed the first line, then came the
two flatboats. He himself, with his guards, his staff and the gentlemen
volunteers, followed with the canoes of Three Rivers on his right and
those of the Indians on his left, while two remaining divisions formed
a rear line.

Thus, with measured paddles, they advanced over the still lake till
they saw a canoe approaching to meet them. It bore several Iroquois
chiefs, who told them that the dignitaries of their nation awaited them
at Cataraqui and offered to guide them to the spot. They entered the
wide mouth of the river and passed along the shore, now covered
by the city of Kingston, till they reached a point at the western end
of Cataraqui bridge. Here they stranded their canoes and disembarked. Baggage was landed, fires lighted, tents pitched and guards

set. Close at hand, under the lee of the forest, were the camping sheds of the Iroquois, who had come to the rendezvous in considerable numbers.

At daybreak of the next morning, the thirteenth of July, the drums beat and the whole party was drawn up under arms. A double line of men extended from the front of Frontenac's tent to the Indian camp, and through the lane thus formed the savage deputies, sixty in number, advanced to the place of council. They could not hide their admiration at the martial array of the French, many of whom were old soldiers of the regiment of Carignan, and when they reached the tent they ejaculated their astonishment at the uniforms of the governor's guard who surrounded it.

Here the ground had been carpeted with the sails of the flatboats, on which the deputies squatted themselves in a ring and smoked their pipes for a time with their usual air of deliberate gravity, while Frontenac, who sat surrounded by his officers, had full leisure to contemplate the formidable adversaries whose mettle was hereafter to put his own to so severe a test.

A chief named Garakontié, a noted friend of the French, at length opened the council in behalf of all the five Iroquois nations, with expressions of great respect and deference towards "Onontio," that is to say, the governor of Canada. Whereupon Frontenac, whose native arrogance where Indians were concerned always took a form which imposed respect without exciting anger, replied:

"Children! Mohawks, Oneidas, Onondagas, Cayugas and Senecas. I am glad to see you here, where I have had a fire lighted for you to smoke by, and for me to talk to you. You have done well, my children, to obey the command of your Father. Take courage: you will hear his word, which is full of peace and tenderness. For do not think that I have come for war. My mind is full of peace, and she walks by my side. Courage, then, children, and take rest."

With that he gave them six fathoms of tobacco, reiterated his assurances of friendship, promised that he would be a kind father so long as they should be obedient children, regretted that he was forced to speak through an interpreter and ended with a gift of guns to the men and prunes and raisins to their wives and children. Here closed this preliminary meeting, the great council being postponed to another day.

During the meeting Raudin, Frontenac's engineer, was tracing out the lines of a fort, after a predetermined plan. The whole party, under the direction of their officers, now set themselves to construct it. Some cut down trees, some dug the trenches, some hewed the palisades, and with such order and alacrity was the work urged on that the Indians were lost in astonishment. Meanwhile, Frontenac spared no pains to make friends of the chiefs, some of whom he had constantly at his table. He fondled the Iroquois children and gave them bread and sweetmeats, and in the evening feasted the squaws to make them dance. The Indians were delighted with these attentions and conceived a high opinion of the new Onontio.

On the seventeenth, when the construction of the fort was well advanced, Frontenac called the chiefs to a grand council, which was held with all possible state and ceremony. His dealing with the Indians on this and other occasions was truly admirable. Unacquainted as he was with them, he seems to have had an instinctive perception of the treatment they required. His predecessors had never ventured to address the Iroquois as "Children," but had always styled them "Brothers," and yet the assumption of paternal authority on the part of Frontenac was not only taken in good part but was received with apparent gratitude. The martial nature of the man, his clear, decisive speech and his frank and downright manner, backed as they were by a display of force which in their eyes was formidable, struck them with admiration and gave tenfold effect to his words of kindness. They thanked him for that which from another they would not have endured.

Frontenac began by again expressing his satisfaction that they had obeyed the commands of their Father and come to Cataraqui to hear what he had to say. Then he exhorted them to embrace Christianity, and on this theme he dwelt at length in words excellently adapted to produce the desired effect—words which it would be most superfluous to tax as insincere, though doubtless they lost nothing in emphasis because in this instance conscience and policy aimed alike. Then, changing his tone, he pointed to his officers, his guard, the long files of the militia and the two flatboats mounted with cannon which lay in the river near by.

"If," he said, "your Father can come so far, with so great a force, through such dangerous rapids, merely to make you a visit of pleasure and friendship, what would he do if you should awaken his anger and make it necessary for him to punish his disobedient children? He is the arbiter of peace and war. Beware how you offend him!"

And he warned them not to molest the Indian allies of the French, telling them sharply that he would chastise them for the least infraction of the peace.

From threats he passed to blandishments and urged them to confide in his paternal kindness, saying that in proof of his affection he was building a storehouse at Cataraqui, where they could be supplied with all the goods they needed without the necessity of a long and dangerous journey. He warned them against listening to bad men, who might seek to delude them by misrepresentations and falsehoods, and he urged them to give heed to none but "men of character, like the Sieur de la Salle." He expressed a hope that they would suffer their children to learn French from the missionaries in order that they and his nephews—meaning the French colonists—might become one people, and he concluded by requesting them to give him a number of their children to be educated in the French manner at Quebec.

This speech, every clause of which was reinforced by abundant presents, was extremely well received, though one speaker reminded him that he had forgotten one important point, inasmuch as he had not told them at what prices they could obtain goods at Cataraqui. Frontenac evaded a precise answer, but promised them that the goods should be as cheap as possible in view of the great difficulty of transportation. As to the request concerning their children, they said that they could not accede to it till they had talked the matter over in their villages, but it is a striking proof of the influence which Frontenac had gained over them that, in the following year, they actually sent several of their children to Quebec to be educated—the girls among the Ursulines and the boys in the household of the governor.

Three days after the council the Iroquois set out on their return, and as the palisades of the fort were now finished and the barracks nearly so, Frontenac began to send his party homeward by detachments. He himself was detained for a time by the arrival of another band of Iroquois from the villages on the north side of Lake Ontario.

He repeated to them the speech he had made to the others, and this final meeting over, he embarked with his guard, leaving a sufficient number to hold the fort, which was to be provisioned for a year by means of a convoy then on its way up the river. Passing the rapids safely, he reached Montreal on the first of August.

His enterprise had been a complete success. He had gained every point and, in spite of the dangerous navigation, had not lost a single canoe. Thanks to the enforced and gratuitous assistance of the inhabitants, the whole had cost the King only about ten thousand francs, which Frontenac had advanced on his credit. Though in a commercial point of view the new establishment was of very questionable benefit to the colony at large, the governor had, nevertheless, conferred an inestimable blessing on all Canada by the assurance he had gained of a long respite from the fearful scourge of Iroquois hostility.

"Assuredly," he writes, "I may boast of having impressed them at once with respect, fear and good will." He adds that the fort at Cataraqui, with the aid of a vessel now building, will command Lake Ontario, keep the peace with the Iroquois and cut off the trade with the English, and he proceeds to say that by another fort at the mouth of the Niagara and another vessel on Lake Erie we, the French, can command all the Upper Lakes. This plan was an essential link in the schemes of La Salle.

Meanwhile, as accomplices, Frontenac and La Salle faced not only the bitter opposition of the traders but the equally bitter enmity of the Church. The Jesuits were no longer supreme in Canada, or in other words, Canada was no longer simply a mission. It had become a colony. Temporal interests and the civil power were constantly gaining ground, and the disciples of Loyola felt that relatively, if not absolutely, they were losing it.

They struggled vigorously to maintain the ascendancy of their Order, or, as they would have expressed it, the ascendancy of religion, but in the older and more settled parts of the colony it was clear that the day of their undivided rule was past. Therefore they looked with redoubled solicitude to their missions in the West. They had been among its first explorers and they hoped that here the Catholic Faith, as represented by Jesuits, might reign with undisputed sway. In Paraguay it was their constant aim to exclude white men from their missions, and in North America, which they dreamed of making another Paraguay, it was the same. They dreaded fur traders, partly because they interfered with their teachings and perverted their converts and partly for other reasons.

But La Salle was a fur trader, and far worse than a fur trader. He aimed at occupation, fortification and settlement. The scope and vigor of his enterprises and the powerful influence that aided them made him a stumbling block in their path. He was their most dangerous rival for the control of the West, and from first to last they set themselves against him.

~~~~~~

CHAPTER 4

The Grand Enterprise Begins

F," WRITES A FRIEND OF LA SALLE, "HE HAD PRE-
ferred gain to glory, he had only to stay at his fort, where he was
making more than twenty-five thousand livres a year." He loved
solitude and he loved power, and at Fort Frontenac, the count's newly
built outpost on Lake Ontario, which the King had given him to command, he had both. The nearest settlement was a week's journey
distant and he was master of all around him.

Within two years he had demolished the original wooden fort, re-
placing it by another much larger, enclosed on the land side by
ramparts and bastions of stone and on the water side by palisades. It
contained a range of barracks of squared timber, a guardhouse, a lodging for officers, a forge, a well, a mill and a bakery. Nine small cannon
were mounted on the walls. Two officers and a surgeon, with ten or
twelve soldiers, made up the garrison, and three or four times that
number of masons, laborers and canoemen were at one time maintained at the place.

Along the shore south of the fort was a small village of French
families, to whom La Salle had granted farms, and farther on a
village of Iroquois, whom he had persuaded to settle there. Near
these villages were the house and chapel of two Récollet friars, Luc
Buisset and Louis Hennepin. More than a hundred French acres of
land had been cleared of wood and planted in part with crops, while
cattle, fowl and swine had been brought up from Montreal. Four
vessels of from twenty-five to forty tons had been built for the lake

and the river, but canoes served best for ordinary uses and La Salle's followers became so skilled in managing them that they were reputed the best canoemen in America. Feudal lord of the forests around him, commander of a garrison raised and paid by himself, founder of the mission and patron of the church, he reigned the autocrat of his lonely little empire.

It was not solely or chiefly for commercial gain that La Salle had established Fort Frontenac. He regarded it as a first step towards greater things, and now, at length, his plans were ripe and his time was come.

In the autumn of 1677 he left the fort in charge of his lieutenant, descended the St. Lawrence to Quebec and sailed for France. He had the patronage of Frontenac and the help of strong friends in Paris. It is said that his enemies denounced him, in advance, as a madman, but a memorial of his which his friends laid before the minister Colbert found a favorable hearing. La Salle seems to have had an interview with the minister in which the proposals of his memorial were somewhat modified, and he soon received in reply a patent from the King.

This patent granted both more and less than the memorial had asked. It authorized La Salle to build and own, not two forts only, but as many as he might see fit, provided that he did so within five years. It gave him, besides, the monopoly of buffalo hides, for which at first he had not petitioned. Nothing was said of colonies. To discover the country, secure it by forts and find, if possible, a way to Mexico was the only object set forth, for Louis XIV always discountenanced settlement in the West, partly as tending to deplete Canada and partly as removing his subjects too far from his paternal control.

La Salle, however, still held to his plan of a commercial and industrial colony, and in connection with it to another purpose, of which his memorial had made no mention. This was the building of a vessel on some branch of the Mississippi, in order to sail down that river to its mouth and open a route to commerce through the Gulf of Mexico. It is evident that this design was already formed, for he had no sooner received his patent than he engaged ship carpenters and procured iron, cordage and anchors, not for one vessel but for two.

The learned Abbé Renaudot helped him with tongue and pen at Paris and seems to have been instrumental in introducing to him a man who afterwards proved invaluable. This was Henri de Tonty, an Italian officer, a protégé of the Prince de Conti, who sent him to La Salle as a person suited to his purposes. Tonty had but one hand, the other having been blown off by a grenade in the Sicilian wars. His father, who had been governor of Gaeta but who had come to France in consequence of political disturbances in Naples, had earned no small reputation as a financier and had invented the form of life insurance called the Tontine.

Besides Tonty, La Salle found in France another ally, La Motte de Lussière, to whom he offered a share in the enterprise, and who joined him at Rochelle, the place of embarkation. Here vexatious delays occurred. Bellinzani, director of trade, who had formerly taken lessons in rascality in the service of Cardinal Mazarin, abused his official position to throw obstacles in the way of La Salle, in order to extort money from him, and he extorted, in fact, a considerable sum which his victim afterwards reclaimed.

It was not till the fourteenth of July, 1678, that La Salle, with Tonty, La Motte and thirty men, set sail for Canada. Two months more elapsed before he reached Quebec. Here, to increase his resources and strengthen his position, he seems to have made a league with several Canadian merchants, some of whom had been his enemies before and were to be so again. Here, too, he found Father Louis Hennepin, who had come down from Fort Frontenac to meet him.

Hennepin was all eagerness to join in the adventure, and to his great satisfaction, La Salle gave him a letter from his Provincial, Father Le Fèvre, containing the coveted permission. Whereupon, to prepare himself, he went into retreat at the Récollet convent of Quebec, where he remained for a time in such prayer and meditation as his nature, the reverse of spiritual, would permit.

Frontenac, always partial to his Order, then invited him to dine at the château, and having visited the bishop and asked his blessing, he went down to the Lower Town and embarked. His vessel was a small birch canoe, paddled by two men. With sandaled feet, a coarse gray capote and peaked hood, the cord of St. Francis about his waist and a rosary and crucifix hanging at his side, the father set forth on his memorable journey. He carried with him the furniture of a portable altar, which in time of need he could strap on his back like a knapsack.

He slowly made his way up the St. Lawrence, stopping here and there, where a clearing and a few log houses marked the feeble beginning of a parish and a seigniory. The settlers, though good Catholics, were too few and too poor to support a priest and hailed the arrival of the friar with delight. He said mass, exhorted a little, as was his custom, and on one occasion baptized a child. At length he reached Montreal, where the enemies of the enterprise enticed away his two canoemen. He succeeded in finding two others with whom he continued his voyage, passed the rapids of the upper St. Lawrence and reached Fort Frontenac at eleven o'clock at night of the second of November, where his brethren of the mission, Ribourde and Buisset, received him with open arms. La Motte, with most of the men, appeared on the eighth, but La Salle and Tonty did not arrive till more than a month later.

This bold, hardy and adventurous friar, the historian of the expedition and a conspicuous actor in it, has unwittingly painted his own portrait with tolerable distinctness. "I always," he says, "felt a strong inclination to fly from the world and live according to the rules of a pure and severe virtue; and it was with this view that I entered the Order of St. Francis." He then speaks of his zeal for the saving of souls, but admits that a passion for travel and a burning desire to visit strange lands had no small part in his inclination for the missions.

Being in a convent in Artois, his Superior sent him to Calais at the season of the herring fishery to beg alms, after the practice of the Franciscans. Here and at Dunkirk he made friends of the sailors and was never tired of their stories. So insatiable, indeed, was his appetite for them that "often," he says, "I hid myself behind tavern doors while the sailors were telling of their voyages. The tobacco smoke made me very sick at the stomach, but notwithstanding, I listened attentively to all they said about their adventures at sea and their travels in distant countries. I could have passed whole days and nights in this way without eating."

He got leave from his superiors to go to Canada, the most adventurous of all the missions, and accordingly sailed in 1675 in the ship which carried La Salle, who had just obtained the grant of Fort Frontenac. On arriving in Canada, he was sent up to Fort Frontenac as a missionary. That wild and remote post was greatly to his liking. He planted a gigantic cross, superintended the building of a chapel for himself and his colleague Buisset and instructed the Iroquois colonists of the place. He visited, too, the neighboring Indian settlements, paddling his canoe in summer when the lake was open and journeying in winter on snowshoes with a blanket slung at his back.

Thus he inured himself to the hardships of the woods and prepared for the execution of the grand plan of discovery which he calls his own—"an enterprise," to borrow his own words, "capable of terrifying anybody but me."

When the later editions of his book describing his travels appeared, doubts had already been expressed of his veracity. "I here protest to you before God," he writes, addressing the reader, "that my narrative is faithful and sincere, and that you may believe everything related in it." And yet this reverend father was the most impudent of liars and the narrative of which he speaks is a rare monument of brazen mendacity. Hennepin, however, had seen and dared much, for among his many failings fear had no part, and where his vanity or his spite was not involved, he often told the truth. His books have their value, with all their enormous fabrications.

La Motte and Hennepin, with sixteen men, went on board the little vessel of ten tons which lay at Fort Frontenac. The friar's two brethren, Buisset and Ribourde, threw their arms about his neck as they bade him farewell, while his Indian proselytes, learning whither he was bound, stood with their hands pressed upon their mouths in amazement at the perils which awaited their ghostly instructor. La Salle, with the rest of the party, was to follow as soon as he could finish his preparations.

It was a boisterous and gusty day, the eighteenth of November. The sails were spread; the shore receded—the stone walls of the fort, the huge cross that the friar had reared, the wigwams, the settlers' cabins, the group of staring Indians on the strand. The lake was rough, and the men, crowded in so small a craft, grew nervous and uneasy. They hugged the northern shore to escape the fury of the wind, which blew savagely from the northeast, while the long gray sweep of naked forests on their right betokened that winter was fast closing in. On the twenty-sixth they reached the neighborhood of the Indian town of Taiaiagon, not far from Toronto, and ran their vessel for safety into the mouth of a river—probably the Humber—where the ice closed about her and they were forced to cut her out with axes.

On the fifth of December they attempted to cross to the mouth of the Niagara, but darkness overtook them and they spent a comfortless night, tossing on the troubled lake, five or six miles from shore. In the morning they entered the mouth of the Niagara and landed on the point at its eastern side, where later stood the historic ramparts of Fort Niagara. Here they found a small village of Senecas, attracted there by the fisheries, who gazed with curious eyes at the vessel and listened in wonder as the voyagers sang *Te Deum* in gratitude for their safe arrival.

Hennepin, with several others, now ascended the river in a canoe to the foot of the mountain ridge of Lewiston, which, stretching on the right hand and on the left, forms the acclivity of a vast plateau, rent with the mighty chasm along which from this point to the cataract, seven miles above, rush with the fury of an Alpine torrent the gathered waters of four inland oceans.

To urge the canoe farther was impossible. He landed with his companions on the west bank, near the foot of that part of the ridge now called Queenstown Heights, climbed the steep ascent and pushed through the wintry forest on a tour of exploration. On his left sank the cliffs, the furious river raging below, till at length, in primeval solitudes unprofaned as yet by the pettiness of man, the imperial cataract burst upon his sight. [In the 1683 edition of his book, Hennepin wrote that the falls was five hundred feet high, but he raised it to six hundred in the edition of 1697.]

The explorers passed three miles beyond it and encamped for the night on the banks of Chippewa Creek, scraping away the snow, which was a foot deep, in order to kindle a fire. In the morning they retraced their steps, startling a number of deer and wild turkeys on their way, and rejoined their companions at the mouth of the river.

La Motte now began the building of a fortified house, some two leagues above the mouth of the Niagara. Hot water was used to soften the frozen ground, but frost was not the only obstacle. The Senecas of the neighboring village betrayed a sullen jealousy at a design which, indeed, boded them no good. Niagara was the key to the four great lakes above, and whoever held possession of it could, in no small measure, control the fur trade of the interior. Occupied by the French, it would in time of peace intercept the trade which the Iroquois carried on between the western Indians and the Dutch and English at Albany, and in time of war threaten them with serious danger.

La Motte saw the necessity of conciliating these formidable neighbors and, if possible, cajoling them to give their consent to the plan. La Salle, indeed, had instructed him to that effect. He resolved on a journey to the great village of the Senecas, and called on Hennepin, who was busied in building a bark chapel for himself, to accompany him. They accordingly set out with several men well armed and equipped, and bearing at their backs presents of very considerable value.

The village was beyond the Genesee, southeast of the site of Rochester. After a march of five days they reached it on the last day of December. They were conducted to the lodge of the great chief, where they were beset by a staring crowd of women and children. Two Jesuits, Raffeix and Julien Garnier, were in the village, and their presence boded no good for the embassy. La Motte, who seems to have had little love for priests of any kind, was greatly annoyed at seeing them, and when the chiefs assembled to hear what he had to say, he insisted that the two fathers should leave the council house. At this, Hennepin, out of respect for his cloth, thought it befitting that he should retire also.

The chiefs, forty-two in number, squatted on the ground, arrayed in ceremonial robes of beaver, wolf or black-squirrel skin. "The senators of Venice," writes Hennepin, "do not look more grave or speak more deliberately than the counsellors of the Iroquois." La Motte's interpreter harangued the attentive conclave, placed gift after gift at their feet—coats, scarlet cloth, hatchets, knives and beads—and used all his eloquence to persuade them that the building of a fort on the banks of the Niagara and a vessel on Lake Erie were measures vital to their interest. They gladly took the gifts, but answered the interpreter's speech with evasive generalities, and having been enter-

211

tained with the burning of an Indian prisoner, the discomfited embassy returned, half famished, to Niagara.

Meanwhile, La Salle and Tonty were on their way from Fort Frontenac, with men and supplies, to join La Motte and his advance party. They were in a small vessel, with a pilot either unskillful or treacherous. On Christmas Eve he was near wrecking them off the Bay of Quinté. On the next day they crossed to the mouth of the Genesee, and La Salle, after some delay, proceeded to the neighboring town of the Senecas, where he appears to have arrived just after the departure of La Motte and Hennepin.

He, too, called them to a council and tried to soothe the extreme jealousy with which they regarded his proceedings. "I told them my plan," he says, "and gave the best pretexts I could, and I succeeded in my attempt." More fortunate than La Motte, he persuaded them to consent to his carrying arms and ammunition by the Niagara portage, building a vessel above the cataract and establishing a fortified warehouse at the mouth of the river.

This success was followed by a calamity. La Salle had gone up the Niagara to find a suitable place for a shipyard when he learned that the pilot in charge of the vessel he had left had disobeyed his orders and ended by wrecking it on the coast. Little was saved except the anchors and cables destined for the new vessel to be built above the cataract. This loss threw him into extreme perplexity, and, as Hennepin says, "would have made anybody but him give up the enterprise."

The whole party was now gathered at the palisaded house which La Motte had built a little below the mountain ridge of Lewiston. They were a motley crew of French, Flemings and Italians, all mutually jealous. La Salle's enemies had tampered with some of the men and none of them seemed to have had much heart for the enterprise. The fidelity even of La Motte was doubtful. "He served me very ill," says La Salle, "and Messieurs de Tonty and de la Forest knew that he did his best to debauch all my men." His health soon failed under the hardships of these winter journeyings, and he returned to Fort Frontenac, half blinded by an inflammation of the eyes.

La Salle, seldom happy in the choice of subordinates, had perhaps in all his company but one man whom he could fully trust, and this was Tonty. He and Hennepin were on indifferent terms. Men thrown together in a rugged enterprise like this quickly learn to know each other, and the vain and assuming friar was not likely to commend himself to La Salle's brave and loyal lieutenant. Hennepin says that it was La Salle's policy to govern through the dissensions of his followers, and from whatever cause, it is certain that those beneath him were rarely in perfect harmony.

A more important work than that of the warehouse at the mouth of the river was now to be begun. This was the building of a vessel above the cataract. The small craft which had brought La Motte and Hennepin with their advance party had been hauled to the foot of the rapids at Lewiston and drawn ashore with a capstan to save her from the drifting ice. Her lading was taken out and must now be carried beyond the cataract to the calm water above. The distance to the destined point was at least twelve miles and the steep heights above Lewiston must first be climbed.

This heavy task was accomplished on the twenty-second of January. The level of the plateau was reached, and the file of burdened men, · some thirty in number, toiled slowly on its way over the snowy plains and through the gloomy forests of spruce and naked oak trees, while Hennepin plodded through the drifts with his portable altar lashed fast to his back. They came at last to the mouth of a stream which entered the Niagara two leagues above the cataract and which was undoubtedly that now called Cayuga Creek.

Trees were felled, the place cleared, and the master carpenter set his shipbuilders at work. Meanwhile two Mohegan hunters attached to the party made bark wigwams to lodge the men. Hennepin had his chapel, apparently of the same material, where he placed his altar, and on Sundays and saints' days said mass, preached and exhorted, while some of the men who knew the Gregorian chant lent their aid at the service. When the carpenters were ready to lay the keel of the vessel, La Salle asked the friar to drive the first bolt, "but the modesty of my religious profession," he says, "compelled me to decline this honor."

Fortunately it was the hunting season of the Iroquois and most of the Seneca warriors were in the forests south of Lake Erie, yet enough remained to cause serious uneasiness. They loitered sullenly about the

213

place, expressing their displeasure at the proceedings of the French. One of them, pretending to be drunk, attacked the blacksmith and tried to kill him, but the Frenchman, brandishing a red-hot bar of iron, held him at bay till Hennepin ran to the rescue, when, as he declares, the severity of his rebuke caused the savage to desist. The work of the shipbuilders advanced rapidly, and when the Indian visitors beheld the vast ribs of the wooden monster their jealousy was redoubled. A squaw told the French that they meant to burn the vessel on the stocks. All now stood anxiously on the watch. Cold, hunger, and discontent found imperfect antidotes in Tonty's energy and Hennepin's sermons.

While La Salle was absent at Fort Frontenac during the winter, Tonty finished the vessel, which was of about forty-five tons' burden. As spring opened, she was ready for launching. The friar pronounced his blessing on her, the assembled company sang *Te Deum,* cannon were fired, and French and Indians, warmed alike by a generous gift of brandy, shouted and yelped in chorus as she glided into the Niagara.

Her builders towed her out and anchored her in the stream, safe at last from incendiary hands, and then, swinging their hammocks under her deck, slept in peace beyond reach of the tomahawk. The Indians gazed on her with amazement. Five small cannon looked out from her portholes and on her prow was carved a portentous monster, the griffin, whose name she bore in honor of the armorial bearings of Frontenac. La Salle had often been heard to say that he would make the griffin fly above the crows, or, in other words, make Frontenac triumph over the Jesuits.

They now took her up the river and made her fast below the swift current at Black Rock. Here they finished her equipment and waited for La Salle's return, but the absent commander did not appear. The spring and more than half of the summer had passed before they saw him again. At length, early in August, he arrived at the mouth of the Niagara, bringing three more friars. Though no friend of the Jesuits, he was zealous for the Faith and was rarely without a missionary in his journeyings. Like Hennepin, the three friars were all Flemings. One of them, Melithon Watteau, was to remain at Niagara. The others, Zenobe Membré and Gabriel Ribourde, were to preach the Faith among the tribes of the West. Ribourde was a hale and cheerful old man of sixty-four. He went four times up and down the Lewiston heights while the men were climbing the steep pathway with their loads. It required four of them, well stimulated with brandy, to carry up the principal anchor destined for the *Griffin.*

La Salle brought a tale of disaster. His enemies, bent on ruining the enterprise, had given out that he was embarked on a harebrained venture from which he would never return. His creditors, excited by rumors set afloat to that end, had seized on all his property in the settled parts of Canada, though seigniory of Fort Frontenac alone would have more than sufficed to pay all his debts.

There was no remedy. To defer the enterprise would have been to give his adversaries the triumph that they sought, and he hardened himself against the blow with his usual stoicism.

On the seventh of August, La Salle and his followers were ready to embark. They sang *Te Deum* and fired their cannon. A fresh breeze sprang up, and with swelling canvas the *Griffin* plowed the virgin waves of Lake Erie, where sail was never seen before. For three days they held their course over these unknown waters, and on the fourth turned northward into the Strait of Detroit.

Here, on the right hand and on the left, lay verdant prairies dotted with groves and bordered with lofty forests. They saw walnut, chestnut and wild plum trees, and oaks festooned with grapevines, herds of deer and flocks of swans and wild turkeys. The bulwarks of the *Griffin* were plentifully hung with game which the men killed on shore, and among the rest with a number of bears, much commended by Hennepin for their want of ferocity and the excellence of their flesh. "Those," he says, "who will one day have the happiness to possess this fertile and pleasant strait will be very much obliged to those who have shown them the way." They crossed Lake St. Clair and still sailed northward against the current till now, sparkling in the sun, Lake Huron spread before them like a sea.

For a time they bore on prosperously. Then the wind died to a calm, then freshened to a gale, then rose to a furious tempest, and the vessel tossed wildly among the short, steep, perilous waves of the raging lake. Even La Salle called on his followers to commend themselves to Heaven. All fell to their prayers but the godless pilot, who was

215

loud in complaint against his commander for having brought him, after the honor he had won on the ocean, to drown at last ignominiously in fresh water. The rest clamored to the saints. St. Anthony of Padua was promised a chapel to be built in his honor if he would save them from their jeopardy, while in the same breath La Salle and the friars declared him patron of their great enterprise.

The saint heard their prayers. The obedient winds were tamed and the *Griffin* plunged on her way through foaming surges that still grew calmer as she advanced. Now the sun shone forth on woody islands, Boise Blanc and Mackinaw and the distant Manitoulins, on the forest wastes of Michigan and the vast blue bosom of the angry lake, and now her port was won and she found her rest behind the point of St. Ignace of Michilimackinac, floating in that tranquil cove where crystal waters cover but cannot hide the pebbly depths beneath. Before her rose the house and chapel of the Jesuits, closed with palisades. On the right was the Huron village, with its bark cabins and its fence of tall pickets; on the left, the square compact houses of the French traders, and not far off, the clustered wigwams of an Ottawa village.

The *Griffin* fired her cannon and the Indians yelped in wonder and amazement. The adventurers landed in state and marched under arms to the bark chapel of the Ottawa village, where they heard mass. La Salle knelt before the altar in a mantle of scarlet bordered with gold. Soldiers, sailors and artisans knelt around him—black Jesuits, gray Récollets, swarthy *voyageurs* and painted savages. It was a devout but motley concourse.

As they left the chapel the Ottawa chiefs came to bid them welcome and the Hurons saluted them with a volley of musketry. They saw the *Griffin* at her anchorage, surrounded by more than a hundred bark canoes, like a Triton among minnows. Yet it was with more wonder than good will that the Indians of the mission gazed on the "floating fort," as they called the vessel. A deep jealousy of La Salle's designs had been infused into them. His own followers, too, had been tampered with.

Anxious and troubled as to the condition of his affairs in Canada, La Salle had meant, after seeing his party safe at Michilimackinac, to leave Tonty to conduct it to the Illinois while he himself returned to the colony. But Tonty had tarried at Ste. Marie, and he had none to trust but himself. Therefore he resolved at all risks to remain with his men. Moreover, he thought that he had detected an intrigue of his enemies to hound on the Iroquois against the Illinois, in order to defeat his plan by involving him in the war.

Early in September he set sail again and, passing westward into Lake Michigan, cast anchor near one of the islands at the entrance of Green Bay. Here, for once, he found a friend in the person of a Potawatomi chief, who had been so wrought upon by the politic kindness of Frontenac that he declared himself ready to die for the children of Onontio. Here, too, he found several of his advance party, who had remained faithful and collected a large store of furs. It would have been better had they proved false, like the rest. La Salle, who asked counsel of no man, resolved in spite of his followers to send back the *Griffin* laden with these furs and others collected on the way to satisfy his creditors. It was a rash resolution, for it involved trusting her to the pilot, who had already proved either incompetent or treacherous.

She fired a parting shot and on the eighteenth of September set sail for Niagara with orders to return to the head of Lake Michigan as soon as she had discharged her cargo. La Salle, with the fourteen men who remained, put out from the island and resumed his voyage in four canoes deeply laden with a forge, tools, merchandise and arms.

The parting was not auspicious. The lake, glassy and calm in the afternoon, was convulsed at night with a sudden storm when the canoes were midway between the island and the main shore. It was with difficulty that they could keep together, the men shouting to each other through the darkness. Hennepin, who was in the smallest canoe with a heavy load and a carpenter for a companion who was awkward at the paddle, found himself in jeopardy which demanded all his nerve.

The voyagers thought themselves happy when they gained at last the shelter of a little sandy cove, where they dragged up their canoes and made their cheerless bivouac in the drenched and dripping forest. Here they spent five days, living on pumpkins and Indian corn, the gift of their Potawatomi friends, and on a Canada porcupine brought in by La Salle's Mohegan hunter.

217

The gale raged meanwhile with relentless fury. They trembled when they thought of the *Griffin*. When at length the tempest lulled, they re-embarked and steered southward along the shore of Wisconsin, but again the storm fell upon them and drove them for safety to a bare, rocky islet. Here they made a fire of driftwood, crouched around it, drew their blankets over their heads and in this miserable plight, pelted with sleet and rain, remained for two days.

At length they were afloat again, but their prosperity was brief. On the twenty-eighth a fierce squall drove them to a point of rocks covered with bushes, where they consumed the little that remained of their provisions. On the first of October they paddled about thirty miles without food, when they came to a village of Potawatomis, who ran down to the shore to help them to land. But La Salle, fearing that some of his men would steal the merchandise and desert to the Indians, insisted on going three leagues farther, to the great indignation of his followers. The lake, swept by an easterly gale, was rolling its waves against the beach like the ocean in a storm. In the attempt to land, La Salle's canoe was nearly swamped. He and his three canoemen leaped into the water and, in spite of the surf, which nearly drowned them, dragged their vessel ashore with all its load. He then went to the rescue of Hennepin, who with his awkward companion was in woeful need of succor.

Father Gabriel, with his sixty-four years, was no match for the surf and the violent undertow. Hennepin, finding himself safe, waded to his relief and carried him ashore on his sturdy shoulders, while the old friar, though drenched to the skin, laughed gaily under his cowl as his brother missionary staggered with him up the beach.

When all were safe ashore, La Salle, who distrusted the Indians they had passed, took post on a hill and ordered his followers to pre-pare their guns for action. Nevertheless, as they were starving, an effort must be risked to gain a supply of food and he sent three men back to the village to purchase it. Well armed but faint with toil and famine, they made their way through the stormy forest bearing a pipe of peace, but on arriving saw that the scared inhabitants had fled. They found, however, a stock of corn, of which they took a portion, leaving goods in exchange, and then set out on their return.

Meanwhile about twenty of the warriors, armed with bows and

218

arrows, approached the camp of the French to reconnoiter. La Salle went out to meet them with some of his men, opened a parley with them and kept them seated at the foot of the hill till his three messengers returned, when on seeing the peace pipe the warriors set up a cry of joy. In the morning they brought more corn to the camp, with a supply of fresh venison, not a little cheering to the exhausted Frenchmen, who in dread of treachery had stood under arms all night.

This was no journey of pleasure. The lake was ruffled with almost ceaseless storms; clouds big with rain above, a turmoil of gray and gloomy waves beneath. Every night the canoes must be shouldered through the breakers and dragged up the steep banks, which as they neared the site of Milwaukee became almost insurmountable. The men paddled all day, with no other food than a handful of Indian corn. They were spent with toil, sick with the haws and wild berries which they ravenously devoured and dejected at the prospect before them. Father Gabriel's good spirits began to fail. He fainted several times from famine and fatigue, but was revived by a certain "confection of Hyacinth," administered by Hennepin, who had a small box of this precious specific.

At length they descried at a distance on the stormy shore two or three eagles among a busy congregation of crows or turkey buzzards. They paddled in all haste to the spot. The feasters took flight and the starved travelers found the mangled body of a deer, lately killed by the wolves. This good luck proved the inauguration of plenty. As they approached the head of the lake, game grew abundant, and with the aid of the Mohegan, there was no lack of bear's meat and venison. They found wild grapes, too, in the woods and gathered them by cutting down the trees to which the vines clung.

While thus employed they were startled by a sight often so fearful in the waste and the wilderness—the print of a human foot. It was clear that Indians were not far off. A strict watch was kept, not without cause, as it proved, for that night, while the sentry thought of little but screening himself and his gun from the floods of rain, a party of Outagamis crept under the bank, where they lurked for some time before he discovered them. Being challenged, they came forward, professing great frendship and pretending to have mistaken the French for Iroquois.

In the morning, however, there was an outcry from La Salle's servant, who declared that the visitors had stolen his coat from under the inverted canoe where he had placed it, while some of the carpenters also complained of being robbed. La Salle well knew that if the theft were left unpunished, worse would come of it. First he posted his men at the woody point of a peninsula, whose sandy neck was interposed between them and the main forest. Then he went forth, pistol in hand, met a young Outagami, seized him and led him prisoner to his camp. This done, he again set out and soon found an Outagami chief—for the wigwams were not far distant—to whom he told what he had done, adding that unless the stolen goods were restored, the prisoner should be killed.

The Indians were in perplexity, for they had cut the coat to pieces and divided it. In this dilemma they resolved, being strong in numbers, to rescue their comrade by force. Accordingly they came down to the edge of the forest or posted themselves behind fallen trees on the banks, while La Salle's men in their stronghold braced their nerves for the fight.

Here three Flemish friars with their rosaries, and eleven Frenchmen with their guns, confronted a hundred and twenty screeching Outagamis. Hennepin, who had seen service and who had always an exhortation at his tongue's end, busied himself to inspire the rest with a courage equal to his own. Neither party, however, had an appetite for the fray. A parley ensued. Full compensation was made for the stolen goods and the aggrieved Frenchmen were further propitiated with a gift of beaver skins.

Their late enemies, now become friends, spent the next day in dances, feasts and speeches. They entreated La Salle not to advance farther, since the Illinois, through whose country he must pass, would be sure to kill him, for, added these friendly counselors, they hated the French because they had been instigating the Iroquois to invade their country. Here was another subject of anxiety. La Salle was confirmed in his belief that his busy and unscrupulous enemies were intriguing for his destruction.

He pushed on, however, circling around the southern shore of Lake Michigan till he reached the mouth of the St. Joseph, called by him the Miamis. Here, by a previous arrangement, Tonty was to have rejoined him with twenty men, making his way from Michilimackinac along the eastern shore of the lake, but the rendezvous was a solitude. Tonty was nowhere to be seen.

It was the first of November. Winter was at hand and the streams would soon be frozen. The men clamored to go forward, urging that they should starve if they could not reach the villages of the Illinois before the tribe scattered for the winter hunt. La Salle was inexorable. If they should all desert, he said, he with his Mohegan hunter and the three friars would still remain and wait for Tonty. The men grumbled but obeyed, and to divert their thoughts he set them at building a fort of timber on a rising ground at the mouth of the river.

They had spent twenty days at this task and their work was well advanced when at length Tonty appeared. He brought with him only half of his men. Provisions had failed and the rest of his party had been left thirty leagues behind, to sustain themselves by hunting. La Salle told him to return and hasten them forward. Tonty set out with two men. A violent north wind arose. He tried to run his canoe ashore through the breakers. The two men could not manage their vessel and he with his one hand could not help them. She swamped, rolling over in the surf. Guns, baggage and provisions were lost and the three voyagers returned to the Miamis, subsisting on acorns by the way. Happily, the men left behind, excepting two deserters, succeeded a few days after in rejoining the party.

Thus was one heavy load lifted from the heart of La Salle. But where was the *Griffin?* Time enough, and more than enough, had passed for her voyage to Niagara and back again. He scanned the dreary horizon with an anxious eye. No returning sail gladdened the watery solitude, and a dark foreboding gathered on his heart. Yet further delay was impossible. He sent back two men to Michilimackinac to meet her, if she still existed, and pilot her to his new fort of the Miamis, and then prepared to ascend the river, whose weedy edges were already glassed with thin flakes of ice.

On the third of December the party re-embarked, thirty-three in all, in eight canoes and ascended the chill current of the St. Joseph, bordered with dreary meadows and bare gray forests. When they approached the site of the present city of South Bend, they looked anxiously along the shore on their right to find the portage or path leading to the headquarters of the Illinois. The Mohegan was absent, hunting, and, unaided by his practiced eye, they passed the path without seeing it. La Salle landed to search the woods. Hours passed and he did not return. Hennepin and Tonty grew uneasy, disembarked, bivouacked, ordered guns to be fired and sent out men to scour the country. Night came, but not their lost leader. Muffled in their blankets and powdered by the thick-falling snowflakes, they sat ruefully speculating as to what had befallen him, nor was it till four o'clock of the next afternoon that they saw him approaching along the margin of the river.

His face and hands were besmirched with charcoal and he was further decorated with two opossums which hung from his belt and which he had killed with a stick as they were swinging head downwards from the bough of a tree, after the fashion of that singular beast. He had missed his way in the forest and had been forced to make a wide circuit around the edge of a swamp, while the snow, of which the air was full, added to his perplexities. Thus he pushed on through the rest of the day and the greater part of the night, till about two o'clock in the morning he reached the river again and fired his gun as a signal to his party. Hearing no answering shot, he pursued his way along the bank, when he presently saw the gleam of a fire among the dense thickets close at hand. Not doubting that he had found the bivouac of his party, he hastened to the spot. To his surprise, no human being was to be seen. Under a tree beside the fire was a heap of dry grass impressed with the form of a man who must have fled but a moment before, for his couch was still warm. It was no doubt an Indian, ambushed on the bank, watching to kill some passing enemy.

La Salle called out in several Indian languages, but there was dead silence all around. He then, with admirable coolness, took possession of the quarters he had found, shouting to their invisible proprietor that he was about to sleep in his bed, piled a barricade of bushes around the spot, rekindled the dying fire, warmed his benumbed hands, stretched himself on the dried grass and slept undisturbed till morning.

The Mohegan had rejoined the party before La Salle's return, and with his aid the portage was soon found. Here the party encamped.

La Salle, who was excessively fatigued, occupied with Hennepin a wigwam covered in the Indian manner with mats of reeds. The cold forced them to kindle a fire, which before daybreak set the mats in a blaze and the two sleepers narrowly escaped being burned along with their hut.

In the morning the party shouldered their canoes and baggage and began their march for the sources of the river Illinois, some five miles distant. Around them stretched a desolate plain, half covered with snow and strewn with the skulls and bones of buffalo, while on its farther verge they could see the lodges of the Miami Indians, who had made this place their abode.

As they filed on their way a man named Duplessis, who bore a grudge against La Salle and now walked just before him, raised his gun to shoot him through the back but was prevented by one of his comrades.

They soon reached a spot where the oozy, saturated soil quaked beneath their tread. All around were clumps of alder bushes, tufts of rank grass and pools of glistening water. In the midst a dark and lazy current, which a tall man might bestride, crept twisting like a snake among the weeds and rushes. Here were the sources of the Kankakee, one of the heads of the Illinois. They set their canoes on this thread of water, embarked their baggage and themselves and pushed down the sluggish streamlet, looking at a little distance like men who sailed on land. Fed by an unceasing tribute of the spongy soil, it quickly widened to a river and they floated on their way through a voiceless, lifeless solitude of dreary oak barrens or boundless marshes overgrown with reeds. At night they built their fire on ground made firm by frost and bivouacked among the rushes.

A few days brought them to a more favored region. On the right hand and on the left stretched the boundless prairie, dotted with leafless groves and bordered by gray wintry forests, scorched by the fires kindled in the dried grass by Indian hunters and strewn with the carcasses and the bleached skulls of innumerable buffalo. Plains were scored with their pathways and the muddy edges of the river were full of their hoofprints. Yet not one was to be seen.

At night the horizon glowed with distant fires and by day the savage hunters could be descried at times roaming on the verge of the prairie.

The men, discontented and half starved, would have deserted to them had they dared. La Salle's Mohegan could kill no game except two lean deer, with a few wild geese and swans. At length, in their straits, they made a happy discovery. It was a buffalo bull, fast mired in a slough. They killed him, lashed a cable about him, and then twelve men dragged out the shaggy monster, whose ponderous carcass demanded their utmost efforts.

The scene changed again as they descended. On either hand ran ranges of woody hills, following the course of the river, and when they mounted to their tops they saw beyond them a rolling sea of dull green prairie, a boundless pasture of the buffalo and the deer.

They passed the site of the future town of Ottawa and saw on their right the high plateau of Buffalo Rock, long a favorite dwelling place of Indians. A league below, the river glided among islands bordered with stately woods. Close on their left towered a lofty cliff, crested with trees that overhung the rippling current, while before them spread the valley of the Illinois in broad low meadows bordered on the right by the graceful hills at whose foot now lies Utica. Along the right bank of the river were clustered the lodges of a great Indian town. Hennepin counted four hundred and sixty of them. In shape they were somewhat like the arched top of a baggage wagon. They were built of a framework of poles, covered with mats of rushes closely interwoven, and each contained three or four fires, of which the greater part served for two families.

Here, then, was the town, but where were the inhabitants? All was silent as the desert. The lodges were empty, the fires dead and the ashes cold. La Salle had expected this, for he knew that in the autumn the Illinois always left their towns for their winter hunting and that the time of their return had not yet come.

Yet he was not the less embarrassed, for he would fain have bought a supply of food to relieve his famished followers. Some of them, searching the deserted town, presently found the *caches,* or covered pits, in which the Indians hid their stock of corn. This was precious beyond measure in their eyes, and to touch it would be a deep offense. La Salle shrank from provoking their anger, which might prove the ruin of his plans, but his necessity overcame his prudence and he took thirty *minots* of corn, hoping to appease the owners by presents.

Thus provided, the party embarked again and resumed their downward voyage.

On New Year's Day, 1680, they landed and heard mass. Then Hennepin wished a happy new year to La Salle first and afterwards to all the men, making them a speech which, as he tells us, was "most touching." He and his two brethren next embraced the whole company in turn, "in a manner," writes the father, "most tender and affectionate," exhorting them at the same time to patience, faith and constancy. Four days after these solemnities they reached the long expansion of the river then called Pimitoui, and now known as Peoria Lake, and leisurely made their way downward to the site of the city of Peoria.

Here, as evening drew near, they saw a faint spire of smoke curling above the gray forest, betokening that Indians were at hand. La Salle, as we have seen, had been warned that these tribes had been taught to regard him as their enemy, and when in the morning he resumed his course he was prepared alike for peace or war.

The shores now approached each other and the Illinois was once more a river, bordered on either hand with overhanging woods. At nine o'clock, doubling a point, he saw about eighty Illinois wigwams on both sides of the river. He instantly ordered the eight canoes to be ranged in line abreast across the stream, Tonty on the right and he himself on the left. The men laid down their paddle and seized their weapons, while in this warlike guise the current bore them swiftly into the midst of the surprised and astounded savages. The camps were in a panic. Warriors whooped and howled; squaws and children screeched in chorus. Some snatched their bows and war clubs; some ran in terror; and in the midst of the hubbub La Salle leaped ashore, followed by his men.

None knew better how to deal with Indians, and he made no sign of friendship, knowing that it might be construed as a token of fear. His little knot of Frenchmen stood, gun in hand, passive yet prepared for battle. The Indians, on their part, rallying a little from their fright, made all haste to proffer peace. Two of their chiefs came forward, holding out the calumet, while another began a loud harangue to check the young warriors who were aiming their arrows from the farther bank. La Salle, responding to these friendly overtures, displayed another calumet, while Hennepin caught several scared children and soothed them with winning blandishments. The uproar was quelled and the strangers were presently seated in the midst of the camp, beset by a throng of wild and swarthy figures.

Food was placed before them, and as the Illinois code of courtesy enjoined, their entertainers conveyed the morsels with their own hands to the lips of these unenviable victims of their hospitality, while others rubbed their feet with bear's grease. La Salle, on his part, made them a gift of tobacco and hatchets and, when he had escaped from their caresses, rose and harangued them. He told them that he had been forced to take corn from their granaries lest his men should die of hunger, but he prayed them not to be offended, promising full restitution or ample payment. He had come, he said, to protect them against their enemies and teach them to pray to the true God. As for the Iroquois, they were subjects of the Great King and therefore brethren of the French, yet nevertheless, should they begin a war and invade the country of the Illinois, he would stand by them, give them guns and fight in their defense, if they would perimt him to build a fort among them for the security of his men.

It was also, he added, his purpose to build a great wooden canoe in which to descend the Mississippi to the sea, and then return, bringing them the goods of which they stood in need. But if they would not consent to his plans and sell provisions to his men, he would pass on to the Osages, who would then reap all the benefits of intercourse with the French while they were left destitute, at the mercy of the Iroquois.

This threat had its effect, for it touched their deep-rooted jealousy of the Osages. They were lavish of promises, and feasts and dances consumed the day. Yet La Salle soon learned that the intrigues of his enemies were still pursuing him.

That evening, unknown to him, a stranger appeared in the Illinois camp. He was a Mascoutin chief named Monso, attended by five or six Miamis and bringing a gift of knives, hatchets and kettles to the Illinois. The chiefs assembled in a secret, nocturnal session, where, smoking their pipes, they listened with open ears to the harangue of the envoys.

Monso told them that he had come in behalf of certain Frenchmen, whom he named, to warn his hearers against the designs of La

Salle, whom he denounced as a partisan and spy of the Iroquois, affirming that he was now on his way to stir up the tribes beyond the Mississippi to join in a war against the Illinois, who, thus assailed from the east and from the west, would be utterly destroyed. There was no hope for them, he added, but in checking the progress of La Salle, or at least retarding it, thus causing his men to desert him. Having thrown his firebrand, Monso and his party left the camp in haste, dreading to be confronted with the object of their aspersions.

In the morning La Salle saw a change in the behavior of his hosts. They looked on him askance, cold, sullen and suspicious. There was one Omawha, a chief, whose favor he had won the day before by the politic gift of two hatchets and three knives, and who now came to him in secret to tell him what had taken place at the nocturnal council. La Salle at once saw in it a device of his enemies, and this belief was confirmed when, in the afternoon, Nicanopé, brother of the head chief, sent to invite the Frenchmen to a feast. They repaired to his lodge, but before dinner was served—that is to say, while the guests, white and red, were seated on mats, each with his hunting knife in his hand and the wooden bowl before him which was to receive his share of the bear's or buffalo's meat, or the corn boiled in fat, with which he was to be regaled—their host arose and began a long speech.

He told the Frenchmen that he had invited them to his lodge less to refresh their bodies with good cheer than to cure their minds of the dangerous purpose which possessed them of descending the Mississippi. Its shores, he said, were beset by savage tribes against whose numbers and ferocity their valor would avail nothing. Its waters were infested by serpents, alligators and unnatural monsters, while the river itself, after raging among rocks and whirlpools, plunged headlong at last into a fathomless gulf which would swallow them and their vessel forever.

La Salle's men were for the most part raw hands, knowing nothing of the wilderness and easily alarmed at its dangers, but there were two among them, old *coureurs de bois,* who unfortunately knew too much. They understood the Indian orator and explained his speech to the rest. As La Salle looked around on the circle of his followers, he read an augury of fresh trouble in their disturbed and rueful visages. He waited patiently, however, till the speaker had ended and then

227

answered him through his interpreter with great composure. First he thanked him for the friendly warning which his affection had impelled him to utter, but, he continued, the greater the danger, the greater the honor, and even if the danger were real, Frenchmen would never flinch from it.

But were not the Illinois jealous? Had they not been deluded by lies? "We were not asleep, my brother, when Monso came to tell you, under cover of night, that we were spies of the Iroquois. The presents he gave you, that you might believe his falsehoods, are at this moment buried in the earth under this lodge. If he told you the truth, why did he skulk away in the dark? Why did he not show himself by day? Do you not see that when we first came among you and your camp was all in confusion, we could have killed you without needing help from the Iroquois? And now, while I am speaking, could we not put your old men to death while your young warriors are all gone away to hunt? If we meant to make war on you, we should need no help from the Iroquois, who have so often felt the force of our arms. Look at what we have brought you. It is not weapons to destroy you, but merchandise and tools for your good. If you still harbor evil thoughts of us, be frank as we are and speak them boldly. Go after this impostor Monso and bring him back, that we may answer him face to face, for he never saw either us or the Iroquois and what can he know of the plots that he pretends to reveal?"

Nicanopé had nothing to reply and, grunting assent in the depths of his throat, made a sign that the feast should proceed.

The French were lodged in huts near the Indian camp, and fearing treachery, La Salle placed a guard at night. On the morning after the feast he came out into the frosty air and looked about him for the sentinels. Not one of them was to be seen. Vexed and alarmed, he entered hut after hut and roused his drowsy followers. Six of the number, including two of the best carpenters, were nowhere to be found. Discontented and mutinous from the first, and now terrified by the fictions of Nicanopé, they had deserted, prefering the hardships of the midwinter forest to the mysterious terrors of the Mississippi.

La Salle mustered the rest before him and inveighed sternly against the cowardice and baseness of those who had thus abandoned him, regardless of his many favors. If any here, he added, are afraid, let them but wait till the spring and they shall have free leave to return to Canada, safely and without dishonor.

This desertion cut him to the heart. It showed him that he was leaning on a broken reed and he felt that, on an enterprise of doubt and peril, there were scarcely four men in his party whom he could trust.

CHAPTER 5

Desperate Journeys

L A SALLE NOW RESOLVED TO LEAVE THE INDIAN camp and fortify himself for the winter in a strong position where his men would be less exposed to dangerous influence and where he could hold his ground against an outbreak of the Illinois or an Iroquois invasion. At the middle of January a thaw broke up the ice which had closed the river and he set out in a canoe, with Hennepin, to visit the site he had chosen for his projected fort.

It was half a league below the camp, on a low hill or knoll, two hundred yards from the southern bank. On either side was a deep ravine and in front a marshy tract, overflowed at high water. There the party was removed. They dug a ditch behind the hill, connecting the two ravines and thus completely isolating it. The hill was nearly square in form. An embankment of earth was thrown up on every side. Its declivities were sloped steeply down to the bottom of the ravines and the ditch, and further guarded by *chevaux-de-frise,* while a palisade twenty-five feet high was planted around the whole. The lodgings of the men, built of musketproof timber, were at two of the angles; the house of the friars at the third; the forge and magazine at the fourth; and the tents of La Salle and Tonty in the area within.

Hennepin laments the failure of wine, which prevented him from saying mass, but every morning and evening he summoned the men to his cabin to listen to prayers and preaching, and on Sundays and fete days they chanted vespers. Father Zenobe usually spent the day in the Indian camp, striving with very indifferent success to win them to the Faith and to overcome the disgust with which their manners and habits inspired him.

Such was the first civilized occupation of the region which now forms the state of Illinois. La Salle christened his new fort Fort Crèvecœur. The name tells of disaster and suffering but does no justice to the ironhearted constancy of the sufferer. Up to this time he had clung to the hope that his vessel, the *Griffin,* might still be safe. Her safety was vital to his enterprise. She had on board articles of the last necessity to him, including the rigging and anchors of another vessel which he was to build at Fort Crèvecœur, in order to descend the Mississippi and sail to the West Indies. But now his last hope had well nigh vanished. Past all reasonable doubt, the *Griffin* was lost, and in her loss he and all his plans seemed ruined alike. Nothing, indeed, was ever heard of her.

One path, beset with hardships and terrors, still lay open to him. He might return on foot to Fort Frontenac and bring back the needful succors. La Salle felt deeply the dangers of such a step. His men were uneasy, discontented and terrified by the stories with which the jealous Illinois still constantly filled their ears of the whirlpools and the monsters of the Mississippi. He dreaded that in his absence they should follow the example of their comrades and desert.

In the midst of his anxieties, a lucky accident gave him the means of disabusing them. He was hunting one day near the fort when he met a young Illinois on his way home, half starved, from a distant war excursion. He had been absent so long that he knew nothing of what had passed between his countrymen and the French. La Salle gave him a turkey he had shot, invited him to the fort, fed him and made him presents. Having thus warmed his heart, he questioned him with apparent carelessness as to the countries he had visited, and especially as to the Mississippi. The young warrior, seeing no reason to disguise the truth, gave him all the information he required. La Salle now made him the present of a hatchet, to engage him to say nothing of what had passed, and leaving him in excellent humor, repaired with some of his followers to the Illinois camp.

Here he found the chiefs seated at a feast of bear's meat and he took his place among them on a mat of rushes. After a pause he charged them with having deceived him about the Mississippi, adding

231

that he knew the river perfectly, having been instructed concerning it by the Master of Life. He then described it to them with so much accuracy that his astonished hearers, conceiving that he owed his knowledge to sorcery, clapped their hands to their mouths in sign of wonder and confessed that all they had said was but an artifice, inspired by their earnest desire that he should remain among them.

At this La Salle's men took heart again, and their courage rose still more when, soon after, a band of Chickasa, Arkansas and Osage warriors from the Mississippi came to the camp on a friendly visit and assured the French not only that the river was navigable to the sea but that the tribes along its banks would give them a warm welcome.

La Salle now had good reason to hope that his followers would neither mutiny nor desert in his absence. One chief purpose of his intended journey was to procure the anchors, cables and rigging of the vessel which he meant to build at Fort Crèvecœur, and he resolved to see her on the stocks before he set out. This was no easy matter, for the pit sawyers had deserted.

"Seeing," he writes, "that I should lose a year if I waited to get others from Montreal, I said one day before my people that I was so vexed to find that the absence of two sawyers would defeat my plans and make all my trouble useless, that I was resolved to try to saw the planks myself, if I could find a single man who would help me with a will."

Two men stepped forward and promised to do their best. They were tolerably successful, and the rest being roused to emulation, the work went on with such vigor that within six weeks the hull of the vessel was half finished. She was of forty tons' burden and was built with high bulwarks to protect those on board from Indian arrows.

La Salle now bethought him that in his absence he might get from Hennepin service of more value than his sermons and he requested him to descend the Illinois and explore it to its mouth. The friar, though hardy and daring, would have excused himself, alleging a troublesome bodily infirmity, but his venerable colleague Ribourde, himself too old for the journey, urged him to go, telling him that if he died by the way his apostolic labors would redound to the glory of God. Father Membré had been living for some time in the Illinois camp and was thoroughly out of humor with the objects of his missionary efforts, of whose obduracy and filth he bitterly complained. Hennepin proposed to take his place, while he should assume the Mississippi adventure, but this Membré declined, preferring to remain where he was.

Hennepin now reluctantly accepted the proposed task. "Anybody but me," he says with his usual modesty, "would have been very much frightened at the dangers of such a journey, and in fact, if I had not placed all my trust in God, I should not have been the dupe of the Sieur de la Salle, who exposed my life rashly."

On the last day of February, Hennepin's canoe lay at the water's edge and the party gathered on the bank to bid him farewell. He had two companions and the canoe was well laden with gifts for the Indians —tobacco, knives, beads, awls and other goods to a very considerable value, supplied at La Salle's cost. "In fact," observes Hennepin, "he is liberal enough towards his friends."

The friar bade farewell to La Salle and embraced all the rest in turn. Father Ribourde gave him his benediction. "Be of good courage and let your heart be comforted," said the excellent old missionary as he spread his hands in benediction over the shaven crown of the reverend traveler. Du Gay and Accau, the companions, plied their paddles. The canoe receded and vanished at length behind the forest, carrying Hennepin to adventures both imaginary and real. He never rejoined La Salle.

On the first of March, before the frost was yet out of the ground, when the forest was still leafless and the oozy prairies still patched with snow, a band of discontented men were again gathered on the shore for another leave-taking. Hard by, the unfinished ship lay on the stocks, white and fresh from the saw and ax, ceaselessly reminding them of the hardship and peril that was in store. Here you would have seen the calm, impenetrable face of La Salle, and with him the Mohegan hunter who seems to have felt towards him that admiring attachment which he could always inspire in his Indian retainers. Besides the Mohegan, four Frenchmen were to accompany him— Hunaut, La Violette, Collin and Dautray.

His parting with Tonty was an anxious one, for each well knew the risks that environed both. Embarking with his followers in two canoes, he made his way upward amid the drifting ice, while the faithful

Italian, with two or three honest men and twelve or thirteen knaves, remained to hold Fort Crèvecœur in his absence.

La Salle well knew what was before him, and nothing but necessity spurred him to this desperate journey. He says that he could trust nobody else to go in his stead, and that unless the articles lost in the *Griffin* were replaced without delay, the expedition would be retarded a full year and he and his associates consumed by its expenses.

"Therefore," he writes to one of them, "though the thaws of approaching spring greatly increased the difficulty of the way, interrupted as it was everywhere by marshes and rivers, to say nothing of the length of the journey, which is about five hundred leagues in a direct line, and the danger of meeting Indians of four or five different nations through whose country we were to pass, as well as an Iroquois army which we knew was coming that way; though we must suffer all the time from hunger; sleep on the open ground, and often without food; watch by night and march by day, loaded with baggage, such as blanket, clothing, kettle, hatchet, gun, powder, lead, and skins to make moccasins; sometimes pushing through thickets, sometimes climbing rocks covered with ice and snow, sometimes wading whole days through marshes where the water was waist-deep or even more, at a season when the snow was not entirely melted—though I knew all this, it did not prevent me from resolving to go on foot to Fort Frontenac, to learn for myself what had become of my vessel, and bring back the things we needed."

The winter had been a severe one, and when an hour after leaving the fort he and his companions reached the still water of Peoria Lake, they found it sheeted with ice from shore to shore. They carried their canoes up the bank, made two rude sledges, placed the light vessels upon them and dragged them to the upper end of the lake, where they encamped. In the morning they found the river still covered with ice, too weak to bear them and too strong to permit them to break a way for the canoes. They spent the whole day in carrying them through the woods, toiling knee-deep in saturated snow. Rain fell in floods and they took shelter at night in a deserted Indian hut.

In the morning, the third of March, they dragged their canoes half a league farther, then launched them and, breaking the ice with clubs and hatchets, forced their way slowly up the stream. Again their progress was barred, and again they took to the woods, toiling onward till a tempest of moist, half-liquid snow forced them to bivouac for the night. A sharp frost followed, and in the morning the white waste around them was glazed with a dazzling crust. Now, for the first time, they could use their snowshoes. Bending to their work, dragging their canoes, which glided smoothly over the polished surface, they journeyed on hour after hour and league after league till they reached at length the great town of the Illinois, still void of its inhabitants.

It was a desolate and lonely scene—the river gliding dark and cold beneath its banks of rushes; the empty lodges, covered with crusted snow; the vast white meadows; the distant cliffs, bearded with shining icicles; and the hills wrapped in forests, which glittered from afar with the icy incrustations that cased each frozen twig. Yet there was life in the savage landscape. The men saw buffalo wading in the snow and they killed one of them. More than this, they discovered the tracks of moccasins. They cut rushes by the edge of the river, piled them on the bank and set them on fire so that the smoke might attract the eyes of savages roaming near.

On the following day, while the hunters were smoking the meat of the buffalo, La Salle went out to reconnoiter and presently met three Indians, one of whom proved to be Chassagoac, the principal chief of the Illinois. La Salle brought them to his bivouac, feasted them, gave them a red blanket, a kettle and some knives and hatchets, made friends with them, promised to restrain the Iroquois from attacking them, told them that he was on his way to the settlements to bring arms and ammunition to defend them against their enemies and, as the result of these advances, gained from the chief a promise that he would send provisions to Tonty's party at Fort Crèvecœur.

On the fifteenth the party set out again, carried their canoes along the bank of the river as far as the rapids above Ottawa, then launched them and pushed their way upward, battling with the floating ice which, loosened by a warm rain, drove down the swollen current in sheets. On the eighteenth they reached a point some miles below the site of Joliet and here found the river once more completely closed. Despairing of further progress by water, they hid their canoes on an island and struck across the country for Lake Michigan.

It was the worst of all seasons for such a journey. The nights were cold, but the sun was warm at noon and the half-thawed prairie was one vast tract of mud, water and discolored, half-liquid snow. On the twenty-second they crossed marshes and inundated meadows, wading to the knee, till at noon they were stopped by a river, perhaps the Calumet. They made a raft of hardwood timber, for there was no other kind, and shoved themselves across. On the next day they could see Lake Michigan dimly glimmering beyond the waste of woods, and after crossing three swollen streams, they reached it at evening.

On the twenty-fourth they followed its shore, till at nightfall they arrived at the fort which they had built in the autumn at the mouth of the St. Joseph. Here La Salle found Chapelle and Leblanc, the two men he had sent to Michilimackinac in search of the *Griffin*. They reported that they had made the circuit of the lake and had neither seen her nor heard tidings of her. Assured of her fate, he ordered them to rejoin Tonty at Fort Crèvecœur, while he pushed onward with his party through the unknown wild of southern Michigan.

"The rain," says La Salle, "which lasted all day, and the raft we were obliged to make to cross the river, stopped us till noon of the twenty-fifth, when we continued our march through the woods, which was so interlaced with thorns and brambles that in two days and a half our clothes were all torn and our faces so covered with blood that we hardly knew each other. On the twenty-eighth we found the woods more open and began to fare better, meeting a good deal of game, which after this rarely failed us; so that we no longer carried provisions with us, but made a meal of roast meat wherever we happened to kill a deer, bear or turkey. These are the choicest feasts on a journey like this; and till now we had generally gone without them, so that we had often walked all day without breakfast.

"The Indians do not hunt in this region, which is debatable ground between five or six nations who are at war, and being afraid of each other, do not venture into these parts except to surprise each other, and always with the greatest precaution and all possible secrecy. The reports of our guns and the carcasses of the animals we killed soon led some of them to find our trail. In fact, on the evening of the twenty-eighth, having made our fire by the edge of a prairie, we were surrounded by them; but as the man on guard waked us, and we posted ourselves behind trees with our guns, these savages, who are called

Wapoos, took us for Iroquois, and thinking that there must be a great many of us because we did not travel secretly, as they do when in small bands, they ran off without shooting their arrows, and gave the alarm to their comrades, so that we were two days without meeting anybody."

La Salle guessed the cause of their fright, and in order to confirm their delusion he drew with charcoal on the trunks of trees from which he had stripped the bark the usual marks of an Iroquois war party, with signs for prisoners and for scalps, after the custom of those dreaded warriors. This ingenious artifice, it turned out, was nearly the destruction of the whole party. He also set fire to the dry grass of the prairies over which he and his men had just passed, thus destroying the traces of their passage.

"We practiced this device every night, and it answered very well so long as we were passing over an open country, but on the thirtieth we got into great marshes, flooded by the thaws, and were obliged to cross them in mud or water up to the waist; so that our tracks betrayed us to a band of Mascoutins who were out after Iroquois. They followed us through these marshes during the three days we were crossing them, but we made no fire at night, contenting ourselves with taking off our wet clothes and wrapping ourselves in our blankets on some dry knoll, where we slept till morning. At last, on the night of the second of April, there came a hard frost and our clothes, which were drenched when we took them off, froze stiff as sticks, so that we could not put them on in the morning without making a fire to thaw them.

"The fire betrayed us to the Indians, who were encamped across the marsh; and they ran towards us with loud cries, till they were stopped halfway by a stream so deep that they could not get over, the ice which had formed in the night not being strong enough to bear them. We went to meet them, within gunshot; and whether our firearms frightened them, or whether they thought us more numerous than we were, or whether they really meant us no harm, they called out, in the Illinois language, that they had taken us for Iroquois, but now saw that we were friends and brothers; whereupon, they went off as they came, and we kept on our way till the fourth, when two of my men fell ill and could not walk."

In this emergency La Salle went in search of some watercourse by

237

which they might reach Lake Erie and soon came upon a small river, which was probably the Huron. Here, while the sick men rested, their companions made a canoe. There were no birch trees and they were forced to use elm bark, which at that early season would not slip freely from the wood until they loosened it with hot water. Their canoe being made, they embarked in it and for a time floated prosperously down the stream, when at length the way was barred by a matted barricade of trees fallen across the water. The sick men could now walk again, and pushing eastward through the forest, the party soon reached the banks of the Detroit.

La Salle directed two of the men to make a canoe and go to Michilimackinac, the nearest harborage. With the remaining two he crossed the Detroit on a raft and, striking a direct line across the country, reached Lake Erie, not far from Point Pelee. Snow, sleet and rain pelted them with little intermission, and when after a walk of about thirty miles they gained the lake, the Mohegan and one of the Frenchmen were attacked with fever and spitting of blood.

Only one man now remained in health. With his aid La Salle made another canoe and, embarking the invalids, pushed for Niagara. It was Easter Monday when they landed at a cabin of logs above the cataract, probably on the spot where the *Griffin* was built. Here several of La Salle's men had been left the year before and here they still remained. They told him woeful news. Not only had he lost the *Griffin* and her lading of ten thousand crowns in value, but a ship from France, freighted with his goods, valued at more than twenty-two thousand livres, had been totally wrecked at the mouth of the St. Lawrence, and of twenty hired men on their way from Europe to join him, some had been detained by his enemy, the intendant Duchesneau, while all but four of the remainder, being told that he was dead, had found means to return home.

His three followers were all unfit for travel; he alone retained his strength and spirit. Taking with him three fresh men at Niagara, he resumed his journey and on the sixth of May descried, looming through floods of rain, the familiar shores of his seigniory and the bastioned walls of Fort Frontenac. During sixty-five days he had toiled almost incessantly, traveling by the course he took about a thousand miles through a country beset with every form of peril and obstruction—

"the most arduous journey," says the chronicler, "ever made by Frenchmen in America."

He had reached his goal, but for him there was neither rest nor peace. Man and Nature seemed in arms against him. His agents had plundered him; his creditors had seized his property; and several of his canoes, richly laden, had been lost in the rapids of the St. Lawrence. He hastened to Montreal, where his sudden advent caused great astonishment, and where, despite his crippled resources and damaged credit, he succeeded within a week in gaining the supplies which he required and the needful succors for the forlorn band on the Illinois. He had returned to Fort Frontenac and was on the point of embarking for their relief when a blow fell upon him more disheartening than any that had preceded.

On the twenty-second of July two *voyageurs,* Messier and Laurent, came to him with a letter from Tonty, who wrote that soon after La Salle's departure nearly all the men had deserted, after destroying Fort Crèvecœur, plundering the magazine and throwing into the river all the arms, goods and stores which they could not carry off.

The messengers who brought this letter were speedily followed by two of the *habitants* of Fort Frontenac, who had been trading on the lakes and who, with a fidelity which the unhappy La Salle rarely knew how to inspire, had traveled day and night to bring him their tidings. They reported that they had met the deserters and that, having been reinforced by recruits gained at Michilimackinac and Niagara, they now numbered twenty men. They had destroyed the fort on the St. Joseph, seized a quantity of furs belonging to La Salle at Michilimackinac and plundered the magazine at Niagara. Here they had separated, eight of them coasting the south side of Lake Ontario to find harborage at Albany, a common refuge at that time of this class of scoundrels, while the remaining twelve in three canoes made for Fort Frontenac along the north shore, intending to kill La Salle as the surest means of escaping punishment.

He lost no time in lamentation. Of the few men at his command he chose nine of the trustiest, embarked with them in canoes and went to meet the marauders. After passing the Bay of Quinté, he took his station with five of his party at a point of land suited to his purpose and detached the remaining four to keep watch. In the morning two canoes

239

were discovered approaching without suspicion, one of them far in advance of the other. As the foremost drew near, La Salle's canoe darted out from under the leafy shore, two of the men handling the paddles while he, with the remaining two, leveled their guns at the deserters and called on them to surrender. Astonished and dismayed, they yielded at once, while two more, who were in the second canoe, hastened to follow their example.

La Salle now returned to the fort with his prisoners, placed them in custody and again set forth. He met the third canoe upon the lake at about six o'clock in the evening. His men vainly plied their paddles in pursuit. The mutineers reached the shore, took post among rocks and trees, leveled their guns and showed fight. Four of La Salle's men made a circuit to gain their rear and dislodge them, on which they stole back to their canoe and tried to escape in the darkness. They were pursued and summoned to yield, but they replied by aiming their guns at their pursuers, who instantly gave them a volley, killed two of them and captured the remaining three. Like their companions, they were placed in custody at the fort to await the arrival of Count Frontenac.

La Salle's best hope was now in Tonty. Could that brave and truehearted officer and the three or four faithful men who had remained with him make good their foothold on the Illinois and save from destruction the vessel on the stocks and the forge and tools so laboriously carried there, then a basis was left on which the ruined enterprise might be built up once more. There was no time to lose. Tonty must be succored soon, or succor would come too late.

La Salle had already provided the necessary material and a few days sufficed to complete his preparations. On the tenth of August he embarked again for the Illinois. With him went his lieutenant La Forest, who held of him in fief an island then called Belle Isle, opposite Fort Frontenac. A surgeon, ship carpenters, joiners, masons, soldiers, *voyageurs* and laborers completed his company, twenty-five men in all, with everything useful for the outfit of the vessel.

His route, though difficult, was not so long as that which he had followed the year before. He ascended the river Humber, crossed to Lake Simcoe and descended the Severn to the Georgian Bay of Lake Huron, followed its eastern shore, coasted the Manitoulin Islands and at length reached Michilimackinac. Here, as usual, all was hostile and

240

he had great difficulty in inducing the Indians, who had been excited against him, to sell him provisions. Anxious to reach his destination, he pushed forward with twelve men, leaving La Forest to bring on the rest.

On the fourth of November he reached the ruined fort at the mouth of the St. Joseph and left five of his party, with the heavy stores, to wait till La Forest should come up, while he himself hastened forward with six Frenchmen and an Indian. A deep anxiety possessed him. The rumor, current for months past, that the Iroquois, bent on destroying the Illinois, were on the point of invading their country had constantly gained strength. Here was a new disaster which, if realized, might involve him and his enterprise in irretrievable wreck.

He ascended the St. Joseph, crossed the portage to the Kankakee and followed its course downward till it joined the northern branch of the Illinois. He had heard nothing of Tonty on the way and neither here nor elsewhere could he discover the smallest sign of the passage of white men. His friend, therefore, if alive, was probably still at his post, and he pursued his course with a mind lightened in some small measure of its load of anxiety.

When last he had passed here all was solitude, but now the scene was changed. The boundless waste was thronged with life. He beheld that wondrous spectacle, the memory of which can quicken pulse and stir the blood after the lapse of years: far and near the prairie was alive with buffalo; now like black specks dotting the distant swells; now trampling by in ponderous columns, or filing in long lines, morning, noon and night, to drink at the river—wading, plunging and snorting in the water; climbing the muddy shores and staring with wild eyes at the passing canoes.

It was an opportunity not to be lost. The party landed and encamped for a hunt. Sometimes they hid under the shelving bank and shot them as they came to drink. Sometimes, flat on their faces, they dragged themselves through the long dead grass till the savage bulls, guardians of the herd, ceased their grazing, raised their huge heads and glared through tangled hair at the dangerous intruders. The hunt was successful. In three days the hunters killed twelve buffalo, besides deer, geese and swans. They cut the meat into thin flakes and dried it in the sun or in the smoke of their fires. The men were in high spirits, delighting in

241

the sport and rejoicing in the prospect of relieving Tonty and his hungry followers with a plentiful supply.

They embarked again and soon approached the great town of the Illinois. The buffalo were far behind and once more the canoes glided on their way through a voiceless solitude. No hunters were seen; no saluting whoop greeted their ears. They passed the cliff afterwards called the Rock of St. Louis, where La Salle had ordered Tonty to build his stronghold, but as he scanned its lofty top he saw no palisades, no cabins, no sign of human hand, and still its primeval crest of forests overhung the gliding river. Now the meadow opened before them where the great town had stood. They gazed, astonished and confounded. All was desolation. The town had vanished and the meadow was black with fire. They plied their paddles, hastened to the spot, landed, and as they looked around their cheeks grew white and the blood was frozen in their veins.

Before them lay a plain once swarming with wild human life and covered with Indian dwellings, now a waste of devastation and death, strewn with heaps of ashes and bristling with the charred poles and stakes which had formed the framework of the lodges. At the points of most of them were stuck human skulls, half picked by birds of prey.

Near at hand was the burial ground of the village. The travelers sickened with horror as they entered its revolting precincts. Wolves in multitudes fled at their approach, while clouds of crows or buzzards, rising from their hideous repast, wheeled above their heads or settled on the naked branches of the neighboring forest. Every grave had been rifled and the bodies flung down from the scaffold where, after the Illinois custom, many of them had been placed. The field was strewn with broken bones and torn and mangled corpses. A hyena warfare had been waged against the dead. La Salle knew the handiwork of the Iroquois. The threatened blow had fallen and the wolfish hordes of the five cantons had fleshed their rabid fangs in a new victim.

As La Salle surveyed the scene of havoc one thought engrossed him: where were Tonty and his men? He searched the Iroquois fort. There were abundant traces of its savage occupants, and among them a few fragments of French clothing. He examined the skulls, but the hair, portions of which clung to nearly all of them, was in every case that of an Indian. Evening came on before he had finished the search. The sun set and the wilderness sank to its savage rest. Night and silence brooded over the waste, where far as the raven could wing his flight stretched the dark domain of solitude and horror.

When daylight returned La Salle told his followers he intended to push forward and directed three of them to await his return near the ruined village. They were to hide themselves on an island, conceal their fire at night, make no smoke by day, fire no guns and keep a close watch. Should the rest of the party arrive, they too were to wait with similar precautions. The baggage was placed in a hollow of the rocks at a place difficult of access, and these arrangements made, La Salle set out on his perilous journey with the four remaining men and the Indian. Each was armed with two guns, a pistol and a sword, and a number of hatchets and other goods were placed in the canoe as presents for Indians whom they might meet.

Several leagues below the village they found, on their right hand close to the river, a sort of island made inaccessible by the marshes and water which surrounded it. Here the flying Illinois had sought refuge with their women and children and the place was full of their deserted huts. On the left bank, exactly opposite, was an abandoned camp of the Iroquois. On the level meadow stood a hundred and thirteen huts, and on the forest trees which covered the hills behind were carved the totems, or insignia, of the chiefs, together with marks to show the number of followers which each had led to the war. La Salle counted five hundred and eighty-two warriors. He found marks, too, for the Illinois killed or captured, but none to indicate that any of the Frenchmen had shared their fate.

As they descended the river they passed on the same day six abandoned camps of the Illinois and opposite to each was a camp of the invaders. The former, it was clear, had retreated in a body, while the Iroquois had followed their march, day by day, along the other bank. La Salle and his men pushed rapidly onward, passed Peoria Lake and soon reached Fort Crèvecœur, which they found, as they expected, demolished by the deserters. The vessel on the stocks was still left entire, though the Iroquois had found means to draw out the iron nails and spikes. On one of the planks were written the words, in French, "We are all savages: *ce* 15, 1680"—the work, no doubt, of the knaves who had pillaged and destroyed the fort.

243

La Salle and his companions hastened on, and during the following day passed four opposing camps of the savage armies. The silence of death now reigned along the deserted river, whose lonely borders, wrapped deep in forests, seemed lifeless as the grave. As they drew near the mouth of the stream they saw a meadow on their right, and on its farthest verge several human figures, erect yet motionless.

They landed and cautiously examined the place. The long grass was trampled down and all around were strewn the relics of the hideous orgies which formed the ordinary sequel of an Iroquois victory. The figures they had seen were the half-consumed bodies of women, still bound to the stakes where they had been tortured. Other sights there were, too revolting for record. All the remains were those of women and children. The men, it seemed, had fled and left them to their fate.

Here again La Salle sought long and anxiously without finding the smallest sign that could indicate the presence of Frenchmen. Once more descending the river, they soon reached its mouth. Before them a broad eddying current rolled swiftly on its way and La Salle beheld the Mississippi—the object of his daydreams, the destined avenue of his ambition and his hopes.

It was no time for reflections. The moment was too engrossing, too heavily charged with anxieties and cares. From a rock on the shore he saw a tree stretched forward above the stream, and stripping off its bark to make it more conspicuous, he hung upon it a board on which he had drawn the figures of himself and his men, seated in their canoe and bearing a pipe of peace. To this he tied a letter for Tonty, informing him that he had returned up the river to the ruined village.

His four men had behaved admirably throughout and they now offered to continue the journey if he saw fit and follow him to the sea, but he thought it useless to go farther and was unwilling to abandon the three men whom he had ordered to await his return. Accordingly, they retraced their course and, paddling at times both day and night, urged their canoe so swiftly that they reached the village in the incredibly short space of four days. [The distance is about two hundred and fifty miles.]

The sky was clear, and as night came on the travelers saw a prodigious comet blazing above this scene of desolation. On that night it was chilling with a superstitious awe the hamlets of New England and the gilded chambers of Versailles, but it is characteristic of La Salle that, beset as he was with perils and surrounded with ghastly images of death, he coolly notes down the phenomenon, not as a portentous messenger of war and woe, but rather as an object of scientific curiosity.

He found his three men safely ensconced upon their island, where they were anxiously looking for his return. After collecting a store of half-burnt corn from the ravaged granaries of the Illinois, the whole party began to ascend the river, and on the sixth of January reached the junction of the Kankakee with the northern branch.

On their way downward they had descended the former stream. They now chose the latter and soon discovered by the margin of the water a rude cabin of bark. La Salle landed and examined the spot, when an object met his eye which cheered him with a bright gleam of hope. It was only a piece of wood, but the wood had been cut with a saw. Tonty and his party, then, had passed this way, escaping from the carnage behind them. Unhappily, they had left no token of their passage at the fork of the two streams, and thus La Salle on his voyage downward had believed them to be still on the river below.

With rekindled hope, the travelers pursued their journey, leaving their canoes and making their way overland towards the fort on the St. Joseph.

"Snow fell in extraordinary quantities all day," writes La Salle, "and it kept falling for nineteen days in succession, with cold so severe that I never knew so hard a winter, even in Canada. We were obliged to cross forty leagues of open country, where we could hardly find wood to warm ourselves at evening, and could get no bark whatever to make a hut, so that we had to spend the night exposed to the furious winds which blow over these plains. I never suffered so much from cold, or had more trouble in getting forward; for the snow was so light, resting suspended as it were among the tall grass, that we could not use snowshoes. Sometimes it was waist deep; and as I walked before my men, as usual, to encourage them by breaking the path, I often had much ado, though I am rather tall, to lift my legs above the drifts, through which I pushed by the weight of my body."

At length they reached their goal and found shelter and safety within the walls of Fort Miami.

CHAPTER 6

~~~~~~

Down the Mississippi

LA SALLE MIGHT HAVE BROODED ON THE REDOUBLED ruin that had befallen him—the desponding friends, the exulting foes, the wasted energies, the crushing load of debt, the stormy past, the black and lowering future. But his mind was of a different temper. He had no thought but to grapple with adversity, and out of the fragments of his ruin to build up the fabric of success.

He would not recoil, but he modified his plans to meet the new contingency. His white enemies had found, or rather perhaps had made, a savage ally in the Iroquois. Their incursions must be stopped or his enterprise would be frustrated, and he thought he saw the means by which this new danger could be converted into a source of strength.

The tribes of the West, threatened by the common enemy, might be taught to forget their mutual animosities and join in a defensive league, with La Salle at its head. They might be colonized around his fort in the valley of the Illinois, where in the shadow of the French flag and with the aid of French allies they could hold the Iroquois in check and acquire in some measure the arts of a settled life. The Franciscan friars could teach them the Faith, and La Salle and his associates could supply them with goods in exchange for the vast harvest of furs which their hunters could gather in these boundless wilds. Meanwhile he would seek out the mouth of the Mississippi, and the furs gathered at his colony in the Illinois would then find a ready passage to the markets of the world.

Thus might this ancient slaughter field of warring savages be redeemed for civilization and Christianity, and a stable settlement, half feudal, half commercial, grow up in the heart of the western wilderness. This plan was only a part of the original scheme of his enterprise, adapted to new and unexpected circumstances, and he now set himself to its execution with his usual vigor.

There were allies close at hand. Near Fort Miami were the huts of twenty-five or thirty savages, exiles from their homes and strangers in this western world. Several of the English colonies, from Virginia to Maine, had of late years been harassed by Indian wars, and the Puritans of New England, above all, had been scourged by the deadly outbreak of King Philip's War. Those engaged in it had paid a bitter price for their brief triumphs. A band of refugees, chiefly Abenakis and Mohegans, driven from their native seats, had roamed into these distant wilds and were wintering in the friendly neighborhood of the French.

La Salle soon won them over to his interests. One of their number was the Mohegan hunter who for two years had faithfully followed his fortunes and who had been four years in the West. He is described as a prudent and discreet young man in whom La Salle had great confidence and who could make himself understood in several western languages belonging, like his own, to the great Algonquin tongue. This devoted henchman proved an efficient mediator with his countrymen. The New England Indians, with one voice, promised to follow La Salle, asking no recompense but to call him their chief and yield to him the love and admiration which he rarely failed to command from this hero-worshiping race.

New allies soon appeared. A Shawanoe chief from the valley of the Ohio, whose following embraced a hundred and fifty warriors, came to ask the protection of the French against the all-destroying Iroquois. "The Shawanoes are too distant," was La Salle's reply, "but let them come to me at the Illinois and they shall be safe." The chief promised to join him in the autumn at Fort Miami with all his band. But more important than all, the consent and co-operation of the Illinois must be gained, and the Miamis, their neighbors and of late their enemies, must be taught the folly of their league with the Iroquois and the necessity of joining in the new confederation.

248

Of late they had been made to see the perfidy of their dangerous allies. A band of the Iroquois, returning from the slaughter of the Tamaroa Illinois, had met and murdered a band of Miamis on the Ohio and had not only refused satisfaction but had intrenched themselves in three rude forts of trees and brushwood in the heart of the Miami country. The moment was favorable for negotiating, but first La Salle wished to open a communication with the Illinois, some of whom had begun to return to the country they had abandoned. With this view, and also it seems to procure provisions, he set out on the first of March with his lieutenant, La Forest, and fifteen men.

The country was sheeted in snow and the party journeyed on snow-shoes but when they reached the open prairies the white expanse glared in the sun with so dazzling a brightness that La Salle and several of the men became snow-blind. They stopped and encamped under the edge of a forest and here La Salle remained in darkness for three days, suffering extreme pain. Meanwhile he sent forward La Forest and most of the men, keeping with him his old attendant Hunaut. Going out in quest of pine leaves, a decoction of which was supposed to be useful in cases of snow blindness, this man discovered the fresh tracks of Indians, followed them and found a camp of Outagamis, or Foxes, from the neighborhood of Green Bay. From them he heard welcome news. They told him that Tonty was safe among the Potawatomis and that Hennepin had passed through their country on his return from among the Sioux.

A thaw took place. The snow melted rapidly, the rivers were opened, the blind men began to recover, and launching the canoes which they had dragged after them, the party pursued their way by water. They soon met a band of Illinois. La Salle gave them presents, condoled with them on their losses and urged them to make peace and alliance with the Miamis. Thus, he said, they could set the Iroquois at defiance, for he himself with his Frenchmen and his Indian friends would make his abode among them, supply them with goods and aid them to defend themselves. They listened, well pleased, promised to carry his message to their countrymen and furnished him with a large supply of corn. Meanwhile he had rejoined La Forest, whom he now sent to Michilimackinac to await Tonty and tell him to remain there till he, La Salle, should arrive.

Having thus accomplished the objects of his journey, he returned to Fort Miami, from where he soon after ascended the St. Joseph to the village of the Miami Indians, on the portage at the head of the Kankakee.

Here he found unwelcome guests. These were three Iroquois warriors who had been for some time in the place and who, as he was told, had demeaned themselves with the insolence of conquerors and spoken of the French with the utmost contempt. He hastened to confront them and told them that now, when he was present, they dared not repeat the calumnies which they had uttered in his absence. They stood abashed and confounded, and during the following night secretly left the town and fled. The effect was prodigious on the minds of the Miamis when they saw that La Salle, backed by ten Frenchmen, could command from their arrogant visitors a respect which they, with their hundreds of warriors, had wholly failed to inspire. Here at the outset was an augury full of promise for the approaching negotiations.

There were other strangers in the town—a band of eastern Indians, more numerous than those who had wintered at the fort. The greater number were from Rhode Island, including probably some of King Philip's warriors. Others were from New York, and others again from Virginia.

La Salle called them to a council, promised them a new home in the West under the protection of the Great King, with rich lands, an abundance of game, and French traders to supply them with the goods which they had once received from the English. Let them but help him to make peace between the Miamis and the Illinois and he would insure for them a future of prosperity and safety. They listened with open ears and promised their aid in the work of peace.

On the next morning the Miamis were called to a grand council. It was held in the lodge of their chief, from which the mats were removed so that the crowd without might hear what was said. La Salle rose and harangued the concourse. Few men were so skilled in the arts of forest rhetoric and diplomacy. He was, to follow his chroniclers, "the greatest orator in North America."

He began with a gift of tobacco, to clear the brains of his auditory. Next, for he had brought a canoeload of presents to support his eloquence, he gave them cloth to cover their dead, coats to dress them, hatchets to build a grand scaffold in their honor and beads, bells and trinkets of all sorts to decorate their relatives at a grand funeral feast. All this was mere metaphor. The living, while appropriating the gifts to their own use, were pleased at the compliment offered to their dead and their delight redoubled as the orator proceeded.

One of their great chiefs had lately been killed, and La Salle, after a eulogy of the departed, declared that he would now raise him to life again—that is, that he would assume his name and give support to his squaws and children. This flattering announcement drew forth an outburst of applause, and when, to confirm his words, his attendants placed before them a huge pile of coats, shirts and hunting knives, the whole assembly exploded in yelps of admiration.

Now came the climax of the harangue, introduced by a further present of six guns: "He who is my master, and the master of all this country, is a mighty chief, feared by the whole world; but he loves peace, and the words of his lips are for good alone. He is called the King of France, and he is the mightiest among the chiefs beyond the great water. His goodness reaches even to your dead, and his subjects come among you to raise them up to life. But it is his will to preserve the life he has given; it is his will that you should obey his laws, and make no war without the leave of Onontio, who commands in his name at Quebec, and who loves all the nations alike, because such is the will of the Great King.

"You ought, then, to live at peace with your neighbors, and above all with the Illinois. You have had causes of quarrel with them; but their defeat has avenged you. Though they are still strong, they wish to make peace with you. Be content with the glory of having obliged them to ask for it. You have an interest in preserving them, since if the Iroquois destroy them, they will next destroy you. Let us all obey the Great King, and live together in peace under his protection. Be of my mind, and use these guns that I have given you, not to make war, but only to hunt and to defend yourselves."

So saying, he gave two belts of wampum to confirm his words, and the assembly dissolved. On the following day the chiefs again convoked it and made their reply in form. It was all that La Salle could have wished. "The Illinois is our brother because he is the son of our Father, the Great King. We make you the master of our beaver and our lands, of our minds and our bodies. We cannot wonder that our brothers from the East wish to live with you. We should have wished so too, if we had known what a blessing it is to be the children of the Great King."

The rest of this auspicious day was passed in feasts and dances, in which La Salle and his Frenchmen all bore part. His new scheme was hopefully begun. It remained to achieve the enterprise, twice defeated, of the discovery of the mouth of the Mississippi—that vital condition of his triumph without which all other success was meaningless and vain.

To this end he must return to Canada, appease his creditors and collect his scattered resources. Towards the end of May he set out in canoes from Fort Miami and reached Michilimackinac after a prosperous voyage. Here, to his great joy, he found Tonty and Zenobe Membré, who had lately arrived from Green Bay. The meeting was one at which even his stoic nature must have melted. Each had for the other a tale of disaster, but when La Salle recounted the long succession of his reverses, it was with the tranquil tone and cheerful look of one who relates the incidents of an ordinary journey. Without loss of time they embarked together for Fort Frontenac, paddled their canoes a thousand miles and safely reached their destination.

At the beginning of the autumn, starting out anew, La Salle was at Toronto, where the long and difficult portage to Lake Simcoe detained him a fortnight, and it was October before he reached Lake Huron. Day after day and week after week the heavy-laden canoes crept on along the lonely wilderness shores, by the monotonous ranks of bristling moss-bearded firs; lake and forest, forest and lake; a dreary scene haunted with yet more deary memories—disasters, sorrows and deferred hopes; time, strength and wealth spent in vain; a ruinous past and a doubtful future; slander, obloquy and hate. With unmoved heart, the patient voyager held his course and drew up his canoes at last on the beach at Fort Miami.

The season was far advanced. On the bare limbs of the forest hung a few withered remnants of its gay autumnal livery, and the smoke crept upward through the sullen November air from the squalid wigwams of La Salle's Abenaki and Mohegan allies. These, his new friends, were savages whose midnight yells had startled the border hamlets of New England, who had danced around Puritan scalps and whom Puritan imaginations painted as incarnate fiends.

La Salle chose eighteen of them, whom he added to the twenty-three Frenchmen who remained with him, some of the rest having deserted and others lagged behind. The Indians insisted on taking their squaws with them. These were ten in number, besides three children. Thus the expedition included fifty-four persons, of whom some were useless and others a burden.

On the twenty-first of December, Tonty and Membré set out from Fort Miami with some of the party in six canoes and crossed to the little river Chicago. La Salle, with the rest of the men, joined them a few days later. It was the dead of winter and the streams were frozen. They made sledges, placed on them the canoes, the baggage and a disabled Frenchman, crossed from the Chicago to the northern branch of the Illinois and filed in a long procession down its frozen course. They reached the site of the great Illinois village, found it tenantless and continued their journey, still dragging their canoes, till at length they reached open water below Lake Peoria.

La Salle had abandoned for a time his original plan of building a vessel for the navigation of the Mississippi. Bitter experience had taught him the difficulty of the attempt and he resolved to trust to his canoes alone. They embarked again, floating prosperously down between the leafless forests that flanked the tranquil river, till on the sixth of February they issued upon the majestic bosom of the Mississippi. Here, for the time, their progress was stopped, for the river was full of floating ice. La Salle's Indians, too, had lagged behind, but within a week all had arrived, the navigation was once more free and they resumed their course.

Towards evening they saw on their right the mouth of a great river, and the clear current was invaded by the headlong torrent of the Missouri, opaque with mud. They built their campfires in the neighboring forest, and at daylight, embarking anew on the dark and mighty stream, drifted swiftly down towards unknown destinies. They passed a deserted town of the Tamaroas, saw three days after the mouth of the Ohio and, gliding by the wastes of bordering swamp, landed on the twenty-fourth of February near the Third Chickasaw Bluffs. They encamped and the hunters went out for game.

Again they embarked, and with every stage of their adventurous progress the mystery of this vast New World was more and more unveiled. More and more they entered the realms of spring. The hazy sunlight, the warm and drowsy air, the tender foliage, the opening flowers betokened the reviving life of Nature. For several days more they followed the writhings of the great river on its tortuous ,course through wastes of swamp and canebrake, till on the thirteenth of March they found themselves wrapped in a thick fog. Neither shore was visible, but they heard on the right the booming of an Indian drum and the shrill outcries of the war dance. La Salle at once crossed to the opposite side, where in less than an hour his men threw up a rude fort of felled trees.

Meanwhile the fog cleared and from the farther bank the astonished Indians saw the strange visitors at their work. Some of the French advanced to the edge of the water and beckoned them to come over. Several of them approached in a wooden canoe to within the distance of a gunshot. La Salle displayed the calumet and sent a Frenchman to meet them. He was well received, and the friendly mood of the Indians being now apparent, the whole party crossed the river. On landing, they found themselves at a town of the Kappa band of the Arkansas, a people dwelling near the mouth of the river which bears their name.

Various were the dances and ceremonies with which they entertained the strangers, who on their part responded with a solemnity which their hosts would have liked less if they had understood it better. La Salle and Tonty, at the head of their followers, marched to the open area in the midst of the village. Here, to the admiration of the gazing crowd of warriors, women and children, a cross was raised bearing the arms of France. Membré, in canonicals, sang a hymn, the men shouted *Vive le Roi* and La Salle in the King's name took formal possession of the country. The friar, not he flatters himself without success, labored to expound by signs the mysteries of the Faith, while La Salle, by methods equally satisfactory, drew from the chief an acknowledgment of fealty to Louis XIV.

After touching at several other towns of this people, the voyagers resumed their course, guided by two of the Arkansas, passed the sites of Vicksburg and Grand Gulf and, about three hundred miles below the Arkansas, stopped by the edge of a swamp on the western side of the river. Here, as their two guides told them, was the path to the great town of the Taensas. Tonty and Membré were sent to visit it. They and their men shouldered their birch canoe through the swamp and launched it on a lake which had once formed a portion of the channel of the river.

In two hours they reached the town, and Tonty gazed at it with astonishment. He had seen nothing like it in America—large, square dwellings built of sun-baked mud mixed with straw, arched over with a dome-shaped roof of canes and placed in regular order around an open area. Two of them were larger and better than the rest. One was the lodge of the chief; the other was the temple, or house of the Sun. They entered the former and found a single room, forty feet square, where in the dim light—for there was no opening but the door—the chief sat awaiting them on a sort of bedstead, three of his wives at his side, while sixty old men wrapped in white cloaks woven of mulberry bark formed his divan. When he spoke his wives howled to do him honor and the assembled councilors listened with the reverence due to a potentate for whom, at his death, a hundred victims were to be sacrificed. He received the visitors graciously and joyfully accepted the gifts which Tonty laid before him.

The chief condescended to visit La Salle at his camp—a favor which he would by no means have granted had the visitors been Indians. A master of ceremonies and six attendants preceded him, to clear the path and prepare the place of meeting. When all was ready, he was seen advancing, clothed in a white robe and preceded by two men bearing white fans, while a third displayed a disk of burnished copper, doubtless to represent the Sun, his ancestor, or, as others will have it, his elder brother. His aspect was marvelously grave and he and La Salle met with gestures of ceremonious courtesy. The interview was very friendly and the chief returned well pleased with the gifts which his entertainer bestowed on him, and which indeed had been the principal motive of his visit.

On the next morning, as they descended the river, they saw a wooden canoe full of Indians, and Tonty gave chase. He had nearly overtaken it when more than a hundred men appeared suddenly on the shore, with bows bent to defend their countrymen. La Salle called out to Tonty to withdraw. He obeyed and the whole party encamped on the opposite bank. Tonty offered to cross the river with a peace pipe, and set out accordingly with a small party of men. When he landed the Indians made signs of friendship by joining their hands, a proceeding by which Tonty, having but one hand, was somewhat embarrassed, but he directed his men to respond in his stead. La Salle and Membré now joined him and went with the Indians to their village, three leagues distant. Here they spent the night.

"The Sieur de la Salle," writes Membré, "whose very air, engaging manners, tact and address attract love and respect alike, produced such an effect on the hearts of these people that they did not know how to treat us well enough."

The Indians of this village were the Natchez and their chief was brother of the great chief, or Sun, of the whole nation. His town was several leagues distant, near the site of the city of Natchez, and there the French repaired to visit him. They saw what they had already seen among the Taensas—a religious and political despotism, a privileged caste descended from the sun, a temple and a sacred fire. La Salle planted a large cross with the arms of France attached in the midst of the town, while the inhabitants looked on with a satisfaction which they would hardly have displayed had they understood the meaning of the act.

The French next visited the Coroas at their village two leagues below, and here they found a reception no less auspicious. On the thirty-first of March, as they approached Red River, they passed in the fog a town of the Oumas and three days later discovered a party of fishermen in wooden canoes among the canes along the margin of the water. They fled at sight of the Frenchmen.

La Salle sent men to reconnoiter, who as they struggled through the marsh were greeted with a shower of arrows, while from the neighboring village of the Quinipissas, invisible behind the canebrake, they heard the sound of an Indian drum and the whoops of the mustering warriors. La Salle, anxious to keep the peace with all the tribes along the river, recalled his men and pursued his voyage. A few leagues below they saw a cluster of Indian lodges on the left bank, apparently void of inhabitants. They landed and found three of them filled with corpses. It was a village of the Tangibao, sacked by their enemies only a few days before.

And now they neared their journey's end. On the sixth of April the river divided itself into three broad channels. La Salle followed that of the west and Dautray that of the east, while Tonty took the middle passage. As he drifted down the turbid current between the low and marshy shores, the brackish water changed to brine and the breeze grew fresh with the salt breath of the sea. Then the broad bosom of the great gulf opened on his sight, tossing its restless billows, limitless, voiceless, lonely as when born of chaos, without a sail, without a sign of life.

La Salle, in a canoe, coasted the marshy borders of the sea and then the reunited parties assembled on a spot of dry ground a short distance above the mouth of the river. Here a column was made ready bearing the arms of France and inscribed with the words "Louis le Grand, Roy de France et de Navarre, Règne; le neuvième Avril 1682."

The Frenchmen were mustered under arms, and while the New England Indians and their squaws looked on in wondering silence, they chanted the *Te Deum,* the *Exaudiat* and the *Domine salvum fac Regem.* Then, amid volleys of musketry and shouts of *Vive le Roi,* La Salle planted the column in its place and, standing near it, recited a long proclamation of possession in a loud voice.

Shouts of *Vive le Roi* and volleys of musketry responded to his words. Then a cross was planted beside the column and a leaden plate buried near it, bearing the arms of France with a Latin inscription, *Ludovicus Magnus regnat.* The weather-beaten voyagers joined their voices in the grand hymn of the *Vexilla Regis:*

> *"The banners of Heaven's King advance,*
> *The mystery of the Cross shines forth . . ."*

and renewed shouts of *Vive le Roi* closed the ceremony.

On that day the realm of France received on parchment a stupendous accession. The fertile plains of Texas; the vast basin of the Mississippi, from its frozen northern springs to the sultry borders of the gulf; from the woody ridges of the Alleghenies to the bare peaks of the Rocky Mountains—a region of savannas and forests, sun-cracked deserts and grassy prairies, watered by a thousand rivers, ranged by a thousand warlike tribes, passed beneath the scepter of the Sultan of Versailles, and all by virtue of a feeble human voice, inaudible at half a mile.

CHAPTER 7

A New Enterprise

COUNT FRONTENAC WAS IN POWER NO LONGER. HE had been recalled to France through the intrigues of the party adverse to La Salle, and Le Febvre de la Barre reigned in his stead. La Barre was an old naval officer of rank, advanced to a post for which he proved himself notably unfit. If he was without the arbitrary passions which had been the chief occasion of the recall of his predecessor, he was no less without his energies and his talents. He showed a weakness and an avarice for which his age may have been in some measure answerable. He was no whit less unscrupulous than his predecessor in his secret violation of the royal ordinances regulating the fur trade, which it was his duty to enforce. Like Frontenac, he took advantage of his position to carry on an illicit traffic with the Indians, but it was with different associates. The late governor's friends were the new governor's enemies, and La Salle, armed with his monopolies, was the object of his special jealousy.

Meanwhile, La Salle, buried in the western wilderness, remained for the time ignorant of La Barre's disposition towards him and made an effort to secure his good will and countenance. He wrote to him from his colony of Fort St. Louis, on Starved Rock, early in the spring of 1683, expressing the hope that he should have from him the same support as from Count Frontenac, "although," he says, "my enemies will try to influence you against me." His attachment to Frontenac, he pursues, has been the cause of all the late governor's enemies turning against him. He then recounts his voyage down the

Mississippi, says that with twenty-two Frenchmen he caused all the tribes along the river to ask for peace, and speaks of his right under the royal patent to build forts anywhere along his route and grant out lands around them, as at Fort Frontenac.

While La Salle was thus writing to La Barre, La Barre was writing to Seignelay, the Marine and Colonial Minister, decrying his correspondent's discoveries and pretending to doubt their reality. "The Iroquois," he adds, "have sworn his (La Salle's) death. The imprudence of this man is about to involve the colony in war." And again he writes, in the following spring, to say that La Salle was with a score of vagabonds at Green Bay, where he set himself up as a king, pillaged his countrymen and put them to ransom, exposed the tribes of the West to the incursions of the Iroquois, and all under pretense of a patent from His Majesty, the provisions of which he grossly abused, but as his privileges would expire on the twelfth of May ensuing, he would then be forced to come to Quebec, where his creditors, to whom he owned more than thirty thousand crowns, were anxiously awaiting him.

Finally, when La Barre had received two letters from La Salle, he sent copies of them to the Minister Seignelay with the following comment: "By the copies of the Sieur de la Salle's letters, you will perceive that his head is turned, and that he has been bold enough to give you intelligence of a false discovery, and that, instead of returning to the colony to learn what the King wishes him to do, he does not come near me, but keeps in the backwoods, five hundred leagues off, with the idea of attracting the inhabitants to him, and building up an imaginary kingdom for himself, by debauching all the bankrupts and idlers of this country. If you will look at the two letters I had from him, you can judge the character of this personage better than I can. Affairs with the Iroquois are in such a state that I cannot allow him to muster all their enemies together and put himself at their head. All the men who brought me news from him have abandoned him, and say not a word about returning, but sell the furs they have brought as if they were their own; so that he cannot hold his ground much longer."

Such calumnies had their effect. The enemies of La Salle had already gained the ear of the King, and he had written in August from

Fontainebleau to his new governor of Canada: "I am convinced, like you, that the discovery of the Sieur de la Salle is very useless, and that such enterprises ought to be prevented in future, as they tend only to debauch the inhabitants by the hope of gain, and to diminish the revenue from beaver skins."

In order to understand the state of affairs at this time, it must be remembered that Dutch and English traders of New York were urging on the Iroquois to attack the western tribes, with the object of gaining, through their conquest, the control of the fur trade of the interior and diverting it from Montreal to Albany. The scheme was full of danger to Canada, which the loss of the trade would have ruined. La Barre and his associates were greatly alarmed at it. Its complete success would have been fatal to their hopes of profit, but they nevertheless wished it such a measure of success as would ruin their rival, La Salle.

Thus no little satisfaction mingled with their anxiety when they heard that the Iroquois were again threatening to invade the Miamis and the Illinois, and thus La Barre, whose duty it was strenuously to oppose the intrigue of the English and use every effort to quiet the ferocious bands whom they were hounding against the Indian allies of the French, was in fact but halfhearted in the work. He cut off La Salle from all supplies, detained the men whom he had sent for succor and at a conference with the Iroquois told them that they were welcome to plunder and kill him.

The old governor and the unscrupulous ring with which he was associated now took a step to which he was doubtless emboldened by the tone of the King's letter in condemnation of La Salle's enterprise. He resolved to seize Fort Frontenac, the property of La Salle, under the pretext that the latter had not fulfilled the conditions of the grant and had not maintained a sufficient garrison.

Two of his associates, La Chesnaye and Le Ber, armed with an order from him, went up and took possession, despite the remonstrances of La Salle's creditors and mortgagees, lived on La Salle's stores, sold for their own profit and (it is said) that of La Barre the provisions sent by the King and turned in the cattle to pasture on the growing crops. La Forest, La Salle's lieutenant, was told that he might retain the command of the fort if he would join the associates, but he refused and sailed in the autumn for France.

Meanwhile La Salle remained at the Illinois in extreme embarrassment, cut off from supplies, robbed of his men who had gone to seek them and disabled from fulfilling the pledges he had given to the surrounding Indians. Such was his position when reports came to Fort St. Louis that the Iroquois were at hand. The Indian hamlets were wild with terror, beseeching him for succor which he had no power to give. Happily, the report proved false. No Iroquois appeared, the threatened attack was postponed and the summer passed away in peace. But La Salle's position, with the governor his declared enemy, was intolerable and untenable and there was no resource but in the protection of the court. Early in the autumn he left Tonty in command of the rock, bade farewell to his savage retainers and descended to Quebec, intending to sail for France.

On his way he met the Chevalier de Baugis, an officer of the King's dragoons, commissioned by La Barre to take possession of Fort St. Louis and bearing letters from the governor ordering La Salle to come to Quebec—a superfluous command, since he was then on his way there.

He smothered his wrath and wrote to Tonty to receive De Baugis well. The chevalier and his party proceeded to the Illinois and took possession of the fort, De Baugis commanding for the governor, while Tonty remained as representative of La Salle. The two officers could not live in harmony, but with the return of spring each found himself in sore need of aid from the other. Towards the end of March the Iroquois attacked their citadel and besieged it for six days, but at length withdrew discomfited, carrying with them a number of Indian prisoners, most of whom escaped from their clutches.

Meanwhile, La Salle had sailed for France.

The news of his discovery and the rumor of his schemes were the talk of a moment among the courtiers and then were forgotten. It was not so with their master, the King. La Salle's friends and patrons did not fail him. A student and a recluse in his youth and a backwoodsman in his manhood, he had what was to him the formidable honor of an interview with royalty itself, and stood with such philosophy as he could command before the gilded armchair where, majestic and awful, the power of France sat embodied. The King listened to all he said, but the results of the interview were kept so secret that it was rumored in the antechambers that his proposals had been rejected.

On the contrary, they had met with more than favor. The moment was opportune for La Salle. The King had long been irritated against the Spaniards because they had not only excluded his subjects from their American ports but forbade them to enter the Gulf of Mexico. Certain Frenchmen who had sailed on this forbidden sea had been seized and imprisoned, and more recently a small vessel of the royal navy had been captured for the same offense. This had drawn from the King a declaration that every sea should be free to all his subjects, and Count d'Estrees was sent with a squadron to the gulf to exact satisfaction of the Spaniards, or fight them if they refused it.

This was in time of peace. War had since arisen between the two crowns and brought with it the opportunity of settling the question forever. In order to do so, the minister Seignelay, like his father Colbert, proposed to establish a French port on the gulf, as a permanent menace to the Spaniards and a basis of future conquest. It was in view of this plan that La Salle's past enterprises had been favored and the proposals he now made were in perfect accord with it.

These proposals were set forth in two memorials. The first of them states that the late Monseigneur Colbert deemed it important for the service of His Majesty to discover a port in the Gulf of Mexico; that to this end the memorialist, La Salle, made five journeys of upwards of five thousand leagues, in great part on foot, and traversed more than six hundred leagues of unknown country, among savages and cannibals, at the cost of a hundred and fifty thousand francs. He now proposes to return by way of the Gulf of Mexico and the mouth of the Mississippi to the countries he has discovered, whence great benefits may be expected: first, the cause of God may be advanced by the preaching of the gospel to many Indian tribes; and secondly, great conquests may be effected for the glory of the King by the seizure of provinces rich in silver mines and defended only by a few indolent and effeminate Spaniards.

The Sieur de la Salle, pursues the memorial, binds himself to be ready for the accomplishment of this enterprise within one year after his arrival on the spot and he asks for this purpose only one vessel and two hundred men, with their arms, munitions, pay and maintenance. When Monseigneur shall direct him, he will give the details of what he proposes. The memorial then describes the boundless extent, the fertility and resources of the country watered by the river Colbert, or Mississippi; the necessity of guarding it against foreigners, who will be eager to seize it now that La Salle's discovery has made it known; and the ease with which it may be defended by one or two forts at a proper distance above its mouth, which would form the key to an interior region eight hundred leagues in extent.

"Should foreigners anticipate us," he adds, "they will complete the ruin of New France, which they already hem in by their establishments of Virginia, Pennsylvania, New England and Hudson's Bay."

The second memorial is more explicit. The place, it says, which the Sieur de la Salle proposes to fortify is on the river Colbert, or Mississippi, sixty leagues above its mouth, where the soil is very fertile, the climate very mild, and whence we, the French, may control the continent—since, the river being narrow, we could defend ourselves by means of fireships against a hostile fleet, while the position is excellent both for attacking an enemy or retreating in case of need.

The neighboring Indians detest the Spaniards but love the French, having been won over by the kindness of the Sieur de la Salle. We could form of them an army of more than fifteen thousand savages who, supported by the French and Abenakis, followers of the Sieur de la Salle, could easily subdue the province of New Biscay (the most northern province of Mexico) where there are but four hundred Spaniards, more fit to work the mines than to fight. On the north of New Biscay lie vast forests, extending to the river Seignelay (Red River), which is but forty or fifty leagues from the Spanish province. This river affords the means of attacking it to great advantage.

In view of these facts, pursues the memorial, the Sieur de la Salle offers, if the war with Spain continues, to undertake this conquest with two hundred men from France. He will take on his way fifty buccaneers at St. Domingo and direct the four thousand Indian warriors at Fort St. Louis of the Illinois to descend the river and join him. He will separate his force into three divisions and attack at the same time the center and the two extremities of the province.

To accomplish this great design, he asks only for a vessel of thirty guns, a few cannon for the forts and power to raise in France two hundred such men as he shall think fit, to be armed, paid and maintained six months at the King's charge. And the Sieur de la Salle binds himself, if the execution of this plan is prevented for more than three years, by peace with Spain, to refund to His Majesty all the costs of the enterprise, on pain of forfeiting to the government the ports he will have established.

Such, in brief, was the substance of this singular proposition. And first it is to be observed that it is based on a geographical blunder, the nature of which is explained by a map of La Salle's discoveries made in that very year. Here the river Seignelay, or Red River, is represented as running parallel to the northern border of Mexico and at no great distance from it—the region now called Texas being almost entirely suppressed. According to the map, New Biscay might be reached from this river in a few days, and after crossing the intervening forests the coveted mines of Ste. Barbe, or Santa Barbara, would be within striking distance.

That La Salle believed in the possibility of invading the Spanish province of New Biscay from Red River there can be no doubt. Neither can it be reasonably doubted that he hoped at some future day to make the attempt, and yet it is incredible that a man in his sober senses could have proposed this scheme with the intention of attempting to execute it at the time and in the manner which he indicates.

This memorial bears some indications of being drawn up in order to produce a certain effect on the minds of the King and his minister. La Salle's immediate necessity was to obtain from them the means for establishing a fort and a colony within the mouth of the Mississippi. This was essential to his own plans, nor did he in the least exaggerate the value of such an establishment to the French nation and the importance of anticipating other powers in the possession of it. But he thought that he needed a more glittering lure to attract the eyes of Louis and Seignelay, and thus it may be he held before them, in a definite and tangible form, the project of Spanish conquest which had haunted his imagination from youth, trusting that the speedy conclusion of peace, which actually took place, would absolve him from the immediate execution of the scheme and give him time, with the means placed at his disposal, to mature his plans and prepare for eventual action.

Even with this madcap enterprise lopped off, La Salle's scheme of Mississippi trade and colonization, perfectly sound in itself, was too vast for an individual—above all, for one crippled and crushed with debt. While he grasped one link of the great chain, another no less essential escaped from his hand; while he built up a colony on the Mississippi, it was reasonably certain that evil would befall his distant colony of the Illinois.

The glittering project which he now unfolded found favor in the eyes of the King and his minister, for both were in the flush of an unparalleled success and looked in the future, as in the past, for nothing but triumphs. They granted more than the petitioner asked, as indeed they well might, if they expected the accomplishment of all that he proposed to attempt. La Forest, La Salle's lieutenant, ejected from Fort Frontenac by La Barre, was now at Paris, and he was dispatched to Canada, empowered to reoccupy in La Salle's name both Fort Frontenac and Fort St. Louis of the Illinois.

La Salle had asked for two vessels and four were given to him. Agents were sent to Rochelle and Rochefort to gather recruits. A hundred soldiers were enrolled, besides mechanics and laborers, and thirty volunteers, including gentlemen and burghers of condition, joined the expedition. And as the plan was one no less of colonization than of war, several families embarked for the new land of promise, as well as a number of girls, lured by the prospect of almost certain matrimony. Nor were missionaries wanting. Among them was La Salle's brother, Cavelier, and two other priests of St. Sulpice. Three Récollets were added: Zenobe Membré, who was then in France, Anastase Douay and Maxime Le Clerc. The principal vessel was the *Joly,* belonging to the royal navy and carrying thirty-six guns. Another armed vessel of six guns was added, together with a storeship and a ketch.

La Salle had asked for sole command of the expedition, with a subaltern officer and one or two pilots to sail the vessels as he should direct. Instead of complying, Seignelay gave the command of the vessels to Beaujeu, a captain of the royal navy, whose authority was restricted to their management at sea, while La Salle was to prescribe the route they were to take and have entire control of the troops and colonists on land. This arrangement displeased both parties. Beaujeu, an old and experienced officer, was galled that a civilian should be set over him—and he, too, a burgher lately ennobled. Nor was La Salle the man to soothe his ruffled spirit.

Preparation dragged slowly on. The season was growing late, the King grew impatient and found fault with the naval intendant. Meanwhile the various members of the expedition had all gathered at Rochelle. Joutel, a fellow townsman of La Salle, returning to his native Rouen after sixteen years in the army, found all astir with the new project. His father had been gardener to Henri Cavelier, La Salle's uncle, and being of an adventurous spirit, he volunteered for the enterprise, of which he was to become the historian. With La Salle's brother, the priest, and two of his nephews, one of whom was a boy of fourteen, Joutel set out for Rochelle, where all were to embark together for their promised land.

CHAPTER 8

La Salle in Texas

THE FOUR SHIPS SAILED FROM ROCHELLE ON THE twenty-fourth of July. Four days after, the *Joly* broke her bowsprit, by design as La Salle fancied. They all put back to Rochefort, where the mischief was quickly repaired and they put to sea again. La Salle and the chief persons of the expedition, with a crowd of soldiers, artisans and women, the destined mothers of Louisiana, were all on board the *Joly*. Beaujeu wished to touch at Madeira to replenish his water casks. La Salle refused, lest by doing so the secret of the enterprise might reach the Spaniards. One Paget, a Huguenot, took up the word in support of Beaujeu. La Salle told him that the affair was none of his, and as Paget persisted with increased warmth and freedom, he demanded of Beaujeu if it was with his consent that a man of no rank spoke to him in that manner. Beaujeu sustained the Huguenot.

"That is enough," returned La Salle, and withdrew into his cabin.

This was not the first misunderstanding, nor was it the last. There was incessant chafing between the two commanders, and the sailors of the *Joly* were soon of one mind with their captain. When the ship crossed the tropic they made ready a tub on deck to baptize the passengers, but La Salle refused to permit it, at which they were highly exasperated, having promised themselves a bountiful ransom in money or liquor from their victims. "Assuredly," says Joutel, "they would gladly have killed us all."

When the ships reached St. Domingo after a wretched voyage of two months, a fresh dispute occurred. It had been resolved at a council of officers to stop at Port de Paix, but Beaujeu, on pretext of a fair wind, ran by that place in the night and cast anchor at Petit Goave, on the other side of the island. La Salle was extremely vexed, for he expected to meet at Port de Paix the Marquis de Saint-Laurent, lieutenant general of the islands, Bégon the intendant and De Cussy, governor of La Tortue, who had orders to supply him with provisions and give him all possible aid.

The *Joly* was alone; the other vessels had lagged behind. She had more than fifty sick men on board, and La Salle was of the number. He sent a messenger to Saint-Laurent, Bégon and Cussy, begging them to come to him, ordered Joutel to get the sick ashore, suffocating as they were in the hot and crowded ship, and caused the soldiers to be landed on a small island in the harbor.

Scarcely had the voyagers sung *Te Deum* for their safe arrival when two of the lagging vessels appeared, bringing tidings that the third, the ketch *St. François,* had been taken by Spanish buccaneers. She was laden with provisions, tools and other necessaries for the colony and the loss was irreparable. Beaujeu was answerable for it, for had he anchored at Port de Paix, it would not have occurred. The lieutenant general, with Bégon and Cussy, who presently arrived, plainly spoke their minds to him.

La Salle's illness increased. "I was walking with him one day," writes Joutel, "when he was seized of a sudden with such a weakness that he could not stand and was obliged to lie down on the ground. When he was a little better, I led him to a chamber of a house that the brothers Duhaut had hired. Here we put him to bed, and in the morning he was attacked by a violent fever." "It was so violent that," says another of his shipmates, "his imagination pictured to him things equally terrible and amazing." He lay delirious in the wretched garret, attended by his brother and one or two others who stood faithful to him.

A goldsmith of the neighborhood, moved at his deplorable condition, offered the use of his house, and Abbé Cavelier had him removed there. But there was a tavern hard by and the patient was tormented with daily and nightly riot. At the height of his fever a party of Beaujeu's sailors spent a night in singing and dancing before the house, and says Cavelier, "The more we begged them to be quiet, the more noise they made."

La Salle lost reason and well nigh life, but at length his mind resumed its balance and the violence of the disease abated. A friendly Capucin friar offered him the shelter of his roof, and two of his men supported him there on foot, giddy with exhaustion and hot with fever. Here he found repose and was slowly recovering when some of his attendants rashly told him of the loss of the ketch *St. François*. The consequence was a critical return of the disease.

There was no one to fill his place. Beaujeu would not; Cavelier could not. Joutel, the gardener's son, was apparently the most trusty man of the company, but the expedition was virtually without a head. The men roamed on shore and plunged into every excess of debauchery, contracting diseases which eventually killed them.

"The air of this place is bad," says Joutel, "so are the fruits; and there are plenty of women worse than either."

It was near the end of November before La Salle could resume the voyage. He was told that Beaujeu had said that he would not wait longer for the storeship *Aimable* and that she might follow as she could. Moreover, La Salle was on ill terms with Aigron, her captain, who had declared that he would have nothing more to do with him. Fearing, therefore, that some mishap might befall her, he resolved to embark in her himself with his brother Cavelier, Membré, Douay and others, the trustiest of his followers.

On the twenty-fifth they set sail, the *Joly* and the little frigate *Belle* following. They coasted the shore of Cuba and landed at the Isle of Pines, where La Salle shot an alligator, which the soldiers ate, and the hunter brought in a wild pig, half of which he sent to Beaujeu. Then they advanced to Cape St. Antoine, where bad weather and contrary winds long detained them. A load of cares oppressed the mind of La Salle, pale and haggard with recent illness, wrapped within his own thoughts and seeking sympathy from none.

At length they entered the Gulf of Mexico, that forbidden sea whence by a Spanish decree, dating from the reign of Philip II, all foreigners were excluded on pain of extermination. Not a man on board knew the secrets of its perilous navigation. Cautiously feeling their way, they held a northwesterly course till on the twenty-eighth of December a sailor at the masthead of the *Aimable* saw land. La Salle and all the pilots had been led to form an exaggerated idea of the force of the easterly currents and they therefore supposed themselves near the Bay of Appalache, when in fact they were much farther westward.

On New Year's Day they anchored three leagues from the shore. La Salle, with the engineer Minet, went to explore it and found nothing but a vast marshy plain, studded with clumps of rushes. Two days after there was a thick fog, and when at length it cleared the *Joly* was nowhere to be seen. La Salle in the *Aimable,* followed closely by the little frigate *Belle,* stood westward along the coast.

When at the mouth of the Mississippi in 1682, he had taken its latitude but unhappily could not determine its longitude, and now every eye on board was strained to detect in the monotonous lines of the low shore some tokens of the great river. In fact, they had already passed it. On the sixth of January a wide opening was descried between two low points of land and the adjacent sea was discolored with mud. "La Salle," writes his brother Cavelier, "has always thought that this was the Mississippi." To all appearance, it was the entrance of Galveston Bay.

He lay there five or six days, waiting in vain for Beaujeu, till at last, thinking that he must have passed westward, he resolved to follow. The *Aimable* and the *Belle* again spread their sails and coasted the shores of Texas. Joutel, with a boat's crew, tried to land, but the sand bars and breakers repelled him. A party of Indians swam out through the surf and were taken on board, but La Salle could learn nothing from them as their language was unknown to him. Again Joutel tried to land, and again the breakers repelled him. He approached as near as he dared and saw vast plains and a dim expanse of forest, buffalo running with their heavy gallop along the shore and deer grazing on the marshy meadows.

Soon after, he succeeded in landing at a point somewhere between Matagorda Island and Corpus Christi Bay. The aspect of the country was not cheering, with its barren plains, its reedy marshes, its interminable oyster beds and broad flats of mud, bare at low tide. Joutel and his men sought in vain for fresh water and, after shooting some geese and ducks, returned to the *Aimable*. Nothing had been seen of

Beaujeu and the *Joly*. The coast was trending southward, and La Salle, convinced that he must have passed the missing ship, turned to retrace his course. He had sailed but a few miles when the wind failed, a fog covered the sea and he was forced to anchor opposite one of the openings into the lagoons north of Mustang Island. At length, on the nineteenth, there came a faint breeze, the mists rolled away before it, and to his great joy he saw the *Joly* approaching.

"His joy," says Joutel, "was short." Beaujeu's lieutenant, Aire, came on board to charge him with having caused the separation, and La Salle retorted by throwing the blame on Beaujeu. Then came a debate as to their position. The priest Esmanville was present and reports that La Salle seemed greatly perplexed. He had more cause for perplexity than he knew, for in his ignorance of the longitude of the Mississippi, he had sailed more than four hundred miles beyond it.

Of this he had not the faintest suspicion. In full sight from his ship lay a reach of those vast lagoons which, separated from the sea by narrow strips of land, line this coast with little interruption from Galveston Bay to the Rio Grande. The idea took possession of him that the Mississippi discharged itself into these lagoons and made its way to the sea through the various openings he had seen along the coast, chief among which was that he had discovered on the sixth, about fifty leagues from the place where he now was.

Yet he was full of doubt as to what he should do. Four days after rejoining Beaujeu, he wrote him the strange request to land the troops that he "might fulfil his commission," that is, that he might set out against the Spaniards.

More than a week passed, a gale had set in, and nothing was done. Then La Salle wrote again, intimating some doubt as to whether he was really at one of the mouths of the Mississippi and saying that, being sure that he had passed the principal mouth, he was determined to go back to look for it. Meanwhile, Beaujeu was in a state of great irritation. The weather was stormy and the coast was dangerous. Supplies were scanty and La Salle's soldiers, still crowded in the *Joly,* were consuming the provisions of the ship. Beaujeu gave vent to his annoyance and La Salle retorted in the same strain.

According to Joutel, he urged the naval commander to sail back in search of the river and Beaujeu refused unless La Salle should give the soldiers provisions. La Salle, he adds, offered to supply them with rations for fifteen days and Beaujeu declared this insufficient.

Impatience to rid himself of his colleague and to command alone no doubt had its influence on the judgment of La Salle. He presently declared that he would land the soldiers and send them along shore till they came to the principal outlet of the river. On this the engineer Minet took up the word. He expressed his doubts as to whether the Mississippi discharged itself into the lagoons at all, represented that even if it did the soldiers would be exposed to great risks and gave as his opinion that all should reembark and continue the search in company. The advice was good, but La Salle resented it as coming from one in whom he recognized no right to give it. "He treated me," complains the engineer, "as if I were the meanest of mankind."

He persisted in his purpose and sent Joutel and Moranget with a party of soldiers to explore the coast. They made their way northeastward along the shore of Matagorda Island till they were stopped on the third day by what Joutel calls a river, but which was in fact the entrance of Matagorda Bay. Here they encamped and tried to make a raft of driftwood.

"The difficulty was," says Joutel, "our great number of men, and the few of them who were fit for anything except eating. As I said before, they had all been caught by force or surprise, so that our company was like Noah's Ark, which contained animals of all sorts." Before their raft was finished they descried to their great joy the ships which had followed them along the coast.

La Salle landed and announced that here was the western mouth of the Mississippi, and the place to which the King had sent him. He said further that he would land all his men and bring the *Aimable* and the *Belle* to the safe harborage within. Beaujeu remonstrated, alleging the shallowness of the water and the force of the currents, but his remonstrance was in vain.

The Bay of St. Louis, now Matagorda Bay, forms a broad and sheltered harbor, accessible from the sea by a narrow passage obstructed by sand bars and by the small island now called Pelican Island. Boats were sent to sound and buoy out the channel, and this was successfully accomplished on the sixteenth of February. The

273

Aimable was ordered to enter, and on the twentieth she weighed anchor. La Salle was on shore watching her. A party of men at a little distance were cutting down a tree to make a canoe. Suddenly some of them ran towards him with terrified faces, crying out that they had been set upon by a troop of Indians who had seized their companions and carried them off. La Salle ordered those about him to take their arms and at once set out in pursuit. He overtook the Indians and opened a parlay with them, but when he wished to reclaim his men he discovered that they had been led away during the conference to the Indian camp, a league and a half distant. Among them was one of his lieutenants, the young Marquis de la Sablonnière.

He was deeply vexed, for the moment was critical, but the men must be recovered and he led his followers in haste towards the camp. Yet he could not refrain from turning a moment to watch the *Aimable* as she neared the shoals, and he remarked with deep anxiety to Joutel, who was with him, that if she held that course she would soon be aground.

They hurried on till they saw the Indian huts. About fifty of them, oven-shaped and covered with mats and hides, were clustered on a rising ground, with their inmates gathered among and around them. As the French entered the camp there was the report of a cannon from seaward.

The startled savages dropped flat with terror. A different fear seized La Salle, for he knew that the shot was a signal of disaster. Looking back, he saw the *Aimable* furling her sails and his heart sank with conviction that she had struck upon the reef. Smothering his distress—she was laden with all the stores of the colony—he pressed forward among the filthy wigwams, whose astonished inmates swarmed about the band of armed strangers, staring between curiosity and fear. La Salle knew those with whom he was dealing and, without ceremony, entered the chief's lodge with his followers. The crowd closed around them, naked men and half-naked women, described by Joutel as of singular ugliness. They gave buffalo meat and dried porpoise to the unexpected guests, but La Salle, racked with anxiety, hastened to close the interview, and having without difficulty recovered the kidnaped men, he returned to the beach, leaving with the Indians as usual an impression of good will and respect.

When he reached the shore he saw his worst fears realized. The *Aimable* lay careened over on the reef, hopelessly aground. Little remained but to endure the calamity with firmness and to save as far as might be the vessel's cargo. This was no easy task. The boat which hung at her stern had been stove in—it is said, by design. Beaujeu sent a boat from the *Joly* and one or more Indian pirogues were procured. La Salle urged on his men with stern and patient energy and a quantity of gunpowder and flour was safely landed. But now the wind blew fresh from the sea, the waves began to rise, a storm came on, and the vessel, rocking to and fro on the sand bar, opened along her side and the ravenous waves were strewn with her treasures.

When the confusion was at its height a troop of Indians came down to the shore, greedy for plunder. The drum was beat; the men were called to arms; La Salle set his trustiest followers to guard the gunpowder, in fear not of the Indians alone but of his own countrymen. On that lamentable night the sentinels walked their rounds through the dreary bivouac among the casks, bales and boxes which the sea had yielded up. Here, too, their fate-hunted chief held his drearier vigil, encompassed with treachery, darkness and the storm.

Not only La Salle but Joutel and others of his party believed that the wreck of the *Aimable* was intentional. Aigron, who commanded her, had disobeyed orders and disregarded signals. Though he had been directed to tow the vessel through the channel, he went in under sail, and though little else was saved from the wreck, his personal property, including even some preserved fruits, was all landed safely. He had long been on ill terms with La Salle.

All La Salle's company were now encamped on the sands at the left side of the inlet where the *Aimable* was wrecked. "They were all," says the engineer Minet, "sick with nausea and dysentery. Five or six died every day, in consequence of brackish water and bad food. There was no grass, but plenty of rushes and plenty of oysters. There was nothing to make ovens, so that they had to eat flour saved from the wreck, boiled into messes of porridge with this brackish water.

"Along the shore were quantities of uprooted trees and rotten logs, thrown up by the sea and the lagoon."

Of these and fragments of the wreck they made a sort of rampart to protect their camp, and here, among tents and hovels, bales, boxes, casks, spars, dismounted cannon and pens for fowls and swine, were gathered the dejected men and homesick women who were to seize New Biscay and hold for France a region large as half Europe. The Spaniards, whom they were to conquer, were they knew not where. They knew not where they were themselves, and for the fifteen thousand Indian allies who were to have joined them, they found two hundred squalid savages, more like enemies than friends.

It was about this time that Beaujeu prepared to return to France. He had accomplished his mission and landed his passengers at what La Salle assured him to be one of the mouths of the Mississippi. His ship was in danger on this exposed and perilous coast and he was anxious to find shelter. He set sail on the twelfth of March, after a leave-taking which was courteous on both sides.

La Salle and his colonists were left alone. Several of them had lost heart and embarked for home with Beaujeu. Among these was Minet the engineer, who had fallen out with La Salle and who when he reached France was imprisoned for deserting him. Even his brother, the priest Jean Cavelier, had a mind to abandon the enterprise, but was persuaded at last to remain, along with his nephew the hot-headed Moranget, and the younger Cavelier, a mere schoolboy. The two Récollet friars, Zenobe Membré and Anastase Douay, the trusty Joutel, a man of sense and observation, and the Marquis de la Sablonnière, a debauched noble whose patrimony was his sword, were now the chief persons of the forlorn company. The rest were soldiers, raw and undisciplined, and artisans, most of whom knew nothing of their vocation. Add to these the miserable families and the infatuated young women who had come to tempt fortune in the swamps and cane-brakes of the Mississippi.

La Salle had found a spot which he thought well fitted for a temporary establishment. It was on the river which he named the La Vache, now the Lavaca, which enters the head of Matagorda Bay, and there he ordered all the women and children and most of the men to remove, while the rest, thirty in number, remained with Joutel at the fort near the mouth of the bay. Here they spent their time in hunting, fishing and squaring the logs of driftwood which the sea washed up in abundance and which La Salle proposed to use in building his new station on the Lavaca.

Thus the time passed till midsummer, when Joutel received orders to abandon his post and rejoin the main body of the colonists. To this end, the little frigate *Belle* was sent down the bay. She was a gift from the King to La Salle, who had brought her safely over the bar and regarded her as a mainstay of his hopes. She now took on board the stores and some of the men, while Joutel with the rest followed along shore to the post on the Lavaca.

Here he found a state of things that was far from cheering. Crops had been sown, but the drought and the cattle had nearly destroyed them. The colonists were lodged under tents and hovels, and the only solid structure was a small square enclosure of pickets, in which the gunpowder and the brandy were stored. The site was good, a rising ground by the river, but there was no wood within the distance of a league and no horses or oxen to drag it. Their work must be done by men. Some felled and squared the timber and others dragged it by main force over the matted grass of the prairie, under the scorching Texan sun. The gun carriages served to make the task somewhat easier, yet the strongest men soon gave out under it.

Joutel went down to the first fort, made a raft and brought up the timber collected there, which proved a most seasonable and useful supply. Palisades and buildings began to rise. The men labored without spirit, yet strenuously, for they labored under the eye of La Salle. The carpenters brought from Rochelle proved worthless, and he himself made the plans of the work, marked out the tenons and mortises and directed the whole.

Death, meanwhile, made withering havoc among his followers, and under the sheds and hovels that shielded them from the sun lay a score of wretches slowly wasting away with the diseases contracted at St. Domingo. Of the soldiers enlisted for the expedition by La Salle's agents, many are affirmed to have spent their lives in begging at the church doors of Rochefort and were consequently incapable of discipline. It was impossible to prevent either them or the sailors from devouring persimmons and other wild fruits to a destructive excess. Nearly all fell ill, and before the summer had passed, the graveyard had thirty more tenants.

The bearing of La Salle did not raise the drooping spirits of his followers. The results of the enterprise had been far different from

277

his hopes, and after a season of flattering promise he had entered again on those dark and obstructed paths which seemed his destined way of life. The present was beset with trouble; the future thick with storms. The consciousness quickened his energies, but it made him stern, harsh and often unjust to those beneath him.

Meanwhile the work was urged on. A large building was finished, constructed of timber, roofed with boards and raw hides and divided into apartments for lodging and other uses. La Salle gave the new establishment his favorite name of Fort St. Louis, and the neighboring bay was also christened after the royal saint.

The scene was not without its charms. Towards the southeast stretched the bay with its bordering meadows, and on the northeast the Lavaca ran along the base of green declivities. Around, far and near, rolled a sea of prairie, with distant forests dim in the summer haze. At times it was dotted with the browsing buffalo, not yet scared from their wonted pastures, and the grassy swells were spangled with the flowers for which Texas is renowed and which now form the gay ornaments of our gardens.

And now, the needful work accomplished and the colony in some measure housed and fortified, its indefatigable chief prepared to renew his quest of the "fatal river," as Joutel repeatedly calls it. It was the last day of October, 1685, when La Salle set out on his great journey of exploration. His brother Cavelier, who had now recovered, accompanied him with fifty men, and five cannon shot from the fort saluted them as they departed. They were lightly equipped, but some of them wore corselets made of staves, to ward off arrows. Descending the Lavaca, they pursued their course eastward on foot along the margin of the bay, while Joutel remained in command of the fort.

Weeks and months dragged on. At the end of March, Joutel, chancing to mount on the roof of one of the buildings, saw seven or eight men approaching over the prairie. He went out to meet them with an equal number, well armed, and as he drew near recognized, with mixed joy and anxiety, La Salle and some of those who had gone with him. His brother Cavelier was at his side, with his cassock so tattered that, says Joutel, "there was hardly a piece left large enough to wrap a farthing's worth of salt. He had an old cap on his head, having lost his hat by the way. The rest were in no better plight, for their shirts were all in rags. Some of them carried loads of meat, because M. de la Salle was afraid that we might not have killed any buffalo. We met with great joy and many embraces. We went into the house and refreshed ourselves with some bread and brandy, as there was no wine left."

La Salle and his companions told their story. They had wandered on through various savage tribes, with whom they had more than one encounter, scattering them like chaff by the terror of their firearms. At length they found a more friendly band and learned much touching the Spaniards, who, they were told, were universally hated by the tribes of that country. It would be easy, said their informants, to gather a host of warriors and lead them over the Rio Grande, but La Salle was in no condition for attempting conquests, and the tribes in whose alliance he had trusted had, a few days before, been at blows with him. The invasion of New Biscay must be postponed to a more propitious day.

Still advancing, he came to a large river which he at first mistook for the Mississippi and, building a fort of palisades, he left here several of his men. The fate of these unfortunates does not appear. He now retraced his steps towards Fort St. Louis and, as he approached it, detached some of his men to look for his vessel, the *Belle,* for whose safety, since the loss of her pilot, he had become very anxious.

On the next day these men appeared at the fort with downcast looks. They had not found the *Belle* at the place where she had been ordered to remain, nor were any tidings to be heard of her. From that hour the conviction that she was lost possessed the mind of La Salle. Surrounded as he was, and had always been, with traitors, the belief now possessed him that her crew had abandoned the colony and made sail for the West Indies or for France. The loss was incalculable. He had relied on this vessel to transport the colonists to the Mississippi, as soon as its exact position could be ascertained, and thinking her a safer place of deposit than the fort, he had put on board of her all his papers and personal baggage, besides a great quantity of stores, ammunition and tools. In truth, she was of the last necessity to the unhappy exiles and their only resource for escape from a position which was fast becoming desperate.

La Salle, as his brother tells us, now fell dangerously ill, the fatigues of his journey, joined to the effects upon his mind of this last disaster, having overcome his strength, though not his fortitude. "In truth," writes the priest, "after the loss of the vessel which deprived us of our only means of returning to France, we had no resource but in the firm guidance of my brother, whose death each of us would have regarded as his own."

No sooner had he recovered than La Salle embraced a resolution which could be the offspring only of a desperate necessity. He determined to make his way by the Mississippi and the Illinois to Canada, from which he might bring succor to the colonists and send a report of their condition to France. The attempt was beset with uncertainties and dangers. The Mississippi was first to be found, then followed through all the perilous monotony of its interminable windings to a goal which was to be but the starting point of a new and not less arduous journey. Cavelier his brother, Moranget his nephew, the friar Anastase Douay and others to the number of twenty were chosen to accompany him.

Every corner of the magazine was ransacked for an outfit. Joutel generously gave up the better part of his wardrobe to La Salle and his two relatives. The scantily furnished chests of those who had died were used to supply the wants of the living. Each man labored with needle and awl to patch his failing garments or supply their place with buffalo or deer skins.

On the twenty-second of April, after mass and prayers in the chapel, they issued from the gate, each bearing his pack and his weapons, some with kettles slung at their backs, some with axes, some with gifts for Indians. In this guise, they held their way in silence across the prairie, while anxious eyes followed them from the palisades of St. Louis, whose inmates, not excepting Joutel himself, seem to have been ignorant of the extent and difficulty of the undertaking.

Leaving the fort, they journeyed towards the northeast over plains green as an emerald with the young verdure of April, till at length they saw, far as the eye could reach, the boundless prairie alive with herds of buffalo. The animals were in one of their tame or stupid moods, and they killed nine or ten of them without the least difficulty, drying the best parts of the meat. They crossed the Colorado on a raft and reached the banks of another river where one of the party, named Hiens, a German of Württemberg and an old buccaneer, was mired and nearly suffocated in a mudhole. Unfortunately, as events proved, he managed to crawl out, and to console him the river was christened with his name. The party made a bridge of trees, on which they crossed in safety.

La Salle now changed their course and journeyed eastward. The travelers soon found themselves in the midst of a numerous Indian population, where they were feasted and caressed without measure. At another village they were less fortunate. The inhabitants were friendly by day and hostile by night. They came to attack the French in their camp, but withdrew, daunted by the menacing voice of La Salle, who had heard them approaching through the canebrake.

La Salle's favorite Shawanoe hunter, Nika, who had followed him from Canada to France, and from France to Texas, was bitten by a rattlesnake, and though he recovered, the accident detained the party for several days. At length they resumed their journey but were stopped by a river, called by Douay "La Rivière des Malheurs." La Salle and Cavelier, with a few others, tried to cross on a raft, which as it reached the channel was caught by a current of marvelous swiftness. Douay and Moranget, watching the transit from the edge of the canebrake, beheld their commander swept down the stream, vanishing in an instant.

All that day they remained with their companions on the bank, lamenting in despair for the loss of their guardian angel, for so Douay calls La Salle. It was fast growing dark, when to their unspeakable relief they saw him advancing with his party along the opposite bank, having succeeded after great exertion in guiding the raft to land.

How to rejoin him was now the question. Douay and his companions, who had tasted no food that day, broke their fast on two young eagles which they knocked out of their nest and then spent the night in rueful consultation as to the means of crossing the river. In the morning they waded into the marsh, the friar with his breviary in his hood to keep it dry, and hacked among the canes till they had gathered enough to make another raft, on which, profiting by La Salle's experience, they safely crossed and rejoined him.

Next they became entangled in a canebrake, where La Salle, as usual with him in such cases, took the lead, a hatchet in each hand, and hewed out a path for his followers. They soon reached the villages of the Cenis Indians, on and near the river Trinity—a tribe then powerful but long since extinct. Nothing could surpass the friendliness of their welcome. The chiefs came to meet them, bearing the calumet and followed by warriors in shirts of embroidered deerskin. Then the whole village swarmed out like bees, gathering around the visitors with offerings of food and all that was precious in their eyes. La Salle was lodged with the great chief, but he compelled his men to encamp at a distance lest the ardor of their gallantry might give occasion of offense.

The lodges of the Cenis, forty or fifty feet high and covered with a thatch of meadow grass, looked like huge beehives. Each held several families, whose fire was in the middle and their beds around the circumference. The spoil of the Spaniards was to be seen on all sides—silver lamps and spoons, swords, old muskets, money, clothing and a bull of the Pope dispensing the Spanish colonists of New Mexico from fasting during summer.

These treasures, as well as their numerous horses, were obtained by the Cenis from their neighbors and allies, the Comanches, that fierce prairie banditti who scourged the Mexican border with their bloody forays. A party of these wild horsemen was in the village. Douay was edified at seeing them make the sign of the cross in imitation of the neophytes of one of the Spanish missions. They enacted, too, the ceremony of the mass, and one of them in his rude way drew a sketch of a picture he had seen in some church which he had pillaged, wherein the friar plainly recognized the Virgin weeping at the foot of the cross.

They invited the French to join them on a raid into New Mexico, and they spoke with contempt of the Spanish creoles, saying that it would be easy to conquer a nation of cowards who make people walk before them with fans to cool them in hot weather.

Soon after leaving the Cenis villages, both La Salle and his nephew Moranget were attacked by fever. This caused a delay of more than two months, during which the party seems to have remained encamped on the Neches, or possibly the Sabine. When at length the invalids had recovered sufficient strength to travel, the stock of ammunition was nearly spent, some of the men had deserted and the condition of the travelers was such that there seemed no alternative but to return to Fort St. Louis. This they accordingly did, greatly aided in their march by the horses bought from the Cenis, and suffering no very serious accident by the way except the loss of La Salle's servant Dumesnil, who was seized by an alligator while attempting to cross the Colorado. Twenty men had gone out with La Salle; only eight returned.

The temporary excitement caused among the colonists by their return soon gave place to a dejection bordering on despair. "This pleasant land," writes Cavelier, "seemed to us an abode of weariness and a perpetual prison." Flattering themselves with the delusion, common to exiles of every kind, that they were objects of solicitude at home, they watched daily with straining eyes for an approaching sail.

The weary precincts of Fort St. Louis, with its fence of rigid palisades, its area of trampled earth, its buildings of weather-stained timber and its well-peopled graveyard without, were hateful to their sight. La Salle had a heavy task to save them from despair. His composure, his unfailing equanimity, his words of encouragement and cheer were the breath of life to this forlorn company, for though he could not impart to minds of less adamantine temper the audacity of hope with which he still clung to the final accomplishment of his purposes, the contagion of his hardihood touched, nevertheless, the drooping spirits of his followers.

The journey to Canada was clearly their only hope, and after a brief rest La Salle prepared to renew the attempt. He proposed that Joutel should this time be of the party and should proceed from Quebec to France with his brother Cavelier to solicit succors for the colony, while he himself returned to Texas.

A new obstacle was presently interposed. La Salle, whose constitution seems to have suffered from his long course of hardships, was attacked in November with hernia. Joutel offered to conduct the party in his stead, but La Salle replied that his own presence was indispensable at the Illinois. He had the good fortune to recover within four or five weeks, sufficiently to undertake the journey, and all in the fort busied themselves in preparing an outfit.

Christmas came, and was solemnly observed. There was a midnight mass in the chapel where Membré, Cavelier, Douay and their priestly brethren stood before the altar in vestments strangely contrasting with the rude temple and the ruder garb of the worshipers. And as Membré elevated the consecrated wafer and the lamps burned dim through the clouds of incense, the kneeling group drew from the daily miracle such consolation as true Catholics alone can know. When Twelfth Night came, all gathered in the hall and cried, after the jovial old custom, "The King drinks," with hearts perhaps as cheerless as their cups, which were filled with cold water.

On the morrow the band of adventurers mustered for the fatal journey. The five horses, bought by La Salle of the Indians, stood in the area of the fort, packed for the march, and here was gathered the wretched remnant of the colony—those who were to go and those who were to stay behind.

La Salle had made them a last address, delivered, we are told, with that winning air which, though alien from his usual bearing, seems to have been at times a natural expression of this unhappy man. It was a bitter parting, one of sighs, tears and embracings—the farewell of those on whose souls had sunk a heavy boding that they would never meet again.

Equipped and weaponed for the journey, the adventurers filed from the gate, crossed the river and held their slow march over the prairies beyond, till intervening woods and hills shut Fort St. Louis forever from their sight.

CHAPTER 9

~~~~~~

The Assassination

THE TRAVELERS WERE CROSSING A MARSHY PRAIRIE towards a distant belt of woods that followed the course of a little river. They led with them their five horses, laden with their scanty baggage and, with what was of no less importance, their stock of presents for Indians. Some wore the remains of the clothing they had worn from France, eked out with deerskins, dressed in the Indian manner, and some had coats of old sailcloth.

Here was La Salle, whom one would have known at a glance as chief of the party; and the priest Cavelier, who seems to have shared not one of the high traits of his younger brother. Here, too, were their nephews, Moranget and the boy Cavelier, now about seventeen years old; the trusty soldier Joutel; and the friar Anastase Douay. Duhaut followed, a man of respectable birth and education; and Liotot, the surgeon of the party. At home they might perhaps have lived and died with a fair repute, but the wilderness is a rude touchstone which often reveals traits that would have lain buried and unsuspected in civilized life.

The German Hiens, the ex-buccaneer, was also of the number. He had probably sailed with an English crew, for he was sometimes known as *Gemme Anglais,* or "English Jen." The Sieur de Marle; Teissier, a pilot; L'Archevêque, a servant of Duhaut; and others, to the number in all of seventeen, made up the party—to which is to be added Nika, La Salle's Shawanoe hunter, who had twice crossed the ocean with him and still followed his fortunes with an admiring though un-demonstrative fidelity.

They passed the prairie and neared the forest. Here they saw buffalo, and the hunters approached and killed several of them. Then they traversed the woods, found and forded the shallow and rushy stream and pushed through the forest beyond till they again reached the open prairie. Heavy clouds gathered over them and it rained all night, but they sheltered themselves under the fresh hides of the buffalo they had killed.

They suffered greatly from the want of shoes and found for a while no better substitute than a casing of raw buffalo hide, which they were forced to keep always wet, as when dry it hardened about the foot like iron. At length they bought dressed deerskin from the Indians, of which they made tolerable moccasins. The rivers, streams and gullies filled with water were without number, and to cross them they made a boat of bullhide, like the "bull boat" later used on the upper Missouri. This did good service because they could carry it with them, with the help of their horses. Two or three men could cross in it at once and the horses swam after them like dogs.

Sometimes they traversed the sunny prairie; sometimes dived into the dark recesses of the forest, where the buffalo, descending daily from their pastures in long files to drink at the river, often made a broad and easy path for the travelers. When foul weather arrested them they built huts of bark and long meadow grass and, safely sheltered, lounged away the day while their horses, picketed nearby, stood steaming in the rain. At night they usually set a rude stockade about their camp, and here, by the grassy border of a brook or at the edge of a grove where a spring bubbled up through the sands, they lay asleep around the embers of their fire while the man on guard listened to the deep breathing of the slumbering horses and the howling of the wolves that saluted the rising moon as it flooded the waste of prairie with pale mystic radiance.

They met Indians almost daily—sometimes a band of hunters, mounted or on foot, chasing buffalo on the plains; sometimes a party of fishermen; sometimes a winter camp on the slope of a hill or under the sheltering border of a forest. They held intercourse with them in the distance by signs. Often they disarmed their distrust and attracted them into their camp, and often they visited them in their lodges, where seated on buffalo robes they smoked with their entertainers, passing the pipe from hand to hand. Cavelier says that they once saw a band of a hundred and fifty mounted Indians attacking a herd of buffalo with lances pointed with sharpened bone. The old priest was delighted with the sport, which he pronounces "the most diverting thing in the world."

On another occasion, when the party were encamped near the village of a tribe which Cavelier calls Sassory, he saw them catch an alligator about twelve feet long, which they proceeded to torture as if he were a human enemy, first putting out his eyes and then leading him to the neighboring prairie where, having confined him by a number of stakes, they spent the entire day in tormenting him.

Holding a northerly course, the travelers crossed the Brazos and reached the waters of the Trinity. The weather was unfavorable, and on one occasion they encamped in the rain during four or five days together. It was not a harmonious company. La Salle's cold and haughty reserve had returned, at least for those of his followers to whom he was not partial. Duhaut and the surgeon Liotot, both of whom were men of some property, had a large pecuniary stake in the enterprise and were disappointed and incensed at its ruinous result. They had a quarrel with young Moranget, whose hot and hasty temper was as little fitted to conciliate as was the harsh reserve of his uncle. Already, at Fort St. Louis, Duhaut had intrigued among the men, and the mild admonition of Joutel had not, it seems, sufficed to divert him from his sinister purposes. Liotot, it is said, had secretly sworn vengeance against La Salle, whom he charged with having caused the death of his brother, or, as some will have it, his nephew. On one of the former journeys this young man's strength had failed, and La Salle having ordered him to return to the fort, he had been killed by Indians on the way.

The party moved again as the weather improved, and on the fifteenth of March encamped within a few miles of a spot which La Salle had passed on his preceding journey and where he had left a quantity of Indian corn and beans in cache, hidden in the ground or in a hollow tree. As provisions were falling short, he sent a party from the camp to find it.

These men were Duhaut, Liotot, Hiens the buccaneer, Teissier, L'Archevêque, Nika the hunter and La Salle's servant Saget. They opened the cache and found the contents spoiled, but as they returned from their bootless errand they saw buffalo and Nika shot two of them. They now encamped on the spot and sent the servant to inform La Salle, in order that he might send horses to bring in the meat. Accordingly, on the next day, he directed Moranget and De Marle, with the necessary horses, to go with Saget to the hunters' camp.

When they arrived they found that Duhaut and his companions had already cut up the meat and laid it upon scaffolds for smoking, though it was not yet so dry as, it seems, this process required. Duhaut and the others had also put by, for themselves, the marrowbones and certain portions of the meat to which, by woodland custom, they had a perfect right. Moranget, whose rashness and violence had once before caused a fatal catastrophe, fell into a most unreasonable fit of rage, berated and menaced Duhaut and his party and ended by seizing upon the whole of the meat, including the reserved portions.

This added fuel to the fire of Duhaut's old grudge against Moranget and his uncle. There is reason to think that he had harbored deadly designs, the execution of which was only hastened by the present outbreak. The surgeon also bore hatred against Moranget, whom he had nursed with constant attention when wounded by an Indian arrow, and who had since repaid him with abuse. These two now took counsel apart with Hiens, Teissier and L'Archevêque, and it was resolved to kill Moranget that night. Nika, La Salle's devoted follower, and Saget, his faithful servant, must die with him. All of the five were of one mind except the pilot Teissier, who neither aided nor opposed the plot.

Night came. The woods grew dark; the evening meal was finished and the evening pipes were smoked. The order of the guard was arranged, and, doubtless by design, the first hour of the night was assigned to Moranget, the second to Saget and the third to Nika. Gun in hand, each stood watch in turn over the silent but not sleeping forms around him, till, his time expiring, he called the man who was to relieve him, wrapped himself in his blanket and was soon buried in a slumber that was to be his last.

Now the assassins rose. Duhaut and Hiens stood with their guns cocked, ready to shoot down any one of the destined victims who should resist or fly. The surgeon, with an ax, stole towards the three sleepers and struck a rapid blow at each in turn. Saget and Nika died with little movement, but Moranget started spasmodically into a sitting posture, gasping and unable to speak, and the murderers compelled De Marle, who was not in their plot, to compromise himself by dispatching him.

The floodgates of murder were open and the torrent must have its way. Vengeance and safety alike demanded the death of La Salle. Hiens alone seems to have hesitated, for he was one of those to whom that stern commander had always been partial. Meanwhile the intended victim was still at his camp about six miles distant. It is easy to picture with sufficient accuracy the features of the scene: the sheds of bark and branches beneath which, among blankets and buffalo robes, camp utensils, packsaddles, rude harness, guns, powder horns and bullet pouches, the men lounged away the hour, sleeping or smoking or talking among themselves; the blackened kettles that hung from tripods of poles over the fires; the Indians strolling about the place or lying, like dogs in the sun, with eyes half shut yet all observant; and in the neighboring meadow, the horses grazing under the eye of a watchman.

It was the eighteenth of March. Moranget and his companions had been expected to return the night before, but the whole day passed and they did not appear. La Salle became very anxious. He resolved to go and look for them but, not well knowing the way, he told the Indians who were about the camp that he would give them a hatchet if they would guide him. One of them accepted the offer and La Salle prepared to set out in the morning, at the same time directing Joutel to be ready to go with him.

Joutel says: "That evening, while we were talking about what could have happened to the absent men, he seemed to have a presentiment of what was to take place. He asked me if I had heard of any machinations against them, or if I had noticed any bad design on the part of Duhaut and the rest. I answered that I had heard nothing except that they sometimes complained of being found fault with so often; and that this was all I knew; besides which, as they were persuaded that I was in his interest, they would not have told me of any bad design they might have. We were very uneasy all the rest of the evening."

In the morning La Salle set out with his Indian guide. He had changed his mind with regard to Joutel, whom he now directed to remain in charge of the camp and to keep a careful watch. He told the friar Anastase Douay to come with him instead of Joutel, whose gun, which was the best in the party, he borrowed for the occasion, as well as his pistol.

The three proceeded on their way—La Salle, the friar and the Indian. "All the way," writes the friar, "he spoke to me of nothing but matters of piety, grace and predestination; enlarging on the debt he owed to God, who had saved him from so many perils during more than twenty years of travel in America. Suddenly, I saw him overwhelmed with a profound sadness, for which he himself could not account. He was so much moved that I scarcely knew him."

He soon recovered his usual calmness and they walked on till they approached the camp of Duhaut, which was on the farther side of a small river. Looking about him with the eye of a woodsman, La Salle saw two eagles circling in the air nearly over him, as if attracted by carcasses of beasts or men. He fired his gun and his pistol, as a summons to any of his followers who might be within hearing. The shots reached the ears of the conspirators. Rightly conjecturing by whom they were fired, several of them led by Duhaut crossed the river at a little distance above, where trees or other intervening objects hid them from sight. Duhaut and the surgeon crouched like Indians in the long, dry, reed-like grass of the last summer's growth, while L'Archevêque stood in sight near the bank.

La Salle, continuing to advance, soon saw him and, calling to him, demanded where was Moranget. The man, without lifting his hat or making any show of respect, replied in an agitated and broken voice, but with a tone of studied insolence, that Moranget was strolling about somewhere. La Salle rebuked and menaced him. He rejoined with increased insolence, drawing back as he spoke towards the ambuscade, while the incensed commander advanced to chastise him. At that moment a shot was fired from the grass, instantly followed by another, and, pierced through the brain, La Salle dropped dead.

The friar at his side stood terror-stricken, unable to advance or to fly, when Duhaut, rising from the ambuscade, called out to him to take courage for he had nothing to fear. The murderers now came forward and with wild looks gathered about their victim.

"There thou liest, great Bashaw! There thou liest!" exclaimed the surgeon Liotot, in base exultation over the unconscious corpse. With mockery and insult they stripped it naked, dragged it into the bushes and left it there, a prey to the buzzards and wolves.

Thus, in the vigor of his manhood, at the age of forty-three, died Robert Cavelier de la Salle, "one of the greatest men," writes Tonty, "of this age," and without question one of the most remarkable explorers whose names live in history.

His faithful officer Joutel thus sketches his portrait: "His firmness, his courage, his great knowledge of the arts and sciences, which made him equal to every undertaking, and his untiring energy, which enabled him to surmount every obstacle, would have won at last a glorious success for his grand enterprise, had not all his fine qualities been counterbalanced by a haughtiness of manner which often made him insupportable, and by a harshness towards those under his command which drew upon him an implacable hatred, and was at last the cause of his death."

The enthusiasm of the disinterested and chivalrous Champlain was not the enthusiasm of La Salle, nor had he any part in the self-devoted zeal of the early Jesuit explorers. He belonged not to the age of the knight-errant and the saint, but to the modern world of practical study and practical action. He was the hero not of a principle nor of a faith, but simply of a fixed idea and a determined purpose. As often happens with concentered and energetic natures, his purpose was to him a passion and an inspiration, and he clung to it with a certain fanaticism of devotion. It was the offspring of an ambition vast and comprehensive, yet acting in the interest both of France and of civilization.

Serious in all things, incapable of the lighter pleasures, incapable of repose, finding no joy but in the pursuit of great designs, too shy for society and too reserved for popularity, often unsympathetic and always seeming so, smothering emotions which he could not utter, schooled to universal distrust, stern to his followers and pitiless to himself, bearing the brunt of every hardship and every danger, demanding of others an equal constancy joined to an implicit deference, heeding no counsel but his own, attempting the impossible and grasping at what was too vast to hold—he contained in his own complex and painful nature the chief springs of his triumphs, his failures and' his death.

To estimate aright the marvels of his patient fortitude, one must follow on his track through the vast scene of his interminable journeyings—those thousands of weary miles of forest, marsh and river, where again and again, in the bitterness of baffled striving, the untiring pilgrim pushed onward towards the goal which he was never to attain.

America owes him an enduring memory, for in this masculine figure is the pioneer who guided her to the possession of her richest heritage.

PART FOUR

Count Frontenac

First Term

COUNT FRONTENAC CAME OF AN ANCIENT AND
noble race, said to have been of Basque origin. His father held
a high post in the household of Louis XIII, who became the child's
godfather and gave him his own name.

At the age of fifteen, the young Louis showed an uncontrollable
passion for the life of a soldier. He was sent to the seat of war in
Holland, to serve under the Prince of Orange. At the age of nineteen,
he was a volunteer at the siege of Hesdin; in the next year he was at
Arras, where he distinguished himself during a sortie of the garrison;
in the next he took part in the siege of Aire; and in the next, in those of
Callioure and Perpignan. At the age of twenty-three, he was made
colonel of the regiment of Normandy, which he commanded in
repeated battles and sieges of the Italian campaign. He was several
times wounded, and in 1646 he had an arm broken at the siege of
Orbitello. In the same year, when twenty-six years old, he was raised to
the rank of *maréchal de camp,* equivalent to that of brigadier general.

In 1669 a Venetian embassy came to France to beg for aid against
the Turks, who for more than two years had attacked Candia in overwhelming force. The ambassadors offered to place their own troops
under French command and they asked Turenne to name a general
officer equal to the task. Frontenac had the signal honor of being
chosen by the first soldier of Europe for this most arduous and difficult
position. He went accordingly. The result increased his reputation for
ability and courage, but Candia was doomed and its chief fortress fell

into the hands of the infidels after a protracted struggle which is said to have cost them a hundred and eighty thousand men.

Three years later, Frontenac received the appointment of Governor and Lieutenant General for the King in all New France. "He was," says Saint-Simon, "a man of excellent parts, living much in society, and completely ruined. He found it hard to bear the imperious temper of his wife; and he was given the government of Canada to deliver him from her, and afford him some means of living."

Frontenac was fifty-two years old when he landed at Quebec. If time had done little to cure his many faults, it had done nothing to weaken the springs of his unconquerable vitality. In his ripe middle age, he was keen, fiery and perversely headstrong.

Had nature disposed him to melancholy, there was much in his position to awaken it. A man of courts and camps, born and bred in the focus of a most gorgeous civilization, he was banished to the ends of the earth, among savage hordes and half-reclaimed forests—to exchange the splendors of St. Germain and the dawning glories of Versailles for a stern gray rock, haunted by somber priests, rugged merchants and traders, blanketed Indians and wild bushrangers.

But Frontenac was a man of action. He wasted no time in vain regrets and set himself to his work with the elastic vigor of youth. His first impressions had been very favorable. As he sailed up the St. Lawrence, the basin of Quebec opened before him and his imagination kindled with the grandeur of the scene. "I never," he wrote, "saw anything more superb than the position of this town. It could not be better situated as the future capital of a great empire."

That Quebec was to become the capital of a great empire there seemed in truth good reason to believe. The young King and his minister Colbert had labored in earnest to build up a new France in the west. For years past, shiploads of emigrants had landed every summer on the strand beneath the rock. All was life and action and the air was full of promise.

Frontenac shared the spirit of the hour. His first step was to survey his government. He talked with traders, colonists and officials; visited seigniories, farms, fishing stations and all the infant industries that the royal agent, Talon, had galvanized into life; examined the new ship on the stocks, admired the structure of the new brewery, went to Three

Rivers to see the iron mines, and then, having acquired a tolerably exact idea of his charge, returned to Quebec. He was well pleased with what he saw, but not with the ways and means of Canadian travel. He thought it strangely unbecoming that a lieutenant general of the King should be forced to crouch on a sheet of bark at the bottom of a birch canoe, scarcely daring to move his head to the right or left lest he should disturb the balance of the fragile vessel.

At Quebec he convoked the council, made them a speech and administered the oath of allegiance. This did not satisfy him. He resolved that all Quebec should take the oath together. It was little but a pretext. Like many of his station, Frontenac was not in full sympathy with the centralizing movement of the time, which tended to level ancient rights, privileges and prescriptions under the ponderous roller of the monarchical administration. He looked back with regret to the day when the three orders of the State—clergy, nobles and commons—had a place and a power in the direction of national affairs. The three orders still subsisted, in form if not in substance, in some of the provinces of France, and Frontenac conceived the idea of reproducing them in Canada.

Not only did he cherish the tradition of faded liberties, but he loved pomp and circumstance above all, when he was himself the central figure in it, and the thought of a royal governor of Languedoc or Brittany presiding over the estates of his province appears to have fired him with emulation.

He had no difficulty in forming his order of the clergy. The Jesuits and the seminary priests supplied material even more abundant than he wished. For the order of the nobles, he found three or four *gentilshommes* at Quebec and these he reinforced with a number of officers.

The third estate consisted of the merchants and citizens, and he formed the members of the council and the magistrates into another distinct body—though, properly speaking, they belonged to the third estate, of which by nature and prescription they were the head.

The Jesuits, glad no doubt to lay him under some slight obligation, lent him their church for the ceremony that he meditated, and aided in decorating it for the occasion. Here, on the twenty-third of October, 1672, the three estates of Canada were convoked, with as much pomp and splendor as circumstances would permit. Then Frontenac, with the ease of a man of the world and the loftiness of a *grand seigneur,* delivered himself of the harangue he had prepared. He wrote exceedingly well. He is said also to have excelled as an orator. Certainly he was never averse to the tones of his own eloquence.

The dispatches in which Frontenac announced to his masters what he had done received in due time their answer. The minister Colbert wrote: "Your assembling of the inhabitants to take the oath of fidelity, and your division of them into three estates, may have had a good effect for the moment; but it is well for you to observe that you are always to follow, in the government of Canada, the forms in use here; and since our kings have long regarded it as good for their service not to convoke the states-general of the kingdom, in order, perhaps, to abolish insensibly this ancient usage, you, on your part, should very rarely, or, to speak more correctly, never, give a corporate form to the inhabitants of Canada. You should even, as the colony strengthens, suppress gradually the office of the syndic, who presents petitions in the name of the inhabitants; for it is well that each should speak for himself, and no one for all."

Here, in brief, is the whole spirit of the French colonial rule in Canada—a government of excellent intentions but of arbitrary methods. Frontenac, filled with the traditions of the past and sincerely desirous of the good of the colony, rashly set himself against the prevailing current. His municipal government and his meetings of citizens were, like his three estates, abolished by a word from the court, which, bold and obstinate as he was, he dared not disobey. Had they been allowed to exist, there can be little doubt that great good would have resulted in Canada.

Frontenac has been called a mere soldier. He was an excellent soldier and more besides. He was a man of vigorous and cultivated mind, penetrating observation and ample travel and experience. His zeal for the colony, however, was often counteracted by the violence of his prejudices, and by two other influences. First, he was a ruined man who meant to mend his fortunes and his wish that Canada should prosper was joined with a determination to reap a goodly part of her prosperity for himself. Again, he could not endure a rival. Opposition maddened him, and when crossed or thwarted, he forgot everything but his passion. Signs of storm quickly showed themselves between him and the intendant Talon, but the danger was averted by the departure of that official for France.

He fared even worse with Talon's successor, Duchesneau, and the years of his first term in the governor's office is a record of increasingly violent quarrels, not only with the intendant but with the clergy, and in fact with everyone who dared to oppose him.

Every ship from Canada brought to the King fresh complaints of Duchesneau against Frontenac, and of Frontenac against Duchesneau. The King replied with rebukes, exhortations and threats to both. At first he had shown a disposition to extenuate and excuse the faults of Frontenac, but every year his letters grew sharper. In 1681 he wrote: "Again I urge you to banish from your mind the difficulties which you have yourself devised against the execution of my orders; to act with mildness and moderation towards all the colonists, and divest yourself entirely of the personal animosities which have thus far been almost your sole motive of action. In conclusion, I exhort you once more to profit well by the directions which this letter contains; since, unless you succeed better herein than formerly, I cannot help recalling you from the command which I have intrusted to you."

The dispute still went on. The autumn ships from Quebec brought back the usual complaints and the long-suffering King at length made good his threat. Both Frontenac and Duchesneau received their recall and they both deserved it.

The last official act of the governor, recorded in the register of the council of Quebec, is the formal declaration that his rank in that body is superior to that of the intendant.

The key to nearly all these disputes lay in the relations between Frontenac and the Church. The fundamental quarrel was generally covered by superficial issues and it was rarely that the governor fell out with anybody who was not in league with the bishop and the Jesuits. "Nearly all the disorders in New France," he writes, "spring from the ambition of the ecclesiastics who want to join to their spiritual authority an absolute power over things temporal, and who persecute all who do not submit entirely to them."

He says that the intendant and the councilors are completely under their control and dare not decide any question against them; that they have spies everywhere, even in his house; that the bishop told him that he could excommunicate even a governor, if he chose; that the missionaries in Indian villages say that they are equals of Onontio and tell their converts that all will go wrong till the priests have the government of Canada; that directly or indirectly they meddle in all civil affairs; that they trade even with the English of New York; that, what with Jesuits, Sulpitians, the bishop, and the seminary of Quebec, they hold two thirds of the good lands of Canada; that, in view of the poverty of the country, their revenues are enormous; that, in short, their object is mastery and that they use all means to compass it.

The recall of the governor was a triumph for the ecclesiastics, offset but slightly by the recall of their instrument, the intendant, who had done his work and whom they needed no longer.

When Frontenac sailed for France, it was a day of rejoicing to more than half the merchants of Canada, and excepting the Récollets, to all the priests. But he left behind him an impression, very general among the people, that if danger threatened the colony, Count Frontenac was the man for the hour.

CHAPTER 2

La Barre and the Iroquois

WHEN THE NEW GOVERNOR LA BARRE, AND THE new intendant Meules, arrived at Quebec, a dismal greeting waited them. All the Lower Town was in ashes except the house of the merchant Aubert de la Chesnaye, standing alone amid the wreck.

On a Tuesday, the fourth of August, at ten o'clock in the evening, the nuns of the Hôtel-Dieu were roused from their early slumbers by shouts, outcries and the ringing of bells; "and," writes one of them, "what was our terror to find it as light as noonday, the flames burned so fiercely and rose so high."

Half an hour before, Chartier de Lotbinière, judge of the King's court, heard the first alarm, ran down the descent now called Mountain Street, and found everything in confusion in the town below. The house of Etienne Planchon was in a blaze. The fire was spreading to those of his neighbors and had just leaped the narrow street to the storehouses of the Jesuits. The season was excessively dry; there were no means of throwing water except kettles and buckets and the crowd was bewildered with excitement and fright.

Men were ordered to tear off roofs and pull down houses, but the flames drove them from their work and by four o'clock in the morning fifty-five buildings were burnt to the ground. They were all of wood, but many of them were storehouses filled with goods, and the property consumed was more in value than all that remained in Canada.

Under these gloomy auspices, Le Febvre de la Barre began his reign. He was an old officer who had achieved notable exploits against

301

the English in the West Indies, but who was now to be put to a test far more severe. He made his lodging in the château while his colleague, Meules, could hardly find a shelter. The buildings of the Upper Town were filled with those whom the fire had made roofless and the intendant was obliged to content himself with a house in the neighboring woods. Here he was ill at ease, for he dreaded an Indian war and the scalping knives of the Iroquois.

So far as his own safety was concerned, his alarm was needless, but not so as regarded the colony with whose affairs he was charged. For those who had eyes to see it, a terror and a woe lowered in the future of Canada. In an evil hour for her, the Iroquois had conquered their southern neighbors, the Andastes, who had long held their ground against them and at one time threatened them with ruin. The hands of the confederates were now free. Their arrogance was redoubled by victory, and having long before destroyed all the adjacent tribes on the north and west, they looked for fresh victims in the wilderness beyond.

Their most easterly tribe, the Mohawks, had not forgotten the chastisement they had received from previous governors. They had learned to fear the French and were cautious in offending them, but it was not so with the remoter Iroquois. Of these, the Senecas at the western end of the "Long House," as they called their fivefold league, were by far the most powerful, for they could muster as many warriors as all the four remaining tribes together and they now sought to draw the confederacy into a series of wars, which, though not directed against the French, threatened soon to involve them. Their first movement westward was against the tribes of the Illinois. They made the valley of the Illinois a desert and returned with several hundred prisoners, of whom they burned those who were useless and incorporated the young and strong into their own tribe.

This movement of the western Iroquois had a double incentive: their love of fighting and their love of gain. It was a war of conquest and of trade. All the five tribes of the league had become dependent on the English and Dutch of Albany for guns, powder, lead, brandy and many other things that they had learned to regard as necessities. Beaver skins alone could buy them, but to the Iroquois the supply of beaver skins was limited. The regions of the west and northwest, the upper Mississippi with its tributaries and, above all, the forests of the upper lakes were occupied by tribes in the interest of the French, whose missionaries and explorers had been the first to visit them, and whose traders controlled their immense annual product of furs.

La Salle, by his newly built fort of St. Louis, engrossed the trade of the Illinois and Miami tribes, while the Hurons and Ottawas gathered about the old mission of Michilimackinac acted as factors for the Sioux, the Winnebagos, and many other remote hordes. Every summer they brought down their accumulated beaver skins to the fair at Montreal, while French bushrangers roving through the wilderness, with or without licenses, collected many more.

It was the purpose of the Iroquois to master all this traffic, conquer the tribes who had possession of it and divert the entire supply of furs to themselves, and through themselves to the English and Dutch. That English and Dutch traders urged them on is affirmed by the French and is very likely. The accomplishment of the scheme would have ruined Canada. Moreover, the Illinois, the Hurons, the Ottawas and all the other tribes threatened by the Iroquois were the allies and "children" of the French, who in honor as in interest were bound to protect them.

La Barre summoned in 1682 the most able and experienced persons in the colony to discuss the state of affairs. Their conclusion was that the Iroquois would attack and destroy the Illinois and, this accomplished, turn upon the tribes of the lakes, conquer or destroy them also and ruin the trade of Canada.

In the spring of 1683, La Barre took a step as rash as it was lawless. He sent the Chevalier de Baugis, lieutenant of his guard, with a considerable number of canoes and men to seize La Salle's fort of St. Louis on the river Illinois—a measure which, while gratifying the passions and the greed of himself and his allies, would greatly increase the danger of rupture with the Iroquois.

Late in the season he dispatched seven canoes and fourteen men, with goods to the value of fifteen or sixteen thousand livres, to trade with the tribes of the Mississippi. As he had sown, so he reaped. The seven canoes passed through the country of the Illinois. A large war party of Senecas and Cayugas invaded it in February. La Barre had told their chiefs that they were welcome to plunder the canoes of La Salle. The Iroquois were not discriminating. They fell upon the gov-

303

ernor's canoes, seized all the goods and captured the men. Then they attacked Baugis at Fort St. Louis. The place, perched on a rock, was strong and they were beaten off, but the act was one of open war.

When La Barre heard the news he was furious. He trembled for the vast amount of goods which he and his fellow speculators had sent to Michilimackinac and the lakes. There was but one resource—to call out the militia, muster the Indian allies, advance to Lake Ontario and dictate peace to the Senecas at the head of an imposing force, or, failing in this, to attack and crush them. A small vessel lying at Quebec was dispatched to France with urgent appeals for immediate aid, though there was little hope that it could arrive in time. Meanwhile, La Barre was left scared, excited and blustering.

The Dutch colony of New Netherland had now become the English colony of New York. Its proprietor, the Duke of York, afterwards James II of England, had appointed Colonel Thomas Dongan its governor. He was a Catholic Irish gentleman of high rank, nephew of the famous Earl of Tyrconnel, and presumptive heir to the earldom of Limerick. He had served in France, was familiar with its language and partial to its King and its nobility, but he nevertheless gave himself with vigor to the duties of his new trust.

The Dutch and English colonists aimed at a share in the western fur trade, hitherto a monopoly of Canada, and it is said that Dutch traders had already ventured among the tribes of the Great Lakes, boldly poaching on the French preserves. Dongan did his utmost to promote their interests, so far at least as was consistent with his instructions from the Duke of York, enjoining him to give the French governor no just cause of offense.

For several years past the Iroquois had made forays against the borders of Maryland and Virginia, plundering and killing the settlers, and a declared rupture between those colonies and the savage confederates had more than once been imminent. The English believed that these hostilities were instigated by the Jesuits in the Iroquois villages. There is no proof whatever of the accusation, but it is certain that it was the interest of Canada to provoke a war which might sooner or later involve New York. In consequence of a renewal of such attacks, Lord Howard of Effingham, governor of Virginia, came to Albany in the summer of 1684 to hold a council with the Iroquois.

The Oneidas, Onondagas and Cayugas were the offending tribes. They all promised friendship for the future. A hole was dug in the courtyard of the council house, each of the three threw a hatchet into it, and Lord Howard and the representative of Maryland added two others. Then the hole was filled, the song of peace was sung, and the high contracting parties stood pledged to mutual accord. The Mohawks were also at the council and the Senecas soon after arrived, so that all the confederacy was present by its deputies.

Not long before, La Barre, then in the heat of his martial preparations, had sent a messenger to Dongan with a letter informing him that, as the Senecas and Cayugas had plundered French canoes and assaulted a French fort, he was compelled to attack them, and asked that the Dutch and English colonists should be forbidden to supply them with arms.

This letter produced two results, neither of·them agreeable to the writer. First, the Iroquois were fully warned of the designs of the French, and secondly, Dongan gained the opportunity he wanted of asserting the claim of his King to sovereignty over the confederacy and possession of the whole country south of the Great Lakes. He added that if the Iroquois had done wrong, he would require them, as British subjects, to make reparation and he urged La Barre, for the sake of peace between the two colonies, to refrain from his intended invasion of British territory.

Dongan next laid before the assembled sachems the complaints made against them in the letter of La Barre. They replied by accusing the French of carrying arms to their enemies, the Illinois and the Miamis. "Onontio," said their orator, "calls us his children and then helps our enemies to knock us in the head."

They were somewhat disturbed at the prospect of La Barre's threatened attack and Dongan seized the occasion to draw from them an acknowledgment of subjection to the Duke of York, promising in return that they should be protected from the French. They did not hesitate.

"We put ourselves," said the Iroquois speaker, "under the great sachem Charles, who lives over the Great Lake, and under the protection of the great Duke of York, brother of your great sachem." But he added a moment after: "Let your friend [King Charles] who lives

305

over the Great Lake know that we are a free people, though united to the English."

They consented that the arms of the Duke of York should be planted in their villages, being told that this would prevent the French from destroying them. Dongan now insisted that they should make no treaty with Onontio without his consent, and he promised that if their country should be invaded he would send four hundred horsemen and as many foot soldiers to their aid.

As for the acknowledgment of subjection to the King and the Duke of York, the Iroquois neither understood its full meaning nor meant to abide by it. What they did clearly understand was that while they recognized Onontio, the governor of Canada, as their father, they recognized Corlaer, the governor of New York, only as their brother. Dongan, it seems, could not or dared not change this mark of equality. He did his best, however, to make good his claims, and sent Arnold Viele, a Dutch interpreter, as his envoy to Onondaga.

The object of Viele was to confirm the Iroquois in their very questionable attitude of subjection to the British Crown, and persuade them to make no treaty or agreement with the French except through the intervention of Dongan, or at least with his consent.

The envoy found two Frenchmen in the town, whose presence boded ill to his errand. The first was the veteran colonist of Montreal, Charles le Moyne, sent by La Barre to invite the Onondagas to a conference. They had known him, in peace or war, for a quarter of a century and they greatly respected him. The other was the Jesuit Jean de Lamberville, who had long lived among them, and knew them better than they knew themselves.

Here, too, was another personage who cannot pass unnoticed. He was a famous Onondaga orator named Otréouati, and called also Big Mouth, whether by reason of the dimensions of that feature or the greatness of the wisdom that issued from it. His contemporary, Baron la Hontan, thinking perhaps that his French name of La Grande Gueule was wanting in dignity, Latinized it into Grangula, and the Scotchman Colden afterwards improved it into Garangula, under which high-sounding appellation Big Mouth has descended to posterity.

He was an astute old savage, well trained in the arts of Iroquois

306

rhetoric and gifted with the power of strong and caustic sarcasm, which has marked more than one of the chief orators of the confederacy. He shared with most of his countrymen the conviction that the earth had nothing so great as the league of the Iroquois, but if he could be proud and patriotic, so too he could be selfish and mean. He valued gifts, attentions and a good meal and would pay for them abundantly in promises, which he kept or not, as his own interests or those of his people might require. He could use bold and loud words in public and then secretly make his peace with those he had denounced. He was so given to rough jokes that the intendant Meules calls him a buffoon, but his buffoonery seems to have been often a cover to his craft.

He had taken a prominent part in the council of the preceding summer at Montreal, and doubtless, as he stood in full dress before the governor and the officers, his head plumed, his face painted, his figure draped in a colored blanket and his feet decked with embroidered moccasins, he was a picturesque and striking object. He was less so as he squatted almost naked by his lodge fire, with a piece of board laid across his lap, chopping rank tobacco with a scalping knife to fill his pipe, and entertaining the grinning circle with grotesque stories and obscene jests.

Though he was not one of the hereditary chiefs, his influence was great. "He has the strongest head and the loudest voice among the Iroquois," wrote Lamberville to La Barre. "He calls himself your best friend . . . He is a venal creature, whom you do well to keep in pay. I assured him I would send him the jerkin you promised." Well as the Jesuit knew the Iroquois, he was deceived if he thought that Big Mouth was securely won.

The first act of Viele was a blunder. He told the Onondagas that the English governor was master of their country, and that as they were subjects of the King of England, they must hold no council with the French without permission. The pride of Big Mouth was touched.

"You say," he exclaimed to the envoy, "that we are subjects of the King of England and the Duke of York, but we say that we are brothers. We must take care of ourselves. The coat-of-arms which you have fastened to that post cannot defend us against Onontio. We tell you that we shall bind a covenant chain to our arm and to his. We shall take the Senecas by one hand and Onontio by the other, and their hatchet and his sword shall be thrown into deep water."

Thus well and manfully did Big Mouth assert the independence of his tribe and proclaim it the arbiter of peace. He told the warriors, moreover, to close their ears to the words of the Dutchman, who spoke as if he were drunk, and it was resolved at last that he, Big Mouth, with an embassy of chiefs and elders, should go with Le Moyne to meet the French governor.

While these things were passing at Onondaga, La Barre had finished his preparations and was now in full campaign. Before setting out, he had written to the minister that he was about to advance on the enemy with seven hundred Canadians, a hundred and thirty regulars, and two hundred mission Indians; that more Indians were to join him on the way; that Du Lhut and La Durantaye were to meet him at Niagara with a body of *coureurs de bois* and Indians from the interior; and that, "when we are all united, we will perish or destroy the enemy."

After a long stay at Montreal, La Barre embarked his little army at La Chine, crossed Lake St. Louis and began the ascent of the upper St. Lawrence. In one of the three companies of regulars which formed a part of the force was a young subaltern, the Baron la Hontan, who has left a lively account of the expedition.

Some of the men were in flatboats and some were in birch canoes. Of the latter was La Hontan, whose craft was paddled by three Canadians. Several times they shouldered it through the forest to escape the turmoil of the rapids. The flatboats could not be so handled and were dragged or pushed up in the shallow water close to the bank by gangs of militiamen, toiling and struggling among the rocks and foam. The regulars, unskilled in such matters, were spared these fatigues, though tormented night and day by swarms of gnats and mosquitoes, objects of La Hontan's bitterest invective. At length the last rapid was passed and they moved serenely on their way, threaded the mazes of the Thousand Islands, entered what is now the harbor of Kingston, and landed under the palisades of Fort Frontenac.

Here the whole force was soon assembled—the regulars in their tents, the Canadian militia and the Indians in huts and under sheds of bark. Of these red allies there were several hundred: Abenakis and

Algonquins from Sillery, Hurons from Lorette, and converted Iroquois from the Jesuit mission of Saut St. Louis, near Montreal.

The camp of the French was on a low, damp plain near the fort, and here a malarious fever presently attacked them, killing many and disabling many more. La Hontan says that La Barre himself was brought by it to the brink of the grave. If he had ever entertained any other purpose than that of inducing the Senecas to agree to a temporary peace, he now completely abandoned it. He dared not even insist that the offending tribe should meet him in council, but hastened to ask the mediation of the Onondagas, which the letters of Lamberville had assured him that they were disposed to offer. He sent Le Moyne to persuade them to meet him on their own side of the lake, and with such of his men as were able to move, crossed to the mouth of Salmon River, then called La Famine.

The name proved prophetic. Provisions fell short from bad management in transportation and the men grew hungry and discontented. September had begun. The place was unwholesome and the malarious fever of Fort Frontenac infected the new encampment. The soldiers sickened rapidly. La Barre, racked with suspense, waited impatiently the return of Le Moyne, who presently appeared at La Famine on the third of the month, bringing with him Big Mouth and thirteen other deputies. La Barre gave them a feast of bread, wine and salmon trout, and on the morning of the fourth the council began.

Before the deputies arrived, the governor had sent the sick men homeward in order to conceal his helpless condition and he now told the Iroquois that he had left his army at Fort Frontenac and had come to meet them attended only by an escort. The Onondaga politician was not to be so deceived. He or one of his party spoke a little French, and during the night, roaming noiselessly among the tents, he contrived to learn the true state of the case from the soldiers.

The council was held on an open spot near the French encampment. La Barre was seated in an armchair. The Jesuit Bruyas stood by him as interpreter and the officers were ranged on his right and left. The Indians sat on the ground in a row opposite the governor, and two lines of soldiers, forming two sides of a square, closed the intervening space.

Among the officers was La Hontan, a spectator of the whole proceeding. He may be called a man in advance of his time, for he had the caustic, skeptical and mocking spirit which a century later marked the approach of the great revolution, but which was not a characteristic of the reign of Louis XIV. He usually told the truth when he had no motive to do otherwise, and yet was capable at times of prodigious mendacity. There is no reason to believe that he indulged in it on the present occasion and his account of what he now saw and heard may probably be taken as substantially correct. According to him, La Barre opened the council as follows:

"The King my master, being informed that the Five Nations of the Iroquois have long acted in a manner adverse to peace, has ordered me to come with an escort to this place, and to send Akouessan [Le Moyne] to Onondaga to invite the principal chiefs to meet me. It is the wish of this great King that you and I should smoke the calumet of peace together, provided that you promise in the name of the Mohawks, Oneidas, Onondagas, Cayugas and Senecas to give entire satisfaction and indemnity to his subjects, and do nothing in future which may occasion rupture."

Then he recounted the offenses of the Iroquois. First, they had maltreated and robbed French traders in the country of the Illinois, "wherefore," said the governor, "I am ordered to demand reparation and in case of refusal to declare war against you.

"The warriors of the Five Nations have introduced the English into the lakes which belong to the King my master, and among the tribes who are his children, in order to destroy the trade of his subjects and seduce these people from the obedience they owe him. I am willing to forget this, but should it happen again, I am expressly ordered to declare war against you.

"The warriors of the Five Nations have made sundry barbarous inroads into the country of the Illinois and Miamis, seizing, binding and leading into captivity an infinite number of these savages in time of peace. They are the children of my King and are not to remain your slaves. They must at once be set free and sent home. If you refuse to do this, I am expressly ordered to declare war against you."

La Barre concluded by assuring Big Mouth, as representing the Five Nations of the Iroquois, that the French would leave them in peace if they made atonement for the past and promised good conduct for the future, but that if they did not heed his words, their villages should be burned and they themselves destroyed. He added, though he knew the contrary, that the governor of New York would join him in war against them.

During the delivery of this martial harangue, Big Mouth sat silent and attentive, his eyes fixed on the bowl of his pipe. When the interpreter had ceased, he rose, walked gravely two or three times around the lines of the assembly, then stopped before the governor, looked steadily at him, stretched his tawny arm, opened his capacious jaws and uttered himself as follows:

"Onontio, I honor you, and all the warriors who are with me honor you. Your interpreter has ended his speech, and now I begin mine. Listen to my words.

"Onontio, when you left Quebec you must have thought that the heat of the sun had burned the forests that make our country inaccessible to the French, or that the lake had overflowed them so that we could not escape from our villages. You must have thought so, Onontio, and curiosity to see such a fire or such a flood must have brought you to this place. Now your eyes are opened, for I and my warriors have come to tell you that the Senecas, Cayugas, Onondagas, Oneidas and Mohawks are all alive. I thank you in their name for bringing back the calumet of peace which they gave to your predecessors, and I give you joy that you have not dug up the hatchet which has been so often red with the blood of your countrymen.

"Listen, Onontio. I am not asleep. My eyes are open, and by the sun that gives me light I see a great captain at the head of a band of soldiers who talks like a man in a dream. He says that he has come to smoke the pipe of peace with the Onondagas, but I see that he came to knock them in the head if so many of his Frenchmen were not too weak to fight. I see Onontio raving in a camp of sick men, whose lives the Great Spirit has saved by smiting them with disease. Our women had snatched war clubs and our children and old men seized bows and arrows to attack your camp, if our warriors had not restrained them, when your messenger Akouessan appeared in our village."

He next justified the pillage of French traders on the ground, very doubtful in this case, that they were carrying arms to the Illinois, enemies of the confederacy, and he flatly refused to make reparation, telling La Barre that even the old men of his tribe had no fear of the

311

French. He also avowed boldly that the Iroquois had conducted English traders to the lakes. "We are born free," he exclaimed. "We depend neither on Onontio nor on Corlaer. We have the right to go wherever we please, to take with us whomever we please, and buy and sell of whomever we please. If your allies are your slaves or your children, treat them like slaves or children, and forbid them to deal with anybody but your Frenchmen.

"We have knocked the Illinois in the head because they cut down the tree of peace and hunted the beaver on our lands. We have done less than the English and the French, who have seized upon the lands of many tribes, driven them away, and built towns, villages and forts in their country.

"Listen, Onontio. My voice is the voice of the Five Tribes of the Iroquois. When they buried the hatchet at Cataraqui [Fort Frontenac] in presence of your predecessor, they planted the tree of peace in the middle of the fort, that it might be a post of traders and not of soldiers. Take care that all the soldiers you have brought with you, shut up in so small a fort, do not choke this tree of peace. I assure you in the name of the Five Tribes that our warriors will dance the dance of the calumet under its branches, and that they will sit quiet on their mats and never dig up the hatchet till their brothers, Onontio and Corlaer, separately or together, make ready to attack the country that the Great Spirit has given to our ancestors."

The session presently closed and La Barre withdrew to his tent where, according to La Hontan, he vented his feelings in invective till reminded that good manners were not to be expected from an Iroquois. Big Mouth, on his part, entertained some of the French at a feast which he opened in person by a dance.

There was another session in the afternoon and the terms of peace were settled in the evening. The tree of peace was planted anew. La Barre promised not to attack the Senecas and Big Mouth, in spite of his former declaration, consented that they should make amends for the pillage of the traders. On the other hand, he declared that the Iroquois would fight the Illinois to the death and La Barre dared not utter a word in behalf of his allies. The Onondaga next demanded that the council fire should be removed from Fort Frontenac to La Famine, in the Iroquois country. This point was yielded without resistance and

La Barre promised to decamp and set out for home on the following morning.

Such was the futile and miserable end of the grand expedition. Even the promise to pay for the plundered goods was contemptuously broken. The honor rested with the Iroquois. They had spurned the French, repelled the claims of the English and by act and word asserted their independence of both.

The treaty made at La Famine was greeted with contumely through all the colony and the next ship from France brought the following letter from the King: "Monsieur de la Barre—Having been informed that your years do not permit you to support the fatigues inseparable from your office of governor and lieutenant general in Canada, I send you this letter to acquaint you that I have selected Monsieur de Denonville to serve in your place; and my intention is that, on his arrival, after resigning to him the command, with all instructions concerning it, you embark for your return to France."

La Barre sailed for home and the Marquis de Denonville, a pious colonel of dragoons, assumed the vacant office.

CHAPTER 3

~~~~~~

Denonville and the Senecas

DENONVILLE EMBARKED AT ROCHELLE IN JUNE with his wife and a part of his family. Saint-Vallier, the destined bishop, was in the same vessel and the squadron carried five hundred soldiers, of whom a hundred and fifty died of fever and scurvy on the way.

Saint-Vallier speaks in glowing terms of the new governor: "He spent nearly all his time in prayer and the reading of good books. The Psalms of David were always in his hands. In all the voyage, I never saw him do anything wrong, and there was nothing in words or acts which did not show a solid virtue and a consummate prudence, as well in the duties of the Christian life as in the wisdom of this world."

Much was expected of Denonville. He was to repair the mischief wrought by his predecessor and restore the colony to peace, strength and security. The King had stigmatized La Barre's treaty with the Iroquois as disgraceful and expressed indignation at his abandonment of the Illinois allies. All this was now to be changed, but it was easier to give the order at Versailles than to execute it in Canada.

Denonville's difficulties were great and his means of overcoming them were small. What he most needed were more troops and more money. The Senecas, insolent and defiant, were still attacking the Illinois; the tribes of the northwest were angry, contemptuous and disaffected; the English of New York were urging claims to the whole country south of the Great Lakes and to a controlling share in all the western fur trade; while the English of Hudson's Bay were competing

314

for the traffic of the northern tribes and the English of New England were seizing upon the fisheries of Acadia, and now and then making piratical descents upon its coast. The great question lay between New York and Canada. Which of these two should gain mastery in the west?

Denonville, like Frontenac, was a man of the army and the court. As a soldier, he had the experience of thirty years of service and he was in high repute not only for piety but for probity and honor. He was devoted to the Jesuits, an ardent servant of the King, a lover of authority, filled with the instinct of subordination and order and, in short, a type of the ideas religious, political and social then dominant in France. He was greatly distressed at the disturbed condition of the colony, while the state of the settlements, scattered in broken lines for two or three hundred miles along the St. Lawrence, seemed to him an invitation to destruction. "If we have a war," he wrote, "nothing can save the country but a miracle of God."

Nothing was more likely than war. Intrigues were on foot between the Senecas and the tribes of the lakes which threatened to render the appeal to arms a necessity to the French. Some of the Hurons of Michilimackinac were bent on allying themselves with the English. "They like the manners of the French," wrote Denonville, "but they like the cheap goods of the English better." The Senecas, in collusion with several Huron chiefs, had captured a considerable number of that tribe and of the Ottawas. The scheme was that these prisoners should be released on condition that the lake tribes should join the Senecas and repudiate their alliance with the French. The governor of New York favored this intrigue to the utmost.

Denonville was quick to see that the peril of the colony rose not from the Iroquois alone, but from the English of New York who prompted them. Dongan understood the situation. He saw that the French aimed at mastering the whole interior of the continent. They had established themselves in the valley of the Illinois, had built a fort on the lower Mississippi, and were striving to entrench themselves at its mouth. They occupied the Great Lakes and it was already evident that as soon as their resources should permit they would seize the avenues of communication throughout the west. In short, the grand scheme of French colonization had begun to declare itself.

315

Dongan entered the lists against them. If his policy should prevail, New France would dwindle to a feeble province on the St. Lawrence; if the French policy should prevail, the English colonies would remain a narrow strip along the sea. Dongan's cause was that of all these colonies, but they all stood aloof and left him to wage the strife alone. Canada was matched against New York, or rather against the governor of New York. The population of the English colony was larger than that of its rival, but except the fur traders, few of the settlers cared much for the questions at issue.

Dongan's chief difficulty, however, rose from the relations of the French and English kings. Louis XIV gave Denonville an unhesitating support. James II, on the other hand, was for a time cautious to timidity. The two monarchs were closely united. Both hated constitutional liberty and both held the same principles of supremacy in Church and State, but Louis was triumphant and powerful while James, in conflict with his subjects, was in constant need of his great ally and dared not offend him.

The royal instructions to Denonville enjoined him to humble the Iroquois, sustain the allies of the colony, oppose the schemes of Dongan and treat him as an enemy if he encroached on French territory. At the same time, the French ambassador at the English court was directed to demand from James II precise orders to the governor of New York for a complete change of conduct in regard to Canada and the Iroquois.

But Dongan, like the French governors, was not easily controlled. In the absence of money and troops, he intrigued busily with his Indian neighbors. "The artifices of the English," wrote Denonville, "have reached such a point that it would be better if they attacked us openly and burned our settlements instead of instigating the Iroquois against us for our destruction. I know beyond a particle of doubt that M. Dongan caused all the five Iroquois nations to be assembled last spring at Orange [Albany] in order to excite them against us, by telling them publicly that I meant to declare war against them."

He says, further, that Dongan supplies them with arms and ammunition, incites them to attack the colony and urges them to deliver Lamberville, the priest at Onondaga, into his hands. "He has sent people at the same time to our Montreal Indians to entice them over to him, promising them missionaries to instruct them, and assuring them that he would prevent the introduction of brandy into their villages. All these intrigues have given me not a little trouble throughout the summer. M. Dongan has written to me and I have answered him as a man may do who wishes to dissimulate and does not feel strong enough to get angry."

The most pressing danger was the defection of the lake tribes. "In spite of the King's edicts," pursues Denonville, "the *coureurs de bois* have carried a hundred barrels of brandy to Michilimackinac in a single year, and their libertinism and debauchery have gone to such an extremity that it is a wonder the Indians have not massacred them all to save themselves from their violence and recover their wives and daughters from them. This, Monseigneur, joined to our failure in the last war, has drawn upon us such contempt among all the tribes that there is but one way to regain our credit, which is to humble the Iroquois by our unaided strength, without asking the help of our Indian allies." And he begs hard for a strong reinforcement of troops.

Without doubt, Denonville was right in thinking that the chastising of the Iroquois, or at least the Senecas, the head and front of mischief, was a matter of the last necessity. A crushing blow dealt against them would restore French prestige, paralyze English intrigue, save the Illinois from destruction and confirm the wavering allies of Canada.

Meanwhile, matters grew from bad to worse. In the north and in the west, there was scarcely a tribe in the French interest which was not either attacked by the Senecas or cajoled by them into alliances hostile to the colony. "We may set down Canada as lost," again writes Denonville, "if we do not make war next year; and yet, in our present disordered state, war is the most dangerous thing in the world. Nothing can save us but the sending out of troops and the building of forts and blockhouses. Yet I dare not begin to build them, for if I do it will bring down all the Iroquois upon us before we are in a condition to fight them."

Nevertheless, he made what preparations he could, begging all the while for more soldiers and carrying on at the same time a correspondence with his rival, Dongan. At first it was courteous on both sides, but it soon grew pungent, and at last acrid.

317

Denonville, vexed and perturbed by his long strife with Dongan and the Iroquois, presently found a moment of comfort in tidings that reached him from the north. Here, as in the west, there was violent rivalry between the subjects of the two crowns. With the help of two French renegades named Radisson and Groseilliers, the English Company of Hudson's Bay, then in its infancy, had established a post near the mouth of Nelson River, on the western shore of that dreary inland sea. The company had also three other posts—called Fort Albany, Fort Hayes and Fort Rupert—at the southern end of the bay.

A rival French company had been formed in Canada under the name of the "Company of the North" and it resolved on an effort to expel its English competitors. Though it was a time of profound peace between the two kings, Denonville warmly espoused the plan, and in the early spring of 1686 he sent the Chevalier de Troyes from Montreal, with eighty or more Canadians, to execute it. With Troyes went Iberville, Sainte-Hélène and Maricourt, three of the sons of Charles le Moyne; and the Jesuit Silvy joined the party as chaplain.

They ascended the Ottawa and thence, from stream to stream and lake to lake, toiled painfully towards their goal. At length they neared Fort Hayes. It was a stockade with four bastions, mounted with cannon. There was a strong blockhouse within, in which the sixteen occupants of the place were lodged, unsuspicious of danger. Troyes approached at night. Iberville and Sainte-Hélène with a few followers climbed the palisade on one side, while the rest of the party burst the main gate with a sort of battering-ram and rushed in, yelling the war whoop. In a moment the door of the blockhouse was dashed open and its astonished inmates captured in their shirts.

The victors now embarked for Fort Rupert, distant forty leagues along the shore. In construction it resembled Fort Hayes. The fifteen traders who held the place were all asleep at night in their blockhouse when the Canadians burst the gate of the stockade and swarmed into the area. One of them mounted by a ladder to the roof of the building and dropped lighted hand grenades down the chimney, which exploded among the occupants and told them unmistakably that something was wrong. At the same time the assailants fired briskly on them through the loopholes and, placing a petard under the walls, threatened to blow them into the air. Five, including a woman, were killed or wounded and the rest cried for quarter.

Meanwhile, Iberville with another party attacked a vessel anchored near the fort and, climbing silently over her side, found the man on watch asleep in his blanket. He sprang up and made fight but they killed him, then stamped on the deck to rouse those below, sabered two of them as they came up the hatchway and captured the rest. Among them was Bridger, governor for the company of all its stations on the bay.

They next turned their attention to Fort Albany, thirty leagues from Fort Hayes in a direction opposite to that of Fort Rupert. Here there were about thirty men, under Henry Sargent, an agent of the company. Surprise was this time impossible, for news of their proceedings had gone before them and Sargent, though no soldier, stood on his defense. The Canadians arrived, some in canoes, some in the captured vessel, bringing ten captured pieces of cannon which they planted in battery on a neighboring hill, well covered by entrenchments from the English shot. Here they presently opened fire, and in an hour the stockade with the houses that it enclosed was completely riddled. The English took shelter in a cellar, nor was it till the fire slackened that they ventured out to show a white flag and ask for a parley. Troyes and Sargent had an interview. The Englishman regaled his conqueror with a bottle of Spanish wine, and after drinking the health of King Louis and King James they settled the terms of capitulation. The prisoners were sent home in an English vessel which soon after arrived and Maricourt remained to command at the bay, while Troyes returned to report his success to Denonville.

This buccaneer exploit exasperated the English public and it became doubly apparent that the state of affairs in America could not be allowed to continue. A conference had been arranged between the two powers even before the news came from Hudson's Bay and Count d'Avaux appeared at London as special envoy of Louis XIV to settle the questions at issue. A treaty of neutrality was signed at Whitehall and commissioners were appointed on both sides.

Pending the discussion, each party was to refrain from acts of hostility or encroachment, and, said the declaration of the commissioners, "to the end the said agreement may have the better effect, we do likewise agree that the said serene kings shall immediately send necessary orders in that behalf to their respective governors in America." Dongan accordingly was directed to keep a friendly correspondence with his rival and take good care to give him no cause of complaint.

More than four months after, Louis XIV sent corresponding instructions to Denonville, but meantime he had sent him troops, money and munitions in abundance and ordered him to attack the Iroquois towns. Whether such a step was consistent with the recent treaty of neutrality may well be doubted, for though James II had not yet formally claimed the Iroquois as British subjects, his representative had done so for years with his tacit approval, and out of this claim had risen the principal differences which it was the object of the treaty to settle.

It was whispered that there was to be war and the rumor was brought to the ears of Dongan by some Canadian deserters. He lost no time in warning the Iroquois and their deputies came to beg for his help. Danger humbled them for the moment. They not only recognized King James as their sovereign but consented at last to call his representative *Father* Corlaer instead of *Brother*. Their father, however, dared not promise them soldiers, though in spite of the recent treaty he caused gunpowder and lead to be given them and urged them to recall the powerful war parties which they had lately sent against the Illinois.

Denonville at length broke silence and ordered the militia to muster. They grumbled and hesitated, for they remembered the failures of La Barre. The governor issued a proclamation, and the bishop a pastoral mandate. There were sermons, prayers and exhortations in all the churches. A revulsion of popular feeling followed and the people, says Denonville, "made ready for the march with extraordinary animation." The Church showered blessings on them as they went and daily masses were ordained for the downfall of the foes of Heaven and of France.

Again the fields about Fort Frontenac were covered with tents, camp sheds and wigwams. Regulars, militia and Indians, there were about two thousand men, and besides these, eight hundred regulars just arrived from France had been left at Montreal to protect the settlers. Fortune thus far had smiled on the enterprise and she now gave Denonville a fresh proof of her favor. On the very day of his arrival, a canoe came from Niagara with news that a large body of allies from the west had reached that place three days before and were waiting his commands. It was more than he had dared to hope. In the preceding autumn he had ordered Tonty, commanding at the Illinois, and La Durantaye, commanding at Michilimackinac, to muster as many *coureurs de bois* and Indians as possible and join him early in July at Niagara. The distances were vast and the difficulties incalculable. In the eyes of the pious governor, their timely arrival was a manifest sign of the favor of Heaven.

At Fort St. Louis of the Illinois, Tonty had mustered sixteen Frenchmen and about two hundred Indians, whom he led across the country to Detroit. Here he found Du Lhut, La Fôret and La Durantaye with a large body of French and Indians from the upper lakes. It had been the work of the whole winter to induce these savages to move. Presents, persuasions and promises had not been spared, and while La Durantaye, aided by the Jesuit Engelran, labored to gain over the tribes of Michilimackinac, the indefatigable Nicolas Perrot was at work among those of the Mississippi and Lake Michigan.

They were of a race unsteady as aspens and fierce as wildcats, full of mutual jealousies, without rulers and without laws, for each was a law to himself. It was difficult to persuade them, and when persuaded, scarcely possible to keep them so. Perrot, however, induced some of them to follow him to Michilimackinac, where many hundreds of Algonquin savages were presently gathered—a perilous crew who changed their minds every day, and whose dancing, singing and yelping might turn at any moment into war whoops against one another or against their hosts, the French.

The Hurons showed more stability and La Durantaye was reasonably sure that some of them would follow him to the war, though it was clear that others were bent on allying themselves with the Senecas and the English. As for the Potawatomis, Sacs, Ojibwas, Ottawas and other Algonquin hordes, no man could foresee what they would do.

La Durantaye and his companions, with a hundred and eighty *coureurs de bois* and four hundred Indians, waited impatiently at Niagara for orders from the governor. A canoe dispatched in haste from Fort Frontenac soon appeared and they were directed to repair

321

at once to the rendezvous at Irondequoit Bay, on the borders of the Seneca country.

Denonville was already on his way there. On the fourth of July he had embarked at Fort Frontenac with four hundred bateaux and canoes, crossed the foot of Lake Ontario, and moved westward along the southern shore. The weather was rough and six days passed before he descried the low headlands of Irondequoit Bay. Far off on the glimmering water he saw a multitude of canoes advancing to meet him. It was the flotilla of La Durantaye. Good management and good luck had so disposed it that the allied bands, concentrating from points more than a thousand miles distant, reached the rendezvous on the same day. This was not all. The Ottawas of Michilimackinac, who refused to follow La Durantaye, had changed their minds the next morning, embarked in a body, paddled up the Georgian Bay of Lake Huron, crossed to Toronto and joined the allies at Niagara. White and red, Denonville now had nearly three thousand men under his command.

All were gathered on the low point of land that separates Irondequoit Bay from Lake Ontario. "Never," says an eyewitness, "had Canada seen such a sight; and never, perhaps, will she see such a sight again. Here was the camp of the regulars from France, with the general's headquarters; the camp of the four battalions of Canadian militia, commanded by the *noblesse* of the country; the camp of the Christian Indians; and farther on, a swarm of savages of every nation. Their features were different and so were their manners, their weapons, their decorations and their dances. They sang and whooped and harangued in every accent and tongue. Most of them wore nothing but horns on their heads and the tails of beasts behind their backs. Their faces were painted red or green, with black or white spots; their ears and noses were hung with ornaments of iron; and their naked bodies were daubed with figures of various sorts of animals."

These were the allies from the upper lakes. The enemy, meanwhile, had taken alarm. Just after the army arrived, three Seneca scouts called from the edge of the woods and demanded what they meant to do. "To fight you, you blockheads," answered a Mohawk Christian attached to the French. A volley of bullets was fired at the scouts, but they escaped and carried the news to their villages. Many of the best warriors were absent. Those who remained, four hundred or four hundred and fifty by their own accounts, and eight hundred by that of the French, mustered in haste, and though many of them were mere boys, they sent off the women and children, hid their most valued possessions, burned their chief town and prepared to meet the invaders.

On the twelfth, at three o'clock in the afternoon, Denonville began his march, leaving four hundred men in a hastily built fort to guard the bateaux and canoes. Troops, officers and Indians all carried their provisions at their backs. Some of the Christian Mohawks guided them, but guides were scarcely needed for a broad Indian trail led from the bay to the great Seneca town, twenty-two miles southward.

They marched three leagues through the open forests of oak and encamped for the night. In the morning the heat was intense. The men gasped in the dead and sultry air of the woods, or grew faint in the pitiless sun as they waded waist-deep through the rank grass of the narrow intervales. They passed safely through two dangerous defiles, and about two in the afternoon began to enter a third. Dense forests covered the hills on either hand.

La Durantaye with Tonty and his cousin Du Lhut led the advance, nor could all Canada have supplied three men better for the' work. Each led his band of *coureurs de bois,* white Indians without discipline and scarcely capable of it, but brave and accustomed to the woods. On their left were the Iroquois converts from the missions of Saut St. Louis and the Mountain of Montreal, fighting under the influence of their ghostly prompters against their own countrymen. On the right were the pagan Indians from the west. The woods were full of these painted specters, grotesquely horrible in horns and tail, and among them flitted the black robe of Father Engelran, the Jesuit of Michilimackinac. Nicolas Perrot and two other bushranging Frenchmen were assigned to command them, but in fact they obeyed no man. These formed the vanguard, eight or nine hundred in all, under an excellent officer, Callières, governor of Montreal.

Behind came the main body under Denonville, each of the four battalions of regulars alternating with a battalion of Canadians. Some of the regulars wore light armor, while the Canadians were in plain attire of coarse cloth or buckskin. Denonville, oppressed by the heat, marched in his shirt. "It is a rough life," wrote the marquis, "to tramp afoot through the woods, carrying one's own provisions in a haversack, devoured by mosquitoes and faring no better than a mere soldier."

With him was the Chevalier de Vaudreuil, who had just arrived from France in command of the eight hundred men left to guard the colony, and who, eager to take part in the campaign, had pushed forward alone to join the army. Here, too, were the Canadian seigniors at the head of their vassals, Berthier, La Valterie, Granville, Longueuil and many more. A guard of rangers and Indians brought up the rear.

Scouts thrown out in front ran back with the report that they had reached the Seneca clearings and had seen no more dangerous enemy than three or four women in the cornfields. This was a device of the Senecas to cheat the French into the belief that the inhabitants were still in the town. It had the desired effect. The vanguard pushed rapidly forward, hoping to surprise the place and ignorant that behind the ridge of thick forests on their right, among a tangled growth of beech trees in the gorge of a brook, three hundred ambushed warriors lay biding their time.

Hurrying forward through the forest, they left the main body behind and soon reached the end of the defile. The woods were still dense on their left and front, but on their right lay a great marsh, covered with alder thickets and rank grass.

Suddenly the air was filled with yells and a rapid though distant fire was opened from the thickets and the forest. Scores of painted savages, stark naked, some armed with swords and some with hatchets, leaped screeching from their ambuscade and rushed against the van. Almost at the same moment a burst of whoops and firing sounded in the defile behind. It was the ambushed three hundred supporting the onset of their countrymen in front, but they had made a fatal mistake. Deceived by the numbers of the vanguard, they supposed it to be the whole army, never suspecting that Denonville was close behind with sixteen hundred men.

It was a surprise on both sides. So dense was the forest that the advancing battalions could see neither the enemy nor one another. Appalled by the din of whoops and firing, redoubled by the echoes of the narrow valley, the whole army was seized with something like a panic. Some of the officers, it is said, threw themselves on the ground in their fright. There were a few moments of intense bewilderment. The various corps became broken and confused, and moved here and there without knowing why.

Denonville behaved with great courage. He ran, sword in hand, to where the uproar was greatest, ordered the drums to beat the charge, turned back the militia of Berthier who were trying to escape, and commanded them and all others whom he met to fire on whatever looked like an enemy. He was bravely seconded by Callières, La Valterie and several other officers. The Christian Iroquois fought well from the first, leaping from tree to tree and exchanging shots and defiance with their heathen countrymen till the Senecas, seeing themselves confronted by numbers that seemed endless, abandoned the field after heavy loss, carrying with them many of their dead and all of their wounded.

Denonville made no attempt to pursue. He had learned the dangers of this blind warfare of the woods and he feared that the Senecas would waylay him again in the labyrinth of bushes that lay between him and the town.

"Our troops," he says, "were all so overcome by the extreme heat and the long march that we were forced to remain where we were till morning. We had the pain of witnessing the usual cruelties of the Indians, who cut the dead bodies into quarters, like butchers' meat, to put into their kettles, and opened most of them while still warm to drink the blood. Our rascally Ottawas particularly distinguished themselves by these barbarities, as well as by cowardice; for they made off in the fight. We had five or six men killed on the spot, and about twenty wounded, among whom were Father Engelran, who was badly hurt by a gunshot. Some prisoners who escaped from the Senecas tell us that they lost forty men killed outright, twenty-five of whom we saw butchered. One of the escaped prisoners saw the rest buried, and he saw also more than sixty very dangerously wounded."

In the morning the troops advanced in order of battle through a marsh covered with alders and tall grass, whence they had no sooner emerged than, says Abbé Belmont, "we began to see the famous Babylon of the Senecas, where so many crimes have been committed, so much blood spilled, and so many men burned. It was a village or

325

town of bark, on the top of a hill. They had burned it a week before. We found nothing in it but the graveyard and the graves, full of snakes and other creatures; a great mask, with teeth and eyes of brass, and a bearskin drawn over it, with which they performed their conjurations." The fire had also spared a number of huge receptacles of bark, still filled with the last season's corn, while the fields around were covered with the growing crop, ripening in the July sun. There were hogs, too, in great number, for the Iroquois did not share the antipathy with which Indians were apt to regard that unsavory animal, and from which certain philosophers have argued their descent from the Jews.

The soldiers killed the hogs, burned the old corn, and hacked down the new with their swords. Next they advanced to an abandoned Seneca fort on a hill half a league distant and burned it, with all that it contained. Ten days were passed in the work of havoc. Three neighboring villages were leveled, and all their fields laid waste. The amount of corn destroyed was prodigious. Denonville reckons it at the absurdly exaggerated amount of twelve hundred thousand bushels.

The Senecas, laden with such of their possessions as they could carry off, had fled to their confederates in the east and Denonville did not venture to pursue them. His men, feasting without stint on green corn and fresh pork, were sickening rapidly and his Indian allies were deserting him.

On the twenty-fourth he withdrew, with all his army, to the fortified post at Irondequoit Bay, whence he proceeded to Niagara, in order to accomplish his favorite purpose of building a fort there. The troops were set at work and a stockade was planted on the point of land at the eastern angle between the river Niagara and Lake Ontario, the site of the ruined fort built by La Salle nine years before. Here he left a hundred men, under the Chevalier de Troyes, and embarking with the rest of the army, descended to Montreal.

The campaign was but half a success. Joined to the capture of the English traders on the lakes, it had indeed prevented the defection of the western Indians and in some slight measure restored their respect for the French—of whom, nevertheless, one of them was heard to say that they were good for nothing but to make war on hogs and corn.

As for the Senecas, they were more enraged than hurt. They could rebuild their bark villages in a few weeks, and though they had lost their harvest, their confederates would not let them starve. A converted Iroquois had told the governor before his departure that if he overset a wasps' nest, he must crush the wasps or they would sting him. Denonville left the wasps alive.

CHAPTER 4

The Iroquois Invasion

W HEN DONGAN HEARD THAT THE FRENCH HAD
invaded the Senecas, seized English traders on the lakes and
built a fort at Niagara, his wrath was kindled anew. He sent to the
Iroquois and summoned them to meet him at Albany; told the assembled chiefs that the late calamity had fallen upon them because
they had held councils with the French without asking his leave; forbade them to do so again, and informed them that as subjects of King
James they must make no treaty except by the consent of his representative, the governor of New York. He declared that the Ottawas
and other remote tribes were also British subjects; that the Iroquois
should unite with them to expel the French from the west; and that all
alike should bring down their beaver skins to the English at Albany.
Moreover, he enjoined them to receive no more French Jesuits into
their towns, and to call home their countrymen whom these fathers had
converted and enticed to Canada.

"Obey my commands," added the governor, "for that is the only
way to eat well and sleep well, without fear or disturbance." The Iroquois, who wanted his help, seemed to assent to all he said. "We will
fight the French," exclaimed their orator, "as long as we have a man
left."

The dispute now assumed a new phase. James II at length consented to own the Iroquois as his subjects, ordering Dongan to protect them and repel the French by force of arms should they attack
them again. At the same time, conferences were opened at London be-

328

tween the French ambassador and the English commissioners appointed to settle the questions at issue. Both disputants claimed the Iroquois as subjects and the contest wore an aspect more serious than before.

The royal declaration was a great relief to Dongan. Thus far he had acted at his own risk. Now he was sustained by the orders of his King. He instantly assumed a warlike attitude, and in the next spring wrote to the Earl of Sunderland that he had been at Albany all winter, with four hundred infantry, fifty horsemen and eight hundred Indians. This was not without cause, for a report had come from Canada that the French were about to march on Albany to destroy it.

Denonville was sorely perplexed. He was hard pressed and eager for peace with the Iroquois at any price, but Dongan was using every means to prevent their treating of peace with the French governor until he had complied with all the English demands. In this extremity, Denonville sent Father Vaillant to Albany in the hope of bringing his intractable rival to conditions less humiliating.

The Jesuit played his part with ability and proved more than a match for his adversary in dialectics, but Dongan held fast to all his demands. Vaillant tried to temporize and asked for a truce, with a view to a final settlement by reference to the two kings. Dongan referred the question to a meeting of Iroquois chiefs, who declared in reply that they would make neither peace nor truce till Fort Niagara was demolished and all the prisoners restored.

Vaillant returned from his bootless errand and a stormy correspondence followed between the two governors. Dongan renewed his demands, then protested his wish for peace, extolled King James for his pious zeal and declared that he was sending over missionaries of his own to convert the Iroquois. What Denonville wanted was not their conversion by Englishmen but their conversion by Frenchmen, and the presence in their towns of those most useful political agents, the Jesuits. He replied angrily, charging Dongan with preventing the conversion of the Iroquois by driving off the French missionaries, and accusing him further of instigating the tribes of New York to attack Canada.

Suddenly there was a change in the temper of his letters. He wrote to his rival in terms of studied civility; declared that he wished he could meet him and consult with him on the best means of advancing the cause of true religion; begged that he would not refuse him his friendship; and thanked him in warm terms for befriending some French prisoners whom he had saved from the Iroquois and treated with great kindness.

This change was due to dispatches from Versailles, in which Denonville was informed that the matters in dispute would soon be amicably settled by the commissioners; that he was to keep on good terms with the English commanders and, what pleased him still more, that the King of England was about to recall Dongan.

In fact, James II had resolved on remodeling his American colonies. New York, New Jersey and New England had been formed into one government under Sir Edmund Andros and Dongan was summoned home, where a regiment was given him with the rank of major general of artillery. Denonville says that in his efforts to extend English trade to the Great Lakes and the Mississippi his late rival had been influenced by motives of personal gain. Be this as it may, he was a bold and vigorous defender of the claims of the British Crown.

Sir Edmund Andros now reigned over New York, and by the terms of his commission, his rule stretched westward to the Pacific. The usual official courtesies passed between him and Denonville, but Andros renewed all the demands of his predecessor, claimed the Iroquois as subjects and forbade the French to attack them. The new governor was worse than the old.

While these things were passing, the state of Canada was deplorable and the position of its governor as mortifying as it was painful. He thought with good reason that the maintenance of the new fort at Niagara was of great importance to the colony and he had repeatedly refused the demands of Dongan and the Iroquois for its demolition. But a power greater than sachems and governors presently intervened. The provisions left at Niagara, though abundant, were atrociously bad. Scurvy and other malignant diseases soon broke out among the soldiers. The Senecas prowled about the place and no man dared venture out for hunting, fishing or firewood. The fort was first a prison, then a hospital, then a charnel house, till before spring the garrison of a hundred men was reduced to ten or twelve.

In this condition they were found towards the end of April by a large war party of friendly Miamis, who entered the place and held it till a French detachment at length arrived for its relief. The garrison of Fort Frontenac had suffered from the same causes, though not to the same degree. Denonville feared that he should be forced to abandon them both. The way was so long and so dangerous, and the governor had grown of late so cautious, that he dreaded the risk of maintaining such remote communications. On second thought, he resolved to keep Frontenac and sacrifice Niagara. He promised Dongan that he would demolish it and he kept his word.

What had brought the marquis to this pass? Famine, destitution, disease and the Iroquois were making Canada their prey. The fur trade had been stopped for two years and the people, bereft of their only means of subsistence, could contribute nothing to their own defense. Above Three Rivers, the whole population was imprisoned in stockade forts hastily built in every seigniory. Here they were safe provided that they never ventured out, but their fields were left untilled and the governor was already compelled to feed many of them at the expense of the King.

The Iroquois roamed among the deserted settlements or prowled like lynxes about the forts, waylaying convoys and killing or capturing stragglers. Their war parties were usually small, but their movements were so mysterious and their attacks so sudden that they spread a universal panic through the upper half of the colony. They were the wasps which Denonville had failed to kill.

But now a new hope dawned on the governor. He had been more active of late in negotiating than in fighting and his diplomacy had prospered more than his arms. Some of the Iroquois entrapped at Fort Frontenac had been given to their Christian relatives in the mission villages. Here they had since remained and Denonville thought that he might use them as messengers to their heathen countrymen. He sent one or more of them to Onondaga with gifts and overtures of peace.

That shrewd old politician, Big Mouth, was still strong in influence at the Iroquois capital and his name was great to the farthest bounds of the confederacy. He knew by personal experience the advantages of a neutral position between the rival European powers, from both of whom he received gifts and attention, and he saw that what was good

331

for him was good for the confederacy, since if it gave itself to neither party, both would court its alliance. In his opinion, it had now leaned long enough towards the English and a change of attitude had become expedient. Therefore, as Denonville promised the return of the prisoners and was plainly ready to make other concessions, Big Mouth, ignoring the prohibitions of Andros, consented to a conference with the French.

He set out at his leisure for Montreal, with six Onondaga, Cayuga and Oneida chiefs, and as no diplomat ever understood better the advantage of negotiating at the head of an imposing force, a body of Iroquois warriors—to the number, it is said, of twelve hundred—set out before him and silently took path to Canada.

The ambassadors paddled across the lake and presented themselves before the commandant of Fort Frontenac, who received them with distinction and ordered Lieutenant Perelle to escort them to Montreal. Scarcely had the officer conducted his august charge five leagues on their way when, to his amazement, he found himself in the midst of six hundred Iroquois warriors, who amused themselves for a time with his terror and then accompanied him as far as Lake St. Francis, where he found another body of savages nearly equal in number. Here the warriors halted and the ambassadors with their escort gravely pursued their way to meet Denonville at Montreal.

Big Mouth spoke haughtily, like a man who knew his power. He told the governor that he and his people were subjects neither of the French nor of the English; that they wished to be friends of both; that they held their country of the Great Spirit; and that they had never been conquered in war. He declared that the Iroquois knew the weakness of the French and could easily exterminate them; that they had formed a plan of burning all the houses and barns of Canada, killing the cattle, setting fire to the ripe grain and then, when the people were starving, attacking the forts; but that he, Big Mouth, had prevented its execution. He concluded by saying that he was allowed but four days to bring back the governor's reply, and that if he were kept waiting longer, he would not answer for what might happen.

Though it appeared by some expressions in his speech that he was ready to make peace only with the French, leaving the Iroquois free to attack the Indian allies of the colony, and though while the ambassadors were at Montreal their warriors on the river above actually killed several of the Indian converts, Denonville felt himself compelled to pretend ignorance of the outrage. A declaration of neutrality was drawn up and Big Mouth affixed to it the figures of sundry birds and beasts as the signatures of himself and his fellow chiefs. He promised, too, that within a certain time deputies from the whole confederacy should come to Montreal and conclude a general peace.

The time arrived and they did not appear. It became known, however, that a number of chiefs were coming from Onondaga to explain the delay and to promise that the deputies would soon follow. The chiefs, in fact, were on their way. They reached La Famine, the scene of La Barre's meeting with Big Mouth, and here an unexpected incident arrested them and completely changed the aspect of affairs.

Among the Hurons of Michilimackinac there was a chief of high renown named Kondiaronk, or the Rat. He was in the prime of life, a redoubted warrior and a sage counselor. The French seem to have admired him greatly. "He is a gallant man," says La Hontan, "if ever there was one," while Charlevoix declares that he was the ablest Indian the French ever knew in America, and that he had nothing of the savage but the name and the dress.

In spite of the father's eulogy, the moral condition of the Rat savored strongly of the wigwam. He had given Denonville great trouble by his constant intrigues with the Iroquois, with whom he had once made a plot for the massacre of his neighbors, the Ottawas, under cover of a pretended treaty. The French had spared no pains to gain him and he had at length been induced to declare for them under a pledge from the governor that the war should never cease till the Iroquois were destroyed. During the summer he raised a party of forty warriors and came down the lakes in quest of Iroquois scalps. On the way he stopped at Fort Frontenac to hear the news, when to his amazement the commandant told him that deputies from Onondaga were coming in a few days to conclude peace and that he had better go home at once.

"It is well," replied the Rat.

He knew that for the Hurons it was not well. He and his tribe stood fully committed to the war and for them peace between the French and the Iroquois would be a signal of destruction, since Denonville could not or would not protect his allies. The Rat paddled off with his warriors. He had secretly learned the route of the expected deputies and he shaped his course not as he had pretended for Michilimackinac but for La Famine, where he knew that they would land. Having reached his destination, he watched and waited four or five days till canoes at length appeared, approaching from the direction of Onondaga. On this, the Rat and his friends hid themselves in the bushes.

The newcomers were the messengers sent as precursors of the embassy. At their head was a famous personage named Decanisora, or Tegannisorens, with whom were three other chiefs and, it seems, a number of warriors. They had scarcely landed when the ambushed Hurons gave them a volley of bullets, killed one of the chiefs, wounded all the rest and then, rushing upon them, seized the whole party, except a warrior who escaped with a broken arm. Having secured his prisoners, the Rat told them that he had acted on the suggestion of Denonville, who had informed him that an Iroquois war party was to pass that way. The astonished captives protested that they were envoys of peace. The Rat put on a look of amazement, then of horror and fury, and presently burst into invectives against Denonville for having made him the instrument of such atrocious perfidy.

"Go, my brothers," he exclaimed, "go home to your people. Though there is war between us, I give you your liberty. Onontio has made me do so black a deed that I shall never be happy again till your five tribes take a just vengeance upon him."

After giving them guns, powder and ball, he sent them on their way, well pleased with him and filled with rage against the governor.

In accordance with Indian usage, however, he kept one of them to be adopted, as he declared, in place of one of his followers whom he had lost in the skirmish. Then, recrossing the lake, he went alone to Fort Frontenac and, as he left the gate to rejoin his party, he said coolly, "I have killed the peace. We shall see how the governor will get out of this business." Then, without loss of time, he repaired to Michilimackinac and gave his Iroquois prisoner to the officer in command.

No news of the intended peace had yet reached that distant outpost, and though the unfortunate Iroquois told the story of his mission and his capture, the Rat declared that it was a crazy invention inspired by the fear of death and the prisoner was immediately shot by a file of soldiers.

The Rat now sent for an old Iroquois who had long been a prisoner at the Huron village, telling him with a mournful air that he was free to return to his people and recount the cruelty of the French, who had put their countryman to death. The liberated Iroquois faithfully acquitted himself of his mission.

One incident seemed for a moment likely to rob the intriguer of the fruits of his ingenuity. The Iroquois who had escaped in the skirmish contrived to reach Fort Frontenac some time after the last visit of the Rat. He told what had happened, and after being treated with utmost attention, he was sent to Onondaga, charged with explanations and regrets. The Iroquois dignitaries seemed satisfied and Denonville wrote to the minister that there was still good hope of peace. He little knew his enemy. They could dissemble and wait, but they neither believed the governor nor forgave him. His supposed treachery at La Famine and his real treachery at Fort Frontenac filled them with a patient but inextinguishable rage. They sent him word that they were ready to renew the negotiations. Then they sent again to say that Andros forbade them. Without doubt they used his prohibition as a pretext.

Months passed and Denonville remained in suspense. He did not trust his Indian allies, nor did they trust him. Like the Rat and his Hurons, they dreaded the conclusion of peace and wished the war to continue that the French might bear the brunt of it and stand between them and the wrath of the Iroquois.

In the direction of the Iroquois there was a long and ominous silence. It was broken at last by the crash of a thunderbolt. On the night between the fourth and fifth of August, a violent hailstorm burst over Lake St. Louis, an expansion of the St. Lawrence a little above Montreal. Concealed by the tempest and the darkness, fifteen hundred warriors landed at La Chine and silently posted themselves about the houses of the sleeping settlers, then screeched the war whoop and began the most frightful massacre in Canadian history. The houses were burned and men, women and children indiscriminately butchered.

In the neighborhood were three stockade forts, called Rémy, Roland and La Présentation, and they all had garrisons. There was also an encampment of two hundred regulars about three miles distant under an officer named Subercase, then absent at Montreal on a visit to Denonville, who had lately arrived with his wife and family. At four o'clock in the morning the troops in this encampment heard a cannon shot from one of the forts. They were at once ordered under arms. Soon after, they saw a man running towards them, just escaped from the butchery. He told his story and passed on with the news to Montreal, six miles distant. Then several fugitives appeared, chased by a band of Iroquois who gave over the pursuit at sight of the soldiers, but pillaged several houses before their eyes.

The day was well advanced before Subercase arrived. He ordered the troops to march. About a hundred armed inhabitants had joined them and they moved together towards La Chine. Here they found the houses still burning and the bodies of their inmates strewn among them or hanging from the stakes where they had been tortured. They learned from a French surgeon, escaped from the enemy, that the Iroquois were all encamped a mile and a half farther on, behind a tract of forest.

Subercase, whose force had been strengthened by troops from the forts, resolved to attack them, and had he been allowed to do so, he would probably have punished them severely for most of them were helplessly drunk with brandy taken from the houses of the traders. Sword in hand, at the head of his men, the daring officer entered the forest, but at that moment a voice from the rear commanded a halt. It was that of the Chevalier de Vaudreuil, just come from Montreal with positive orders from Denonville to run no risks and stand solely on the defensive. Subercase was furious. High words passed between him and Vaudreuil, but he was forced to obey.

The troops were led back to Fort Roland, where about five hundred regulars and militia were now collected under command of Vaudreuil. On the next day eighty men from Fort Rémy attempted to join them, but the Iroquois had slept off the effect of their orgies and were again on the alert. The unfortunate detachment was set upon by a host of savages and cut to pieces in full sight of Fort Roland. All were killed or captured except Le Moyne de Longueuil and a few others, who escaped within the gate of Fort Rémy.

Montreal was wild with terror. It had been fortified with palisades since the war began, but though there were troops in the town under the governor himself, the people were in mortal dread. No attack was made either on the town or on any of the forts and such of the inhabitants as could reach them were safe, while the Iroquois held undisputed possession of the open country, burned all the houses and barns over an extent of nine miles and roamed in small parties, pillaging and scalping, over more than twenty miles.

There is no mention of their having encountered opposition, nor do they seem to have met with any loss but that of some warriors killed in the attack on the detachment from Fort Rémy, and that of three drunken stragglers who were caught and thrown into a cellar in Fort La Présentation. When they came to their senses, they defied their captors and fought with such ferocity that it was necessary to shoot them.

At length most of the invaders took to their canoes and recrossed Lake St. Louis in a body, giving ninety yells to show that they had ninety prisoners in their clutches. This was not all, for the whole number carried off was more than a hundred and twenty, besides about two hundred who had the good fortune to be killed on the spot.

As the Iroquois passed the forts, they shouted, "Onontio, you deceived us and now we have deceived you." Towards evening they encamped on the farther side of the lake and began to torture and devour their prisoners. On that miserable night stupefied and speechless groups stood gazing from the strand of La Chine at the lights that gleamed along the distant shore of Chateaugay, where their friends, wives, parents or children agonized in the fires of the Iroquois, and scenes were enacted of indescribable and nameless horror.

The greater part of the prisoners were, however, reserved to be distributed among the towns of the confederacy, and there tortured for the diversion of the inhabitants. While some of the invaders went home to celebrate their triumph, others roamed in small parties through all the upper parts of the colony, spreading universal terror.

Canada lay bewildered and benumbed under the shock of this calamity, but the cup of her misery was not full. There was revolution in England. James II, the friend and ally of France, had been driven from his kingdom and William of Orange had seized his vacant throne. Soon there came news of war between the two crowns. The Iroquois

337

alone had brought the colony to the brink of ruin, and now they would be supported by the neighboring British colonies, rich, strong and populous, compared with impoverished and depleted Canada.

A letter of recall for Denonville was already on its way. His successor arrived in October, and the marquis sailed for France.

~~~~~~

CHAPTER 5

Frontenac's Return

THE SUN OF LOUIS XIV HAD REACHED ITS ZENITH. From a morning of unexampled brilliancy it had mounted to the glare of a cloudless noon, but the hour of its decline was near. The mortal enemy of France was on the throne of England, turning against her from that new point of vantage all the energies of his unconquerable genius. An invalid built the Bourbon monarchy and another invalid battered and defaced the imposing structure—two potent and daring spirits in two frail bodies, Richelieu and William of Orange.

But there was one corner of the world where Louis's emblem, the sun, would not shine on him. He had done his best for Canada and had got nothing for his pains but news of mishaps and troubles. He was growing tired of the colony which he had nursed with paternal fondness and he was more than half angry with it because it did not prosper. Denonville's letters had grown worse and worse, and though he had not yet heard of the last great calamity, he was sated with ill tidings already.

Count Frontenac stood before him. Since his recall he had lived at court, needy and no longer in favor, but he had influential friends and an intriguing wife, always ready to serve him. The King knew his merits as well as his faults, and in the desperate state of his Canadian affairs he had been led to the resolution of restoring him to the command from which, for excellent reasons, he had removed him seven years before. He now told him that, in his belief, the charges brought against him were without foundation. "I send you back to Canada," he is reported to have said, "where I am sure that you will serve me as well as you did before; and I ask nothing more of you."

The post was not a tempting one to a man in his seventieth year. Alone and unsupported—for the King, with Europe rising against him, would give him no more troops—he was to restore the prostrate colony to hope and courage and fight two enemies with a force that had proved no match for one of them alone. The audacious count trusted himself and undertook the task, received the royal instructions and took his last leave of the master whom even he after a fashion honored and admired.

Frontenac made sail for Quebec, and stopping by the way at Isle Percée, learned from Récollet missionaries the irruption of the Iroquois at Montreal. He hastened on, but the wind was against him and the autumn woods were turning brown before he reached his destination.

It was evening when he landed, amid fireworks, illuminations and the firing of cannon. All Quebec came to meet him by torchlight. The members of the council offered their respects and the Jesuits made him a harangue of welcome. It was but a welcome of words. They and the councilors had done their best to have him recalled and hoped that they were rid of him forever, but now he was among them again, rasped by the memory of real or fancied wrongs.

The count, however, had no time for quarreling. The King had told him to bury old animosities and forget the past, and for the present he was too busy to break the royal injunction. He caused boats to be made ready, and in spite of incessant rains pushed up the river to Montreal. Here he found Denonville and his frightened wife. Everything was in confusion. The Iroquois were gone, leaving dejection and terror behind them. Frontenac reviewed the troops. There were seven or eight hundred of them in the town, the rest being in garrison at the various forts. Then he repaired to what was once La Chine and surveyed the miserable waste of ashes and desolation that spread for miles around.

To his extreme disgust, he learned that Denonville had sent a Canadian officer by secret paths to Fort Frontenac, with orders to Valrenne, the commandant, to blow it up and return with his garrison to Montreal. Frontenac had built the fort, had given it his own name, and had cherished it with a paternal fondness, reinforced by strong hopes of making money out of it. For its sake he had become the butt of scandal and opprobrium, but not the less had he always stood its strenuous and passionate champion. An Iroquois envoy had lately with great insolence demanded its destruction of Denonville, and this alone, in the eyes of Frontenac, was ample reason for maintaining it at any cost. He still had hopes that it might be saved, and with all the energy of youth he proceeded to collect canoes, men, provisions and arms; battled against dejection, insubordination and fear, and in a few days dispatched a convoy of three hundred men to relieve the place and stop the execution of Denonville's orders.

His orders had been but too promptly obeyed. The convoy was scarcely gone an hour when, to Frontenac's unutterable wrath, Valrenne appeared with his garrison. He reported that he had set fire to everything in the fort that would burn, sunk the three vessels belonging to it, thrown the cannon into the lake, mined the walls and bastions and left matches burning in the powder magazine. When he and his men were five leagues on their way to Montreal, a dull and distant explosion told them that the mines had sprung. It proved afterwards that the destruction was not complete and the Iroquois took possession of the abandoned fort, with a large quantity of stores and munitions left by the garrison in their too hasty retreat.

So desperate were the needs of the colony and so great the contempt with which the Iroquois regarded it that it almost needed a miracle either to carry on war or make peace. What Frontenac most earnestly wished was to keep the Iroquois quiet and so leave his hands free to deal with the English. This was not easy, to such a pitch of audacity had late events raised them. Neither his temper nor his convictions would allow him to beg peace of them, like his predecessor, but he had inordinate trust in the influence of his name and he now took a course which he hoped might answer his purpose without increasing their insolence.

The perfidious folly of Denonville in seizing their countrymen at Fort Frontenac had been a prime cause of their hostility, and at the request of the late governor the surviving captives, thirteen in all, had been taken from the galleys, gorgeously clad in French attire, and sent back to Canada in the ship which carried Frontenac. Among them was a famous Cayuga war chief called Ourehaoué, whose loss had infuriated the Iroquois. Frontenac gained his good will on the voyage, and when they reached Quebec, he lodged him in the château and treated him with such kindness that the chief became his devoted admirer and friend. As his influence was great among his people, Frontenac hoped that he might use him with success to bring about an accommodation.

He placed three of the captives at the disposal of the Cayuga, who forthwith sent them to Onondaga with a message which the governor had dictated, and which was to the following effect: "The great Onontio, whom you all know, has come back again. He does not blame you for what you have done, for he looks upon you as foolish children and blames only the English, who are the cause of your folly and have made you forget your obedience to a father who has always loved and never deceived you. He will permit me, Ourehaoué, to return to you as soon as you will come to ask for me—not as you have spoken of late, but like children speaking to a father."

Frontenac hoped that they would send an embassy to reclaim their chief and thus give him an opportunity to use personal influence over them. With the three released captives, he sent an Iroquois convert named Cut Nose with a wampum belt to announce his return.

When the deputation arrived at Onondaga and made known their errand, the Iroquois magnates, with their usual deliberation, deferred answering till a general council of the confederacy should have time to assemble and meanwhile they sent messengers to ask the mayor of Albany and others of their Dutch and English friends to come to the meeting. They did not comply, merely sending the government interpreter with a few Mohawk Indians to represent their interests.

On the other hand, the Jesuit Milet, who had been captured a few months before, adopted and made an Oneida chief, used every effort to second the designs of Frontenac. The authorities of Albany tried in vain to induce the Iroquois to place him in their hands. They understood their interests too well and held fast to the Jesuit.

The grand council took place at Onondaga on the twenty-second of January. Eighty chiefs and sachems, seated gravely on mats around the council fire, smoked their pipes in silence for a while, till at length an

342

Onondaga orator rose and announced that Frontenac, the old Onontio, had returned with Ourehaoué and twelve more of their captive friends; that he meant to rekindle the council fire at Fort Frontenac, and that he invited them to meet him there.

"Ho, ho, ho!" returned the eighty senators from the bottom of their throats. It was the unfailing Iroquois response to a speech. Then Cut Nose, the governor's messenger, addressed the council: "I advise you to meet Onontio as he desires. Do so, if you wish to live." He presented a wampum belt to confirm his words and the conclave again returned the same guttural ejaculation. "Ourehaoué sends you this," continued Cut Nose, presenting another belt of wampum. "By it he advises you to listen to Onontio, if you wish to live."

When the messenger from Canada had ceased, the messenger from Albany, a Mohawk Indian, rose and repeated word for word a speech confided to him by the mayor of that town, urging the Iroquois to close their ears against the invitation of Onontio.

Next rose one Cannehoot, a sachem of the Senecas, charged with matters of grave import, for they involved no less than the revival of that scheme, so perilous to the French, of the union of the tribes of the Great Lakes in a triple alliance with the Iroquois and the English. These lake tribes, disgusted with the French, who under Denonville had left them to the mercy of the Iroquois, had been impelled both by their fears and their interests to make new advances to the confederacy, and had first addressed themselves to the Senecas, whom they had most cause to dread. They had given up some of the Iroquois prisoners in their hands and promised soon to give up the rest. A treaty had been made and it was this event which the Seneca sachem now announced to the council.

Having told the story to his assembled colleagues, he exhibited and explained the wampum belts and other tokens brought by the envoys from the lakes, who represented nine distinct tribes or bands from the region of Michilimackinac. By these tokens, the nine tribes declared that they came to learn wisdom of the Iroquois and the English; to wash off the war paint, throw down the tomahawk, smoke the pipe of peace and unite with them as one body. "Onontio is drunk," was the interpretation of the fourth wampum belt, "but we, the tribes of

343

Michilimackinac, wash our hands of all his actions. Neither we nor you must defile ourselves by listening to him."

When the Seneca sachem had ended, and when the ejaculations that echoed his words had ceased, the belts were hung up before all the assembly, then taken down again and distributed among the sachems of the five Iroquois tribes, excepting one, which was given to the messenger from Albany. Thus was concluded the triple alliance, which to Canada meant no less than ruin.

"Brethren," said an Onondaga sachem, "we must hold fast to our brother Quider [Peter Schuyler, mayor of Albany] and look on Onontio as our enemy, for he is a cheat."

Then they invited the interpreter from Albany to address the council, which he did, advising them not to listen to the envoys from Canada. When he had ended, they spent some time in consultation among themselves and at length agreed on the following message, addressed to Corlaer, or New York, and to Kinshon, the Fish, by which they meant New England, the authorities of which had sent them the image of a fish as a token of alliance:

"Brethren, our council-fire burns at Albany. We will not go to meet Onontio at Fort Frontenac. We will hold fast to the old chain of peace with Corlaer, and we will fight with Onontio. Brethren, we are glad to hear that you are preparing to make war on Canada, but tell us no lies. Brother Kinshon, we hear that you mean to send soldiers against the Indians to the eastward, but we advise you, now that we are all united against the French, to fall upon them at once. Strike at the root. When the trunk is cut down, all the branches fall with it. Courage, Corlaer! courage, Kinshon! Go to Quebec in the spring; take it, and you will have your feet on the necks of the French and all their friends."

Then they consulted together again and agreed on the following answer to Ourehaoué and Frontenac: "Ourehaoué, the whole council is glad to hear that you have come back. Onontio, you have told us that you have come back again and brought with you thirteen of our people who were carried prisoners to France. We are glad of it. You wish to speak with us at Cataraqui [Fort Frontenac]. Don't you know that your council-fire there is put out? It is quenched in blood. You must first send home the prisoners. When our brother Ourehaoué is returned to us, then we will talk with you of peace. You must send him and the others home this very winter. We now let you know that we have made peace with the tribes of Michilimackinac. You are not to think, because we return you an answer, that we have laid down the tomahawk. Our warriors will continue the war till you send our countrymen back to us."

The messengers from Canada returned with this reply. Unsatisfactory as it was, such a quantity of wampum was sent with it as showed plainly the importance attached by the Iroquois to the matters in question.

Encouraged by a recent success against the English, and still possessed with an overweening confidence in his influence over the confederates, Frontenac resolved that Ourehaoué should send them another message. The chief, whose devotion to the count never wavered, accordingly dispatched four envoys with a load of wampum belts, expressing his astonishment that his countrymen had not seen fit to send a deputation of chiefs to receive him from the hands of Onontio, and calling upon them to do so without delay, lest he should think that they had forgotten him.

Along with the messengers, Frontenac ventured to send the Chevalier d'Aux, a half-pay officer, with orders to observe the disposition of the Iroquois and impress them in private talk with a sense of the count's power, of his good will to them and of the wisdom of coming to terms with him lest, like an angry father, he should be forced at last to use the rod. The chevalier's reception was a warm one. They burned two of his attendants, forced him to run the gantlet, and after a vigorous thrashing sent him prisoner to Albany.

The last failure was worse than the first. The count's name was great among the Iroquois, but he had trusted its power too far.

CHAPTER 6

Three War Parties

FRONTENAC RESOLVED TO TAKE THE OFFENSIVE— not against the Iroquois, who seemed invulnerable as ghosts, but against the English. By striking a few sharp and rapid blows, he hoped to teach both friends and foes that Onontio was still alive. The effect of his return had already begun to appear and the energy and fire of the undaunted veteran had shot new life into the dejected population. He formed three war parties of picked men, one at Montreal, one at Three Rivers and one at Quebec. The first was to strike at Albany, the second at the border settlements of New Hampshire and the third at those of Maine.

That of Montreal was ready first. It consisted of two hundred and ten men, of whom ninety-six were Indian converts, chiefly from the two mission villages of Saut St. Louis and the Mountain of Montreal. They were Christian Iroquois whom the priests had persuaded to leave their homes and settle in Canada, to the great indignation of their heathen countrymen and the great annoyance of the English colonists, to whom they were a constant menace. When Denonville attacked the Senecas they had joined him, but of late they had shown reluctance to fight their heathen kinsmen, with whom the French even suspected them of collusion. Against the English, however, they willingly took up the hatchet.

The French of the party were for the most part *coureurs de bois*. As the sea is the sailor's element, so the forest was theirs. Their merits were hardihood and skill in woodcraft; their chief faults were insubordination and lawlessness. They had shared the general demoralization that followed the inroad of the Iroquois, and under Denonville had proved mutinous and unmanageable.

In the best times it was a hard task to command them, and one that needed not bravery alone but tact, address and experience. Under a chief of such a stamp they were admirable bushfighters and such were those now chosen to lead them. D'Ailleboust de Mantet and Le Moyne de Sainte-Hélène, the brave son of Charles le Moyne, had the chief command, supported by the brothers Le Moyne d'Iberville and Le Moyne de Bienville, with Repentigny de Montesson, Le Ber du Chesne and others of the sturdy Canadian *noblesse,* nerved by adventure and trained in Indian warfare.

It was the depth of winter when they began their march, striding on snowshoes over the vast white field of the frozen St. Lawrence, each with the hood of his blanket coat drawn over his head, a gun in his mittened hand, a knife, a hatchet, a tobacco pouch and a bullet pouch at his belt, a pack on his shoulders and his inseparable pipe hung at his neck in a leather case. They dragged their blankets and provisions over the snow on Indian sledges. Crossing the forest to Chambly, they advanced four or five days up the frozen Richelieu and the frozen Lake Champlain, and then stopped to hold a council.

Frontenac had left the precise point of attack at the discretion of the leaders and thus far the men had been ignorant of their destination. The Indians demanded to know it. Mantet and Sainte-Hélène replied that they were going to Albany. The Indians demurred. "How long is it," asked one of them, "since the French grew so bold?" The commanders answered that to regain the honor of which their late misfortunes had robbed them, the French would take Albany or die in the attempt. The Indians listened sullenly; the decision was postponed and the party moved forward again.

When after eight days they reached the Hudson and found the place where two paths diverged, the one for Albany and the other for Schenectady, they all without further words took the latter. Indeed, to attempt Albany would have been an act of desperation.

The march was horrible. There was a partial thaw and they waded knee-deep through the half-melted snow and the mingled ice, mud and water of the gloomy swamps. So painful and so slow was their progress

347

that it was nine days more before they reached a point two leagues from Schenectady. The weather had changed again and a cold, gusty snowstorm pelted them.

It was one of those days when the trees stand white as specters in the sheltered hollows of the forest, and bare and gray on the wind-swept ridges. The men were half dead with cold, fatigue and hunger. It was four in the afternoon of the eighth of February. The scouts found an Indian hut and in it were four Iroquois squaws, whom they captured. There was a fire in the wigwam and the shivering Canadians crowded about it, stamping their chilled feet and warming their be-numbed hands over the blaze. The Christian chief of the Saut St. Louis, known as Le Grand Agnié, or the Great Mohawk, by the French, and called Kryn by the Dutch, harangued his followers and exhorted them to wash out their wrongs in blood. Then they all ad-vanced again and about dark reached the river Mohawk, a little above the village.

A Canadian named Gignières, who had gone with nine Indians to reconnoiter, now returned to say that he had been within sight of Schenectady and had seen nobody. Their purpose had been to post-pone the attack till two o'clock in the morning, but the situation was intolerable and the limit of human endurance was reached. They could not make fires and they must move on or perish.

Guided by the frightened squaws, they crossed the Mohawk on the ice, toiling through the drifts amid the whirling snow that swept down the valley of the darkened stream, till about eleven o'clock they descried through the storm the snow-beplastered palisades of the village. Such was their plight that some of them afterwards declared that they would all have surrendered if an enemy had appeared to summon them.

Schenectady was the farthest outpost of the colony of New York. Westward lay the Mohawk forests; Orange, or Albany, was fifteen miles or more towards the southeast. The village was oblong in form and enclosed by a palisade which had two gates, one towards Albany and the other towards the Mohawks. There was a blockhouse near the eastern gate, occupied by eight or nine Connecticut militiamen under Lieutenant Talmage. There were also about thirty friendly Mohawks in the place on a visit.

The inhabitants, who were all Dutch, were in a state of discord and confusion. The revolution in England had produced a revolution in New York. The demagogue Jacob Leisler had got possession of Fort William and was endeavoring to master the whole colony. Albany was in the hands of the anti-Leisler or conservative party, represented by a convention of which Peter Schuyler was the chief. The Dutch of Schenectady for the most part favored Leisler, whose emissaries had been busily at work among them, but their chief magistrate, John Sander Glen, a man of courage and worth, stood fast for the Albany convention, and in consequence the villagers had threatened to kill him. Talmage and his Connecticut militia were under orders from Albany, and therefore, like Glen, they were under the popular ban.

In vain the magistrate and the officer entreated the people to stand on their guard. They turned the advice to ridicule, laughed at the idea of danger, left both their gates wide open and placed there, it is said, two snow images as mock sentinels. A French account declares that the village contained eighty houses, which is certainly an exaggeration. There had been some festivity during the evening, but it was now over and the primitive villagers, fathers, mothers, children and infants lay buried in sleep. They were simple peasants and rude woodsmen, but with human affections and capable of human woe.

The French and Indians stood before the open gate, with its blind and dumb warder, the mock sentinel of snow. Iberville went with a detachment to find the Albany gate and bar it against the escape of fugitives, but he missed it in the gloom and hastened back. The assailants were now formed into two bands, Sainte-Hélène leading the one and Mantet the other. They passed through the gate together in dead silence. One turned to the right and the other to the left and they filed around the village between the palisades and the houses till the two leaders met at the farther end. Thus the place was completely surrounded. The signal was then given. They all screeched the war whoop together, burst in the doors with hatchets, and fell to their work.

Roused by the infernal din, the villagers leaped from their beds. For some it was but a momentary nightmare of fright and horror, ended by the blow of the tomahawk. Others were less fortunate. Neither women nor children were spared. "No pen can write, and no tongue express," wrote Schuyler, "the cruelties that were committed."

349

There was little resistance except at the blockhouse, where Talmage and his men made a stubborn fight, but the doors were at length forced open, the defenders killed or taken and the building set on fire. Adam Vrooman, one of the villagers, saw his wife shot and his child brained against the doorpost, but he fought so desperately that the assailants promised him his life. Orders had been given to spare Peter Tasse-maker, the dominie or minister, from whom it was thought that valuable information might be obtained, but he was hacked to pieces and his house burned. Some, more agile or more fortunate than the rest, escaped at the eastern gate and fled through the storm to seek shelter at Albany or at houses along the way.

Sixty persons were killed outright, of whom thirty-eight were men and boys, ten were women, and twelve were children. The number captured appears to have been between eighty and ninety. The thirty Mohawks in the town were treated with studied kindness by the victors, who declared that they had no quarrel with them, but only with the Dutch and English.

The massacre and pillage continued two hours. Then the prisoners were secured, sentinels posted, and the men told to rest and refresh themselves. In the morning a small party crossed the river to the house of Glen, which stood on a rising ground half a mile distant. It was loopholed and palisaded and Glen had mustered his servants and tenants, closed his gates and prepared to defend himself. The French told him to fear nothing, for they had orders not to hurt a chicken of his, whereupon, after requiring them to lay down their arms, he allowed them to enter. They urged him to go with them to the village and he complied, they on their part leaving one of their number as a hostage in the hands of his followers.

Iberville appeared at the gate with the Great Mohawk and, drawing his commission from the breast of his coat, told Glen that he was specially charged to pay a debt which the French owed him. On several occasions he had saved the lives of French prisoners in the hands of the Mohawks, and he with his family and, above all, his wife had shown them the greatest kindness. He was now led before the crowd of wretched prisoners and told that not only were his own life and property safe, but that all his kindred should be spared. Glen stretched his privilege to the utmost, till the French Indians, disgusted at his multiplied demands for clemency, observed that everybody seemed to be his relation.

Some of the houses had already been burned. Fire was now set to the rest, excepting one in which a French officer lay wounded, another belonging to Glen, and three or four more which he begged the victors to spare. At noon Schenectady was in ashes. Then the French and Indians withdrew, laden with booty. Thirty or forty captured horses dragged their sledges and a troop of twenty-seven men and boys were driven prisoners into the forest. About sixty old men, women and children were left behind without further injury in order, it is said, to conciliate the Mohawks in the place who had joined with Glen in begging that they might be spared. Of the victors, only two had been killed.

The war party which attacked Schenectady was but one of three which Frontenac had sent against the English borders. The second, aimed at New Hampshire, left Three Rivers on the twenty-eighth of January, commanded by François Hertel. It consisted of twenty-four Frenchmen, twenty Abenakis of the Sokoki band, and five Algonquins. After three months of excessive hardship in the vast and rugged wilderness that intervened, they approached the little settlement of Salmon Falls on the stream which separates New Hampshire from Maine.

Through snow and ice and storm, Hertel and his band moved on their prey. On the night of the twenty-seventh of March, they lay hidden in the forest that bordered the farms and clearings of Salmon Falls. Their scouts reconnoitered the place and found a fortified house with two stockade forts, built as a refuge for the settlers in case of alarm.

Towards daybreak, Hertel, dividing his followers into three parties, made a sudden and simultaneous attack. The settlers, unconscious of danger, were in their beds. No watch was kept, even in the so-called forts, and when the French and Indians burst in, there was no time for their few tenants to gather for defense. The surprise was complete, and after a short struggle the assailants were successful at every point. They next turned upon the scattered farms of the neighborhood, burned houses, barns and cattle, and laid the entire settlement in ashes. About thirty persons of both sexes and all ages were tomahawked or shot, and fifty-four, chiefly women and children, were made prisoners.

Two Indian scouts now brought word that a party of English was advancing to the scene of havoc from Piscataqua, or Portsmouth, not many miles distant. Hertel called his men together and began his retreat. The pursuers, a hundred and forty in number, overtook him about sunset at Wooster River, where the swollen stream was crossed by a narrow bridge. Hertel and his followers made a stand on the farther bank, killed and wounded a number of the English as they attempted to cross, kept up a brisk fire on the rest, held them in check till night and then continued their retreat. The prisoners, or some of them, were given to the Indians, who tortured one or more of the men and killed and tormented children and infants with a cruelty not always equaled by their heathen countrymen.

Hertel continued his retreat to one of the Abenaki villages on the Kennebec. Here he learned that a band of French and Indians had lately passed southward on their way to attack the English fort at Casco Bay, on the site of Portland. Leaving at the village his eldest son, who had been badly wounded at Wooster River, he set out to join them with thirty-six of his followers.

The band in question was Frontenac's third war party. It consisted of fifty French and sixty Abenakis from the mission of St. Francis and it had left Quebec in January under a Canadian officer named Portneuf, and his lieutenant Courtemanche. They advanced at their leisure, often stopping to hunt, till in May they were joined on the Kennebec by a large body of Indian warriors. On the twenty-fifth, Portneuf encamped in the forest near the English forts, with a force which, including Hertel's party, the Indians of the Kennebec and another band led by Saint-Castin from the Penobscot, amounted to between four and five hundred men.

Fort Loyal was a palisade work with eight cannon, standing on rising ground by the shore of the bay at what is now the foot of India Street in the city of Portland. Not far distant were four blockhouses and a village which they were designed to protect. These, with the fort, were occupied by about a hundred men, chiefly settlers of the neighborhood under Captain Sylvanus Davis, a prominent trader.

Around lay rough and broken fields stretching to the skirts of the forest half a mile distant.

Some of Portneuf's scouts met a straggling Scotchman and could not resist the temptation of killing him. Their scalp yells alarmed the garrison and thus the advantage of surprise was lost. Davis resolved to keep his men within their defenses and to stand on his guard, but there was little or no discipline in the yeoman garrison and thirty young volunteers under Lieutenant Thaddeus Clark sallied out to find the enemy.

They were too successful, for as they approached the top of a hill near the woods, they observed a number of cattle staring with a scared look at some object on the farther side of a fence, and rightly judging that those they sought were hidden there, they raised a cheer and ran to the spot. They were met by a fire so close and deadly that half their number were shot down. A crowd of Indians leaped the fence and rushed upon the survivors, who ran for the fort, but only four, all of whom were wounded, succeeded in reaching it.

The men in the blockhouses withdrew under cover of night to Fort Loyal, where the whole force of the English was now gathered, along with their frightened families. Portneuf determined to besiege the place in form, and after burning the village and collecting tools from the abandoned blockhouses, he opened his trenches in a deep gully within fifty yards of the fort, where his men were completely protected. They worked so well that in three days they had wormed their way close to the palisade, and covered as they were in their burrows, they had lost scarcely a man while their enemies suffered severely.

They now summoned the fort to surrender. Davis asked for a delay of six days, which was refused, and in the morning the fight began again. For a time the fire was sharp and heavy. The English wasted much powder in vain efforts to dislodge the besiegers from their trenches, till at length, seeing a machine loaded with a tar barrel and other combustibles shoved against their palisades, they asked for a parley. Up to this time Davis had supposed that his assailants were all Indians, the French being probably dressed and painted like their red allies.

"We demanded," he says, "if there were any French among them, and if they would give us quarter. They answered that they were

Frenchmen, and that they would give us good quarter. Upon this, we sent out to them again to known from whence they came, and if they would give us good quarter for our men, women, and children, both wounded and sound, and [to demand] that we should have liberty to march to the next English town, and have a guard for our defense and safety; then we would surrender; and also that the governour of the French should hold up his hand and swear by the great and ever living God that the several articles should be performed; all which he did solemnly swear."

The survivors of the garrison now filed through the gate and laid down their arms. They with their women and children were thereupon abandoned to the Indians, who murdered many of them and carried off the rest. When Davis protested against this breach of faith, he was told that he and his countrymen were rebels against their lawful King, James II. After spiking the cannon, burning the fort and destroying all the neighboring settlements, the triumphant allies departed for their respective homes, leaving the slain unburied where they had fallen.

The triumphant success of his three war parties produced on the Canadian people all the effect Frontenac had expected. This effect was very apparent, even before the last two victories had become known.

"You cannot believe, Monseigneur," wrote the governor, speaking of the capture of Schenectady, "the joy that this slight success has caused, and how much it contributes to raise the people from their dejection and terror."

CHAPTER 7

Massachusetts Attacks Quebec

WHEN FRONTENAC SENT HIS WAR PARTIES against New York and New England, it was in the hope not only of reanimating the Canadians, but also of teaching the Iroquois that they could not safely rely on English aid, and of inciting the Abenakis to renew their attacks on the border settlements. He imagined, too, that the British colonies could be chastised into prudence and taught a policy of conciliation towards their Canadian neighbors, but he mistook the character of these bold and vigorous though not martial communities.

The plan of a combined attack on Canada seems to have been first proposed by the Iroquois, and New York and the several governments of New England, smarting under French and Indian attacks, hastened to embrace it. Early in May, a congress of their delegates was held in the city of New York. It was agreed that the colony of that name should furnish four hundred men, and Massachusetts, Plymouth and Connecticut three hundred and fifty-five jointly, while the Iroquois afterwards added their worthless pledge to join the expedition with nearly all their warriors. The colonial militia were to rendezvous at Albany and advance upon Montreal by way of Lake Champlain. Mutual jealousies made it difficult to agree upon a commander, but Fitz-John Winthrop of Connecticut was at length placed at the head of the feeble and discordant band.

While Montreal was thus assailed by land, Massachusetts and the other New England colonies were invited to attack Quebec by sea—a task formidable in difficulty and in cost, and one that imposed on them an inordinate share in the burden of the war. Massachusetts hesitated. She had no money and she was already engaged in a less remote and less critical enterprise. During the winter her commerce had suffered from French cruisers, which found convenient harborage at Port Royal, whence also the hostile Indians were believed to draw supplies. Seven vessels, with two hundred and eighty-eight sailors, were impressed and from four to five hundred militiamen were drafted for the service.

That rugged son of New England, Sir William Phips, was appointed to the command. He sailed from Nantasket at the end of April, reached Port Royal on the eleventh of May, landed his militia and summoned Meneval, the governor, to surrender. The fort, though garrisoned by about seventy soldiers, was scarcely in condition to repel an assault and Meneval yielded without resistance, first stipulating, according to French accounts, that private property should be respected, the church left untouched and the troops sent to Quebec or to France.

It was found, however, that during the parley a quantity of goods, belonging partly to the King and partly to merchants of the place, had been carried off and hidden in the woods. Phips thought this a sufficient pretext for plundering the merchants, imprisoning the troops and desecrating the church. "We cut down the cross," writes one of his followers, "rifled their church, pulled down their high altar and broke their images." The houses of the two priests were also pillaged. The people were promised security to life, liberty and property on condition of swearing allegiance to King William and Queen Mary, "which," says the journalist, "they did with great acclamation," and thereupon they were left unmolested.

The lawful portion of the booty included twenty-one pieces of cannon, with a considerable sum of money belonging to the King. The smaller articles, many of which were taken from the merchants and from such of the settlers as refused the oath, were packed in hogsheads and sent on board the ships.

Phips took no measures to secure his conquest, though he commissioned a president and six councilors, chosen from the inhabitants, to govern the settlement till further orders from the Crown or from the authorities of Massachusetts. The president was directed to constrain nobody in the matter of religion and he was assured of protection and support so long as he remained "faithful to our government," that is, the government of Massachusetts. The little Puritan commonwealth already gave itself airs of sovereignty.

Phips now sent Captain Alden, who had already taken possession of Saint-Castin's post at Penobscot, to seize upon La Hêve, Chedabucto and other stations on the southern coast. Then, after providing for the reduction of the settlements at the head of the Bay of Fundy, he sailed with the rest of the fleet for Boston, where he arrived triumphant on the thirtieth of May, bringing with him, as prisoners, the French governor, fifty-nine soldiers and the two priests, Petit and Trouvé. Massachusetts had made an easy conquest of all Acadia; a conquest, however, which she had neither the men nor the money to secure by sufficient garrisons.

Phips was a rude sailor, bluff, prompt and choleric. He never gave proof of intellectual capacity, and such of his success in life as he did not owe to good luck was due probably to an energetic and adventurous spirit, aided by a blunt frankness of address that pleased the great and commended him to their favor. Two years after the expedition to Port Royal, the King, under the new charter, made him governor of Massachusetts—a post for which, though totally unfit, he had been recommended by the elder Mather, who, like his son Cotton, expected to make use of him.

New England writers describe him as honest in private dealings, but in accordance with his coarse nature, he seems to have thought that anything is fair in war. On the other hand, he was warmly patriotic and was almost as ready to serve New England as to serve himself.

When Phips returned from Port Royal, he found Boston alive with martial preparation. A bold enterprise was afoot. Massachusetts of her own motion had resolved to attempt the conquest of Quebec. She and her sister colonies had not yet recovered from the exhaustion of King Philip's War, and still less from the disorders that attended the expulsion of the royal governor and his adherents. The public treasury was empty and the recent expeditions against the eastern Indians had been supported by private subscription.

Worse yet, New England had no competent military commander. The Puritan gentlemen of the original emigration, some of whom were as well fitted for military as for civil leadership, had passed from the stage, and by a tendency which circumstances made inevitable, they had left none behind them equally qualified. The great Indian conflict of fifteen years before had, it is true, formed good partisan chiefs and proved that the New England yeoman, defending his family and his hearth, was not to be surpassed in stubborn fighting, but since Andros and his soldiers had been driven out, there was scarcely a single man in the colony of the slightest training or experience in regular war.

Up to this moment, New England had never asked help of the mother country. When thousands of savages burst on her defenseless settlements, she had conquered safety and peace with her own blood and her own slender resources, but now, as the proposed capture of Quebec would inure to the profit of the British Crown, Bradstreet and his council thought it not unfitting to ask for a supply of arms and ammunition, of which they were in great need. The request was refused and no aid of any kind came from the English government, whose resources were engrossed by the Irish war.

While waiting for the reply, the colonial authorities urged on their preparations in the hope that the plunder of Quebec would pay the expenses of its conquest. Humility was not among the New England virtues, and it was thought a sin to doubt that God would give his chosen people the victory over papists and idolaters, yet no pains were spared to insure the divine favor. A proclamation was issued calling the people to repentance; a day of fasting was ordained; and as Mather expresses it, "the wheel of prayer was kept in continual motion."

The chief difficulty was to provide funds. An attempt was made to collect a part of the money by private subscription, but as this plan failed, the provisional government, already in debt, strained its credit yet further and borrowed the needful sums.

Thirty-two trading and fishing vessels, great and small, were impressed for the service. The largest was a ship called the *Six Friends,* engaged in the dangerous West India trade and carrying forty-four guns. A call was made for volunteers and many enrolled themselves, but as more were wanted, a press was ordered to complete the number. So rigorously was it applied that, what with voluntary and enforced enlistment, one town, that of Gloucester, was deprived of two thirds of its able-bodied men.

There was not a moment of doubt as to the choice of a commander, for Phips was imagined to be the very man for the work. One John Walley, a respectable citizen of Barnstable, was made second in command with the modest rank of major and a sufficient number of shipmasters, merchants, master mechanics and substantial farmers were commissioned as subordinate officers.

About the middle of July the committee charged with the preparations reported that all was ready. Still there was a long delay. The vessel sent early in spring to ask aid from England had not returned. Phips waited for her as long as he dared and the best of the season was over when he resolved to put to sea. The rustic warriors, duly formed into companies, were sent on board and the fleet sailed from Nantasket on the ninth of August. Including sailors, it carried twenty-two hundred men, with provisions for four months, but insufficient ammunition and no pilot for the St. Lawrence.

While Massachusetts was making ready to conquer Quebec by sea, the militia of the land expedition against Montreal had mustered at Albany. Their strength was even less than was at first proposed, for after the disaster at Casco, Massachusetts and Plymouth had recalled their contingents to defend their frontiers. The rest, decimated by dysentery and smallpox, began their march to Lake Champlain with bands of Mohawk, Oneida and Mohegan allies. The western Iroquois were to join them at the lake and the combined force was then to attack the head of the colony while Phips struck at its heart.

Meanwhile, Frontenac had gone with the intendant Champigny to Montreal, the chief point of danger. Here he arrived on the thirty-first of July, 1690, and a few days after, the officer commanding the fort at La Chine sent him a messenger in hot haste with the startling news that Lake St. Louis was "all covered with canoes."

Nobody doubted that the Iroquois were upon them again. Cannon were fired to call in the troops from the detached posts, when alarm was suddenly turned to joy by the arrival of other messengers to announce that the newcomers were not enemies but friends. They were the Indians of the upper lakes, descending from Michilimackinac to trade at Montreal. Nothing so auspicious had happened since Frontenac's return. Despairing of an English market for their beaver skins, they had come as of old to seek one from the French.

On the next day they all came down the rapids and landed near the town. There were fully five hundred of them—Hurons, Ottawas, Ojibwas, Potawatomis, Crees and Nipissings—with a hundred and ten canoes laden with beaver skins to the value of nearly a hundred thousand crowns.

Nor was this all. A few days after, La Durantaye, late commander at Michilimackinac, arrived with fifty-five more canoes, manned by French traders and filled with the valuable furs. The stream of wealth dammed back so long was flowing upon the colony at the moment when it was most needed. Never had Canada known a more prosperous trade than now in the midst of her danger and tribulation. It was a triumph for Frontenac. If his policy had failed with the Iroquois, it had found a crowning success among the tribes of the lakes.

Having painted, greased and befeathered themselves, the Indians gathered for the grand council which always preceded the opening of the market. The Ottawa orator spoke of nothing but trade and, with a regretful memory of the cheapness of English goods, begged that the French would sell them at the same rate. The Huron touched upon politics and war, declaring that he and his people had come to visit their old father and listen to his voice, being well assured that he would never abandon them, as others had done, nor fool away his time like Denonville in shameful negotiations for peace, and he exhorted Frontenac to fight, not the English only, but the Iroquois also, till they were brought to reason.

"If this is not done," he said, "my father and I shall both perish, but come what may, we will perish together."

"I answered," writes Frontenac, "that I would fight the Iroquois till they came to beg for peace, and that I would grant them no peace that did not include all my children, both white and red, for I was the father of both alike."

Now ensued a curious scene. Frontenac took a hatchet, brandished it in the air, and sang a war song. The principal Frenchmen present followed his example. The Christian Iroquois of the two neighboring missions rose and joined them, and so also did the Hurons and the Algonquins of Lake Nipissing, stamping and screeching like a troop of madmen, while the governor led the dance, whooping like the rest.

His predecessor would have perished rather than play such a part in such company, but the punctilious old courtier was himself half Indian at heart, as much at home in a wigwam as in the halls of princes. Another man would have lost respect in Indian eyes by such a performance. In Frontenac, it roused his audience to enthusiasm. They snatched the proffered hatchet and promised war to the death.

Then came a solemn war feast. Two oxen and six large dogs had been chopped to pieces for the occasion and boiled with a quantity of prunes. Two barrels of wine with abundant tobacco were also served out to the guests, who devoured the meal in a species of frenzy. All seemed eager for war except the Ottawas, who had not forgotten their late dalliance with the Iroquois. A Christian Mohawk of the Saut St. Louis called them to another council and demanded that they should explain clearly their position. Thus pushed to the wall, they no longer hesitated but promised like the rest to do all that their father should ask.

Their sincerity was soon put to the test. An Iroquois convert called La Plaque, a notorious reprobate though a good warrior, had gone out as a scout in the direction of Albany. On the day when the market opened and trade was in full activity, the buyers and sellers were suddenly startled by the sound of the death yell. They snatched their weapons, and for a moment all was confusion, when La Plaque, who had probably meant to amuse himself at their expense, made his appearance and explained that the yells proceeded from him. The news that he brought, however, was sufficiently alarming.

He declared that he had been at Lake St. Sacrement, or Lake George, and had seen there a great number of men making canoes as if about to advance on Montreal. Frontenac thereupon sent the Chevalier de Clermont to scout as far as Lake Champlain. Clermont soon sent back one of his followers to announce that he had discovered a party of the enemy, and that they were already on their way down the Richelieu. Frontenac ordered cannon to be fired to call in the troops, crossed the St. Lawrence, followed by all the Indians, and encamped with twelve hundred men at La Prairie to meet the expected attack. He waited in vain. All was quiet and the Ottawa scouts reported that they could find no enemy.

Three days passed. The Indians grew impatient and wished to go home. Neither English nor Iroquois had shown themselves and Frontenac, satisfied that their strength had been exaggerated, left a small force at La Prairie, recrossed the river and distributed the troops again among the neighboring parishes to protect the harvesters. He now gave ample presents to his departing allies, whose chiefs he had entertained at his own table and to whom, says Charlevoix, he bade farewell "with those engaging manners which he knew so well how to assume when he wanted to gain anybody to his interest." Scarcely were they gone when the distant cannon of La Prairie boomed a sudden alarm.

The men whom La Plaque had seen near Lake George were a part of the combined force of Connecticut and New York, destined to attack Montreal. They had made their way along Wood Creek to the point where it widens into Lake Champlain and here they had stopped. Disputes between the men of the two colonies, internal quarrels in the New York militia, who were divided between the two factions engendered by the late revolution, the want of provisions, the want of canoes and the ravages of smallpox had ruined an enterprise which had been mismanaged from the first.

There was no birchbark to make more canoes, and owing to the lateness of the season, the bark of the elms would not peel. Such of the Iroquois as had joined them were cold and sullen, and news came that the three western tribes of the confederacy, terrified by the smallpox, had refused to move. It was impossible to advance and Winthrop, the commander, gave orders to return to Albany, leaving Phips to conquer Canada alone.

Frontenac was at Montreal on October 10 when a messenger arrived in haste at three o'clock in the afternoon and gave him a letter from Prévost, town major of Quebec. It was to the effect that an Abenaki Indian had just come overland from Acadia with news that some of his tribe had captured an English woman near Portsmouth who told them that a great fleet had sailed from Boston to attack Quebec.

Frontenac, not easily alarmed, doubted the report. Nevertheless, he embarked at once with the intendant in a small vessel, which proved to be leaky and was near foundering with all on board. He then took a canoe and towards evening set out again for Quebec, ordering some two hundred men to follow him.

On the next day he met another canoe, bearing a fresh message from Prévost, who announced that the English fleet had been seen in the river and that it was already above Tadoussac. Frontenac now sent back Captain de Ramsay with orders to Callières, governor of Montreal, to descend immediately to Quebec with all the force at his disposal and to muster the inhabitants on the way.

Then he pushed on with the utmost speed. The autumnal storms had begun and the rain pelted him without ceasing, but on the morning of the fourteenth he neared the town. The rocks of Cape Diamond towered before him; the St. Lawrence lay beneath them, lonely and still, and the Basin of Quebec outspread its broad bosom, a solitude without a sail.

Frontenac had arrived in time. He landed at the Lower Town and the troops and the armed inhabitants came crowding to meet him. He was delighted at their ardor. Shouts, cheers and the waving of hats greeted the old man as he climbed the steep ascent of Mountain Street. Fear and doubt seemed banished by his presence. Even those who hated him rejoiced at his coming and hailed him as a deliverer.

He went at once to inspect the fortifications. Since the alarm a week before, Prévost had accomplished wonders and not only completed the works begun in the spring but added others to secure a place which was a natural fortress in itself.

Two days passed in completing the defenses, under the eye of the governor. Men were flocking in from the parishes far and near, and on the evening of the fifteenth, about twenty-seven hundred, regulars and militia, were gathered within the fortifications, besides the armed peasantry of Beauport and Beaupré, who were ordered to watch the river below the town and resist the English, should they attempt to land.

At length, before dawn on the morning of the sixteenth, the sentinels on the Saut au Matelot could descry the slowly moving lights of distant vessels. At daybreak the fleet was in sight. Sail after sail passed the Point of Orleans and glided into the Basin of Quebec. The excited spectators on the rock counted thirty-four of them. Four were large ships, several others were of considerable size and the rest were brigs, schooners and fishing craft, all thronged with men.

As he sailed into the Basin of Quebec, after a protracted voyage, Phips beheld one of the grandest scenes on the western continent—the wide expanse of waters, the lofty promontory beyond and the opposing heights of Levi; the cataract of Montmorenci, the distant range of the Laurentian Mountains, the warlike rock with its diadem of walls and towers, the roofs of the Lower Town clustering on the strand beneath, the Château St. Louis perched at the brink of the cliff, and over it the white banner, spangled with fleur-de-lis, flaunting defiance in the clear autumnal air. Perhaps, as he gazed, a suspicion seized him that the task he had undertaken was less easy than he had thought, but he had conquered once by a simple summons to surrender and he resolved to try its virtue again.

The fleet anchored a little below Quebec, and towards ten o'clock the French saw a boat put out from the admiral's ship, bearing a flag of truce. Four canoes went from the Lower Town and met it midway. It brought a subaltern officer, who announced himself as the bearer of a letter from Sir William Phips to the French commander. He was taken into one of the canoes and paddled to the quay, after being completely blindfolded by a bandage which covered half his face. Prévost received him as he landed and ordered two sergeants to take him by the arms and lead him to the governor.

His progress was neither rapid nor direct. They drew him here and there, delighting to make him clamber in the dark over every possible obstruction, while a noisy crowd hustled him and laughing women called him Colin Maillard, the name of the chief player in blindman's buff. Amid a prodigious hubbub, intended to bewilder him and impress him with a sense of immense warlike preparation, they dragged him over the three barricades of Mountain Street and brought him at last into a large room of the château. Here they took the bandage from his eyes.

He stood for a moment with an air of astonishment and some confusion. The governor stood before him, haughty and stern, surrounded by French and Canadian officers—Maricourt, Sainte-Hélène, Longueuil, Villebon, Valrenne, Bienville and many more—bedecked with gold lace and silver lace, perukes and powder, plumes and ribbons, and all the martial foppery in which they took delight, and regarding the envoy with keen, defiant eyes.

After a moment he recovered his breath and his composure, saluted Frontenac and, expressing a wish that the duty assigned him had been of a more agreeable nature, handed him the letter of Phips. Frontenac gave it to an interpreter, who read it aloud in French that all might hear.

When the reading was finished, the Englishman pulled his watch from his pocket and handed it to the governor. Frontenac could not, or pretended that he could not, see the hour. The messenger thereupon told him that it was ten o'clock and that he must have his answer before eleven. A general cry of indignation arose and Valrenne called out that Phips was nothing but a pirate and that his man ought to be hanged. Frontenac contained himself for a moment and then said to the envoy:

"I will not keep you waiting so long. Tell your general that I do not recognize King William, and that the Prince of Orange, who so styles himself, is a usurper who has violated the most sacred laws of blood in attempting to dethrone his father-in-law. I know no King of England but King James. Your general ought not to be surprised at the hostilities which he says that the French have carried on in the colony of Massachusetts, for as the King my master has taken the King of England under his protection, and is about to replace him on his throne by force of arms, he might have expected that his Majesty would order me to make war on a people who have rebelled against their lawful prince."

Then, turning with a smile to the officers about him: "Even if your general offered me conditions a little more gracious, and if I had a mind to accept them, does he suppose that these brave gentlemen would give their consent and advise me to trust a man who broke his agreement with the governor of Port Royal, or a rebel who has failed in his duty to his King and forgotten all the favors he had received from him, to follow a prince who pretends to be the liberator of England and the defender of the faith, and yet destroys the laws and privileges of the kingdom and overthrows its religion? The divine justice which your general invokes in his letter will not fail to punish such acts severely."

The messenger seemed astonished and startled, but he presently asked if the governor would give him his answer in writing.

"No," returned Frontenac, "I will answer your general only by the mouths of my cannon, that he may learn that a man like me is not to be summoned after this fashion. Let him do his best, and I will do mine." And he dismissed the Englishman abruptly. He was again blindfolded, led over the barricades, and sent back to the fleet by the boat that brought him.

Phips had often given proof of personal courage, but for the past three weeks his conduct seems that of a man conscious that he is charged with a work too large for his capacity. He had spent a good part of his time in holding councils of war, and now, when he heard the answer of Frontenac, he called another to consider what should be done.

A plan of attack was at length arranged. The militia were to be landed on the shore of Beauport, which was just below Quebec, though separated from it by the St. Charles. They were then to cross this river by a ford practicable at low water, climb the heights of Ste. Geneviève, and gain the rear of the town. The small vessels of the fleet were to aid the movement by ascending the St. Charles as far as the ford, holding the enemy in check by their fire and carrying provisions, ammunition and intrenching tools for the use of the land troops.

When these had crossed and were ready to attack Quebec in the rear, Phips was to cannonade it in front and land two hundred men under cover of his guns to effect a diversion by storming the barricades. Some of the French prisoners, from whom their captors appear to have received a great deal of correct information, told the admiral that there was a place a mile or two above the town where the heights might be scaled and the rear of the fortifications reached from a direction opposite to that proposed. This was precisely the movement by which Wolfe afterwards gained his memorable victory, but Phips chose to abide by the original plan.

While the plan was debated, the opportunity for accomplishing it ebbed away. It was still early when the messenger returned from Quebec, but before Phips was ready to act, the day was on the wane and the tide was against him. He lay quietly at his moorings, when in the evening a great shouting, mingled with the roll of drums and the sound of fifes, was heard from the Upper Town. The English officers asked their prisoner, Granville, what it meant.

"Ma foi, messieurs," he replied, "you have lost the game. It is the governor of Montreal with the people from the country above. There is nothing for you now but to pack and go home."

In fact, Callières had arrived with seven or eight hundred men, many of them regulars. With these were bands of *coureurs de bois* and other young Canadians, all full of fight, singing and whooping with martial glee as they passed the western gate and trooped down St. Louis Street.

The next day was gusty and blustering and still Phips lay quiet, waiting on the winds and the waves. A small vessel, with sixty men on board under Captain Ephraim Savage, ran in towards the shore of Beauport to examine the landing and stuck fast in the mud. The Canadians plied her with bullets and brought a cannon to bear on her. They might have waded out and boarded her, but Savage and his men kept up so hot a fire that they forbore the attempt, and when the tide rose, she floated again.

There was another night of tranquillity, but at about eleven on Wednesday morning the French heard the English fifes and drums in full action, while repeated shouts of "God save King William!" rose from all the vessels. This lasted an hour or more, after which a great number of boats, loaded with men, put out from the fleet and rowed rapidly towards the shore of Beauport.

The tide was low and the boats grounded before reaching the landing place. The French on the rock could see the troops through telescopes, looking in the distance like a swarm of black ants as they waded through mud and water and formed in companies along the strand. They were some thirteen hundred in number and were commanded by Major Walley.

Frontenac had sent three hundred sharpshooters under Sainte-Hélène to meet them and hold them in check. A battalion of troops followed, but long before they could reach the spot, Sainte-Hélène's men, with a few militia from the neighboring parishes and a band of Huron warriors from Lorette, threw themselves into the thickets along the front of the English and opened a distant but galling fire upon the compact bodies of the enemy.

Walley ordered a charge. The New England men rushed in a disorderly manner but with great impetuosity up the rising ground, received two volleys, which failed to check them, and drove back the assailants in some confusion. They turned, however, and fought in Indian fashion with courage and address, leaping and dodging among trees, rocks and bushes, firing as they retreated and inflicting more harm than they received.

Towards evening they disappeared and Walley, whose men had been much scattered in the desultory fight, drew them together as well as he could and advanced towards the St. Charles in order to meet the vessels which were to aid him in passing the ford. Here he posted sentinels and encamped for the night.

He had lost four killed and about sixty wounded and imagined that he had killed twenty or thirty of the enemy. In fact, however, their loss was much less, though among the killed was a valuable officer, the Chevalier de Clermont, and among the wounded the veteran captain of Beauport, Juchereau de Saint-Denis, more than sixty-four years of age. In the evening a deserter came to the English camp and brought the unwelcome intelligence that there were three thousand armed men in Quebec.

Meanwhile, Phips, whose fault hitherto had not been an excess of promptitude, grew impatient and made a premature movement inconsistent with the preconcerted plan. He left his moorings, anchored his largest ships before the town and prepared to cannonade it. But the fiery veteran who watched him from the Château St. Louis anticipated him and gave him the first shot. Phips replied furiously, opening fire with every gun that he could bring to bear, while the rock paid him back in kind and belched flame and smoke from all its batteries. So fierce and rapid was the firing that La Hontan compares it to volleys of musketry and old officers who had seen many sieges declared that they had never known the like. The din was prodigious, reverberated from the surrounding heights and rolled back from the distant mountains in one continuous roar.

On the part of the English, however, surprisingly little was accomplished besides noise and smoke. The practice of their gunners was so bad that many of their shot struck harmlessly against the face of the cliff. Their guns, too, were very light and appear to have been charged with a view to the most rigid economy of gunpowder, for the balls failed to pierce the stone walls of the buildings and did so little damage that, as the French boasted, twenty crowns would have repaired it all. Night came at length and the turmoil ceased.

Phips lay quiet till daybreak, when Frontenac sent a shot to waken him and the cannonade began again. Sainte-Hélène had returned from Beauport and he, with his brother Maricourt, took charge of the two batteries of the Lower Town, aiming the guns in person and throwing balls of eighteen and twenty-four pounds with excellent precision against the four largest ships of the fleet. One of their shots cut the flagstaff of the admiral and the cross of St. George fell into the river. It drifted with the tide towards the north shore, whereupon several Canadians paddled out in a birch canoe, secured it and brought it back in triumph.

On the spire of the cathedral in the Upper Town had been hung a picture of the Holy Family as an invocation of divine aid. The Puritan gunners wasted their ammunition in vain attempts to knock it down. That it escaped their malice was ascribed to miracle, but the miracle would have been greater if they had hit it.

At length one of the ships which had suffered most hauled off and abandoned the fight. That of the admiral had fared little better and now her condition grew desperate. With her rigging torn, her mainmast half cut through, her mizzenmast splintered, her cabin pierced and her hull riddled with shot, another volley seemed likely to sink her, when Phips ordered her to be cut loose from her moorings and she drifted out of fire, leaving cable and anchor behind. The remaining ships soon gave over the conflict and withdrew to stations where they could neither do harm nor suffer it.

Phips had thrown away nearly all his ammunition in this futile and disastrous attack, which should have been deferred till the moment when Walley, with his land force, had gained the rear of the town. Walley lay in his camp, his men wet, shivering with cold, famished and sickening with the smallpox. Food and all other supplies were to have been brought him by the small vessels, which should have entered the mouth of the St. Charles and aided him to cross it. But he waited for them in vain. Every vessel that carried a gun had busied itself in cannonading and the rest did not move. There appears to have been insubordination among the masters of these small craft, some of whom, being owners or part owners of the vessels they commanded, were probably unwilling to run them into danger.

Walley was no soldier, but he saw that to attempt the passage of the river without aid, under the batteries of the town and in the face of forces twice as numerous as his own, was not an easy task. Frontenac, on his part, says that he wished him to do so, knowing that the attempt would ruin him.

The New England men were eager to push on, but the night of Thursday, the day of Phips's repulse, was so cold that ice formed more than an inch in thickness and the half-starved militia suffered intensely. Six fieldpieces, with their ammunition, had been sent ashore, but they were nearly useless as there were no means of moving them. Half a barrel of musket powder and one biscuit for each man were also landed, and with this meager aid Walley was left to capture Quebec. He might, had he dared, have made a dash across the ford on the morning of Thursday and assaulted the town in the rear while Phips was cannonading it in front, but his courage was not equal to so desperate a venture. The firing ceased and the possible opportunity was lost.

The citizen soldier despaired of success, and on the morning of Friday he went on board the admiral's ship to explain his situation. While he was gone, his men put themselves in motion and advanced along the borders of the St. Charles towards the ford. Frontenac, with three battalions of regular troops, went to receive them at the crossing, while Sainte-Hélène, with his brother Longueuil, passed the ford with a body of Canadians and opened fire on them from the neighboring thickets. Their advance parties were driven in and there was a hot skirmish, the chief loss falling on the New England men, who were fully exposed. On the side of the French, Sainte-Hélène was mortally wounded and his brother was hurt by a spent ball.

Towards evening the Canadians withdrew and the English encamped for the night. Their commander presently rejoined them. The admiral had given him leave to withdraw them to the fleet and boats were accordingly sent to bring them off, but as these did not arrive till about daybreak, it was necessary to defer the embarkation till the next night.

At dawn Quebec was all astir with the beating of drums and the ringing of bells. The New England drums replied, and Walley drew up his men under arms, expecting an attack, for the town was so near that the hubbub of voices from within could plainly be heard. The noise gradually died away, and except for a few shots from the ramparts, the invaders were left undisturbed.

Walley sent two or three companies to beat up the neighboring thickets, where he suspected that the enemy was lurking. On the way they had the good luck to find and kill a number of cattle, which they cooked and ate on the spot, whereupon, being greatly refreshed and invigorated, they dashed forward in complete disorder and were soon met by the fire of the ambushed Canadians. Several more companies were sent to their support and the skirmishing became lively. Three detachments from Quebec had crossed the river and the militia of Beauport and Beaupré had hastened to join them. They fought like Indians, hiding behind trees or throwing themselves flat among the bushes and laying repeated ambuscades as they slowly fell back. At length they all made a stand on a hill behind the buildings and fences of a farm and here they held their ground till night, while the New England men taunted them as cowards who would never fight except under cover.

Walley, who with his main body had stood in arms all day, now called in the skirmishers and fell back to the landing place, where as soon as it grew dark the boats arrived from the fleet. The sick men, of whom there were many, were sent on board and then, amid floods of rain, the whole force embarked in noisy confusion, leaving behind them in the mud five of their cannon.

Hasty as was their parting, their conduct on the whole had been creditable and La Hontan, who was in Quebec at the time, says of them: "They fought vigorously, though as ill-disciplined as men gathered together at random could be, for they did not lack courage, and if they failed, it was by reason of their entire ignorance of discipline, and because they were exhausted by the fatigues of the voyage."

Of Phips he speaks with contempt and says that he could not have served the French better if they had bribed him to stand all the while with his arms folded. Some allowance should, nevertheless, be made him for the unmanageable character of the force under his command, the constitution of which was fatal to military subordination.

On Sunday, the morning after the re-embarkation, Phips called a

371

council of officers and it was resolved that the men should rest for a day or two, that there should be a meeting for prayer, and that if ammunition enough could be found, another landing should be attempted. But the rough weather prevented the prayer meeting and the plan of a new attack was fortunately abandoned.

Quebec remained in agitation and alarm till Tuesday, when Phips weighed anchor and disappeared with all his fleet behind the Island of Orleans. He did not go far, as indeed he could not, but stopped four leagues below to mend rigging, fortify wounded masts and stop shot-holes. Subercase had gone with a detachment to watch the retiring enemy and Phips was repeatedly seen among his men on a scaffold at the side of his ship, exercising his old trade of carpenter.

This delay was turned to good use by an exchange of prisoners. Chief among those in the hands of the French was Captain Davis, late commander at Casco Bay, and there were also two young daughters of Lieutenant Clark, who had been killed at the same place. Frontenac himself had humanely ransomed these children from the Indians and Madame de Champigny, wife of the intendant, had with equal kindness bought from them a little girl named Sarah Gerrish and placed her in charge of the nuns at the Hôtel-Dieu, who had become greatly attached to her, while she, on her part, left them with reluctance. The French had the better in these exchanges, receiving able-bodied men and returning, with the exception of Davis, only women and children.

The heretics were gone and Quebec breathed freely again. Her escape had been a narrow one. Not that three thousand men, in part regular troops, defending one of the strongest positions on the continent and commanded by Frontenac could not defy the attacks of two thousand raw fishermen and farmers, led by an ignorant civilian, but the numbers which were a source of strength were at the same time a source of weakness. Nearly all the adult males of Canada were gathered at Quebec and there was imminent danger of starvation. Cattle from the neighboring parishes had been hastily driven into the town, but there was little other provision, and before Phips retreated the pinch of famine had begun. Had he come a week earlier or stayed a week later, the French themselves believed that Quebec would have fallen—in the one case for want of men, and in the other for want of food.

Phips returned crestfallen to Boston late in November and one by one the rest of the fleet came straggling after him, battered and weather-beaten. Some did not appear till February and three or four never came at all. The autumn and early winter were unusually stormy. Captain Rainsford, with sixty men, was wrecked on the Island of Anticosti, where more than half their number died of cold and misery. In the other vessels, some were drowned, some frostbitten, and above two hundred killed by smallpox and fever.

At Boston, all was dismay and gloom. The Puritan bowed before "this awful frown of God" and searched his conscience for the sin that had brought upon him so stern a chastisement. Massachusetts, already impoverished, found herself in extremity. The war, instead of paying for itself, had burdened her with an additional debt of fifty thousand pounds. The sailors and soldiers were clamorous for their pay, and to satisfy them, the colony was forced for the first time in its history to issue a paper currency.

Massachusetts had made her usual mistake. She had confidently believed that ignorance and inexperience could match the skill of a tried veteran and that the rude courage of her fishermen and farmers could triumph without discipline or leadership.

The conditions of her material prosperity were adverse to efficiency in war. A trading republic, without trained officers, may win victories, but it wins them either by accident or by an extravagant outlay in money and life.

CHAPTER 8

The Battle with the Onondagas

THE WAR WITH ENGLAND AND THE IROQUOIS STILL
went on. The contest for territorial mastery was fourfold: first,
for the control of the west; secondly, for that of Hudson's Bay; thirdly,
for that of Newfoundland; and lastly, for that of Acadia. All these vast
and widely sundered regions were included in the government of Frontenac. Each division of the war was distinct from the rest and each
had a character of its own. As the contest for the west was wholly with
New York and her Iroquois allies, so the contest for Acadia was
wholly with the "Bostonnais," or people of New England.

But in Hudson's Bay, Newfoundland and Acadia the issues of the
war were unimportant compared with the momentous question whether
France or England should be mistress of the west—that is to say, of
the whole interior of the continent. The result hung, for the present, on
the relations of the French with the Iroquois and the tribes of the
lakes, the Illinois and the valley of the Ohio, but above all, on their
relations with the Iroquois; for could they be conquered or won over,
it would be easy to deal with the rest.

Frontenac was meditating a grand effort to inflict such castigation as
would bring them to reason, when one of their chiefs named Tareha
came to Quebec with overtures of peace. The Iroquois had lost many
of their best warriors. The arrival of troops from France had discouraged them; the war had interrupted their hunting; and having no
furs to barter with the English, they were in want of arms, ammunition
and all the necessaries of life. Moreover, Father Milet, nominally a

prisoner among them but really an adopted chief, had used all his influence to bring about a peace and the mission of Tareha was the result.

Frontenac received him kindly. "My Iroquois children have been drunk, but I will give them an opportunity to repent. Let each of your five nations send me two deputies and I will listen to what they have to say."

They would not come but sent him instead an invitation to meet them and their friends, the English, in a general council at Albany, a proposal which he rejected with contempt. Then they sent another deputation, partly to him and partly to their Christian countrymen of the Saut and the Mountain, inviting all alike to come and treat with them at Onondaga. Frontenac, adopting the Indian fashion, kicked away their wampum belts, rebuked them for tampering with the mission Indians, and told them that they were rebels, bribed by the English, adding that if a suitable deputation should be sent to Quebec to treat squarely of peace he still would listen, but that if they came back with any more such proposals as they had just made they should be roasted alive.

A few weeks later the deputation appeared. It consisted of two chiefs of each nation, headed by the renowned orator Decanisora. The council was held in the hall of the supreme council at Quebec. The dignitaries of the colony were present, with priests, Jesuits, Récollets, officers and the Christian chiefs of the Saut and the Mountain. The appearance of the ambassadors bespoke their destitute plight, for they were all dressed in shabby deerskins and old blankets, except Decanisora, who was attired in a scarlet coat laced with gold, given him by the governor of New York. Colden, who knew him in his old age, describes him as a tall, well-formed man, with a face not unlike the busts of Cicero.

"He spoke," says the French reporter, "with as perfect a grace as is vouchsafed to an uncivilized people." He buried the hatchet, covered the blood that had been spilled, opened the roads and cleared the clouds from the sun. In other words, he offered peace. But he demanded at the same time that it should include the English.

Frontenac replied, in substance: "My children are right to come submissive and repentant. I am ready to forgive the past and hang up

375

the hatchet, but the peace must include all my other children, far and near. Shut your ears to English poison. The war with the English has nothing to do with you, and only the great kings across the sea have power to stop it. You must give up all your prisoners, both French and Indian, without one exception. I will then return mine, and make peace with you, but not before."

He then entertained them at his own table, gave them a feast described as "magnificent" and bestowed gifts so liberally that the tattered ambassadors went home in embroidered coats, laced shirts and plumed hats. They were pledged to return with the prisoners before the end of the season and they left two hostages as security.

Meanwhile, the authorities of New York tried to prevent the threatened peace. First, Major Peter Schuyler convoked the chiefs at Albany and told them that if they went to ask peace in Canada they would be slaves forever. The Iroquois declared that they loved the English, but they repelled every attempt to control their action. Then Fletcher, the governor, called a general council at the same place and told them that they should not hold councils with the French, or that if they did so, they should hold them at Albany in presence of the English. Again they asserted their rights as an independent people.

"Corlaer," said their speaker, "has held councils with our enemies, and why should not we hold councils with his?" Yet they were strong in assurances of friendship and declared themselves "one head, one heart, one blood, and one soul with the English." Their speaker continued: "Our only reason for sending deputies to the French is that we are brought so low, and none of our neighbors help us, but leave us to bear all the burden of the war. Our brothers of New England, Pennsylvania, Maryland and Virginia, all of their own accord took hold of the covenant chain and called themselves our allies, but they have done nothing to help us, and we cannot fight the French alone because they are always receiving soldiers from beyond the Great Lake. Speak from your heart, brother: will you and your neighbors join with us and make strong war against the French? If you will, we will break off all treaties and fight them as hotly as ever; but if you will not help us, we must make peace."

Nothing could be more just than these reproaches, and if the English governor had answered by a vigorous attack on the French forts south of the St. Lawrence, the Iroquois warriors would have raised the hatchet again with one accord. But Fletcher was busy with other matters and he had, besides, no force at his disposal but four companies—the only British regulars on the continent, defective in numbers, ill appointed and mutinous. Therefore he answered not with acts, but with words. The negotiation with the French went on and Fletcher called another council. It left him in a worse position than before. The Iroquois again asked for help. He could not promise it, but was forced to yield the point and tell them that he consented to their making peace with Onontio.

It is certain that they wanted peace, but equally certain that they did not want it to be lasting and sought nothing more than a breathing time to regain their strength. Even now some of them were for continuing the war, and at the great council at Onondaga, where the matter was debated, the Onondagas, Oneidas and Mohawks spurned the French proposals and refused to give up their prisoners. The Cayugas and some of the Senecas were of another mind and agreed to a partial compliance with Frontenac's demands. The rest seem to have stood passive in the hope of gaining time.

They were disappointed. In vain the Seneca and Cayuga deputies buried the hatchet at Montreal and promised that the other nations would soon do likewise. Frontenac was not to be deceived. He would accept nothing but the frank fulfillment of his conditions, refused the proffered peace and told his Indian allies to wage war to the knife. There was a dog feast and a war dance and the strife began anew.

In all these conferences the Iroquois had stood by their English allies with a fidelity not too well merited. But though they were loyal towards the English, they had acted with duplicity towards the French, and while treating of peace with them had attacked some of their Indian allies and intrigued with others. They pursued with more persistency than ever the policy they had adopted in the time of La Barre—that is, to persuade or frighten the tribes of the west to abandon the French, join hands with them and the English, and send their furs to Albany instead of Montreal, for the sagacious confederates knew well that if the trade were turned into this new channel their local position would enable them to control it. Their scheme was good, but with whatever consistency their chiefs and elders might pursue it, the

377

wayward ferocity of their young warriors crossed it incessantly and murders alternated with intrigues.

On the other hand, the western tribes, who since the war had been but ill supplied with French goods and French brandy, knew that they could have English goods and English rum in great abundance and at far less cost, and thus, in spite of hate and fear, the intrigue went on. Michilimackinac was the focus of it, but it pervaded all the west.

The position of Frontenac was one of great difficulty, the more so because the internal quarrels of his allies excessively complicated the mazes of forest diplomacy. This heterogeneous multitude, scattered in tribes and groups of tribes over two thousand miles of wilderness, was like a vast menagerie of wild animals. The lynx bristled at the wolf and the panther grinned fury at the bear, in spite of all his efforts to form them into a happy family under his paternal rule.

One course alone was now left to Frontenac and this was to strike the Iroquois with a blow heavy enough to humble them, and teach the wavering hordes of the west that he was, in truth, their father and their defender. Nobody knew so well as he the difficulties of the attempt and, deceived perhaps by his own energy, he feared that in his absence on a distant expedition the governor of New York would attack Montreal. Therefore he had begged for more troops. About three hundred were sent him, and with these he was forced to content himself.

He had waited also for another reason. In his belief the re-establishment of Fort Frontenac, abandoned in a panic by Denonville, was necessary to the success of a campaign against the Iroquois. A party in the colony vehemently opposed the measure on the ground that the fort would be used by the friends of Frontenac for purposes of trade. It was, nevertheless, very important if not essential for holding the Iroquois in check. They themselves felt it to be so, and when they heard that the French intended to occupy it again, they appealed to the governor of New York, who told them that if the plan were carried into effect he would march to their aid with all the power of his government. He did not, and perhaps could not, keep his word.

In the question of Fort Frontenac, as in everything else, the opposition to the governor, always busy and vehement, found its chief representative in the intendant, who told the minister that the policy of Frontenac was all wrong; that the public good was not its object; that he disobeyed or evaded the orders of the King; and that he had suffered the Iroquois to delude him by false overtures of peace.

The representations of the intendant and his faction had such effect that Ponchartrain wrote to the governor that the plan of re-establishing Fort Frontenac "must absolutely be abandoned." Frontenac, bent on accomplishing his purpose, and doubly so because his enemies opposed it, had anticipated the orders of the minister and sent seven hundred men to Lake Ontario to repair the fort. The day after they left Montreal the letter of Ponchartrain arrived. The intendant demanded their recall. Frontenac refused. The fort was repaired, garrisoned and victualed for a year.

A successful campaign was now doubly necessary to the governor, for by this alone could he hope to avert the consequences of his audacity. He waited no longer, but mustered troops, militia and Indians and marched to attack the Iroquois.

On the fourth of July, 1696, Frontenac left Montreal at the head of about twenty-two hundred men. On the nineteenth he reached Fort Frontenac, and on the twenty-sixth he crossed to the southern shore of Lake Ontario. A swarm of Indian canoes led the way. Next followed two battalions of regulars in bateaux, commanded by Callières. Then more bateaux, laden with cannon, mortars and rockets; then Frontenac himself, surrounded by the canoes of his staff and his guard; then eight hundred Canadians, under Ramesay; while more regulars and more Indians, all commanded by Vaudreuil, brought up the rear.

In two days they reached the mouth of the Oswego. Strong scouting parties were sent out to scour the forests in front, while the expedition slowly and painfully worked its way up the stream. Most of the troops and Canadians marched through the matted woods along the banks, while the bateaux and canoes were pushed, rowed, paddled or dragged forward against the current. On the evening of the thirtieth they reached the falls, where the river plunged over ledges of rock which completely stopped the way. The work of "carrying" was begun at once.

The Indians and Canadians carried the canoes to the navigable water above and gangs of men dragged the bateaux up the portage path on rollers. Night soon came and the work was continued till ten o'clock by torchlight. Frontenac would have passed on foot like the rest, but the Indians would not have it so. They lifted him in his canoe upon their shoulders and bore him in triumph, singing and yelling, through the forest and along the margin of the rapids, the blaze of the torches lighting the strange procession, where plumes of officers and uniforms of the governor's guard mingled with the feathers and scalp locks of naked savages.

When the falls were passed, the troops pushed on as before along the narrow stream and through the tangled labyrinths on either side, till on the first of August they reached Lake Onondaga and with sails set the whole flotilla glided before the wind and landed the motley army on a rising ground half a league from the salt springs of Salina. The next day was spent in building a fort to protect the canoes, bateaux and stores, and as evening closed, a ruddy glow above the southern forest told them that the town of Onondaga was on fire.

The Marquis de Crisasy was left with a detachment to hold the fort, and at sunrise on the fourth the army moved forward in order of battle. The governor, enfeebled by age, was carried in an armchair, while Callières, disabled by gout, was mounted on a horse, brought for the purpose in one of the bateaux. To Subercase fell the hard task of directing the march among the dense columns of the primeval forest, by hill and hollow, over rocks and fallen trees, through swamps, brooks and gullies, among thickets, brambles and vines.

It was but eight or nine miles to Onondaga, but they were all day in reaching it and evening was near when they emerged from the shadows of the forest into the broad light of the Indian clearing. The maize fields stretched before them for miles, and in the midst lay the charred and smoking ruins of the Iroquois capital. Not an enemy was to be seen, but they found the dead bodies of two murdered French prisoners. Scouts were sent out, guards were set and the disappointed troops encamped on the maize fields.

Onondaga, formerly an open town, had been fortified by the English, who had enclosed it with a double range of strong palisades, forming a rectangle, flanked by bastions at the four corners and surrounded by an outer fence of tall poles. The place was not defensible against cannon and mortars and the four hundred warriors belonging to it had been but slightly reinforced from the other tribes of the confederacy, each of which feared that the French attack might be directed against itself. On the approach of an enemy of five times their number, they had burned their town and retreated southward into distant forests.

The troops were busied for two days in hacking down the maize, digging up the caches, or hidden stores of food, and destroying their contents. The neighboring tribe of the Oneidas sent a messenger to beg peace. Frontenac replied that he would grant it on condition that they all should migrate to Canada and settle there and Vaudreuil, with seven hundred men, was sent to enforce the demand.

Meanwhile, a few Onondaga stragglers had been found, and among them, hidden in a hollow tree, a withered warrior eighty years old and nearly blind. Frontenac would have spared him, but the Indian allies, Christians from the mission villages, were so eager to burn him that it was thought inexpedient to refuse them. They tied him to the stake and tried to shake his constancy by every torture that fire could inflict, but not a cry nor a murmur escaped him. He defied them to do their worst, till enraged at his taunts, one of them gave him a mortal stab.

"I thank you," said the old stoic with his last breath, "but you ought to have finished as you began and killed me by fire. Learn from me, you dogs of Frenchmen, how to endure pain; and you, dogs of dogs, their Indian allies, think what you will do when you are burned like me."

Vaudreuil and his detachment returned within three days, after destroying Oneida, with all the growing corn, and seizing a number of chiefs as hostages for the fulfillment of the demands of Frontenac. There was some thought of marching on Cayuga, but the governor judged it to be inexpedient, and as it would be useless to chase the fugitive Onondagas, nothing remained but to return home.

What Frontenac feared had come to pass. The enemy had saved themselves by flight and his expedition, like that of Denonville, was but half successful. He took care, however, to announce it to the King as a triumph. The King highly commended him and sent him the cross of the Military Order of St. Louis.

Callières, who deserved it less, had received it several years before, but he had not found or provoked so many defamers. Frontenac complained to the minister that his services had been slightly and tardily requited. This was true and it was due largely to the complaints excited by his own perversity and violence. These complaints still continued, but the fault was not all on one side and Frontenac himself often had just reason to retort them.

Most of these quarrels, however trivial in themselves, had a solid foundation and were closely connected with the great question of the control of the west. As to the measures to be taken, two parties divided the colony—one consisting of the governor and his friends, and the other of the intendant, the Jesuits and such of the merchants as were not in favor with Frontenac.

His policy was to protect the Indian allies at all risks; to repel by force, if necessary, every attempt of the English to encroach on the territory in dispute; and to occupy it by forts which should be at once posts of war and commerce and places of rendezvous for traders and *voyageurs*. Champigny and his party denounced this system; urged that the forest posts should be abandoned; that both garrisons and traders should be recalled; that the French should not go to the Indians, but that the Indians should come to the French; that the fur trade of the interior should be carried on at Montreal; and that no Frenchman should be allowed to leave the settled limits of the colony except the Jesuits and persons in their service, who, as Champigny insisted, would be able to keep the Indians in the French interest without the help of soldiers.

In vain Frontenac represented that to abandon the forest posts would be to resign to the English the trade of the interior country, and at last the country itself. The royal ear was open to his opponents and the royal instincts reinforced their arguments.

The King, enamored of subordination and order, wished to govern Canada as he governed a province of France and this could be done only by keeping the population within prescribed bounds. Therefore he commanded that licenses for the forest trade should cease, that the forest posts should be abandoned and destroyed, that all Frenchmen should be ordered back to the settlements, and that none should return under pain of the galleys. An exception was made in favor of the Jesuits, who were allowed to continue their western missions, subject to restrictions designed to prevent them from becoming a cover for illicit fur trade.

Frontenac was also directed to make peace with the Iroquois, even if necessary without including the western allies of France—that is, he was authorized by Louis XIV to pursue the course which had discredited and imperiled the colony under the rule of Denonville.

The intentions of the King did not take effect. The policy of Frontenac was the true one, whatever motives may have entered into his advocacy of it. In view of the geographical, social, political and commercial conditions of Canada, the policy of his opponents was impracticable and nothing less than a perpetual cordon of troops could have prevented the Canadians from escaping to the backwoods. In spite of all the evils that attended the forest posts, it would have been a blunder to abandon them. This quickly became apparent. Champigny himself saw the necessity of compromise. The instructions of the King were scarcely given before they were partially withdrawn and they soon became a dead letter. Even Fort Frontenac was retained after repeated directions to abandon it. The policy of the governor prevailed. The colony returned to its normal methods of growth, and so continued to the end.

Now came the question of peace with the Iroquois, to whose mercy Frontenac was authorized to leave his western allies. He was the last man to accept such permission. Since the burning of Onondaga, the Iroquois negotiations with the western tribes had been broken off and several fights had occurred in which the confederates had suffered loss and been roused to vengeance. This was what Frontenac wanted, but at the same time it promised him fresh trouble, for while he was determined to prevent the Iroquois from making peace with the allies without his authority, he was equally determined to compel them to do so with it. There must be peace, though not till he could control its conditions.

The Onondaga campaign, unsatisfactory as it was, had had its effect. Several Iroquois chiefs came to Quebec with overtures of peace. They brought no prisoners, but promised to bring them in the spring, and one of them remained as a hostage that the promise should be kept.

It was nevertheless broken under English influence, and instead of a solemn embassy, the council of Onondaga sent a messenger with a wampum belt to tell Frontenac that they were all so engrossed in bewailing the recent death of Black Kettle, a famous war chief, that they had no strength to travel. They begged that Onontio would return the hostage and send to them for the French prisoners. The messenger further declared that, though they would make peace with Onontio, they would not make it with his allies.

Frontenac threw back the peace belt into his face. "Tell the chiefs that if they must needs stay at home to cry about a trifle, I will give them something to cry for. Let them bring me every prisoner, French and Indian, and make a treaty that shall include all my children, or they shall feel my tomahawk again."

Then, turning to a number of Ottawas who were present: "You see that I can make peace for myself when I please. If I continue the war, it is only for your sake. I will never make a treaty without including you, and recovering your prisoners like my own."

Thus the matter stood when a great event took place. Early in February a party of Dutch and Indians came to Montreal with news that peace had been signed in Europe, and at the end of May, Major Peter Schuyler, accompanied by Dellius, the minister of Albany, arrived with copies of the treaty in French and Latin. The scratch of a pen at Ryswick had ended the conflict in America, as far at least as concerned the civilized combatants.

In November 1698, when the last ship had gone and Canada was sealed from the world for half a year, a mortal illness fell upon the governor. On the twenty-second he had strength enough to dictate his will, seated in an easy chair in his chamber at the château. His colleague and adversary, Champigny, often came to visit him and did all in his power to soothe his last moments. The reconciliation between them was complete. One of his Récollet friends, Father Olivier Goyer, administered extreme unction, and on the afternoon of the twenty-eighth he died, in perfect composure and full possession of his faculties. He was in his seventy-eighth year.

From the first, Frontenac had set himself in opposition to the most influential of the Canadian clergy. When he came to the colony, their power in the government was still enormous and even the most devout of his predecessors had been forced into conflict with them to defend the civil authority. But when Frontenac entered the strife, he brought into it an irritability, a jealous and exacting vanity, a love of rule and a passion for having his own way, even in trifles, which made him the most exasperating of adversaries. Hence it was that many of the clerical party felt towards him a bitterness that was far from ending with his life.

Frontenac's own acts and words best paint his character and it is needless to enlarge upon it. What perhaps may be least forgiven him is the barbarity of the warfare that he waged and the cruelties that he permitted. He had seen too many towns sacked to be much subject to the scruples of modern humanitarianism, yet he was no whit more ruthless than his times and his surroundings and some of his contemporaries find fault with him for not allowing more Indian captives to be tortured.

If he was a hot and pertinacious foe, he was also a fast friend, and he excited love and hatred in about equal measure. His attitude towards public enemies was always proud and peremptory, yet his courage was guided by so clear a sagacity that he never was forced to recede from the position he had taken. Towards Indians he was an admirable compound of sternness and conciliation. Of the immensity of his services to the colony, there can be no doubt. He found it, under Denonville, in humiliation and terror; and he left it in honor and almost in triumph.

Greatness must be denied him, but a more remarkable figure, in its bold and salient individuality and sharply marked light and shadow, is nowhere seen in American history.

CHAPTER 9

Peace

IT DID NOT NEED THE PRESENCE OF FRONTENAC TO cause snappings and sparks in the highly electrical atmosphere of New France. Callières took his place as governor ad interim and in due time received a formal appointment to the office. Apart from the wretched state of his health, undermined by gout and dropsy, he was in most respects well fitted for it. But his deportment at once gave umbrage to the excitable Champigny, who declared that he had never seen such hauteur since he came to the colony.

Another official was still more offended. "Monsieur de Frontenac," he says, "was no sooner dead than trouble began. Monsieur de Callières, puffed up by his new authority, claims honors due only to a marshal of France. It would be a different matter if he, like his predecessor, were regarded as the father of the country and the love and delight of the Indian allies. At the review at Montreal he sat in his carriage and received the incense offered him with as much composure and coolness as if he had been some divinity of this New World." In spite of these complaints, the court sustained Callières and authorized him to enjoy the honors that he had assumed.

His first and chief task was to finish the work that Frontenac had shaped out and bring the Iroquois to such submission as the interests of the colony and its allies demanded. The fierce confederates admired the late governor and, if they themselves are to be believed, could not help lamenting him. But they were emboldened by his death and the difficulty of dealing with them was increased by it. Had they been sure

386

of effectual support from the English, there can be little doubt that they would have refused to treat with the French, of whom their distrust was extreme.

They persisted in asserting their independence of each of the rival powers and played the one against the other in order to strengthen their position with both. When Bellomont required them to surrender their French prisoners to him, they answered: "We are the masters; our prisoners are our own. We will keep them or give them to the French, if we choose." At the same time they told Callières that they would bring them to the English at Albany, and invited him to send his agents there to receive them.

They were much disconcerted, however, when letters were read to them which showed that, pending the action of commissioners to settle the dispute, the two Kings had ordered their respective governors to refrain from all acts of hostility and join forces, if necessary, to compel the Iroquois to keep quiet. This, with their enormous losses and their desire to recover their people held captive in Canada, led them at last to serious thoughts of peace.

Resolving at the same time to try the temper of the new Onontio and yield no more than was absolutely necessary, they sent him but six ambassadors and no prisoners. The ambassadors marched in single file to the place of council, while their chief who led the way sang a dismal song of lamentation for the French slain in the war, calling on them to thrust their heads aboveground, behold the good work of peace and banish every thought of vengeance.

Callières proved, as they had hoped, less inexorable than Frontenac. He accepted their promises and consented to send for the prisoners in their hands on condition that within thirty-six days a full deputation of their principal men should came to Montreal. The Jesuit Bruyas, the Canadian Maricourt and a French officer named Joncaire went back with them to receive the prisoners.

The history of Joncaire was a noteworthy one. The Senecas had captured him some time before, tortured his companions to death, and doomed him to the same fate. As a preliminary torment, an old chief tried to burn a finger of the captive in the bowl of his pipe, on which Joncaire knocked him down. If he had begged for mercy, their hearts would have been flint, but the warrior crowd were so pleased with this proof of courage that they adopted him as one of their tribe and gave him an Iroquois wife. He lived among them for many years and gained a commanding influence which proved very useful to the French.

When he, with Bruyas and Maricourt, approached Onondaga, which had long before risen from its ashes, they were greeted with a fusillade of joy and regaled with the sweet stalks of young maize, followed by the more substantial refreshment of venison and corn beaten together into a pulp and boiled. The chiefs and elders seemed well inclined to peace, and though an envoy came from Albany to prevent it, he behaved with such arrogance that, far from dissuading his auditors, he confirmed them in their resolve to meet Onontio at Montreal.

They seemed willing enough to give up their French prisoners, but an unexpected difficulty arose from the prisoners themselves. They had been adopted into Iroquois families, and having become attached to the Indian life, they would not leave it. Some of them hid in the woods to escape their deliverers, who with their best efforts could collect but thirteen, all women, children and boys. With these they returned to Montreal, accompanied by a peace embassy of nineteen Iroquois.

Peace, then, was made. "I bury the hatchet," said Callières, "in a deep hole, and over the hole I place a great rock, and over the rock I turn a river, that the hatchet may never be dug up again."

The famous Huron, Kondiaronk, or the Rat, was present, as were also a few Ottawas, Abenakis and converts of the Saut and the Mountain. Sharp words passed between them and the ambassadors, but at last they all laid down their hatchets at the feet of Onontio and signed the treaty together. It was but a truce, and a doubtful one. More was needed to confirm it and the following August was named for a solemn act of ratification.

Father Engelran was sent to Michilimackinac, while Courtemanche spent the winter and spring in toilsome journeyings among the tribes of the west. Such was his influence over them that he persuaded them all to give up their Iroquois prisoners and send deputies to the grand council. Engelran had had scarcely less success among the northern tribes, and early in July a great fleet of canoes, conducted by Courtemanche and filled with chiefs, warriors and Iroquois prisoners, paddled down the lakes for Montreal.

Meanwhile Bruyas, Maricourt and Joncaire had returned on the same errand to the Iroquois towns, but as far as prisoners were concerned, their success was no greater than before. Whether French or Indian, the chiefs were slow to give them up, saying that they had all been adopted into families who would not part with them unless consoled for the loss by gifts. This was true, but it was equally true of the other tribes, whose chiefs had made the necessary gifts and recovered the captive Iroquois. Joncaire and his colleagues succeeded, however, in leading a large deputation of chiefs and elders to Montreal.

Courtemanche, with his canoe fleet from the lakes, was not far behind, and when their approach was announced, the chronicler La Potherie, full of curiosity, went to meet them at the mission village of Saut. First appeared the Iroquois, two hundred in all, firing their guns as their canoes drew near, while the mission Indians ranged along the shore returned the salute. The ambassadors were conducted to a capacious lodge, where for a quarter of an hour they sat smoking with immovable composure. Then a chief of the mission made a speech, and then followed a feast of boiled dogs. In the morning they descended the rapids to Montreal and in due time the distant roar of the saluting cannon told of their arrival.

They had scarcely left the village when the river was covered with the canoes of the western and northern allies. There was another fusillade of welcome as the heterogeneous company landed and marched to the great council house. The calumet was produced and twelve of the assembled chiefs sang a song, each rattling at the same time a dried gourd half full of peas. Six large kettles were next brought in, containing several dogs and a bear suitably chopped to pieces, which, being ladled out to the guests, were dispatched in an instant, and a solemn dance and a supper of boiled corn closed the festivity.

The strangers embarked again on the next day and the cannon of Montreal greeted them as they landed before the town. A great quantity of evergreen boughs had been gathered for their use, and of these they made their wigwams outside the palisades. Before the opening of the grand council, a multitude of questions must be settled, jealousies soothed and complaints answered.

Callières had no peace. He was busied for a week in giving audience

389

to the deputies. There was one question which agitated them all and threatened to rekindle the war. Kondiaronk, the Rat, the foremost man among all the allied tribes, gave utterance to the general feeling:

"My father, you told us last autumn to bring you all the Iroquois prisoners in our hands. We have obeyed and brought them. Now let us see if the Iroquois have also obeyed and brought you our people whom they captured during the war. It they have done so, they are sincere; if not, they are false. But I know that they have not brought them. I told you last year that it was better that they should bring their prisoners first. You see now how it is, and how they have deceived us."

The complaint was just and the situation became critical. The Iroquois deputies were invited to explain themselves. They stalked into the council room with their usual haughty composure and readily promised to surrender the prisoners in future, but offered no hostages for their good faith.

The Rat, who had counseled his own and other tribes to bring their Iroquois captives to Montreal, was excessively mortified at finding himself duped. He came to a later meeting, when this and other matters were to be discussed, but he was so weakened by fever that he could not stand. An armchair was brought him and, seated in it, he harangued the assembly for two hours amid a deep silence, broken only by ejaculations of approval from his Indian hearers. When the meeting ended, he was completely exhausted and, being carried in his chair to the hospital, he died about midnight.

He was a great loss to the French, for though he had caused the massacre of La Chine, his services of late years had been invaluable. In spite of his unlucky name, he was one of the ablest North American Indians on record, as appears by his remarkable influence over many tribes, and by the respect, not to say admiration, of his French contemporaries.

The French charged themselves with the funeral rites, carried the dead chief to his wigwam, stretched him on a robe of beaver skin and left him lying there in state, swathed in a scarlet blanket, with a kettle, a gun and a sword at his side for his use in the world of spirits. This was a concession to the superstition of his countrymen, for the Rat was a convert and went regularly to mass.

Even the Iroquois, his deadliest foes, paid tribute to his memory.

Sixty of them came in solemn procession and ranged themselves around the bier, while one of their principal chiefs pronounced a harangue in which he declared that the sun had covered his face that day in grief for the loss of the great Huron.

He was buried on the next morning. Saint-Ours, senior captain, led the funeral train with an escort of troops, followed by sixteen Huron warriors in robes of beaver skin, marching four and four, with faces painted black and guns reversed. Then came the clergy and then six war chiefs carrying the coffin. It was decorated with flowers, and on it lay a plumed hat, a sword and a gorget. Behind it were the brother and sons of the dead chief and files of Huron and Ottawa warriors, while Madame de Champigny, attended by Vaudreuil and all the military officers, closed the procession.

After the service, the soldiers fired three volleys over the grave and a tablet was placed upon it, carved with the words, *"Cy git le Rat, chef des Hurons."*

All this ceremony pleased the allied tribes and helped to calm their irritation. Every obstacle being at length removed or smoothed over, the fourth of August was named for the grand council. A vast oblong space was marked out on a plain near the town and enclosed with a fence of branches. At one end was a canopy of boughs and leaves, under which were seats for the spectators. Troops were drawn up in line along the sides; the seats under the canopy were filled by ladies, officials and the chief inhabitants of Montreal; Callières sat in front, surrounded by interpreters; and the Indians were seated on the grass around the open space.

There were more than thirteen hundred of them, gathered from a distance of full two thousand miles—Hurons and Ottawas from Michilimackinac, Ojibwas from Lake Superior, Crees from the remote north, Potawatomis from Lake Michigan, Mascutins, Sacs, Foxes, Winnebagoes and Menominies from Wisconsin, Miamis from the St. Joseph, Illinois from the river Illinois, Abenakis from Acadia, and many allied hordes of less account. Each savage was painted with diverse hues and patterns and each was clad in his dress of ceremony, leathern shirts fringed with scalp locks, colored blankets or robes of bison hide and beaver skin, bristling crests of hair or long lank tresses, eagle feathers or horns of beasts.

391

Pre-eminent among them all sat their valiant and terrible foes, the warriors of the confederacy. "Strange," exclaims La Potherie, "that four or five thousand should make a whole new world tremble. New England is but too happy to gain their good graces; New France is often wasted by their wars, and our allies dread them over an extent of more than fifteen hundred leagues." It was more a marvel than he knew, for he greatly overrates their number.

Callières opened the council with a speech in which he told the assembly that, since but few tribes were represented at the treaty of the year before, he had sent for them all to ratify it; that he now threw their hatchets and his own into a pit so deep that nobody could find them; that henceforth they must live like brethren; and if by chance one should strike another, the injured brother must not revenge the blow but come for redress to him, Onontio, their common father. Nicolas Perrot and the Jesuits who acted as interpreters repeated the speech in five different languages, and to confirm it, thirty-one wampum belts were given to the thirty-one tribes present.

Then each tribe answered in turn. First came Hassaki, chief of an Ottawa band known as Cut Tails. He approached with a majestic air, his long robe of beaver skin trailing on the grass behind him. Four Iroquois captives followed, with eyes bent on the ground, and when he stopped before the governor, they seated themselves at his feet.

"You asked us for our prisoners," he said, "and here they are. I set them free because you wish it, and I regard them as my brothers." Then turning to the Iroquois deputies: "Know that if I pleased I might have eaten them, but I have not done as you would have done. Remember this when we meet, and let us be friends." The Iroquois ejaculated their approval.

Next came a Huron chief, followed by eight Iroquois prisoners, who, as he declared, had been bought at great cost in kettles, guns and blankets from the families who had adopted them. "We thought that the Iroquois would have done by us as we have done by them, and we were astonished to see that they had not brought us our prisoners. Listen to me, my father, and you Iroquois, listen! I am not sorry to make peace, since my father wishes it, and I will live in peace with him and with you."

Thus, in turn, came the spokesmen of all the tribes, delivering their prisoners and making their speeches. The Miami orator said: "I am very angry with the Iroquois, who burned my son some years ago, but today I forget all that. My father's will is mine. I will not be like the Iroquois, who have disobeyed his voice." The orator of the Mississagas came forward, crowned with the head and horns of a young bison bull, and, presenting his prisoners, said: "I place them in your hands. Do with them as you like. I am only too proud that you count me among your allies."

The chief of the Foxes now rose from his seat at the farther end of the enclosure and walked sedately across the whole open space towards the stand of spectators. His face was painted red and he wore an old French wig with its abundant curls in a state of complete entanglement. When he reached the chair of the governor, he bowed and lifted the wig like a hat, to show that he was perfect in French politeness. There was a burst of laughter from the spectators, but Callières, with ceremonious gravity, begged him to put it on again, which he did, and proceeded with his speech, the pith of which was briefly as follows: "The darkness is gone, the sun shines bright again, and now the Iroquois is my brother."

Then came a young Algonquin war chief, dressed like a Canadian but adorned with a drooping red feather and a tall ridge of hair like the crest of a cock. It was he who slew Black Kettle, that redoubted Iroquois whose loss filled the confederacy with mourning and who exclaimed as he fell, "Must I, who have made the whole earth tremble, now die by the hand of a child!" The young chief spoke concisely and to the purpose: "I am not a man of counsel: it is for me to listen to your words. Peace has come, and now let us forget the past."

When he and all the rest had ended, the orator of the Iroquois strode to the front and in brief words gave their adhesion to the treaty: "Onontio, we are pleased with all you have done, and we have listened to all you have said. We assure you by these four belts of wampum that we will stand fast in our obedience. As for the prisoners whom we have not brought you, we place them at your disposal and you will send and fetch them."

The calumet was lighted. Callières, Champigny and Vaudreuil drew the first smoke, then the Iroquois deputies, and then all the tribes in turn. The treaty was duly signed, the representative of each tribe affixing his mark in the shape of some bird, beast, fish, reptile, insect, plant or nondescript object.

"Thus," says La Potherie, "the labors of the late Count Frontenac were brought to a happy consummation."

The work of Frontenac was indeed finished, though not as he would have finished it. Callières had told the Iroquois that till they surrendered their Indian prisoners he would keep in his own hands the Iroquois prisoners surrendered by the allied tribes.

To this the spokesman of the confederacy coolly replied: "Such a proposal was never made since the world began. Keep them, if you like. We will go home and think no more about them, but if you gave them to us without making trouble and gave us our son Joncaire at the same time, we should have no reason to distrust your sincerity, and should all be glad to send you back the prisoners we took from your allies."

Callières yielded, persuaded the allies to agree to the conditions, gave up the prisoners and took an empty promise in return. It was a triumph for the Iroquois, who meant to keep their Indian captives and did in fact keep nearly all of them.

The chief objects of the late governor were gained. The power of the Iroquois was so far broken that they were never again very formidable to the French. Canada had confirmed her Indian alliances and rebutted the English claim to sovereignty over the five tribes, with all the consequences that hung upon it.

By the treaty of Ryswick, the great questions at issue in America were left to the arbitration of future wars, and meanwhile, as time went on, the policy of Frontenac developed and ripened. Detroit was occupied by the French, the passes of the west were guarded by forts, another New France grew up at the mouth of the Mississippi and lines of military communication joined the Gulf of Mexico with the Gulf of St. Lawrence, while the colonies of England lay passive between the Alleghenies and the sea till roused by the trumpet that sounded with wavering notes on many a bloody field to peal at last in triumph from the Heights of Abraham.

PART FIVE

A Half Century of Conflict

CHAPTER 1

Queen Anne's War

THE WAR WHICH IN THE BRITISH COLONIES WAS called Queen Anne's War, and in England the War of the Spanish Succession, was the second of a series of four conflicts which ended in giving to Great Britain a maritime and colonial preponderance over France and Spain. As far as the colonies and the sea are concerned, these several wars may be regarded as a single protracted one, broken by intervals of truce. The three earlier of them, it is true, were European contests, begun and waged on European disputes. Their American part was incidental and apparently subordinate, yet it involved questions of prime importance in the history of the world.

The war of the Spanish Succession sprang from the ambition of Louis XIV. At the beginning of his reign two roads lay before him and it was a momentous question for posterity, as for his own age, which one of them he would choose—whether he would follow the wholesome policy of his great minister Colbert, or obey his own vanity and arrogance and plunge France into exhausting wars; whether he would hold to the principle of tolerance embodied in the Edict of Nantes, or do the work of fanaticism and priestly ambition.

The one course meant prosperity, progress and the rise of a middle class; the other meant bankruptcy and the Dragonades—and this was the King's choice. Crushing taxation, misery and ruin followed, till France burst out at last in a frenzy, drunk with the wild dreams of Rousseau. Then came the Terror and the Napoleonic Wars, and reaction on reaction, revolution on revolution.

Louis placed his grandson on the throne of Spain and insulted England by acknowledging as her rightful King the son of James II, whom she had deposed. Then England declared war. Canada and the northern British colonies had had but a short breathing time since the Peace of Ryswick. Both were tired of slaughtering each other and both needed rest. Yet before the declaration of war, the Canadian officers of the Crown prepared, with their usual energy, to meet the expected crisis.

While the New England colonies, and especially Massachusetts and New Hampshire, had most cause to deprecate a war, the prospect of one was also extremely unwelcome to the people of New York. The conflict lately closed had borne hard upon them through the attacks of the enemy, and still more through the derangement of their industries. They were distracted, too, with the factions rising out of the recent revolution under Jacob Leisler. New York had been the bulwark of the colonies farther south, who, feeling themselves safe, had given their protector little help and that little grudgingly, seeming to regard the war as no concern of theirs. Three thousand and fifty-one pounds, provincial currency, was the joint contribution of Virginia, Maryland, East Jersey and Connecticut to the aid of New York during five years of the late war. Massachusetts could give nothing, even if she would, her hands being full with the defense of her own borders.

Colonel Quary wrote to the Board of Trade that New York could not bear alone the cost of defending herself; that the other colonies were "stuffed with commonwealth notions" and were "of a sour temper in opposition to government," so that Parliament ought to take them in hand and compel each to do its part in the common cause. To this Lord Cornbury adds that Rhode Island and Connecticut are even more stubborn than the rest, hate all true subjects of the Queen, and will not give a farthing to the war so long as they can help it. Each province lived in selfish isolation, recking little of its neighbor's woes.

The forts were no better than their garrisons. The governor complains that those of Albany and Schenectady "are so weak and ridiculous that they look more like pounds for cattle than forts." At Albany the rotten stockades were falling from their own weight.

If New York had cause to complain of those whom she sheltered, she herself gave cause for complaint to those who sheltered her. The

Five Nations of the Iroquois had always been her allies against the French, had guarded her borders and fought her battles. What they wanted in return were gifts, attentions, just dealings and active aid in war, but they got them in scant measure. Their treatment by the province was shortsighted, if not ungrateful.

New York was a mixture of races and religions not yet fused into a harmonious body politic, divided in interests and torn with internal disputes. Its Assembly was made up in large part of men unfitted to pursue a consistent scheme of policy, or spend the little money at their disposal on any objects but those of present and visible interest. The royal governors, even when personally competent, were hampered by want of means and by factious opposition.

The Five Nations were robbed by land speculators, cheated by traders and feebly supported in their constant wars with the French. Spasmodically, on occasions of crisis, they were summoned to Albany, soothed with such presents as could be got from unwilling legislators, or now and then from the Crown, and exhorted to fight vigorously in the common cause. The case would have been far worse but for a few patriotic men, with Peter Schuyler at their head, who understood the character of these Indians and labored strenuously to keep them in what was called their allegiance.

The proud and fierce confederates had suffered greatly in the late war. Their numbers had been reduced about one half and they now counted little more than twelve hundred warriors. They had learned a bitter and humiliating lesson and their arrogance had changed to distrust and alarm. Though hating the French, they had learned to respect their military activity and prowess and to look askance on the Dutch and English, who rarely struck a blow in their defense and suffered their hereditary enemy to waste their fields and burn their towns.

The English called the Five Nations British subjects, on which the French taunted them with being British slaves and told them that the King of England had ordered the governor of New York to poison them. This invention had great effect. The Iroquois capital, Onondaga, was filled with wild rumors. The credulous savages were tossed among doubts, suspicions and fears. Some were in terror of poison, and some of witchcraft. They believed that the rival European nations had leagued to destroy them and divide their lands, and that they were be-witched by sorcerers, both French and English.

After the Peace of Ryswick, and even before it, the French governor kept agents among them. Some of these were soldiers, like Joncaire, Maricourt or Longueuil, and some were Jesuits like Bruyas, Lamber-ville or Vaillant. The Jesuits showed their usual ability and skill in their difficult and perilous task. The Indians derived various ad-vantages from their presence, which they regarded also as a flattering attention, while the English, jealous of their influence, made feeble attempts to counteract it by sending Protestant clergymen to Onon-daga.

The aims of the propagandists on both sides were secular. The French wished to keep the Five Nations neutral in the event of another war; the English wished to spur them to active hostility. But while the former pursued their purpose with energy and skill, the efforts of the latter were intermittent and generally feeble.

The "Far Indians," or "Upper Nations," as the French called them, consisted of the tribes of the Great Lakes and adjacent regions, Ottawas, Potawatomis, Sacs, Foxes, Sioux and many more. It was from these that Canada drew the furs by which she lived. Most of them were nominal friends and allies of the French, who in the interest of trade strove to keep these wildcats from tearing one another's throats, and who were in constant alarm lest they should again come to blows with their old enemies, the Five Nations, in which case they would call on Canada for help, thus imperiling those pacific relations with the Iroquois confederacy which the French were laboring con-stantly to secure.

In regard to the "Far Indians," the French, the English and the Five Iroquois Nations all had distinct and opposing interests. The French wished to engross their furs, either by inducing the Indians to bring them down to Montreal or by sending traders into their country to buy them. The English, with a similar object, wished to divert the "Far Indians" from Montreal and draw them to Albany, but this did not suit the purpose of the Five Nations, who, being sharp politicians and keen traders as well as bold and enterprising warriors, wished to act as middlemen between the beaver-hunting tribes and the Albany merchants, well knowing that good profit might thus accrue.

The Dutch traders of Albany and the importing merchants who supplied them with Indian goods had a strong interest in preventing active hostilities with Canada, which would have spoiled their trade. So, too, and for similar reasons, had influential persons in Canada. The French authorities, moreover, thought it impolitic to harass the frontiers of New York by war parties, since the Five Nations might come to the aid of their Dutch and English allies, and so break the peaceful relations which the French were anxious to maintain with them.

Thus it happened that during the first six or seven years of the eighteenth century there was a virtual truce between Canada and New York and the whole burden of the war fell upon New England, or rather upon Massachusetts, with its outlying district of Maine and its small and weak neighbor, New Hampshire.

For untold ages Maine had been one unbroken forest and it was so still. Only along the rocky seaboard or on the lower waters of one or two great rivers a few rough settlements had gnawed slight indentations into this wilderness of woods, and a little farther inland some dismal clearing around a blockhouse or stockade let in the sunlight to a soil that had lain in shadow time out of mind.

The life and light of this grim solitude were in its countless streams and lakes, from little brooks stealing clear and cold under the alders, full of the small fry of trout, to the mighty arteries of the Penobscot and the Kennebec; from the great reservoir of Moosehead to a thousand nameless ponds shining in the hollow places of the forest.

It had its beasts of prey—wolves, savage, cowardly and mean; bears, gentle and mild compared to their grisly relatives of the Far West, vegetarians when they could do no better and not without something grotesque and quaint in manners and behavior; sometimes, though rarely, the strong and sullen wolverine; frequently the lynx; and now and then the fierce and agile cougar.

The human denizens of this wilderness were no less fierce, and far more dangerous. These were the various tribes and sub-tribes of the Abenakis, whose villages were on the Saco, the Kennebec, the Penobscot and the other great watercourses. Most of them had been converted by the Jesuits, and as we have seen already, some had been persuaded to remove to Canada, like the converted Iroquois of

401

Caughnawaga. The rest remained in their native haunts, where, under the direction of their missionaries, they could be used to keep the English settlements in check.

They had plied their tomahawks busily in William and Mary's War, and when Queen Anne's War was declared on the fourth of May 1702, the Abenakis again assumed a threatening attitude.

In June of the next year Dudley, governor of Massachusetts, called the chiefs of the various bands to a council at Casco. Here presently appeared the Norridgewocks from the Kennebec, the Penobscots and Androscoggins from the rivers that bear their names, the Penacooks from the Merrimac, and the Pequawkets from the Saco, all well armed and daubed with ceremonial paint. The principals among them, gathered under a large tent, were addressed by Dudley in a conciliatory speech.

Their orator replied that they wanted nothing but peace, and that their thoughts were as far from war as the sun was from the earth—words which they duly confirmed by a belt of wampum. Presents were distributed among them and received with apparent satisfaction, while two of their principal chiefs, known as Captain Samuel and Captain Bomazeen, declared that several French missionaries had lately come among them to excite them against the English, but that they were "firm as mountains," and would remain so "as long as the sun and moon endured." They ended the meeting with dancing, singing and whoops of joy, followed by a volley of musketry, answered by another from the English.

It was discovered, however, that the Indians had loaded their guns with ball, intending, as the English believed, to murder Dudley and his attendants if they could have done so without danger to their chiefs, whom the governor had prudently kept about him. It was afterwards found, if we may believe a highly respectable member of the party, that two hundred French and Indians were on their way, "resolved to seize the governor, council and gentlemen, and then to sacrifice the inhabitants at pleasure," but when they arrived, the English officials had been gone three days.

Within six weeks after this Treaty of Casco, every unprotected farmhouse in Maine was in a blaze. The settlements of Maine, confined to the southwestern corner of what is now the state of Maine, extended along the coast in a feeble and broken line from Kittery to Casco. Ten years of murderous warfare had almost ruined them. East of the village of Wells little was left except one or two forts and the so-called "garrisons," which were private houses pierced with loopholes and having an upper story projecting over the lower, so that the defenders could fire down on assailants battering the door or piling fagots against the walls. A few were fenced with palisades.

These fortified houses were very rarely attacked, except by surprise and treachery. In case of alarm, such of the inhabitants as found time took refuge in them with their families and left their dwellings to the flames, for the first thought of the settler was to put his women and children beyond reach of the scalping knife. There were several of these asylums in different parts of Wells, and without them the place must have been abandoned. In the little settlement of York, farther westward, there were five of them.

Wells was a long, straggling settlement, consisting at the beginning of William and Mary's War of about eighty houses and log cabins strung at intervals along the north side of the rough track known as the King's Road, which ran parallel to the sea. Behind the houses were rude, half-cleared pastures, and behind these again the primeval forest. The cultivated land was on the south side of the road. In front of the houses and beyond it spread great salt marshes, bordering the sea and haunted by innumerable gamebirds. The settlements of Maine were a dependency of Massachusetts—a position that did not please their inhabitants, but which they accepted because they needed the help of their Puritan neighbors, from whom they differed widely both in their qualities and in their faults. The Indian wars that checked their growth had kept them in a condition more than half barbarous. They were a hard-working and hard-drinking race, for though tea and coffee were scarcely known, the land flowed with New England rum, which was ranked among the necessaries of life. The better sort could read and write in a bungling way, but many were wholly illiterate and it was not till long after Queen Anne's War that the remoter settlements established schools, taught by poor students from Harvard or less competent instructors, and held at first in private houses or under sheds.

In spite of efforts to maintain public worship, Wells was far from being a religious community, nor was it a peaceful one. Gossip and

403

scandal ran riot; social jealousies abounded; and under what seemed entire democratic equality, the lazy, drunken and shiftless envied the industrious and thrifty. Wells was infested, moreover, by several "frightfully turbulent women," as the chronicle styles them, from whose rabid tongues the minister himself did not always escape, and once in its earlier days the town had been indicted for not providing a ducking stool to correct these breeders of discord.

On the tenth of August 1703 these rugged borderers were about their usual callings, unconscious of danger, the women at their household work, the men in the fields or on the more distant salt marshes. The wife of Thomas Wells had reached the time of her confinement and her husband had gone for a nurse.

Some miles east of Wells's cabin lived Stephen Harding—hunter, blacksmith and tavern keeper, a sturdy, good-natured man who loved the woods and whose frequent hunting trips sometimes led him nearly to the White Mountains. Distant gunshots were heard from the westward and his quick eye presently discovered Indians approaching, on which he told his frightened wife to go with their infant to a certain oak tree beyond the creek, while he waited to learn whether the strangers were friends or foes.

That morning several parties of Indians had stolen out of the dismal woods behind the houses and farms of Wells and approached different dwellings of the far-extended settlement at about the same time. They entered the cabin of Thomas Wells, where his wife lay in the pains of childbirth, and murdered her and her two small children. At the same time they killed Joseph Sayer, a neighbor of Wells, with all his family.

Meanwhile Stephen Harding, having sent his wife and child to a safe distance, returned to his blacksmith's shop, and seeing nobody, gave a defiant whoop, on which four Indians sprang at him from the bushes. He escaped through a back door of the shop, eluded his pursuers and found his wife and child in a cornfield, where the woman had fainted with fright. They spent the night in the woods, and on the next day, after a circuit of nine miles, reached the palisaded house of Joseph Storer.

They found the inmates in distress and agitation. Storer's daughter Mary, a girl of eighteen, was missing. The Indians had caught her, and afterwards carried her prisoner to Canada. Samuel Hill and his family were captured, and the younger children butchered. But it is useless to record the names and fate of the sufferers. Thirty-nine in all, chiefly women and children, were killed or carried off and then the Indians disappeared as quickly and silently as they had come, leaving many of the houses in flames.

This raid upon Wells was only part of a combined attack on all the settlements from that place to Casco. Those eastward of Wells had been abandoned in the last war, excepting the forts and fortified houses, but the inhabitants, reassured no doubt by the Treaty of Casco, had begun to return.

On this same day, the tenth of August, they were startled from their security. A band of Indians mixed with Frenchmen fell upon the settlements about the stone fort near the falls of the Saco, killed eleven persons, captured twenty-four, and vainly attacked the fort itself. Others surprised the settlers at a place called Spurwink and killed or captured twenty-two. Others, again, destroyed the huts of the fishermen at Cape Porpoise and attacked the fortified house at Winter Harbor, the inmates of which, after a brave resistance, were forced to capitulate. The settlers at Scarborough were also in a fortified house, where they made a long and obstinate defense till help at last arrived.

Nine families were settled at Purpooduck Point, near the present city of Portland. They had no place of refuge, and the men, being, no doubt, fishermen, were all absent when the Indians burst into the hamlet, butchered twenty-five women and children and carried off eight.

The fort at Casco, or Falmouth, was held by Major March, with thirty-six men. He had no thought of danger when three well-known chiefs from Norridgewock appeared with a white flag and asked for an interview. As they seemed to be alone and unarmed, he went to meet them, followed by two or three soldiers and accompanied by two old men named Phippeny and Kent, inhabitants of the place.

They had hardly reached the spot when the three chiefs drew hatchets from under a kind of mantle which they wore and sprang upon them, while other Indians ambushed near by leaped up and joined in the attack. The two old men were killed at once, but March, who was noted for strength and agility, wrenched a hatchet from one of his assailants and kept them all at bay till Sergeant Hook came to his aid with a file of men and drove them off.

They soon reappeared, burned the deserted cabins in the neighborhood and beset the garrison in numbers that continually increased till in a few days the entire force that had been busied in ravaging the scattered settlements was gathered around the place. It consisted of about five hundred Indians of several tribes and a few Frenchmen under an officer named Beaubassin.

Being elated with past successes, they laid siege to the fort, sheltering themselves under a steep bank by the waterside and burrowing their way towards the rampart. March could not dislodge them and they continued their approaches till the third day, when Captain Southack, with the Massachusetts armed vessel known as the *Province Galley,* sailed into the harbor, recaptured three small vessels that the Indians had taken along the coast and destroyed a great number of their canoes, on which they gave up their enterprise and disappeared.

Such was the beginning of Queen Anne's War.

The whole number of persons killed and carried off during the August attacks did not much exceed one hundred and sixty and these were of both sexes and all ages, from octogenarians to newborn infants. The able-bodied men among them were few, as most of the attacks were made upon unprotected houses in the absence of the head of the family, and the only fortified place captured was the garrison house at Winter Harbor, which surrendered on terms of capitulation. The instruments of this ignoble warfare and the revolting atrocities that accompanied it were all, or nearly all, converted Indians of the missions.

One of the objects was, no doubt, to check the progress of the English settlements, but, says Charlevoix, "the essential point was to commit the Abenakis in such a manner that they could not draw back. This object was constantly kept in view."

The French claimed at this time that the territory of Acadia reached as far westward as the Kennebec, which therefore formed, in their view, the boundary between the rival nations. They trusted in the Abenakis to defend this assumed line of demarcation. But the Abenakis sorely needed English guns, knives, hatchets and kettles and nothing but the utmost vigilance could prevent them from coming to terms with those who could supply their necessities.

Thus the policy of the French authorities on the frontier of New England was the opposite of their policy on the frontier of New York. They left the latter undisturbed, lest by attacking the Dutch and English settlers they should stir up the Five Nations to attack Canada, while on the other hand they constantly spurred the Abenakis against New England in order to avert the dreaded event of their making peace with her.

The attack on Wells, Casco and the intervening settlements was followed by murders and depredations that lasted through the autumn and extended along two hundred miles of frontier. By far the most dangerous and harassing attacks were those of small parties skulking under the edge of the forest, or lying hidden for days together, watching their opportunity to murder unawares, and vanishing when they had done so.

Against such an enemy there was no defense. The Massachusetts government sent a troop of horse to Portsmouth and another to Wells. These had the advantage of rapid movement in case of alarm along the roads and forest paths from settlement to settlement, but once in the woods, their horses were worse than useless and they could only fight on foot. Fighting, however, was rarely possible, for on reaching the scene of action they found nothing but mangled corpses and burning houses.

The murders and burnings along the borders were destined to continue with little variety and little interruption during ten years. It was a repetition of what the pedantic Cotton Mather calls *Decennium luctuosum,* or the "woful decade" of William and Mary's War. The wonder is that the outlying settlements were not abandoned. These ghastly, insidious and ever-present dangers demanded a more obstinate courage than the hottest battle in the open field.

CHAPTER 2

The Conquest of Acadia

ABOUT 1708 A SCHEME WAS FORMED FOR THE PERMA-
nent riddance of New England from war parties by the conquest
of Canada. The prime mover in it was Samuel Vetch. He came of a
respectable Scotch family. His grandfather, his father, three of his
uncles and one of his brothers were Covenanting ministers who had
suffered some persecution under Charles II. He himself was destined
for the ministry, but his inclinations being in no way clerical, he and
his brother William got commissions in the army and took an active
part in the war that ended with the Peace of Ryswick.

William Vetch died at sea and Samuel repaired to New York, where
he married a daughter of Robert Livingston, one of the chief men of
the colony, and engaged largely in the Canadian trade. From New
York he went to Boston, where he was living when the War of the
Spanish Succession began.

During his several visits to Canada he had carefully studied the St.
Lawrence and its shores, and boasted that he knew them better than
the Canadians themselves. He was impetuous, sanguine, energetic and
headstrong, astute withal, and full of ambition. A more vigorous agent
for the execution of the proposed plan of conquest could not have
been desired.

The General Court of Massachusetts, contrary to its instinct and
its past practice, resolved in view of the greatness of the stake to ask
this time for help from the mother country and Vetch sailed for England, bearing an address to the Queen, begging for an armament to

408

aid in the reduction of Canada and Acadia. The scheme waxed broader yet in the ardent brain of the agent. He proposed to add New-foundland to the other conquests, and when all was done in the North, to sail to the Gulf of Mexico and wrest Pensacola from the Spaniards, by which means, he writes, "Her Majesty shall be sole empress of the vast North American continent." The idea was less visionary than it seems. Energy, helped by reasonable good luck, might easily have made it a reality, as far as the possessions of France were concerned.

The court granted all that Vetch asked. On the eleventh of March he sailed for America, fully empowered to carry his plans into execution, and with the assurance that when Canada was conquered he should be its governor. A squadron bearing five regiments of regular troops was promised. The colonies were to muster their forces in all haste. New York was directed to furnish eight hundred men; New Jersey, two hundred; Pennsylvania, a hundred and fifty; and Connecticut, three hundred and fifty—the whole to be at Albany by the middle of May and to advance on Montreal by way of Wood Creek and Lake Champlain as soon as they should hear that the squadron had reached Boston. Massachusetts, New Hampshire and Rhode Island were to furnish twelve hundred men, to join the regulars in attacking Quebec by way of the St. Lawrence.

Vetch sailed from Portsmouth in the ship *Dragon,* accompanied by Colonel Francis Nicholson, late lieutenant governor of New York, who was to take an important part in the enterprise. The squadron with the five regiments was to follow without delay. The weather was bad and the *Dragon,* beating for five weeks against head winds, did not enter Boston harbor till the evening of the twenty-eighth of April 1709. Vetch, chafing with patience, for every moment was precious, sent off expresses that same night to carry the Queen's letters to the governors of Rhode Island, Connecticut, New Jersey and Pennsylvania. Dudley and his council met the next morning, and to them Vetch delivered the royal message, which was received, he says, "with the dutiful obedience becoming good subjects, and all the marks of joy and thankfulness."

Vetch, Nicholson and the Massachusetts authorities quickly arranged their plans. An embargo was laid on the shipping; provision was made for raising men and supplies and providing transportation.

When all was prepared, the two emissaries hired a sloop for New York, and touching on the way at Rhode Island, found it in the throes of the annual election of governor. Yet every warlike preparation was already made and Vetch and his companion sailed at once for New Haven to meet Saltonstall, the newly elected governor of Connecticut. Here, too, all was ready and the envoys, well pleased, continued their voyage to New York, which they reached on the eighteenth of May. The governor, Lord Lovelace, had lately died and Colonel Ingoldsby, the lieutenant governor, acted in his place. The Assembly was in session, and being summoned to the council chamber, the members were addressed by Vetch and Nicholson with excellent effect.

In accepting the plan of conquest, New York completely changed front. She had thus far stood neutral, leaving her neighbors to defend themselves and carrying on an active trade with the French and their red allies. Still, it was her interest that Canada should become English, thus throwing open to her the trade of the Western tribes, and the promises of aid from England made the prospects of the campaign so flattering that she threw herself into the enterprise, though not without voices of protest. For while the frontier farmers and some prominent citizens like Peter Schuyler thought that the time for action had come, the Albany traders and their allies, who fattened on Canadian beaver, were still for peace at any price.

With Pennsylvania and New Jersey the case was different. The one, controlled by non-combatant Quakers and safe from French war parties, refused all aid, while the other, in less degree under the same military blight, would give no men, though granting a slow and reluctant contribution of three thousand pounds, taking care to suppress on the record every indication that the money was meant for military uses. New York, on the other hand, raised her full contingent, and Massachusetts and New Hampshire something more, being warm in the faith that their borders would be plagued with war parties no longer.

It remained for New York to gain the help of the Five Nations of the Iroquois, to which end Abraham Schuyler went to Onondaga, well supplied with presents. The Iroquois capital was now, as it had been for years, divided between France and England. French interests were represented by the two Jesuits, Mareuil and Jacques Lamberville.

410

The skillful management of Schuyler, joined to his gifts and his rum, presently won over so many to the English party and raised such excitement in the town that Lamberville thought it best to set out for Montreal with news of what was going on. The intrepid Joncaire, agent of France among the Senecas, was scandalized at what he calls the Jesuit's flight, and wrote to the commandant of Fort Frontenac that its effect on the Indians was such that he, Joncaire, was in peril of his life. Yet he stood his ground and managed so well that he held the Senecas firm in their neutrality.

Lamberville's colleague, Mareuil, whose position was still more critical, was persuaded by Schuyler that his only safety was in going with him to Albany, which he did, and on this the Onondagas, excited by rum, plundered and burned the Jesuit mission house and chapel. Clearly the two priests at Onondaga were less hungry for martyrdom than their murdered brethren Jogues, Brébeuf, Lalemant and Charles Garnier. But it is to be remembered that the Canadian Jesuit of the first half of the seventeenth century was before all things an apostle and his successor of a century later was before all things a political agent.

As for the Five Nations, that once haughty confederacy, in spite of divisions and waverings, had conceived the idea that its true policy lay, not in siding with either of the European rivals, but in making itself important to both, and courted and caressed by both. While some of the warriors sang the war song at the prompting of Schuyler, they had been but halfhearted in doing so, and even the Mohawks, nearest neighbors and best friends of the English, sent word to their Canadian kindred, the Caughnawagas, that they took up the hatchet only because they could not help it.

The attack on Canada by way of the Hudson and Lake Champlain was to have been commanded by Lord Lovelace or some officer of his choice, but as he was dead, Ingoldsby, his successor in the government of the province, jointly with the governors of several adjacent colonies who had met at New York, appointed Colonel Nicholson in his stead.

Nicholson went to Albany, from which he moved up the Hudson with about fifteen hundred men, built a stockade fort opposite Saratoga and another at the spot known as the Great Carrying Place. This latter he called Fort Nicholson, a name which it afterwards exchanged for that of Fort Lydius and later still for that of Fort Edward, which the town that occupies the site owns to this day. From there he cut a rough roadway through the woods to where Wood Creek, choked with beaver dams, writhed through flat green meadows, walled in by rock and forest. Here he built another fort, which was afterwards rebuilt and named Fort Anne. Wood Creek led to Lake Champlain, and Lake Champlain to Chambly and Montreal, the objective points of the expedition.

All was astir at the camp. Flatboats and canoes were made and stores brought up from Albany, till everything was ready for an advance the moment word should come that the British fleet had reached Boston. Vetch, all impatience, went there to meet it, as if his presence could hasten its arrival.

Reports of Nicholson's march to Wood Creek had reached Canada and Vaudreuil sent Ramesay, governor of Montreal, with fifteen hundred troops, Canadians and Indians, to surprise his camp. Ramesay's fleet of canoes had reached Lake Champlain and was halfway to the mouth of Wood Creek when his advance party was discovered by English scouts, and the French commander began to fear that he should be surprised in his turn. In fact, some of his Indians were fired upon from an ambuscade.

All was now doubt, perplexity and confusion. Ramesay landed at the narrows of the lake, a little south of the place now called Crown Point. Here, in the dense woods, his Indians fired on some Canadians whom they took for English. This nearly produced a panic. "Every tree seemed an enemy," writes an officer present. Ramesay lost himself in the woods and could not find his army. One Deruisseau, who had gone out as a scout, came back with the report that nine hundred Englishmen were close at hand. Seven English canoes did in fact appear, supported, as the French in their excitement imagined, by a numerous though invisible army in the forest, but being fired upon and seeing that they were entering a hornet's nest, the English sheered off. Ramesay having at last found his army, and order being gradually restored, a council of war was held, after which the whole force fell back to Chambly, having accomplished nothing.

Great was the alarm in Canada when it became known that the enemy aimed at nothing less than the conquest of the colony. One

La Plaine spread a panic at Quebec by reporting that forty-five leagues below he had seen eight or ten ships under sail and heard the sound of cannon. It was afterwards surmised that the supposed ships were points of rocks seen through the mist at low tide, and the cannon the floundering of whales at play.

Quebec, however, was all excitement in expectation of attack. The people of the Lower Town took refuge on the rock above; the men of the neighboring parishes were ordered within the walls; and the women and children, with the cattle and horses, were sent to hiding places in the forest. There had been no less consternation at Montreal, caused by exaggerated reports of Iroquois hostility and the movements of Nicholson. It was even proposed to abandon Chambly and Fort Frontenac and concentrate all available forces to defend the heart of the colony. "A most bloody war is imminent," wrote Vaudreuil to the minister Ponchartrain.

The British squadron, with the five regiments on board, was to have reached Boston by the middle of May. On the twentieth of that month the whole contingent of Massachusetts, New Hampshire and Rhode Island was encamped by Boston harbor with transports and stores, ready to embark for Quebec at ten hours' notice.

When Vetch, after seeing everything in readiness at New York, returned to Boston on the third of July, he found the New England levies encamped there still, drilled diligently every day by officers whom he had brought from England for the purpose. "The bodies of the men," he writes to Lord Sunderland, "are in general better than in Europe, and I hope their courage will prove so too; so that nothing in human probability can prevent the success of this glorious enterprise but the too late arrival of the fleet." But of the fleet there was no sign.

Time passed and still no ships appeared. Vetch wrote again: "I shall only presume to acquaint your Lordship how vastly uneasy all her Majesty's loyall subjects here on this continent are. Pray God hasten the fleet." Dudley, scarcely less impatient, wrote to the same effect. It was all in vain and the soldiers remained in their camp, monotonously drilling day after day through all the summer and half the autumn.

At length, on the eleventh of October, Dudley received a letter from Lord Sunderland, informing him that the promised forces had been sent to Portugal to meet an exigency of the European war. They were to have reached Boston by the middle of May. Sunderland's notice of the change of destination was not written till the twenty-seventh of July, and was eleven weeks on its way, thus imposing on the colonists a heavy and needless tax in time, money, temper, and, in the case of the expedition against Montreal, health and life. What was left of Nicholson's force had fallen back before Sunderland's letter came, making a scapegoat of the innocent Vetch, cursing him and wishing him hanged.

In New England the disappointment and vexation were extreme. But not to lose all the fruits of their efforts, the governors of Massachusetts, Connecticut, New Hampshire and Rhode Island met and resolved to attack Port Royal if the captains of several British frigates then at New York and Boston would take part in the enterprise. To the disgust of the provincials, the captains with one exception refused, on the score of the late season and the want of orders.

A tenacious energy has always been a characteristic of New England and the hopes of the colonists had been raised too high to be readily abandoned. Port Royal was in their eyes a pestilent nest of privateers and pirates that preyed on the New England fisheries, and on the refusal of the naval commanders to join in an immediate attack, they offered to the court to besiege the place themselves next year if they could count on the help of four frigates and five hundred soldiers, to be at Boston by the end of March. The Assembly of Massachusetts requested Nicholson, who was on the point of sailing for Europe, to beg Her Majesty to help them in an enterprise which would be so advantageous to the Crown, "and which, by the long and expensive war, we are so impoverished and enfeebled as not to be in a capacity to effect."

Nicholson sailed in December and Peter Schuyler soon followed. New York, having once entered on the path of war, saw that she must continue in it, and to impress the Five Nations with the might and majesty of the Queen and so dispose them to hold fast to the British cause, Schuyler took five Mohawk chiefs with him to England. One died on the voyage. The rest arrived safe and their appearance was the sensation of the hour. They were clad, at the Queen's expense, in strange and gay attire, invented by the costumer of one of the theaters;

were lodged and feasted as the guests of the nation; driven about London in coaches with liveried servants; conducted to dockyards, arsenals and reviews, and saluted with cannon by ships of war. The Duke of Shrewsbury presented them to Queen Anne—one as emperor of the Mohawks and the other three as kings—and the Archbishop of Canterbury solemnly gave each of them a Bible. Steele and Addison wrote essays about them and the Dutch artist Verelst painted their portraits, which were engraved in mezzotint.

Their presence and the speech made in their name before the court seem to have had no small effect in drawing attention to the war in America and inclining the ministry towards the proposals of Nicholson. These were accepted and he sailed for America commissioned to command the enterprise against Port Royal, with Vetch as adjutant general.

Though the English ministry had promised aid, it was long in coming. The Massachusetts Assembly had asked that the ships should be at Boston before the end of March, but it was past the middle of May before they sailed from Plymouth. Then towards midsummer a strange spasm of martial energy seems to have seized the ministry, for Viscount Shannon was ordered to Boston with an additional force, commissioned to take the chief command and attack not Port Royal, but Quebec. This ill-advised change of plan seems to have been reconsidered; at least, it came to nothing.

Meanwhile, the New England people waited impatiently for the retarded ships. No order had come from England for raising men and the colonists resolved this time to risk nothing till assured that their labor and money would not be wasted. At last, not in March but in July, the ships appeared. Then all was astir with preparation.

Autumn had begun before all was ready. Connecticut, New Hampshire and Rhode Island sent their contingents; there was a dinner at the Green Dragon Tavern in honor of Nicholson, Vetch and Sir Charles Hobby, the chief officers of the expedition, and on the eighteenth of September the whole put to sea.

On the twenty-fourth the squadron sailed into the narrow entrance of Port Royal, where the tide runs like a millstream. One vessel was driven upon the rocks and twenty-six men were drowned. The others got in safely and anchored above Goat Island, in sight of the French fort. They consisted of three fourth-rates, the *Dragon,* the *Chester* and the *Falmouth;* two fifth-rates, the *Lowestoffe* and the *Feversham;* the province galley, one bomb ketch, twenty-four small transports, two or three hospital ships, a tender and several sloops carrying timber to make beds for cannon and mortars. The landing force consisted of four hundred British marines and about fifteen hundred provincials, divided into four battalions. Its unnecessary numbers were due to the belief of Nicholson that the fort had been reinforced and strengthened.

In the afternoon of the twenty-fifth they were all on shore—Vetch with his two battalions on the north side and Nicholson with the other two on the south. Vetch marched to his camping ground, on which, in the words of Nicholson's journal, "the French began to fire pretty thick." On the next morning Nicholson's men moved towards the fort, hacking their way through the woods and crossing the marshes of Allen's River, while the French fired briskly with cannon from the ramparts and small arms from the woods, houses and fences. They were driven back and the English advance guard intrenched itself within four hundred yards of the works.

Several days passed in landing artillery and stores, cannonading from the fort and shelling from the English bomb ketch, when on the twenty-ninth Ensign Perelle, with a drummer and a flag of truce, came to Nicholson's tent, bringing a letter from Subercase, who begged him to receive into his camp and under his protection certain ladies of the fort who were distressed by the bursting of the English shells.

The conduct of Perelle was irregular, as he had not given notice of his approach by beat of drum and got himself and his attendants blind-folded before entering the camp. Therefore Nicholson detained him, sending back an officer of his own with a letter to the effect that he would receive the ladies and lodge them in the same house with the French ensign, "for the Queen, my royal mistress, hath not sent me hither to make war against women." Subercase on his part detained the English officer and wrote to Nicholson:

Sir—You have one of my officers, and I have one of yours; so that now we are equal. However, that hinders me not from believing that once you have given me your word, you will keep it very exactly. On that ground I now write to tell you, sir, that to prevent the spilling of both English and French blood, I am ready to hold up both hands for a capitulation that will be honorable to both of us.

In view of which agreement, he adds that he defers sending the ladies to the English camp.

Another day passed during which the captive officers on both sides were treated with much courtesy. On the next morning, Sunday, October 1, the siege guns, mortars and coehorns were in position, and after some firing on both sides Nicholson sent Colonel Tailor and Captain Abercrombie with a summons to surrender the fort. Subercase replied that he was ready to listen to proposals. The firing stopped, and within twenty-four hours the terms were settled. The garrison were to march out with the honors of war and to be carried in English ships to Rochelle or Rochefort. The inhabitants within three miles of the fort were to be permitted to remain, if they chose to do so, unmolested in their homes during two years, on taking an oath of allegiance and fidelity to the Queen.

Two hundred provincials marched to the fort gate and formed in two lines on the right and left. Nicholson advanced between the ranks, with Vetch on one hand and Sir Charles Hobby on the other, followed by all the field officers. Subercase came to meet them and gave up the keys, with a few words of compliment. The French officers and men marched out with shouldered arms, drums beating and colors flying, saluting the English commander as they passed. Then the English troops marched in, raised the union flag and drank the Queen's health amid a general firing of cannon from the fort and ships. Nicholson changed the name of Port Royal to Annapolis Royal, and Vetch, already commissioned as governor, took command of the new garrison, which consisted of two hundred British marines and two hundred and fifty provincials who had offered themselves for the service.

The English officers gave a breakfast to the French ladies in the fort. Sir Charles escorted Madame de Bonaventure and the rest followed in due order of precedence, but as few of the hosts could speak French and few of the guests could speak English, the entertainment could hardly have been a lively one.

The French officers and men in the fort when it was taken were but two hundred and fifty-eight. Some of the soldiers and many of the armed inhabitants deserted during the siege, which no doubt hastened the surrender, for Subercase, a veteran of more than thirty years' service, had borne fair repute as a soldier.

Port Royal had twice before been taken by New England men, once under Major Sedgwick in 1654 and again under Sir William Phips in the last war, and in each case it had been restored to France by treaty. This time England kept what she had got, and as there was no other place of strength in the province, the capture of Port Royal meant the conquest of Acadia.

CHAPTER 3

~~~~~~

Walker's Expedition

ENGLAND WAS TIRING OF THE CONTINENTAL WAR, the costs of which threatened ruin. Marlborough was rancorously attacked and his most stanch supporters, the Whigs, had given place to the Tories, led by the Lord Treasurer Harley and the Secretary of State St. John, soon afterwards Lord Bolingbroke. Never was party spirit more bitter and the new ministry found a congenial ally in the coarse and savage but powerful genius of Swift, who, incensed by real or imagined slights from the late minister, Godolphin, gave all his strength to the winning side.

The prestige of Marlborough's victories was still immense. Harley and St. John dreaded it as their chief danger, and looked eagerly for some means of counteracting it. Such means would be supplied by the conquest of New France. To make America a British continent would be an achievement almost worth Blenheim or Ramillies, and one, too, in which Britain alone would be the gainer, whereas the enemies of Marlborough, with Swift at their head, contended that his greatest triumphs turned more to the profit of Holland or Germany than of England. Moreover, to send a part of his army across the Atlantic would tend to cripple his movements and diminish his fame.

St. John entered with ardor into the scheme. Seven veteran regiments, five of which were from the army in Flanders, were ordered to embark. But in the choice of commanders the judgment of the ministers was not left free; there were influences that they could not disregard. The famous Sarah, Duchess of Marlborough, lately the favorite

419

of the feeble but willful Queen, had lost her good graces and given place to Mrs. Masham, one of the women of her bedchamber. The new favorite had a brother, John Hill, known about the court as Jack Hill, whom Marlborough had pronounced good for nothing but who had been advanced to the rank of colonel, and then of brigadier, through the influence of Mrs. Masham, and though his agreeable social qualities were his best recommendation, he was now appointed to command the troops on the Canadian expedition. It is not so clear why the naval command was given to Admiral Sir Hovenden Walker, a man whose incompetence was soon to become notorious.

Extreme care was taken to hide the destination of the fleet. Even the Lords of the Admiralty were kept ignorant of it. Some thought the ships bound for the West Indies, some for the South Sea. Nicholson was sent to America with orders to the several colonies to make ready men and supplies. He landed at Boston on the eighth of June. The people of the town, who were nearly all Whigs, were taken by surprise, expecting no such enterprise on the part of the Tory ministry, and their perplexity was not diminished when they were told that the fleet was at hand and that they were to supply it forthwith with provisions for ten weeks.

There was no time to lose. The governors of New York, Connecticut and Rhode Island were summoned to meet at New London and Dudley and Nicholson went there to join them. Here plans were made for the double attack, for while Walker and Hill were to sail up the St. Lawrence against Quebec, Nicholson, as in the former attempt, was to move against Montreal by way of Lake Champlain. In a few days the arrangements were made and the governors hastened back to their respective posts.

When Dudley reached Boston, he saw Nantasket Roads crowded with transports and ships of war and the pastures of Noddle's Island studded with tents. The fleet had come on the twenty-fourth, having had what the admiral calls "by the blessing of God a favorable and extraordinary passage, being but seven weeks and two days between Plymouth and Nantasket."

The admiral and the general had been welcomed with all honor. The provincial secretary, with two members of the Council, conducted them to town amid salutes from the batteries of Copp's Hill and Fort

Hill and the Boston militia regiment received them under arms, after which they were feasted at the principal tavern and accompanied in ceremony to the lodgings provided for them.

When the troops were disembarked and the tents pitched, curious townspeople and staring rustics crossed to Noddle's Island, now East Boston, to gaze with wonder on a military pageant the like of which New England had never seen before. Yet their joy at this unlooked-for succor was dashed with deep distrust and jealousy. They dreaded these new and formidable friends, with their imperious demeanor and exacting demands. The British officers, on their part, were no better pleased with the colonists.

Some coolness on the part of the Bostonians was not unnatural. But whatever may have been the popular feeling, the provincial authorities did their full part towards supplying the needs of the newcomers, for Dudley, with his strong Tory leanings, did not share the prevailing jealousy and the country members of the Assembly were anxious before all things to be delivered from war parties. The problem was how to raise the men and furnish the supplies in the least possible time.

The action of the Assembly, far from betraying any slackness, was worthy of a military dictatorship. All ordinary business was set aside. Bills of credit for forty thousand pounds were issued to meet the needs of the expedition. It was ordered that the prices of provisions and other necessaries of the service should stand fixed at the point where they stood before the approach of the fleet was known. Sheriffs and constables, jointly with the Queen's officers, were ordered to search all the town for provisions and liquors, and if the owners refused to part with them at the prescribed prices, to break open doors and seize them.

Stringent and much-needed acts were passed against harboring deserters. Provincial troops, in greater number than the ministry had demanded, were ordered to be raised at once and quartered upon the citizens, with or without their consent, at the rate of eightpence a day for each man. Warrants were issued for impressing pilots, and also mechanics and laborers who, in spite of Puritan scruples, were required to work on Sundays.

Such measures, if imposed by England, would have roused the most

421

bitter resentment. Even when ordered by their own representatives, they caused a sullen discontent among the colonists and greatly increased the popular dislike of their military visitors. It was certain that when the expedition sailed and the operation of the new enactments ceased, prices would rise and hence the compulsion to part with goods at low fixed rates was singularly trying to the commercial temper. It was a busy season, too, for the farmers and they showed no haste to bring their produce to the camp.

Though many of the principal inhabitants bound themselves by mutual agreement to live on their family stores of salt provisions in order that the troops might be better supplied with fresh, this failed to soothe the irritation of the British officers, aggravated by frequent desertions, which the colonists favored, and by the impossibility of finding pilots familiar with the St. Lawrence. Some, when forced into the service, made their escape, to the great indignation of Walker, who wrote to the governor: "Her Majesty will resent such actions in a very signal manner; and when it shall be represented that the people live here as if there were no king in Israel, but every one does what seems right in his own eyes, measures will be taken to put things upon a better foot for the future."

At length, however, every preparation was made, the supplies were all on board, and after a grand review of the troops on the fields of Noddle's Island, the whole force set sail on the thirtieth of July, the provincials wishing them success and heartily rejoicing that they were gone.

The fleet consisted of nine ships of war and two bomb ketches, with about sixty transports, storeships, hospital ships and other vessels, British and provincial. They carried the seven British regiments, numbering with the artillery train about fifty-five hundred men, besides six hundred marines and fifteen hundred provincials, counting with the sailors nearly twelve thousand in all.

Vetch commanded the provincials, having been brought from Annapolis for that purpose. The great need was for pilots. Every sailor in New England who had seen the St. Lawrence had been pressed into the service, though each and all declared themselves incapable of conducting the fleet to Quebec. Several had no better knowledge of the river than they had picked up when serving as soldiers under Phips twenty-one years before. The best among them was the veteran Captain Bonner, who afterwards amused his old age by making a plan of Boston, greatly prized by connoisseurs in such matters. Vetch had studied the St. Lawrence in his several visits to Quebec, but, like Bonner, he had gone up the river only in sloops or other small craft, and was, moreover, no sailor.

One of Walker's ships, the *Chester,* sent in advance to cruise in the gulf, had captured a French vessel commanded by one Paradis, an experienced old voyager who knew the river well. He took a bribe of five hundred pistoles to act as pilot, but the fleet would have fared better perhaps if he had refused the money. He gave such dismal accounts of the Canadian winter that the admiral could see nothing but ruin ahead, even if he should safely reach his destination.

All went well till the eighteenth of August, when there was a strong head wind and the ships ran into the Bay of Gaspé. Two days after, the wind shifted to the southeast and they set sail again, Walker in his flagship, the *Edgar,* being at or near the head of the fleet. On the evening of the twenty-second they were at some distance above the great island of Anticosti. The river here is about seventy miles wide and no land had been seen since noon of the day before. There was a strong east wind, with fog. Walker thought that he was not far from the south shore, when in fact he was at least fifty miles from it and more than half that distance north of his true course.

At eight in the evening the admiral signaled the fleet to bring to, under mizzen and main topsails, with heads turned southward. At half-past ten, Paddon, the captain of the *Edgar,* came to tell him that he saw land which he supposed must be the south shore, on which Walker, in a fatal moment, signaled for the ships to wear and bring to, with heads northward. He then turned into his berth and was falling asleep when a military officer, Captain Goddard, of Seymour's regiment, hastily entered and begged him to come on deck, saying that there were breakers on all sides.

Walker, scornful of a landsman and annoyed at being disturbed, answered impatiently and would not stir. Soon after, Goddard appeared again and implored him for heaven's sake to come up and see for himself, or all would be lost. At the same time the admiral heard a great noise and trampling, on which he turned out of his berth, put on his dressing gown and slippers, and going in this attire on deck, found a scene of fright and confusion.

At first he could see nothing and shouted to the men to reassure them, but just then the fog opened, the moon shone out and the breaking surf was plainly visible to leeward. The French pilot, who at first could not be found, now appeared on deck and declared, to the astonishment of both the admiral and Captain Paddon that they were off the north shore. Paddon, in his perplexity, had ordered an anchor to be let go. Walker directed the cable to be cut, and making all sail, succeeded in beating to windward and gaining an offing.

The ship that carried Colonel King, of the artillery, had a narrow escape. King says that she anchored in a driving rain, "with a shoal of rocks on each quarter within a cable's length of us, which we plainly perceived by the waves breaking over them in a very violent manner." They were saved by a lull in the gale, for if it had continued with the same violence, he pursues, "our anchors could not have held, and the wind and the vast seas which ran would have broke our ship into ten thousand pieces against the rocks. All night we heard nothing but ships firing and showing lights, as in the utmost distress."

Vetch, who was on board the little frigate *Despatch,* says that he was extremely uneasy at the course taken by Walker on the night of the storm. "I told Colonel Dudley and Captain Perkins, commander of the *Despatch,* that I wondered what the Flag meant by that course, and why he did not steer west and west-by-south." The *Despatch* kept well astern and so escaped the danger. Vetch heard, through the fog, guns firing signals of distress, but three days passed before he knew how serious the disaster was. The ships of war had all escaped, but eight British transports, one storeship and one sutler's sloop were dashed to pieces. "It was lamentable to hear the shrieks of the sinking, drowning, departing souls," writes the New England commissary Sheaf, who was very near sharing their fate.

The disaster took place at and near a rocky island, with adjacent reefs, lying off the north shore and called Isle aux Œufs. On the second day after it happened, Walker was told by the master of one of the wrecked transports that eight hundred and eighty-four soldiers had been lost and he gives this hasty estimate in his published *Journal,* though he says in his introduction to it that the total loss of officers, soldiers and sailors was scarcely nine hundred. According to a later and more trustworthy statement, the loss of the troops was twenty-nine officers, six hundred and seventy-six sergeants, corporals, drummers and private soldiers, and thirty-five women attached to the regiments —a total of seven hundred and forty lives. The loss of the sailors is not given, but it could scarcely have exceeded two hundred.

The fleet spent the next two days in standing to and fro between the northern and southern shores, with the exception of some of the smaller vessels employed in bringing off the survivors from the rock of Isle aux Œufs. The number thus saved was, according to Walker, four hundred and ninety-nine. On the twenty-fifth he went on board the general's ship, the *Windsor,* and Hill and he resolved to call a council of war. In fact, Hill had already got his colonels together. Signals were made for the captains of the men of war to join them and the council began.

Jack Hill, the man about town placed in high command by the influence of his sister, the Queen's tirewoman, had now an opportunity to justify his appointment and prove his mettle. Many a man of pleasure and fashion, when put to the proof, has revealed the latent hero within him, but Hill was not one of them. Both he and Walker seemed to look for nothing but a pretext for retreat, and when manhood is conspicuously wanting in the leaders, a council of war is rarely disposed to supply it.

The pilots were called in and examined and they all declared themselves imperfectly acquainted with the St. Lawrence, which, as some of the captains observed, they had done from the first. Sir William Phips, with pilots still more ignorant, had safely carried his fleet to Quebec in 1690, as Walker must have known, for he had with him Phips's journal of the voyage. The expedition had lost about a twelfth part of its soldiers and sailors, besides the transports that carried them. With this exception there was no reason for retreat which might not as well have been put forward when the fleet left Boston. All the warships were safe and the loss of men was not greater than might have happened in a single battle.

Hill says that Vetch, when asked if he would pilot the fleet to Quebec, refused to undertake it, but Vetch himself gives his answer as follows: "I told him [the admiral] I never was bred to sea, nor was it any part of my province; but I would do my best by going ahead and showing them where the difficulty of the river was, which I knew pretty well." The naval captains, however, resolved that by reason of the ignorance of the pilots and the dangerous currents, it was impossible to go up to Quebec. So discreditable a backing out from a great enterprise will hardly be found elsewhere in English annals.

The fleet retraced its course to the gulf, and then steered for Spanish River—now the harbor of Sydney—in the island of Cape Breton, the admiral consoling himself with the reflection that the wreck was a blessing in disguise and a merciful intervention of Providence to save the expedition from the freezing, starvation and cannibalism which his imagination had conjured up.

The frigate *Sapphire* was sent to Boston with news of the wreck and the retreat, which was at once dispatched to Nicholson, who, if he continued his movement on Montreal, would now be left to conquer Canada alone. His force consisted of about twenty-three hundred men, white and red, and when the fatal news reached him he was encamped on Wood Creek, ready to pass Lake Champlain. Captain Butler, a New York officer at the camp, afterwards told Kalm, the Swedish naturalist, that when Nicholson heard what had happened, he was beside himself with rage, tore off his wig, threw it on the ground and stamped upon it, crying out, "Roguery! Treachery!" When his fit was over, he did all that was now left for him to do—burned the wooden forts he had built, marched back to Albany and disbanded his army, after leaving a hundred and fifty men to protect the frontier against scalping parties.

Quebec was not ungrateful. A solemn mass was ordered every month during a year, to be followed by the song of Moses after the destruction of Pharaoh and his host. Amazing reports were spread concerning the losses of the English. About three thousand of "these wretches"—so the story ran—died after reaching land, without counting the multitudes drowned in the attempt, and even this did not satisfy divine justice, for God blew up one of the ships by lightning during the storm.

Vessels were sent to gather up the spoils of the wreck and they came back, it was reported, laden with marvelous treasures, including rich clothing, magnificent saddles, plate, silver-hilted swords and the like, bringing also the gratifying announcement that though the autumn tides had swept away many corpses, more than two thousand still lay on the rocks, naked and in attitudes of despair.

CHAPTER 4

Louisiana

THE GREAT EUROPEAN WAR WAS DRAWING TO AN end in 1712, and with it the American war, which was but its echo. An avalanche of defeat and disaster had fallen upon the old age of Louis XIV and France was burdened with an insupportable load of debt.

Political changes in England came to her relief. Fifty years later, when the elder Pitt went out of office and Bute came in, France had cause to be grateful, for the peace of 1763 was far more favorable to her than it would have been under the imperious war minister. It was the same in 1712. The Whigs who had fallen from power would have wrung every advantage from France; the triumphant Tories were eager to close with her on any terms not so easy as to excite popular indignation. The result was the Treaty of Utrecht, which satisfied none of the allies of England and gave to France conditions more favorable than she had herself proposed two years before. The fall of Godolphin and the disgrace of Marlborough were a godsend to her.

Yet in America Louis XIV made important concessions. The Five Nations of the Iroquois were acknowledged to be British subjects and this became in future the preposterous foundation for vast territorial claims of England. Hudson Bay, Newfoundland and Acadia, "according to its ancient limits," were also given over by France to her successful rival, though the King parted from Acadia with a reluctance shown by the great offers he made for permission to retain it.

But while the Treaty of Utrecht seemed to yield so much, and yielded so much in fact, it staved off the settlement of questions absolutely necessary for future peace. The limits of Acadia, the boundary line between Canada and the British colonies, and the boundary between those colonies and the great western wilderness claimed by France were all left unsettled, since the attempt to settle them would have rekindled the war. The peace left the embers of war still smoldering, sure to burst into flame when the time should come. The next thirty years were years of chronic, smothered war, disguised but never quite at rest.

The standing subjects of dispute were three, very different in importance. First, the question of Acadia: whether the treaty gave England a vast country, or only a strip of seacoast. Next, that of northern New England and the Abenaki Indians, many of whom French policy still left within the borders of Maine, and whom both powers claimed as subjects or allies. Last and greatest was the question of whether France or England should hold the valleys of the Mississippi and the Great Lakes, and with them the virtual control of the continent. This was the triple problem that tormented the northern English colonies for more than a generation, till it found a solution at last in the Seven Years' War.

The vast western regions were scantily peopled by savage hordes, whose increase was stopped by incessant mutual slaughter. This wild population had various centers or rallying points, usually about the French forts, which protected them from enemies and supplied their wants. Thus the Potawatomis, Ottawas and Hurons were gathered about Detroit, and the Illinois about Fort St. Louis, on the river Illinois, where Henri de Tonty and his old comrade La Forest, with fifteen or twenty Frenchmen, held a nominal monopoly of the neighboring fur trade. Another focus of Indian population was near the Green Bay of Lake Michigan, and on Fox River, which enters it. Here were grouped the Sacs, Winnebagoes and Menominies, with the Outagamies, or Foxes, a formidable tribe which were the source of endless trouble to the French, particularly around Detroit.

The constant aim of the Canadian authorities was to keep these western savages at peace among themselves, while preventing their establishing relations of trade with the Five Nations and carrying their furs to them in exchange for English goods.

This was a delicate task, but far down the great river that split the continent and flowed from these wild lands to the gulf the French had to contend with an equally difficult colonial problem. The problem began with an event which took place at the beginning of the eighteenth century, an event that was to have a great influence on the future of French America. This was the occupation by France of the mouth of the Mississippi and the vindication of her claim to the vast and un-defined regions which La Salle had called Louisiana.

La Salle's schemes had failed, but they were revived seven years after his death by his lieutenant, the gallant and faithful Henri de Tonty, who urged the seizure of Louisiana for three reasons: first, as a base of attack upon Mexico; secondly, as a depot for the furs and lead ore of the interior; and thirdly as the only means of preventing the English from becoming masters of the West.

Three years later, the Sieur de Rémonville, a friend of La Salle, proposed the formation of a company for the settlement of Louisiana, and called for immediate action as indispensable to anticipate the English. The English were, in fact, on the point of taking possession of the mouth of the Mississippi, and were prevented only by the prompt intervention of the rival nation.

If they had succeeded, colonies would have grown up on the Gulf of Mexico after the type of those already planted along the Atlantic. Voluntary immigrants would have brought to a new home their old inheritance of English freedom; would have ruled themselves by laws of their own making, through magistrates of their own choice; would have depended on their own efforts and not on government help, in the invigorating consciousness that their destinies were in their own hands and that they themselves and not others were to gather the fruits of their toils. Out of conditions like these would have sprung communities not brilliant but healthy, orderly, well rooted in the soil and of hardy and vigorous growth.

But the principles of absolutism and not those of a regulated liberty were to rule in Louisiana. The new French colony was to be the child of the Crown. Cargoes of emigrants, willing or unwilling, were to be shipped by authority to the fever-stricken banks—cargoes made up in part of those whom fortune and their own defects had sunk to dependence; to whom labor was strange and odious, but who dreamed

430

of gold mines and pearl fisheries, and wealth to be won in the New World and spent in the Old; who wore the shackles of a paternal despotism which they were told to regard as of divine institution; who were at the mercy of military rulers set over them by the King, and agreeing in nothing except in enforcing the mandates of arbitrary power and the withering maxim that the labor of the colonist was due, not to himself but to his masters.

In 1698 the gallant Le Moyne d'Iberville, who has been called the Cid, or, more fitly, the Jean Bart of Canada, offered to carry out the schemes of La Salle and plant a colony in Louisiana. One thing had become clear: France must act at once or lose the Mississippi. Already there was a movement in London to seize upon it, under a grant to two noblemen.

Iberville's offer was accepted. He was ordered to build a fort at the mouth of the great river and leave a garrison to hold it. He sailed with two frigates, the *Badine* and the *Marin,* and towards the end of January 1699 reached Pensacola. Here he found two Spanish ships, which would not let him enter the harbor. Spain, no less than England, was bent on making good her claim to the Mississippi and the Gulf of Mexico and the two ships had come from Vera Cruz on this errand. Three hundred men had been landed and a stockade fort was already built.

Iberville left the Spaniards undisturbed and unchallenged, and felt his way westward along the coasts of Alabama and Mississippi, exploring and sounding as he went. At the beginning of March his boats were caught in a strong muddy current of fresh water and he saw that he had reached the object of his search, the "fatal river" of the unfortunate La Salle. He entered it, encamped on the night of the third twelve leagues above its mouth, climbed a solitary tree and could see nothing but broad flats of bushes and canebrakes.

Still pushing upward against the current, he reached in eleven days a village of the Bayagoula Indians, where he found the chief attired in a blue capote, which was probably put on in honor of the white strangers, and which, as the wearer declared, had been given him by Henri de Tonty on his descent of the Mississippi in search of La Salle, thirteen years before.

Young Le Moyne de Bienville, who accompanied his brother Iberville in a canoe, brought him some time after a letter from Tonty which the writer had left in the hands of another chief, to be delivered to La Salle in case of his arrival, and which Bienville had bought for a hatchet. Iberville welcomed it as convincing proof that the river he had entered was in truth the Mississippi. After pushing up the stream till the twenty-fourth, he returned to the ships by way of Lake Maurepas and Pontchartrain.

Iberville now repaired to the harbor of Biloxi, on the coast of the present state of Mississippi. Here he built a small stockade fort, where he left eighty men under the Sieur de Sauvolle to hold the country for Louis XIV, and this done, he sailed for France. Thus the first foundations of Louisiana were laid in Mississippi.

Bienville, whom his brother had left at Biloxi as second in command, was sent by Sauvolle on an exploring expedition up the Mississippi with five men in two canoes. At the bend of the river now called English Turn—*Tour à l'Anglais*—below the site of New Orleans, he found an English corvette of ten guns, having as passengers a number of French Protestant families taken on board from the Carolinas, with the intention of settling on the Mississippi.

The commander, Captain Louis Bank, declared that his vessel was one of three sent from London by a company formed jointly of Englishmen and Huguenot refugees for the purpose of founding a colony. Though not quite sure that they were upon the Mississippi, they were on their way up the stream to join a party of Englishmen said to be among the Chickasaws, with whom they were trading for Indian slaves. Bienville assured Bank that he was not upon the Mississippi, but on another river belonging to King Louis, who had a strong fort there and several settlements. "The too-credulous Englishman," says a French writer, "believed these inventions and turned back."

First, however, a French engineer in the service of Bank contrived to have an interview with Bienville and gave him a petition to the King of France, signed by four hundred Huguenots who had taken refuge in the Carolinas after the revocation of the Edict of Nantes. The petitions begged that they might have leave to settle in Louisiana, with liberty of conscience, under the French Crown. In due time they got their answer. The King replied, through the minister Ponchartrain, that he had not expelled heretics from France in order that they should set up a republic in America. Thus, by the bigotry that had been the bane of Canada and of France herself, Louis XIV threw away the opportunity of establishing a firm and healthy colony at the mouth of the Mississippi.

So threatening was the danger that England would seize the country that Iberville had scarcely landed in France when he was sent back with a reinforcement. The colonial views of the King may be gathered from his instructions to his officer. Iberville was told to seek out diligently the best places for establishing pearl fisheries, though it was admitted that the pearls of Louisiana were uncommonly bad. He was also to catch bison calves, make a fenced park to hold them, and tame them for the sake of their wool, which was reputed to be of value for various fabrics. Above all, he was to look for mines, the finding of which the document declares to be "la grande affaire."

On the eighth of January, Iberville reached Biloxi and soon after went up the Mississippi to that remarkable tribe of sun worshipers, the Natchez, whose villages were on or near the site of the city that now bears their name. Some thirty miles above he found a kindred tribe, the Taensas, whose temple took fire during his visit, when to his horror he saw five living infants thrown into the flames by their mothers to appease the angry spirits. Retracing his course, he built a wooden redoubt near one of the mouths of the Mississippi to keep out the dreaded English.

Besides Biloxi and Mobile Bay, the French formed a third establishment at Dauphin Island. The Mississippi itself, which may be called the vital organ of the colony, was thus far neglected, being occupied by no settlement and guarded only by the redoubt which Iberville had built.

Of the emigrants sent out by the court to the new land of promise, the most valuable by far were a number of Canadians who had served under Iberville at Hudson Bay. The rest were largely of the sort who are described by that officer as "beggars sent out to enrich themselves," and who expected the government to feed them while they looked for pearls and gold mines. The paternal providence of Versailles, mindful of their needs, sent them in 1704 a gift of twenty marriageable girls,

433

described as "nurtured in virtue and piety, and accustomed to work." Twenty-three more came in the next year from the same benignant source, besides seventy-five soldiers, five priests and two nuns. Food, however, was not sent in proportion to the consumers, and as no crops were raised in Louisiana, famine and pestilence followed till the starving colonists were forced to live on shellfish picked up along the shores.

The colonists felt no confidence in the future of Louisiana, as its prospects failed to improve by 1712. The King was its sole support and if, as was likely enough, he should tire of it, their case would be deplorable. While Bienville ruled over them, they used him as their scapegoat, but that which made the colony languish was not he but the vicious system it was his business to enforce. The royal edicts and arbitrary commands that took the place of law proceeded from masters thousands of miles away, who knew nothing of the country, could not understand its needs and scarcely tried to do so.

In 1711, though the mischievous phantom of gold and silver mines still haunted the colony, we find it reported that the people were beginning to work and were planting tobacco. The King, however, was losing patience with a dependency that cost him endless expense and trouble and brought little or nothing in return, and this at a time when he had a costly and disastrous war on his hands, and was in no mood to bear supernumerary burdens.

The plan of giving over a colony to a merchant, or a company of merchants, was not new. It had been tried in other French colonies with disastrous effect. Yet it was now tried again. Louisiana was farmed out for fifteen years to Antoine Crozat, a wealthy man of business. The countries made over to him extended from the British colonies on the east to New Mexico on the west and the Rio del Norte on the south, including the entire region watered by the Mississippi, the Missouri, the Ohio and their tributaries as far north as the Illinois. In comparison with this immense domain, which was all included under the name of Louisiana, the present state so called is but a small patch on the American map.

While Louisiana was thus handed over to a speculator for a term of years, it needed no prophet to foretell that he would get all he could out of it and put as little into it as possible. When Crozat took possession of the colony, the French court had been thirteen years at work in building it up. The result of its labors was a total population, including troops, government officials and clergy, of three hundred and eighty souls, of whom one hundred and seventy were in the King's pay.

Only a few of the colonists were within the limits of the present Louisiana. The rest lived in or around the feeble stockade forts at Mobile, Biloxi, Ship Island and Dauphin Island. This last station had been partially abandoned, but some of the colonists proposed to return to it in order to live by fishing, and only waited, we are told, for help from the King. This incessant dependence on government relaxed the fibers of the colony and sapped its lifeblood.

The indefatigable curé De La Vente sent to Ponchartrain in 1714 a memorial, in the preamble of which he says that since Monsieur le Ministre wishes to be informed exactly of the state of things in Louisiana, he, La Vente, has the honor, with malice to nobody, to make known the pure truth, after which he goes on to say that the inhabitants "are nearly all drunkards, gamblers, blasphemers and enemies of everything good," and he proceeds to illustrate the statement with many particulars.

As the inhabitants were expected to work for Crozat and not for themselves, it naturally followed that they would not work at all and idleness produced the usual results.

The yearly shipment of girls continued, but there was difficulty in finding husbands for them. The reason was not far to seek. Duclos, the intendant, reports the arrival of an invoice of twelve of them, "so ugly that the inhabitants are in no hurry to take them." The Canadians, who formed the most vigorous and valuable part of the population, much preferred Indian squaws. "It seems to me," pursues the intendant, "that in the choice of girls, good looks should be more considered than virtue."

This latter requisite seems, at the time, to have found no more attention than the other, since the candidates for matrimony were drawn from the Parisian hospitals and houses of correction, from the former of which Crozat was authorized to take one hundred girls a year "in order to increase the population." These hospitals were compulsory asylums for the poor and vagrant of both sexes, of whom the great Hôpital Général of Paris contained at one time more than six thousand.

Crozat had built his chief hopes of profit on a trade, contraband or otherwise, with the Mexican ports. But the Spanish officials, faithful instruments of the exclusive policy of their government, would not permit it and were so vigilant that he could not elude them. At the same time, to his vexation, he found that the King's officers in Louisiana, with more address or better luck and in contempt of his monopoly, which it was their business to protect, carried on for their own profit a small smuggling trade with Vera Cruz. He complained that they were always thwarting his agents and conspiring against his interests.

At last, finding no resource left but an unprofitable trade with the Indians, he gave up his charter, which had been a bane to the colony and a loss to himself. Louisiana returned to the Crown and was soon passed over to the new Mississippi Company, called also the Western Company.

When Crozat resigned his charter, Louisiana by the highest estimates contained about seven hundred souls, including soldiers but not blacks or Indians. Crozat's successors, however, say that the whole number of whites, men, women and children, was not above four hundred. When the Mississippi Company took the colony in charge, it was but a change of despots. Louisiana was a prison. But while no inhabitant could leave it without permission of the authorities, all Jews were expelled and all Protestants excluded. The colonists could buy nothing except from the agents of the company, and sell nothing except to the same all-powerful masters, always at prices fixed by them. Foreign vessels were forbidden to enter any port of Louisiana, on pain of confiscation.

The company, which was invested with sovereign powers, began its work by sending to Louisiana three companies of soldiers and sixty-nine colonists. Its wisest act was the removal of the governor, L'Épinay, and the reappointment of Bienville in his place. Bienville immediately sought out a spot for establishing a permanent station on the Mississippi. Fifty men were set to clear the ground, and in spite of an inundation which overflowed it for a time, the feeble foundations of New Orleans were laid. Louisiana, hitherto diffused through various petty cantonments far and near, had at last a capital, or the germ of one.

It was the sixth of September 1717 when the charter of the Mississippi Company was entered in the registers of the Parliament of Paris, and from that time forward, before the offices of the company in the Rue Quincampoix, crowds of crazed speculators jostled and fought from morning till night to get their names inscribed among the stockholders.

Within five years after, the huge glittering bubble had burst. The shares, each one of which had seemed a fortune, found no more purchasers, and in its fall the company dragged down with it its ally and chief creditor, the bank. All was dismay and despair, except among those who had sold out in time and turned delusive paper into solid values.

The bursting of the Mississippi bubble did not change the principles of administration in Louisiana. The settlers, always looking to France to supply their needs and protect them against their own improvidence, were in the habit of butchering for food the livestock sent them for propagation. The remedy came in the shape of a royal edict forbidding any colonist to kill, without permission of the authorities, any cow, sheep or lamb belonging to himself, on pain of a fine of three hundred livres, or to kill any horse, cow or bull belonging to another on pain of death.

Authority and order were the watchwords and disorder was the rule. The agents of power quarreled among themselves, except when they leagued together to deceive their transatlantic masters and cover their own misdeeds. Each maligned the other and it was scarcely possible for the King or the company to learn the true state of affairs in their distant colony.

In this state of things, the directors of the Mississippi Company, whose affairs had gone from bad to worse, declared that they could no longer bear the burden of Louisiana and begged the King to take it off their hands. The colony was therefore transferred from the mercantile despotism of the company to the paternal despotism of the Crown and it profited by the change. Commercial monopoly was abolished. Trade between France and Louisiana was not only permitted but encouraged by bounties and exemption from duties, and

437

instead of paying to the company two hundred per cent of profit on indispensable supplies, the colonists now got them at a reasonable price.

With the help of industrious nursing—or, one might almost say, in spite of it—Louisiana began at last to strike roots into the soil and show signs of growth, though feebly as compared with its sturdy rivals along the Atlantic seaboard, which had cost their King nothing and had been treated, for the most part, with the coolest neglect. Cavelier de la Salle's dream of planting a firm settlement at the mouth of the Mississippi, and utilizing by means of it the resources of the vast interior, was after half a century in some measure realized. New France (using that name in its broadest geographical sense) had now two heads, Canada and Louisiana—one looking upon the Gulf of St. Lawrence and the other upon the Gulf of Mexico.

Canada was not without jealousy of her younger and weaker sister, lest she might draw away, as she had begun to do at the first, some of the most active and adventurous elements of the Canadian population; lest she might prove a competitor in the fur trade; and lest she should encroach on the Illinois and other western domains, which the elder and stronger sister claimed as her own. These fears were not unfounded, yet the vital interests of the two French colonies were the same and each needed the help of the other in the prime and all-essential task of keeping the British colonies in check. The chiefs of Louisiana looked forward to a time when the great southern tribes— Creeks, Cherokees, Choctaws and even the dreaded Chickasaws— won over by French missionaries to the Church and therefore to France, should be turned against the encroaching English to stop their westward progress and force them back to the borders of the Atlantic.

Meanwhile the chiefs of Canada were maturing the plan—pursued with varying assiduity, but always kept in view—of connecting the two vital extremities of New France by a chain of forts to control the passes of the West, keep communications open and set English invasion at defiance.

CHAPTER 5

~~~~~~

The Chain of Posts

ON MAPS OF BRITISH AMERICA IN THE EARLIER part of the eighteenth century, one sees the eastern shore from Maine to Georgia garnished with ten or twelve colored patches, very different in shape and size and defined more or less distinctly by dividing lines which, in some cases, are prolonged westward till they touch the Mississippi or even cross it, and stretch indefinitely towards the Pacific. These patches are the British provinces and the westward prolongation of their boundary lines represents their several claims to vast interior tracts, founded on ancient grants but not made good by occupation or vindicated by any exertion of power.

These English communities took little thought of the region beyond the Alleghenies. Each lived a life of its own, shut within its own limits, not dreaming of a future collective greatness to which the possession of the West would be a necessary condition. No conscious community of aims and interest held them together, nor was there any authority capable of uniting their forces and turning them to a common object.

Some of the servants of the Crown had urged the necessity of joining them all under a strong central government as the only means of making them loyal subjects and arresting the encroachments of France, but the scheme was plainly impracticable. Each province remained in jealous isolation, busied with its own work, growing in strength in the capacity of self-rule and the spirit of independence, and stubbornly resisting all exercise of authority from without.

439

If the English-speaking populations flowed westward, it was in obedience to natural laws, for the King did not aid the movement, the royal governors had no authority to do so, and the colonial assemblies were too much engrossed with immediate local interests. The power of these colonies was that of a rising flood slowly invading and conquering by the unconscious force of its own growing volume, unless means could be found to hold it back by dams and embankments within appointed limits.

In the French colonies all was different. Here the representatives of the Crown were men bred in an atmosphere of broad ambition and masterful and far-reaching enterprise. Achievement was demanded of them. They recognized the greatness of the prize, studied the strong and weak points of their rivals and with a cautious forecast and a daring energy set themselves to the task of defeating them.

If the English colonies were comparatively strong in numbers, their numbers could not be brought into action, while if the French forces were small, they were vigorously commanded and always ready at a word. It was union confronting division, energy confronting apathy, military centralization opposed to industrial democracy, and for a time the advantage was all on one side.

The demands of the French were sufficiently comprehensive. They repented of their enforced concessions at the Treaty of Utrecht, and, in spite of that compact, maintained that with a few local and trivial exceptions, the whole North American continent except Mexico was theirs of right, while their opponents seemed neither to understand the situation nor see the greatness of the stakes at issue.

France had been advised that she should not trust solely to the justice of her claims, but should back right with might and build forts on the Niagara, the Ohio, the Tennessee and the Alabama, as well as at other commanding points, to shut out the English from the West. Of these positions, Niagara was the most important, for the possession of it would close the access to the Upper Lakes and stop the western tribes on their way to trade at Albany.

For gaining the consent of the Five Nations to the building of a French fort at Niagara, Governor Vaudreuil trusted chiefly to his agent among the Senecas, the bold, skillful and indefatigable Joncaire, who was naturalized among that tribe, the strongest of the confederacy.

440

Governor Hunter of New York sent Peter Schuyler and Philip Livingston to counteract his influence.

The Five Nations, who conscious of declining power seemed ready at this time to be all things to all men, declared that they would prevent the French from building at Niagara which, as they said, would "shut them up as in a prison." Not long before, however, they had sent a deputation to Montreal to say that the English made objection to Joncaire's presence among them, but that they were masters of their land and hoped that the French agent would come as often as he pleased, and they begged that the new King of France would take them under his protection. Accordingly, Vaudreuil sent them a present, with a message to the effect that they might plunder such English traders as should come among them.

Yet so jealous were the Iroquois of a French fort at Niagara that they sent three Seneca chiefs to see what was going on there. The chiefs found a few Frenchmen in a small blockhouse, or loopholed storehouse, which they had just built near Lewiston Heights. The three Senecas requested them to demolish it and go away, which the Frenchmen refused to do, upon which the Senecas asked the English envoys, Schuyler and Livingston, to induce the governor of New York to destroy the obnoxious building.

In short, the Five Nations wavered incessantly between their two European neighbors, and changed their minds every day. The skill and perseverance of the French emissaries so far prevailed at last that the Senecas consented to the building of a fort at the mouth of the Niagara, where Denonville had built one in 1687, and thus that important pass was made tolerably secure.

Meanwhile the English of New York, or rather Burnet, their governor, were not idle. Burnet was on ill terms with his assembly, which grudged him all help in serving the province whose interests it was supposed to represent. Burnet's plan was to build a fortified trading house at Oswego, on Lake Ontario, in the belief that the western Indians, who greatly preferred English goods and English prices, would pass Niagara and bring their furs to the new post.

He got leave from the Five Nations to execute his plan, bought canoes, hired men and built a loopholed house of stone on the site of the present city of Oswego. As the Assembly would give no money,

Burnet furnished it himself, and though the object was one of the greatest importance to the province, he was never fully repaid. A small garrison for the new post was drawn from the four independent companies maintained in the province at the charge of the Crown.

The establishment of Oswego greatly alarmed and incensed the French and a council of war at Quebec resolved to send two thousand men against it. But Vaudreuil's successor, the Marquis de Beauharnois, learning that the court was not prepared to provoke a war, contented himself with sending a summons to the commanding officer to abandon and demolish the place within a fortnight. To this no attention was given, and, as Burnet had foreseen, Oswego became the great center of Indian trade while Niagara, in spite of its more favorable position, was comparatively slighted by the western tribes. The chief danger rose from the obstinate prejudice of the Assembly, which in its disputes with the royal governor would give him neither men nor money to defend the new post.

The Canadian authorities, who saw in Oswego an intrusion on their domain and a constant injury and menace, could not attack it without bringing on a war, and therefore tried to persuade the Five Nations to destroy it, an attempt which completely failed. They then established a trading post at Toronto, in the vain hope of stopping the northern tribes on their way to the more profitable English market, and they built two armed vessels at Fort Frontenac to control the navigation of Lake Ontario.

Meanwhile, in another quarter, the French made an advance far more threatening to the English colonies than Oswego was to their own. They had already built a stone fort at Chambly, which covered Montreal from any English attack by way of Lake Champlain. As that lake was the great highway between the rival colonies, the importance of gaining full mastery of it was evident. It was rumored in Canada that the English meant to seize and fortify the place called Scalp Point by the French and Crown Point by the English, where the lake suddenly contracts to the proportions of a river, so that a few cannon would stop the passage.

As early as 1726 the French made an attempt to establish themselves on the east side of the lake opposite Crown Point, but were deterred by the opposition of Massachusetts. This eastern shore was, however, claimed not only by Massachusetts but by her neighbor, New Hampshire, with whom she presently fell into a dispute about the ownership, and as a writer of the time observes, "while they were quarreling for the bone, the French ran away with it."

At length, in 1731, the French took post on the western side of the lake and began to intrench themselves at Crown Point, which was within the bounds claimed by New York. But that province, being then engrossed not only by her chronic dispute with her governor but by a quarrel with her next neighbor, New Jersey, slighted the danger from the common enemy and left the French to work their will.

It was Saint-Luc de la Corne, Lieutenant du Roy at Montreal, who pointed out the necessity of fortifying this place in order to anticipate the English, who, as he imagined, were about to do so—a danger which was probably not imminent since the English colonies, as a whole, could not and would not unite for such a purpose, while the individual provinces were too much absorbed in their own internal affairs and their own jealousies and disputes to make the attempt. La Corne's suggestion found favor at court and the governor of Canada was ordered to occupy Crown Point.

The Sieur de la Fresnière was sent there with troops and workmen and a fort was built and named Fort Frédéric. It contained a massive stone tower, mounted with cannon to command the lake, which is here but a musket shot wide. Thus was established an advanced post of France, a constant menace to New York and New England, both of which denounced it as an outrageous encroachment on British territory but could not unite to rid themselves of it.

While making this bold push against their neighbors of the South, the French did not forget the West, and towards the middle of the century they had occupied points controlling all the chief waterways between Canada and Louisiana. Niagara held the passage from Lake Ontario to Lake Erie. Detroit closed the entrance to Lake Huron and Michilimackinac guarded the point where Lake Huron is joined by Lakes Michigan and Superior; while the fort called La Baye, at the head of Green Bay, stopped the way to the Mississippi by Marquette's old route of Fox River and the Wisconsin. Another route to the Mississippi was controlled by a post on the Maumee to watch the carrying-place between that river and the Wabash, and by another on the Wabash where Vincennes now stands. La Salle's route, by way of the Kankakee and the Illinois, was barred by a fort on the St. Joseph, and even if, in spite of these obstructions, an enemy should reach the Mississippi by any of its northern affluents, the cannon of Fort Chartres would prevent him from descending it.

These various western forts, except Fort Chartres and Fort Niagara, which were afterwards rebuilt, the one in stone and the other in earth, were stockades of no strength against cannon. Slight as they were, their establishment was costly, and as the King, to whom Canada was a yearly loss, grudged every franc spent upon it, means were contrived to make them self-supporting. Each of them was a station of the fur trade and the position of most of them had been determined more or less with a view to that traffic. Hence they had no slight commercial value.

In some of them the Crown itself carried on trade through agents who usually secured a lion's share of the profits. Others were farmed out to merchants at a fixed sum. In others again, the commanding officer was permitted to trade on condition of maintaining the post, paying the soldiers and supporting a missionary, while in one case, at least, he was subjected to similar obligations though not permitted to trade himself but only to sell trading licenses to merchants. These methods of keeping up forts and garrisons were of course open to prodigious abuses and roused endless jealousies and rivalries.

France had now occupied the valley of the Mississippi and joined with loose and uncertain links her two colonies of Canada and Louisiana. But the strength of her hold on these regions of unkempt savagery bore no proportion to the vastness of her claims or the growing power of the rivals who were soon to contest them.

~~~~~~

CHAPTER 6

The Capture of Louisbourg

LOUISBOURG WAS A STANDING MENACE TO ALL THE northern British colonies. This fort, on the southeastern point of Isle Royale, lying east of Acadia and separated from it by the narrow Strait of Canseau, commanded the chief entrance of the gulf and river of St. Lawrence. It was reputed the strongest fortress, French or British, in North America, with the possible exception of Quebec, which owed its chief strength to nature and not to art.

It was the only French naval station on the continent, and was such a haunt of privateers that it was called the American Dunkirk. It commanded the chief entrance of Canada, and threatened to ruin the fisheries, which were nearly as vital to New England as was the fur trade to New France. The French government had spent twenty-five years in fortifying it and the cost of its powerful defenses—constructed after the system of Vauban—was reckoned at thirty million livres.

This was the fortress which William Vaughan of Damariscotta now advised Governor Shirley to attack with fifteen hundred raw New England militia. Vaughan was born at Portsmouth in 1703, and graduated from Harvard College nineteen years later. His father, also a graduate of Harvard, was for a time lieutenant governor of New Hampshire. Soon after leaving college the younger Vaughan, a youth of restless and impetuous activity, established a fishing station on the island of Matinicus, off the coast of Maine, and afterwards became the owner of most of the land on both sides of the little river Damariscotta, where he built a garrison house, or wooden fort, established a considerable settlement and carried on an extensive trade in fish and timber.

Being interested in the fisheries, Vaughan was doubly hostile to Louisbourg, their worst enemy. He found a willing listener in the governor, William Shirley. Shirley was an English barrister who had come to Massachusetts in 1731 to practice his profession and seek his fortune. After filling various offices with credit, he was made governor of the province in 1741, and had discharged his duties with both tact and talent. He was able, sanguine and a sincere well-wisher to the province, though gnawed by an insatiable hunger for distinction. He thought himself a born strategist, and was possessed by a propensity for contriving military operations, which finally cost him dear.

It took all of Vaughan's impetuous and irrepressible energy, with Shirley's enthusiastic help, to get the Massachusetts Assembly's approval of his plan to attack Louisbourg. It was carried by a single vote on the second attempt, and even this result was said to be due to the accident of a member in opposition, who fell and broke his leg as he was hastening to the House.

The die was cast and now doubt and hesitation vanished. All alike set themselves to push on the work. Shirley wrote to all the colonies, as far south as Pennsylvania, to ask for co-operation. All excused themselves except Connecticut, New Hampshire and Rhode Island, and the whole burden fell on the four New England colonies. These, and Massachusetts above all, blazed with pious zeal, for as the enterprise was directed against Roman Catholics, it was supposed in a peculiar manner to commend itself to heaven. There were prayers without ceasing in churches and families and all was ardor, energy and confidence, while the other colonies looked on with distrust, dashed with derision.

When Benjamin Franklin, in Philadelphia, heard what was afoot, he wrote to his brother in Boston: "Fortified towns are hard nuts to crack, and your teeth are not accustomed to it; but some seem to think that forts are as easy taken as snuff."

It was difficult to choose a leader. The colony had been at peace for twenty years, and except some grizzled Indian fighters of the last war and some survivors of the Carthagena expedition, nobody had seen service. Few knew well what a fortress was and nobody knew how to attack one. Courage, energy, good sense and popularity were the best qualities to be hoped for in the leader. Popularity was indispensable, for the soldiers were all to be volunteers and they would not enlist under a commander whom they did not like. Shirley's choice was William Pepperrell, a merchant of Kittery.

Pepperrell was the son of a Welshman who migrated in early life to the Isles of Shoals and thence to Kittery, where by trade, shipbuilding and the fisheries, he made a fortune, most of which he left to his son William. The young Pepperrell learned what little was taught at the village school, supplemented by a private tutor whose instructions, however, did not perfect him in English grammar. In the eyes of his self-made father, education was valuable only so far as it could make a successful trader, and on this point he had reason to be satisfied, as his son passed for many years as the chief merchant in New England. He dealt in ships, timber, naval stores, fish and miscellaneous goods brought from England and he also greatly prospered by successful land purchases, becoming owner of the greater part of the growing towns of Saco and Scarborough.

At once a provincial magnate and the great man of a small rustic village, his manners are said to have answered to both positions. Certainly they were such as to make him popular. But whatever he became as a man, he learned nothing to fit him to command an army and lay siege to Louisbourg.

However, Shirley's choice of a commander was perhaps the best that could have been made, for Pepperrell joined to an unusual popularity as little military incompetency as anybody else who could be had. Popularity was indispensable and even company officers were appointed with an eye to it. Many of these were well-known men in rustic neighborhoods, who had raised companies in the hope of being commissioned to command them. Others were militia officers recruiting under orders of the governor.

As the three provinces contributing soldiers recognized no common authority nearer than the King, Pepperrell received three different commissions as lieutenant general, one from the governor of Massachusetts and the others from the governors of Connecticut and New Hampshire, while Wolcott, commander of the Connecticut forces, was commissioned as major general by both the governor of his own province and that of Massachusetts. When the levies were complete, it was found that Massachusetts had contributed about 3,300 men, Connecticut 516, and New Hampshire 304 in her own pay, besides 150 paid by her wealthier neighbor. Rhode Island had lost faith and disbanded her 150 men, but afterwards raised them again, though too late to take part in the siege.

Each of the four New England colonies had a little navy of its own, consisting of from one to three or four small armed vessels, and as privateering—which was sometimes a euphemism for piracy where Frenchmen and Spaniards were concerned—was a favorite occupation, it was possible to extemporize an additional force in case of need. For a naval commander, Shirley chose Captain Edward Tyng, who had signalized himself in the past summer by capturing a French privateer of greater strength than his own.

Within seven weeks after Shirley issued his proclamation for volunteers, the preparations were all made and the unique armament was afloat. Transports, such as they were, could be had in abundance, for the harbors of Salem and Marblehead were full of fishing vessels thrown out of employment by the war. These were hired and insured by the province for the security of the owners. There was a great dearth of cannon. The few that could be had were too light, the heaviest being of twenty-two-pound caliber. New York lent ten eighteen-pounders to the expedition. But the adventurers looked to the French for their chief supply. A detached work near Louisbourg called the Grand, or Royal, Battery was known to be armed with thirty heavy pieces and these it was proposed to capture and turn against the town—which, as Hutchinson remarks, was "like selling the skin of the bear before catching him."

It was clear that the expedition must run for luck against risks of all kinds. Those whose hopes were highest based them on a belief in the special and direct interposition of Providence; others were sanguine through ignorance and provincial self-conceit. As soon as the troops were embarked, Shirley wrote to the ministers of what was going on, telling them that, accidents apart, four thousand New England men would land on Cape Breton in April, and that even should they fail to capture Louisbourg, he would answer for it that they would lay the town in ruins, retake Canseau, do other good service to his Majesty and then come safe home. On receiving this communication, the government resolved to aid the enterprise if there should yet be time, and accordingly ordered several ships of war to sail for Louisbourg.

The sarcastic Dr. Douglas, then living at Boston, writes that the expedition had a lawyer for contriver, a merchant for general, and farmers, fishermen and mechanics for soldiers. In fact, it had something of the character of broad farce, to which Shirley himself, with all his ability and general good sense, was a chief contributor. He wrote to the Duke of Newcastle that though the officers had no experience and the men no discipline, he would take care to provide against these defects—meaning that he would give exact directions how to take Louisbourg. Accordingly, he drew up copious instructions to that effect.

On the twenty-fourth of March the fleet, consisting of about ninety transports escorted by the provincial cruisers, sailed from Nantasket Roads, followed by prayers and benedictions and also by toasts drunk with cheers in bumpers of rum punch.

On board one of the transports was Seth Pomeroy, gunsmith at Northampton and now major of Willard's Massachusetts regiment, later a hero of the Seven Years' War and of the Revolution. The voyage caused the miserable gunsmith to write that he and the other landsmen were "Sick, day and night, so bad that I have not words to set it forth." But on Friday, April 5, Pomeroy's vessel entered the harbor of Canseau, about fifty miles from Louisbourg. Here was the English fishing hamlet, the seizure of which by the French had first provoked the expedition. The place now quietly changed hands again. Sixty-eight of the transports lay here at anchor and the rest came dropping in from day to day, sorely buffeted but all safe.

On Monday, the twenty-second, a clear, cold, windy day, a large ship under British colors sailed into the harbor and proved to be the frigate *Eltham*, escort to the annual mast fleet from New England. On orders from Commander Warren, she had left her charge in waiting and sailed for Canseau to join the expedition, bringing the unexpected and welcome news that Warren himself would soon follow. On the next day, to the delight of all, he appeared in the ship *Superbe*, of

449

sixty guns, accompanied by the *Launceston* and the *Mermaid,* of forty guns each. Here was force enough to oppose any ships likely to come to the aid of Louisbourg and Warren, after communicating with Pepperrell, sailed to blockade the port, along with the provincial cruisers, which by order of Shirley were placed under his command.

The transports lay at Canseau nearly three weeks, waiting for the ice to break up. The time was passed in drilling the raw soldiers and forming them into divisions of four and six hundred each, according to the directions of Shirley. At length, on Friday the twenty-seventh, they heard that Gabarus Bay was free from ice, and on the morning of the twenty-ninth, with the first fair wind, they sailed out of Canseau harbor, expecting to reach Louisbourg at nine in the evening, as prescribed in the governor's recipe for taking Louisbourg "while the enemy were asleep."

But a lull in the wind defeated this plan, and after sailing all day they found themselves becalmed towards night. It was not till the next morning that they could see the town, no very imposing spectacle for the buildings, with a few exceptions, were small and the massive ramparts that belted them round rose to no conspicuous height.

It was about the twenty-fifth of March when the garrison first saw the provincial cruisers hovering off the mouth of the harbor. They continued to do so at intervals till daybreak of the thirtieth of April, when the whole fleet of transports appeared standing towards Flat Point, which projects into Gabarus Bay, three miles west of the town. On this, Chevalier Duchambon, the governor, sent Morpain, captain of a privateer or "corsair," to oppose the landing. He had with him eighty men and was to be joined by forty more already on the watch near the supposed point of disembarkation. At the same time cannon were fired and alarm bells rung in Louisbourg to call in the militia of the neighborhood.

Pepperrell managed the critical work of landing with creditable skill. The rocks and the surf were more dangerous than the enemy. Several boats filled with men rowed towards Flat Point, but on a signal from the flagship *Shirley,* rowed back again, Morpain flattering himself that his appearance had frightened them off. Being joined by several other boats, the united party, a hundred men in all, pulled for another landing place called Freshwater Cove, or Anse de la Cormorandière, two miles farther up Gabarus Bay. Morpain and his party ran to meet them, but the boats were first in the race and as soon as the New England men got ashore they rushed upon the French, killed six of them, captured as many more, including an officer named Boularderie, and put the rest to flight, with the loss on their own side of two men slightly wounded. Further resistance to the landing was impossible, for a swarm of boats pushed against the rough and stony beach, the men dashing through the surf, till before night about two thousand were on shore. The rest, or about two thousand more, landed at their leisure on the next day.

Duchambon says that soon after the English landed, he got a letter from Thierry, the captain in command of the royal battery, advising that the cannon should be spiked and the works blown up. It was then, according to the governor, that a council was called and a unanimous vote passed to follow Thierry's advice, on the ground that the defenses of the battery were in bad condition and that the four hundred men posted there could not stand against three or four thousand. The engineer Verrier opposed the blowing up of the works and they were therefore left untouched.

Thierry and his garrison came off in boats, after spiking the cannon in a hasty way without stopping to knock off the trunnions or burn the carriages. They threw their loose gunpowder into the well but left behind a good number of cannon cartridges, two hundred and eighty large bombshells and other ordnance stores, invaluable both to the enemy and to themselves.

Brigadier Waldo was sent to occupy the battery with his regiment and Major Seth Pomeroy, the gunsmith, with twenty soldier mechanics was set at drilling out the spiked touchholes of the cannon. There were twenty-eight forty-two-pounders and two eighteen-pounders. Several were ready for use the next morning, and immediately opened on the town, which, writes a soldier in his diary, "damaged the houses and made the women cry." "The enemy," says another contemporary account, "saluted us with our own cannon, and made a terrific fire, smashing everything within range."

The English occupation of the Grand Battery may be called the decisive event of the siege, and there seems no doubt that the French could have averted the disaster long enough to make it of little help to the invaders.

The English landed their cannon near Flat Point, but before they could be turned against the Grand Battery they had to be dragged four miles over hills and rocks, through spongy marshes and jungles of matted evergreens. This would have required a week or more. The alternative was an escalade, in which the undisciplined assailants would no doubt have met a bloody rebuff. Thus this Grand Battery, which, says Wolcott, "is in fact a fort," might at least have been held long enough to save the munitions and stores and effectually disable the cannon, which supplied the English with the only artillery they had that was competent to the work before them. The hasty abandonment of this important post was not Duchambon's only blunder, but it was the worst of them all.

Pepperrell writes in ardent words of the cheerfulness of his men "under almost incredible hardships." Shoes and clothing failed till many were in tatters and many barefooted, yet they toiled on with unconquerable spirit and within four days had planted a battery of six guns on Green Hill, which was about a mile from the King's bastion of Louisbourg. In another week they had dragged four twenty-two-pound cannon and ten coehorns—gravely called "cowhorns" by the bucolic Pomeroy—six or seven hundred yards farther, and planted them within easy range of the citadel. Two of the cannon burst and were replaced by four more and a large mortar, which burst in its turn, and Shirley was begged to send another.

Meanwhile a battery, chiefly of coehorns, had been planted on a hillock four hundred and forty yards from the West Gate, where it greatly annoyed the French, and on the next night an advanced battery was placed just opposite the same gate, scarcely two hundred and fifty yards from it. This West Gate, the principal gate of Louisbourg, opened upon the tract of high, firm ground that lay on the left of the besiegers, between the marsh and the harbor, an arm of which here extended westward beyond the town into what was called the Barachois, a salt pond formed by a projecting spit of sand.

On the side of the Barachois farthest from the town was a hillock on which stood the house of a habitant named Martissan. Here on the twentieth of May a fifth battery was planted, consisting of two of the

French forty-two-pounders taken in the Grand Battery, to which three others were afterwards added. Each of these heavy pieces was dragged to its destination by a team of three hundred men over rough and rocky ground swept by the French artillery. This fifth battery, called the Northwest, or Titcomb's, proved most destructive to the fortress.

All these operations were accomplished with the utmost ardor and energy, but with a scorn of rule and precedent that astonished and bewildered the French. The raw New England men went their own way, laughed at trenches and zigzags and persisted in trusting their lives to the night and the fog.

The scarcity of good gunners was one of the chief difficulties of the besiegers. As privateering, and piracy also, against Frenchmen and Spaniards was a favorite pursuit in New England, there were men in Pepperrell's army who knew how to handle cannon, but their number was insufficient and the general sent a note to Warren, begging that he would lend him a few experienced gunners to teach their trade to the raw hands at the batteries. Three or four were sent and they found apt pupils.

The cannon could be loaded only under a constant fire of musketry, which the enemy briskly returned. The French practice was excellent. A soldier who in bravado mounted the rampart and stood there for a moment was shot dead with five bullets. The men on both sides called to each other in scraps of bad French or broken English, while the French drank ironical healths to the New England men and gave them bantering invitations to breakfast.

It is said in proof of the orderly conduct of the men that not one of them was punished during all the siege, but this shows the mild and conciliating character of the general quite as much as any peculiar merit of the soldiers. The state of things in and about the camp was compared by the caustic Dr. Douglas to "a Cambridge Commencement," which academic festival was then attended by much rough frolic and boisterous horseplay among the disorderly crowds, white and black, bond and free, who swarmed among the booths on Cambridge Common.

While the cannon bellowed in the front, frolic and confusion reigned at the camp, where the men raced, wrestled, pitched quoits, fired at marks—though there was no ammunition to spare—and ran after the

French cannon balls, which were carried to the batteries to be returned to those who sent them.

Yet through all these gambols ran an undertow of enthusiasm, born in brains still fevered from the "Great Awakening." The New England soldier, a growth of sectarian hotbeds, fancied that he was doing the work of God. The army was Israel and the French were Canaanitish idolators. Red-hot Calvinism, acting through generations, had modified the transplanted Englishman and the descendant of the Puritans was never so well pleased as when teaching their duty to other people, whether by pen, voice or bombshells. The ragged artillerymen, battering the walls of papistical Louisbourg, flattered themselves with the notion that they were champions of gospel truth.

Barefoot and tattered, they toiled on with indomitable pluck and cheerfulness, doing the work which oxen could not do, with no comfort but their daily dram of New England rum as they plodded through the marsh and over rocks, dragging the ponderous guns through fog and darkness.

Frequent councils of war were held in solemn form at headquarters. On the seventh of May a summons to surrender was sent to Duchambon, who replied that he would answer with his cannon. Two days after, we find in the record of the council the following startling entry: "Advised unanimously that the Town of Louisbourg be attacked by storm this Night." Vaughan was a member of the board and perhaps his impetuous rashness had turned the heads of his colleagues. To storm the fortress at that time would have been a desperate attempt for the best-trained and best-led troops. There was as yet no breach in the walls, nor the beginning of one, and the French were so confident in the strength of their fortifications that they boasted that women alone could defend them. Nine in ten of the besiegers had no bayonets, many had no shoes, and it is said that the scaling ladders brought from Boston were ten feet too short.

Perhaps it was unfortunate for the French that the army was more prudent than its leaders, and another council being called on the same day, it was "Advised, That, inasmuch as there appears a great Dissatisfaction in many of the officers and Soldiers at the designed attack of the Town by Storm this Night, the said Attack be deferred for the present."

On the nineteenth of May a fierce cannonade was heard from the harbor and a large French ship of war was seen hotly engaged with several vessels of the squadron. She was the *Vigilant,* carrying sixty-four guns and five hundred and sixty men, and commanded by the Marquis de la Maisonfort. She had come from France with munitions and stores, when on approaching Louisbourg she met one of the English cruisers. Being no match for her, the British or provincial frigate kept up a running fight and led her towards the English fleet. The *Vigilant* soon found herself beset by several other vessels, and after a gallant resistance and the loss of eighty men, struck her colors.

Nothing could be more timely for the New England army, whose ammunition and provisions had sunk perilously low. The French prize now supplied their needs, and drew from an inhabitant of the fortress the mournful comment, "We were victims devoted to appease the wrath of Heaven, which turned our own arms into weapons for our enemies."

Gridley's artillery at Lighthouse Point was now doing its best, dropping bombshells with such precision into the island battery that the French soldiers were sometimes seen running into the sea to escape the explosions. Many of the island guns were dismounted and the place was fast becoming untenable. At the same time the English batteries on the land side were pushing their work of destruction with relentless industry and walls and bastions crumbled under their fire.

Pepperrell and Warren, after a restrained argument, at length came to an understanding as to a joint attack by land and water. The island battery was by this time crippled and the town batteries that commanded the interior of the harbor were nearly destroyed. It was agreed that Warren, whose squadron was now increased by recent arrivals to eleven ships besides the provincial cruisers, should enter the harbor with the first fair wind, cannonade the town and attack it in boats, while Pepperrell stormed it from the land side. Warren was to hoist a Dutch flag under his pennant at his main topgallant masthead as a signal that he was about to sail in and Pepperrell was to answer by three columns of smoke, marching at the same time towards the walls with drums beating and colors flying.

The French saw with dismay a large quantity of fascines carried to the foot of the glacis, ready to fill the ditch, and their scouts came in with reports that more than a thousand scaling ladders were lying behind the ridge of the nearest hill. Toil, loss of sleep and the stifling air of the casemates, in which they were forced to take refuge, had sapped the strength of the besieged. The town was a ruin. Only one house was untouched by shot or shell.

La Perelle, the French officer, delivered a note from Duchambon, directed to both Pepperrell and Warren and asking for a suspension of arms to enable him to draw up proposals for capitulation. Warren chanced to be on shore when the note came and the two commanders answered jointly that it had come in good time, as they had just resolved on a general attack, and that they would give the governor till eight o'clock of the next morning to make his proposals.

They came in due time, but were of such a nature that Pepperrell refused to listen to them and sent back Bonaventure, the officer who brought them, with counter-proposals. These were terms which Duchambon had already rejected on the seventh of May, with added conditions such as, among others, that no officer, soldier or inhabitant of Louisbourg should bear arms against the King of England or any of his allies for the space of a year. Duchambon stipulated, as the condition of his acceptance, that his troops should march out of the fortress with their arms and colors. To this both the English commanders consented, Warren observing to Pepperrell "the uncertainty of our affairs, that depend so much on wind and weather, makes it necessary not to stickle at trifles."

The articles were signed on both sides, and on the seventeenth the ships sailed peacefully into the harbor, while Pepperrell with a part of his ragged army entered the south gate of the town. "Never was a place more mal'd [mauled] with cannon and shells," he writes to Shirley, "neither have I red in History of any troops behaving with greater courage. We gave them about nine thousand cannon balls and six hundred bombs." Thus this unique military performance ended in complete and astonishing success.

According to English accounts, the French had lost about three hundred men during the siege, but their real loss seems to have been not much above a third of that number. On the side of the besiegers, the deaths from all causes were only a hundred and thirty, about thirty of which were from disease. The French used their muskets to good purpose, but their mortar practice was bad and close as was the advanced battery to their walls, they often failed to hit it, while the ground on both sides of it looked like a plowed field from the bursting of their shells. Their surrender was largely determined by want of ammunition, as, according to one account, the French had but thirty-seven barrels of gunpowder left, in which particular the besiegers fared little better.

The New England men had been full of confidence in the result of the proposed assault and a French writer says that the timely capitulation saved Louisbourg from a terrible catastrophe. Yet, ill-armed and disorderly as the besiegers were, it may be doubted whether the quiet ending of the siege was not as fortunate for them as for their foes.

Pepperrell celebrated the victory by a dinner to the commodore and his officers. As the redoubtable Parson Moody was the general's chaplain and the oldest man in the army, he expected to ask a blessing at the board, and was in fact invited to do so, to the great concern of those who knew his habitual prolixity and dreaded its effect on the guests. At the same time, not one of them dared rasp his irritable temper by any suggestion of brevity and hence they came in terror to the feast, expecting an invocation of a good half-hour, ended by open revolt of the hungry Britons.

To their surprise and relief, Moody said: "Good Lord, we have so much to thank thee for that time will be too short, and we must leave it for eternity. Bless our food and fellowship upon this joyful occasion, for the sake of Christ our Lord. Amen." And with that he sat down.

When the volunteers exchanged their wet and dreary camp for what they expected to be the comfortable quarters of the town, they were disgusted to see the houses still occupied by the owners, and to find themselves forced to stand guard at the doors to protect them. They were not, and perhaps could not be, long kept in order, and when, in accordance with the capitulation, the inhabitants had been sent on board vessels for transportation to France, discipline gave way and General Wolcott records that while Moody was preaching on a Sunday in the garrison chapel, there was "excessive stealing in every part of the town." Little, however, was left to steal.

But if the army found only meager gleanings, the navy reaped a rich harvest. French ships, instead of being barred out of the harbor, were now lured to enter it. The French flag was kept flying over the town, and in this way prizes were entrapped to the estimated value of a million sterling, half of which went to the Crown and the rest to the British officers and crews, the army getting no share whatever.

The news that Louisbourg was taken reached Boston at one o'clock in the morning of the third of July by a vessel sent express. A din of bells and cannon proclaimed it to the slumbering townsmen, and before the sun rose the streets were filled with shouting crowds. At night every window shone with lamps and the town was ablaze with fireworks and bonfires. The next Thursday was appointed a day of general thanksgiving for a victory believed to be the direct work of Providence. New York and Philadelphia also hailed the great news with illuminations, ringing of bells and firing of cannon.

In England the tidings were received with astonishment and a joy that was dashed with reflections on the strength and mettle of colonists supposed already to aspire to independence. Pepperrell was made a baronet and Warren an admiral. The merchant soldier was commissioned colonel in the British Army and a regiment given him, while a similar recognition was granted to the lawyer Shirley.

CHAPTER 7

Fort Massachusetts

THE SETTLEMENTS OF MASSACHUSETTS HAD PUSHED
westward by 1745 and begun to invade the beautiful region of
mountains and valleys that now forms Berkshire. Villages, or rudi-
ments of villages, had grown up on the Housatonic and an establishment had been attempted at Pontoosuc, now Pittsfield, on the extreme
western limits of the province.

The position of these new settlements was critical, for the enemy
could reach them with little difficulty by way of Lake Champlain and
Wood Creek. The Massachusetts government was not unmindful of
them, and when war again broke out, three wooden forts were built
for their protection, forming a line of defense westward from North-
field on the northern frontier of the province. One of these forts was
in the present town of Heath, and was called Fort Shirley; another,
named Fort Pelham, was in the present town of Rowe; while the
third, Fort Massachusetts, was farther westward in what is now the
town of Adams, then known as East Hoosac. Two hundred men from
the militia were taken into pay to hold these posts and patrol the
intervening forests.

These forts were pitifully exposed to French and Indian attack, like
so much of New England, and in 1746 Governor Shirley had devised
a plan for capturing Fort Frédéric, or Crown Point, built by the
French at the narrows of Lake Champlain, and commanding ready
access for war parties to New York and New England.

The approach of a fleet commanded by the Duc D'Anville had de-

459

feated that plan, but rumors of it had reached Canada and excited great alarm. Large bodies of men were ordered to Lake Champlain to protect the threatened fort. The two brothers De Muy were already on the lake with a numerous party of Canadians and Indians, both Christian and heathen, and Rigaud de Vaudreuil, town major of Three Rivers, was ordered to follow with a still larger force, repel any English attack, or, if none should be made, take the offensive and strike a blow at the English frontier. [French writers always call him Rigaud, to distinguish him from his brother, Pierre Rigaud de Vaudreuil-Cavagnal, afterwards governor of Canada, who is usually mentioned as Vaudreuil.]

On the third of August, Rigaud left Montreal with a fleet of canoes carrying what he calls his army, and on the twelfth he encamped on the east side of the lake, at the mouth of Otter Creek. There was rain, thunder and a violent wind all night, but the storm ceased at daybreak, and embarking again, they soon saw the octagonal stone tower of Fort Frédéric.

The party set up their tents and wigwams near the fort, and on the morning of the sixteenth the elder De Muy arrived with a reinforcement of sixty Frenchmen and a band of Indians. They had just returned from an incursion towards Albany and reported that all was quiet in those parts, and that Fort Frédéric was in no danger.

Now, to their great satisfaction, Rigaud and his band saw themselves free to take the offensive. The question was, where to strike. The Indians held council after council, made speech after speech, and agreed on nothing. Rigaud gave them a wampum belt and told them that he meant to attack Corlaer, that is, Schenectady, at which they seemed well pleased and sang war songs all night.

In the morning they changed their minds and begged him to call the whole army to a council for debating the question. It appeared that some of them, especially the Iroquois converts of Caughnawaga, disapproved of attacking Schenectady because some of their Mohawk relatives were always making visits there and might be inadvertently killed by the wild western Indians of Rigaud's party. Now all was doubt again, for as Indians are as unstable as water, it was no easy task to hold them to any plan of action.

The Abenakis proposed a solution of the difficulty. They knew the New England border well, for many of them had lived upon it before the war, on terms of friendly intercourse with the settlers. They now drew upon the floor of the council room a rough map of the country, on which was seen a certain river, and on its upper waters a fort which they recommended as a proper object of attack. The river was that eastern tributary of the Hudson which the French called the Kaské-kouké, the Dutch the Schaticook, and the English the Hoosac. The fort was Fort Massachusetts, the most westerly of the three posts lately built to guard the frontier. "My father," said the Abenaki spokesman to Rigaud, "it will be easy to take this fort and make great havoc on the lands of the English. Deign to listen to your children and follow our advice."

Seeing his Indians well pleased with the proposal to march for the Hoosac, Rigaud gladly accepted it, on which whoops, yelps and war songs filled the air. Hardly, however, was the party on its way when the Indians changed their minds again and wanted to attack Saratoga, but Rigaud told them that they had made their choice and must abide by it, to which they assented and gave him no further trouble.

On the twentieth of August they all embarked and paddled southward, passed the lonely promontory where Fort Ticonderoga was afterwards built, and held their course till the lake dwindled to a mere canal creeping through the weedy marsh then called the Drowned Lands.

Rigaud stopped at a place known as East Bay, at the mouth of a stream that joins Wood Creek, just north of the present town of Whitehall. Here he left the younger De Muy, with thirty men, to guard the canoes. The rest of the party, guided by a brother of the slain Cadenaret, filed southward on foot along the base of Skene Mountain that overlooks Whitehall. They counted about seven hundred men, of whom five hundred were French and a little above two hundred were Indians.

After a march of four days they encamped on the twenty-sixth by a stream which ran into the Hudson and was no doubt the Batten Kill, known to the French as *la rivière de Saratogue*. Being nearly opposite Saratoga, where there was then a garrison, they changed their course on the twenty-seventh from south to southeast, the better to

461

avoid scouting parties which might discover their trail and defeat their plan of surprise.

Early on the next day they reached the Hoosac, far above its mouth, and now their march was easier, "for," says Rigaud, "we got out of the woods and followed a large road that led up the river." In fact, there seem to have been two roads, one on each side of the Hoosac, for the French were formed into two brigades, one of which, under the Sieur de la Valterie, filed along the right bank of the stream, and the other, under the Sieur de Sabrevois, along the left, while the Indians marched on the front, flanks and rear. They passed deserted houses and farms belonging to Dutch settlers from the Hudson, for the Hoosac in this part of its course was in the province of New York. They did not stop to burn barns and houses, but they killed poultry, hogs, a cow and a horse to supply themselves with meat.

Before night they had passed the New York line and they made their camp in or near the valley where Williamstown and Williams College now stand. Here they were joined by the Sieurs Beaubassin and La Force, who had gone forward with eight Indians to reconnoiter. Beaubassin had watched Fort Massachusetts from a distance and had seen a man go up into the watchtower but could discover no other sign of alarm. Apparently the fugitive Dutch farmers had not taken pains to warn the English garrison of the coming danger, for there was a coolness between the neighbors.

The chaplain said mass next morning and the party marched in a brisk rain up the Williamstown Valley, till after advancing about ten miles they encamped again. Fort Massachusetts was only three or four miles distant. Rigaud held a talk with the Abenaki chiefs who had acted as guides, and it was agreed that the party should stop in the woods near the fort, make scaling ladders, battering rams to burst the gates, and other things needful for a grand assault, to take place before daylight. But their plan failed through the impetuosity of the young Indians and Canadians, who were so excited at the first glimpse of the watchtower of the fort that they dashed forward, as Rigaud says, "like lions."

From this one might fairly expect to see the fort assaulted at once, but by the maxims of forest war this would have been reprehensible rashness and nothing of the kind was attempted. The assailants spread to right and left, squatted behind stumps and opened a distant and harmless fire, accompanied with unearthly yells and howlings.

The garrison of the fort, when complete, consisted of fifty-one men, under Captain Ephraim Williams, who has left his name to Williamstown and Williams College, of the latter of which he was the founder. He was born at Newton, near Boston; was a man vigorous in body and mind; better acquainted with the world than most of his countrymen, having followed the seas in his youth and visited England, Spain and Holland; frank and agreeable in manners, well fitted for such a command and respected and loved by his men.

When a recent proposed invasion of Canada was preparing, he and some of his men went to take part in it and had not yet returned. The fort was left in charge of a sergeant, John Hawks, of Deerfield, with men too few for the extent of the works and a supply of ammunition nearly exhausted. Canada being then put on the defensive, the frontier forts were thought safe for a time.

On the Saturday before Rigaud's arrival Hawks had sent Thomas Williams, the surgeon, brother of the absent captain, to Deerfield with a detachment of fourteen men to get a supply of powder and lead. This detachment reduced the entire force, including Hawks himself and Norton, the chaplain, to twenty-two men, half of whom were disabled with dysentery, from which few of the rest were wholly free. There were also in the fort three women and five children.

Sergeant Hawks, the provisional commander, was according to tradition a tall man with sunburnt features, erect, spare, very sinewy and strong and of a bold and resolute temper. He had need to be so. As there was nothing but a log fence between him and his enemy, it was clear that they could hew or burn a way through it, or climb over it with no surprising effort of valor.

Rigaud had planned a general assault under cover of night, but had been thwarted by the precipitancy of the young Indians and Canadians. These now showed no inclination to depart from the cautious maxims of forest warfare. They made a terrific noise, but when they came within gunshot of the fort, it was by darting from stump to stump with a quick zigzag movement that made them more difficult to hit than birds on the wing. The best moment for a shot was when they reached a stump and stopped for an instant to duck and hide behind

it. By seizing this fleeting opportunity, Hawks himself put a bullet
into the breast of an Abenaki chief from St. Francis, "which ended his
days," says the chaplain.

In view of the nimbleness of the assailants, a charge of buckshot
was found more to the purpose than a bullet. Besides the slain
Abenaki, Rigaud reports sixteen Indians and Frenchmen wounded,
which under the circumstances was good execution for ten farmers
and a minister, for Chaplain Norton loaded and fired with the rest.
Rigaud himself was one of the wounded, having been hit in the arm
and sent to the rear as he stood giving orders on the rocky hill about
forty rods from the fort.

But the supply of ammunition in the fort had sunk so low that
Hawks was forced to give the discouraging order not to fire except
when necessary to keep the enemy in check, or when the chance of
hitting him should be unusually good. Such of the sick men as were
strong enough aided the defense by casting bullets and buckshot.

The outrageous noise lasted till towards nine in the evening, when
the assailants greeted the fort with a general war whoop and repeated
it three or four times. Then a line of sentinels was placed around it
to prevent messengers from carrying the alarm to Deerfield or Albany.

The evening was dark and cloudy. The lights of a camp could be
seen by the river towards the southeast, and those of another near the
swamp towards the west. There was a sound of axes, as if the enemy
were making scaling ladders for a night assault, but it was found that
they were cutting fagots to burn the wall. Hawks ordered every tub
and bucket to be filled with water, in preparation for the crisis.

Rigaud spent the night in preparing for a decisive attack, "being resolved to open trenches two hours before sunrise and push them to the
foot of the palisade, so as to place fagots against it, set them on fire,
and deliver the fort a prey to the fury of the flames." It began to rain
and he determined to wait till morning. That the commander of seven
hundred French and Indians should resort to such elaborate devices to
subdue a sergeant, seven militiamen and a minister—for this was now
the effective strength of the besieged—was no small compliment to the
spirit of the defense.

The firing was renewed in the morning, but there was no attempt
to open trenches by daylight. Two men were sent up into the watch-

tower and about eleven o'clock one of them, Thomas Knowlton, was shot through the head. The number of effectives was thus reduced to eight, including the chaplain.

Norton, the chaplain, says that about noon the French "desired to parley," and that "we agreed to it." He says further that the sergeant, with himself and one or two others, met Rigaud outside the gate, and that the French commander promised "good quarter" to the besieged if they would surrender, with the alternative of an assault if they would not. The sergeant promised an answer within two hours, and going back to the fort with his companions, examined their means of defense. He found that they had left but three or four pounds of gunpowder and about as much lead. Hawks called a council of his effective men. Norton prayed for divine aid and guidance and then they fell to considering the situation.

"Had we all been in health, or had there been only those eight of us that were in health, I believe every man would willingly have stood it out to the last. For my part, I should," writes the manful chaplain. But besides the sick and wounded, there were three women and five children, who, if the fort were taken by assault, would no doubt be butchered by the Indians, but who might be saved by a capitulation.

Hawks resolved to make the best terms he could. He had defended his post against prodigious odds for twenty-eight hours. Rigaud promised that all in the fort should be treated with humanity as prisoners of war, and exchanged at the first opportunity. He also promised that none of them should be given to the Indians, though he had lately assured his savage allies that they should have their share of the prisoners.

At three o'clock the principal French officers were admitted into the fort and the French flag was raised over it. The Indians and Canadians were excluded, on which some of the Indians pulled out several of the stones that formed the foundation of the wall, crawled through, opened the gates and let in the whole crew. They raised a yell when they saw the blood of Thomas Knowlton trickling from the watchtower where he had been shot, then rushed up to where the corpse lay, brought it down, scalped it and cut off the head and arms. The fort was then plundered, set on fire and burned to the ground.

On the return home, writes Rigaud: "I divided my army between the two sides of the Kaskékouké and ordered them to do what I had not permitted to be done before we reached Fort Massachusetts. Every house was set on fire, and numbers of domestic animals of all sorts were killed. French and Indians vied with each other in pillage, and I made them enter the [valleys of all the] little streams that flow into the Kaskékouké and lay waste everything there. . . . Wherever we went we made the same havoc, laid waste both sides of the river, through twelve leagues of fertile country, burned houses, barns, stables and even a meetinghouse—in all, above two hundred establishments—killed all the cattle and ruined all the crops. Such, Monseigneur, was the damage I did our enemies during the eight or nine days I was in their country." As the Dutch settlers had escaped, there was no resistance.

In due time the prisoners reached Montreal, whence they were sent to Quebec, and in the course of the next year those who remained alive were exchanged and returned to New England. Fort Massachusetts was soon rebuilt by the province and held its own thenceforth till the war was over. Sergeant Hawks became a lieutenant colonel and took a creditable part in the last French war.

For two years after the incursion of Rigaud the New England borders were scourged with partisan warfare, bloody, monotonous and futile, with no event that needs recording and no result beyond a momentary check to the progress of settlement. At length, in July 1748, news came that the chief contending powers had come to terms of agreement, and in the next October the Peace of Aix-la-Chapelle was signed.

Both nations were tired of the weary and barren conflict, with its enormous cost and its vast entail of debt. It was agreed that all conquests should be mutually restored. The chief conquest of England was Louisbourg, with the island of Cape Breton, won for her by the farmers and fishermen of New England. When the preliminaries of peace were under discussion, Louis XV had demanded the restitution of the lost fortress and George II is said to have replied that it was not his to give, having been captured by the people of Boston. But his sense of justice was forced to yield to diplomatic necessity, for Louisbourg was the indispensable price of peace. To the indignation of the northern provinces, it was restored to its former owners.

"The British ministers," says Smollett, "gave up the important island of Cape Breton in exchange for a petty factory in the East Indies" (Madras), and the King deigned to send two English noblemen to the French court as security for the bargain.

Peace returned to the tormented borders. The settlements advanced again and the colonists found a short breathing space against the great conclusive struggle of the Seven Years' War.

PART SIX

Montcalm and Wolfe

CHAPTER 1

On the Eve of War

I T IS THE NATURE OF GREAT EVENTS TO OBSCURE THE great events that came before them. The Seven Years' War in Europe is seen but dimly through revolutionary convulsions and Napoleonic tempests, and the same contest in America is half lost to sight behind the storm cloud of the War of Independence. Few even now see the momentous issues involved in it, or the greatness of the danger that it averted. The strife that armed all the civilized world began here.

"Such was the complication of political interests," says Voltaire, "that a cannon shot fired in America could give the signal that set Europe in a blaze." Not quite. It was not a cannon shot but a volley from the hunting pieces of a few backwoodsmen, commanded by a Virginian youth, George Washington.

To us of this day, the result of the American part of the war seems a foregone conclusion. It was far from being so, and very far from being so regarded by our forefathers. The numerical superiority of the British colonies was offset by organic weaknesses fatal to vigorous and united action. Nor at the outset did they or the mother country aim at conquering Canada, but only at pushing back her boundaries.

Canada—using the name in its restricted sense—was a position of great strength, and even when her dependencies were overcome, she could hold her own against forces far superior. Armies could reach her only by three routes: the Lower St. Lawrence on the east, the Upper St. Lawrence on the west, and Lake Champlain on the south. The first access was guarded by a fortress almost impregnable by nature, and the second by a long chain of dangerous rapids, while the third offered a series of points easy to defend. During this same war, Frederick of Prussia held his ground triumphantly against greater odds, though his kingdom was open on all sides to attack.

It was the fatuity of Louis XV and his Pompadour that made the conquest of Canada possible. Had they not broken the traditional policy of France, allied themselves to Austria, her ancient enemy, and plunged needlessly into the European war, the whole force of the kingdom would have been turned from the first to the humbling of England and the defense of the French colonies. The French soldiers left dead on inglorious Continental battlefields could have saved Canada and perhaps made good her claim to the vast territories of the West.

But there were other contingencies. The possession of Canada was a question of diplomacy as well as of war. If England conquered her, she might restore her, as she had lately restored Cape Breton. She had an interest in keeping France alive on the American continent. More than one clear eye saw, at the middle of the last century, that the subjection of Canada would lead to a revolt of the British colonies. So long as an active and enterprising enemy threatened their borders, they could not break with the mother country because they needed her help. And if the arms of France had prospered in the other hemisphere; if she had gained in Europe or Asia territories with which to buy back what she had lost in America, then in all likelihood Canada would have passed again into her hands.

The most momentous and far-reaching question ever brought to issue on this continent was: Shall France remain here, or shall she not? If, by diplomacy or war, she had preserved only half, or less than half, of her American possessions, then a barrier would have been set to the spread of the English-speaking races; there would have been no Revolutionary War; and for a long time, at least, no independence. It was not a question of scanty populations strung along the banks of the St. Lawrence. It was—or under a government of any worth it would have been—a question of the armies and generals of France. America owes much to the imbecility of Louis XV and the ambitious vanity and personal dislikes of his mistress.

The Seven Years' War made England what she became. It crippled the commerce of her rival, ruined France in two continents and blighted her as a colonial power. It gave England the control of the seas and the mastery of North America and India, made her the first of commercial nations and prepared that vast colonial system that planted new Englands in every quarter of the globe. And while it made England a great power, it supplied to the United States the indis-pensable condition of their greatness, if not of their national existence.

When the peace of Aix-la-Chapelle was signed, the Marquis de la Galissonière ruled over Canada. Like all the later Canadian governors, he was a naval officer, and a few years after, he made himself famous by a victory near Minorca over the English admiral Byng—an achieve-ment now remembered chiefly by the fate of the defeated commander, judicially murdered as the scapegoat of an imbecile ministry. La Galissonière was a humpback, but his deformed person was animated by a bold spirit and a strong and penetrating intellect. He was the chief representative of the American policy of France.

He felt that, cost what it might, she must hold fast to Canada and link her to Louisiana by chains of forts strong enough to hold back the British colonies and cramp their growth by confinement within narrow limits, while French settlers, sent from the mother country, should spread and multiply in the broad valleys of the interior. It is true, he said, that Canada and her dependencies have always been a burden, but they are necessary as a barrier against English ambition, and to abandon them is to abandon ourselves, for if we suffer our enemies to become masters in America, their trade and naval power will grow to vast proportions and they will draw from their colonies a wealth that will make them preponderant in Europe.

The treaty had done nothing to settle the vexed question of bound-aries between France and her rival. It had only staved off the in-evitable conflict. Meanwhile the English traders were crossing the mountains from Pennsylvania and Virginia, poaching on the domain which France claimed as hers, ruining the French fur trade, seducing the Indian allies of Canada and stirring them up against her. Worse still, English land speculators were beginning to follow. Something must be done, and that promptly, to drive back the intruders and vindicate French rights in the valley of the Ohio.

473

French America had two heads: one among the snows of Canada, and one among the canebrake of Louisiana; one communicating with the world through the Gulf of St. Lawrence, and the other through the Gulf of Mexico. These vital points were feebly connected by a chain of military posts—slender and often interrupted—circling through the wilderness nearly three thousand miles. Midway between Canada and Louisiana lay the valley of the Ohio. If the English should seize it, they would sever the chain of posts and cut French America asunder. If the French held it and intrenched themselves well along its eastern limits, they would shut their rivals between the Alleghenies and the sea, control all the tribes of the West, and turn them in case of war against the English borders—a frightful and insupportable scourge.

The Indian population of the Ohio and its northern tributaries was relatively considerable. The upper or eastern half of the valley was occupied by mingled hordes of Delawares, Shawanoes, Wyandots and Iroquois, or Indians of the Five Nations, who had migrated there from their ancestral abodes within the present limits of the state of New York, and who were called Mingoes by the English traders. Along with them were a few wandering Abenakis, Nipissings and Ottawas. Farther west, on the waters of the Miami, the Wabash and other neighboring streams, was the seat of a confederacy formed of the various bands of the Miamis and their kindred or affiliated tribes. Still farther west, towards the Mississippi, were the remnants of the Illinois.

France had done little to make good her claims to this grand domain. East of the Miami she had no military post whatever. Westward, on the Maumee, there was a small wooden fort, another on the St. Joseph, and two on the Wabash. On the meadows of the Mississippi, in the Illinois country, stood Fort Chartres, a much stronger work and one of the chief links of the chain that connected Quebec with New Orleans. Its four stone bastions were impregnable to musketry, and here in the depths of the wilderness there was no fear that cannon would be brought against it. It was the center and citadel of a curious little forest settlement, the only vestige of civilization through all this region.

At Kaskaskia, extended along the borders of the stream, were seventy or eighty French houses; thirty or forty at Cahokia, opposite the site of St. Louis; and a few more at the intervening hamlets of St.

Philippe and Prairie à la Roche—a picturesque but thriftless population, mixed with Indians, totally ignorant, busied partly with the fur
trade and partly with the raising of corn for the market of New Orleans. They communicated with it by means of a sort of row galley of
eighteen or twenty oars, which made the voyage twice a year and
usually spent ten weeks on the return up the river.

The Pope and the Bourbons had claimed this wilderness for seventy
years and had done scarcely more for it than the Indians, its natural
owners. Of the western tribes, even of those living at the French posts,
the Hurons or Wyandots alone were Christian. The devoted zeal of
the early missionaries and the politic efforts of their successors had
failed alike. The savages of the Ohio and the Mississippi, instead of
being tied to France by the mild bonds of the faith, were now in a
state which the French called defection or revolt: that is, they received
and welcomed the English traders.

These traders came in part from Virginia, but chiefly from Pennsylvania. Dinwiddie, governor of Virginia, says of them: "They appear to
me to be in general a set of abandoned wretches," and Hamilton, governor of Pennsylvania, replies: "I concur with you in opinion that they
are a very licentious people." Indian traders, of whatever nation, were
rarely models of virtue, and these without doubt were rough and lawless men, with abundant blackguardism and few scruples.

Not all of them, however, are to be thus qualified. Some were of a
better stamp, among whom were Christopher Gist, William Trent and
George Croghan. These and other chief traders hired men on the
frontiers, crossed the Alleghenies with goods packed on the backs of
horses, descended into the valley of the Ohio and journeyed from
stream to stream and village to village along the Indian trails, with
which all this wilderness was seamed and which the traders widened to
make them practicable. More rarely, they carried their goods on horses
to the upper waters of the Ohio and embarked them in large wooden
canoes, in which they descended the main river and ascended such
of its numerous tributaries as were navigable. They were bold and
enterprising and French writers, with alarm and indignation, declare
that some of them had crossed the Mississippi and traded with the
distant Osages. It is said that about three hundred of them came over
the mountains every year.

All looked well for the English in the West, but under this fair outside lurked hidden danger. The Miamis were hearty in the English cause, and so perhaps were the Shawanoes, but the Delawares had not forgotten the wrongs that drove them from their old abodes east of the Alleghenies, while the Mingoes, or emigrant Iroquois, like their brethren of New York, felt the influence of Joncaire and other French agents, who spared no efforts to seduce them.

Still more baneful to British interests were the apathy and dissensions of the British colonies themselves. The Ohio Company had built a trading house at Will's Creek, a branch of the Potomac, to which the Indians resorted in great numbers, whereupon the jealous traders of Pennsylvania told them that the Virginians meant to steal away their lands. This confirmed what they had been taught by the French emissaries, whose intrigues it powerfully aided. The governors of New York, Pennsylvania and Virginia saw the importance of Indian alliances and felt their own responsibility in regard to them, but they could do nothing without their assemblies. Those of New York and Pennsylvania were composed largely of tradesmen and farmers, absorbed in local interests and possessed by two motives—the saving of the people's money, and opposition to the governor, who stood for the royal prerogative.

A large part of the valley of the Ohio, including the site of the proposed establishment, was claimed by both Pennsylvania and Virginia and each feared that whatever money it might spend there would turn to the profit of the other. This was not the only evil that sprang from uncertain ownership. "Till the line is run between the two provinces," says Dinwiddie, governor of Virginia, "I cannot appoint magistrates to keep the traders in good order." Hence they did what they pleased, and often gave umbrage to the Indians.

Clinton, of New York, appealed to his Assembly for means to assist Pennsylvania in "securing the fidelity of the Indians on the Ohio" and the Assembly refused. "We will take care of our Indians, they may take care of theirs." Such was the spirit of their answer. He wrote to the various provinces, inviting them to send commissioners to meet the tribes at Albany, "in order to defeat the designs and intrigues of the French." All turned a deaf ear except Massachusetts, Connecticut and South Carolina, who sent the commissioners but supplied them very meagerly with the indispensable presents. Clinton says further: "The Assembly of this province have not given one farthing for Indian affairs, nor for a year past have they provided for the subsistence of the garrison at Oswego, which is the key for the commerce between the colonies and the inland nations of Indians."

In the heterogeneous structure of the British colonies, their clashing interests, their internal disputes and the misplaced economy of penny-wise and shortsighted assemblymen, lay the hope of France. The rulers of Canada knew the vast numerical preponderance of their rivals, but with their centralized organization they felt themselves more than a match for any one English colony alone.

They hoped to wage war under the guise of peace, and to deal with the enemy in detail; and they at length perceived that the fork of the Ohio, so strangely neglected by the English, formed together with Niagara the key of the Great West. Could France hold these two controlling passes firmly, she might almost boast herself mistress of the continent.

~~~~~~

CHAPTER 2

Washington and the Conflict for the West

THE IROQUOIS, OR FIVE NATIONS, SOMETIMES
called Six Nations after the Tuscarora joined them, had been a
power of high importance in American international politics. In a certain sense they may be said to have held the balance between their
French and English neighbors, but their relative influence had of late
declined. So many of them had emigrated and joined the tribes of the
Ohio that the center of Indian population had passed to that region.
Nevertheless, the Five Nations were still strong enough in their ancient
abodes to make their alliance an object of the utmost consequence to
both the European rivals. At the western end of their "Long House,"
or belt of confederated villages, Joncaire intrigued to gain them for
France, while in the east he was counteracted by a young colonel of
militia, William Johnson, who lived on the Mohawk and was already
well skilled in managing Indians.

In former times the French had hoped to win over the Five Nations
in a body by wholesale conversion to the Faith, but the attempt had
failed. They had, however, made within their own limits an asylum for
such converts as they could gain, whom they collected together at
Caughnawaga, near Montreal, to the number of about three hundred
warriors. These could not be trusted to fight their kinsmen but willingly
made forays against the English borders. Caughnawaga, like various
other Canadian missions, was divided between the Church, the army
and the fur trade. It had a chapel, fortifications and storehouses; two
Jesuits, an officer and three chief traders. Of these last, two were

maiden ladies, the Demoiselles Desauniers; and of the Jesuits, their friend Father Tournois was their partner in business. They carried on by means of the mission Indians, and in collusion with influential persons in the colony, a trade with the Dutch at Albany, illegal but very profitable. Besides this Iroquois mission, which was chiefly composed of Mohawks and Oneidas, another was now begun farther westward to win over the Onondagas, Cayugas and Senecas. This was the establishment of Father Piquet.

Piquet was a man in the prime of life, of an alert, vivacious countenance, by no means unprepossessing; an enthusiastic schemer with great executive talents; ardent, energetic, vain, self-confident and boastful. The enterprise seems to have been of his own devising, but it found warm approval from the government.

La Présentation, as he called the new mission, stood on the bank of the river Oswegatchie, where it enters the St. Lawrence. Here the rapids ceased and navigation was free to Lake Ontario. The place commanded the main river and could bar the way to hostile war parties or contraband traders. Rich meadows, forests and abundance of fish and game made it attractive to Indians and the Oswegatchie gave access to the Iroquois towns. Piquet had chosen his site with great skill.

His activity was admirable. His first stockade was burned by Indian incendiaries, but it rose quickly from its ashes and within a year or two the mission of La Présentation had a fort of palisades flanked with blockhouses, a chapel, a storehouse, a barn, a stable, ovens, a sawmill, broad fields of corn and beans, and three villages of Iroquois containing, in all, forty-nine bark lodges, each holding three or four families, more or less converted to the Faith, and as time went on this number increased. The governor had sent a squad of soldiers to man the fort and five small cannon to mount upon it. The place was as safe for the new proselytes as it was convenient and agreeable. The Pennsylvanian interpreter, Conrad Weiser, was told at Onondaga, the Iroquois capital, that Piquet had made a hundred converts from that place alone, and that, "having clothed them all in very fine clothes, laced with silver and gold, he took them down and presented them to the French governor at Montreal, who received them very kindly and made them large presents."

Such were some of the temporal attractions of La Présentation. The nature of the spiritual instruction bestowed by Piquet and his fellow priests may be partly inferred from the words of a proselyte warrior, who declared with enthusiasm that he had learned from the Sulpitian missionary that the King of France was the eldest son of the wife of Jesus Christ. This, of course, he took in a literal sense, the mystic idea of the Church as the spouse of Christ being beyond his savage comprehension. The effect was to stimulate his devotion to the Great Onontio beyond the sea and to the lesser Onontio who represented him as governor of Canada.

In the course of a long journey in 1751 to muster recruits for his mission, Piquet made the entire circuit of Lake Ontario. Beyond lay four other inland oceans, to which Fort Niagara was the key. As that all-essential post controlled the passage from Ontario to Erie, so did Fort Detroit control that from Erie to Huron, and Fort Michilimackinac that from Huron to Michigan, while Fort Ste. Marie at the outlet of Lake Superior had lately received a garrison and changed from a mission and trading station to a post of war. This immense extent of inland navigation was safe in the hands of France as long as she held Niagara. If Niagara were lost, not only the lakes but also the valley of the Ohio would be lost with it.

Next in importance was Detroit. This was not a military post alone but also a settlement, and except the hamlets about Fort Chartres, the only settlement that France owned in all the West. There were, it is true, only a few families there, but the hope of growth seemed good, for to those who liked a wilderness home, no spot in America had more attraction. The white flag of the Bourbons floated over the compact little palisaded town, with its population of soldiers and fur traders, and from the blockhouses which served as bastions, one saw on either hand the small solid dwellings of the *habitants,* ranged at intervals along the margin of the water, while at a little distance three Indian villages—Ottawa, Potawatomi and Wyandot—curled their wigwam smoke into the pure summer air.

By 1750, La Galissonière no longer governed Canada. He had been honorably recalled and the Marquis de la Jonquière sent in his stead. La Jonquière, like his predecessor, was a naval officer of high repute. He was tall and imposing in person and of undoubted capacity and courage, but old and, according to his enemies, very avaricious. The colonial minister gave him special instructions regarding that thorn in the side of Canada, Oswego. To attack it openly would be indiscreet, as the two nations were at peace, but there was a way of dealing with it less hazardous, if not more lawful. This was to attack it vicariously by means of the Iroquois.

La Jonquière immediately involved himself in frequent disputes with the English, but these were not his only source of trouble. His superiors at Versailles would not adopt his views and looked on him with distrust. He advised the building of forts near Lake Erie and his advice was rejected. "Niagara and Detroit," he was told, "will secure forever our communications with Louisiana." "His Majesty," again wrote the colonial minister, "thought that expenses would diminish after the peace, but on the contrary, they have increased. There must be great abuses. You and the intendant must look to it."

Great abuses there were, and of the money sent to Canada for the service of the King, the larger part found its way into the pockets of peculators. The colony was eaten to the heart with official corruption and the center of it was François Bigot, the intendant. The minister directed La Jonquière's attention to certain malpractices which had been reported to him, and the old man, deeply touched, replied: "I have reached the age of sixty-six years and there is not a drop of blood in my veins that does not thrill for the service of my King. I will not conceal from you that the slightest suspicion on your part against me would cut the thread of my days."

Perplexities increased; affairs in the West grew worse and worse. La Jonquière wrote: "I cannot express how much this business troubles me; it robs me of sleep; it makes me ill." Another letter of rebuke presently came from Versailles. "Last year you wrote that you would soon drive the English from the Ohio, but private letters say that you have done nothing. This is deplorable. If not expelled, they will seem to acquire a right against us. Send force enough at once to drive them off, and cure them of all wish to return."

La Jonquière answered with bitter complaints and begged to be recalled. His health, already shattered, was ruined by fatigue and vexation and he took to his bed. Before spring he was near his end. It is said that, though very rich, his habits of thrift so possessed his

481

last hours that, seeing wax candles burning in his chamber, he ordered others of tallow to be brought instead as being good enough to die by. Thus frugally lighted on its way, his spirit fled. The Baron de Longueuil took his place till a new governor should arrive.

Sinister tidings came thick from the West. Raymond, commandant at the French fort on the Maumee, close to the center of intrigue, wrote: "My people are leaving me for Detroit. Nobody wants to stay here and have his throat cut. All the tribes who go to the English at Pickawillany come back loaded with gifts. I am too weak to meet the danger. Instead of twenty men, I need five hundred. . . . We have made peace with the English, yet they try continually to make war on us by means of the Indians; they intend to be masters of all this upper country. The tribes here are leaguing together to kill all the French, that they may have nobody on their lands but their English brothers. This I am told by Coldfoot, a great Miami chief, whom I think an honest man, if there is any such thing among Indians. . . . If the English stay in this country we are lost. We must attack and drive them out." And he tells of war belts sent from tribe to tribe, and rumors of plots and conspiracies far and near.

Without doubt, the English traders spared no pains to gain over the Indians by fair means or foul, sold them goods at low rates, made ample gifts and gave gunpowder for the asking. Saint-Ange, who commanded at Vincennes, wrote that a storm would soon burst on the heads of the French. Joncaire reported that all the Ohio Indians sided with the English. Longueuil informed the minister that the Miamis had scalped two soldiers; that the Piankishaws had killed seven Frenchmen; and that a squaw who had lived with one of the slain declared that the tribes of the Wabash and Illinois were leaguing with the Osages for a combined insurrection. Every letter brought news of murder. Smallpox had broken out at Detroit.

"It is to be wished," says Longueuil, "that it would spread among our rebels; it would be fully as good as an army. . . . We are menaced with a general outbreak, and even Toronto is in danger. . . . Before long the English on the Miami will gain over all the surrounding tribes, get possession of Fort Chartres, and cut our communications with Louisiana."

The moving spirit of disaffection was the chief called Old Britain, or the Demoiselle, and its focus was his town of Pickawillany, on the Miami. At this place it is said that English traders sometimes mustered to the number of fifty or more. "It is they," wrote Longueuil, "who are the instigators of revolt and the source of all our woes." Whereupon the colonial minister reiterated his instructions to drive them off and plunder them, which he thought would "effectually disgust them" and bring all trouble to an end.

La Jonquière's remedy had been more heroic, for he had ordered Céloron de Bienville, a valiant captain, to attack the English and their red allies alike and he charged that officer with arrogance and disobedience because he had not done so. It is not certain that obedience was easy, for though a strong body of militia was sent up to Detroit to aid the stroke, besides the garrison of regulars, the Indians of that post, whose co-operation was thought necessary, proved halfhearted, intractable and even touched with disaffection.

Thus the enterprise languished till, in June of 1752, aid came from another quarter. Charles Langlade, a young French trader married to a squaw at Green Bay and strong in influence with the tribes of that region, came down the lakes from Michilimackinac with a fleet of canoes manned by two hundred and fifty Ottawa and Ojibwa warriors; stopped a while at Detroit; then embarked again, paddled up the Maumee to Raymond's fort at the portage and let his greased and painted rabble through the forest to attack the Demoiselle and his English friends.

They approached Pickawillany at about nine o'clock on the morning of the twenty-first. The scared squaws fled from the cornfields into the town, where the wigwams of the Indians clustered about the fortified warehouse of the traders. Of these there were at the time only eight in the place. Most of the Indians also were gone on their summer hunt, though the Demoiselle remained with a band of his tribesmen. Great was the screeching of war whoops and clatter of guns. Three of the traders were caught outside the fort. The remaining five closed the gate and stood on their defense. The fight was soon over. Fourteen Miamis were shot down, the Demoiselle among the rest. The five white men held out till the afternoon, when three of them surrendered and two made their escape. One of the English prisoners being wounded, the victors stabbed him to death. Seventy years of missionaries had not weaned them from cannibalism and they boiled and ate the Demoiselle.

The captive traders, plundered to the skin, were carried by Langlade to Duquesne, the new governor, who highly praised the bold leader of the enterprise and recommended him to the minister for such reward as befitted one of his station. "As he is not in the King's service and has married a squaw, I will ask for him only a pension of two hundred francs, which will flatter him infinitely."

The Marquis Duquesne, sprung from the race of the great naval commander of that name, had arrived towards midsummer and he began his rule by a general review of troops and militia. His lofty bearing offended the Canadians, but he compelled their respect and, according to a writer of the time, showed from the first that he was born to command. He presently took in hand an enterprise which his predecessor would probably have accomplished, had the home government encouraged him. Duquesne, profiting by the infatuated neglect of the British provincial assemblies, prepared to occupy the upper waters of the Ohio and secure the passes with forts and garrisons. Thus the Virginian and Pennsylvanian traders would be debarred all access to the West and the tribes of that region, bereft of English guns, knives, hatchets and blankets, English gifts and English cajoleries, would be thrown back to complete dependence on the French. The moral influence, too, of such a movement would be incalculable, for the Indian respects nothing so much as a display of vigor and daring, backed by force.

In short, the intended enterprise was a master stroke and laid the ax to the very root of disaffection. It is true that, under the treaty, commissioners had been long in session at Paris to settle the question of American boundaries, but there was no likelihood that they would come to an agreement, and if France would make good her western claims, it behooved her while there was yet time to prevent her rival from fastening a firm grasp on the countries in dispute.

Duquesne mustered the colony troops and ordered out the Canadians. With the former he was but half satisfied. With the latter he was delighted and he praises highly their obedience and alacrity. "I had not the least trouble in getting them to march. They came on the minute, bringing their own guns, though many people tried to excite them to revolt; for the whole colony opposes my operations."

The expedition set out early in the spring of 1753. The whole force was not much above a thousand men, increased by subsequent detachments to fifteen hundred, but to the Indians it seemed a mighty host and one of their orators declared that the lakes and rivers were covered with boats and soldiers from Montreal to Presqu'isle. Some Mohawk hunters by the St. Lawrence saw them as they passed and hastened home to tell the news to Johnson, whom they wakened at midnight "whooping and hollowing in a frightful manner," as Johnson described it to Clinton. Lieutenant Holland at Oswego saw a fleet of canoes upon the lake and was told by a roving Frenchman that they belonged to an army of six thousand men going to the Ohio "to cause all the English to quit those parts."

The main body of the expedition landed at Presqu'isle, on the southeastern shore of Lake Erie, where the city of Erie now stands. Duquesne calls the harbor "the finest in nature." Here they built a fort of squared chestnut logs, and when it was finished they cut a road of several leagues through the woods to Rivière aux Bœufs, now French Creek. At the farther end of this road they began another wooden fort and called it Fort Le Bœuf. From there, when the water was high, they could descend French Creek to the Allegheny and follow that stream to the main current of the Ohio.

It was heavy work to carry the cumbrous load of baggage across the portages. Much of it is said to have been superfluous, consisting of velvets, silks and other useless and costly articles, sold to the King at enormous prices as necessaries of the expedition. The weight of the task fell on the Canadians, who worked with cheerful hardihood and did their part to admiration.

Marin, commander of the expedition, a gruff, choleric old man of sixty-three, but full of force and capacity, spared himself so little that he was struck down with dysentery and, refusing to be sent home to Montreal, was before long in a dying state. His place was taken by Chevalier Péan, of whose private character there is little good to be said, but whose conduct as an officer was such that Duquesne calls him a prodigy of talents, resources and zeal.

485

The subalterns deserve no such praise. They disliked the service and made no secret of their discontent. Rumors of it filled Montreal and Duquesne wrote to Marin: "I am surprised that you have not told me of this change. Take note of the sullen and discouraged faces about you. This sort are worse than useless. Rid yourself of them at once; send them to Montreal, that I may make an example of them."

Péan wrote at the end of September that Marin was in extremity, and the governor, disturbed and alarmed, for he knew the value of the sturdy old officer, looked anxiously for a successor. He chose another veteran, Legardeur de Saint-Pierre, who had just returned from a journey of exploration towards the Rocky Mountains, and whom Duquesne now ordered to the Ohio.

Meanwhile the effects of the expedition had already justified it. At first the Indians of the Ohio had shown a bold front. One of them, a chief whom the English called the Half-King, came to Fort Le Bœuf and ordered the French to leave the country, but was received by Marin with such contemptuous haughtiness that he went home shedding tears of rage and mortification. The western tribes were daunted. The Miamis, but yesterday fast friends of the English, made humble submission to the French and offered them two English scalps to signalize their repentance, while the Sacs, Potawatomis and Ojibwas were loud in professions of devotion. Even the Iroquois, Delawares and Shawanoes on the Allegheny had come to the French camp and offered their help in carrying the baggage. It needed only perseverance and success in the enterprise to win over every tribe from the mountains to the Mississippi.

To accomplish this and to curb the English, Duquesne had planned a third fort, at the junction of French Creek with the Allegheny, or at some point lower down. Then, leaving the three posts well garrisoned, Péan was to descend the Ohio with the whole remaining force, impose terror on the wavering tribes and complete their conversion. Both plans were thwarted. The fort was not built, nor did Péan descend the Ohio. Fevers, lung diseases and scurvy made such deadly havoc among troops and Canadians that the dying Marin saw with bitterness that his work must be left half done. Three hundred of the best men were kept to garrison Forts Presqu'isle and Le Bœuf, and then as winter approached, the rest were sent back to Montreal.

When they arrived, the governor was shocked at their altered looks. "I reviewed them and could not help being touched by the pitiable state to which fatigues and exposures had reduced them. Past all doubt, if these emaciated figures had gone down the Ohio as intended, the river would have been strewn with corpses, and the evil-disposed savages would not have failed to attack the survivors, seeing that they were but specters."

Legardeur de Saint-Pierre arrived at the end of autumn and made his quarters at Fort Le Bœuf. The surrounding forests had dropped their leaves and in gray and patient desolation bided the coming winter. Chill rains drizzled over the gloomy "clearing" and drenched the palisades and log-built barracks, raw from the ax. Buried in the wilderness, the military exiles resigned themselves as they might to months of monotonous solitude.

Just after sunset on the eleventh of December, 1753, a tall youth came out of the forest on horseback, attended by a companion much older and rougher than himself, and followed by several Indians and four or five white men with pack horses. Officers from the fort went out to meet the strangers, and wading through mud and sodden snow, they entered at the gate. On the next day the young leader of the party, with the help of an interpreter, for he spoke no French, had an interview with the commandant and gave him a letter from Governor Dinwiddie. Saint-Pierre and the officer next in rank, who knew a little English, took it to another room to study it at their ease, and in it, all unconsciously, they read a name destined to stand one of the noblest in the annals of mankind, for it introduced Major George Washington, adjutant general of the Virginia militia.

Dinwiddie, jealously watchful of French aggression, had learned through traders and Indians that a strong detachment from Canada had entered the territories of the King of England and built forts on Lake Erie and on a branch of the Ohio. He wrote to challenge the invasion and summon the invaders to withdraw, and he could find none so fit to bear his message as a young man of twenty-one. It was this rough Scotchman who launched Washington on his illustrious career.

Washington set out for the trading station of the Ohio Company on Will's Creek, and from there at the middle of November, struck into the wilderness with Christopher Gist as a guide; Vanbraam, a Dutchman, as French interpreter; Davison, a trader, as Indian interpreter; and four woodsmen as servants.

Washington describes Legardeur de Saint-Pierre as "an elderly gentleman with much the air of a soldier." The letter sent him by Dinwiddie expressed astonishment that his troops should build forts upon lands "so notoriously known to be the property of the Crown of Great Britain."

"I must desire you," continued the letter, "to acquaint me by whose authority and instructions you have lately marched from Canada with an armed force and invaded the King of Great Britain's territories. It becomes my duty to require your peaceable departure, and that you would forbear prosecuting a purpose so interruptive of the harmony and good understanding which His Majesty is desirous to continue and cultivate with the Most Christian King. I persuade myself you will receive and entertain Major Washington with the candor and politeness natural to your nation; and it will give me the greatest satisfaction if you return him with an answer suitable to my wishes for a very long and lasting peace between us."

Saint-Pierre took three days to frame the answer. In it he said that he should send Dinwiddie's letter to the Marquis Duquesne and wait his orders, and that meanwhile he should remain at his post, according to the commands of his general. "I made it my particular care," so the letter closed, "to receive Mr. Washington with a distinction suitable to your dignity as well as his own quality and great merit."

No form of courtesy had, in fact, been wanting. "He appeared to be extremely complaisant," says Washington, "though he was exerting every artifice to set our Indians at variance with us. I saw that every stratagem was practiced to win the Half-King to their interest." Neither gifts nor brandy were spared and it was only by the utmost pains that Washington could prevent his red allies from staying at the fort, conquered by French blandishments.

On his return he found the horses so weak that, to arrive the sooner, he left them and their drivers in charge of Vanbraam and pushed forward on foot, accompanied by Gist alone. Each was wrapped to the throat in an Indian "matchcoat," with a gun in his hand and a pack at his back. Passing an old Indian hamlet called Murdering Town, they had an adventure which threatened to make good the name. A French

Indian, whom they met in the forest, fired at them, pretending that his gun had gone off by chance. They caught him and Gist would have killed him, but Washington interposed and they let him go. Then, to escape pursuit from his tribesmen, they walked all night and all the next day.

This brought them to the banks of the Allegheny. They hoped to have found it dead frozen, but it was all alive and turbulent, filled with ice sweeping down the current. They made a raft, shoved out into the stream, and were soon caught helplessly in the drifting ice. Washington, pushing hard with his setting pole, was jerked into the freezing river, but caught a log of the raft and dragged himself out. By no efforts could they reach the farther bank or regain that which they had left, but they were driven against an island, where they landed and left the raft to its fate.

The night was excessively cold and Gist's feet and hands were badly frostbitten. In the morning the ice had set and the river was a solid floor. They crossed it and succeeded in reaching the house of the trader Fraser, on the Monongahela. It was the middle of January when Washington arrived at Williamsburg and made his report to Dinwiddie.

Robert Dinwiddie was lieutenant governor of Virginia in place of the titular governor, Lord Albemarle, whose post was a sinecure. He had been clerk in a government office in the West Indies, then surveyor of customs in the "Old Dominion," a position in which he made himself cordially disliked, and when he rose to the governorship he carried his unpopularity with him. Yet Virginia and all the British colonies owed him much, for though past sixty, he was the most watchful sentinel against French aggression and its most strenuous opponent.

He deserves admiration for the energy with which he opposed the public enemy, under the most discouraging circumstances. He invited the Indians to meet him in council at Winchester, and as bait to attract them, coupled the message with a promise of gifts. He sent circulars from the King to the neighboring governors, calling for supplies, and wrote letter upon letter to rouse them to effort. He wrote also the more distant governors, Delancey of New York and Shirley of Massachusetts, begging them to make what he called a "faint" against Canada, to prevent the French from sending so large a force to the Ohio. It was to the nearer colonies, from New Jersey to South Carolina, that he looked for direct aid and their several governors were all more or less active to procure it. But as most of them had some standing dispute with their assemblies, they could get nothing except on terms with which they would not, and sometimes could not, comply.

As the lands invaded by the French belonged to one of the two rival claimants, Virginia and Pennsylvania, the other colonies had no mind to vote money to defend them. Pennsylvania herself refused to move. Hamilton, her governor, could do nothing against the placid obstinacy of the Quaker non-combatants and the stolid obstinacy of the German farmers who chiefly made up his Assembly. North Carolina alone answered the appeal and gave money enough to raise three or four hundred men. Two independent companies maintained by the King in New York, and one in South Carolina, had received orders from England to march to the scene of action, and in these, with the scanty levies of his own and the adjacent province, lay Dinwiddie's only hope. With men abundant and willing, there were no means to put them into the field, and no commander whom they would all obey.

From the brick house at Williamsburg pompously called the Governor's Palace, Dinwiddie dispatched letters, orders, couriers to hasten the tardy reinforcements of North Carolina and New York and push on the raw soldiers of the Old Dominion, who now numbered three hundred men. They were called the Virginia regiment and Joshua Fry, an English gentleman bred at Oxford, was made their colonel, with Washington as next in command.

Fry was at Alexandria with half the so-called regiment, trying to get it into marching order; Washington, with the other half, had pushed forward to the Ohio Company's storehouse at Will's Creek, which was to form a base of operations. His men were poor whites, brave but hard to discipline, without tents—ill-armed and ragged as Falstaff's recruits. Besides these, a band of backwoodsmen under Captain Trent had crossed the mountains in February to build a fort at the forks of the Ohio, where Pittsburgh now stands—a spot which Washington had examined when on his way to Fort Le Bœuf, and which he had reported as the best for the purpose. The hope was that Trent would fortify himself before the arrival of the French, and that Washington and Fry would join him in time to secure the position. Trent had begun the fort, but for some unexplained reason had gone back to Will's Creek, leaving Ensign Ward with forty men to work upon it.

Their labors were suddenly interrupted. On the seventeenth of April a swarm of bateaux and canoes came down the Allegheny, bringing, according to Ward, more than a thousand Frenchmen, though in reality not much above five hundred, who landed, planted cannon against the incipient stockade and summoned the ensign to surrender on pain of what might ensue. He complied and was allowed to depart with his men. Retracing his steps over the mountains, he reported his mishap to Washington, while the French demolished his unfinished fort, began a much larger and better one and named it Fort Duquesne.

They had acted with their usual promptness. Their governor, a practiced soldier, knew the value of celerity and had set his troops in motion with the first opening of spring. He had no refractory assembly to hamper him, no lack of money, for the King supplied it, and all Canada must march at his bidding. Thus, while Dinwiddie was still toiling to muster his raw recruits, Duquesne's lieutenant, Contrecœur, successor of Saint-Pierre, had landed at Presqu'isle with a much greater force, in part regulars and in part Canadians.

The seizure of a king's fort by planting cannon against it and threatening it with destruction was in Dinwiddie's eyes a beginning of hostilities on the part of the French and henceforth both he and Washington acted much as if war had been declared. From their station at Will's Creek, the distance by the traders' path to Fort Duquesne was about a hundred and forty miles. Midway was a branch of the Monongahela called Redstone Creek, at the mouth of which the Ohio Company had built another storehouse. Dinwiddie ordered all the forces to cross the mountains and assemble at this point until they should be strong enough to advance against the French.

The movement was critical in presence of an enemy as superior in discipline as he was in numbers, while the natural obstacles were great. A road for cannon and wagons must be cut through a dense forest and over two ranges of high mountains, besides countless hills and streams. Washington set all his force to the work and they spent a fortnight in making twenty miles.

Towards the end of May, however, Dinwiddie learned that he had crossed the main ridge of the Alleghenies and was encamped with a hundred and fifty men near the parallel ridge of Laurel Hill, at a place called the Great Meadows. Trent's backwoodsmen had gone off in disgust; Fry, with the rest of the regiment, was still far behind; and Washington was daily expecting an attack. Close upon this a piece of good news, or what seemed such, came over the mountains and gladdened the heart of the governor. He heard that a French detachment had tried to surprise Washington, and that he had killed or captured the whole. The facts were as follows.

Washington was on the Youghiogheny, a branch of the Monongahela, exploring it in hopes that it might prove navigable, when a messenger came to him from his old comrade, the Half-King, who was on the way to join him. The message was to the effect that the French had marched from their fort and meant to attack the first English they should meet. A report came soon after that they were already at the ford of the Youghiogheny, eighteen miles distant.

Washington at once repaired to the Great Meadows, a level tract of grass and bushes bordered by wooded hills and traversed in one part by a gully, which with a little labor the men turned into an intrenchment, at the same time cutting away the bushes and clearing what the young commander called "a charming field for an encounter."

Parties were sent out to scour the woods, but they found no enemy. Two days passed. On the morning of the twenty-seventh, Christopher Gist, who had lately made a settlement on the farther side of Laurel Hill, twelve or thirteen miles distant, came to the camp with news that fifty Frenchmen had been at his house towards noon of the day before and would have destroyed everything but for the intervention of two Indians whom he had left in charge during his absence. Washington sent seventy-five men to look for the party, but the search was vain, the French having hidden themselves so well as to escape any eye but that of an Indian.

In the evening a runner came from the Half-King, who was encamped with a few warriors some miles distant. He had sent to tell Washington that he had found the tracks of two men and traced them towards a dark glen in the forest, where in his belief all the French were lurking.

Washington seems not to have hesitated a moment. Fearing a stratagem to surprise his camp, he left his main force to guard it and at ten o'clock set out for the Half-King's wigwams at the head of forty men. The night was rainy and the forest, to use his own words, "as black as pitch." "The path," he continues, "was hardly wide enough for one man; we often lost it, and could not find it again for fifteen or twenty minutes, and we often tumbled over each other in the dark."

Seven of his men were lost in the woods and left behind. The rest groped their way all night and reached the Indian camp at sunrise. A council was held with the Half-King and he and his warriors agreed to join in striking the French. Two of them led the way. The tracks of the two French scouts seen the day before were again found, and marching in single file, the party pushed through the forest into the rocky hollow where the French were supposed to be concealed.

They were there in fact, and they snatched their guns the moment they saw the English. Washington gave the word to fire. A short fight ensued. Coulon de Jumonville, an ensign in command, was killed with nine others. Twenty-two were captured and none escaped but a Canadian who had fled at the beginning of the fray. After it was over, the prisoners told Washington that the party had been sent to bring him a summons from Contrecœur, the commandant at Fort Duquesne.

Five days before, Contrecœur had sent Jumonville to scour the country as far as the dividing ridge of the Alleghenies. Under him were another officer, three cadets, a volunteer, an interpreter and twenty-eight men. He was provided with a written summons, to be delivered to any English he might find. It required them to withdraw from the domain of the King of France, and threatened compulsion by force of arms in case of refusal. But before delivering the summons Jumonville was ordered to send two couriers back with all speed to Fort Duquesne to inform the command that he had found the English, and to acquaint him when he intended to communicate with them. It is difficult to imagine any object for such an order except that of enabling Contrecœur to send to the spot whatever force might be needed to attack the English on their refusal to withdraw.

Jumonville had sent the two couriers and had hidden himself, apparently to wait the result. He lurked nearly two days within five miles of Washington's camp, sent out scouts to reconnoiter it, but gave no notice of his presence; played to perfection the part of a

493

skulking enemy and brought destruction on himself by conduct which can only be ascribed to a sinister motive on the one hand, or to extreme folly on the other. French deserters told Washington that the party came as spies and were to show the summons only if threatened by a superior force. This last assertion is confirmed by the French officer Pouchot, who says that Jumonville, seeing himself the weaker party, tried to show the letter he had brought.

French writers say that, on first seeing the English, Jumonville's interpreter called out that he had something to say to them, but Washington, who was at the head of his men, affirms this to be absolutely false. The French say further that Jumonville was killed in the act of reading the summons. This is also denied by Washington, and rests only on the assertion of the Canadian who ran off at the outset, and on the alleged assertion of Indians who, if present at all, which is unlikely, escaped like the Canadian before the fray began.

Coolness of judgment, a profound sense of public duty and a strong self-control were even then the characteristics of Washington, but he was scarcely twenty-two, was full of military ardor and was vehement and fiery by nature. Yet it is far from certain that, even when age and experience had ripened him, he would have forborne to act as he did, for there was every reason for believing that the designs of the French were hostile, and though by passively waiting the event he would have thrown upon them the responsibility of striking the first blow, he would have exposed his small party to capture or destruction by giving them time to gain reinforcements from Fort Duquesne.

It was inevitable that the killing of Jumonville should be greeted in France by an outcry of real or assumed horror, but the Chevalier de Lévis, second in command to Montcalm, probably expresses the true opinion of Frenchmen best fitted to judge when he calls it "a pretended assassination." Judge it as we may, this obscure skirmish began the war that set the world on fire.

Washington returned to the camp at the Great Meadows, and expecting soon to be attacked, sent for reinforcements to Colonel Fry, who was lying dangerously ill at Will's Creek. Then he set his men to work at an intrenchment, which he named Fort Necessity and which must have been of the slightest, as they finished it within three days.

The Half-King now joined him, along with the female potentate known as Queen Alequippa and some thirty Indian families. A few days after, Gist came from Will's Creek with news that Fry was dead. Washington succeeded to the command of the regiment, the remaining three companies of which presently appeared and joined their comrades, raising the whole number to three hundred. Next arrived the independent company from South Carolina and the Great Meadows became an animated scene, with the wigwams of the Indians, the campsheds of the rough Virginians, the cattle grazing on the tall grass or drinking at the lazy brook that traversed it; the surrounding heights and forests; and over all, four miles away, the lofty green ridge of Laurel Hill.

The presence of the company of regulars was a doubtful advantage. Captain Mackay, its commander, holding his commission from the King, thought himself above any officer commissioned by the governor. There was great courtesy between him and Washington, but Mackay would take no orders, not even the countersign, from the colonel of volunteers. Nor would his men work, except for an additional shilling a day. To give this was impossible, both from want of money and from the discontent it would have bred in the Virginians, who worked for nothing besides their daily pay of eightpence.

Washington, already a leader of men, possessed himself in a patience extremely difficult to his passionate temper, but the position was untenable and the presence of the military drones demoralized his soldiers. Therefore, leaving Mackay at the Meadows, he advanced towards Gist's settlement, cutting a wagon road as he went.

On reaching the settlement the camp was formed and an intrenchment thrown up. Deserters had brought news that strong reinforcements were expected at Fort Duquesne and friendly Indians repeatedly warned Washington that he would soon be attacked by overwhelming numbers. Forty Indians from the Ohio came to the camp and several days were spent in councils with them, but they proved for the most part to be spies of the French. The Half-King stood fast by the English and sent out three of his young warriors as scouts.

Reports of attack thickened. Mackay and his men were sent for and they arrived on the twenty-eighth of June. A council of war was held at Gist's house, and as the camp was commanded by neighboring heights, it was resolved to fall back. The horses were so few that the

Virginians had to carry much of the baggage on their backs and drag nine swivels over the broken and rocky road. The regulars, though they also were raised in the provinces, refused to give the slightest help.

Toiling on for two days, they reached the Great Meadows on the first of July. The position, though perhaps the best in the neighborhood, was very unfavorable and Washington would have retreated farther but for the condition of his men. They were spent with fatigue and there was no choice but to stay and fight.

Strong reinforcements had been sent to Fort Duquesne in the spring and the garrison now consisted of about fourteen hundred men. When news of the death of Jumonville reached Montreal, Coulon de Villiers, brother of the slain officer, was sent to the spot with a body of Indians from all the tribes in the colony. He made such speed that at eight o'clock in the morning of the twenty-sixth of June he reached the fort with his motley following. Here he found that five hundred Frenchmen and a few Ohio Indians were on the point of marching against the English, under Chevalier le Mercier, but in view of his seniority in rank and his relationship to Jumonville, the command was now transferred to Villiers.

The march was postponed. The newly arrived warriors were called to council and Contrecœur thus harangued them: "The English have murdered my children; my heart is sick; tomorrow I shall send my French soldiers to take revenge. And now, men of the Saut St. Louis, men of the Lake of Two Mountains, Hurons, Abenakis, Iroquois of La Présentation, Nipissings, Algonquins and Ottawas—I invite you all by this belt of wampum to join your French father and help him to crush the assassins. Take this hatchet, and with it two barrels of wine for a feast."

Both hatchet and wine were cheerfully accepted. Then Contrecœur turned to the Delawares, who were also present: "By these four strings of wampum I invite you, if you are true children of Onontio, to follow the example of your brethren." And with some hesitation they also took up the hatchet.

The party set out on the next morning, paddled their canoes up the Monongahela, encamped, heard mass, and on the thirtieth reached the deserted storehouse of the Ohio Company at the mouth of Redstone Creek. It was a building of solid logs, well loopholed for musketry.

496

To please the Indians by asking their advice, Villiers called all the chiefs to council, which being concluded to their satisfaction, he left a sergeant's guard at the storehouse to watch the canoes and began his march through the forest.

The path was so rough that at the first halt the chaplain declared he could go no farther and turned back for the storehouse, though not till he had absolved the whole company in a body. Thus lightened of their sins, they journeyed on, constantly sending out scouts.

On the second of July they reached the abandoned camp of Washington at Gist's settlement and here they bivouacked, tired and drenched all night by rain. At daybreak they marched again and passed through the gorge of Laurel Hill. It rained without ceasing, but Villiers pushed his way through the dripping forest to see the place, half a mile from the road, where his brother had been killed and where several bodies still lay unburied. They had learned from a deserter the position of the enemy and Villiers filled the woods in front with a swarm of Indian scouts. The crisis was near. He formed his men in column and ordered every officer to his place.

Washington's men had had a full day at Fort Necessity, but they spent it less in resting from their fatigue than in strengthening their rampart with logs. The fort was a simple square enclosure, with a trench said by a French writer to be only knee-deep. On the south, and partly on the west, there was an exterior embankment, which seems to have been made, like a rifle pit, with the ditch inside. The Virginians had but little ammunition and no bread whatever, living chiefly on fresh beef. They knew the approach of the French, who were reported to Washington as nine hundred strong, besides Indians.

Towards eleven o'clock a wounded sentinel came in with news that they were close at hand and they presently appeared at the edge of the woods, yelling and firing from such a distance that their shot fell harmless. Washington drew up his men on the meadow before the fort, thinking, he says, that the enemy, being greatly superior in force, would attack at once, and choosing for some reason to meet them on the open plain.

But Villiers had other views. "We approached the English," he writes, "as near as possible, without uselessly exposing the lives of the King's subjects" and he and his followers made their way through the forest till they came opposite the fort, where they stationed themselves on two densely wooded hills, adjacent though separated by a small brook. One of these was about a hundred paces from the English and the other about sixty. Their position was such that the French and Indians, well sheltered by trees and bushes, and with the advantage of higher ground, could cross their fire upon the fort and enfilade a part of it. Washington had meanwhile drawn his followers within the intrenchment and the firing now began on both sides.

Rain fell all day. The raw earth of the embankment was turned to soft mud and the men in the ditch of the outwork stood to the knee in water. The swivels brought back from the camp at Gist's farm were mounted on the rampart, but the gunners were so ill protected that the pieces were almost silenced by the French musketry. The fight lasted nine hours. At times the fire on both sides was nearly quenched by the showers and the bedrenched combatants could do little but gaze at each other through a gray veil of mist and rain. Towards night, however, the fusillade revived and became sharp again until dark. At eight o'clock the French called out to propose a parley.

Villiers thus gives his reasons for these overtures: "As we had been wet all day by the rain, as the soldiers were very tired, as the savages said that they would leave us the next morning, and as there was a report that drums and the firing of cannon had been heard in the distance, I proposed to M. Le Mercier to offer the English a conference." He says further that ammunition was falling short, and that he thought the enemy might sally in a body and attack him. The English, on their side, were in a worse plight. They were half starved, their powder was nearly spent, their guns were foul, and among them all they had but two screw rods to clean them.

In spite of his desperate position, Washington declined the parley, thinking it a pretext to introduce a spy, but when the French repeated their proposal and requested that he send an officer to them, he could hesitate no longer. There were but two men with him who knew French, Ensign Peyroney, who was disabled by a wound, and the Dutchman, Captain Vanbraam. To him the unpalatable errand was assigned.

After a long absence he returned with articles of capitulation offered by Villiers, and while the officers gathered about him in the rain, he read and interpreted the paper by the glimmer of a sputtering candle kept alight with difficulty. Objection was made to some of the terms and they were changed. Vanbraam, however, apparently anxious to get the capitulation signed and the affair ended, mistranslated several passages and rendered the words *l'assassinat du Sieur de Jumonville* as "the death of the Sieur de Jumonville."

As thus understood, the articles were signed about midnight. They provided that the English should march out with drums beating and the honors of war, carrying with them one of their swivels and all their other property; that they should be protected against insult from French or Indians; that the prisoners taken in the affair of Jumonville should be set free; and that two officers should remain as hostages for their safe return to Fort Duquesne.

White men and red, it seems clear that the French force was more than twice that of the English, while they were better posted and better sheltered, keeping all day under cover and never showing themselves on the open meadow. There were no Indians with Washington. Even the Half-King held aloof, though being of a caustic turn, he did not spare his comments on the fight, telling Conrad Weiser, the provincial interpreter, that the French behaved like cowards and the English like fools.

In the early morning the fort was abandoned and the retreat began. The Indians had killed all the horses and cattle and Washington's men were so burdened with the sick and wounded, whom they were obliged to carry on their backs, that most of the baggage was perforce left behind. Even then they could march but a few miles and then encamped to wait for wagons. The Indians increased the confusion by plundering and threatening an attack. They knocked to pieces the medicine chest, thus causing great distress to the wounded, two of whom they murdered and scalped. For a time there was danger of panic, but order was restored and the wretched march began along the forest road that led over the Alleghenies, fifty-two miles to the station at Will's Creek.

Whatever may have been the feelings of Washington, he has left no record of them. His immense fortitude was doomed to severer trials in the future, yet perhaps this miserable morning was the darkest of his life. He was deeply moved by sights of suffering and all around him were wounded men borne along in torture, and weary men staggering under the living load. His pride was humbled and his young ambition seemed blasted in the bud. It was the fourth of July.

Villiers went back exultant to Fort Duquesne, burning on his way the buildings of Gist's settlement and the storehouse at Redstone Creek. Not an English flag now waved beyond the Alleghenies.

CHAPTER 3

~~~~~~

Braddock's Campaign

TO THE NORTHERN PROVINCES CANADA WAS AN OLD
and pestilent enemy. Those towards the south scarcely knew
her by name, and the idea of French aggression on their borders was
so novel and strange that they admitted it with difficulty. Mind and
heart were engrossed in strife with their governors—the universal
struggle for virtual self-rule. But the war was often waged with a
passionate stupidity. The colonist was not then an American. He was
simply a provincial, and a narrow one. The time was yet distant when
these dissevered and jealous communities would weld themselves into
one broad nationality, capable at need of the mightiest efforts to purge
itself of disaffection and vindicate its commanding unity.

In the interest of that practical independence which they had so
much at heart, two conditions were essential to the colonists. The one
was a field for expansion and the other was mutual help. Their first
necessity was to rid themselves of the French, who by shutting them
between the Alleghenies and the sea would cramp them into perpetual
littleness. With France on their backs, growing while they had no room
to grow, they must remain in helpless wardship, dependent on England,
whose aid they would always need; but with the West open before
them, their future was their own. King and Parliament would respect
perforce the will of a people spread from the ocean to the Mississippi
and united in action as in aims.

But in the middle of that century, the vision of the ordinary colonist
rarely reached so far. The immediate victory over a governor, however

slight the point at issue, was more precious in his eyes than the remote though decisive advantage which he saw but dimly.

The governors, representing the central power, saw the situation from the national point of view. Several of them, notably Dinwiddie and Shirley, were filled with wrath at the proceedings of the French and the former was exasperated beyond measure at the supineness of the provinces. He had spared no effort to rouse them, and had failed. His instincts were on the side of authority, but under the circumstances it is hardly to be imputed to him as a very deep offense against human liberty that he advised the compelling of the colonies to raise men and money for their own defense, and proposed, in view of their "intolerable obstinacy and disobedience to his Majesty's commands," that Parliament should tax them half-a-crown a head. The approaching war offered to the party of authority temptations from which the colonies might have saved it by opening their purse strings without waiting to be told.

The home government, on its part, was but halfhearted in the wish that they should unite in opposition to the common enemy. It was very willing that the several provinces should give money and men, but not that they should acquire military habits and a dangerous capacity of acting together.

There was one kind of union, however, so obviously necessary and at the same time so little to be dreaded that the British Cabinet, instructed by the governors, not only assented to it but urged it. This was joint action in making treaties with the Indians. The practice of separate treaties, made by each province in its own interest, had bred endless disorders. The adhesion of all the tribes had been so shaken and the efforts of the French to alienate them were so vigorous and effective that not a moment was to be lost.

Joncaire had gained over most of the Senecas, Piquet was drawing the Onondagas more and more to his mission and the Dutch of Albany were alienating their best friends, the Mohawks, by encroaching on their lands. Their chief, Hendrick, came to New York with a deputation of the tribe to complain of their wrongs, and finding no redress, went off in anger, declaring that the convenant chain was broken. The authorities, in alarm, called William Johnson to their aid. He succeeded in soothing the exasperated chief and then proceeded to the confederate council at Onondaga, where he found the assembled sachems full of anxieties and doubts.

"We don't know what you Christians, English and French, intend," said one of their orators. "We are so hemmed in by you both that we have hardly a hunting place left. In a little while, if we find a bear in a tree, there will immediately appear an owner of the land to claim the property and hinder us from killing it, by which we live. We are so perplexed between you that we hardly know what to say or think."

No man had such power over the Five Nations as Johnson. His dealings with them were at once honest, downright and sympathetic. They loved and trusted him as much as they detested the Indian commissioners at Albany, whom the province of New York had charged with their affairs, and who, being traders, grossly abused their office.

It was to remedy this perilous state of things that the Lords of Trade and Plantations directed the several governors to urge on their assemblies the sending of commissioners to make a joint treaty with the wavering tribes. Seven of the provinces, New York, Pennsylvania, Maryland and the four New England colonies, acceded to the plan and sent to Albany, the appointed place of meeting, a body of men who for character and ability had never had an equal on the continent, but whose powers from their respective assemblies were so cautiously limited as to preclude decisive action.

They met in the courthouse of the little frontier city. A large "chain belt" of wampum was provided, on which the King was symbolically represented, holding in his embrace the colonies, the Five Nations, and all their allied tribes. This was presented to the assembled warriors, with a speech in which the misdeeds of the French were not forgotten. The chief, Hendrick, made a much better speech in reply.

"We do now solemnly renew and brighten the covenant chain. We shall take the chain belt to Onondaga, where our council fire always burns, and keep it so safe that neither thunder nor lightning shall break it." The commissioners had blamed them for allowing so many of their people to be drawn away to Piquet's mission. "It is true," said the orator, "that we live disunited. We have tried to bring back our brethren, but in vain; for the governor of Canada is like a wicked, deluding spirit. You ask why we are so dispersed. The reason is that you have neglected us for these three years past." Here he took a stick and threw it behind him. "You have thus thrown us behind your back; whereas the French are a subtle and vigilant people, always using their utmost endeavors to seduce and bring us over to them."

He then told them that it was not the French alone who invaded the country of the Indians. "The governor of Virginia and the governor of Canada are quarreling about lands which belong to us, and their quarrel may end in our destruction." And he closed with a burst of sarcasm. "We would have taken Crown Point [in the last war] but you prevented us. Instead, you burned your own fort at Saratoga and ran away from it—which was a shame and a scandal to you. Look about your country and see: you have no fortifications; no, not even in this city. It is but a step from Canada here, and the French may come and turn you out of doors. You desire us to speak from the bottom of our hearts and we shall do it. Look at the French: they are men; they are fortifying everywhere. But you are all like women, bare and open, without fortifications."

The congress now occupied itself with another matter. Its members were agreed that great danger was impending; that without wise and just treatment of the tribes the French would gain them all, build forts along the back of the British colonies and, by means of ships and troops from France, master them one by one unless they would combine for mutual defense. The necessity of some form of union had at length begun to force itself upon the colonial mind.

A rough woodcut had lately appeared in the *Pennsylvania Gazette,* figuring the provinces under the not very flattering image of a snake cut to pieces, with the motto, "Join, or die." A writer of the day held up the Five Nations for emulation, observing that if ignorant savages could confederate, British colonists might do as much.

Franklin, the leading spirit of the congress, now laid before it his famous project of union, which has been too often described to need much notice here. Its fate is well known. The Crown rejected it because it gave too much power to the colonies; the colonies, because it gave too much power to the Crown, and because it required each of them to transfer some of its functions of self-government to a central council.

Even if some plan of union had been agreed upon, long delay must have followed before its machinery could be set in motion, and meantime there was need of immediate action. War parties of Indians from Canada, set on, it was thought, by the governor, were already burning and murdering among the border settlements of New York and New Hampshire. In the south Dinwiddie grew more and more alarmed, "for the French are like so many locusts; they are collected in bodies in a most surprising manner; their number now on the Ohio is from twelve hundred to fifteen hundred." He writes to Lord Granville that, in his opinion, they aim to conquer the continent and that "the obstinacy of this stubborn generation" exposes the country "to the most merciless rage of a rapacious enemy."

Dinwiddie turned all his hopes to the home government, again recommended a tax by Act of Parliament, and begged in repeated letters for arms, munitions and two regiments of infantry. His petition was not made in vain.

England at this time presented the phenomenon of a prime minister who could not command the respect of his own servants. A more preposterous figure than the Duke of Newcastle never stood at the head of a great nation. He had a feverish craving for place and power, joined to a total unfitness for both. He was an adept in personal politics, and was so busied with the arts of winning and keeping office that he had no leisure, even if he had had ability, for the higher work of government. He was restless, quick in movement, rapid and confused in speech, lavish of worthless promises, always in a hurry and at once headlong, timid and rash.

"A borrowed importance and real insignificance," says Walpole, who knew him well, "gave him the perpetual air of a solicitor. . . . He had no pride, though infinite self-love. He loved business immoderately; yet was only always doing it, never did it. When left to himself, he always plunged into difficulties, and then shuddered for the consequences."

Walpole gives an anecdote showing the state of his ideas on colonial matters. General Ligonier suggested to him that Annapolis ought to be defended. "To which he replied with his lisping, evasive hurry: 'Annapolis, Annapolis! Oh, yes, Annapolis must be defended; to be sure, Annapolis should be defended—where is Annapolis?' "

His wealth, county influence, flagitious use of patronage and long-practiced skill in keeping majorities in the House of Commons by means that would not bear the light made his support necessary to Pitt himself, and placed a fantastic political jobber at the helm of England in a time when she needed a patriot and a statesman. Newcastle was the growth of the decrepitude and decay of a great party, which had fulfilled its mission and done its work. But if the Whig soil had become poor for a wholesome crop, it was never so rich for toadstools.

Sir Thomas Robinson held the Southern Department, charged with the colonies, and Lord Mahon remarks of him that the duke had achieved the feat of finding a secretary of state more incapable than himself. The Duke of Cumberland commanded the army—an indifferent soldier, though a brave one; harsh, violent and headlong. Anson, the celebrated navigator, was First Lord of the Admiralty, a position in which he disappointed everybody.

In France the true ruler was Madame Pompadour, once the King's mistress, now his procuress and a sort of feminine prime minister. Machault d'Arnouville was at the head of the Marine and Colonial Department. The diplomatic representatives of the two crowns were more conspicuous for social than for political talents. Of Mirepoix, French ambassador at London, Marshal Saxe had once observed: "It is a good appointment; he can teach the English to dance."

The rival nations differed widely in military and naval strength. England had afloat more than two hundred ships of war, some of them of great force, while the navy of France counted little more than half the number. On the other hand, England had reduced her army to eighteen thousand men and France had nearly ten times as many under arms. Both alike were weak in leadership. That rare son of the tempest, a great commander, was to be found in neither of them since the death of Saxe.

When on the fourteenth of November, 1754, the King made his opening speech to the Houses of Parliament, he congratulated them on the prevailing peace and assured them that he should improve it to promote the trade of his subjects, "and protect those possessions which constitute one great source of their wealth." America was not mentioned, but his hearers understood him and made a liberal grant for the service of the year.

Two regiments, each of five hundred men, had already been ordered to sail for Virginia, where their numbers were to be raised by enlistment to seven hundred. Major General Braddock, a man after the Duke of Cumberland's own heart, was appointed to the chief command. The two regiments—the forty-fourth and the forty-eighth—embarked at Cork in the middle of January. The soldiers detested the service and many had deserted. More would have done so had they foreseen what awaited them.

William Shirley, son of the governor of Massachusetts, was Braddock's secretary, and after an acquaintance of some months wrote to his friend Governor Morris, of Pennsylvania: "We have a general most judiciously chosen for being disqualified for the service he is employed in in almost every respect. He may be brave for aught I know, and he is honest in pecuniary matters." The astute Franklin, who also had good opportunity of knowing him, says: "This general was, I think, a brave man, and might probably have made a good figure in some European war. But he had too much self-confidence; too high an opinion of the validity of regular troops; too mean a one of both Americans and Indians."

Horace Walpole, in his function of gathering and immortalizing the gossip of his time, has left a sharply drawn sketch of Braddock in two letters to Sir Horace Mann, written in the summer of this year: "I love to give you an idea of our characters as they rise upon the stage of history. Braddock is a very Iroquois in disposition. He had a sister who, having gamed away all her little fortune at Bath, hanged herself with a truly English deliberation, leaving only a note upon the table with those lines: 'To die is landing on some silent shore,' etc. When Braddock was told of it, he only said: 'Poor Fanny! I always thought she would play till she would be forced to tuck herself up.' "

Walpole continues: "But a more ridiculous story of Braddock, and which is recorded in heroics by Fielding in his 'Covent Garden Tragedy,' was an amorous discussion he had formerly with a Mrs. Upton, who kept him. He had gone the greatest lengths with her pin-money, and was still craving. One day, that he was very pressing, she pulled out her purse and showed him that she had but twelve or fourteen shillings left. He twitched it from her: 'Let me see that.' Tied up at the other end, he found five guineas. He took them, tossed the empty purse in her face, saying, 'Did you mean to cheat me?' and never went near her more. Now you are acquainted with General Braddock."

Whatever were his failings, he feared nothing and his fidelity and honor in the dischage of public trusts were never questioned. "Desperate in his fortune, brutal in his behavior, obstinate in his sentiments," again writes Walpole, "he was still intrepid and capable." He was a veteran in years and in service, having entered the Coldstream Guards as ensign in 1710.

The transports bringing the two regiments from Ireland all arrived safely at Hampton and were ordered to proceed up the Potomac to Alexandria, where a camp was to be formed. There, towards the end of March, went Braddock himself, along with Keppel and Dinwiddie, in the governor's coach; while his aide-de-camp, Orme, his secretary, Shirley, and the servants of the party followed on horseback.

Braddock had sent for the elder Shirley and other provincial governors to meet him in council, and on the fourteenth of April they assembled in a tent of the newly formed encampment. Here was Dinwiddie, who thought his troubles at an end and saw in the red-coated soldiery the near fruition of his hopes. Here, too, was his friend and ally, Dobbs of North Carolina; with Morris of Pennsylvania, fresh from Assembly quarrels; Sharpe of Maryland, who, having once been a soldier, had been made a sort of provisional commander-in-chief before the arrival of Braddock; and the ambitious Delancey of New York, who had lately led the opposition against the governor of that province and now filled the office himself—a position that needed all his manifold adroitness.

But next to Braddock, the most noteworthy man present was Shirley, governor of Massachusetts. There was a fountain of youth in this old lawyer. A few years before, when he was boundary commissioner in Paris, he had had the indiscretion to marry a young Catholic French girl, the daughter of his landlord, and now, when more than sixty years old, he thirsted for military honors and delighted in contriving operations of war.

He and Lawrence, governor of Nova Scotia, had concerted an attack on the French fort of Beauséjour, and jointly with others in New England, he had planned the capture of Crown Point, the key of Lake

Champlain. By these two strokes and by fortifying the portage between the Kennebec and the Chaudière, he thought that the northern colonies would be saved from invasion and placed in a position to become themselves invaders. Then, by driving the enemy from Niagara, securing that important pass and thus cutting off the communication between Canada and her interior dependencies, all the French posts in the West would die of inanition.

In order to commend these schemes to the home government, he had painted in gloomy colors the dangers that beset the British colonies. Our Indians, he said, will all desert us if we submit to French encroachment. Some of the provinces are full of Negro slaves, ready to rise against their masters, and of Roman Catholics, Jacobites, indented servants and other dangerous persons who would aid the French in raising a servile insurrection. Pennsylvania is in the hands of Quakers, who will not fight, and of Germans, who are likely enough to join the enemy. The Dutch of Albany would do anything to save their trade. A strong force of French regulars might occupy that place without resistance, then descend the Hudson and, with the help of a naval force, capture New York and cut the British colonies asunder.

The plans against Crown Point and Beauséjour had already found approval of the home government and the energetic support of all the New England colonies. Preparation for them was in full activity, and it was with great difficulty that Shirley had disengaged himself from these cares to attend the council at Alexandria. He and Dinwiddie stood in the front of opposition to French designs. As they both defended the royal prerogative and were strong advocates of taxation by Parliament, they have found scant justice from American writers. Yet the British colonies owed them a debt of gratitude and the American states owe it still.

Braddock laid his instructions before the council and Shirley found them entirely to his mind, while the general, on his part, fully approved the schemes of the governor. The plan of the campaign was settled. The French were to be attacked at four points at once. The two British regiments lately arrived were to advance on Fort Duquesne; two new regiments, known as Shirley's and Pepperrell's just raised in the provinces and taken into the King's pay, were to reduce Niagara; a body of provincials from New England, New York and New Jersey was to seize Crown Point; and another body of New England men to capture Beauséjour and bring Acadia to complete subjection.

Braddock himself was to lead the expedition against Fort Duquesne. He asked Shirley, who though a soldier only in theory had held the rank of colonel since the last war, to charge himself with that against Niagara, and Shirley eagerly assented. The movement on Crown Point was entrusted to Colonel William Johnson, by reason of his influence over the Indians and his reputation for energy, capacity and faithfulness. Lastly, the Acadian enterprise was assigned to Lieutenant Colonel Monckton, a regular officer of merit.

To strike this fourfold blow in time of peace was a scheme worthy of Newcastle and of Cumberland. The pretext was that the positions to be attacked were all on British soil; that in occupying them the French had been guilty of invasion; and that to expel the invaders would be an act of self-defense. Yet in regard to two of these positions, the French, if they had no other right, might at least claim one of prescription. Crown Point had been twenty-four years in their undisturbed possession, while it was three quarters of a century since they first occupied Niagara, and though New York claimed the ground, no serious attempt had been made to dislodge them.

Shirley hastened back to New England, burdened with the preparation for three expeditions and the command of one of them. Johnson, who had been in the camp though not in the council, went back to Albany, provided with a commission as sole superintendent of Indian affairs and charged besides with the enterprise against Crown Point, while an express was dispatched to Monckton at Halifax with orders to set at once to his work of capturing Beauséjour.

In regard to Braddock's part of the campaign, there had been a serious error. If, instead of landing in Virginia and moving on Fort Duquesne by the long and circuitous route of Will's Creek, the two regiments had disembarked at Philadelphia and marched westward, the way would have been shortened and would have lain through one of the richest and most populous districts on the continent, filled with supplies of every kind. In Virginia, on the other hand, and in the adjoining province of Maryland, wagons, horses and forage were scarce. The enemies of the administration ascribed this blunder to the influence of the Quaker merchant, John Hanbury, whom the Duke of

Newcastle had consulted as a person familiar with American affairs. Hanbury, who was a prominent stockholder in the Ohio Company and who traded largely in Virginia, saw it for his interest that the troops should pass that way, and is said to have brought the duke to this opinion. A writer of the time thinks that if they had landed in Pennsylvania, forty thousand pounds would have been saved in money, and six weeks in time.

Not only were supplies scarce, but the people showed such unwillingness to furnish them and such apathy in aiding the expedition that even Washington was provoked to declare that "they ought to be chastised." Many of them thought that the alarm about French encroachment was a device of designing politicians; and they did not awake to a full consciousness of the peril till it was forced upon them by a deluge of calamities, produced by the purblind folly of their own representatives, who, instead of frankly promoting the expedition, displayed a perverse and exasperating narrowness which chafed Braddock to fury.

The quartermaster general, Sir John Sinclair, "stormed like a lion rampant," but with small effect. Contracts broken or disavowed, want of horses, want of wagons, want of forage, want of wholesome food or sufficient food of any kind caused such delay that the report of it reached England and drew from Walpole the comment that Braddock was in no hurry to be scalped. In reality he was maddened with impatience and vexation.

A powerful ally presently came to his aid in the shape of Benjamin Franklin, then postmaster general of Pennsylvania. He and his son had visited the camp and found the general waiting restlessly for the report of the agents whom he had sent to collect wagons. "I stayed with him," says Franklin, "several days, and dined with him daily. When I was about to depart, the returns of wagons to be obtained were brought in, by which it appeared that they amounted only to twenty-five, and not all of these were in serviceable condition." On this the general and his officers declared that the expedition was at an end, and denounced the ministry for sending them into a country void of the means of transportation.

Franklin remarked that it was a pity they had not landed in Pennsylvania, where almost every farmer had a wagon. Braddock caught

511

eagerly at his words and begged that he would use his influence to enable the troops to move. Franklin went back to Pennsylvania, issued an address to the farmers appealing to their interest and their fears, and in a fortnight procured a hundred and fifty wagons, with a large number of horses. Braddock, grateful to his benefactor and enraged at everybody else, pronounced him "almost the only instance of ability and honesty I have known in these provinces." More wagons and more horses gradually arrived and at the eleventh hour the march began.

On the tenth of May, Braddock reached Will's Creek, where the whole force was now gathered, having marched there by detachments along the banks of the Potomac. This old trading station of the Ohio Company had been transformed into a military post and named Fort Cumberland. During the past winter the independent companies which had failed Washington in his need had been at work here to prepare a base of operations for Braddock. Their axes had been of more avail than their muskets. A broad wound had been cut in the bosom of the forest and the murdered oaks and chestnuts turned into ramparts, barracks and magazines.

Fort Cumberland was an enclosure of logs set upright in the ground, pierced with loopholes and armed with ten small cannon. It stood on a rising ground near the point where Will's Creek joined the Potomac and the forest girded it like a mighty hedge, or rather like a paling of gaunt brown stems upholding a canopy of green. All around spread illimitable woods, wrapping hill, valley and mountain. The spot was an oasis in a desert of leaves—if the name oasis can be given to anything so rude and harsh. In this rugged area, or "clearing," all Braddock's force was now assembled, amounting, regulars, provincials and sailors, to about twenty-two hundred men.

There was great show of discipline and little real order. Braddock's executive capacity seems to have been moderate, and his dogged, imperious temper, rasped by disappointments, was in constant irritation. "He looks upon the country, I believe," writes Washington, "as void of honor or honesty. We have frequent disputes on this head, which are maintained with warmth on both sides, especially on his, as he is incapable of arguing without it, or giving up any point he asserts, be it ever so incompatible with reason or common sense."

Captain Robert Orme was aide-de-camp to Braddock and author of a copious and excellent journal of the expedition. His portrait, painted at full length by Sir Joshua Reynolds, shows him standing by his horse, a gallant young figure, with a face pale yet rather handsome, booted to to the knee, his scarlet coat, ample waistcoat and small three-cornered hat all heavy with gold lace. The general had two other aides-de-camp, Captain Roger Morris and Colonel George Washington, whom he had invited, in terms that do him honor, to become one of his military family.

It was the tenth of June before the army was well on its march. Three hundred axmen led the way to cut and clear the road, and the long train of pack horses, wagons and cannon toiled on behind, over the stumps, roots and stones of the narrow track, the regulars and provincials marching in the forest close on either side. Squads of men were thrown out on the flanks and scouts ranged the woods to guard against surprise, for with all his scorn of Indians and Canadians, Braddock did not neglect reasonable precautions.

Thus, foot by foot, they advanced into the waste of lonely mountains that divided the streams flowing to the Atlantic from those flowing to the Gulf of Mexico—a realm of forests ancient as the world. The road was but twelve feet wide and the line of march often extended four miles. It was like a thin, long, parti-colored snake, red, blue and brown, trailing slowly through the depth of leaves, creeping round inaccessible heights, crawling over ridges, moving always in dampness and shadow, by rivulets and waterfalls, crags and chasms, gorges and shaggy steeps. In glimpses only, through jagged boughs and flickering leaves, did this wild primeval world reveal itself, with its dark green mountains flecked with the morning mist and its distant summits penciled in dreamy blue.

The army passed the main Allegheny, Meadow Mountain and Great Savage Mountain, and traversed the funereal pine forest afterwards called the Shades of Death. No attempt was made to interrupt their march, though the commandant of Fort Duquesne had sent out parties for that purpose. A few French and Indians hovered about them, now and then scalping a straggler or inscribing filthy insults on trees, while others fell upon the border settlements which the advance of the troops had left defenseless. Here they were more successful, butchering about thirty persons, chiefly women and children.

It was the eighteenth of June before the army reached a place called the Little Meadows, less than thirty miles from Fort Cumberland. Fever and dysentery among the men and the weakness and worthlessness of many of the horses, joined to the extreme difficulty of the road, so retarded them that they could move scarcely more than three miles a day.

Braddock consulted with Washington, who advised him to leave the heavy baggage to follow as it could and push forward with a body of chosen troops. This counsel was given in view of a report that five hundred regulars were on the way to reinforce Fort Duquesne. It was adopted. Colonel Dunbar was left to command the rear division, whose powers of movement were now reduced to the lowest point. The advance corps, consisting of about twelve hundred soldiers, besides officers and drivers, began its march on the nineteenth with such artillery as was thought indispensable, thirty wagons and a large number of pack horses.

"The prospect," writes Washington to his brother, "conveyed infinite delight to my mind, though I was excessively ill at the time. But this prospect was soon clouded, and my hopes brought very low indeed when I found that, instead of pushing on with vigor without regarding a little rough road, they were halting to level every mole-hill, and to erect bridges over every brook, by which means we were four days in getting twelve miles."

It was not till the seventh of July that they neared the mouth of Turtle Creek, a stream entering the Monongahela about eight miles from the French fort. The way was direct and short but would lead them through a difficult country and a defile so perilous that Braddock resolved to ford the Monongahela to avoid this danger, and then ford it again to reach his destination.

Fort Duquesne stood on the point of land where the Allegheny and the Monongahela join to form the Ohio, and where now stands Pittsburgh. At that early day a white flag fluttering over a cluster of palisades and embankments betokened the first intrusions of civilized men upon a scene which, a few months before, breathed the repose of a virgin wilderness, voiceless but for the lapping of waves upon the pebbles, or the note of some lonely bird. But now the sleep of ages was broken and bugle and drum told the astonished forest that its doom was pronounced and its days numbered.

The garrison consisted of a few companies of the regular troops stationed permanently in the colony, and to these were added a considerable number of Canadians. Contrecœur still held the command. Under him were three other captains, Beaujeu, Dumas and Ligneris. Besides the troops and Canadians, eight hundred Indian warriors, mustered from far and near, had built their wigwams and campsheds on the open ground or under the edge of the neighboring woods, very little to the advantage of the young corn. Some were baptized savages settled in Canada—Caughnawagas from Saut St. Louis, Abenakis from St. Francis and Hurons from Lorette, whose chief bore the name of Anastase, in honor of that Father of the Church. The rest were unmitigated heathen—Potawatomis and Ojibwas from the northern lakes under Charles Langlade, the same bold partisan who had led them three years before to attack the Miamis at Pickawillany; Shawanoes and Mingoes from the Ohio; and Ottawas from Detroit, commanded, it is said, by that most redoubtable of savages, Pontiac.

An Indian had brought the report that the English were approaching and the Chevalier de la Perade was sent out to reconnoiter. He returned with news that they were not far distant. On the eighth of July, the brothers Normanville went out and found that they were within six leagues of the fort. The French were in great excitement and alarm, but Contrecœur at length took a resolution, which seems to have been inspired by Beaujeu. It was determined to meet the enemy on the march and ambuscade them if possible at the crossing of the Monongahela, or some other favorable spot.

Beaujeu proposed the plan to the Indians and offered them the war hatchet, but they would not take it. "Do you want to die, my father, and sacrifice us besides?" That night they held a council, and in the morning again refused to go. Beaujeu did not despair. "I am determined," he exclaimed, "to meet the English. What! will you let your father go alone?" The greater part caught fire at his words, promised to follow him, and put on their war paint. Beaujeu received the communion, then dressed himself like a savage and joined the clamorous throng.

Band after band, they filed off along the forest track that led to the

515

ford of the Monongahela. They numbered six hundred and thirty-seven, and with them went thirty-six French officers and cadets, seventy-two regular soldiers and a hundred and forty-six Candians, or about nine hundred in all. At eight o'clock the tumult was over. The broad clearing lay lonely and still, and Contrecœur, with what was left of his garrison, waited in suspense for the issue.

It was near one o'clock when Braddock crossed the Monongahela for the second time. If the French made a stand anywhere, it would be, he thought, at the fording place, but Lieutenant Colonel Gage, whom he sent across with a strong advance party, found no enemy and quietly took possession of the farther shore. Then the main body followed.

To impose on the imagination of the French scouts, who were doubtless on the watch, the movement was made with studied regularity and order. The sun was cloudless and the men were inspirited by the prospect of near triumph. Washington afterwards spoke with admiration of the spectacle. The music, the banners, the mounted officers, the troop of light cavalry, the naval detachment, the red-coated regulars, the blue-coated Virginians, the wagons and tumbrils, cannon, howitzers and coehorns, the train of pack horses and the droves of cattle passed in long procession through the rippling shallows and slowly entered the bordering forest. Here, when all were over, a short halt was ordered for rest and refreshment.

Beaujeu had spent half the day in marching seven miles and was more than a mile from the fording place when the British reached the eastern shore. The delay, from whatever cause arising, cost him the opportunity of laying an ambush either at the ford or in the gullies and ravines that channeled the forest through which Braddock was now on the point of marching.

Not far from the bank of the river, and close by the British line of march, there was a clearing and a deserted house that had once belonged to the trader Fraser. Washington remembered it well. It was here that he found rest and shelter on the winter journey homeward from his mission to Fort Le Bœuf. He was in no less need of rest at this moment, for recent fever had so weakened him that he could hardly sit his horse. From Fraser's house to Fort Duquesne the distance was eight miles by a rough path, along which the troops were now beginning to move after their halt. It ran inland for a little, then curved to the left and followed a course parallel to the river along the base of a line of steep hills that here bordered the valley. These and all the country were buried in dense and heavy forest, choked with bushes and the carcasses of fallen trees.

Braddock has been charged with marching blindly into an ambuscade, but it was not so. There was no ambuscade, and had there been one, he would have found it. It is true that he did not reconnoiter the woods very far in advance of the head of the column, yet with this exception, he made elaborate dispositions to prevent surprise.

Gage, with his advance column, had just passed a wide and bushy ravine that crossed their path, and the van of the main column was on the point of entering it, when the guides and light horsemen in the front suddenly fell back and the engineer Gordon, then engaged in marking out the road, saw a man, dressed like an Indian but wearing the gorget of an officer, bounding forward along the path. He stopped when he discovered the head of the column, turned and waved his hat. The forest behind was swarming with French and savages. At the signal of the officer, who was probably Beaujeu, they yelled the war whoop, spread themselves to right and left and opened a sharp fire under cover of the trees.

Gage's column wheeled deliberately into line and fired several volleys with great steadiness against the now invisible assailants. Few of them were hurt. The trees caught the shot, but the noise was deafening under the dense arches of the forest. The greater part of the Canadians fled shamefully. Volley followed volley, and at the third Beaujeu dropped dead. Gage's two cannon were now brought to bear, on which the Indians, like the Canadians, gave way in confusion, but did not, like them, abandon the field. The close scarlet ranks of the English were plainly to be seen through the trees and the smoke. They were moving forward, cheering lustily and shouting, "God save the King!" Dumas, now chief in command, thought that all was lost. "I advanced," he says, "with the assurance that comes from despair, exciting by voice and gesture the few soldiers that remained. The fire of my platoon was so sharp that the enemy seemed astonished."

The Indians, encouraged, began to rally. The French officers who commanded them showed admirable courage and address, and while

Dumas and Ligneris, with the regulars and what was left of the Canadians, held the ground in front, the savage warriors, screeching their war cries, swarmed through the forest along both flanks of the English, hid behind trees, bushes and fallen trunks, or crouched in gullies and ravines and opened a deadly fire on the helpless soldiery, who, themselves completely visible, could see no enemy and wasted volley after volley on the impassive trees. The most destructive fire came from a hill on the English right, where the Indians lay in multitudes, firing from their lurking places on the living target below. But the invisible death was everywhere, in front, flank and rear. The British cheer was heard no more. The troops broke their ranks and huddled together in a bewildered mass, shrinking from the bullets that cut them down by scores.

When Braddock heard the firing in the front, he pushed forward with the main body to the support of Gage, leaving four hundred men in the rear, under Sir Peter Halket, to guard the baggage. At the moment of his arrival Gage's soldiers had abandoned their two cannon and were falling back to escape the concentrated fire of the Indians. Meeting the advancing troops, they tried to find cover behind them. This threw the whole into confusion. The men of the two regiments became mixed together and in a short time the entire force, except the Virginians and the troops left with Halket, were massed in several dense bodies within a small space of ground, facing some one way and some another, and all alike exposed without shelter to the bullets that pelted them like hail.

Both men and officers were new to this blind and frightful warfare of the savage in his native woods. To charge the Indians in their hiding places would have been useless. They would have eluded pursuit with the agility of wildcats and swarmed back, like angry hornets, the the moment that it ceased. The Virginians alone were equal to the emergency. Fighting behind trees like the Indians themselves, they might have held the enemy in check till order could be restored had not Braddock, furious at a proceeding that shocked all his ideas of courage and discipline, ordered them with oaths to form into line.

A body of them under Captain Waggoner made a dash for a fallen tree lying in the woods, far out towards the lurking places of the Indians, and crouching behind the huge trunk, opened fire. But the regulars, seeing the smoke among the bushes, mistook their best friends for the enemy, shot at them from behind, killed many and forced the rest to return. A few of the regulars also tried in their clumsy way to fight behind trees, but Braddock beat them with his sword and compelled them to stand with the rest, an open mark for the Indians.

The panic increased. The soldiers crowded together and the bullets spent themselves in a mass of human bodies. Commands, entreaties and threats were lost upon them. "We would fight," some of them answered, "if we could see anybody to fight with." Nothing was visible but puffs of smoke. Officers and men who had stood all the afternoon under fire afterwards declared that they could not be sure they had seen a single Indian.

Braddock ordered Lieutenant Colonel Burton to attack the hill, where the puffs of smoke were thickest and the bullets most deadly. With infinite difficulty that brave officer induced a hundred men to follow him, but he was soon disabled by a wound, and they all faced about. The artillerymen stood for some time by their guns, which did great damage to the trees and little to the enemy. The mob of soldiers, stupefied with terror, stood panting, their foreheads beaded with sweat, loading and firing mechanically, sometimes into the air, sometimes among their own comrades, many of whom they killed. The ground, strewn with dead and wounded men, the bounding of maddened horses, the clatter and roar of musketry and cannon, mixed with the spiteful report of rifles and the yells that rose from the indefatigable throats of six hundred unseen savages, formed a chaos of anguish and terror scarcely paralleled even in Indian war.

"I cannot describe the horrors of that scene," one of Braddock's officers wrote three weeks after. "No pen could do it. The yell of the Indians is fresh on my ear, and the terrific sound will haunt me till the hour of my dissolution."

Braddock showed a furious intrepidity. Mounted on horseback, he dashed to and fro, storming like a madman. Four horses were shot under him and he mounted a fifth. Washington seconded his chief with equal courage. He escaped as by a miracle. Two horses were killed under him and four bullets tore his clothes. The conduct of the British officers was above praise. Nothing could surpass their undaunted self-

519

devotion, and in their vain attempts to lead on the men, the havoc among them was frightful.

Sir Peter Halket was shot dead. His son, a lieutenant in his regiment, stooping to raise the body of his father, was shot dead in turn. Young Shirley, Braddock's secretary, was pierced through the brain. Orme and Morris, his aides-de-camp, Sinclair, the quartermaster general, Gates and Gage, both afterwards conspicuous on opposite sides in the War of the Revolution, and Gladwin, who eight years later defended Detroit against Pontiac, were all wounded. Of eighty-six officers, sixty-three were killed or disabled, while out of thirteen hundred and seventy-three non-commissioned officers and privates, only four hundred and fifty-nine came off unharmed.

Braddock saw that all was lost. To save the wreck of his force from annihilation, he at last commanded a retreat, and as he and such of his officers as were left strove to withdraw the half-frenzied crew in some semblance of order, a bullet struck him down. The gallant bulldog fell from his horse, shot through the arm into the lungs. It is said, though on evidence of no weight, that the bullet came from one of his own men. Be this as it may, there he lay among the bushes, bleeding, gasping, unable even to curse. He demanded to be left where he was. Captain Stewart and another provincial bore him between them to the rear.

It was about this time that the mob of soldiers, having been three hours under fire and having spent their ammunition, broke away in a blind frenzy, rushed back towards the ford, "and when," says Washington, "we endeavored to rally them, it was with as much success as if we had attempted to stop the wild bears of the mountains." They dashed across, helter-skelter, plunging through the water to the farther bank, leaving wounded comrades, cannon, baggage, the military chest and the general's papers a prey to the Indians. About fifty of these followed to the edge of the river. Dumas and Ligneris, who had now only about twenty Frenchmen with them, made no attempt to pursue and went back to the fort because, says Contrecœur, so many of the Canadians had "retired at the first fire." The field, abandoned to the savages, was a pandemonium of pillage and murder.

The loss of the French was slight but fell chiefly on the officers, three of whom were killed and four wounded. Of the regular soldiers, all but four escaped untouched. The Canadians suffered still less in proportion to their numbers, only five of them being hurt. The Indians, who won the victory, bore the principal loss.

In the pain and languor of a mortal wound, Braddock showed unflinching resolution. His bearers stopped with him at a favorable spot beyond the Monongahela and here he hoped to maintain his position till the arrival of Dunbar. By the efforts of the officers about a hundred men were collected around him, but to keep them there was impossible. Within an hour they abandoned him and fled like the rest. Gage, however, succeeded in rallying about eighty beyond the other fording place, and Washington, on an order from Braddock, spurred his jaded horse towards the camp of Dunbar to demand wagons, provisions and hospital stores.

Fright overcame fatigue. The fugitives toiled on all night, pursued by specters of horror and despair, hearing still the war whoops and the shrieks, possessed with the one thought of escape from this wilderness of death. In the morning some order was restored. Braddock was placed on a horse; then, the pain being insufferable, he was carried on a litter, Captain Orme having bribed the carriers by the promise of a guinea and a bottle of rum apiece. Early in the succeeding night, such as had not fainted on the way reached the deserted farm of Gist. Here they met wagons and provisions, with a detachment of soldiers sent by Dunbar, whose camp was six miles farther on, and Braddock ordered them to go to the relief of the stragglers left behind.

At noon of that day a number of wagoners and pack-horse drivers had come to Dunbar's camp with wild tidings of rout and ruin. More fugitives followed, and soon after a wounded officer was brought in on a sheet. The drums beat to arms. The camp was in commotion and many soldiers and teamsters took to flight in spite of the sentinels, who tried in vain to stop them. There was a still more disgraceful scene on the next day, after Braddock, with the wreck of his force, had arrived. Orders were given to destroy such of the wagons, stores and ammunition as could not be carried back at once to Fort Cumberland.

Whether Dunbar or the dying general gave these orders is not clear, but it is certain that they were executed with shameful alacrity. More than a hundred wagons were burned; cannon, coehorns and shells were burst or buried; barrels of gunpowder were staved and the contents thrown into a brook; provisions were scattered through the woods and swamps. Then the whole command began its retreat over the mountains to Fort Cumberland, sixty miles distant. This proceeding, for which, in view of the condition of Braddock, Dunbar must be held answerable, excited the utmost indignation among the colonists. If he could not advance, they thought, he might at least have fortified himself and held his ground till the provinces could send him help, thus covering the frontier and holding French war parties in check.

Braddock's last moment was near. Orme, who, though himself severely wounded, was with him till his death, told Franklin that he was totally silent all the first day, and at night said only, "Who would have thought it?" All the next day he was again silent, till at last he muttered, "We shall better know how to deal with them another time," and died a few minutes after. He had nevertheless found breath to give orders at Gist's for the succor of the men who had dropped on the road. It is said, too, that in his last hours "he could not bear the sight of a red coat," but murmured praises of "the blues," or Virginians, and said that he hoped he should live to reward them.

He died at about eight o'clock in the evening of Sunday, the thirteenth. Dunbar had begun his retreat that morning and was then encamped near the Great Meadows. On Monday the dead commander was buried in the road, and men, horses and wagons passed over his grave, effacing every sign of it, lest the Indians should find and mutilate the body.

After these tragic events, the frontier was left unguarded, and soon, as Dinwiddie had foreseen, there burst upon it a storm of blood and fire.

CHAPTER 4

The Acadians Exiled

BY THE PLAN WHICH THE DUKE OF CUMBERLAND had ordained and Braddock had announced in the council at Alexandria, four blows were to be struck at once to force back the French boundaries, lop off the dependencies of Canada and reduce her from a vast territory to a petty province. The first stroke had failed and had shattered the hand of the striker. It remains to see what fortune awaited the others.

Shirley had already discussed his plans for the invasion of Acadia with his Assembly in secret session, and found them of one mind with himself. Preparation was nearly complete and the men raised for the expedition before the council at Alexandria recognized it as a part of a plan of the summer campaign.

The French fort of Beauséjour, mounted on its hill between the marshes of Missaguash and Tantemar, was a regular work pentagonal in form, with solid earthen ramparts, bomb-proofs and an armament of twenty-four cannon and one mortar. The commandant, Duchambon de Vergor, a captain in the colony regulars, was a dull man of no education, of stuttering speech, unpleasing countenance and doubtful character. He owed his place to the notorious intendant Bigot, who, it is said, was in his debt for disreputable service in an affair of gallantry, and who had ample means of enabling his friends to enrich themselves by defrauding the King. Beauséjour was one of those plague spots of official corruption which dotted the whole surface of New France.

523

An entire heartlessness marked the dealings of the French authorities with the Acadians. They were treated as mere tools of policy, to be used, broken, and flung away. Yet in using them, the sole condition of their efficiency was neglected. The French government, cheated of enormous sums by its own ravenous agents, grudged the cost of sending a single regiment to the Acadian border. Thus unsupported, the Acadians remained in fear and vacillation, aiding the French but feebly, though a ceaseless annoyance and menace to the English.

This was the state of affairs at Beauséjour while Shirley and Lawrence, the governor of Nova Scotia, were planning its destruction. Lawrence had empowered his agent, Monckton, to draw without limit on two Boston merchants, Apthorp and Hancock. Shirley, as commander-in-chief of the province of Massachusetts, commissioned John Winslow to raise two thousand volunteers.

Winslow was sprung from the early governors of Plymouth colony, but though well-born he was ill-educated, which did not prevent him from being both popular and influential. He had strong military inclinations, had led a company of his own raising in a luckless attack on Carthagena, had commanded the force sent in the preceding summer to occupy the Kennebec and on various other occasions had left his Marshfield farm to serve his country. The men enlisted readily at his call and were formed into a regiment, of which Shirley made himself the nominal colonel. It had two battalions, of which Winslow, as lieutenant colonel, commanded the first and George Scott the second, both under the orders of Monckton.

Country villages far and near, from the western borders of the Connecticut to uttermost Cape Cod, lent soldiers to the new regiment. The muster rolls preserve their names, vocations, birthplaces and abode. Obadiah, Nehemiah, Jedediah, Jonathan, Ebenezer, Joshua and the like Old Testament names abound upon the list. Some are set down as "farmers," "yeomen," or "husbandmen"; others as "shopkeepers," others "fishermen" and many as "laborers," while a great number were handicraftsmen of various trades, from blacksmiths to wigmakers. They mustered at Boston early in April, where clothing, haversacks and blankets were served out to them at the charge of the King, and the crooked streets of the New England capital were filled with staring young rustics.

On the next Saturday, the following mandate went forth: "The men will behave very orderly on the Sabbath Day, and either stay on board their transports, or else go to church, and not stroll up and down the streets." The transports, consisting of about forty sloops and schooners, lay at Long Wharf, and here on Monday a grand review took place, to the gratification, no doubt, of a populace whose amusements were few. All was ready except the muskets, which were expected from England but did not come. Hence the delay of a month, threatening to ruin the enterprise. When Shirley returned from Alexandria he found, to his disgust, that the transports still lay at the wharf where he had left them on his departure.

The muskets arrived at length and the fleet sailed on the twenty-second of May, 1755. Three small frigates, the *Success,* the *Mermaid* and the *Siren,* commanded by the ex-privateersman Captain Rous, acted as convoy, and on the twenty-sixth the whole force safely reached Annapolis. After some delay they sailed up the Bay of Fundy, and at sunset on the first of June anchored within five miles of the hill of Beauséjour.

At two o'clock on the next morning a party of Acadians from Chipody roused Vergor with the news. In great alarm he sent a messenger to Louisbourg to beg for help, and ordered all the fighting men of the neighborhood to repair to the fort. They counted in all between twelve and fifteen hundred, but they had no appetite for war. The force of the invaders daunted them and the hundred and sixty regulars who formed the garrison of Beauséjour were too few to revive their confidence. Those who had crossed from the English side dreaded what might ensue should they be caught in arms, and to prepare an excuse beforehand, they begged Vergor to threaten them with punishment if they disobeyed his order. He willingly complied, promised to have them killed if they did not fight, and assured them at the same time that the English could never take the fort. Three hundred of them thereupon joined the garrison, and the rest, hiding their families in the woods, prepared to wage guerrilla war against the invaders.

Monckton, with all his force, landed unopposed and encamped at night on the fields around Fort Lawrence, from which he could contemplate Fort Beauséjour at his ease. The regulars of the English garrison joined the New England men, and then on the morning of the fourth, they marched to the attack.

Their course lay along the south bank of the Missaguash, to where it was crossed by a bridge called Pont-à-Buot. This bridge had been destroyed and on the farther bank there was a large blockhouse and a breastwork of timber defended by four hundred regulars, Acadians and Indians. They lay silent and unseen till the head of the column reached the opposite bank, then raised a yell and opened fire, causing some loss. Three fieldpieces were brought up, the defenders were driven out and a bridge was laid under a spattering fusillade from behind bushes, which continued till the English had crossed the stream. Without further opposition, they marched along the road to Beauséjour, and turning to the right, encamped among the woody hills half a league from the fort. That night there was a grand illumination, for Vergor set fire to the church and all the houses outside the ramparts.

The English spent some days in preparing their camp and reconnoitering the ground. Then Scott, with five hundred provincials, seized upon a ridge within easy range of the works. An officer named Vannes came out to oppose him with a hundred and eighty men, boasting that he would do great things, but on seeing the enemy, quietly returned to become the laughingstock of the garrison.

The fort fired furiously, but with little effect. During the night of the thirteenth, Winslow, with a part of his own battalion, relieved Scott and planted in the trenches two small mortars, brought to the camp on carts. On the next day they opened fire. One of them was disabled by the French cannon, but Captain Hazen brought up two more of larger size on ox wagons, and in spite of heavy rain, the fire was brisk on both sides.

Within the fort there was little promise of a strong defense. The Acadians thought more of escape than of fighting. Some of them vainly begged to be allowed to go home; others went off without leave, which was not difficult since only one side of the place was attacked. Even among the officers there were some in whom interest was stronger than honor, and who would rather rob the King than die for him. The general discouragement was redoubled when, on the fourteenth, a letter came from the commandant of Louisbourg to say that he could send no help, as British ships blocked the way.

On the morning of the sixteenth a mischance befell, recorded in these words in the diary of Surgeon John Thomas: "One of our large shells fell through what they called their bomb-proof, where a number of their officers were sitting, killed six of them dead, and one Ensign Hay, which the Indians had took prisoner a few days agone and carried to the fort." The party was at breakfast when the unwelcome visitor burst in. Just opposite was a second bomb-proof, where was Vergor himself, with the infamous priest Le Loutre, another priest, and several officers who felt that they might at any time share the same fate.

The effect was immediate. The English, who had not yet got a single cannon into position, saw to their surprise a white flag raised on the rampart. Some officers of the garrison protested against surrender, and Le Loutre, who thought that he had everything to fear at the hands of the victors, exclaimed that it was better to be buried under the ruins of the fort than to give it up. But all was in vain and the valiant Vannes was sent out to propose terms of capitulation.

They were rejected, and others offered to the following effect: the garrison to march out with honors of war and to be sent to Louisbourg at the charge of the King of England, but not to bear arms in America for the space of six months; the Acadians to be pardoned the part they had just borne in the defense, "seeing that they had been compelled to take arms on pain of death."

Confusion reigned all day at Beauséjour. The Acadians went home loaded with plunder. The French officers were so busy in drinking and pillaging that they could hardly be got away to sign the capitulation. At the appointed hour, seven in the evening, Scott marched in with a body of provincials, raised the British flag on the ramparts and saluted it by a general discharge of the French cannon, while Vergor, as a last act of hospitality, gave a supper to the officers.

Fort Gaspereau, at Baye Verte, twelve miles distant, was summoned by letter to surrender. Villeray, its commandant, at once complied and Winslow went with a detachment to take possession. Nothing remained but to occupy the French post at the mouth of the St. John. Captain Rous, relieved at last from inactivity, was charged with the task, and on the thirtieth he appeared off the harbor, manned his boats and rowed for shore. The French burned their fort and withdrew beyond his reach. A hundred and fifty Indians, suddenly converted from enemies to pretended friends, stood on the strand firing their guns into the air as a salute and declaring themselves brothers of the English.

All Acadia was now in British hands. Fort Beauséjour became Fort Cumberland—the second fort in America that bore the name of the royal duke.

Now began the first act of a deplorable drama. Monckton and his small body of regulars had pitched their tents under the walls of Beauséjour. Winslow and Scott, with the New England troops, lay not far off. There was little intercourse between the two camps. The British officers bore themselves toward those of the provincials with a supercilious coldness common enough on their part throughout the war. July had passed in what Winslow calls "an indolent manner," with prayers every day in the Puritan camp, when early in August Monckton sent for him and made an ominous declaration.

"The said Monckton was so free as to acquaint me that it was determined to remove all the French inhabitants out of the province, and that he should send for all the adult males from Tantemar, Chipody, Aulac, Beauséjour and Baye Verte to read the Governor's orders; and when that was done, was determined to retain them all prisoners in the fort. And this is the first conference of a public nature I have had with the colonel since the reduction of Beauséjour; and I apprehend that no officer of either corps has been made more free with."

Monckton sent accordingly to all the neighboring settlements, commanding the male inhabitants to meet him at Beauséjour. Scarcely a third part of their number obeyed. These arrived on the tenth and were told to stay all night under the guns of the fort. What then befell them will appear from an entry in the diary of Winslow under date of August eleventh:

"This day was one extraordinary to the inhabitants of Tantemar, Oueskak, Aulac, Baye Verte, Beauséjour, and places adjacent; the male inhabitants, or the principal of them, being collected together in Fort Cumberland to hear the sentence, which determined their property, from the Governor and Council of Halifax; which was that they were declared rebels, their lands, goods, and chattels forfeited to the Crown, and their bodies to be imprisoned. Upon which the gates of the fort were shut, and they all confined, to the amount of four hundred men and upwards." Parties were sent to gather more, but caught very few, the rest escaping to the woods.

Some of the prisoners were no doubt among those who had joined the garrison at Beauséjour and had been pardoned for doing so by the terms of the capitulation. It was held, however, that though forgiven this special offense they were not exempted from the doom that had gone forth against the great body of their countrymen. We must look closely at the motives and execution of this stern sentence.

At any time up to the spring of 1755, the emigrant Acadians were free to return to their homes on taking the ordinary oath of allegiance required of British subjects. The English authorities of Halifax used every means to persuade them to do so, yet the greater part refused. This was due not only to Le Loutre and his brother priests, backed by the military power, but also to the bishop of Quebec, who enjoined the Acadians to demand of the English certain concessions, the chief of which were that the priests should exercise their functions without being required to ask leave of the governor, and that the inhabitants should not be called upon for military service of any kind. The bishop added that the provisions of the Treaty of Utrecht were insufficient, and that others ought to be exacted. The oral declaration of the English authorities, that for the present the Acadians should not be required to bear arms, was not thought enough. They, or rather their prompters, demanded a written pledge.

The refusal to take the oath without reservation was not confined to the emigrants. Those who remained in the peninsula equally refused it, though most of them were born and had always lived under the British flag. Far from pledging themselves to complete allegiance, they showed continual signs of hostility. In May three pretended French deserters were detected among them inciting them to take arms against the English.

On the capture of Beauséjour, the British authorities found themselves in a position of great difficulty. The New England troops were enlisted for the year only and could not be kept in Acadia. It was likely that the French would make a strong effort to recover the province, sure as they were of support from the great body of its people. The presence of this disaffected population was for the French commanders a continual inducement to invasion and Lawrence was not strong enough to cope at once with attack from without and insurrection from within.

Shirley had held for some time that there was no safety for Acadia but in ridding it of the Acadians. He had lately proposed that the lands of the district of Chignecto, abandoned by their emigrant owners, should be given to English settlers, who would act as a check and a counterpoise to the neighboring French population. This advice had not been acted upon. Nevertheless Shirley and his brother governor of Nova Scotia were kindred spirits and inclined to similar measures. Colonel Charles Lawrence had not the good nature and conciliatory temper which marked his predecessors, Cornwallis and Hopson. His energetic will was not apt to relent under the softer sentiments and the behavior of the Acadians was fast exhausting his patience.

In fact, the Acadians, while calling themselves neutrals, were an enemy encamped in the heart of the province. That is the sum of the reasons which explain and palliate a measure too harsh and indiscriminate to be wholly justified.

If they were sent to Canada, Cape Breton or the neighboring islands, they would strengthen the enemy and still threaten the province. It was therefore resolved to distribute them among the various English colonies, and to hire vessels for the purpose with all dispatch.

The oath, the refusal of which had brought such consequences, was a simple pledge of fidelity and allegiance to King George II and his successors. Many of the Acadians had already taken an oath of fidelity, though with the omission of the word "allegiance," and as they insisted, with a saving clause exempting them from bearing arms. The effect of this was that they did not regard themselves as British subjects and claimed, falsely as regards most of them, the character of neutrals.

It was to put an end to this anomalous state of things that the oath without reserve had been demanded of them. Their rejection of it, reiterated in full view of the consequences, is to be ascribed partly to a fixed belief that the English would not execute their threats, partly to ties of race and kin, but mainly to superstition. They feared to take part with heretics against the King of France, whose cause they had been taught to regard as one with the cause of God. They were constrained by the dread of perdition.

Instructions were sent to Winslow to secure the inhabitants on or near the Basin of Mines and place them on board transports, which he was told would soon arrive from Boston. His orders were stringent: "If you find that fair means will not do with them, you must proceed by the most vigorous measures possible, not only in compelling them to embark, but in depriving those who shall escape of all means of shelter or support, by burning their houses and by destroying everything that may afford them the means of subsistence in the country." Similar orders were given to Major Handfield, the regular officer in command at Annapolis.

On the fourteenth of August, Winslow set out from his camp at Fort Beauséjour, or Cumberland, on his unenviable errand. He had with him but two hundred and ninety-seven men. His mood of mind was not serene. He was chafed because the regulars had charged his men with stealing sheep and he was doubly vexed by an untoward incident that happened on the morning of his departure. He had sent forward his detachment under Adams, the senior captain, and they were marching by the fort with drums beating and colors flying when Monckton sent out his aide-de-camp with a curt demand that the colors should be given up, on the ground that they ought to remain with the regiment.

Thus ruffled in spirit, Winslow embarked with his men and sailed down Chignecto Channel to the Bay of Fundy. Here, while they waited the turn of the tide to enter the Basin of Mines, the shores of Cumberland lay before them, dim in the hot and hazy air, and the promontory of Cape Split, like some misshapen monster of primeval chaos, stretched its portentous length along the glimmering sea, with head of yawning rock and ridgy back bristled with forests.

Borne on the rushing flood, they soon drifted through the inlet, glided under the rival promontory of Cape Blomedon, passed the red sandstone cliffs of Lyon's Cove and descried the mouths of the rivers Canard and Des Habitants, where fertile marshes, diked against the tide, sustained a numerous and thriving population. Before them spread the boundless meadows of Grand Pré, waving with harvests or alive with grazing cattle. The green slopes behind were dotted with the simple dwellings of the Acadian farmers and the spire of the village church rose against a background of woody hills. It was a peace-

531

ful, rural scene, soon to become one of the most wretched spots on earth.

Winslow did not land for the present, but held his course to the estuary of the river Pisiquid, since called the Avon. Here, where the town of Windsor now stands, there was a stockade called Fort Edward, where a garrison of regulars under Captain Alexander Murray kept watch over the surrounding settlements. The New England men pitched their tents on shore, while the sloops that had brought them slept on the soft bed of tawny mud left by the fallen tide.

Winslow found a warm reception, for Murray and his officers had been reduced too long to their own society not to welcome the coming of strangers. The two commanders conferred together. Both had been ordered by Lawrence to "clear the whole country of such bad subjects," and the methods of doing so had been outlined for their guidance.

Having come to some understanding with his brother officer concerning the duties imposed on both, and begun an acquaintance which soon grew cordial on both sides, Winslow embarked again and retraced his course to Grand Pré, the station which the governor had assigned him.

As the men of the settlement greatly outnumbered his own, Winslow set his followers to surrounding the camp with a stockade. Card playing was forbidden, because it encouraged idleness, and pitching quoits in camp, because it spoiled the grass. Presently there came a letter from Lawrence expressing a fear that the fortifying of the camp might alarm the inhabitants. To which Winslow replied that the making of the stockade had not alarmed them in the least, since they took it as a proof that the detachment was to spend the winter with them, and he added that as the harvest was not yet got in he and Murray had agreed not to publish the governor's commands till the next Friday. He concludes: "Although it is a disagreeable part of duty we are put upon, I am sensible it is a necessary one, and shall endeavor strictly to obey your Excellency's orders."

On the thirtieth, Murray, whose post was not many miles distant, made him a visit. They agreed that Winslow should summon all the male inhabitants about Grand Pré to meet him at the church and hear the King's orders, and that Murray should do the same for those

around Fort Edward. Winslow then called in his three captains—
Adams, Hobbs and Osgood—made them swear secrecy and laid before
them his instructions and plans, which latter they approved.

On the next day, Sunday, Winslow and doctor, whose name was
Whitworth, made a tour of the neighborhood with an escort of fifty
men and found a great quantity of wheat still on the fields. On Tuesday, Winslow "set out in a whaleboat with Dr. Whitworth and
Adjutant Kennedy, to consult with Captain Murray in this critical
conjuncture." They agreed that three in the afternoon of Friday should
be the time of assembling; then between them they drew up a summons
to the inhabitants, and got one Beauchamp, a merchant, to "put it into
French." A similar summons was drawn up in the name of Murray for
the inhabitants of the district of Fort Edward.

The inhabitants appeared at the hour appointed, to the number of
four hundred and eighteen men. Winslow ordered a table to be set in
the middle of the church and placed on it his instructions and the
address he had prepared. Here he took his stand in his laced uniform,
with one or two subalterns from the regulars at Fort Edward, and such
of the Massachusetts officers as were not on guard duty—strong,
sinewy figures, bearing no doubt, more or less distinctly, the peculiar
stamp with which toil, trade and Puritanism had imprinted the features
of New England. Their commander was not of the prevailing type. He
was fifty-three years of age, with double chin, smooth forehead, arched
eyebrows, close powdered wig and round, rubicund face, from which
the weight of an odious duty had probably banished the smirk of self-
satisfaction that dwelt there at other times. Nevertheless, he had manly
and estimable qualities. The congregation of peasants, clad in rough
homespun, turned their sunburned faces upon him, anxious and intent, and Winslow "delivered them by interpreters the King's
orders . . ."

He then declared them prisoners of the King. "They were greatly
struck," he says, "at this determination, though I believe they did not
imagine that they were actually to be removed." After delivering the
address, he returned to his quarters at the priest's house, where he was
followed by some of the elder prisoners, who begged leave to tell their
families what had happened, "since they were fearful that the surprise
of their detention would quite overcome them." Winslow consulted

with his officers and it was arranged that the Acadians should choose twenty of their number each day to revisit their homes, the rest being held answerable for their return.

"Thus," says of the diary of the commander, "ended the memorable fifth of September, a day of great fatigue and trouble."

Winslow had some cause for anxiety. He had captured more Acadians since the fifth, and had now in charge nearly five hundred ablebodied men, with scarcely three hundred to guard them. As they were allowed daily exercise in the open air, they might by a sudden rush get possession of arms and make serious trouble.

On the Wednesday after the scene in the church, some unusual movements were observed among them and Winslow and his officers became convinced that they could not safely be kept in one body. Five vessels, lately arrived from Boston, were lying within the mouth of the neighboring river. It was resolved to place fifty of the prisoners on board each of these and keep them anchored in the Basin. The soldiers were all ordered under arms and posted in an open space beside the church and behind the priest's house. The prisoners were then drawn up before them, ranked six deep, the young unmarried men, as the most dangerous, being told off and placed on the left, to the number of a hundred and forty-one. Captain Adams, with eighty men, was then ordered to guard them to the vessels.

Though the object of the movement had been explained to them, they were possessed with the idea that they were to be torn from their families and sent away at once and they all, in great excitement, refused to go. Winslow told them that there must be no parley or delay, and as they still refused, a squad of soldiers advanced towards them with fixed bayonets, while he himself, laying hold of the foremost young man, commanded him to move forward. "He obeyed; and the rest followed, though slowly, and went off praying, singing, and crying, being met by the women and children all the way (which is a mile and a half) with great lamentation, upon their knees, praying."

When the escort returned, about a hundred of the married men were ordered to follow the first party, and "the ice being broken," they readily complied. The vessels were anchored at a little distance from shore and six soldiers were placed on board each of them as a guard. The prisoners were offered the King's rations but preferred to be supplied by their families, who, it was arranged, should go in boats to visit them every day, "and thus," says Winslow, "ended this troublesome job." He was not given to effusions of feeling, but he wrote to Major Handfield: "This affair is more grievous to me than any service I was ever employed in."

The provisions for the vessels which were to carry the prisoners did not come, nor did the vessels themselves, excepting the five already at Grand Pré. In vain Winslow wrote urgent letters to George Saul, the commissary, to bring the supplies at once. Murray, at Fort Edward, though with less feeling than his brother officer, was quite as impatient of the burden of suffering humanity on his hands. "I am amazed what can keep the transports and Saul. Surely our friend at Chignecto is willing to give us as much of our neighbors' company as he well can." Saul came at last with a shipload of provisions, but the lagging transports did not appear. Winslow grew heartsick at the daily sight of miseries which he himself had occasioned.

After weeks of delay, seven transports came from Annapolis and Winslow sent three of them to Murray, who joyfully responded: "Thank God, the transports are come at last. So soon as I have shipped off my rascals, I will come down and settle matters with you, and enjoy ourselves a little."

Winslow prepared for the embarkation. The Acadian prisoners and their families were divided into groups answering to their several villages, in order that those of the same village might, as far as possible, go in the same vessel. It was also provided that the members of each family should remain together and notice was given them to hold themselves in readiness. "But even now," he writes, "I could not persuade the people I was in earnest."

Their doubts were soon ended. The first embarkation took place on the eighth of October, under which date the diary contains this entry: "Began to embark the inhabitants, who went off very solentarily [sic] and unwillingly, the women in great distress, carrying off their children in their arms; others carrying their decrepit parents in their carts, with all their goods; moving in great confusion, and appeared a scene of woe and distress."

At the beginning of November, Winslow reported that he had sent off fifteen hundred and ten persons in nine vessels, and that more than six hundred still remained in his district. The last of these were not embarked till late in December. Murray finished his part of the work at the end of October, having sent from the district of Fort Edward eleven hundred persons in four frightfully crowded transports. At the close of that month sixteen hundred and sixty-four had been sent from the district of Annapolis, where many others escaped to the woods. A detachment which was ordered to seize the inhabitants of the district of Cobequid failed entirely, finding the settlements abandoned.

In the country about Fort Cumberland, Monckton, who directed the operation in person, had very indifferent success, catching in all but little more than a thousand. Le Guerne, missionary priest in this neighborhood, gives a characteristic and affecting incident of the embarkation:

"Many unhappy women, carried away by excessive attachment to their husbands, whom they had been allowed to see too often, and closing their ears to the voice of religion and their missionary, threw themselves blindly and despairingly into the English vessels. And now was seen the saddest of spectacles, for some of these women, solely from a religious motive, refused to take with them their grown-up sons and daughters." They would expose their own souls to perdition among heretics, but not those of their children.

When all, or nearly all, had been sent off from the various points of departure, such of the houses and barns as remained standing were burned, in obedience to the orders of Lawrence, that those who had escaped might be forced to come in and surrender themselves. The whole number removed from the province, men, women and children, was a little above six thousand. Many remained behind, and while some of these withdrew to Canada, Isle St. Jean and other distant retreats, the rest lurked in the woods or returned to their old haunts, from which they waged for several years a guerrilla warfare against the English. Yet their strength was broken, and they were no longer a danger to the province.

Of their exiled countrymen, one party overpowered the crew of the vessel that carried them, ran her ashore at the mouth of the St. John and escaped. The rest were distributed among the colonies from Massachusetts to Georgia, the master of each transport having been provided with a letter from Lawrence addressed to the governor of the province to which he was bound, and desiring him to receive the unwelcome strangers. The provincials were vexed at the burden imposed upon them, and though the Acadians were not in general ill-treated, their lot was a hard one. Still more so was that of those among them who escaped to Canada.

Many of the exiles eventually reached Louisiana, where their descendants formed a numerous and distinct population. Some, after incredible hardship, made their way back to Acadia, where after the peace they remained unmolested and, with those who had escaped seizure, became the progenitors of the present Acadians, now settled in various parts of the British maritime provinces, notably at Madawaska, on the upper St. John, and at Clare, in Nova Scotia. Others were sent from Virginia to England, and others again, after the complete conquest of the country, found refuge in France.

Whatever judgment may be passed on the cruel measure of wholesale expatriation, it was not put in execution till every resource of patience and persuasion had been tried in vain. The agents of the French court, civil, military and ecclesiastical, had made some sort of force a necessity. By vile practices they had produced in Acadia a state of things intolerable, and impossible of continuance. They conjured up the tempest, and when it burst on the heads of the unhappy people, they gave no help.

The government of Louis XV began with making the Acadians its tools, and ended with making them its victims.

~~~~~~

CHAPTER 5

Dieskau

HE NEXT STROKE OF THE CAMPAIGN WAS TO BE
the capture of Crown Point, that dangerous neighbor which for
a quarter of a century had threatened the northern colonies. Shirley,
in January of 1755, had proposed an attack on it to the ministry, and
in February, without waiting their reply, he laid the plan before his
Assembly. They accepted it and voted money for the pay and maintenance of twelve hundred men, provided the adjacent colonies would
contribute in due proportion.

Massachusetts showed a military activity worthy of the reputation
she had won. Forty-five hundred of her men, or one in eight of her
adult males, volunteered to fight the French and enlisted for the various
expeditions, some in the pay of the province and some in that of the
King.

It remained to name a commander for the Crown Point enterprise.
Nobody had power to do so, for Braddock was not yet come, but that
time might not be lost, Shirley, at the request of his Assembly, took
the responsibility on himself. If he had named a Massachusetts officer,
it would have roused the jealousy of the other New England colonies
and he therefore appointed William Johnson of New York, thus gratifying that important province and pleasing the Five Nations, who at
this time looked on Johnson with even more than usual favor. In reply
to his request, Connecticut voted twelve hundred men, New Hampshire five hundred and Rhode Island four hundred, all at their own
charge, while New York a little later promised eight hundred more.

In April, when Braddock and the council at Alexandria approved the plan and the commander, Shirley gave Johnson the commission of major general of the levies of Massachusetts and the governors of the other provinces contributing to the expedition gave him similar commissions for their respective contingents. Never did general take the field with authority so heterogeneous.

Johnson had never seen service and knew nothing of war. By birth he was Irish, of good family, being nephew of Admiral Sir Peter Warren, who, owning extensive wild lands on the Mohawk, had placed the young man in charge of them nearly twenty years before. Johnson was born to prosper. He had ambition, energy, an active mind, a tall, strong person, a rough, jovial temper and a quick adaptation to his surroundings. He could drink flip with Dutch boors, or Madeira with royal governors. He liked the society of the great, would intrigue and flatter when he had an end to gain, and foil a rival without looking too closely at the means. But compared with the Indian traders who infested the border, he was a model of uprightness.

He lived by the Mohawk in a fortified house which was a stronghold against foes and a scene of hospitality to friends both white and red. Here—for his tastes were not fastidious—presided for many years a Dutch or German wench whom he finally married, and after her death a young Mohawk squaw took her place.

Over his neighbors, the Indians of the Five Nations, and all others of their race with whom he had to deal, he acquired a remarkable influence. He liked them, adopted their ways and treated them kindly or sternly as the case required, but always with a justice and honesty in strong contrast with the rascalities of the commission of Albany traders who had lately managed their affairs, and whom they so detested that one of their chiefs called them "not men, but devils." When Johnson was made Indian superintendent there was joy through all the Iroquois confederacy. When, in addition, he was made a general, he assembled the warriors in council to engage them to aid the expedition.

This meeting took place at his own house, known as Fort Johnson, and as more than eleven hundred Indians appeared at his call, his larder was sorely taxed to entertain them. The speeches were interminable. Johnson, a master of Indian rhetoric, knew his audience too well not to contest with them the palm of insufferable prolixity.

The climax was reached on the fourth day, when he threw down the war belt. An Oneida chief took it up. Stevens, the interpreter, began the war dance and the assembled warriors howled in chorus. Then a tub of punch was brought in and they all drank the King's health. They showed less alacrity, however, to fight his battles and scarcely three hundred of them would take the warpath. Too many of their friends and relatives were enlisted for the French.

While the British colonists were preparing to attack Crown Point, the French of Canada were preparing to defend it. Duquesne, recalled from his post, had resigned the government to the Marquis de Vaudreuil, who had at his disposal the battalions of regulars that had sailed in the spring from Brest under Baron Dieskau. His first thought was to use them for the capture of Oswego, but the letters of Braddock, found on the battlefield, warned him of the design against Crown Point, while a reconnoitering party which had gone as far as the Hudson brought back news that Johnson's forces were already in the field. Therefore the plan was changed and Dieskau was ordered to lead the main body of his troops not to Lake Ontario, but to Lake Champlain.

He passed up the Richelieu and embarked in boats and canoes for Crown Point. The veteran knew that the foes with whom he had to deal were but a mob of countrymen. He doubted not of putting them to rout, and meant never to hold his hand till he had chased them back to Albany. "Make all haste," Vaudreuil wrote to him, "for when you return we shall send you to Oswego to execute our first design."

Johnson on his part was preparing to advance. In July about three thousand provincials were encamped near Albany, some on the "Flats" above the town and some on the meadows below. There, too, came a swarm of Johnson's Mohawks—warriors, squaws and children. They adorned the general's face with war paint and he danced the war dance. Then with his sword he cut the first slice from the ox that had been roasted whole for their entertainment. "I shall be glad," wrote the surgeon of a New England regiment, "if they fight as eagerly as they ate their ox and drank their wine."

Above all things the expedition needed promptness, yet everything moved slowly. Five popular legislatures controlled the troops and the supplies. Connecticut had refused to send her men till Shirley promised that her commanding officer should rank next to Johnson. The whole movement was for some time at a deadlock because the five governments could not agree about their contributions of artillery and stores. The New Hampshire regiment had taken a short cut for Crown Point across the wilderness of Vermont, but had been recalled in time to save them from probable destruction. They were now with the rest in the camp at Albany, in such distress for provisions that a private subscription was proposed for their relief.

Johnson's army, crude as it was, had in it good material. Here was Phineas Lyman, of Connecticut, second in command, once a tutor at Yale College and more recently a lawyer, a raw soldier but a vigorous and brave one; Colonel Moses Titcomb of Massachusetts, who had fought with credit at Louisbourg; and Ephraim Williams, also colonel of a Massachusetts regiment, a tall and portly man who had been a captain in the last war, member of the General Court and deputy sheriff. He made his will in the camp at Albany and left a legacy to found the school which has since become Williams College. His relative Stephen Williams was chaplain of his regiment, and his brother Thomas was its surgeon.

Seth Pomeroy, gunsmith at Northampton, who like Titcomb had seen service at Louisbourg, was its lieutenant colonel. He had left a wife at home, an excellent matron, to whom he was continually writing affectionate letters, mingling household cares with news of the camp, and charging her to see that their eldest boy Seth, then in college at New Haven, did not run off to the army. Pomeroy had with him his brother Daniel, and this, he thought, was enough.

Here, too, was a man whose name is still a household word in New England—the sturdy Israel Putnam, private in a Connecticut regiment; and another as bold as he, John Stark, lieutenant in the New Hampshire levies and the future victor of Bennington.

The soldiers were no soldiers, but farmers and farmers' sons who had volunteered for the summer campaign. One of the corps had a blue uniform faced with red. The rest wore their daily clothing. Blankets had been served out to them by the several provinces, but the greater part brought their own guns, some under the penalty of a fine if they came without them, and some under the inducement of a reward. They had no bayonets but carried hatchets in their belts as a sort of substitute. At their sides were slung powder horns, on which in the leisure of the camp they carved quaint devices with the points of their jackknives. They came chiefly from plain New England homesteads—rustic abodes, unpainted and dingy, with long well-sweeps, capacious barns, rough fields of pumpkins and corn and vast kitchen chimneys, above which in winter hung squashes to keep them from frost, and guns to keep them from rust.

Johnson had sent four Mohawk scouts to Canada. They returned on the twenty-first of August with the report that the French were all astir with preparation, and that eight thousand men were coming to defend Crown Point. A council of war was called and it was resolved to send to the several colonies for reinforcements. Meanwhile the main body had moved up the river to the spot called the Great Carrying Place, where Lyman had begun a fortified storehouse, which his men called Fort Lyman, but which was afterwards named Fort Edward. Two Indian trails led from this point to the waters of Lake Champlain, one by way of Lake George and the other by way of Wood Creek.

There was doubt which course the army should take. A road was begun to Wood Creek, then it was countermanded and a party was sent to explore the path to Lake George. "With submission to the general officers," Surgeon Williams writes, "I think it a very grand mistake that the business of reconnoitering was not done months agone." It was resolved at last to march for Lake George. Gangs of axmen were sent to hew out the way, and on the twenty-sixth two thousand men were ordered to the lake, while Colonel Blanchard of New Hampshire remained with five hundred to finish and defend Fort Lyman.

The train of Dutch wagons, guarded by the homely soldiery, jolted slowly over the stumps and roots of the newly made road and the regiments followed at their leisure. The hardships of the way were not without their consolations. The jovial Irishman who held the chief command made himself very agreeable to the New England officers. "We went on about four or five miles," says Pomeroy in his journal, "then stopped, ate pieces of broken bread and cheese, and drank some fresh lemon-punch and the best of wine with General Johnson and some of the field officers." It was the same on the next day. "Stopped about noon and dined with General Johnson by a small brook under a tree; ate a good dinner of cold boiled and roast venison; drank good fresh lemon-punch and wine."

That afternoon they reached their destination, fourteen miles from Fort Lyman. The most beautiful lake in America lay before them, then more beautiful than now in the wild charm of untrodden mountains and virgin forests. "I have given it the name of Lake George," wrote Johnson to the Lords of Trade, "not only in honor of His Majesty, but to ascertain his undoubted dominion here."

His men made their camp on a piece of rough ground by the edge of the water, pitching their tents among the stumps of the newly felled trees. In their front was a forest of pitch pine; on their right, a marsh choked with alders and swamp maples; on their left, the low hill where Fort George was afterwards built; and at their rear, the lake.

Little was done to clear the forest in front, though it would give excellent cover to an enemy. Nor did Johnson take much pains to learn the movements of the French in the direction of Crown Point, though he sent scouts towards South Bay and Wood Creek. Every day stores and bateaux, or flatboats, came on wagons from Fort Lyman and preparation moved on with the leisure that had marked it from the first. About three hundred Mohawks came to the camp and were regarded by the New England men as nuisances. On Sunday the gray-haired Stephen Williams preached to these savage allies a long Calvinistic sermon which must have sorely perplexed the interpreter whose business it was to turn it into Mohawk, and in the afternoon young Chaplain Newell, of Rhode Island, expounded to the New England men the somewhat untimely text, "Love your enemies."

On the next Sunday, September seventh, Williams preached again, this time to the whites, from a text in Isaiah. It was a peaceful day, fair and warm, with a few light showers, yet not wholly a day of rest, for two hundred wagons came up from Fort Lyman, loaded with bateaux. After the sermon there was an alarm. An Indian scout came in about sunset and reported that he had found the trail of a body of men moving from South Bay towards Fort Lyman. Johnson called for a volunteer to carry a letter of warning to Colonel Blanchard, the commander. A wagoner named Adams offered himself for the perilous service, mounted and galloped along the road with the letter. Sentries were posted and the camp fell asleep.

While Johnson lay at Lake George, Dieskau prepared a surprise for him. The German baron had reached Crown Point at the head of three thousand five hundred and seventy-three men, regulars, Canadians and Indians. He had no thought of waiting there to be attacked. The troops were told to hold themselves ready to move at a moment's notice. Officers—so ran the order—will take nothing with them but one spare shirt, one spare pair of shoes, a blanket, a bearskin and provisions for twelve days. Indians are not to amuse themselves by taking scalps till the enemy is entirely defeated, since they can kill ten men in the time required to scalp one. Then Dieskau moved on, with nearly all his force, to Carillon, or Ticonderoga, a promontory commanding both the routes by which alone Johnson could advance, that of Wood Creek and that of Lake George.

The Indian allies were commanded by Legardeur de Saint-Pierre, the officer who had received Washington on his embassy to Fort Le Bœuf. These unmanageable warriors were a constant annoyance to Dieskau, being a species of humanity quite new to him. "They drive us crazy," he says, "from morning till night. There is no end to their demands. They have already eaten five oxen and as many hogs, without counting the kegs of brandy they have drunk. In short, one needs the patience of an angel to get on with these devils; and yet one must always force himself to seem pleased with them."

They would scarcely even go out as scouts. At last, however, on the fourth of September, a reconnoitering party came in with a scalp and an English prisoner caught near Fort Lyman. He was questioned under the threat of being given to the Indians for torture if he did not tell the truth, but nothing daunted, he invented a patriotic falsehood, and thinking to lure his captors into a trap, told them that the English army had fallen back to Albany, leaving five hundred men at Fort Lyman, which he represented as indefensible.

Dieskau resolved on a rapid movement to seize the place. At noon of the same day, leaving a part of his force at Ticonderoga, he embarked the rest in canoes and advanced along the narrow prolongation of Lake Champlain that stretched southward through the wilderness to where the town of Whitehall now stands. He soon came to a point where the lake dwindled to a mere canal, while two mighty rocks, capped with stunted forests, faced each other from the opposing banks.

544

Here he left an officer named Roquemaure with a detachment of troops, and again advanced along a belt of quiet water traced through the midst of a deep marsh, green at that season with sedge and water-weeds, and known to the English as the Drowned Lands. Beyond, on either hand, crags feathered with birch and fir, or hills mantled with woods, looked down on the long procession of canoes.

As they neared the site of Whitehall, a passage opened on the right, the entrance to a sheet of lonely water slumbering in the shadow of woody mountains and forming the lake then, as now, called South Bay. They advanced to its head, landed where a small stream enters it, left the canoes under a guard and began their march through the forest. They counted in all two hundred and sixteen regulars of the battalions of Languedoc and La Reine, six hundred and eighty-four Canadians and about six hundred Indians. Every officer and man carried provisions for eight days in his knapsack. They encamped at night by a brook, and in the morning, after hearing mass, marched again. The evening of the next day brought them near the road that led to Lake George. Fort Lyman was but three miles distant.

A man on horseback galloped by. It was Adams, Johnson's unfortunate messenger. The Indians shot him and found the letter in his pocket. Soon after, ten or twelve wagons appeared in charge of mutinous drivers who had left the English camp without orders. Several of them were shot, two were taken and the rest ran off. The two captives declared that, contrary to the assertion of the prisoner at Ticonderoga, a large force lay encamped at the lake.

The Indians now held a council and presently gave out that they would not attack the fort, which they thought well supplied with cannon, but that they were willing to attack the camp at Lake George. Remonstrance was lost upon them. Dieskau was not young, but he was daring to rashness and inflamed to emulation by the victory over Braddock. The enemy were reported to outnumber him greatly, but his Canadian advisers had assured him that the English colony militia were the worst troops on the face of the earth. "The more there are," he said to the Canadians and Indians, "the more we shall kill," and in the morning the order was given to march for the lake.

They moved rapidly on through the waste of pines and soon entered the rugged valley that led to Johnson's camp. On their right was a gorge where, shadowed in bushes, gurgled a gloomy brook, and beyond rose the cliffs that buttressed the rocky heights of French Mountain, seen by glimpses between the boughs. On their left rose gradually the lower slopes of West Mountain. All was rock, thicket and forest. There was no open space but the road along which the regulars marched, while the Canadians and Indians pushed their way through the woods in such order as the broken ground would permit.

They were three miles from the lake when their scouts brought in a prisoner who told them that a column of English troops was approaching. Dieskau's preparations were quickly made. While the regulars halted on the road, the Canadians and Indians moved to the front, where most of them hid in the forest along the slopes of West Mountain and the rest lay close among the thickets on the other side. Thus, when the English advanced to attack the regulars in front, they would find themselves caught in a double ambush. No sight or sound betrayed the snare, but behind every bush crouched a Canadian or a savage, with gun cocked and ears intent, listening for the tramp of the approaching column.

The wagoners who escaped the evening before had reached the camp about midnight and reported that there was a war party on the road near Fort Lyman. Johnson had at this time twenty-two hundred effective men, besides his three hundred Indians. He called a council of war in the morning and a resolution was taken which can only be explained by a complete misconception as to the force of the French. It was determined to send out two detachments of five hundred men each, one towards Fort Lyman and the other towards South Bay, the object being, according to Johnson, "to catch the enemy in their retreat."

Hendrick, chief of the Mohawks, a brave and sagacious warrior, expressed his dissent after a fashion of his own. He picked up a stick and broke it. Then he picked up several sticks and showed that together they could not be broken. The hint was taken and the two detachments were joined in one. Still the old savage shook his head. "If they are to be killed," he said, "they are too many; if they are to fight, they are too few."

Nevertheless, he resolved to share their fortunes, and mounting a gun carriage, he harangued his warriors with a voice so animated and gestures so expressive that the New England officers listened in admiration, though they understood not a word. One difficulty remained. He was too old and fat to go afoot, but Johnson lent him a horse which he bestrode and trotted to the head of the column, followed by two hundred of his warriors as fast as they could grease, paint and befeather themselves.

It was soon after eight o'clock when Ephraim Williams left the camp with his regiment, marched a little distance, and then waited for the rest of the detachment under Lieutenant Colonel Whiting. Thus Dieskau had full time to lay his ambush. When Whiting came up, the whole moved on together, so little conscious of danger that no scouts were thrown out in front or flank, and in full security, they entered the fatal snare.

Before they were completely involved in it, the sharp eye of old Hendrick detected some sign of an enemy. At that instant, whether by accident or design, a gun was fired from the bushes. It is said that Dieskau's Iroquois, seeing Mohawks, their relatives, in the van, wished to warn them of danger. If so, the warning came too late. The thickets on the left blazed out a deadly fire and the men fell by scores. In the words of Dieskau, the head of the column "was doubled up like a pack of cards."

Hendrick's horse was shot down and the chief was killed with a bayonet as he tried to rise. Williams, seeing a rising ground on his right, made for it, calling on his men to follow, but as he climbed the slope, guns flashed from the bushes and a shot through the brain laid him dead.

The men in the rear pressed forward to support their comrades, when a hot fire was suddenly opened on them from the forest along their right flank. Then there was a panic. Some fled outright and the whole column recoiled. The van now became the rear and all the force of the enemy rushed upon it, shouting and screeching. There was a moment of total confusion, but a part of Williams's regiment rallied under command of Whiting and covered the retreat, fighting behind trees like Indians, and firing and falling back by turns, bravely aided by some of the Mohawks and by a detachment which Johnson sent to their aid.

"And a very handsome retreat they made," writes Pomeroy, "and so continued till they came within about three quarters of a mile of our camp. This was the last fire our men gave our enemies, which killed great numbers of them; they were seen to drop as pigeons." So ended the fray long known in New England fireside story as the "bloody morning scout."

Dieskau now ordered a halt and sounded his trumpets to collect his scattered men. His Indians, however, were sullen and unmanageable and the Canadians also showed signs of wavering. The veteran who commanded them all, Legardeur de Saint-Pierre, had been killed. At length they were persuaded to move again, the regulars leading the way.

About an hour after Williams and his men had begun their march, a distant rattle of musketry was heard at the camp, and as it grew nearer and louder, the listeners knew that their comrades were on the retreat. Then, at the eleventh hour, preparations were begun for defense.

A sort of barricade was made along the front of the camp, partly of wagons and partly of inverted bateaux, but chiefly of the trunks of trees hastily hewn down in the neighboring forest and laid end to end in a single row. The line extended from the southern slopes of the hill on the left across a tract of rough ground to the marshes on the right. The forest, choked with bushes and clumps of rank ferns, was within a few yards of the barricade and there was scarcely time to hack away the intervening thickets. Three cannon were planted to sweep the road that descended through the pines and another was dragged up to the ridge of the hill.

The defeated party began to come in: first, scared fugitives both white and red; then gangs of men bringing the wounded; and at last, an hour and a half after the first fire was heard, the main detachment was seen marching in compact bodies down the road.

Five hundred men were detailed to guard the flanks of the camp. The rest stood behind the wagons or lay flat behind the logs and inverted bateaux, the Massachusetts men on the right and the Connecticut men on the left. Besides Indians, this actual fighting force was between sixteen and seventeen hundred rustics, very few of whom had been under fire before that morning.

They were hardly at their posts when they saw ranks of white-

coated soldiers moving down the road and bayonets that to them
seemed innumerable glittering between the boughs. At the same time
a terrific burst of war whoops rose along the front, and in the words of
Pomeroy, "the Canadians and Indians, helter-skelter, the woods full
of them, came running with undaunted courage right down the hill
upon us, expecting to make us flee." Some of the men grew uneasy,
while the chief officers, sword in hand, threatened instant death to any
who should stir from their posts. If Dieskau had made an assault at
that instant, there could be little doubt of the result.

This he well knew, but he was powerless. He had his small force of
regulars well in hand, but the rest, red and white, were beyond control, scattering through the woods and swamps, shouting, yelling and
firing from behind trees. The regulars advanced with intrepidity
towards the camp where the trees were thin, deployed and fired by
platoons, till Captain Eyre, who commanded the artillery, opened on
them with grape, broke their ranks and compelled them to take to
cover. The fusillade was now general on both sides and soon grew
furious.

"Perhaps," Seth Pomeroy wrote to his wife two days after, "the
hailstones from heaven were never much thicker than their bullets
came; but, blessed be God! that did not in the least daunt or disturb
us."

Johnson received a flesh wound in the thigh and spent the rest of
the day in his tent. Lyman took command and it is a marvel that he
escaped alive, for he was four hours in the heat of the fire, directing
and animating the men.

As the wounded men were carried to the rear, the wagoners about
the camp took their guns and powder horns and joined in the fray. A
Mohawk, seeing one of these men still unarmed, leaped over the barricade, tomahawked the nearest Canadian, snatched his gun and darted
back unhurt. The brave savage found no imitators among his tribesmen, most of whom did nothing but utter a few war whoops, saying
that they had come to see their English brothers fight. Some of the
French Indians opened a distant flank fire from the high ground beyond the swamp on the right, but were driven off by a few shells
dropped among them.

Dieskau had directed his first attack against the left and center of

Johnson's position. Making no impression here, he tried to force the right, where lay the regiments of Titcomb, Ruggles and Williams. The fire was hot for about an hour. Titcomb was shot dead, a rod in front of the barricade, firing from behind a tree like a common soldier.

At length Dieskau, exposing himself within short range of the English line, was hit in the leg. His adjutant, Montreuil, himself wounded, came to his aid and was washing the injured limb with brandy when the unfortunate commander was again hit in the knee and thigh. He seated himself behind a tree, while the adjutant called two Canadians to carry him to the rear. One of them was instantly shot down. Montreuil took his place, but Dieskau refused to be moved, bitterly denounced the Canadians and Indians and ordered the adjutant to leave him and lead the regulars in a last effort against the camp.

It was too late. Johnson's men, singly or in small squads, were already crossing their row of logs and in a few moments the whole dashed forward with a shout, falling upon the enemy with hatchets and the butts of their guns. The French and their allies fled.

The wounded general still sat helpless by the tree when he saw a soldier aiming at him. He signed to the man not to fire, but he pulled trigger, shot him across the hips, leaped upon him and ordered him in French to surrender.

"I said," writes Dieskau, " 'You rascal, why did you fire? You see a man lying in his blood on the ground, and you shoot him!' He answered: 'How did I know that you had not got a pistol? I had rather kill the devil than have the devil kill me.' 'You are a Frenchman?' I asked. 'Yes,' he replied, 'it is more than ten years since I left Canada,' whereupon several others fell on me and stripped me. I told them to carry me to their general, which they did. On learning who I was, he sent for surgeons, and though wounded himself, refused all assistance till my wounds were dressed."

It was near five o'clock when the final rout took place. Some time before, several hundred of the Canadians and Indians had left the field and returned to the scene of the morning fight, to plunder and scalp the dead. They were resting themselves near a pool in the forest, close beside the road, when their repose was interrupted by a volley of bullets. It was fired by a scouting party from Fort Lyman, chiefly backwoodsmen under Captains Folsom and McGinnis. The assailants were greatly outnumbered, but after a hard fight the Canadians and Indians broke and fled. McGinnis was mortally wounded. He continued to give orders till the firing was over, then fainted and was carried, dying, to the camp. The bodies of the slain, according to tradition, were thrown into the pool, which bears to this day the name of Bloody Pond.

The various bands of fugitives rejoined each other towards night and encamped in the forest, then made their way round the southern shoulder of French Mountain till, in the next evening, they reached their canoes. Their plight was deplorable, for they had left their knapsacks behind and were spent with fatigue and famine.

Meanwhile their captive general was not yet out of danger. The Mohawks were furious at their losses in the ambush of the morning, and above all at the death of Hendrick. Scarcely were Dieskau's wounds dressed when several of them came into the tent. There was a long and angry dispute in their own language between them and Johnson, after which they went out very sullenly. Dieskau asked what they wanted.

"What do they want?" returned Johnson. "To burn you, by God, eat you and smoke you in their pipes, in revenge for three or four of their chiefs that were killed. But never fear. You shall be safe with me, or else they shall kill us both."

The Mohawks soon came back and another talk ensued, excited at first and then more calm, till at length the visitors, seemingly appeased, smiled, gave Dieskau their hands in sign of friendship and quietly went out again. Johnson warned him that he was not yet safe, and when the prisoner, fearing that his presence might incommode his host, asked to be removed to another tent, a captain and fifty men were ordered to guard him.

In the morning an Indian, alone and apparently unarmed, loitered about the entrance and the stupid sentinel let him pass in. He immediately drew a sword from under a sort of cloak which he wore and tried to stab Dieskau, but was prevented by the colonel to whom the tent belonged, who seized upon him, took away his sword and pushed him out.

As soon as his wounds would permit, Dieskau was carried on a litter, strongly escorted, to Fort Lyman, whence he was sent to Albany and afterwards to New York. In the spring of 1757 he sailed for England. He was afterwards a long time at Bath, for the benefit of the waters. In 1760 the famous Diderot met him at Paris, cheerful and full of anecdote, though wretchedly shattered by his wounds. He died a few years later.

The English loss in killed, wounded and missing was two hundred and sixty-two, and that of the French by their own account, two hundred and twenty-eight—a somewhat modest result of five hours' fighting. The English loss was chiefly in the ambush of the morning, where the killed greatly outnumbered the wounded because those who fell and could not be carried away were tomahawked by Dieskau's Indians. In the fight at the camp, both Indians and Canadians kept themselves so well under cover that it was very difficult for the New England men to pick them off, while they on their part lay close behind their row of logs. On the French side, the regular officers and troops bore the brunt of the battle and suffered the chief loss, nearly all of the former and nearly half of the latter being killed or wounded.

Johnson did not follow up his success. He says that his men were tired. Yet five hundred of them had stood still all day and boats enough for their transportation were lying on the beach. Ten miles down the lake, a path led over a gorge of the mountains to South Bay, where Dieskau had left his canoes and provisions. It needed but a few hours to reach and destroy them, but no such attempt was made.

The Crown Point expedition was a failure disguised under an incidental success. The northern provinces, especially Massachusetts and Connecticut, did what they could to forward it, and after the battle sent a herd of raw recruits to the scene of action.

Shirley wrote to Johnson from Oswego, declared that his reasons for not advancing were insufficient and urged him to push on for Ticonderoga at once. Johnson replied that he had not wagons enough, and that his troops were ill-clothed, ill-fed, discontented, insubordinate and sickly. He complained that discipline was out of the question, because the officers were chosen by popular election; that many of them were no better than the men, unfit for command, and like so many "heads of a mob." The reinforcements began to come in, till in October there were thirty-six hundred men in the camp, and as most of them wore summer clothing and had but one thin domestic blanket, they were half frozen in the chill autumn nights.

552

The army lay more than a month longer at the lake, while the disgust of the men increased daily under the rains, frosts and snows of a dreary November. The men grew more and more unruly, and went off in squads without asking leave.

A difficult question arose: Who should stay for the winter to garrison the new forts, and who should command them? It was settled at last that a certain number of soldiers from each province should be assigned to this ungrateful service, and that Massachusetts should have the first officer, Connecticut the second and New York the third. Then the camp broke up. "Thursday the 27th," wrote the chaplain in his almanac, "we set out about ten of the clock, marched in a body, about three thousand, the wagons and baggage in the center, our colonel much insulted by the way."

The soldiers dispersed to their villages and farms, where on blustering winter nights, by the blazing logs of New England hearthstones, they told their friends and neighbors the story of the campaign.

CHAPTER 6

~~~~~~

Montcalm

ON THE EIGHTEENTH OF MAY, 1756, ENGLAND AT length declared war, after a year of open hostility. She had attacked France by land and sea, turned loose her ships to prey on French commerce, and brought some three hundred prizes into her ports. It was the act of a weak government, supplying by spasms of violence what it lacked in considerate resolution.

France, no match for her amphibious enemy in the game of marine depredation, cried out in horror and, to emphasize her complaints and signalize a pretended good faith which her acts had belied, ostentatiously released a British frigate captured by her cruisers. She in her turn declared war on the ninth of June and now began the most terrible conflict of the eighteenth century, one that convulsed Europe and shook America, India, the coasts of Africa and the islands of the sea.

In Europe the ground was trembling already with the coming earthquake. Such smothered discords, such animosities, ambitions, jealousies, possessed the rival governments; such entanglements of treaties and alliances, offensive or defensive, open or secret—that a blow at one point shook the whole fabric. Hanover, like the heel of Achilles, was the vulnerable part for which England was always trembling. Therefore she made a defensive treaty with Prussia, by which each party bound itself to aid the other, should its territory be invaded. England thus sought a guarantee against France, and Prussia against Russia.

Prussia had need.. Her King, Frederick the Great, had drawn upon himself an avalanche. Three women—two empresses and a concubine —controlled the forces of the three great nations, Austria, Russia and France, and they all hated him: Elizabeth of Russia by reason of a distrust fomented by secret intrigue and turned into gall by the biting tongue of Frederick himself, who had gibed at her amours, compared her to Messalina, and called her *"infâme catin du Nord";* Maria Theresa of Austria because she saw in him a rebellious vassal of the Holy Roman Empire, and above all because he had robbed her of Silesia; Madame de Pompadour because when she sent him a message of compliment, he answered, *"Je ne la connais pas,"* forbade his ambassador to visit her, and in his mocking wit spared neither her nor her royal lover. Feminine pique, revenge or vanity had then at their service the mightiest armaments of Europe.

The recovery of Silesia and the punishment of Frederick for his audacity in seizing it possessed the mind of Maria Theresa with the force of a ruling passion. To these ends she had joined herself in secret league with Russia, and now at the prompting of her minister Kaunitz, she courted the alliance of France. It was a reversal of the hereditary policy of Austria, joining hands with an old and deadly foe and spurning England, of late her most trusty ally. But France could give powerful aid against Frederick, and hence Maria Theresa, virtuous as she was high-born and proud, stooped to make advances to the all-powerful mistress of Louis XV, wrote her flattering letters and addressed her, it is said, as *"Ma chère cousine."*

Pompadour was delighted and could hardly do enough for her imperial friend. She ruled the King and could make and unmake ministers at will. They hastened to do her pleasure, disguising their subserviency by dressing it out in specious reasons of state. A conference at her summer house, called Babiole, "Bauble," prepared the way for a treaty which involved the nation in the anti-Prussian war and made it the instrument of Austria in the attempt to humble Frederick—an attempt which, if successful, would give the hereditary enemy of France a predominance over Germany. France engaged to aid the cause with twenty-four thousand men, but in the zeal of her rulers began with a hundred thousand.

Thus the three great powers stood leagued against Prussia. Sweden and Saxony joined them and the Empire itself, of which Prussia was a part, took arms against its obnoxious member.

Henceforth France was to turn her strength against her European foes and the American war, the occasion of the universal outbreak, was to hold in her eyes a second place. The reasons were several: the vanity of Pompadour, infatuated by the advances of the Empress-Queen, and eager to secure her good graces; the superstition of the King; the anger of both against Frederick; the desire of D'Argenson, minister of war, that the army and not the navy should play the foremost part; and the passion of courtiers and nobles, ignorant of the naval service, to win laurels in a continental war. All these conspired to one end.

It was the interest of France to turn her strength against her only dangerous rival, to continue as she had begun in building up a naval power that could face England on the seas and sustain her own rising colonies in America, India and the West Indies. For she too might have multiplied herself, planted her language and her race over all the globe and grown with the growth of her children had she not been at the mercy of an effeminate profligate, a mistress turned procuress, and the favorites to whom they delegated power.

Still, something must be done for the American war; at least there must be a new general to replace Dieskau. None of the court favorites wanted a command in the backwoods, and the minister of war was free to choose whom he would. His choice fell on Louis Joseph, Marquis de Montcalm-Gozon de Saint-Véran.

Montcalm was born in the south of France, at the Château of Candiac, near Nîmes, on the twenty-ninth of February, 1712. At the age of six he was placed in the charge of one Dumas, a natural son of his grandmother. This man, a conscientious pedant, with many theories of education, ruled his pupil stiffly, and before the age of fifteen, gave him a good knowledge of Latin, Greek and history. Young Montcalm had a taste for books, continued his reading in such intervals of leisure as camps and garrisons afforded and cherished to the end of his life the ambition of becoming a member of the Academy. Yet, with all his liking for study, he sometimes revolted against the sway of the pedagogue who wrote letters of complaint to his father protesting against the "judgments of the vulgar, who, contrary to the experience of ages, say that if children are well reproved they will correct their faults."

So refractory was he at times that his master dispaired. "M. de Montcalm," Dumas informs the father, "has great need of docility, industry and willingness to take advice. What will become of him?" The pupil, aware of these aspersions, met them by writing to his father his own ideas of what his aims should be:

"First, to be an honorable man, of good morals, brave, and a Christian. Secondly, to read in moderation; to know as much Greek and Latin as most men of the world; also the four rules of arithmetic, and something of history, geography, and French and Latin *belles lettres,* as well as to have a taste for the arts and sciences. Thirdly, and above all, to be obedient, docile, and very submissive to your orders and those of my dear mother; and also to defer to the advice of M. Dumas. Fourthly, to fence and ride as well as my small abilities will permit."

At fifteen he joined the army as ensign in the regiment of Hainaut. Two years after, his father bought him a captaincy and he was first under fire at the siege of Philipsbourg. His father died in 1735 and left him heir to a considerable landed estate, much embarrassed by debt. The Marquis de la Fare, a friend of the family, soon after sought for him an advantageous marriage to strengthen his position and increase his prospects of promotion and he accordingly espoused Mademoiselle Angélique Louise Talon du Boulay, a union which brought him influential alliances and some property. Madame de Montcalm bore him ten children, of whom only two sons and four daughters were living in 1752.

His family seat was Candiac, where in the intervals of campaigning he found repose with his wife, his children and his mother, who was a woman of remarkable force of character and who held great influence over her son. He had a strong attachment to this home of his childhood, and in after years, out of the midst of the American wilderness, his thoughts turned longingly towards it.

In 1741 Montcalm took part in the Bohemian campaign. He was made colonel of the regiment of Auxerrois two years later and passed unharmed through the severe campaign of 1744. In the next year he fought in Italy under Maréchal de Maillebois. In 1746, at the disasterous action under the walls of Piacenza, where he twice rallied his regiment, he received five saber cuts, two of which were in the head, and was made prisoner. Returning to France on parole, he was promoted in the year following to the rank of brigadier, and being soon after exchanged, rejoined the army and was again wounded by a musket shot.

The peace of Aix-la-Chapelle now gave him a period of rest. At length, being on a visit to Paris late in the autumn of 1755, the minister D'Argenson hinted to him that he might be appointed to command the troops in America. He heard no more of the matter till, after his return home, he received from D'Argenson a letter dated at Versailles the twenty-fifth of January, at midnight.

"Perhaps, monsieur," it began, "you did not expect to hear from me again on the subject of the conversation I had with you the day you came to bid me farewell at Paris. Nevertheless I have not forgotten for a moment the suggestion I then made you, and it is with the greatest pleasure that I announce to you that my views have prevailed. The King has chosen you to command his troops in North America, and will honor you on your departure with the rank of major general."

The Chevalier de Lévis, afterwards Marshal of France, was named as his second in command with the rank of brigadier, and the Chevalier de Bourlamaque as his third, with the rank of colonel. But what especially pleased him was the appointment of his eldest son to command a regiment in France. He set out from Candiac for the court, and occupied himself on the way with reading Charlevoix. "I take great pleasure in it," he writes from Lyons to his mother. "He gives a pleasant account of Quebec. But be comforted; I shall always be glad to come home."

At the end of March, Montcalm with all his following was ready to embark, and three ships of the line, the *Léopard,* the *Héros* and the *Illustre,* fitted out as transports, were ready to receive the troops, while the general, with Lévis and Bourlamaque, were to take passage in the frigates *Licorne, Sauvage* and *Sirène.* "I like the Chevalier de Lévis," says Montcalm, "and I think he likes me." His first aide-de-camp, Bougainville, pleased him, if possible, still more.

The troops destined for Canada were only two battalions, one belonging to the regiment of La Sarre and the other to that of Royal

Roussillon. Louis XV and Pompadour sent a hundred thousand men to fight the battles of Austria and could spare but twelve hundred to reinforce New France. These troops marched into Brest at early morning, breakfasted in the town and went at once on board the transports "with an incredible gaiety," says Bougainville. Montcalm and he embarked in the *Licorne* and sailed on the third of April, leaving Lévis and Bourlamaque to follow a few days after.

The voyage was a rough one. "I have been fortunate," writes Montcalm to his wife, "in not being ill nor at all incommoded by the heavy gale we had in Holy Week. It was not so with those who were with me, especially M. Estève, my secretary, and Joseph, who suffered cruelly—seventeen days without being able to take anything but water. The season was very early for such a hard voyage, and it was fortunate that the winter has been so mild. We had very favorable weather till Monday the twelfth; but since then till Saturday evening we had rough weather, with a gale that lasted ninety hours, and put us in real danger. The forecastle was always under water, and the waves broke twice over the quarter-deck. From the twenty-seventh of April to the evening of the fourth of May we had fogs, great cold, and an amazing quantity of icebergs. On the thirtieth, when luckily the fog lifted for a time, we counted sixteen of them. The day before, one drifted under the bowsprit, grazed it, and might have crushed us if the deck-officer had not called out quickly, *Luff*.

"After speaking of our troubles and sufferings, I must tell you of our pleasures, which were fishing for cod and eating it. The taste is exquisite. The head, tongue and liver are morsels worthy of an epicure. Still, I would not advise anybody to make the voyage for their sake. My health is as good as it has been for a long time. I found it a good plan to eat little and take no supper; a little tea now and then, and plenty of lemonade. Nevertheless I have taken very little liking for the sea, and think that when I shall be so happy as to rejoin you I shall end my voyages there. I don't know when this letter will go. I shall send it by the first ship that returns to France, and keep on writing till then. It is pleasant, I know, to hear particulars about the people one loves, and I thought that my mother and you, my dearest and most beloved, would be glad to read all these dull details. We heard mass on Easter Day. All the week before, it was impossible, because the ship rolled so that I could hardly keep my legs. If I had dared, I think I should have had myself lashed fast. I shall not soon forget that Holy Week."

This letter was written on the eleventh of May in the St. Lawrence, where the ship lay at anchor ten leagues below Quebec, stopped by ice from proceeding farther. Montcalm made his way to the town by land, and soon after learned with great satisfaction that the other ships were safe in the river below.

Vaudreuil, the governor general, was at Montreal and Montcalm sent a courier to inform him of his arrival. He soon went there in person and the two men met for the first time. The new general was not welcome to Vaudreuil, who had hoped to command the troops himself and had represented to the court that it was needless and inexpedient to send out a general officer from France. The court had not accepted his views and hence it was with more curiosity than satisfaction that he greeted the colleague who had been assigned him.

He saw before him a man of small stature, with a lively countenance, a keen eye, and in moments of animation, rapid, vehement utterance and nervous gesticulation. Montcalm, we may suppose, regarded the governor with no less attention. Pierre François Rigaud, Marquis de Vaudreuil, was the son of Philippe de Vaudreuil, who had governed Canada early in the century, and he himself had been governor of Louisiana. He had not the force of character which his position demanded, lacked decision in times of crisis, and though tenacious of authority, was more jealous in asserting than self-reliant in exercising it. One of his traits was a sensitive egotism, which made him forward to proclaim his own part in every success, and to throw on others the burden of every failure. He was facile by nature and capable of being led by such as had skill and temper for the task. But the impetuous Montcalm was not of their number and the fact that he was born in France would in itself have thrown obstacles in his way to the good graces of the governor.

Vaudreuil, Canadian by birth, loved the colony and its people, and distrusted Old France and all that came out of it. He had been bred, moreover, to the naval service, and like other Canadian governors, his official correspondence was with the minister of marine, while that of

Montcalm was with the minister of war. Even had Nature made him less suspicious, his relations with the general would have been critical. Montcalm commanded the regulars from France, whose very presence was in the eyes of Vaudreuil an evil, though a necessary, one. Their chief was, it is true, subordinate to him by virtue of his office of governor, yet it was clear that for the conduct of the war the trust of the government was mainly in Montcalm and the minister of war had even suggested that he should have the immediate command, not only of the troops from France, but of the colony regulars and the militia.

An order of the King to this effect was sent to Vaudreuil, with instructions to communicate it to Montcalm or withhold it, as he should think best. He lost no time in replying that the general "ought to concern himself with nothing but the command of the troops from France," and he returned the order to the minister who sent it. The governor and the general represented the two parties which were soon to divide Canada—those of New France and of Old.

A like antagonism was seen in the forces commanded by the two chiefs. These were of three kinds, the *troupes de terre,* troops of the line, or regulars from France; the *troupes de la marine,* or colony regulars; and lastly the militia. The first consisted of the four battalions that had come over with Dieskau and the two that had come with Montcalm, comprising in all a little less than three thousand men. Besides these, the battalions of Artois and Bourgogne, to the number of eleven hundred men, were in garrison at Louisbourg. All these troops wore a white uniform, faced with blue, red, yellow or violet, a black three-cornered hat and gaiters, generally black, from the foot to the knee.

The subaltern officers in the French service were very numerous and were drawn chiefly from the class of lesser nobles. A well-informed French writer calls them "a generation of *petits-maîtres,* dissolute, frivolous, heedless, light-witted; but brave always, and ready to die with their soldiers, though not to suffer with them." In fact, the course of the war was to show plainly that in Europe the regiments of France were no longer what they had once been. It was not so with those who fought in America. Here, for enduring gallantry, officers and men alike deserve nothing but praise.

561

The *troupes de la marine* had for a long time formed the permanent military establishment of Canada. Though attached to the naval department, they served on land and were employed as a police within the limits of the colony, or as garrisons of the outlying forts, where their officers busied themselves more with fur trading than with their military duties. Then they had become ill-disciplined and inefficient, till the hard hand of Duquesne restored them to order.

Their uniform was not unlike that of the troops attached to the War Department, being white with black facings. They were enlisted for the most part in France, but when their term of service expired, and even before, in time of peace they were encouraged to become settlers in the colony, as was also the case with their officers, of whom a great part were of European birth. Thus the relations of the *troupes de la marine* with the colony were close and they formed a sort of connecting link between the troops of the line and the native militia. Besides these colony regulars, there was a company of colonial artillery, consisting this year of seventy men and replaced in 1757 by two companies of fifty men each.

All the effective male population of Canada, from fifteen years to sixty, was enrolled in the militia and called into service at the will of the governor. They received arms, clothing, equipment and rations from the King, but no pay, and instead of tents they made themselves huts of bark or branches. The best of them were drawn from the upper parts of the colony, where habits of bushranging were still in full activity.

Their fighting qualities were much like those of the Indians, whom they rivaled in endurance and in the arts of forest war. As bushfighters they had few equals. They fought well behind earthworks, and were good at a surprise or sudden dash, but for regular battle on the open field they were of small account, being disorderly and apt to break and take to cover at the moment of crisis. They had no idea of the great operations of war. At first they despised the regulars for their ignorance of woodcraft and thought themselves able to defend the colony alone, while the regulars regarded them in turn with a contempt no less unjust. They were excessively given to gasconade and every true Canadian boasted himself a match for three Englishmen at least.

To the white fighting force of the colony are to be added the red men. The most trusty of them were the mission Indians, living within or near the settled limits of Canada, chiefly the Hurons of Lorette, the Abenakis of St. Francis and Batiscan, the Iroquois of Caughnawaga and La Présentation, and the Iroquois and Algonquins at the Two Mountains on the Ottawa. Besides these, all the warriors of the West and North, from Lake Superior to the Ohio, and from the Alleghenies to the Mississippi, were now at the beck of France. As to the Iroquois or Five Nations who still remained in their ancient seats within the present limits of New York, their power and pride had greatly fallen, and crowded as they were between the French and the English, they were in a state of vacillation, some leaning to one side, some to the other, and some to each in turn. As a whole, the best that France could expect from them was neutrality.

The military situation was somewhat perplexing. Iroquois spies had brought reports of great preparations on the part of the English. As neither party dared offend these wavering tribes, their warriors could pass with impunity from one to the other, and were paid by each for bringing information, not always trustworthy. They declared that the English were gathering in force to renew the attempt made by Johnson the year before against Crown Point and Ticonderoga, as well as that made by Shirley against Forts Frontenac and Niagara.

Vaudreuil had spared no effort to meet the double danger. Lotbinière, a Canadian engineer, had been busied during the winter in fortifying Ticonderoga, while Pouchot, a captain in the battalion of Béarn, had rebuilt Niagara and two French engineers were at work in strengthening the defenses of Frontenac. The governor even hoped to take the offensive, anticipate the movements of the English, capture Oswego and obtain the complete command of Lake Ontario. Early in the spring a blow had been struck which materially aided these schemes.

The English had built two small forts to guard the Great Carrying Place on the route to Oswego. One of these, Fort Williams, was on the Mohawk; the other, Fort Bull, a mere collection of storehouses surrounded by a palisade, was four miles distant on the bank of Wood Creek. Here a great quantity of stores and ammunition had imprudently been collected against the opening campaign.

In February, Vaudreuil sent Léry, a colony officer, with three hundred and sixty-two picked men, soldiers, Canadians and Indians, to seize these two posts. Towards the end of March, after extreme hardship, they reached the road that connected them, and at half-past five in the morning captured twelve men going with wagons to Fort Bull. Learning from them the weakness of that place, they dashed forward to surprise it.

The thirty provincials of Shirley's regiment who formed the garrison had barely time to shut the gate, while the assailants fired on them through the loopholes, of which they got possession in the tumult. Léry called on the defenders to yield, but they refused and pelted the French for an hour with bullets and hand grenades. The gate was at last beaten down with axes and they were summoned again, but again they refused and fired hotly through the opening. The French rushed in, shouting *"Vive le Roi,"* and a frightful struggle followed. All the garrison were killed, except two or three who hid themselves till the slaughter was over. The fort was set on fire and blown to atoms by the explosion of the magazines and Léry then withdrew, not venturing to attack Fort Williams. Johnson, warned by Indians of the approach of the French, had pushed up the Mohawk with reinforcements, but came too late.

Vaudreuil, who always exaggerates any success in which he has had part, says that, besides bombs, bullets, cannon balls and other munitions, forty-five thousand pounds of gunpowder were destroyed on this occasion. It is certain that damage enough was done to retard English operations in the direction of Oswego sufficiently to give the French time for securing all their posts on Lake Ontario. Before the end of June this was in good measure done.

The battalion of Béarn lay encamped before the now strong fort of Niagara and the battalions of Guienne and La Sarre, with a body of Canadians, guarded Frontenac against attack. Those of La Reine and Languedoc had been sent to Ticonderoga, while the governor, with Montcalm and Lévis, still remained at Montreal watching the turn of events. Here, too, came the intendant François Bigot, the most accomplished knave in Canada, yet indispensable for his vigor and executive skill; Bougainville, who had disarmed the jealousy of Vaudreuil and now stood high in his good graces; and the adjutant general, Montreuil, clearly a vain and pragmatic personage, who, having come to Canada with Dieskau the year before, thought it behooved him to give the general the advantage of his experience.

Indians presently brought word that ten thousand English were coming to attack Ticonderoga. A reinforcement of colony regulars was at once dispatched to join the two battalions already there; a third battalion, Royal Roussillon, was sent after them. The militia were called out and ordered to follow with all speed, while both Montcalm and Lévis hastened to the supposed scene of danger. They embarked in canoes on the Richelieu, coasted the shore of Lake Champlain, passed Fort Frederic or Crown Point, where all was activity and bustle, and reached Ticonderoga at the end of June. They found the fort, on which Lotbinière had been at work all winter, advanced towards completion.

Ticonderoga was now the most advanced position of the French and Crown Point, which had before held that perilous honor, was in the second line. Lévis, to whom had been assigned the permanent command of this post of danger, set out on foot to explore the neighboring woods and mountains, and slept out several nights before he reappeared at the camp.

"I do not think," says Montcalm, "that many high officers in Europe would have occasion to take such tramps as this. I cannot speak too well of him. Without being a man of brilliant parts, he has good experience, good sense, and a quick eye; and, though I had served with him before, I never should have thought that he had such promptness and efficiency. He has turned his campaigns to good account."

Lévis writes of his chief with equal warmth. "I do not know if the Marquis de Montcalm is pleased with me, but I am sure that I am very much so with him, and shall always be charmed to serve under his orders. It is not for me, Monseigneur, to speak to you of his merit and his talents. You know him better than anybody else; but I may have the honor of assuring that he has pleased everybody in this colony, and manages affairs with the Indians extremely well."

The danger from the English proved to be still remote and there was ample leisure in the camp. Duchat, a young captain in the battalion of Languedoc, used it in writing to his father a long account of what he saw about him—the forests full of game; the ducks, geese and partridges; the prodigious flocks of wild pigeons that darkened the air; the bears, the beavers; and above all the Indians, their canoes, dress, ball play and dances. "We are making here," says the military prophet, "a place that history will not forget. . . ."

CHAPTER 7

The Fall of Oswego

S HIRLEY RETURNED FROM A BOOTLESS OSWEGO
campaign at the end of 1755 and called a council of war at New
York to lay before it his scheme for the next summer's operations. It
was a comprehensive one: to master Lake Ontario by an overpowering
naval force and seize the French forts upon it, Niagara, Frontenac and
Toronto; attack Ticonderoga and Crown Point on the one hand and
Fort Duquesne on the other, and at the same time perplex and divide
the enemy by an inroad down the Chaudière upon the settlements
about Quebec.

The council approved the scheme, but to execute it the provinces
must raise at least sixteen thousand men. This they refused to do.
Pennsylvania and Virginia would take no active part, and were content with defending themselves. The attack on Fort Duquesne was
therefore abandoned, as was also the diversion towards Quebec. The
New England colonies were discouraged by Johnson's failure to take
Crown Point, doubtful of the military abilities of Shirley, and embarrassed by the debts of the last campaign. But when they learned
that Parliament would grant a sum of money in partial compensation
for their former sacrifices, they plunged into new debts without
hesitation and raised more men than the general had asked, though
with their usual jealousy, they provided that their soldiers should be
employed for no other purpose than the attack on Ticonderoga and
Crown Point.

Shirley chose John Winslow to command them, and gave him a commission to that effect, while he, to clinch his authority, asked and obtained supplementary commissions from every government that gave men to the expedition. For the movement against the forts of Lake Ontario, which Shirley meant to command in person, he had the remains of his own and Pepperrell's regiments, the two shattered battalions brought over by Braddock, the "Jersey Blues," four provincial companies from North Carolina and the four King's companies of New York. His first care was to recruit their ranks and raise them to their full complement, which when effected would bring them up to the insufficient strength of about forty-four hundred men.

While he was struggling with contradictions and cross-purposes, a withering blow fell upon him; he learned that he was superseded in the command. A cabal formed against him had won over Sir Charles Hardy, the new governor of New York, and had painted Shirley's conduct in such colors that the ministry removed him.

It was essential for the campaign that a successor should be sent at once, to form plans on the spot and make preparations accordingly. The ministry were in no such haste. It was presently announced that Colonel Daniel Webb would be sent to America, followed by General James Abercrombie, who was to be followed in turn by the Earl of Loudon, the destined commander-in-chief. Shirley was to resign his command to Webb, Webb to Abercrombie, and Abercrombie to Loudon. It chanced that the two former arrived in June at about the same time, while the earl came in July, and meanwhile it devolved on Shirley to make ready for them. Unable to divine what their plans would be, he prepared the campaign in accordance with his own.

His star, so bright a twelvemonth before, was now miserably dimmed. In both his public and private life he was the butt of adversity. He had lost two promising sons in the war; he had made a mortifying failure as a soldier; and triumphant enemies were rejoicing in his fall. It is to the credit of his firmness and his zeal in the cause that he set himself to his task with as much vigor as if he, and not others, were to gather the fruits. His chief care was for his favorite enterprise in the direction of Lake Ontario. Making Albany his headquarters, he rebuilt the fort at the Great Carrying Place destroyed in March by the French, sent troops to guard the perilous route to Oswego and gathered provisions and stores at the posts along the way.

Meanwhile the New England men, strengthened by the levies of New York, were mustering at Albany for the attack on Crown Point. At the end of May they moved a short distance up the Hudson and encamped at a place called Half-Moon, where the navigation was stopped by rapids. Here and at the posts above were gathered something more than five thousand men, as raw and untrained as those led by Johnson in the summer before.

From Winslow's headquarters at Half-Moon a road led along the banks of the Hudson to Stillwater, from which there was a water carriage to Saratoga. Here stores were again placed in wagons and carried several miles to Upper Falls, from there by boat to Fort Edward, and then fourteen miles across country to Fort William Henry at Lake George, where the army was to embark for Ticonderoga. Each of the points of transit below Fort Edward was guarded by a stockade and two or more companies of provincials. They were much pestered by Indians, who now and then scalped a straggler and escaped with their usual nimbleness. From time to time strong bands of Canadians and Indians approached by way of South Bay or Wood Creek and threatened more serious mischief. It is surprising that some of the trains were not cut off, for the escorts were often reckless and disorderly to the last degree.

Colonel Jonathan Bagley commanded at Fort William Henry, where gangs of men were busied under his eye in building three sloops and making several hundred whaleboats to carry the army to Ticonderoga. The season was advancing fast and Winslow urged him to hasten on the work, to which the humorous Bagley answered: "Shall leave no stone unturned; every wheel shall go that rum and human flesh can move."

The English were fast learning the art of forest war and the partisan chief, Captain Robert Rogers, began already to be famous. On the seventeenth of June he and his band lay hidden in the bushes within the outposts of Ticonderoga and made a close survey of the fort and surrounding camps. His report was not cheering. Winslow's so-called army had now grown to nearly seven thousand men and these, it was plain, were not too many to drive the French from their stronghold.

While Winslow pursued his preparations, tried to settle disputes of rank among the colonels of the several colonies and strove to bring order out of the little chaos of his command, Sir William Johnson was engaged in a work for which he was admirably fitted. This was the attaching of the Five Nations to the English interest. Along with his patent of baronetcy, which reached him about this time, he received direct from the Crown the commission of "Colonel, Agent, and Sole Superintendent of the Six Nations and other Northern Tribes." Henceforth he was independent of governors and generals, and responsible to the court alone.

His task was a difficult one. The Five Nations would fain have remained neutral and let the European rivals fight it out, but on account of their local position they could not. The exactions and lies of the Albany traders, the frauds of land speculators, the contradictory action of the different provincial governments, joined to English weakness and mismanagement in the last war, all conspired to alienate them and to aid the efforts of the French agents, who cajoled and threatened them by turns. But for Johnson these intrigues would have prevailed. He had held a series of councils with them at Fort Johnson during the winter, and not only drew from them a promise to stand by the English, but persuaded all the confederated tribes except the Cayugas to consent that the English should build forts near their chief towns, under the pretext of protecting them from the French.

In June he went to Onondaga, well escorted, for the way was dangerous. This capital of the confederacy was under a cloud. It had just lost one Red Head, its chief sachem, and first of all it behooved the baronet to condole their affliction. The ceremony was long, with compliments, lugubrious speeches, wampum belts, the scalp of an enemy to replace the departed and a final glass of rum for each of the assembled mourners. The conferences lasted a fortnight, and when Johnson took his leave, the tribes stood pledged to lift the hatchet for the English.

When he returned to Fort Johnson a fever seized him and he lay helpless for a time, then rose from his sickbed to meet another congregation of Indians. These were deputies of the Five Nations, with Mohegans from the Hudson, and Delawares and Shawanoes from the Susquehanna, whom he had persuaded to visit him in hope that he might induce them to cease from murdering the border settlers. All their tribesmen were in arms against the English, but he prevailed at last and they accepted the war belt at his hands.

But would the Indians keep their word? It was more than doubtful. While some of them treated with him on the Mohawk, others treated with Vaudreuil at Montreal. A display of military vigor on the English side, crowned by some signal victory, would alone make their alliance sure.

What Shirley longed for was the collecting of a body of Five Nation warriors at Oswego to aid him in his cherished enterprise against Niagara and Frontenac. The warriors had promised him to come, but there was small hope that they would do so. Meanwhile he was at Albany pursuing his preparations, posting his scanty force in the forts newly built on the Mohawk and the Great Carrying Place and sending forward stores and provisions.

Having no troops to spare for escorts, he invented a plan which, like everything he did, was bitterly criticized. He took into pay two thousand boatmen, gathered from all parts of the country, including many whalemen from the eastern coasts of New England, divided them into companies of fifty, armed each with a gun and a hatchet and placed them under the command of Lieutenant Colonel John Bradstreet. Thus organized, they would, he hoped, require no escort. Bradstreet was a New England officer who had been a captain in the last war, somewhat dogged and self-opinionated but brave, energetic and well fitted for this kind of service.

In May, Vaudreuil sent Coulon de Villiers with eleven hundred soldiers, Canadians and Indians, to harass Oswego and cut its communications with Albany. Nevertheless Bradstreet safely conducted a convoy of provisions and military stores to the garrison, and on the third of July set out on his return with the empty boats.

The party were pushing their way up the river in three divisions. The first of these, consisting of a hundred boats and three hundred men with Bradstreet at their head, were about nine miles from Oswego when, at three in the afternoon, they received a heavy volley from the forest on the east bank. It was fired by a part of Villiers's command, consisting by English accounts of about seven hundred men. A considerable number of the boatmen were killed or disabled and the others made for the shelter of the western shore. Some prisoners were taken in the confusion, and if the French had been content to stop here, they might fairly have claimed a kind of victory, but eager to push

571

their advantage, they tried to cross under cover of an island just above.

Bradstreet saw the movement and landed on the island with six or eight followers, among whom was young Captain Schuyler, afterwards General Schuyler of the Revolution. Their fire kept the enemy in check till others joined them, to the number of about twenty. These beat back the French a second and a third time and they now gave over the attempt and made for another ford at some distance above. Bradstreet saw their intention, and collecting two hundred and fifty men, was about to advance up the west bank to oppose them when Dr. Kirkland, a surgeon, came to tell him that the second division of boats had come up and that the men had landed. Bradstreet ordered them to stay where they were and defend the lower crossing, then hastened forward. But when he reached the upper ford, the French had passed the river and were ensconced in a pine swamp near the shore. Here he attacked them and both parties fired at each other from behind trees for an hour, with little effect. Bradstreet at length encouraged his men to make a rush at the enemy, who were put to flight and driven into the river, where many were shot or drowned as they tried to cross.

Another party of the French had meanwhile passed by a ford still higher up to support their comrades, but the fight was over before they reached the spot and they in their turn were set upon and driven back across the stream. Half an hour after, Captain Patten arrived from Onondaga with the grenadiers of Shirley's regiment, and late in the evening two hundred men came from Oswego to reinforce the victors. In the morning Bradstreet prepared to follow the French to their camp, twelve miles distant, but was prevented by a heavy rain which lasted all day. On the Monday following, he and his men reached Albany, bringing two prisoners, eighty French muskets and many knapsacks picked up in the woods. He had lost between sixty and seventy killed, wounded and taken.

The success of Bradstreet silenced for a time the enemies of Shirley. His cares, however, redoubled. He was anxious for Oswego, as the two prisoners declared that the French meant to attack it instead of waiting to be attacked from it. Nor was the news from that quarter reassuring. The engineer, Mackellar, wrote that the works were incapable of defense and Colonel Mercer, the commandant, reported general discontent in the garrison.

Captain John Vicars, an invalid officer of Shirley's regiment, arrived at Albany with yet more deplorable accounts. He had passed the winter at Oswego, where he declared the dearth of food to have been such that several councils of war had been held on the question of abandoning the place from sheer starvation. More than half his regiment died of hunger or disease, and in his own words, "had the poor fellows lived they must have eaten one another." Some of the men were lodged in barracks, though without beds, while many lay all winter in huts on the bare ground. Scurvy and dysentery made frightful havoc.

Through the spring and early summer, Shirley was gathering recruits, often of the meanest quality, and sending them to Oswego to fill out the two emaciated regiments. The place must be defended at any cost. Its fall would ruin not only the enterprise against Niagara and Frontenac, but also that against Ticonderoga and Crown Point, since having nothing more to fear on Lake Ontario, the French could unite their whole force on Lake Champlain, whether for defense or attack.

Towards the end of June, Abercrombie and Webb arrived at Albany, bringing a reinforcement of nine hundred regulars, consisting of Otway's regiment, or a part of it, and a body of Highlanders. Shirley resigned his command and Abercrombie requested him to go to New York, wait there till Lord Loudon arrived, and lay before him the state of affairs. Shirley waited till the twenty-third of July, when the earl at length appeared. He was a rough Scotch lord, hot and irascible, and the communications of his predecessor made, no doubt, in a manner somewhat pompous and self-satisfied, did not please him.

Loudon sailed up the Hudson in no placid mood. On reaching Albany, he abandoned the attempt against Niagara and Frontenac, and resolved to turn his whole force against Ticonderoga. Then he was met by an obstacle that both perplexed and angered him. By a royal order lately issued, all general and field officers with provincial commissions were to take rank only as eldest captains when serving in conjunction with regular troops. Hence the whole provincial army, as Winslow observes, might be put under the command of any British major.

The announcement of this regulation naturally caused great discontent. The New England officers held a meeting and voted with one voice that in their belief its enforcement would break up the provincial army and prevent the raising of another. Loudon, hearing of this, desired Winslow to meet him at Albany for a conference on the subject. There Winslow went with some of his chief officers.

The earl asked them to dinner and there was much talk, with no satisfactory result, whereupon, somewhat chafed, he required Winslow to answer in writing, yes or no, whether the provincial officers would obey the commander-in-chief and act in conjunction with the regulars. Thus forced to choose between acquiescence and flat mutiny, they declared their submission to his orders, at the same time asking as a favor that they might be allowed to act independently, to which Loudon gave for the present an unwilling assent.

Winslow by this time had made a forward movement and was now at Lake George with nearly half his command, while the rest were at Fort Edward under Lyman, or in detachments at Saratoga and the other small posts below.

At the beginning of August, Winslow wrote to the committees of the several provinces: "It looks as if it won't be long before we are fit for a remove"—that is, for an advance on Ticonderoga. On the twelfth Loudon sent Webb with the forty-fourth regiment and some of Bradstreet's boatmen to reinforce Oswego. They had been ready for a month, but confusion and misunderstanding arising from the change of command had prevented their departure.

Yet the utmost anxiety had prevailed for the safety of that important post, and on the twenty-eight Surgeon Thomas Williams wrote: "Whether Oswego is yet ours is uncertain. Would hope it is, as the reverse would be such a terrible shock as the country never felt, and may be a sad omen of what is coming upon poor sinful New England. Indeed, we can't expect anything but to be severely chastened till we are humbled for our pride and haughtiness."

His foreboding proved true. Webb had scarcely reached the Great Carrying Place when tidings of disaster fell upon him like a thunder-bolt. The French had descended in force upon Oswego, taken it with all its garrison, and as report ran, were advancing into the province six thousand strong.

Wood Creek had just been cleared, with great labor, of the trees that choked it. Webb ordered others to be felled and thrown into the stream to stop the progress of the enemy, then with shameful precipitation he burned the forts of the Carrying Place and retreated down the Mohawk to German Flats. Loudon ordered Winslow to think no more of Ticonderoga, but to stay where he was and hold the French in check. All was astonishment and dismay at the sudden blow.

This is how the catastrophe befell.

Since Vaudreuil became chief of the colony he had nursed the plan of seizing Oswego, yet hesitated to attempt it. Montcalm declares that he confirmed the governor's wavering purpose, but Montcalm himself had hesitated. In July, however, there came exaggerated reports that the English were moving upon Ticonderoga in greatly increased numbers and both Vaudreuil and the general conceived that a feint against Oswego would draw off the strength of the assailants, and if promptly and secretly executed, might even be turned successfully into a real attack.

Vaudreuil thereupon recalled Montcalm from Ticonderoga. Leaving that post in the keeping of Lévis and three thousand men, he embarked on Lake Champlain, rowed day and night, and reached Montreal on the nineteenth. Troops were arriving from Quebec and Indians from the far West. A band of Menominies from beyond Lake Michigan, naked, painted, plumed, greased, stamping, uttering sharp yelps, shaking feathered lances, brandishing tomahawks, danced the war dance before the governor, to the thumping of the Indian drum. Bougainville looked on astonished and thought of the Pyrrhic dance of the Greeks.

Montcalm and he left Montreal on the twenty-first, and reached Fort Frontenac in eight days. Rigaud, brother of the governor, had gone there some time before and crossed with seven hundred Canadians to the south side of the lake, where Villiers was encamped at Niaouré Bay, now Sackett's Harbor, with such of his detachment as war and disease had spared. Rigaud relieved him and took command of the united bands. With their aid the engineer, Descombles, reconnoitered the English forts and came back with the report that success was certain. It was but a confirmation of what had already been learned from deserters and prisoners, who declared that the main fort was but a loopholed wall held by six or seven hundred men, ill-fed, discontented and mutinous. Others said that they had been driven to desert by the want of good food, and that within a year twelve hundred men had died of disease at Oswego.

The battalions of La Sarre, Guienne and Béarn, with the colony regulars, a body of Canadians and about two hundred and fifty Indians, were destined for the enterprise. The whole force was a little above three thousand, abundantly supplied with artillery. La Sarre and Guienne were already at Fort Frontenac. Béarn was at Niagara, where the expedition arrived in a few days, much buffeted by the storms of Lake Ontario.

On the fourth of August all was ready. Montcalm embarked at night with the first division, crossed in darkness to Wolf Island, lay hidden there all day, and embarking again in the evening, joined Rigaud at Niaouré Bay at seven o'clock on the morning of the sixth. The second division followed, with provisions, hospital train and eighty artillery boats, and on the eighth all were united at the bay. On the ninth Rigaud, covered by the universal forest, marched in advance to protect the landing of the troops. Montcalm followed with the first division, and coasting the shore in bateaux, landed at midnight of the tenth within half a league of the first English fort. Four cannon were planted in battery upon the strand and the men bivouacked by their boats. So skillful were the assailants and so careless the assailed that the English knew nothing of their danger till the morning, when a reconnoitering canoe discovered the invaders. Two armed vessels soon came to cannonade them, but their light guns were no match for the heavy artillery of the French and they were forced to keep the offing.

Descombles, the engineer, went before dawn to reconnoiter the fort with several other officers and a party of Indians. While he was thus employed, one of these savages, hungry for scalps, took him in the gloom for an Englishman and shot him dead. Captain Pouchot, of the battalion of Béarn, replaced him and the attack was pushed vigorously. The Canadians and Indians, swarming through the forest, fired all day on the fort under cover of the trees. The second division came up with twenty-two more cannon and at night the first parallel was marked out at a hundred and eighty yards from the rampart. Stumps were grubbed up, fallen trunks shoved aside and a trench dug, sheltered by fascines, gabions and a strong abatis.

THE FALL OF OSWEGO

Fort Ontario, counted as the best of the three forts at Oswego, stood on a high plateau at the east or right side of the river where it entered the lake. It was in the shape of a star and was formed of trunks of trees set upright in the ground, hewn flat on two sides and closely fitted together—an excellent defense against musketry or swivels, but worthless against cannon. The garrison, three hundred and seventy in all, were the remnant of Pepperrell's regiment, joined to raw recruits lately sent up to fill the places of the sick and dead. They had eight small cannon and a mortar, with which on the next day, Friday the thirteenth, they kept up a brisk fire till towards night, when after growing more rapid for a time, it ceased and the fort showed no sign of life.

Not a cannon had yet opened on them from the trenches, but it was certain that, with the French artillery once in action, their wooden rampart would be shivered to splinters. Thus it was that Colonel Mercer, commandant at Oswego, thinking it better to lose the fort than to lose both fort and garrison, signaled to them from across the river to abandon their position and join him on the other side. Boats were sent to bring them off and they passed over unmolested after spiking their cannon and firing off their ammunition or throwing it into the well.

The fate of Oswego was now sealed. The principal work, called Old Oswego or Fort Pepperrell, stood at the mouth of the river on the west side, nearly opposite Fort Ontario and less than five hundred yards distant from it. The trading house, which formed the center of the place, was built of rough stone laid in clay and the wall which enclosed it was of the same materials; both would crumble in an instant at the touch of a twelve-pound shot. Towards the west and south they had been protected by an outer line of earthworks, mounted with cannon and forming an intrenched camp, while the side towards Fort Ontario was left wholly exposed in the rash confidence that this work, standing on the opposite heights, would guard against attack from that quarter.

On the hill, a fourth of a mile beyond Old Oswego, stood the unfinished stockade called New Oswego, Fort George or, by reason of its worthlessness, Fort Rascal. It had served as a cattle pen before the French appeared, but was now occupied by a hundred and fifty Jersey provincials. Old Oswego with its outwork was held by Shirley's regiment, chiefly invalids and raw recruits, to whom were now joined the garrison of Fort Ontario and a number of sailors, boatmen and laborers.

Montcalm lost no time. As soon as darkness set in he began a battery at the brink of the height on which stood the captured fort. His whole force toiled all night, digging, setting gabions and dragging up cannon, some of which had been taken from Braddock. Before daybreak twenty heavy pieces had been brought to the spot and nine were already in position. The work had been so rapid that the English imagined their enemies to number six thousand at least. The battery soon opened fire. Grape and round shot swept the intrenchment and crashed through the rotten masonry. The English, says a French officer, "were exposed to their shoe buckles." Their artillery was pointed the wrong way, in expectation of an attack, not from the east but from the west. They now made a shelter of pork barrels, three high and three deep, planted cannon behind them and returned the French fire with some effect.

Early in the morning Montcalm had ordered Rigaud to cross the river with the Canadians and Indians. There was a ford three quarters of a league above the forts and here they passed over unopposed, the English not having discovered the movement. The only danger was from the river. Some of the men were forced to swim, others waded to the waist and others to the neck, but they all crossed safely and presently showed themselves at the edge of the woods, yelling and firing their guns, too far for much execution but not too far to discourage the garrison.

The garrison were already disheartened. Colonel Mercer, the soul of the defense, had just been cut in two by a cannon shot while directing the gunners. Up to this time the defenders had behaved with spirit, but despair now seized them, increased by the screams and entreaties of the women, of whom there were more than a hundred in the place. There was a council of officers and then the white flag was raised. Bougainville went to propose terms of capitulation. "The cries, threats, and hideous howlings of our Canadians and Indians," says Vaudreuil, "made them quickly decide." "This," observes the Reverend Father Claude Godefroy Cocquard, "reminds me of the fall of Jericho before the shouts of the Israelites." The English surrendered prisoners of war, to the number, according to the governor, of sixteen hundred, which included the sailors, laborers and women.

The Canadians and Indians broke through all restraint and fell to plundering. There was an opening of rum barrels and a scene of drunkenness in which some of the prisoners had their share, while others tried to escape in the confusion and were tomahawked by the excited savages. Many more would have been butchered but for the efforts of Montcalm, who by unstinted promises succeeded in appeasing his ferocious allies, whom he dared not offend. "It will cost the King," he says, "eight or ten thousand livres in presents."

The loss on both sides is variously given. By the most trustworthy accounts, that of the English did not reach fifty killed, and that of the French was still less. In the forts and vessels were found above a hundred pieces of artillery, most of them swivels and other light guns, with a large quantity of powder, shot and shell. The victors burned the forts and the vessels on the stocks, destroyed such provisions and stores as they could not carry away and made the place a desert. The priest Piquet, who had joined the expedition, planted amid the ruin a tall cross, graven with the words *In hoc signo vincunt,* and near it was set a pole bearing the arms of France, with the inscription, *Manibus date lilia plenis.* Then the army decamped, loaded with prisoners and spoil, descended to Montreal, hung the captured flags in the churches and sang Te Deum in honor of their triumph.

It was the greatest triumph that French arms had yet achieved in America. The defeat of Braddock was an Indian victory; this last exploit was the result of bold enterprise and skillful tactics. With its laurels came its fruits. Hated Oswego had been laid in ashes and the would-be assailants forced to a vain and hopeless defense. France had conquered the undisputed command of Lake Ontario and her communications with the West were safe. A small garrison at Niagara and another at Frontenac would now hold those posts against any effort that the English could make this year and the whole French force could concentrate at Ticonderoga, repel the threatened attack and perhaps retort it by seizing Albany.

If the English, on the other side, had lost a great material advantage, they had lost no less in honor. The news of the surrender was received with indignation in England and in the colonies. Yet the behavior of the garrison was not so discreditable as it seemed. The position was indefensible and they could have held out at best but a few days more. They yielded too soon, but unless Webb had come to their aid, which was not to be expected, they must have yielded at last.

The French had scarcely gone when two English scouts, Thomas Harris and James Conner, came with a party of Indians to the scene of desolation. The ground was strewn with broken casks and bread sodden with rain. The remains of burnt bateaux and whaleboats were scattered along the shore. The great stone trading house in the old fort was a smoking ruin; Fort Rascal was still burning on the neighboring hill; Fort Ontario was a mass of ashes and charred logs, and by it stood two poles on which were written words which the visitors did not understand. They went back to Fort Johnson with their story and Oswego reverted for a time to the bears, foxes and wolves.

~~~~~~

CHAPTER 8

Partisan War

A SENSE OF POWERLESSNESS ARISING FROM A WANT of union spread alarm through the northern and middle colonies after the fall of Oswego and drew these desponding words from William Livingston, of New Jersey: "The colonies are nearly exhausted, and their funds already anticipated by expensive unexecuted projects. Jealous are they of each other; some ill-constituted, others shaken with intestine divisions, and, if I may be allowed the expression, parsimonious even to prodigality. Our assemblies are diffident of their governors, governors despise their assemblies; and both mutually misrepresent each other to the Court of Great Britain."

In spite of these difficulties, Loudon now had about ten thousand men at his command, though not all fit for duty. They were posted from Albany to Lake George. The earl himself was at Fort Edward, while about three thousand of the provincials still lay, under Winslow, at the lake. Montcalm faced them at Ticonderoga with five thousand three hundred regulars and Canadians, in a position where they could defy three times their number.

"The sons of Belial are too strong for me," jocosely wrote Winslow and he set himself to intrenching his camp, then had the forest cut down for the space of a mile from the lake to the mountains, so that the trees, lying in what he calls a "promiscuous manner," formed an almost impenetrable abatis. An escaped prisoner told him that the French were coming to visit him with fourteen thousand men, but Montcalm thought no more of stirring than Loudon himself, and each stood watching the other, with the lake between them, till the season closed.

Meanwhile the western borders were still ravaged by the tomahawk. New York, New Jersey, Pennsylvania, Maryland and Virginia all writhed under the infliction. Each had made a chin of blockhouses and wooden forts to cover its frontier and manned them with disorderly bands, lawless and almost beyond control. The case was at the worst in Pennsylvania, where the tedious quarreling of governor and Assembly, joined to the doggedly pacific attitude of the Quakers, made vigorous defense impossible.

The waters and mountains of Lake George, and not the western borders, were the chief center of partisan war. Ticonderoga was a hornet's nest, pouring out swarms of savages to infest the highways and byways of the wilderness. The English at Fort William Henry, having few Indians, could not retort in kind, but they kept their scouts and rangers in active movement.

Few were so conspicuous as the blunt and sturdy Israel Putnam. Winslow writes in October that he has just returned from the best "scout" yet made, and that being a man of strict truth, he may be entirely trusted. Putnam had gone with six followers down Lake George in a whaleboat to a point on the east side, opposite the present village of Hague, hid the boat, crossed northeasterly to Lake Champlain, three miles from the French fort, climbed the mountain that overlooks and made a complete reconnaissance. Then he approached, chased three Frenchmen who escaped within the lines, climbed the mountain again and, moving westward along the ridge, made a minute survey of every outpost between the fort and Lake George.

Early in September of 1756 a band of New England rangers came to Winslow's camp with three prisoners taken within the lines of Ticonderoga. Their captain was Robert Rogers, of New Hampshire, a strong, well-knit figure, in dress and appearance more woodsman than soldier, with a clear, bold eye and features that would have been good but for the ungainly proportions of the nose. He had passed his boyhood in the rough surroundings of a frontier village. Growing to manhood, he engaged in some occupation which, he says, led him to frequent journeyings in the wilderness between the French and English settlements and gave him a good knowledge of both. It taught him.

582

also to speak a little French. He does not disclose the nature of this mysterious employment, but there can be little doubt that it was a smuggling trade with Canada.

His character leaves much to be desired. He had been charged with forgery, or complicity in it, seems to have had no scruple in matters of business, and after the war was accused of treasonable dealings with the French and Spaniards in the West. He was ambitious and violent, yet able in more ways than one, by no means uneducated, and so skilled in woodcraft, so energetic and resolute, that his services were invaluable. In recounting his own adventures, his style is direct, simple, without boasting, and to all appearance without exaggeration.

During the past summer he had raised a band of men, chiefly New Hampshire borderers, and made a series of daring excursions which gave him a prominent place in this hardy byplay of war. In the spring of the present year, 1756, he raised another company and was commissioned as its captain, with his brother Richard as his first lieutenant and the intrepid John Stark as his second. In July still another company was formed, and Richard Rogers was promoted to command it. Before the following spring there were seven such, and more were afterwards added, forming a battalion dispersed on various service, but all under the orders of Robert Rogers, with the rank of major. These rangers wore a sort of woodland uniform, which varied in the different companies, and were armed with smoothbore guns, loaded with buckshot, bullets, or sometimes both.

The best of them were commonly employed on Lake George, and nothing can surpass the adventurous hardihood of their lives. Summer and winter, day and night, were alike to them. Embarked in whale-boats or birch canoes, they glided under the silent moon or in the languid glare of a breathless August day, when islands floated in dreamy haze and the hot air was thick with odors of the pine, or in the bright October, when the jay screamed from the woods, squirrels gathered their winter hoard and congregated blackbirds chattered farewell to their summer haunts; when gay mountains basked in light, maples dropped leaves of rustling gold, sumachs glowed like rubies under the dark green of the unchanging spruce and mossed rocks with all their painted plumage lay double in the watery mirror.

Or, in the tomblike silence of the winter forest, with breath frozen on his beard, the ranger strode on snowshoes over the spotless drifts and, like Dürer's knight, a ghastly death stalked ever at his side. There were those among them for whom this stern life had a fascination that made all other existence tame.

Rogers and his men had been in active movement since midwinter. In January they skated down Lake George, passed Ticonderoga, hid themselves by the forest road between that post and Crown Point, intercepted two sledges loaded with provisions and carried the drivers to Fort William Henry. In February they climbed a hill near Crown Point and made a plan of the works, then lay in ambush by the road from the fort to the neighboring village, captured a prisoner, burned houses and barns, killed fifty cattle and returned without loss. At the end of the month they went again to Crown Point, burned more houses and barns and reconnoitered Ticonderoga on the way back.

Such excursions were repeated throughout the spring and summer. The reconnaissance of Ticonderoga and the catching of prisoners there for the sake of information were always capital objects. The valley, four miles in extent, that lay between the foot of Lake George and the French fort was at this time guarded by four distinct outposts or fortified camps. Watched as it was at all points, and ranged incessantly by Indians in the employ of France, Rogers and his men knew every yard of the ground.

On a morning in May he lay in ambush with eleven followers on a path between the fort and the nearest camp. A large body of soldiers passed. The rangers counted a hundred and eighteen and lay close in their hiding place. Soon after came a party of twenty-two. They fired on them, killed six, captured one and escaped with him to Fort William Henry.

In October, Rogers was passing with twenty men in two whaleboats through the seeming solitude of the Narrows when a voice called to them out of the woods. It was that of Captain Shepherd, of the New Hampshire regiment, who had been captured two months before and had lately made his escape. He told them that the French had the fullest information of the numbers and movements of the English; that letters often reached them from within the English lines; and that Lydius, a Dutch trader at Albany, was their principal correspondent.

Arriving at Ticonderoga, Rogers cautiously approached the fort till

584

about noon he saw a sentinel on the road leading to the woods. Followed by five of his men, he walked directly towards him. The man challenged and Rogers answered in French. Perplexed for a moment, the soldier suffered him to approach, till, seeing his mistake, he called out in amazement, *"Qui êtes-vous?"* "Rogers" was the answer, and the sentinel was seized, led in hot haste to the boats and carried to the English fort, where he gave important information.

An exploit of Rogers towards midsummer greatly perplexed the French. He embarked at the end of June with fifty men in five whale-boats, made light and strong expressly for this service, rowed about ten miles down Lake George, landed on the east side, carried the boats six miles over a gorge of the mountains, launched them again in South Bay and rowed down the narrow prolongation of Lake Champlain under cover of darkness.

At dawn they were within six miles of Ticonderoga. They landed, hid their boats and lay close all day. Embarking again in the evening, they rowed with muffled oars under the shadow of the eastern shore and passed so close to the French fort that they heard the voices of the sentinels calling the watchword. In the morning they had left it five miles behind. Again they hid in the woods, and from their lurking place saw bateaux passing, some northward and some southward, along the narrow lake. Crown Point was ten or twelve miles farther on. They tried to pass it after nightfall, but the sky was too clear and the stars too bright, and as they lay hidden the next day nearly a hundred boats passed before them on the way to Ticonderoga. Some other boats which appeared about noon landed near them and they watched the soldiers at dinner, within a musket shot of their lurking place.

The next night was more favorable. They embarked at nine in the evening, passed Crown Point unseen and hid themselves as before, ten miles below. It was the seventh of July. Thirty boats and a schooner passed them, returning towards Canada. On the next night they rowed fifteen miles farther and then sent men to reconnoiter. They reported a schooner at anchor about a mile off. They were preparing to board her when two sloops appeared, coming up the lake at but a short distance from the land. They gave them a volley and called on them to surrender, but the crews put off in boats and made for the opposite shore. They followed and seized them. Out of twelve men, their fire had killed three and wounded two, one of whom, says Rogers in his report, "could not march, therefore we put an end to him, to prevent discovery." They sank the vessels, which were laden with wine, brandy and flour, hid their boats on the west shore and returned on foot with their prisoners.

Some weeks after, Rogers returned to the place where he had left the boats, embarked in them, reconnoitered the lake nearly to St. John, hid them again eight miles north of Crown Point, took three prisoners near that post and carried them to Fort William Henry. In the next month the French found several English boats in a small cove north of Crown Point. Bougainville propounds five different hypotheses to account for their being there, and exploring parties were sent out in the vain attempt to find some water passage by which they could have reached the spot without passing under the guns of two French forts.

The French, on their side, still kept their war parties in motion, and Vaudreuil faithfully chronicled in his dispatches every English scalp they brought in. He believed in Indians and sent them to Ticonderoga in numbers that were sometimes embarrassing. Even Potawatomis from Lake Michigan were prowling about Winslow's camp and silently killing his sentinels with arrows while their medicine men remained at Ticonderoga practicing sorcery and divination to aid the warriors or learn how it fared with them.

Till November the hostile forces continued to watch each other from the opposite ends of Lake George. On the first of the month, however, the French began to move off towards Canada, and before many days Ticonderoga was left in the keeping of five or six companies. Winslow's men followed their example. Major Eyre, with four hundred regulars, took possession of Fort William Henry and the provincials marched for home, their ranks thinned by camp diseases and smallpox.

Major Eyre and his soldiers, in their wilderness exile by the borders of Lake George, whiled the winter away with few other excitements than the evening howl of wolves from the frozen mountains or some nocturnal savage shooting at a sentinel from behind a stump on the moonlit fields of snow.

The winter dragged slowly away and the ice of Lake George, cracking with change of temperature, uttered its strange cry of agony, heralding that dismal season when winter begins to relax its grip but spring still holds aloof; when the sap stirs in the sugar maples but the buds refuse to swell, and even the catkins of the willows will not burst their brown integuments; when the forest is patched with snow, though on its sunny slopes one hears in the stillness the whisper of trickling waters that ooze from the half-thawed soil and saturated beds of fallen leaves; when clouds hang low on the darkened mountains and cold mists entangle themselves in the tops of the pines; now a dull rain, now a sharp morning frost and now a storm of snow powdering the waste and wrapping it again in the pall of winter.

In this cheerless season, on St. Patrick's Day, the seventeenth of March, the Irish soldiers who formed a part of the garrison of Fort William Henry were paying homage to their patron saint in libations of heretic rum, the product of New England stills, and it is said that John Stark's rangers forgot theological differences in their zeal to share the festivity. The story adds that they were restrained by their commander and that their enforced sobriety proved the saving of the fort. This may be doubted, for without counting the English soldiers of the garrison who had no special call to be drunk that day, the fort was in no danger till twenty-four hours after, when the revelers had had time to rally from their pious carouse.

Whether rangers or British soldiers, it is certain that watchmen were on the alert during the night between the eighteenth and nineteenth and that towards one in the morning they heard a sound of axes far down the lake, followed by the faint glow of a distant fire. The inference was plain that an enemy was there and that the necessity of warming himself had overcome his caution. Then all was still for some two hours, when, listening in the pitchy darkness, the watchers heard the footsteps of a great body of men approaching on the ice, which at the time was bare of snow. The garrison were at their posts and all the cannon on the side towards the lake vomited grape- and round-shot in the direction of the sound, which thereafter was heard no more.

Those who had made it were a detachment, called by Vaudreuil an army, sent by him to seize the English fort. Shirley had planned a similar stroke against Ticonderoga a year before, but the provincial levies had come in so slowly and the ice had broken up so soon that the scheme was abandoned.

Vaudreuil was more fortunate. The whole force, regulars, Canadians and Indians, was ready to his hand. No pains were spared in equipping them. Overcoats, blankets, bearskins to sleep on, tarpaulins to sleep under, spare moccasins, spare mittens, kettles, axes, needles, awls, flint and steel and many miscellaneous articles were provided, to be dragged by the men on light Indian sledges, along with provisions for twelve days. The cost of the expedition is set at a million francs. To the disgust of the officers from France, the governor named his brother Rigaud for the chief command, and before the end of February the whole party was on its march along the ice of Lake Champlain.

They rested nearly a week at Ticonderoga, where no less than three hundred short scaling ladders, so constructed that two or more could be joined in one, had been made for them, and here, too, they received a reinforcement, which raised their number to sixteen hundred. Then, marching three days along Lake George, they neared the fort on the evening of the eighteenth and prepared for a general assault before daybreak.

The garrison, including rangers, consisted of three hundred and forty-six effective men. The fort was not strong and a resolute assault by numbers so superior must, it seems, have overpowered the defenders, but the Canadians and Indians who composed most of the attacking force were not suited for such work, and disappointed in his hope of a surprise, Rigaud withdrew them at daybreak, after trying in vain to burn the buildings outside.

A few hours after, the whole body reappeared, filing off to surround the fort, on which they kept up a brisk but harmless fire of musketry. In the night they were heard again on the ice, approaching as if for an assault, and the cannon, firing towards the sound, again drove them back. There was silence for a while till tongues of flame lighted up the gloom and two sloops, icebound in the lake, and a large number of bateaux on the shore were seen to be on fire. A party sallied to save them, but it was too late. In the morning they were all consumed and the enemy had vanished.

It was Sunday, the twentieth. Everything was quiet till noon, when the French filed out of the woods and marched across the ice in procession, ostentatiously carrying their scaling ladders and showing themselves to the best effect. They stopped at a safe distance, fronting towards the fort, and several of them advanced, waving a red flag. An officer with a few men went to meet them and returned bringing Le Mercier, chief of the Canadian artillery, who, being led blindfold into the fort, announced himself as bearer of a message from Rigaud.

He was conducted to the room of Major Eyre, where all the British officers were assembled, and after mutual compliments he invited them to give up the place peaceably, promising the most favorable terms and threatening a general assault and massacre in case of refusal. Eyre said that he should defend himself to the last, and the envoy, again blindfolded, was led back to whence he came.

The whole French force now advanced as if to storm the works, and the garrison prepared to receive them. Nothing came of it but a fusillade, to which the British made no reply. At night the French were heard advancing again and each man nerved himself for the crisis. The real attack, however, was not against the fort but against the buildings outside, which consisted of several storehouses, a hospital, a sawmill and the huts of the rangers, besides a sloop on the stocks and piles of planks and cordwood. Covered by the night, the assailants crept up with fagots of resinous sticks, placed them against the farther side of the buildings, kindled them and escaped before the flames rose, while the garrison, straining their ears in the thick darkness, fired wherever they heard a sound.

Before morning all around them was in a blaze and they had much ado to save the fort barracks from the shower of burning cinders. At ten o'clock the fires had subsided and a thick fall of snow began, filling the air with a restless chaos of large moist flakes. This lasted all day and all the next night, till the ground and the ice were covered to a depth of three feet and more. The French lay close in their camps till a little before dawn on Tuesday morning, when twenty volunteers from the regulars made a bold attempt to burn the sloop on the stocks, with several storehouses and other structures, and several hundred scows and whaleboats which had thus far escaped. They were only in part successful, but they fired the sloop and some buildings near it and stood far out on the ice watching the flaming vessel, a superb bonfire amid the wilderness of snow. The spectacle cost the volunteers a fourth of their number killed and wounded.

On Wednesday morning the sun rose bright on a scene of wintry splendor and the frozen lake was dotted with Rigaud's retreating followers, toiling towards Canada on snowshoes. Before they reached it many of them were blinded for a while by the insufferable glare and their comrades led them homeward by the hand.

CHAPTER 9

~~~~~~

Fort William Henry

S PRING CAME AT LAST, AND THE DUTCH BURGHERS
of Albany heard, faint from the far height, the clamor of the wild
fowl, streaming in long files northward to their summer home. As the
aerial travelers winged their way, the seat of war lay spread beneath
them like a map.

First the blue Hudson, slumbering among its forests, with the forts
along its banks, Half-Moon, Stillwater, Saratoga and the geometric
lines and earthen mounds of Fort Edward. Then a broad belt of dingy
evergreen, and beyond, released from wintry fetters, the glistening
breast of Lake George, with Fort William Henry at its side, amid
charred ruins and a desolation of prostrate forests. From there the
lake stretched northward, like some broad river, trenched between
mountain ranges still leafless and gray. Then they looked down on
Ticonderoga, with the flag of the Bourbons like a flickering white
speck waving on its ramparts; and next on Crown Point with its tower
of stone.

Lake Champlain now spread before them, widening as they flew:
on the left, the mountain wilderness of the Adirondacks, like a stormy
sea congealed; on the right, the long procession of the Green Mountains; and far beyond, on the dim verge of the eastern sky, the White
Mountains throned in savage solitude. They passed over the bastioned
square of Fort St. John, Fort Chambly guarding the rapids of the
Richelieu, and the broad belt of the St. Lawrence, with Montreal

591

seated on its bank. Here we leave them, to build their nests and hatch their brood among the fens of the lonely North.

French prospects, on the whole, were hopeful that spring. The victory at Oswego had wrought marvels among the Indians, inspired the faithful, confirmed the wavering and daunted the ill-disposed. The whole West was astir, ready to pour itself again in blood and fire against the English border, and even the Cherokees and Choctaws, old friends of the British colonies, seemed on the point of turning against them.

The Five Nations were half won for France. In November a large deputation of them came to renew the chain of friendship at Montreal. "I have laid Oswego in ashes," said Vaudreuil, "the English quail before me. Why do you nourish serpents in your bosom? They mean only to enslave you." The deputies trampled under foot the medals the English had given them and promised the "Devourer of Villages," for so they styled the governor, that they would never more lift the hatchet against his children. The chief difficulty was to get rid of them, for, being clothed and fed at the expense of the King, they were in no haste to take leave, and learning that New Year's Day was a time of visits, gifts and health-drinking, they declared that they would stay to share its pleasures, which they did, to their own satisfaction and the annoyance of those who were forced to entertain them and their squaws.

An active siding with France was to be expected only from the western bands of the Confederacy. Neutrality alone could be hoped for from the others, who were too near the English safely to declare against them, while from one of the tribes, the Mohawks, even neutrality was doubtful.

Vaudreuil, while disliking the French regulars, felt that he could not dispense with them and had asked for a reinforcement. His request was granted and the colonial minister informed him that twenty-four hundred men had been ordered to Canada to strengthen the colony regulars and the battalions of Montcalm. This, according to the estimate of the minister, would raise the regular force in Canada to sixty-six hundred rank and file.

The announcement was followed by another, less agreeable. It was to the effect that a formidable squadron was fitting out in British ports. Was Quebec to be attacked, or Louisbourg? Louisbourg was beyond reach of succor from Canada. It must rely on its own strength and on help from France. But so long as Quebec was threatened, all the troops in the colony must be held ready to defend it and the hope of attacking England in her own domains must be abandoned. Till these doubts were solved, nothing could be done, and hence great activity in catching prisoners for the sake of news. A few were brought in, but they knew no more of the matter than the French themselves and Vaudreuil and Montcalm rested for a while in suspense.

The truth, had they known it, would have gladdened their hearts. The English preparations were aimed at Louisbourg. In the autumn before, Loudon, prejudiced against all plans of his predecessor, Shirley, proposed to the ministry a scheme of his own, involving a possible attack on Quebec but with the reduction of Louisbourg as its immediate object—an important object, no doubt, but one that had no direct bearing on the main question of controlling the interior of the continent.

Pitt, then for a brief space at the head of the government, accepted the suggestion and set himself to executing it, but he was hampered by opposition and early in April was forced to resign. Then followed a contest of rival claimants to office, and the war against France was made subordinate to disputes of personal politics. Meanwhile one Florence Hensey, a spy at London, had informed the French court that a great armament was fitting out for America, though he could not tell its precise destination. Without loss of time, three French squadrons were sent across the Atlantic with orders to rendezvous at Louisbourg, the conjectured point of attack.

The English were as tardy as their enemies were prompt. Everything depended on speed, yet their fleet, under Admiral Holbourne, consisting of fifteen ships of the line and three frigates, with about five thousand troops on board, did not get to sea till the fifth of May, when it made sail for Halifax, where Loudon was to meet it with additional forces.

Loudon had drawn off the best part of the troops from the northern frontier and they were now at New York waiting for embarkation. That the design might be kept secret, he laid an embargo on colonial shipping, a measure which exasperated the colonists without answering its purpose.

Now ensued a long delay, during which the troops, the provincial levies, the transports destined to carry them and the ships of war which were to serve as escort all lay idle. In the interval Loudon showed great activity in writing dispatches and other avocations more or less proper to a commander, being always busy without, according to Franklin, accomplishing anything. One Innis, who had come with a message from the governor of Pennsylvania and had waited more than a fortnight for the general's reply, remarked of him that he was like St. George on a tavern sign, always on horseback and never riding on.

Yet nobody longed more than he to reach the rendezvous at Halifax. He was waiting for news of Holbourne and he waited in vain. He knew only that a French fleet had been seen off the coast strong enough to overpower his escort and sink all his transports. But the season was growing late; he must act quickly if he was to act at all.

He and Sir Charles Hardy agreed between them that the risk must be run, and on the twentieth of June the whole force put to sea. They met no enemy and entered Halifax harbor on the thirtieth. Holbourne and his fleet had not yet appeared, but his ships soon came straggling in, and before the tenth of July all were at anchor before the town.

Then there was more delay. The troops, nearly twelve thousand in all, were landed and weeks were spent in drilling them and planting vegetables for their refreshment. Sir Charles Hay was put under arrest for saying that the nation's money was spent in sham battles and raising cabbages. Some attempts were made to learn the state of Louisbourg, and Captain Gorham, of the rangers, who reconnoitered it from a fishing vessel, brought back an imperfect report, upon which, after some hesitation, it was resolved to proceed to the attack.

The troops were embarked again and all was ready, when on the fourth of August a sloop came from Newfoundland bringing letters found on board a French vessel lately captured. From these it appeared that all three of the French squadrons were united in the harbor of Louisbourg, to the number of twenty-two ships of the line, besides several frigates, and that the garrison had been increased to a total force of seven thousand men, ensconced in the strongest fortress of the continent. So far as concerned the naval force, the account was true. La Motte, the French admiral, had with him a fleet carrying an

594

aggregate of thirteen hundred and sixty cannon, anchored in a sheltered harbor under the guns of the town.

Success was now hopeless and the costly enterprise was at once abandoned. Loudon with his troops sailed back for New York, and Admiral Holbourne, who had been joined by four additional ships, steered for Louisbourg in hopes that the French fleet would come out and fight him. He cruised off the port, but La Motte did not accept the challenge.

The elements declared for France. A September gale, of fury rare even on that tempestuous coast, burst upon the British fleet. "It blew a perfect hurricane," says the unfortunate admiral, "and drove us right on shore." One ship was dashed on the rocks, two leagues from Louisbourg. A shifting of the wind in the nick of time saved the rest from total wreck. Nine were dismasted. Others threw their cannon into the sea. Not one was left fit for immediate action, and had La Motte sailed out of Louisbourg he would have had them all at his mercy.

Delay, the source of most of the disasters that befell England and her colonies in this dismal epoch, was the ruin of the Louisbourg expedition. The greater part of La Motte's fleet reached its destination a full month before that of Holbourne. Had the reverse taken place, the fortress must have fallen. As it was, the ill-starred attempt, drawing off the British forces from the frontier, where they were needed most, did for France more than she could have done for herself, and gave Montcalm and Vaudreuil the opportunity to execute a scheme which they had nursed since the fall of Oswego.

The time was come not only to strike the English on Lake George, but perhaps to seize Fort Edward and carry terror to Albany itself. Only one difficulty remained, the want of provisions. Agents were sent to collect corn and bacon among the inhabitants; the curés and militia captains were ordered to aid in the work and enough was presently found to feed twelve thousand men for a month.

The emissaries of the governor had been busy all winter among the tribes of the West and North, and more than a thousand savages, lured by the prospect of gifts, scalps and plunder, were now encamped at Montreal. Many of them had never visited a French settlement before. All were eager to see Montcalm, whose exploit in taking Oswego had inflamed their imagination, and one day, on a visit of ceremony, an orator from Michilimackinac addressed the general thus: "We wanted to see this famous man who tramples the English under his feet. We thought we should find him so tall that his head would be lost in the clouds. But you are a little man, my Father. It is when we look into your eyes that we see the greatness of the pine tree and the fire of the eagle."

Soon Canadians and Indians were moving by detachments up Lake Champlain. Fleets of bateaux and canoes followed each other day by day along the capricious lake, in calm or storm, sunshine or rain, till towards the end of July the whole force was gathered at Ticonderoga, the base of the intended movement. Bourlamaque had been there since May with the battalions of Béarn and Royal Roussillon, finishing the fort, sending out war parties and trying to discover the force and designs of the English at Fort William Henry.

Here now was gathered a martial population of eight thousand men, including the brightest civilization and the darkest barbarism: from the scholar-soldier Montcalm and his no less accomplished aide-de-camp; from Lévis, conspicuous for graces of person; from a throng of courtly young officers, who would have seemed out of place in that wilderness had they not done their work so well in it; from these to the foulest man-eating savage of the uttermost northwest.

Of Indian allies there were nearly two thousand. One of their tribes, the Iowas, spoke a language which no interpreter understood, and they all bivouacked where they saw fit, for no man could control them.

Preparations were urged on with the utmost energy. Provisions, camp equipage, ammunition, cannon and bateaux were dragged by gangs of men up the road from the camp of Lévis to the head of the rapids. The work went on through heat and rain, by day and night, till at the end of July all was done.

Brandy being prudently denied them, the Indian allies grew restless and the greater part paddled up the lake. They encamped to wait the arrival of the army and amused themselves meantime with killing rattlesnakes, there being a populous den of those reptiles among the neighboring rocks.

Montcalm sent a circular letter to the regular officers, urging them to dispense for a while with luxuries and even comforts. "We have but few bateaux, and these are so filled with stores that a large division of the army must go by land," and he directed that everything not absolutely necessary should be left behind and that a canvas shelter to every two officers should serve them for a tent and a bearskin for a bed. "Yet I do not forbid a mattress," he adds. "Age and infirmities may make it necessary to some, but I shall not have one myself, and make no doubt that all who can will willingly imitate me."

The bateaux lay ready by the shore but could not carry the whole force, and Lévis received orders to march by the side of the lake with twenty-five hundred men, Canadians, regulars and Iroquois. He set out at daybreak of the thirtieth of July, his men carrying nothing but their knapsacks, blankets and weapons. Guided by the unerring Indians, they climbed the steep gorge at the side of Rogers Rock, gained the valley beyond and marched southward along a Mohawk trail which threaded the forest in a course parallel to the lake. The way was of the roughest. Many straggled from the line and two officers completely broke down. The first destination of the party was the mouth of Ganouskie Bay, now called Northwest Bay, where they were to wait for Montcalm and kindle three fires as a signal that they had reached the rendezvous.

Montcalm left a detachment to hold Ticonderoga, and then on the first of August, at two in the afternoon, he embarked with all his remaining force. Including those with Lévis, the expedition counted about seventy-six hundred men, of whom more than sixteen hundred were Indians. At five in the afternoon they reached the place where the Indians, having finished their rattlesnake hunt, were smoking their pipes and waiting for the army. The red warriors embarked and joined the French flotilla, and now as evening drew near was seen one of those wild pageantries of war which Lake George has often witnessed.

A restless multitude of birch canoes, filled with painted savages, glided by shores and islands like troops of swimming waterfowl. Two hundred and fifty bateaux came next, moved by sail and oar, some bearing the Canadian militia and some the battalions of Old France in trim and gay attire: first, La Reine and Languedoc; then the colony regulars; then La Sarre and Guienne; then the Canadian brigade of Courtemanche; then the cannon and mortars, each on a platform sustained by two bateaux lashed side by side and rowed by the militia of Saint-Ours; then the battalions of Béarn and Royal Roussillon; then the Canadians of Gaspé, with the provision bateaux and the field hospital; and lastly a rear guard of regulars closed the line.

So, under the flush of sunset, they held their course along the romantic lake, to play their part in the historic drama that lends a stern enchantment to its fascinating scenery. They passed the Narrows in mist and darkness, and when a little before dawn they rounded the high promontory of Tongue Mountain, they saw far on the right three fiery sparks shining through the gloom. These were the signal fires of Lévis, to tell them that he had reached the appointed spot. Canoes and bateaux were drawn up on the beach and the united forces made their bivouac together.

About ten o'clock at night two boats set out from Fort William Henry to reconnoiter. They were passing a point of land on their left, two miles or more down the lake, when the men on board descried through the gloom a strange object against the bank and they rowed towards it to learn what it might be. It was an awning over the bateaux that carried Roubaud and his brother missionaries.

As the rash oarsmen drew near, the bleating of a sheep in one of the French provision boats warned them of danger, and turning, they pulled for their lives towards the eastern shore. Instantly more than a thousand Indians threw themselves into their canoes and dashed in hot pursuit, making the lake and the mountains ring with the din of their war whoops.

The fugitives had nearly reached land when their pursuers opened fire. They replied, shot one Indian dead and wounded another, then snatched their oars again and gained the beach. But the whole savage crew was upon them. Several were killed, three were taken, and the rest escaped in the dark woods. The prisoners were brought before Montcalm and gave him valuable information on the strength and position of the English.

As the sun rose above the eastern mountains the French camp was all astir. The column of Lévis, with Indians to lead the way, moved through the forest towards the fort and Montcalm followed with the main body. Then the artillery boats rounded the point that had hid them from the sight of the English, saluting them as they did so with musketry and cannon, while a host of savages put out upon the lake, ranged their canoes abreast in a line from shore to shore and advanced slowly with measured paddle strokes and yells of defiance.

The position of the enemy was full in sight before them. At the head of the lake, towards the right, stood the fort, close to the edge of the water. On its left was a marsh; then the rough piece of ground where Johnson had encamped two years before; then a low, flat, rocky hill, crowned with an intrenched camp; and lastly, on the extreme left, another marsh. Far around the fort and up the slopes of the western mountain the forest had been cut down and burned and the ground was cumbered with blackened stumps and charred carcasses and limbs of fallen trees, strewn in savage disorder one upon another. This was the work of Winslow the autumn before.

Distant shouts and war cries, the clatter of musketry, white puffs of smoke in the dismal clearing and along the scorched edge of the bordering forest told that Lévis's Indians were skirmishing with parties of the English who had gone out to save the cattle roaming in the neighborhood and burn some outbuildings that would have favored the besiegers. Others were taking down the tents that stood on a plateau near the foot of the mountain on the right and moving them to the intrenchment on the hill. The garrison sallied from the fort to support their comrades and for a time the firing was hot.

A brave Scotch veteran, Lieutenant Colonel Monro, of the thirty-fifth regiment, was in command of the fort. General Webb lay fourteen miles distant at Fort Edward, with twenty-six hundred men, chiefly provincials. On the twenty-fifth of July he had made a visit to Fort William Henry, examined the place, given some orders and returned on the twenty-ninth. He then wrote to the governor of New York, telling him that the French were certainly coming, begging him to send up the militia and saying: "I am determined to march to Fort William Henry with the whole army under my command as soon as I shall hear of the farther approach of the enemy."

Instead of doing so he waited three days and then sent up a detachment of two hundred regulars under Lieutenant Colonel Young and eight hundred Massachusetts men under Colonel Frye. This raised the force at the lake to twenty-two hundred, including sailors and mechanics, and reduced that of Webb to sixteen hundred, besides

599

half as many more distributed at Albany and the intervening forts. If, according to his spirited intention, he should go to the rescue of Monro, he must leave some of his troops behind him to protect the lower posts from a possible French inroad by way of South Bay. Thus his power of aiding Monro was slight, so rashly had Loudon, intent on Louisbourg, left this frontier open to attack.

When the skirmishing around the fort was over, La Corne, with a body of Indians, occupied the road that led to Fort Edward and Lévis encamped hard by to support him, while Montcalm proceeded to examine the ground and settle his plan of attack. He made his way to the rear of the intrenched camp and reconnoitered it, hoping to carry it by assault, but it had a breastwork of stones and logs and he thought the attempt too hazardous. The ground where he stood was that where Dieskau had been defeated, and as the fate of his predecessor was not of flattering augury, he resolved to besiege the fort in form.

He chose for the site of his operations the ground now covered by the village of Caldwell. A little to the north of it was a ravine, beyond which he formed his main camp, while Lévis occupied a tract of dry ground beside the marsh from which he could easily move to intercept succors from Fort Edward on the one hand or repel a sortie from Fort William Henry on the other. A brook ran down the ravine and entered the lake at a small cove protected from the fire of the fort by a point of land, and at this place, still called Artillery Cove, Montcalm prepared to debark his cannon and mortars.

Having made his preparations, he sent Fontbrune, one of his aides-de-camp, with a letter to Monro. "I owe it to humanity," he wrote, "to summon you to surrender. At present I can restrain the savages, and make them observe the terms of a capitulation, as I might not have power to do under other circumstances; and an obstinate defense on your part could only retard the capture of the place a few days, and endanger an unfortunate garrison which cannot be relieved, in consequence of the dispositions I have made. I demand a decisive answer within an hour."

Monro replied that he and his soldiers would defend themselves to the last. While the flags of truce were flying, the Indians swarmed over the fields before the fort, and when they learned the result an

Abenaki chief shouted in broken French: "You won't surrender, eh! Fire away then, and fight your best; for if I catch you, you shall get no quarter." Monro emphasized his refusal by a general discharge of his cannon.

The trenches were opened on the night of the fourth—a task of extreme difficulty, as the ground was covered by a profusion of half-burned stumps, roots, branches and fallen trunks. Eight hundred men toiled till daylight with pick, spade and ax, while the cannon from the fort flashed through the darkness and grape- and round-shot whistled and screamed over their heads. Some of the English balls reached the camp beyond the ravine and disturbed the slumbers of the officers off duty as they lay wrapped in their blankets and bearskins. Before daybreak the first parallel was made, a battery was nearly finished on the left and another was begun on the right. The men now worked under cover, safe in their burrows; one gang relieved another and the work went on all day.

The Indians were far from doing what was expected of them. Instead of scouting in the direction of Fort Edward to learn the movements of the enemy and prevent surprise, they loitered about the camp and in the trenches or amused themselves by firing at the fort from behind stumps and logs. Some, in imitation of the French, dug little trenches for themselves, in which they wormed their way towards the rampart and now and then picked off an artilleryman, not without loss on their own side.

On the afternoon of the fifth Montcalm invited them to a council, gave them belts of wampum and mildly remonstrated with them. "Why expose yourselves without necessity? I grieve bitterly over the losses that you have met, for the least among you is precious to me. No doubt it is a good thing to annoy the English, but that is not the main point. You ought to inform me of everything the enemy is doing and always keep parties on the road between the two forts." And he gently hinted that their place was not in his camp but in that of Lévis, where missionaries were provided for such of them as were Christians, and food and ammunition for them all.

They promised, with excellent docility, to do everything he wished, but added that there was something on their hearts. Being encouraged to relieve themselves of the burden, they complained that they had not been consulted as to the management of the siege but were expected to obey orders like slaves. "We know more about fighting in the woods than you," said their orator; "ask our advice and you will be the better for it."

Montcalm assured them that if they had been neglected, it was only through the hurry and confusion of the time; expressed high appreciation of their talents for bushfighting, promised them ample satisfaction and ended by telling them that in the morning they should hear the big guns. This greatly pleased them, for they were extremely impatient for the artillery to begin.

About sunrise the battery of the left opened with eight heavy cannon and a mortar, joined on the next morning by the battery of the right, with eleven pieces more. The fort replied with spirit. The cannon thundered all day, and from a hundred peaks and crags the astonished wilderness roared back the sound. The Indians were delighted. They wanted to point the guns, and to humor them they were now and then allowed to do so. Others lay behind logs and fallen trees and yelled their satisfaction when they saw the splinters fly from the wooden rampart.

Day after day the weary roar of the distant cannonade fell on the ears of Webb in his camp at Fort Edward. "I have not as yet received the least reinforcement," he writes to Loudon; "this is the disagreeable situation we are at present in. The fort, by the heavy firing we hear from the lake, is still in our possession; but I fear it cannot long hold out against so warm a cannonading if I am not reinforced by a sufficient number of militia to march to their relief."

The militia were coming, but it was impossible that many could reach him in less than a week. Those from New York alone were within call and two thousand of them arrived soon after he sent Loudon the above letter. Then, by stripping all the forts below, he could bring together forty-five hundred men, while several French deserters assured him that Montcalm had nearly twelve thousand. To advance to the relief of Monro with a force so inferior, through a defile of rocks, forests and mountains, made by nature for ambuscades —and this, too, with troops who had neither the steadiness of regulars nor the bushfighting skill of Indians—was an enterprise for firmer nerve than his.

By this time the sappers had worked their way to the angle of the lake, where they were stopped by a marshy hollow, beyond which was a tract of high ground, reaching to the fort and serving as the garden of the garrison. Logs and fascines in large quantities were thrown into the hollow and hurdles were laid over them to form a causeway for the cannon. Then the sap was continued up the acclivity beyond, a trench was opened in the garden and a battery begun not two hundred and fifty yards from the fort.

The Indians, in great number, crawled forward among the beans, maize and cabbages and lay there ensconced. On the night of the seventh, two men came out of the fort, apparently to reconnoiter with a view to a sortie, when they were greeted by a general volley and a burst of yells which echoed among the mountains, followed by responsive whoops pealing through the darkness from the various camps and lurking places of the savage warriors far and near.

The position of the besieged was now deplorable. More than three hundred of them had been killed and wounded; smallpox was raging in the fort; the place was a focus of infection and the casemates were crowded with the sick. A sortie from the intrenched camp and another from the fort had been repulsed with loss. All their large cannon and mortars had been burst or disabled by shot; only seven small pieces were left fit for service and the whole of Montcalm's thirty-one cannon and fifteen mortars and howitzers would soon open fire, while the walls were already breached and an assault was imminent. Through the night of the eighth they fired briskly from all their remaining pieces. In the morning the officers held a council and all agreed to surrender if honorable terms could be had. A white flag was raised, a drum was beat, and Lieutenant Colonel Young, mounted on horseback, for a shot in the foot had disabled him from walking, went to the tent of Montcalm, followed by a few soldiers.

It was agreed that the English troops should march out with the honors of war and be escorted to Fort Edward by a detachment of French troops; that they should not serve for eighteen months; and that all French prisoners captured in America since the war began should be given up within three months. The stores, munitions and artillery were to be the prize of the victors, except one fieldpiece which the garrison were to retain in recognition of their brave defense.

603

Before signing the capitulation, Montcalm called the Indian chiefs to council and asked them to consent to the conditions and promise to restrain their young warriors from any disorder. They approved everything and promised everything. The garrison then evacuated the fort and marched to join their comrades in the intrenched camp, which was included in the surrender.

No sooner were they gone than a crowd of Indians clambered through the embrasures in search of rum and plunder. All the sick men unable to leave their beds were instantly butchered. There was little left to plunder, and the Indians, joined by the more lawless of the Canadians, turned their attention to the intrenched camp, where all the English were now collected.

The French guard stationed there could not or would not keep out the rabble. By the advice of Montcalm the English stove their rum barrels, but the Indians were drunk already with homicidal rage and the glitter of their vicious eyes told of the devil within. They roamed among the tents, intrusive, insolent, their visages besmirched with war paint, grinning like fiends as they handled, in anticipation of the knife, the long hair of cowering women, of whom, as well as of children, there were many in the camp, all crazed with fright.

The confusion in the camp lasted through the afternoon. "The Indians," says Bougainville, "wanted to plunder the chests of the English; the latter resisted; and there was fear that serious disorder would ensue. The Marquis de Montcalm ran there immediately and used every means to restore tranquillity: prayers, threats, caresses, interposition of the officers and interpreters who have some influence over these savages." "We shall be but too happy if we can prevent a massacre. Detestable position! of which nobody who has not been in it can have any idea, and which makes victory itself a sorrow to the victors. The Marquis spared no efforts to prevent the rapacity of the savages and, I must say it, of certain persons associated with them, from resulting in something worse than plunder. At nine o'clock in the evening, order seemed restored. The Marquis even induced the Indians to promise that, besides the escort agreed upon in the capitulation, two chiefs for each tribe should accompany the English on their way to Fort Edward."

He also ordered La Corne and the other Canadian officers attached to the Indians to see that no violence took place. He might well have done more. In view of the disorders of the afternoon, it would not have been too much if he had ordered the whole body of regular troops, whom alone he could trust for the purpose, to hold themselves ready to move to the spot in case of outbreak and shelter their defeated foes behind a hedge of bayonets.

Bougainville was not to see what ensued, for Montcalm now sent him to Montreal as a special messenger to carry news of the victory. He embarked at ten o'clock. Returning daylight found him far down the lake, and as he looked on its still bosom flecked with mists and its quiet mountains sleeping under the flush of dawn, there was nothing in the wild tranquillity of the scene to suggest the tragedy which even then was beginning on the shore he had left behind.

The English in their camp had passed a troubled night, agitated by strange rumors. In the morning something like a panic seized them, for they distrusted not the Indians only but the Canadians. In their haste to be gone, they got together at daybreak, before the escort of three hundred regulars had arrived. They had their muskets but no ammunition, and few or none of the provincials had bayonets. Early as it was, the Indians were on the alert, and indeed since midnight great numbers of them had been prowling about the skirts of the camp, showing, says Colonel Frye, "more than usual malice in their looks."

Seventeen wounded men of his regiment lay in huts, unable to join the march. In the preceding afternoon Miles Whitworth, the regimental surgeon, had passed them over to the care of a French surgeon, according to an agreement made at the time of the surrender, but the Frenchman being absent, the other remained with them, attending to their wants. The French surgeon had caused special sentinels to be posted for their protection. These were now removed at the moment when they were needed most, upon which, about five o'clock in the morning, the Indians entered the huts, dragged out the inmates and tomahawked and scalped them all before the eyes of Whitworth and in presence of La Corne and other Canadian officers, as well as of a French guard stationed within forty feet of the spot; and declares the surgeon under oath, "none, either officer or soldier, protected the said wounded men." The opportune butchery relieved them of a troublesome burden.

A scene of plundering now began. The escort had by this time arrived, and Monro complained to the officers that the capitulation was broken but got no other answer than advice to give up the baggage to the Indians in order to appease them. To this the English at length agreed, but it only increased the excitement of the mob. They demanded rum, and some of the soldiers, afraid to refuse, gave it to them from their canteens, thus adding fuel to the flame.

When, after much difficulty, the column at last got out of the camp and began to move along the road that crossed the rough plain between the intrenchment and the forest, the Indians crowded upon them, impeded their march, snatched caps, coats and weapons from men and officers, tomahawked those that resisted and, seizing upon shrieking women and children, dragged them off or murdered them on the spot. It is said that some of the interpreters secretly fomented the disorder.

Suddenly there rose the screech of the war whoop. At this signal of butchery, which was given by Abenaki Christians from the mission of the Penobscot, a mob of savages rushed upon the New Hampshire men at the rear of the column and killed or dragged away eighty of them. A frightful tumult ensued, when Montcalm, Lévis, Bourlamaque and many other French officers, who had hastened from their camp on the first news of disturbance, threw themselves among the Indians and by promises and threats tried to allay their frenzy.

"Kill me, but spare the English who are under my protection!" exclaimed Montcalm.

He took from one of them a young officer whom the savage had seized, upon which several other Indians immediately tomahawked their prisoners lest they too should be taken from them. One writer says that a French grenadier was killed and two wounded in attempting to restore order, but the statement is doubtful.

The English seemed paralyzed and fortunately did not attempt a resistance, which, without ammunition as they were, would have ended in a general massacre. Their broken column straggled forward in wild disorder, amid the din of whoops and shrieks, till they reached the French advance guard, which consisted of Canadians, and here they demanded protection from the officers, who refused to give it, telling them that they must take to the woods and shift for themselves. Frye was seized by a number of Indians, who, brandishing spears and tomahawks, threatened him with death and tore off his clothing, leaving nothing but breeches, shoes and shirt. Repelled by the officers of the guard, he made for the woods. A Connecticut soldier who was present says of him that he leaped upon an Indian who stood in his way, disarmed and killed him and then escaped, but Frye himself does not mention the incident. Captain Burke, also of the Massachusetts regiment, was stripped of all his clothes after a violent struggle, then broke loose, gained the woods, spent the night shivering in the thick grass of a marsh and on the next day reached Fort Edward.

Jonathan Carver, a provincial volunteer, declares that when the tumult was at its height he saw officers of the French Army walking about at a little distance and talking with seeming unconcern. Three or four Indians seized him, brandished their tomahawks over his head and tore off most of his clothes, while he vainly claimed protection from a sentinel, who called him an English dog and violently pushed him back among his tormentors. Two of them were dragging him towards the neighboring swamp when an English officer, stripped of everything but his scarlet breeches, ran by. One of Carver's captors sprang upon him but was thrown to the ground, whereupon the other went to the aid of his comrade and drove his tomahawk into the back of the Englishman.

As Carver turned to run, an English boy about twelve years old clung to him and begged for help. They ran on together for a moment, until the boy was seized, dragged from his protector and, as Carver judged by his shrieks, was murdered. He himself escaped to the forest and after three days of famine reached Fort Edward.

The bonds of discipline seem for the time to have been completely broken, for while Montcalm and his chief officers used every effort to restore order, even at the risk of their lives, many other officers, chiefly of the militia, failed atrociously to do their duty. How many English were killed it is impossible to tell with exactness. Roubaud says that he saw forty or fifty corpses scattered about the field. Lévis says fifty, which does not include the sick and wounded murdered in the camp and fort. It is certain that six or seven hundred persons were carried off, stripped and otherwise maltreated. Montcalm succeeded in recovering more than four hundred of them in the course of the day, and many of the French officers did what they could to relieve their wants by buying back from their captors the clothing that had been torn from them.

Many of the fugitives had taken refuge in the fort, where Monro himself had gone to demand protection for his followers, and here Roubaud presently found a crowd of half-frenzied women crying in anguish for husbands and children. All the refugees and redeemed prisoners were afterwards conducted to the intrenched camp, where food and shelter were provided for them and a strong guard set for their protection until the fifteenth, when they were sent under an escort to Fort Edward. Here cannon had been fired at intervals to guide those who had fled to the woods, from which they came dropping in from day to day, half dead with famine.

On the morning after the massacre the Indians decamped in a body and set out for Montreal, carrying with them their plunder and some two hundred prisoners, who, it is said, could not be got out of their hands. The soldiers were set to the work of demolishing the English fort, and the task occupied several days. The barracks were torn down and the huge pine logs of the rampart thrown into a heap. The dead bodies that filled the casemates were added to the mass and fire was set to the whole. The mighty funeral pyre blazed all night. Then, on the sixteenth, the army re-embarked. The din of ten thousand combatants, the rage, the terror, the agony, were gone, and no living thing was left but the wolves that gathered from the mountains to feast upon the dead.

CHAPTER 10

Winter of Discontent

WEBB HAD REMAINED AT FORT EDWARD IN mortal dread of attack. Johnson had joined him with a band of Mohawks, and on the day when Fort William Henry surrendered there had been some talk of attempting to throw succors into it by night. Then came the news of its capture, and now, when it was too late, tumultuous mobs of militia came pouring in from the neighboring provinces.

In a few days thousands of them were bivouacked on the fields about Fort Edward, doing nothing, disgusted and mutinous, declaring that they were ready to fight but not to lie still without tents, blankets or kettles. Webb writes on the fourteenth that most of those from New York had deserted, threatening to kill their officers if they tried to stop them. Delancey ordered them to be fired upon. A sergeant was shot, others were put under arrest, and all was disorder till the seventeenth, when Webb, learning that the French were gone, sent them back to their homes.

Close on the fall of Fort William Henry came crazy rumors of disaster, running like wildfire through the colonies. The number and ferocity of the enemy were grossly exaggerated; there was a cry that they would seize Albany and New York itself, while it was reported that Webb, as much frightened as the rest, was for retreating to the Highlands of the Hudson. This was the day after the capitulation, when only a part of the militia had yet appeared. If Montcalm had seized the moment and marched that afternoon to Fort Edward, it is not impossible that in the confusion he might have carried it by a *coup de main*.

Here was an opportunity for Vaudreuil and he did not fail to use it. Jealous of his rival's exploit, he spared no pains to tarnish it, complaining that Montcalm had stopped halfway on the road to success and, instead of following his instructions, had contented himself with one victory when he should have gained two. But the governor had enjoined upon him as a matter of the last necessity that the Canadians should be at their homes before September to gather the crops, and he would have been the first to complain had the injunction been disregarded. To besiege Fort Edward was impossible, as Montcalm had no means of transporting cannon there, and to attack Webb without them was a risk which he had not the rashness to incur.

It was Bougainville who first brought Vaudreuil the news of the success on Lake George. A day or two after his arrival, the Indians, who had left the army after the massacre, appeared at Montreal, bringing about two hundred English prisoners. The governor rebuked them for breaking the capitulation, on which the heathen savages of the West declared that it was not their fault but that of the converted Indians, who in fact had first raised the war whoop. Some of the prisoners were presently bought from them at the price of two kegs of brandy each, and the inevitable consequences followed.

"I thought," writes Bougainville, "that the Governor would have told them they should have neither provisions nor presents till all the English were given up; that he himself would have gone to their huts and taken the prisoners from them; and that the inhabitants would be forbidden, under the severest penalties, from selling or giving them brandy. I saw the contrary; and my soul shuddered at the sights my eyes beheld. On the fifteenth, at two o'clock, in the presence of the whole town, they killed one of the prisoners, put him into the kettle, and forced his wretched countrymen to eat of him." The intendant Bigot, the friend of the governor, confirms this story, and another French writer says that they "compelled mothers to eat the flesh of their children."

Bigot declares that guns, canoes and other presents were given to the western tribes before they left Montreal and he adds, "they must be sent home satisfied at any cost." Such were the pains taken to preserve allies who were useful chiefly through the terror inspired by their diabolical cruelties.

This time their ferocity cost them dear. They had dug up and scalped the corpses in the graveyard of Fort William Henry, many of which were remains of victims of the smallpox, and the savages caught the disease, which is said to have made great havoc among them.

Vaudreuil, in reporting what he calls "my capture of Fort William Henry," takes great credit to himself for his "generous procedures" towards the English prisoners; alluding, it seems, to his having bought some of them from the Indians with the brandy which was sure to cause the murder of others. His obsequiousness to his red allies did not cease with permitting them to kill and devour before his eyes those whom he was bound in honor and duty to protect. "He let them do what they pleased," says a French contemporary; "they were seen roaming about Montreal, knife in hand, threatening everybody and often insulting those they met. When complaint was made, he said nothing. Far from it; instead of reproaching them, he loaded them with gifts, in the belief that their cruelty would then relent."

Nevertheless, in about a fortnight all, or nearly all, the surviving prisoners were bought out of their clutches, and then after a final distribution of presents and a grand debauch at La Chine, the whole savage rout paddled for their villages.

While Montcalm was passing a winter of discontent in Montreal, the prospects of the next campaign began to open. Captain Pouchot had written from Niagara that three thousand savages were waiting to be let loose against the English borders. "What a scourge!" exclaims Bougainville. "Humanity groans at being forced to use such monsters. What can be done against an invisible enemy, who strikes and vanishes, swift as the lightning? It is the destroying angel."

Captain Hebecourt kept watch and ward at Ticonderoga, begirt with snow and ice and much plagued by English rangers who sometimes got into the ditch itself. This was to reconnoiter the place in preparation for a winter attack which Loudon had planned, but which, like the rest of his schemes, fell to the ground. Towards midwinter a band of these intruders captured two soldiers and butchered some fifteen cattle close to the fort, leaving tied to the horns of one of them a note addressed to the commandant in these terms: "I am obliged to you, sir, for the rest you have allowed me to take and the fresh meat you have sent me. I shall take good care of my prisoners. My compliments to the Marquis of Montcalm. Signed, Rogers."

A few weeks later Hebecourt had his revenge. About the middle of March a report came to Montreal that a large party of rangers had been cut to pieces a few miles from Ticonderoga and that Rogers himself was among the slain. This last announcement proved false, but the rangers had suffered a crushing defeat.

Colonel Haviland, commanding at Fort Edward, sent a hundred and eighty of them, men and officers, on a scouting party towards Ticonderoga, and Captain Pringle and Lieutenant Roche, of the twenty-seventh regiment, joined them as volunteers, no doubt through a love of hardy adventure, which was destined to be fully satisfied. Rogers commanded the whole. They passed down Lake George on the ice under cover of night, and then, as they neared the French outposts, pursued their way by land behind Rogers Rock and the other mountains of the western shore.

On the preceding day, the twelfth of March, Hebecourt had received a reinforcement of two hundred mission Indians and a body of Canadians. The Indians had no sooner arrived than, though nominally Christians, they consulted the spirits, by whom they were told that the English were coming. On this they sent out scouts, who came back breathless, declaring that they had found a great number of snowshoe tracks. The superhuman warning being thus confirmed, the whole body of Indians, joined by a band of Canadians and a number of volunteers from the regulars, set out to meet the approaching enemy and took their way up the valley of Trout Brook, a mountain gorge that opens from the west upon the valley of Ticonderoga.

Towards three o'clock on the afternoon of that day, Rogers had reached a point nearly west of the mountain that bears his name. The rough and rocky ground was buried four feet in snow and all around stood the gray trunks of the forest, bearing aloft their skeleton arms and tangled intricacy of leafless twigs. Close on the right was a steep hill, and at a little distance on the left was the brook, lost under ice and snow. A scout from the front told Rogers that a party of Indians was approaching along the bed of the frozen stream, on which he ordered his men to halt, face to that side and advance cautiously. The Indians

612

soon appeared and received a fire that killed some of them and drove back the rest in confusion.

Not suspecting that they were but an advance guard, about half the rangers dashed in pursuit and were soon met by the whole body of the enemy. The woods rang with yells and musketry. In a few minutes some fifty of the pursuers were shot down and the rest driven back in disorder upon their comrades. Rogers formed them all on the slope of the hill, and here they fought till sunset with stubborn desperation, twice repulsing the overwhelming numbers of the assailants and thwarting all their efforts to gain the heights in the rear. The combatants were often not twenty yards apart and sometimes they were mixed together.

At length a large body of Indians succeeded in turning the right flank of the rangers. Lieutenant Phillips and a few men were sent by Rogers to oppose the movement, but they quickly found themselves surrounded, and after a brave defense surrendered on a pledge of good treatment. Rogers now advised the volunteers, Pringle and Roche, to escape while there was time, and offered them a sergeant as guide, but they gallantly resolved to stand by him. Eight officers and more than a hundred rangers lay dead and wounded in the snow.

Evening was near and the forest was darkening fast when the few survivors broke and fled. Rogers with about twenty followers escaped up the mountain and, gathering others about him, made a running fight against the Indian pursuers, reached Lake George, not without fresh losses, and after two days of misery regained Fort Edward with the remnant of his band. The enemy on their part suffered heavily, the chief loss falling on the Indians, who to revenge themselves murdered all the wounded and nearly all the prisoners and, tying Lieutenant Phillips and his men to trees, hacked them to pieces.

Captain Pringle and Lieutenant Roche had become separated from the other fugitives and, ignorant of woodcraft, they wandered by moonlight amid the desolation of rocks and snow till early in the night they met a man whom they knew as a servant of Rogers and who said that he could guide them to Fort Edward. One of them had lost his snowshoes in the fight, and crouching over a miserable fire of broken sticks, they worked till morning to make a kind of substitute with forked branches, twigs and a few leather strings. They had no hatchet

613

to cut firewood, no blankets, no overcoats and no food except part of a bologna sausage and a little ginger which Pringle had brought with him. There was no game; not even a squirrel was astir, and their chief sustenance was juniper berries and the inner bark of trees.

But their worse calamity was the helplessness of their guide. His brain wandered, and while always insisting that he knew the country well, he led them during four days here and there among a labyrinth of nameless mountains, climbing over rocks, wading through snowdrifts, struggling among fallen trees, till on the fifth day they saw with despair that they had circled back to their own starting point.

On the next morning, when they were on the ice of Lake George not far from Rogers Rock, a blinding storm of sleet and snow drove in their faces. Spent as they were, it was death to stop, and bending their heads against the blast, they fought their way forward, now on the ice and now in the adjacent forest, till in the afternoon the storm ceased and they found themselves on the bank of an unknown stream.

It was the outlet of the lake, for they had wandered into the valley of Ticonderoga and were not three miles from the French fort. In crossing the torrent Pringle lost his gun and was near losing his life. All three of the party were drenched to the skin and, becoming now for the first time aware of where they were, they resolved on yielding themselves prisoners to save their lives.

Night, however, again found them in the forest. Their guide became delirious, saw visions of Indians all around and, murmuring incoherently, straggled off a little way, seated himself in the snow and was soon dead. The two officers, themselves but half alive, walked all night around a tree to keep the blood in motion.

In the morning, again toiling on, they presently saw the fort across the intervening snow fields and approached it, waving a white handkerchief. Several French officers dashed towards them at full speed and reached them in time to save them from the clutches of the Indians, whose camps were near at hand. They were kindly treated, recovered from the effects of their frightful ordeal and were afterwards exchanged. Pringle lived to an old age and died in 1800, senior major general of the British Army.

~~~~~~

Louisbourg

THE STORMY COAST OF CAPE BRETON IS INDENTED by a small landlocked bay, between which and the ocean lies a tongue of land dotted with a few grazing sheep and intersected by rows of stone that mark more or less distinctly the lines of what once were streets. Green mounds and embankments of earth enclose the whole space, and beneath the highest of them yawn arches and caverns of ancient masonry. This grassy solitude was once the "Dunkirk of America." The vaulted caverns where the sheep find shelter from the rain were casemates where terrified women sought refuge from storms of shot and shell, and the shapeless green mounds were citadel, bastion, rampart and glacis.

Here stood Louisbourg, and not all the efforts of its conquerors nor all the havoc of succeeding times have availed to efface it. Men in hundreds toiled for months with lever, spade and gunpowder in the work of destruction, and for more than a century it has served as a stone quarry, but the remains of its vast defenses still tell their tale of human valor and human woe.

Stand on the mounds that were once the King's Bastion. The glistening sea spreads eastward three thousand miles and its waves meet their first rebuff against this iron coast. Lighthouse Point is white with foam; jets of spray spout from the rocks of Goat Island; mist curls in clouds from the seething surf that lashes the crags of Black Point and the sea boils like a caldron among the reefs by the harbor's mouth; but on the calm water within, the small fishing vessels rest tranquil at their moorings. Beyond lies a hamlet of fishermen by the edge of the water, and a few scattered dwellings dot the rough hills, bristled with stunted firs, that gird the quiet basin, while close at hand, within the precinct of the vanished fortress, stand two small farmhouses. All else is a solitude of ocean, rock, marsh and forest.

At the beginning of June, 1758, the place wore another aspect. Since the peace of Aix-la-Chapelle vast sums had been spent in repairing and strengthening it, and Louisbourg was the strongest fortress in French or British America. Nevertheless, it had its weaknesses. The original plan of the works had not been fully carried out, and owing, it is said, to the bad quality of the mortar, the masonry of the ramparts was in so poor a condition that it had been replaced in some parts with fascines.

The circuit of the fortifications was more than a mile and a half and the town contained about four thousand inhabitants. The best buildings in it were the convent, the hospital, the King's storehouses and the chapel and governor's quarters, which were under the same roof. Of the private houses, only seven or eight were of stone, the rest being humble wooden structures suited to a population of fishermen.

The garrison consisted of the battalions of Artois, Bourgogne, Cambis and Volontaires Etrangers, with two companies of artillery and twenty-four of colony troops from Canada—in all, three thousand and eighty regular troops, besides officers; and to these were added a body of armed inhabitants and a band of Indians. In the harbor were five ships of the line and seven frigates, carrying in all five hundred and forty-four guns and about three thousand men. Two hundred and nineteen cannon and seventeen mortars were mounted on the walls and outworks. Of these last the most important were the Grand Battery on the shore of the harbor opposite its mouth and the Island Battery on the rocky islet at its entrance.

The strongest front of the works was on the land side, along the base of the peninsular triangle on which the town stood. This front, about twelve hundred yards in extent, reached from the sea on the left to the harbor on the right and consisted of four bastions with their connecting curtains, the Princess's, the Queen's, the King's and the Dauphin's. The King's Bastion formed part of the citadel. The glacis before it sloped down to an extensive marsh, which with an adjacent

616

pont completely protected this part of the line. On the right, however, towards the harbor, the ground was high enough to offer advantages to an enemy, as was also the case to a lesser degree on the left, towards the sea. The best defense of Louisbourg was the craggy shore, which for leagues on either hand was accessible only at a few points and even there with difficulty. All these points were watched vigilantly.

There had been signs of the enemy from the first opening of spring. In the intervals of fog, rain and snow squalls, sails were seen hovering on the distant sea, and during the latter part of May a squadron of nine ships cruised off the mouth of the harbor, appearing and disappearing, sometimes driven away by gales, sometimes lost in fogs and sometimes approaching to within cannon shot of the batteries. Their object was to blockade the port, in which they failed, for French ships had come in at intervals till twelve of them lay safe anchored in the harbor, with more than a year's supply of provisions for the garrison.

At length, on the first of June, the southeastern horizon was white with a cloud of canvas. The long-expected crisis was come. Drucour, the governor, sent two thousand regulars with about a thousand militia and Indians to guard the various landing places, and the rest, aided by the sailors, remained to hold the town.

Meanwhile in England the Great Commoner, Pitt, had become Secretary of State, with full control of the war and foreign affairs. He had reversed England's downward course, and with the opening of the year 1758 her continental victories began. But it was towards America that Pitt turned his heartiest efforts. His first aim was to take Louisbourg, as a step towards taking Quebec; then Ticonderoga, that thorn in the side of the northern colonies; and lastly Fort Duquesne, the Key to the Great West.

He recalled Loudon, for whom he had a fierce contempt, but there were influences which he could not disregard, and Major General Abercrombie, who was next in order of rank, an indifferent soldier though a veteran in years, was allowed to succeed him and lead in person the attack on Ticonderoga. Pitt hoped that Brigadier Lord Howe, an admirable officer who was joined with Abercrombie, would be the real commander and make amends for all the shortcomings of his chief.

To command the Louisbourg expedition, Colonel Jeffrey Amherst was recalled from the German war and made at one leap a major general. He was energetic and resolute, somewhat cautious and slow, but with a bulldog tenacity of grip. Under him were three brigadiers, Whitmore, Lawrence and Wolfe. The third expedition, that against Fort Duquesne, was given to Brigadier John Forbes, whose qualities well fitted him for the task.

During his first short term of office Pitt had given a new species of troops to the British Army. These were the Scotch Highlanders, who had risen against the House of Hanover in 1745 and would rise against it again should France accomplish her favorite scheme of throwing a force into Scotland to excite another insurrection for the Stuarts. But they would be useful to fight the French abroad, though dangerous as their possible allies at home; and two regiments of them were now ordered to America.

Delay had been the ruin of the last year's attempt against Louisbourg. This time preparation was urged on apace, and before the end of winter two fleets had put to sea: one, under Admiral Boscawen, was destined for Louisbourg; while the other, under Admiral Osborn, sailed for the Mediterranean to intercept the French fleet of Admiral La Clue, who was about to sail from Toulon for America.

At the end of May, Admiral Boscawen was at Halifax with twenty-three ships of the line, eighteen frigates and fireships and a fleet of transports, on board of which were eleven thousand and six hundred soldiers, all regulars, except five hundred provincial rangers. Amherst had not yet arrived, and on the twenty-eighth Boscawen, in pursuance of his orders and to prevent loss of time, put to sea without him. But scarcely had the fleet sailed out of Halifax when they met the ship that bore the expected general. Amherst took command of the troops and the expedition held its way till the second of June, when they saw the rocky shore line of Cape Breton and descried the masts of the French squadron in the harbor of Louisbourg.

Boscawen sailed into Gabarus Bay. The sea was rough, but in the afternoon Amherst, Lawrence and Wolfe, with a number of naval officers, reconnoitered the shore in boats, coasting it for miles and approaching it as near as the French batteries would permit. The rocks were white with surf and every accessible point was strongly guarded. Boscawen saw little chance of success. He sent for his captains and

618

consulted them separately. They thought, like him, that it would be rash to attempt a landing and proposed a council of war. One of them alone, an old sea officer named Ferguson, advised his commander to take the responsibility himself, hold no council and make the attempt at every risk. Boscawen took his advice and declared that he would not leave Gabarus Bay till he had fulfilled his instructions and set the troops on shore.

West of Louisbourg there were three accessible places, Freshwater Cove, four miles from the town, and Flat Point and White Point, which were nearer, the last being within a mile of the fortifications. East of the town there was an inlet called Lorambec, also available for landing. In order to distract the attention of the enemy, it was resolved to threaten all these places and to form the troops into three divisions, two of which, under Lawrence and Whitmore, were to advance towards Flat Point and White Point, while a detached regiment was to make a feint at Lorambec. Wolfe, with the third division, was to make the real attack and try to force a landing at Freshwater Cove, which as it proved was the most strongly defended of all.

When on shore Wolfe was a habitual invalid, and when at sea every heave of the ship made him wretched, but his ardor was unquenchable. Before leaving England he wrote to a friend: "Being of the profession of arms, I would seek all occasions to serve; and therefore have thrown myself in the way of the American war, though I know that the very passage threatens my life, and that my constitution must be utterly ruined and undone."

On the next day, the third, the surf was so high that nothing could be attempted. On the fourth there was a thick fog and a gale. The frigate *Trent* struck on a rock and some of the transports were near being stranded. On the fifth there was another fog and a raging surf. On the sixth there was fog, with rain in the morning and better weather towards noon, whereupon the signal was made and the troops entered the boats; but the sea rose again and they were ordered back to the ships. On the seventh more fog and more surf till night, when the sea grew calmer and orders were given for another attempt. At two in the morning of the eighth the troops were in the boats again.

At daybreak the frigates of the squadron, anchoring before each point of real or pretended attack, opened a fierce cannonade on the

French intrenchments, and a quarter of an hour after, the three divisions rowed towards the shore. That of the left, under Wolfe, consisted of four companies of grenadiers, with the light infantry and New England rangers, followed and supported by Fraser's Highlanders and eight more companies of grenadiers. They pulled for Freshwater Cove. Here there was a crescent-shaped beach, a quarter of a mile long, with rocks at each end. On the shore above, about a thousand Frenchmen, under Lieutenant Colonel de Saint-Julien, lay behind intrenchments covered in front by spruce and fir trees, felled and laid on the ground with the tops outward. Eight cannon and swivels were planted to sweep every part of the beach and its approaches, and these pieces were masked by young evergreens stuck in the ground before them.

, The English were allowed to come within close range unmolested. Then the batteries opened and a deadly storm of grape and musketry was poured upon the boats. It was clear in an instant that to advance farther would be destruction, and Wolfe waved his hand as a signal to sheer off. At some distance on the right, and little exposed to the fire, were three boats of light infantry under Lieutenants Hopkins and Brown and Ensign Grant, who, mistaking the signal or willfully misinterpreting it, made directly for the shore before them.

It was a few rods east of the beach, a craggy coast and a strand strewn with rocks and lashed with breakers, but sheltered from the cannon by a small projecting point. The three officers leaped ashore, followed by their men. Wolfe saw the movement and hastened to support it. The boat of Major Scott, who commanded the light infantry and rangers, next came up and was stove in an instant, but Scott gained the shore, climbed the crags and found himself with ten men in front of some seventy French and Indians. Half his followers were killed and wounded and three bullets were shot through his clothes, but with admirable gallantry he held his ground till others came to his aid.

The remaining boats now reached the landing. Many were stove among the rocks and others were overset; some of the men were dragged back by the surf and drowned; some lost their muskets and were drenched to the skin, but the greater part got safe ashore. Among the foremost was seen the tall, attenuated form of Brigadier Wolfe, armed with nothing but a cane, as he leaped into the surf and climbed the crags with his soldiers. As they reached the top they formed in compact order and attacked and carried with the bayonet the nearest French battery, a few rods distant. The division of Lawrence soon came up, and as the attention of the enemy was now distracted, they made their landing with little opposition at the farther end of the beach, where they were followed by Amherst himself.

The French, attacked on right and left and fearing, with good reason, that they would be cut off from the town, abandoned all their cannon and fled into the woods. About seventy of them were captured and fifty killed. The rest, circling among the hills and around the marshes, made their way to Louisbourg, and those at the intermediate posts joined their flight. The English followed through a matted growth of firs till they reached the cleared ground, when the cannon opening on them from the ramparts stopped the pursuit. The first move of the great game was played and won.

Amherst made his camp just beyond range of the French cannon, and Flat Point Cove was chosen as the landing place of guns and stores. Clearing the ground, making roads and pitching tents filled the rest of the day. At night there was a glare of flames from the direction of the town. The French had abandoned the Grand Battery after setting fire to the buildings in it and to the houses and fish stages along the shore of the harbor.

During the following days stores were landed as fast as the surf would permit, but the task was so difficult that from first to last more than a hundred boats were stove in accomplishing it, and such was the violence of the waves that none of the siege guns could be got ashore till the eighteenth. The camp extended two miles along a stream that flowed down to the cove among the low, woody hills that curved around the town and harbor. Redoubts were made to protect its front and blockhouses to guard its left and rear from the bands of Acadians known to be hovering in the woods.

Wolfe, with twelve hundred men, made his way six or seven miles round the harbor, took possession of the battery at Lighthouse Point which the French had abandoned, planted guns and mortars and opened fire on the Island Battery that guarded the entrance. Other guns were placed at different points along the shore and soon opened on the French ships. The ships and batteries replied. The artillery fight raged night and day, till on the twenty-fifth the island guns were dismounted and silenced. Wolfe then strengthened his posts, secured his communications and returned to the main army in front of the town.

Amherst had reconnoitered the ground and chosen a hillock at the edge of the marsh, less than half a mile from the ramparts, as the point for opening his trenches. A road with an epaulement to protect it must first be made to the spot, and as the way was over a tract of deep mud covered with waterweeds and moss, the labor was prodigious. A thousand men worked at it day and night under the fire of the town and ships.

When the French looked landward from their ramparts they could see scarcely a sign of the impending storm. Behind them Wolfe's cannon were playing busily from Lighthouse Point and the heights around the harbor, but before them the broad, flat marsh and the low hills seemed almost a solitude. Two miles distant they could descry some of the English tents, but the greater part were hidden by the inequalities of the ground.

Various courtesies were exchanged between the two commanders. Drucour, on occasion of a flag of truce, wrote to Amherst that there was a surgeon of uncommon skill in Louisbourg whose services were at the command of any English officer who might need them. Amherst on his part sent to his enemy letters and messages from wounded Frenchmen in his hands, adding his compliments to Madame Drucour with an expression of regret for the disquiet to which she was exposed, begging her at the same time to accept a gift of pineapples from the West Indies. She returned his courtesy by sending him a basket of wine, after which amenities the cannon roared again. Madame Drucour was a woman of heroic spirit. Every day she was on the ramparts, where her presence roused the soldiers to enthusiasm, and every day with her own hand she fired three cannon to encourage them. But the English lines grew closer and closer and their fire more and more destructive.

On the eighth of July news came that the partisan Boishébert was approaching with four hundred Acadians, Canadians and Micmacs to attack the English outposts and detachments. He did little or nothing, however, besides capturing a few stragglers. On the sixteenth, early in the evening, a party of English led by Wolfe dashed forward, drove off a band of French volunteers, seized a rising ground called Hauteur-de-la-Potence, or Gallows Hill, and began to intrench themselves scarcely three hundred yards from the Dauphin's Bastion. The town opened on them furiously with grapeshot, but in the intervals of the firing the sound of their picks and spades could plainly be heard. In the morning they were seen throwing up earth like moles as they burrowed their way forward, and on the twenty-first they opened another parallel within two hundred yards of the rampart. Still their sappers pushed on. Every day they had more guns in position, and on right and left their fire grew hotter. Their pickets made a lodgment along the foot of the glacis and fired up the slope at the French in the covered way.

In the citadel, of which the King's Bastion formed the front, there was a large oblong stone building containing the chapel, lodgings for men and officers and at the southern end the quarters of the governor. On the morning of the twenty-second a shell fell through the roof among a party of soldiers in the chamber below, burst and set the place on fire. In half an hour the chapel and all the northern part of the building were in flames, and no sooner did the smoke rise above the bastion than the English threw into it a steady shower of missiles. Yet soldiers, sailors and inhabitants hastened to the spot and labored desperately to check the fire. They saved the end occupied by Drucour and his wife, but all the rest was destroyed.

Under the adjacent rampart were the casemates, one of which was crowded with wounded officers and the rest with women and children seeking shelter in these subterranean dens. Before the entrances there was a long barrier of timber to protect them from exploding shells, and as the wind blew the flames towards it there was danger that it would take fire and suffocate those within. They rushed out, crazed with fright, and ran here and there with outcries and shrieks amid the storm of iron.

In the neighboring Queen's Bastion was a large range of barracks built of wood by the New England troops after their capture of the fortress in 1745. So flimsy and combustible was it that the French writers call it a "house of cards" and "a paper of matches." Here were lodged the greater part of the garrison, but such was the danger of fire that they were now ordered to leave it, and they accordingly lay in the streets or along the foot of the ramparts, under shelters of timber which gave some little protection against bombs.

The order was well timed, for on the night after the fire in the King's Bastion a shell filled with combustibles set this building also in flames. A fearful scene ensued. All the English batteries opened upon it. The roar of mortars and cannon, the rushing and screaming of round shot and grape, the hissing of fuses and the explosion of grenades and bombs mingled with a storm of musketry from the covered way and trenches, while by the glare of the conflagration the English regiments were seen drawn up in battle array before the ramparts, as if preparing for an assault.

The position of the besieged was deplorable. Nearly a fourth of their number were in the hospitals, while the rest, exhausted with incessant toil, could find no place to snatch an hour of sleep, "and yet," says an officer, "they still show ardor." "Today," he says again on the twenty-fourth, "the fire of the place is so weak that it is more like funeral guns than a defense." On the front of the town only four cannon could fire at all. The rest were either dismounted or silenced by the musketry from the trenches.

"There is not a house in the place," says the diary just quoted, "that has not felt the effects of this formidable artillery. From yesterday morning till seven o'clock this evening we reckon that a thousand or twelve hundred bombs, great and small, have been thrown into the town, accompanied all the time by the fire of forty pieces of cannon, served with an activity not often seen. The hospital and the houses around it, which also serve as hospitals, are attacked with cannon and mortar. The surgeon trembles as he amputates a limb amid cries of *Gare la bombe!* and leaves his patient in the midst of the operation, lest he should share his fate. The sick and wounded, stretched on mattresses, utter cries of pain which do not cease till a shot or the bursting of a shell ends them." On the twenty-sixth the last cannon was silenced in front of the town and the English batteries had made a breach which seemed practicable for assault.

After some parley, however, Drucour was persuaded to capitulate. The articles stipulated that the garrison should be sent to England, prisoners of war, in British ships; that all artillery, arms, munitions and stores, both in Louisbourg and elsewhere on the island of Cape Breton, as well as on Isle St. Jean, now Prince Edward's Island, should be given up intact; that the gate of the Dauphin's Bastion should be delivered to the British troops at eight o'clock in the morning; and that the garrison should lay down their arms at noon. The victors, on their part, promised to give the French sick and wounded the same care as their own and to protect private property from pillage.

Drucour signed the paper at midnight, and in the morning a body of grenadiers took possession of the Dauphin's Gate. The rude soldiery poured in, swarthy with wind and sun and begrimed with smoke and dust; the garrison, drawn up on the esplanade, flung down their muskets and marched from the ground with tears of rage; the cross of St. George floated over the shattered rampart, and Louisbourg, with the two great islands that depended on it, passed to the British Crown. Guards were posted, a stern discipline was enforced and perfect order maintained. The conquerors and the conquered exchanged greetings and the English general was lavish of courtesies to the brave lady who had aided the defense so well. "Every favor she asked was granted," says a Frenchman present.

Drucour and his garrison had made a gallant defense. It had been his aim to prolong the siege till it should be too late for Amherst to co-operate with Abercrombie in an attack on Canada, and in this at least he succeeded.

The fall of the French stronghold was hailed in England with noisy rapture. Addresses of congratulation to the King poured in from all the cities of the kingdom, and the captured flags were hung in St. Paul's amid the roar of cannon and the shouts of the populace. The provinces shared these rejoicings. Sermons of thanksgiving resounded from countless New England pulpits.

The ardent and indomitable Wolfe had been the life of the siege. Wherever there was need of a quick eye, a prompt decision and a bold dash, there his lank figure was always in the front. Yet he was only half pleased with what had been done. The capture of Louisbourg, he thought, should be but the prelude of greater conquests, and he had hoped that the fleet and army would sail up the St. Lawrence and attack Quebec. Impetuous and impatient by nature, and irritable with disease, he chafed at the delay that followed the capitulation.

Amherst, with such speed as his deliberate nature would permit, sailed with six regiments for Boston to reinforce Abercrombie at Lake George, while Wolfe set out on an errand but little to his liking. He had orders to proceed to Gaspé, Miramichi and other settlements on the Gulf of St. Lawrence, destroy them and disperse their inhabitants, a measure of needless and unpardonable rigor, which, while detesting it, he executed with characteristic thoroughness.

"Sir Charles Hardy and I," he wrote to his father, "are preparing to rob the fishermen of their nets and burn their huts. When that great exploit is at an end, I return to Louisbourg, and thence to England." Having finished the work, he wrote to Amherst: "Your orders were carried into execution. We have done a great deal of mischief, and spread the terror of His Majesty's arms through the Gulf, but have added nothing to the reputation of them." The destruction of property was great, yet as Knox writes, "he would not suffer the least barbarity to be committed upon the persons of the wretched inhabitants."

He returned to Louisbourg and sailed for England to recruit his shattered health for greater conflicts.

CHAPTER 12

~~~~~~

The Battle for Ticonderoga

IN JUNE OF 1758 THE COMBINED BRITISH AND PROVIN-
cial force which Abercrombie was to lead against Ticonderoga
was gathered at the head of Lake George, while Montcalm lay at its
outlet around the walls of the French stronghold with an army not
one fourth so numerous. Vaudreuil had devised a plan for saving
Ticonderoga by a diversion into the valley of the Mohawk under
Lévis, Rigaud and Longueuil, with sixteen hundred men who were to
be joined by as many Indians. The English forts of that region were to
be attacked, Schenectady threatened and the Five Nations compelled to
declare for France. Thus, as the governor gave out, the English would
be forced to cease from aggression, leave Montcalm in peace and think
only of defending themselves.

The proposed movement promised, no doubt, great advantages, but
it was not destined to take effect. Some rangers taken on Lake George
by a partisan officer named Langy declared with pardonable exaggeration that twenty-five or thirty thousand men would attack Ticonderoga in less than a fortnight. Vaudreuil saw himself forced to
abandon his Mohawk expedition and to order Lévis and his followers,
who had not yet left Montreal, to reinforce Montcalm. Why they did
not go at once is not clear. The governor declares that there were not
boats enough. From whatever cause, there was a long delay and Montcalm was left to defend himself as he could.

He hesitated whether he should not fall back to Crown Point. The
engineer, Lotbinière, opposed the plan, as did also Le Mercier. It was

but a choice of difficulties, and he stayed at Ticonderoga. His troops were disposed as they had been in the summer before, one battalion, that of Berry, being left near the fort while the main body under Montcalm himself was encamped by the sawmill at the falls, and the rest under Bourlamaque occupied the head of the portage, with a small advanced force at the landing place on Lake George. It remained to determine at which of these points he should concentrate them and make his stand against the English. Ruin threatened him in any case. Each position had its fatal weakness or its peculiar danger, and his best hope was in the ignorance or blundering of his enemy. He seems to have been several days in a state of indecision.

On the afternoon of the fifth of July the partisan Langy, who had again gone out to reconnoiter towards the head of Lake George, came back in haste with the report that the English were embarked in great force. Montcalm sent a canoe down Lake Champlain to hasten Lévis to his aid and ordered the battalion of Berry to begin a breastwork and abatis on the high ground in front of the fort. That they were not begun before shows that he was in doubt as to his plan of defense, and that his whole army was not now set to work at them shows that his doubt was still unsolved.

It was nearly a month since Abercrombie had begun his camp at the head of Lake George. Here, on the ground where Johnson had beaten Dieskau, where Montcalm had planted his batteries and Monro vainly defended the wooden ramparts of Fort William Henry, were now assembled more than fifteen thousand men, and the shores, the foot of the mountains and the broken plains between them were studded thick with tents. Of regulars there were six thousand three hundred and sixty-seven, officers and soldiers, and of provincials nine thousand and thirty-four. To the New England levies, or at least to their chaplains, the expedition seemed a crusade against the abomination of Babylon, and they discoursed in their sermons of Moses sending forth Joshua against Amalek.

Abercrombie, raised to his place by political influence, was little but the nominal commander. Pitt meant that the actual command of the army should be in the hands of Brigadier Lord Howe, and he was in fact its real chief, "the noblest Englishman that has appeared in my time, and the best soldier in the British army," says Wolfe. And he elsewhere speaks of him as "that great man." Abercrombie testifies to the universal respect and love with which officers and men regarded him, and Pitt calls him "a character of ancient times; a complete model of military virtue."

High as this praise is, it seems to have been deserved. The young nobleman, who was then in his thirty-fourth year, had the qualities of a leader of men. The army felt him, from general to drummer boy. He was its soul, and while breathing into it his own energy and ardor and bracing it by stringent discipline, he broke through the traditions of the service and gave it new shapes to suit the time and place.

He made officers and men throw off all useless encumbrances, cut their hair close, wear leggings to protect them from briers, brown the barrels of their muskets and carry in their knapsacks thirty pounds of meal, which they cooked for themselves, so that according to an admiring Frenchman, they could live a month without their supply trains. He made himself greatly beloved by the provincial officers, with many of whom he was on terms of intimacy, and he did what he could to break down the barriers between the colonial soldiers and the British regulars.

On the evening of the fourth of July, baggage, stores and ammunition were all on board the boats, and the whole army embarked on the morning of the fifth. The arrangements were perfect. Each corps marched without confusion to its appointed station on the beach and the sun was scarcely above the ridge of French Mountain when all were afloat. A spectator watching them from the shore says that when the fleet was three miles on its way the surface of the lake at that distance was completely hidden from sight. There were nine hundred bateaux, a hundred and thirty-five whaleboats, and a large number of heavy flatboats carrying the artillery. The whole advanced in three divisions, the regulars in the center and the provincials on the flanks. Each corps had its flags and its music. The day was fair and men and officers were in the highest spirits.

Before ten o'clock they began to enter the Narrows and the boats of the three divisions extended themselves into long files as the mountains closed on either hand upon the contracted lake. From front to rear the line was six miles long. The spectacle was superb: the brightness of the summer day; the romantic beauty of the scenery; the sheen and sparkle of those crystal waters; the countless islets, tufted with pine, birch and fir; the bordering mountains, with their green summits and sunny crags; the flash of oars and glitter of weapons; the banners, the varied uniforms and the notes of bugle, trumpet, bagpipe and drum answered and prolonged by a hundred woodland echoes. "I never beheld so delightful a prospect," wrote a wounded officer at Albany a fortnight after.

Rogers with the rangers, and Gage with the light infantry, led the way in whaleboats, followed by Bradstreet with his corps of boatmen, armed and drilled as soldiers. Then came the main body. The central column of regulars was commanded by Lord Howe, his own regiment, the fifty-fifth, in the van, followed by the Royal Americans, the twenty-seventh, forty-fourth, forty-sixth and eightieth infantry, and the Highlanders of the forty-second, with their major, Duncan Campbell of Inverawe, silent and gloomy amid the general cheer, for his soul was dark with foreshadowings of death.

With this central column came what are described as two floating castles, which were no doubt batteries to cover the landing of the troops. On the right hand and the left were the provincials, uniformed in blue, regiment after regiment, from Massachusetts, Connecticut, New York, New Jersey and Rhode Island. Behind them all came the bateaux, loaded with stores and baggage, and the heavy flatboats that carried the artillery, while a rear guard of provincials and regulars closed the long procession.

At five in the afternoon they reached Sabbath Day Point, twenty-five miles down the lake, where they stopped till late in the evening, waiting for the baggage and artillery, which had lagged behind, and here Lord Howe, lying on a bearskin by the side of the ranger John Stark, questioned him as to the position of Ticonderoga and its best points of approach.

At about eleven o'clock they set out again, and at daybreak entered what was then called the Second Narrows, that is to say, the contraction of the lake where it approaches its outlet. Close on their left, ruddy in the warm sunrise, rose the vast bare face of Rogers Rock, from which a French advance party, under Langy and an officer named Trepezec, was watching their movements.

Lord Howe, with Rogers and Bradstreet, went in whaleboats to reconnoiter the landing. At the place which the French called the Burned Camp, where Montcalm had embarked the summer before, they saw a detachment of the enemy too weak to oppose them. Their men landed and drove them off. At noon the whole army was on shore. Rogers, with a party of rangers, was ordered forward to reconnoiter and the troops were formed for the march.

From this part of the shore a plain covered with forest stretched northwestward half a mile or more to the mountains behind which lay the valley of Trout Brook. On this plain the army began its march in four columns, with the intention of passing round the western bank of the river of the outlet, since the bridge over it had been destroyed.

Rogers, with the provincial regiments of Fitch and Lyman, led the way at some distance before the rest. The forest was extremely dense and heavy and so obstructed with undergrowth that it was impossible to see more than a few yards in any direction, while the ground was encumbered with fallen trees in every stage of decay. The ranks were broken and the men struggled on as they could in dampness and shade, under a canopy of boughs that the sun could scarcely pierce. The difficulty increased when, after advancing about a mile, they came upon undulating and broken ground. They were now not far from the upper rapids of the outlet. The guides became bewildered in the maze of trunks and boughs. The marching columns were confused and fell in one upon the other. They were in the strange situation of an army lost in the woods.

The advanced party of French under Langy and Trepezec, about three hundred and fifty in all, regulars and Canadians, had tried to retreat, but before they could do so the whole English Army had passed them, landed and placed itself between them and their countrymen. They had no resource but to take to the woods. They seem to have climbed the steep gorge at the side of Rogers Rock and followed the Indian path that led to the valley of Trout Brook, thinking to descend it and, by circling along the outskirts of the valley of Ticonderoga, reach Montcalm's camp at the sawmill.

Langy was used to bushranging, but he too became perplexed in the blind intricacies of the forest. Towards the close of the day he and his men had come out from the valley of Trout Brook and were near the junction of that stream with the river of the outlet, in a state of some anxiety for they could see nothing but brown trunks and green boughs. Could any of them have climbed one of the great pines that here and there reared their shaggy spires high above the surrounding forest, they would have discovered where they were but would have gained not the faintest knowledge of the enemy.

Out of the woods on the right they would have seen a smoke rising from the burning huts of the French camp at the head of the portage, which Bourlamaque had set on fire and abandoned. At a mile or more in front, the sawmill at the falls might perhaps have been described, and by glimpses between the trees, the tents of the neighboring camp where Montcalm still lay with his main force. All the rest seemed lonely as the grave; mountain and valley lay wrapped in primeval woods and none could have dreamed that, not far distant, an army was groping its way, buried in foliage; no rumbling of wagons and artillery trains, for none were there; all silent but the cawing of some crow flapping his black wings over the sea of treetops.

Lord Howe, with Major Israel Putnam and two hundred rangers, was at the head of the principal column, which was a little in advance of the three others. Suddenly the challenge *Qui vive?* rang sharply from the thickets in front. *Français!* was the reply.

Langy's men were not deceived: they fired out of the bushes. The shots were returned, a hot skirmish followed, and Lord Howe dropped dead, shot through the breast. All was confusion. The dull, vicious reports of musketry in thick woods, at first few and scattering, then in fierce and rapid volleys, reached the troops behind. They could hear, but could see nothing. Already harassed and perplexed, they became perturbed. For all they knew, Montcalm's whole army was upon them. Nothing prevented a panic but the steadiness of the rangers, who maintained the fight alone till the rest came back to their senses.

Rogers, with his reconnoitering party and the regiments of Fitch and Lyman, were at no great distance in front. They all turned on hearing the musketry, and thus the French were caught between two fires. They fought with desperation. About fifty of them at length escaped; a hundred and forty-eight were captured and the rest killed or drowned in trying to cross the rapids. The loss of the English was small in numbers but immeasurable in the death of Howe.

"The fall of this noble and brave officer," says Rogers, "seemed to produce an almost general languor and consternation through the whole army." "In Lord Howe," writes another contemporary, Major Thomas Mante, "the soul of General Abercrombie's army seemed to expire. From the unhappy moment the General was deprived of his advice, neither order nor discipline was observed, and a strange kind of infatuation usurped the place of resolution." The death of one man was the ruin of fifteen thousand.

The effect of the loss was seen at once. The army was needlessly kept under arms all night in the forest, and in the morning was ordered back to the landing whence it came. Towards noon, however, Bradstreet was sent with a detachment of regulars and provincials to take possession of the sawmill at the falls, which Montcalm had abandoned the evening before. Bradstreet rebuilt the bridges destroyed by the retiring enemy and sent word to his commander that the way was open, on which Abercrombie again put his army in motion, reached the falls late in the afternoon and occupied the deserted encampment of the French.

Montcalm with his main force had held this position at the falls through most of the preceding day, doubtful, it seems, to the last whether he should not make his final stand there. Bourlamaque was for doing so, but two old officers, Bèrnes and Montguy, pointed out the danger that the English would occupy the neighboring heights, whereupon Montcalm at length resolved to fall back. The camp was broken up at five o'clock. Some of the troops embarked in bateaux, while others marched a mile and a half along the forest road, passed the place where the battalion of Berry was still at work on the breastwork begun in the morning and made their bivouac a little farther on, upon the cleared ground that surrounded the fort.

The peninsula of Ticonderoga consists of a rocky plateau, with low ground on each side, bordering Lake Champlain on the one hand and the outlet of Lake George on the other. The fort stood near the end of the peninsula, which points towards the southeast. From there, as one goes westward, the ground declines a little and then slowly rises till, about half a mile from the fort, it reaches its greatest elevation and begins still more gradually to decline again. Thus a ridge is formed across the plateau between the steep declivities that sink to the low grounds on right and left.

Some weeks before, a French officer named Hugues had suggested the defense of this ridge by means of an abatis. Montcalm approved his plan, and now at the eleventh hour he resolved to make his stand here. The two engineers, Pontleroy and Desandrouin, had already traced the outline of the works, and the soldiers of the battalion of Berry had made some progress in constructing them.

At dawn of the seventh, while Abercrombie, fortunately for his enemy, was drawing his troops back to the landing place, the whole French Army fell to their task. The regimental colors were planted along the line and the officers, stripped to the shirt, took ax in hand and labored with their men. The trees that covered the ground were hewn down by thousands, the tops lopped off and the trunks piled one upon another to form a massive· breastwork. The line followed the top of the ridge, along which it zigzagged in such a manner that the whole front could be swept by flank fires of musketry and grape.

Montcalm had done what he could, but the danger of his position was inevitable and extreme. His hope lay in Abercrombie and it was a hope well founded. The action of the English general answered the utmost wishes of his enemy.

Abercrombie had been told by his prisoners that Montcalm had six thousand men and that three thousand more were expected every hour. Therefore he was in haste to attack before these succors could arrive. As was the general, so was the army. "I believe," writes an officer, "we were one and all infatuated by a notion of carrying every obstacle by a mere *coup de mousqueterie.*" Leadership perished with Lord Howe and nothing was left but blind, headlong valor.

Clerk, chief engineer, was sent to reconnoiter the French works from Mount Defiance and came back with the report that, to judge from what he could see, they might be carried by assault. Then, without waiting to bring up his cannon, Abercrombie prepared to storm the lines.

. The French finished their breastwork and abatis on the evening of the seventh, encamped behind them, slung their kettles and rested after their heavy toil. Lévis had not yet appeared, but at twilight one of his officers, Captain Pouchot, arrived with three hundred regulars and announced that his commander would come before morning with a hundred more.

The reinforcement, though small, was welcome and Lévis was a host in himself. Pouchot was told that the army was half a mile off. There he repaired, made his report to Montcalm and looked with amazement at the prodigious amount of work accomplished in one day. Lévis himself arrived in the course of the night and approved the arrangement of the troops. They lay behind their lines till daybreak; then the drums beat and they formed in order of battle.

Soon after nine o'clock a distant and harmless fire of small arms began on the slopes of Mount Defiance. It came from a party of Indians who had just arrived with Sir William Johnson, and who, after amusing themselves in this manner for a time, remained for the rest of the day safe spectators of the fight. The soldiers worked undisturbed till noon, when volleys of musketry were heard from the forest in front. It was the English light troops driving in the French pickets. A cannon was fired as a signal to drop tools and form for battle. The white uniforms lined the breastwork in a triple row, with the grenadiers behind them as a reserve and the second battalion of Berry watching the flanks and rear.

Meanwhile the English Army had moved forward from its camp by the sawmill. First came the rangers, the light infantry and Bradstreet's armed boatmen, who, emerging into the open space, began a spattering fire. Some of the provincial troops followed, extending from left to right and opening fire in turn. Then the regulars, who had formed in columns of attack under cover of the forest, advanced their solid red masses into the sunlight and, passing through the intervals between the provincial regiments, pushed forward to the assault.

Across the rough ground, with its maze of fallen trees whose leaves hung withering in the July sun, they could see the top of the breastwork but not the men behind it. Then, in an instant, all the line was obscured by a gush of smoke, a crash of exploding firearms tore the air and grapeshot and musket balls swept the whole space like a tempest; "a damnable fire," says an officer who heard them screaming about his ears.

The English had been ordered to carry the works with the bayonet, but their ranks were broken by the obstructions through which they struggled in vain to force their way, and they soon began to fire in turn. The storm raged in full fury for an hour. The assailants pushed

635

close to the breastwork, but there they were stopped by the bristling mass of sharpened branches, which they could not pass under the murderous cross fires that swept them from front and flank. At length they fell back, exclaiming that the works were impregnable. Abercrombie, who was at the sawmill a mile and a half in the rear, sent orders to attack again, and again they came on as before.

The scene was frightful: masses of infuriated men who could not go forward and would not go back, straining for an enemy they could not reach and firing on an enemy they could not see; caught in the entanglement of fallen trees; tripped by briers, stumbling over logs, tearing through boughs; shouting, yelling, cursing and pelted all the while with bullets that killed them by scores, stretched them on the ground or hung them on jagged branches in strange attitudes of death. The provincials supported the regulars with spirit and some of them forced their way to the foot of the wooden wall.

The French fought with the intrepid gaiety of their nation and shouts of *Vive le Roi* and *Vive notre Général!* mingled with the din of musketry. Montcalm, with his coat off, for the day was hot, directed the defense of the center and repaired to any part of the line where the danger for the time seemed greatest. He is warm in praise of his enemy and declares that between one and seven o'clock they attacked him six successive times. Early in the action Abercrombie tried to turn the French left by sending twenty bateaux, filled with troops, down the outlet of Lake George. They were met by the fire of the volunteers stationed to defend the low ground on that side and, still advancing, came within range of the cannon of the fort, which sank two of them and drove back the rest.

Towards five o'clock two English columns joined in a most determined assault on the extreme right of the French, defended by the battalions of Guienne and Béarn. The danger for a time was imminent. Montcalm hastened to the spot with the reserves. The assailants hewed their way to the foot of the breastwork, and though again and again repulsed, they again and again renewed the attack.

The Highlanders fought with stubborn and unconquerable fury. "Even those who were mortally wounded," writes one of their lieutenants, "cried to their companions not to lose a thought upon them, but to follow their officers and mind the honor of their country. Their ardor was such that it was difficult to bring them off." Their major, Campbell of Inverawe, found his foreboding true. He received a mortal shot and his clansmen bore him from the field. Twenty-five of their officers were killed or wounded and half the men fell under the deadly fire that poured from the loopholes. Captain John Campbell and a few followers tore their way through the abatis, climbed the breastwork, leaped down among the French and were bayoneted there.

As the colony troops and Canadians on the low ground were left undisturbed, Lévis sent them an order to make a sortie and attack the left flank of the charging columns. They accordingly posted themselves among the trees along the declivity and fired upwards at the enemy, who presently shifted their position to the right, out of the line of shot. The assault still continued, but in vain, and at six there was another effort, equally fruitless.

From this time till half-past seven a lingering fight was kept up by the rangers and other provincials, firing from the edge of the woods and from behind the stumps, bushes and fallen trees in front of the lines. Its only objects were to cover their comrades, who were collecting and bringing off the wounded, and to protect the retreat of the regulars, who fell back in disorder to the falls. As twilight came on, the last combatant withdrew and none were left but the dead.

Abercrombie had lost in killed, wounded and missing nineteen hundred and forty-four officers and men. The loss of the French, not counting that of Langy's detachment, was three hundred and seventy-seven. Bourlamaque was dangerously wounded; Bougainville slightly; and the hat of Lévis was twice shot through.

Montcalm, with a mighty load lifted from his soul, passed along the lines and gave the tired soldiers the thanks they nobly deserved. Beer, wine and food were served out to them and they bivouacked for the night on the level ground between the breastwork and the fort. The enemy had met a terrible rebuff, yet the danger was not over. Abercrombie still had more than thirteen thousand men and he might renew the attack with cannon.

But on the morning of the ninth a band of volunteers who had gone out to watch him brought back the report that he was in full retreat. The sawmill at the falls was on fire and the last English soldier was gone. On the morning of the tenth, Lévis, with a strong detachment, followed the road to the landing place and found signs that a panic had overtaken the defeated troops. They had left behind several hundred barrels of provisions and a large quantity of baggage, while in a marshy place that they had crossed was found a considerable number of their shoes, which had stuck in the mud and which they had not stopped to recover. They had embarked on the morning after the battle and retreated to the head of the lake in a disorder and dejection wofully contrasted with the pomp of their advance.

A gallant army was sacrificed by the blunders of its chief.

~~~~~~

Canada Imperiled

ARLY IN SEPTEMBER, ABERCROMBIE'S MELANCHOLY
camp was cheered with the tidings that the important French
post of Fort Frontenac, which controlled Lake Ontario, which had
baffled Shirley in his attempt against Niagara and given Montcalm the
means of conquering Oswego, had fallen into British hands. "This is a
glorious piece of news, and may God have all the glory of the same!"
writes Chaplain Cleaveland in his diary.

Lieutenant Colonel Bradstreet had planned the stroke long before
and proposed it first to Loudon, then to Abercrombie. Loudon accepted
it, but his successor received it coldly, though Lord Howe was warm
in its favor. At length, under the pressure of a council of war,
Abercrombie consented that the attempt should be made and gave
Bradstreet three thousand men, nearly all provincials. With these he
made his way up the Mohawk and down the Onondaga to the lonely
and dismal spot where Oswego had once stood. By dint of much
persuasion a few Oneidas joined him, though like most of the Five
Nations they had been nearly lost to the English through the effects of
the defeat at Ticonderoga.

On the twenty-second of August his fleet of whaleboats and bateaux
pushed out on Lake Ontario and, three days after, landed near the
French fort. On the night of the twenty-sixth Bradstreet made a
lodgment within less than two hundred yards of it, and early in the
morning De Noyan, the commandant, surrendered himself and his
followers, numbering a hundred and ten soldiers and laborers, pris-

oners of war. With them were taken nine armed vessels, carrying from eight to eighteen guns and forming the whole French naval force on Lake Ontario. The crews escaped.

An enormous quantity of provisions, naval stores, munitions and Indian goods intended for the supply of the western posts fell into the hands of the English, who kept what they could carry off and burned the rest. In the fort were found sixty cannon and sixteen mortars, which the victors used to batter down the walls, and then, reserving a few of the best, knocked off the trunnions of the others.

The Oneidas were bent on scalping some of the prisoners. Bradstreet forbade it. They begged that he would do as the French did—turn his back and shut his eyes—but he forced them to abstain from all violence and consoled them by a lion's share of the plunder. In accordance with the orders of Abercrombie, the fort was dismantled and all the buildings in or around it burned, as were also the vessels, except the two largest, which were reserved to carry off some of the captured goods. Then, with boats deeply laden, the detachment returned to Oswego, where after unloading and burning the two vessels, they proceeded towards Albany, leaving a thousand of their number at the new fort which Brigadier Stanwix was building at the Great Carrying Place of the Mohawk.

Next to Louisbourg, this was the heaviest blow that the French had yet received. Their command of Lake Ontario was gone. New France was cut in two, and unless the severed parts could speedily reunite, all the posts of the interior would be in imminent jeopardy. If Bradstreet had been followed by another body of men to reoccupy and rebuild Oswego, thus recovering a harbor on Lake Ontario, all the captured French vessels could have been brought there and the command of this island sea assured at once.

Even as it was, the advantages were immense. A host of savage warriors, thus far inclined to France or wavering between the two belligerents, stood henceforth neutral or gave themselves to England, while Fort Duquesne, deprived of the supplies on which it depended, could make but faint resistance to its advancing enemy.

Amherst, with five regiments from Louisbourg, came early in October to join Abercrombie at Lake George and the two commanders discussed the question of again attacking Ticonderoga. Both thought the season too late. A fortnight after, a deserter brought news that Montcalm was breaking up his camp. Abercrombie followed his example. The opposing armies filed off each to its winter quarters and only a few scouting parties kept alive the embers of war on the waters and mountains of Lake George.

Meanwhile, Brigadier Forbes was climbing the Alleghenies, hewing his way through the forests of western Pennsylvania and toiling inch by inch towards his goal of Fort Duquesne.

Forbes had embarked on his campaign as the result of a changed political and tactical situation. During the last year Loudon, filled with vain schemes against Louisbourg, had left the French scalping parties to their work of havoc on the western borders. In Virginia, Washington still toiled at his hopeless task of defending with a single regiment a forest frontier of more than three hundred miles, and in Pennsylvania the Assembly thought more of quarreling with their governor than of protecting the tormented settlers.

Fort Duquesne, the source of all the evil, was left undisturbed. In vain Washington urged the futility of defensive war and the necessity of attacking the enemy in his stronghold. His position, trying at the best, was made more so by the behavior of Dinwiddie. That crusty Scotchman had conceived a dislike of him and sometimes treated him in a manner that must have been unspeakably galling to the proud and passionate young man who, nevertheless, unconquerable in his sense of public duty, curbed himself to patience, or the semblance of it.

Dinwiddie was now gone and a new governor had taken his place. The conduct of the war, too, had changed. In the plans of Pitt, the capture of Fort Duquesne held an important place. Forbes, who was charged with it, was a Scotch veteran, forty-eight years of age, who had begun life as a student of medicine and who ended it as an able and faithful soldier. Though a well-bred man of the world, his tastes were simple. He detested ceremony and dealt frankly and plainly with the colonists, who both respected and liked him.

In April of 1758 he was in Philadelphia waiting for his army, which as yet had no existence, for the provincials were not enlisted and an expected battalion of Highlanders had not arrived. It was the end of June before they were all on the march, and meanwhile the general was attacked with a painful and dangerous malady which would have totally disabled a less resolute man.

His force consisted of provincials from Pennsylvania, Virginia, Maryland and North Carolina, with twelve hundred Highlanders of Montgomery's regiment and a detachment of Royal Americans, amounting in all, with wagoners and camp followers, to between six and seven thousand men.

The Royal American regiment was a new corps raised in the colonies largely from among the Germans of Pennsylvania. Its officers were from Europe and conspicuous among them was Lieutenant Colonel Henry Bouquet, a brave and accomplished Swiss, who commanded one of the four battalions of which the regiment was composed.

Early in July he was encamped with the advance guard at the hamlet of Raystown, now the town of Bedford, among the eastern heights of the Alleghenies. Here his tents were pitched in an opening of the forest by the banks of a small stream, and Virginians in hunting shirts, Highlanders in kilt and plaid and Royal Americans in regulation scarlet labored at throwing up intrenchments and palisades, while around stood the silent mountains in their mantles of green.

Now rose the question whether the army should proceed in a direct course to Fort Duquesne, hewing a new road through the forest, or march thirty-four miles to Fort Cumberland and thence follow the road made by Braddock. It was the interest of Pennsylvania that Forbes should choose the former route, and of Virginia that he should choose the latter. The Old Dominion did not wish to see a highway cut for her rival to those rich lands of the Ohio which she called her own.

Washington, who was then at Fort Cumberland with a part of his regiment, was earnest for the old road, and in an interview with Bouquet midway between that place and Raystown he spared no effort to bring him to the same opinion. But the quartermaster general, Sir John Sinclair, who was supposed to know the country, had advised the Pennsylvania route and both Bouquet and Forbes were resolved to take it. It was shorter and, when once made, would furnish readier and more abundant supplies of food and forage, but to make it would consume a vast amount of time and labor.

Washington foretold the ruin of the expedition unless it took Braddock's road. Ardent Virginian as he was, there is no cause to believe that his decision was based on any but military reasons. Forbes thought otherwise and found great fault with him. Bouquet did him more justice. "Colonel Washington," he writes to the general, "is filled with a sincere zeal to aid the expedition, and is ready to march with equal activity by whatever way you choose."

The fate of Braddock had impressed itself on all the army and inspired a caution that was but too much needed. Except for Washington's men and a few others among the provincials, the whole, from general to drummer boy, were total strangers to that insidious warfare of the forest in which their enemies, red and white, had no rival. Instead of marching, like Braddock, at one stretch for Fort Duquesne, burdened with a long and cumbrous baggage train, it was the plan of Forbes to push on by slow stages, establishing fortified magazines as he went, and at last, when within easy distance of the fort, to advance upon it with all his force, as little impeded as possible with wagons and packhorses.

He bore no likeness to his predecessor except in determined resolution and he did not hesitate to embrace military heresies which would have driven Braddock to fury. To Bouquet, in whom he placed a well-merited trust, he wrote: "I have been long in your opinion of equipping numbers of our men like the savages, and I fancy Colonel Burd, of Virginia, has most of his best people equipped in that manner. In this country we must learn the art of war from enemy Indians, or anybody else who has seen it carried on here."

His provincials displeased him, not without reason, for the greater part were but the crudest material for an army, unruly and recalcitrant to discipline. Some of them came to the rendezvous at Carlisle with old province muskets, the locks tied on with a string. Others brought fowling pieces of their own and others carried nothing but walking sticks, while many had never fired a gun in their lives. Forbes reported to Pitt that their officers, except a few in the higher ranks, were "an extremely bad collection of broken innkeepers, horsejockeys and Indian traders," nor is he more flattering towards the men, though as to some of them he afterwards changed his mind.

While Bouquet was with the advance at Raystown, Forbes was still in Philadelphia, trying to bring the army into shape and collecting provisions, horses and wagons, much vexed meantime by the Assembly, whose tedious disputes about taxing the proprietaries greatly obstructed the service. "No sergeant or quartermaster of a regiment," he says, "is obliged to look into more details than I am; and if I did not see to everything myself, we should never get out of this town."

July had begun before he could reach the frontier village of Carlisle, where he found everything in confusion. After restoring some order, he wrote to Bouquet: "I have been and still am but poorly, with a cursed flux, but shall move day after tomorrow." He was doomed to disappointment, and it was not till the ninth of August that he sent another letter from the same place to the same military friend. "I am now able to write after three weeks of a most violent and tormenting distemper, which, thank God, seems now much abated as to pain, but has left me as weak as a newborn infant. However, I hope to have strength enough to set out from this place on Friday next."

The disease was an inflammation of the stomach and other vital organs, and when he should have been in bed, with complete repose of body and mind, he was racked continually with the toils and worries of a most arduous campaign.

Forbes was in total ignorance of the strength and movements of the enemy. The Indians reported their numbers to be at least equal to his own, but nothing could be learned from them with certainty by reason of their inveterate habit of lying. Several scouting parties of whites were therefore sent forward, of which the most successful was that of a young Virginian officer, accompanied by a sergeant and five Indians.

At a little distance from the French fort the Indians stopped to paint themselves and practice incantations. The chief warrior of the party then took certain charms from an otter-skin bag and tied them about the necks of the other Indians. On that of the officer he hung the otter skin itself, while to the sergeant he gave a small packet of paint from the same mystic receptacle. "He told us," reports the officer, "that none of us could be shot, for those things would turn the balls from us; and then shook hands with us, and told us to go and fight like men." Thus armed against fate, they mounted the high ground afterwards called Grant's Hill, where, covered by trees and bushes, they had a good view of the fort and saw plainly that the reports of the French force were greatly exaggerated.

Meanwhile Bouquet's men pushed on the heavy work of road making up the main range of the Alleghenies and, what proved far worse, the parallel mountain ridge of Laurel Hill, hewing, digging, blasting, laying fascines and gabions to support the track along the sides of steep declivities or worming their way like moles through the jungle of swamp and forest. Forbes described the country to Pitt as an "immense uninhabited wilderness, overgrown everywhere with trees and brushwood, so that nowhere can one see twenty yards." In truth, as far as eye or mind could reach, a prodigious forest vegetation spread its impervious canopy over hill, valley and plain and wrapped the stern and awful waste in the shadows of the tomb.

Having secured his magazines at Raystown and built a fort there named Fort Bedford, Bouquet made a forward movement of some forty miles, crossed the main Allegheny and Laurel Hill and, taking post on a stream called Loyalhannon Creek, began another depot of supplies as a base for the final advance on Fort Duquesne, which was scarcely fifty miles distant.

Vaudreuil had learned from prisoners the march of Forbes and with his usual egotism announced to the colonial minister what he had done in consequence. "I have sent reinforcements to M. de Ligneris, who commands there." "I have done the impossible to supply him with provisions, and I am now sending them in abundance, in order that the troops I may perhaps have occasion to send to drive off the English may not be delayed." "A stronger fort is needed on the Ohio; but I cannot build one till after the peace; then I will take care to build such a one as will thenceforth keep the English out of that country." Some weeks later he was less confident, and very anxious for news from Ligneris.

He says that he has sent him all the succors he could and ordered troops to go to his aid from Niagara, Detroit and Illinois, as well as the militia of Detroit, with the Indians there and elsewhere in the West—Hurons, Ottawas, Potawatomis, Miamis and other tribes. What he fears is that the English will not attack the fort till all these Indians have grown tired of waiting and have gone home again. This was precisely the intention of Forbes, and the chief object of his long delays.

Meanwhile, Major Grant of the Highlanders had urged Bouquet to send him to reconnoiter Fort Duquesne, capture prisoners, and strike a blow that would animate the assailants and discourage the assailed. Bouquet, forgetting his usual prudence, consented, and Grant set out from the camp at Loyalhannon with about eight hundred men, Highlanders, Royal Americans and provincials.

On the fourteenth of September, at two in the morning, he reached the top of the rising ground thenceforth called Grant's Hill, half a mile or more from the French fort. The forest and the darkness of the night hid him completely from the enemy. He ordered Major Lewis, of the Virginians, to take with him half the detachment, descend to the open plain before the fort and attack the Indians known to be encamped there, after which he was to make a feigned retreat to the hill, where the rest of the troops were to lie in ambush and receive the pursuers.

Lewis set out on his errand while Grant waited anxiously for the result. Dawn was near and all was silent, till at length Lewis returned and incensed his commander by declaring that his men had lost their way in the dark woods and fallen into such confusion that the attempt was impracticable. The morning twilight now began, but the country was wrapped in thick fog.

Grant abandoned his first plan and sent a few Highlanders into the cleared ground to burn a warehouse that had been seen there. He was convinced that the French and their Indians were too few to attack him, though their numbers in fact were far greater than his own. Infatuated with this idea, and bent on taking prisoners, he had the incredible rashness to divide his force in such a way that the several parts could not support each other. Lewis, with two hundred men, was sent to guard the baggage two miles in the rear, where a company of Virginians under Captain Bullitt was already stationed. A hundred Pennsylvanians were posted far off on the right, towards the Allegheny, while Captain Mackenzie, with a detachment of Highlanders, was sent to the left towards the Monongahela.

Then, the fog having cleared a little, Captain Macdonald, with another company of Highlanders, was ordered into the open plain to

646

reconnoiter the fort and make a plan of it, Grant himself remaining on the hill with a hundred of his own regiment and a company of Maryland men. "In order to put on a good countenance," he says, "and convince our men they had no reason to be afraid, I gave directions to our drums to beat the reveille. The troops were in an advantageous post and I must own I thought we had nothing to fear."

Macdonald was at this time on the plain, midway between the woods and the fort and in full sight of it. The roll of the drums from the hill was answered by a burst of war whoops and the French came swarming out like hornets, many of them in their shirts, having just leaped from their beds. They all rushed upon Macdonald and his men, who met them with a volley that checked their advance, on which they surrounded him at a distance and tried to cut off his retreat. The Highlanders broke through and gained the woods, with the loss of their commander, who was shot dead. A crowd of French followed close and soon put them to rout, driving them and Mackenzie's party back to the hill where Grant was posted.

Here there was a hot fight in the forest, lasting about three quarters of an hour. At length the force of numbers, the novelty of the situation and the appalling yells of the Canadians and Indians completely overcame the Highlanders, so intrepid in the ordinary situations of war. They broke away in a wild and disorderly retreat. "Fear," says Grant, "got the better of every other passion; and I trust I shall never again see such a panic among troops."

His only hope was in the detachment he had sent to the rear under Lewis to guard the baggage. But Lewis and his men, when they heard the firing in front, had left their post and pushed forward to help their comrades, taking a straight course through the forest, while Grant was retreating along the path by which he had advanced the night before. Thus they missed each other, and when Grant reached the spot where he expected to find Lewis, he saw to his dismay that nobody was there but Captain Bullitt and his company.

He cried in despair that he was a ruined man, not without reason, for the whole body of French and Indians was upon him. Such of his men as held together were forced towards the Allegheny and, writes Bouquet, "would probably have been cut to pieces but for Captain Bullitt and his Virginians, who kept up the fight against the whole

French force till two thirds of them were killed." They were offered quarter but refused it, and the survivors were driven at last into the Allegheny, where some were drowned and others swam over and escaped. Grant was surrounded and captured, and Lewis, who presently came up, was also made prisoner, along with some of his men, after a stiff resistance. Thus ended this mismanaged affair, which cost the English two hundred and seventy-three killed, wounded and taken. The rest got back safe to Loyalhannon.

The invalid general was deeply touched by this reverse yet expressed himself with a moderation that does him honor. He wrote to Bouquet from Raystown: "Your letter of the seventeenth I read with no less surprise than concern, as I could not believe that such an attempt would have been made without my knowledge and concurrence. The breaking in upon our fair and flattering hopes of success touches me most sensibly. There are two wounded Highland officers just now arrived, who give so lame an account of the matter that one can draw nothing from them, only that my friend Grant most certainly lost his wits, and by his thirst of fame brought on his own perdition, and ran great risk of ours."

The French pushed their advantage with spirit. Early in October a large body of them hovered in the woods about the camp at Loyalhannon, drove back a detachment sent against them, approached under cover of the trees and, though beaten off, withdrew deliberately after burying their dead and killing great numbers of horses and cattle. But with all their courageous energy, their position was desperate. The militia of Louisiana and the Illinois left the fort in November and went home; the Indians of Detroit and Wabash would stay no longer, and worse yet, the supplies destined for Fort Duquesne had been destroyed by Bradstreet at Fort Frontenac. Hence Ligneris was compelled by prospective starvation to dismiss the greater part of his force and await the approach of his enemy with those that remained.

His enemy was in a plight hardly better than his own. Autumnal rains, uncommonly heavy and persistent, had ruined the newly cut road. On the mountains the torrents tore it up, and in the valleys the wheels of the wagons and cannon churned it into soft mud. The horses, overworked and underfed, were fast breaking down. The forest had little food for them and they were forced to drag their own oats and corn, as well as supplies for the army, through two hundred miles of wilderness. In the wretched condition of the road this was no longer possible. The magazines of provisions formed at Raystown and Loyal-hannon to support the army on its forward march were emptied faster than they could be filled.

Early in October the elements relented. The clouds broke, the sky was bright again and the sun shone out in splendor on mountains radiant in the livery of autumn. A gleam of hope revisited the heart of Forbes. It was but a flattering illusion. The sullen clouds returned and a chill, impenetrable veil of mist and rain hid the mountains and the trees. Dejected Nature wept and would not be comforted. Above, below, around, all was trickling, oozing, pattering, gushing.

In the miserable encampments the starved horses stood steaming in the rain and the men crouched disgusted under their dripping tents, while the drenched picket guard in the neighboring forest paced dole-fully through black mire and spongy mosses. The rain turned to snow. The descending flakes clung to the many-colored foliage or melted from sight in the trench of half-liquid clay that was called a road. The wheels of the wagons sank in it to the hub, and to advance or retreat was alike impossible.

In the beginning of November, Forbes was carried to Loyalhannon, where the whole army was then gathered. There was a council of officers and they resolved to attempt nothing more that season, but a few days later three prisoners were brought in who reported the defenseless condition of the French, on which Forbes gave orders to advance again. The wagons and all the artillery, except a few light pieces, were left behind, and on the eighteenth of November, twenty-five hundred picked men marched for Fort Duquesne, without tents or baggage and burdened only with knapsacks and blankets. Washington and Colonel Armstrong, of the Pennsylvanians, had opened a way for them by cutting a road to within a day's march of the French fort.

On the evening of the twenty-fourth the detachment encamped among the hills of Turkey Creek, and the men on guard heard at midnight a dull and heavy sound booming over the western woods. Was it a magazine exploded by accident, or were the French blowing up their works?

In the morning the march was resumed, a strong advance guard leading the way. Forbes came next, carried in his litter, and the troops followed in three parallel columns, the Highlanders in the center under Montgomery, their colonel, and the Royal Americans and provincials on the right and left, under Bouquet and Washington. Thus, guided by the tap of the drum at the head of each column, they moved slowly through the forest, over damp, fallen leaves, crisp with frost, beneath an endless entanglement of bare gray twigs that sighed and moaned in the bleak November wind.

It was dusk when they emerged upon the open plain and saw Fort Duquesne before them, with its background of wintry hills beyond the Monongahela and the Allegheny. During the last three miles they had passed the scattered bodies of those slain two months before at the defeat of Grant, and it is said that, as they neared the fort, the Highlanders were goaded to fury at seeing the heads of their slaughtered comrades stuck on poles, round which the kilts were hung derisively, in imitation of petticoats.

Their rage was vain; the enemy was gone. Only a few Indians lingered about the place, who reported that the garrison, to the number of four or five hundred, had retreated, some down the Ohio, some overland towards Presq'isle, and the rest, with their commander, up the Allegheny to Venango, called by the French, Fort Machault. They had burned the barracks and storehouses and blown up the fortifications.

The first care of the victors was to provide defense and shelter for those of their number on whom the dangerous task was to fall of keeping what they had won. A stockade was planted around a cluster of traders' cabins and soldiers' huts, which Forbes named Pittsburg, in honor of the great minister. It was not till the next autumn that General Stanwix built, hard by, the regular fortified work called Fort Pitt.

Captain West, brother of Benjamin West, the painter, led a detachment of Pennsylvanians, with Indian guides, through the forests of the Monongahela to search for the bones of those who had fallen under Braddock. In the heart of the savage wood they found them in abundance, gnawed by wolves and foxes and covered with the dead leaves of four successive autumns.

Major Halket, of Forbes's staff, had joined the party, and with the help of an Indian who was in the fight, he presently found two skeletons lying under a tree. In one of them he recognized, by a peculiarity of the teeth, the remains of his father, Sir Peter Halket, and in the other he believed that he saw the bones of a brother who had fallen at his father's side. The young officer fainted at the sight. The two skeletons were buried together, covered with a Highland plaid, and the Pennsylvanian woodsmen fired a volley over the grave. The rest of the bones were undistinguishable and, being carefully gathered up, they were all interred in a deep trench dug in the freezing ground.

The work of the new fort was pushed on apace and the task of holding it for the winter was assigned to Lieutenant Colonel Mercer, of the Virginians, with two hundred provincials. The number was far too small. It was certain that, unless vigorously prevented by a counterattack, the French would gather in early spring from all their nearer western posts, Niagara, Detroit, Presq'isle, Le Bœuf and Venango, to retake the place, but there was no food for a larger garrison and the risk must be run. The rest of the troops, with steps quickened by hunger, began their homeward march early in December.

No sooner was his work done than Forbes fell into a state of entire prostration, so that for a time he could neither write a letter nor dictate one. He managed, however, two days after reaching Fort Duquesne, to send Amherst a brief notice of his success, adding: "I shall leave this place as soon as I am able to stand; but God knows when I shall reach Philadelphia, if I ever do."

On the way back a hut with a chimney was built for him at each stopping place, and on the twenty-eighth of December, Major Halket writes from Tomahawk Camp: "How great was our disappointment, on coming to this ground last night, to find that the chimney was unlaid, no fire made, nor any wood cut that would burn. This distressed the General to the greatest degree, by obliging him after his long journey to sit above two hours without any fire, exposed to a snowstorm which had very near destroyed him entirely; but with great difficulty, by the assistance of some cordials, he was brought to."

At length, carried all the way in his litter, he reached Philadelphia, where after lingering through the winter he died in March and was buried with military honors in the chancel of Christ Church.

If his achievement was not brilliant, its solid value was above price. It opened the Great West to English enterprise, took from France half her savage allies and relieved the western borders from the scourge of Indian war. From southern New York to North Carolina the frontier populations had cause to bless the memory of the steadfast and all-enduring soldier.

So ended the campaign of 1758. The center of the French had held its own triumphantly at Ticonderoga, but their left had been forced back by the capture of Louisbourg and their right by that of Fort Duquesne, while their entire right wing had been well nigh cut off by the destruction of Fort Frontenac. The outlook was dark.

~~~~~~

The Brink of Ruin

NEVER WAS GENERAL IN A MORE CRITICAL POSI-
tion than I was: God has delivered me; his be the praise! He
gives me health, though I am worn out with labor, fatigue, and miserable dissensions that have determined me to ask for my recall. Heaven
grant that I may get it!"

Thus wrote Montcalm to his mother after his triumph at Ticonderoga. That great exploit had entailed a train of vexations, for it
stirred the envy of Vaudreuil, more especially because it was due to
the troops of the line, with no help from Indians and very little from
Canadians. The governor assured the colonial minister that the victory
would have bad results, though he gives no hint what these might be;
that Montcalm had mismanaged the whole affair; that he would have
been beaten but for the manifest interposition of Heaven; and finally,
that he had failed to follow his (Vaudreuil's) directions and had therefore enabled the English to escape. The real directions of the governor,
dictated perhaps by dread lest his rival should reap laurels, were to
avoid a general engagement, and it was only by ignoring them that
Abercrombie had been routed.

After the battle a sharp correspondence passed between the two
chiefs. The governor, who had left Montcalm to his own resources
before the crisis, sent him Canadians and Indians in abundance after
it was over and, while he cautiously refrained from committing himself
by positive orders, repeated again and again that if these reinforcements were used to harass Abercrombie's communications, the whole

English Army would fall back to the Hudson and leave baggage and artillery a prey to the French. These preposterous assertions and tardy succors were thought by Montcalm to be a device for giving color to the charge that he had not only failed to deserve victory but had failed also to make use of it.

Vaudreuil grew more and more bitter. "As the King has intrusted this colony to me," he wrote, "I cannot help warning you of the unhappy consequences that would follow if the Marquis de Montcalm should remain here. I shall keep him by me till I receive your orders. It is essential that they reach me early." "I pass over in silence all the infamous conduct and indecent talk he has held or countenanced; but I should be wanting in my duty to the King if I did not beg you to ask for his recall."

He does not say what is meant by infamous conduct and indecent talk, but the allusion is probably to irreverent utterances touching the governor in which the officers from France were apt to indulge, not always without the knowledge of their chief. Vaudreuil complained of this to Montcalm, adding, "I am greatly above it, and I despise it." To which the general replied: "You are right to despise gossip, supposing that there has been any. For my part, though I hear that I have been torn to pieces without mercy in your presence, I do not believe it."

Vaudreuil's cup of bitterness was full when letters came from Versailles ordering him to defer to Montcalm on all questions of war or of civil administration bearing upon war. He had begged hard for his rival's recall, and in reply his rival was set over his head.

Some of the byplay of the quarrel may be seen in Montcalm's familiar correspondence with Bourlamaque. One day the governor, in his own house, brought up the old complaint that Montcalm, after taking Fort William Henry, did not take Fort Edward also. The general, for the twentieth time, gave good reasons for not making the attempt. "I ended," he tells Bourlamaque, "by saying quietly that when I went to war I did the best I could; and that when one is not pleased with one's lieutenants, one had better take the field in person. He was very much moved, and muttered between his teeth that perhaps he would; at which I said that I should be delighted to serve under him. Madame de Vaudreuil wanted to put in her word. I said:

'Madame, saving due respect, permit me to have the honor to say that ladies ought not to talk war.' She kept on. I said: 'Madame, saving due respect, permit me to have the honor to say that if Madame de Montcalm were here, and heard me talking war with Monsieur le Marquis de Vaudreuil, she would remain silent.' This scene was in presence of eight officers, three of them belonging to the colony troops; and a pretty story they will make of it."

Never was dispute more untimely than that between these ill-matched colleagues. The position of the colony was desperate. Thus far the Canadians had never lost heart, but had obeyed with admirable alacrity the governor's call to arms, borne with patience the burdens and privations of the war and submitted without revolt to the exactions and oppressions of Cadet and his crew; loyal to their native soil, loyal to their Church, loyal to the wretched government that crushed and belittled them. When the able-bodied were ordered to the war, where four fifths of them were employed in the hard and tedious work of transportation, the women, boys and old men tilled the fields and raised a scanty harvest, which always might be, and sometimes was, taken from them in the name of the King. Yet the least destitute among them were forced every winter to lodge soldiers in their houses, for each of whom they were paid fifteen francs a month in return for substance devoured and wives and daughters debauched.

By indefatigable lying, by exaggerating every success and covering over every reverse, Vaudreuil deceived the people and in some measure himself. He had in abundance the Canadian gift of gasconade and boasted to the colonial minister that one of his countrymen was a match for from three to ten Englishmen. It is possible that he almost believed it, for the midnight surprise of defenseless families and the spreading of panics among scattered border settlements were inseparable from his idea of war. Hence the high value he set on Indians, who in such work outdid the Canadians themselves. Sustained by the intoxication of flattering falsehoods, and not doubting that the blunders and weakness of the first years of the war gave the measure of English efficiency, the colonists had never suspected that they could be subdued.

But now there was a change. The reverses of the last campaign, hunger, weariness and possibly some incipient sense of atrocious misgovernment, began to produce their effect, and some, especially in the towns, were heard to murmur that further resistance was useless. The Canadians, though brave and patient, needed, like Frenchmen, the stimulus of success. "The people are alarmed," said the modest governor, "and would lose courage if my firmness did not rekindle their zeal to serve the King."

The condition of Canada was indeed deplorable. The St. Lawrence was watched by British ships; the harvest was meager; a barrel of flour cost two hundred francs; most of the cattle and many of the horses had been killed for food. The people lived chiefly on a pittance of salt cod or on rations furnished by the King; all prices were inordinate; the officers from France were starving on their pay, while a legion of indigenous and imported scoundrels fattened on the general distress. "What a country!" exclaims Montcalm. "Here all the knaves grow rich, and the honest men are ruined."

The only hope was in a strong appeal to the court, and Montcalm thought himself fortunate in persuading Vaudreuil to consent that Bougainville should be commissioned to make it, seconded by Doreil. They were to sail in different ships, in order that at least one of them might arrive safe.

Vaudreuil gave Bougainville a letter introducing him to the colonial minister in high terms of praise: "He is in all respects better fitted than anybody else to inform you of the state of the colony. I have given him my instructions, and you can trust entirely in what he tells you." Concerning Doreil he wrote to the minister of war: "I have full confidence in him, and he may be entirely trusted. Everybody here likes him." While thus extolling the friends of his rival, the governor took care to provide against the effects of his politic commendations and wrote thus to his patron, the colonial minister: "In order to condescend to the wishes of M. de Montcalm, and leave no means untried to keep in harmony with him, I have given letters to MM. Doreil and Bougainville; but I have the honor to inform you, Monseigneur, that they do not understand the colony, and to warn you that they are creatures of M. de Montcalm."

Both Bougainville and Doreil escaped the British cruisers and safely reached Versailles, where in the slippery precincts of the court, as new to him as they were treacherous, the young aide-de-camp justified all the confidence of his chief. He had interviews with the ministers, the King and, more important than all, with Madame de Pompadour, whom he succeeded in propitiating, though not, it seems, without difficulty and delay.

France, unfortunate by land and sea, with finances ruined and navy crippled, had gained one brilliant victory and she owed it to Montcalm. She could pay for it in honors, if in nothing else. Montcalm was made lieutenant general, Lévis major general, Bourlamaque brigadier and Bougainville colonel and chevalier of St. Louis, while Vaudreuil was solaced with the grand cross of that order. But when the two envoys asked substantial aid for the imperiled colony, the response was chilling. The colonial minister, Berryer, prepossessed against Bougainville by the secret warning of Vaudreuil, received him coldly and replied to his appeal for help: "Eh, monsieur, when the house is on fire one cannot occupy one's self with the stable."

"At least, monsieur, nobody will say that you talk like a horse," was the irreverent answer.

Bougainville laid four memorials before the court, in which he showed the desperate state of the colony and its dire need of help. Thus far, he said, Canada has been saved by the dissensions of the English colonies, but now for the first time they are united against her and prepared to put forth their strength. And he begged for troops, arms, munitions, food and a squadron to defend the mouth of the St. Lawrence.

The reply, couched in a letter to Montcalm, was to the effect that it was necessary to concentrate all the strength of the kingdom for a decisive operation in Europe; that, therefore, the aid required could not be sent; and that the King trusted everything to his zeal and generalship, joined with the valor of the victors of Ticonderoga. All that could be obtained was between three and four hundred recruits for the regulars, sixty engineers, sappers and artillerymen, and gunpowder, arms and provisions sufficient, along with the supplies brought over by the contractor Cadet, to carry the colony through the next campaign.

Again Bougainville crossed the Atlantic and sailed up the St. Lawrence as the portentous spring of 1759 was lowering over the dissolving snows of Canada. With him came a squadron bearing the supplies and the petty reinforcements which the court had vouchsafed. "A little is precious to those who have nothing," said Montcalm on receiving them.

Dispatches from the ministers gave warning of a great armament fitted out in English ports for an attack on Quebec, while a letter to the general from the Maréchal de Belleisle, minister of war, told what was expected of him and why he and the colony were abandoned to their fate.

"If we sent a large reinforcement of troops," said Belleisle, "there would be great fear that the English would intercept them on the way; and as the King could never send you forces equal to those which the English are prepared to oppose to you, the attempt would have no other effect than to excite the Cabinet of London to increased efforts for preserving its superiority on the American continent.

"As we must expect the English to turn all their force against Canada, and attack you on several sides at once, it is necessary that you limit your plans of defense to the most essential points and those most closely connected, so that, being concentrated within a smaller space, each part may be within reach of support and succor from the rest. How small soever may be the space you are able to hold, it is indispensable to keep a footing in North America, for if we once lose the country entirely, its recovery will be almost impossible.

"The King counts on your zeal, courage, and persistency to accomplish this object, and relies on you to spare no pains and no exertions. Impart this resolution to your chief officers, and join with them to inspire your soldiers with it. I have answered for you to the King; I am confident that you will not disappoint me, and that for the glory of the nation, the good of the state, and your own preservation, you will go to the utmost extremity rather than submit to conditions as shameful as those imposed at Louisbourg, the memory of which you will wipe out."

"We will save this unhappy colony, or perish," was the answer of Montcalm.

It was believed that Canada would be attacked with at least fifty thousand men. Vaudreuil had caused a census to be made of the governments of Montreal, Three Rivers and Quebec. It showed a little more than thirteen thousand effective men. To these were to be added thirty-five hundred troops of the line, including the late reinforcement, fifteen hundred colony troops, a body of irregulars in Acadia and the militia and *coureurs de bois* of Detroit and the other upper posts, along with from one to two thousand Indians who could still be counted on.

Great as was the disparity of numbers, there was good hope that the center of the colony could be defended, for the only avenues by which an enemy could approach were barred by the rock of Quebec, the rapids of the St. Lawrence and the strong position of Isle-aux-Noix, at the outlet of Lake Champlain. Montcalm had long inclined to the plan of concentration enjoined on him by the minister of war. Vaudreuil was of another mind. He insisted on still occupying Acadia and the forts of the upper country: matters on which he and the general exchanged a correspondence that widened the breach between them.

Should every effort of resistance fail and the invaders force their way into the heart of Canada, Montcalm proposed the desperate resort of abandoning the valley of the St. Lawrence, descending the Mississippi with his troops and as many as possible of the inhabitants and making a last stand for France among the swamps of Louisiana. But even as Montcalm planned, the instruments of Canada's undoing were being forged in the English camp.

Captain John Knox, of the forty-third regiment, had spent the winter in garrison at Fort Cumberland, on the hill of Beauséjour. For nearly two years he and his comrades had been exiles amid the wilds of Nova Scotia, and the monotonous inaction was becoming insupportable. The great marsh of Tantemar on the one side and that of Missaguash on the other, two vast flat tracts of glaring snow, bounded by dark hills of spruce and fir, were hateful to their sight. Shooting, fishing or skating were a dangerous relief, for the neighborhood was infested by "vermin," as they called the Acadians and their Micmac allies.

In January four soldiers and a ranger were waylaid not far from the fort, disabled by bullets and then scalped alive. They were found the next morning on the snow, contorted in the agonies of death and frozen like marble statues.

St. Patrick's Day brought more cheerful excitements. The Irish officers of the garrison gave their comrades a feast, having laid in during the autumn a stock of frozen provisions, that the festival of their saint might be duly honored. All was hilarity at Fort Cumberland, where it is recorded that punch to the value of twelve pounds sterling, with a corresponding supply of wine and beer, was consumed on this joyous occasion.

About the middle of April a schooner came up the bay, bringing letters that filled men and officers with delight. The regiment was ordered to hold itself ready to embark for Louisbourg and join an expedition to the St. Lawrence, under command of Major General Wolfe. All that afternoon the soldiers were shouting and cheering in their barracks, and when they mustered for the evening roll call there was another burst of huzzas.

They waited in expectancy nearly three weeks and then the transports which were to carry them arrived, bringing the provincials who had been hastily raised in New England to take their place. These Knox describes as a mean-looking set of fellows, of all ages and sizes, and without any kind of discipline, adding that their officers are sober, modest men, who though of confined ideas, talk very clearly and sensibly and make a decent appearance in blue, faced with scarlet, though the privates have no uniform at all.

At last the forty-third set sail, the cannon of the fort saluting them and the soldiers cheering lustily, overjoyed to escape from their long imprisonment. A gale soon began; the transports became separated. Knox's vessel sheltered herself for a time in Passamaquoddy Bay, then passed the Grand Menan and steered southward and eastward along the coast of Nova Scotia. A calm followed the gale, and they moved so slowly that Knox beguiled the time by fishing over the stern and caught a halibut so large that he was forced to call for help to pull it in. Then they steered northeastward, now lost in fogs and now tossed mercilessly on those boisterous waves, till on the twenty-fourth of May they saw a rocky and surf-lashed shore, with a forest of masts rising to all appearance out of it. It was the British fleet in the landlocked harbor of Louisbourg.

On the left, as they sailed through the narrow passage, lay the town, scarred with shot and shell, the red cross floating over its battered ramparts; and around in a wide semicircle rose the bristling backs of rugged hills, set thick with dismal evergreens. They passed the great ships of the fleet and anchored among the other transports towards the head of the harbor. It was not yet free from ice, and the floating masses lay so thick in some parts that the reckless sailors, returning from leave on shore, jumped from one to another to regain their ships.

There was a review of troops and Knox went to see it, but it was over before he reached the place, where he was presently told of a characteristic reply just made by Wolfe to some officers who had apologized for not having taught their men the new exercise.

"Poh, poh! New exercise—new fiddlestick. If they are otherwise well disciplined and will fight, that's all I shall require of them."

Knox does not record his impressions of his new commander, but they must have been disappointing. He called him afterwards a British Achilles, but in person at least Wolfe bore no likeness to the son of Peleus, for never was the soul of a hero cased in a frame so incongruous. The forehead and chin receded; the nose, slightly upturned, formed with the other features the point of an obtuse triangle; the mouth was by no means shaped to express resolution; and nothing but the clear, bright and piercing eye bespoke the spirit within. On his head he wore a black three-cornered hat; his red hair was tied in a queue behind; his narrow shoulders, slender body and long, thin limbs were cased in a scarlet frock, with broad cuffs and ample skirts that reached the knee; while on his left arm he wore a band of crepe in mourning for his father, of whose death he had heard a few days before.

James Wolfe was in his thirty-third year. His father was an officer of distinction, Major General Edward Wolfe, and he himself, a delicate and sensitive child but an impetuous and somewhat headstrong youth, had served the King since the age of fifteen. From childhood he had dreamed of the army and the wars. At sixteen he was in Flanders, adjutant of his regiment, discharging the duties of the post in a way that gained him early promotion and, along with a painstaking assiduity, showing a precocious faculty for commanding men.

He passed with credit through several campaigns, took part in the victory of Dettingen and then went to Scotland to fight at Culloden. Next we find him at Stirling, Perth and Glasgow, always ardent and always diligent, constant in military duty and giving his spare hours to mathematics and Latin. He presently fell in love and, being disappointed, plunged into a variety of dissipations contrary to his usual habits, which were far above the standard of that profligate time.

At twenty-three he was a lieutenant colonel, commanding his regiment in the then dirty and barbarous town of Inverness, amid a disaffected and turbulent population whom it was his duty to keep in order: a difficult task, which he accomplished so well as to gain the special commendation of the King and even the good will of the Highlanders themselves. He was five years among these northern hills, battling with ill-health and restless under the intellectual barrenness of his surroundings.

He got leave of absence and spent six months in Paris, where he was presented at court and saw much of the best society. This did not prevent him from working hard to perfect himself in French, as well as in horsemanship, fencing, dancing and other accomplishments, and from earnestly seeking an opportunity to study the various armies of Europe. In this he was thwarted by the stupidity and prejudice of the commander-in-chief, and he made what amends he could by extensive reading in all that bore on military matters.

His martial instincts were balanced by strong domestic inclinations. He was fond of children, and after his disappointment in love used to say that they were the only true inducement to marriage. He was a most dutiful son and wrote continually to both his parents. Sometimes he would philosophize on the good and ill of life; sometimes he held questionings with his conscience; and once he wrote to his mother in a strain of self-accusation not to be expected from a bold and determined soldier.

His nature was a compound of tenderness and fire, which last sometimes showed itself in sharp and unpleasant flashes. His excitable temper was capable almost of fierceness and he could now and then be needlessly stern, but towards his father, mother and friends he was a model of steady affection. He made friends readily and kept them, and was usually a pleasant companion, though subject to sallies of imperious irritability which occasionally broke through his strong sense of good breeding. For this his susceptible constitution was largely answerable, for he was a living barometer, and his spirits rose and fell with every change of weather.

In spite of his impatient outbursts, the officers whom he had commanded remained attached to him for life, and in spite of his rigorous discipline, he was beloved by his soldiers, to whose comfort he was always attentive. Frankness, directness, essential good feeling and a high integrity atoned for all his faults.

His intrepidity was complete. No form of death had power to daunt him. Once and again, when bound on some deadly enterprise of war, he calmly counts the chances whether or not he can compel his feeble body to bear him on till the work is done. A frame so delicately strung could not have been insensible to danger, but forgetfulness of self and the absorption of every faculty in the object before him shut out the sense of fear. He seems always to have been at his best in the thick of battle; most complete in his mastery over himself and over others.

His part in the taking of Louisbourg greatly increased his reputation. After his return he went to Bath to recruit his health, and it seems to have been here that he wooed and won Miss Katherine Lowther, daughter of an ex-governor of Barbadoes and sister of the future Lord Lonsdale. A betrothal took place and Wolfe wore her portrait till the night before his death.

It was a little before this engagement that he wrote to his friend Lieutenant Colonel Rickson: "I have this day signified to Mr. Pitt that he may dispose of my slight carcass as he pleases, and that I am ready for any undertaking within the compass of my skill and cunning. I am in a very bad condition both with the gravel and rheumatism, but I had much rather die than decline any kind of service that offers. If I followed my own taste it would lead me into Germany. However, it is not our part to choose, but to obey. My opinion is that I shall join the army in America."

Pitt chose him to command the expedition then fitting out against Quebec, made him a major general, though to avoid giving offense to older officers he was to hold that rank in America alone, and permitted him to choose his own staff. Appointments made for merit and through routine and patronage shocked the Duke of Newcastle, to whom a man like Wolfe was a hopeless enigma, and he told George II that Pitt's new general was mad. "Mad, is he?" returned the old King. "Then I hope he will bite some others of my generals."

At the end of January the fleet was almost ready and Wolfe wrote to his uncle Walter: "I am to act a greater part in this business than

663

I wished. The backwardness of some of the older officers has in some measure forced the Government to come down so low. I shall do my best, and leave the rest to fortune, as perforce we must when there are not the most commanding abilities. We expect to sail in about three weeks. A London life and little exercise disagrees entirely with me, but the sea still more. If I have health and constitution enough for the campaign, I shall think myself a lucky man; what happens afterward is of no great consequence."

He sent to his mother an affectionate letter of farewell, went to Spithead, embarked with Admiral Saunders in the ship *Neptune* and set sail on the seventeenth of February. In a few hours the whole squadron was at sea, the transports, the frigates and the great line-of-battle ships, with their ponderous armament and their freight of rude humanity armed and trained for destruction, while on the heaving deck of the *Neptune,* wretched with seasickness and racked with pain, stood the gallant invalid who was master of it all.

The fleet consisted of twenty-two ships of the line, with frigates, sloops of war and a great number of transports. When Admiral Saunders arrived with his squadron off Louisbourg he found the entrance blocked by ice and was forced to seek harborage at Halifax. The squadron of Admiral Holmes, which had sailed a few days earlier, proceeded to New York to take on board troops destined for the expedition, while the squadron of Admiral Durell steered for the St. Lawrence to intercept the expected ships from France.

In May the whole fleet, except the ten ships with Durell, was united in the harbor of Louisbourg. Twelve thousand troops were to have been employed for the expedition, but several regiments expected from the West Indies were for some reason countermanded, while the accessions from New York and the Nova Scotia garrisons fell far short of the looked-for numbers. Three weeks before leaving Louisbourg, Wolfe writes to his uncle Walter that he has an army of nine thousand men. The actual number seems to have been somewhat less.

"Our troops are good," he informs Pitt, "and if valor can make amends for the want of numbers, we shall probably succeed."

Three brigadiers, all in the early prime of life, held command under him: Monckton, Townshend and Murray. They were all his superiors in birth, and one of them, Townshend, never forgot that he was so.

"George Townshend," says Walpole, "has thrust himself again into the service; and, as far as wrongheadedness will go, is very proper for a hero." The same caustic writer says further that he was of "a proud, sullen and contemptuous temper" and that he "saw everything in an ill-natured and ridiculous light."

Though his perverse and envious disposition made him a difficult colleague, Townshend had both talents and energy, as also had Monckton, the same officer who commanded at the capture of Beauséjour in 1755. Murray, too, was well matched to the work in hand, in spite of some lingering remains of youthful rashness.

On the sixth of June the last ship of the fleet sailed out of Louisbourg harbor, the troops cheering and the officers drinking to the toast "British colors on every French fort, port and garrison in America." The ships that had gone before lay to till the whole fleet was reunited and then all steered together for the St. Lawrence.

From the headland of Cape Egmont the Micmac hunter, gazing far out over the shimmering sea, saw the horizon flecked with their canvas wings as they bore northward on their errand of havoc.

Wolfe at Quebec

IN EARLY SPRING OF 1759 THE CHIEFS OF CANADA met at Montreal to settle a plan of defense. What at first they most dreaded was an advance of the enemy by way of Lake Champlain. Bourlamaque, with three battalions, was ordered to take post at Ticonderoga, hold it if he could or, if overborne by numbers, fall back to Isle-aux-Noix, at the outlet of the lake. La Corne was sent with a strong detachment to intrench himself at the head of the rapids of the St. Lawrence and oppose any hostile movement from Lake Ontario. Every able-bodied man in the colony, and every boy who could fire a gun, was to be called to the field.

Vaudreuil sent a circular letter to the militia captains of all the parishes, with orders to read it to the parishioners. It exhorted them to defend their religion, their wives, their children and their goods from the fury of the heretics; declared that he, the governor, would never yield up Canada on any terms whatever; and ordered them to join the army at once, leaving none behind but the old, the sick, the women and the children.

It was in the midst of all these preparations that Bougainville arrived from France with news that a great fleet was on its way to attack Quebec. The town was filled with consternation mixed with surprise, for the Canadians had believed that the dangerous navigation of the St. Lawrence would deter their enemies from the attempt. "Everybody," writes one of them, "was stupefied at an enterprise that seemed so bold."

666

In a few days a crowd of sails was seen approaching. They were not enemies, but friends. It was the fleet of the contractor Cadet, commanded by an officer named Kanon and loaded with supplies for the colony. They anchored in the harbor, eighteen sail in all, and their arrival spread universal joy. Before the first of June five more ships had come safely into port.

When the news brought by Bougainville reached Montreal nearly the whole force of the colony, except the detachments of Bourlamaque and La Corne, was ordered to Quebec. Montcalm hastened there and Vaudreuil followed. The governor-general wrote to the minister in his usual strain, as if all the hope of Canada rested in him. Such, he says, was his activity that, though very busy, he reached Quebec only a day and a half after Montcalm and, on arriving, learned from his scouts that English ships of war had already appeared at Isle-aux-Coudres. These were the squadrons of Admiral Durell.

"I expect," Vaudreuil goes on, "to be sharply attacked, and that our enemies will make their most powerful efforts to conquer this colony, but there is no ruse, no resource, no means which my zeal does not suggest to lay snares for them, and finally, when the exigency demands it, to fight them with an ardor, and even a fury, which exceeds the range of their ambitious designs. The troops, the Canadians, and the Indians are not ignorant of the resolution I have taken, and from which I shall not recoil under any circumstance whatever. The burghers of this city have already put their goods and furniture in places of safety. The old men, women, and children hold themselves ready to leave town. My firmness is generally applauded. It has penetrated every heart; and each man says aloud: 'Canada, our native land, shall bury us under its ruins before we surrender to the English.' This is decidedly my own determination, and I shall hold to it inviolably."

Five battalions from France, nearly all the colony troops and the militia from every part of Canada poured into Quebec, along with a thousand or more Indians, who at the call of Vaudreuil came to lend their scalping knives to the defense. Such was the ardor of the people that boys of fifteen and men of eighty were to be seen in the camp. Isle-aux-Coudres and Isle d'Orléans were ordered to be evacuated and an excited crowd on the rock of Quebec watched hourly for the approaching fleet.

Days passed and weeks passed, yet it did not appear. Meanwhile Vaudreuil held council after council to settle a plan of defense. They were strange scenes: a crowd of officers of every rank, mixed pell-mell in a small room, pushing, shouting, elbowing each other, interrupting each other, till Montcalm in despair took each aside after the meeting was over and made him give his opinion in writing.

He himself had at first proposed to encamp the army on the Plains of Abraham and the meadows of the St. Charles, making that river his line of defense, but he changed his plan and, with the concurrence of Vaudreuil, resolved to post his whole force on the St. Lawrence below the city, with his right resting on the St. Charles and his left on the Montmorenci. Here, accordingly, the troops and militia were stationed as they arrived.

Early in June, standing at the northeastern brink of the rock of Quebec, one could have seen the whole position at a glance. On the curving shore from the St. Charles to the rocky gorge of the Montmorenci, a distance of seven or eight miles, the whitewashed dwellings of the parish of Beauport stretched down the road in a double chain and the fields on both sides were studded with tents, huts and Indian wigwams. Along the borders of the St. Lawrence, as far as the eye could distinguish them, gangs of men were throwing up redoubts, batteries and lines of intrenchment. About midway between the two extremities of the encampment ran the little river of Beauport, and on the rising ground just beyond it stood a large stone house, round which the tents were thickly clustered, for here Montcalm had made his headquarters.

A boom of logs chained together was drawn across the mouth of the St. Charles, which was further guarded by two hulks mounted with cannon. The bridge of boats that crossed the stream nearly a mile above formed the chief communication between the city and the camp. Its head toward Beauport was protected by a strong and extensive earthwork, and the banks of the stream on the Quebec side were also intrenched to form a second line of defense in case the position at Beauport should be forced.

In the city itself every gate except the Palace Gate, which gave access to the bridge, was closed and barricaded. A hundred and six cannon were mounted on the walls. A floating battery of twelve heavy pieces, a number of gunboats, eight fire ships and several fire rafts formed the river defenses. The largest merchantmen of Kanon's fleet were sacrificed to make the fire ships, and the rest, along with the frigates that came with them, were sent for safety up the St. Lawrence beyond the river Richelieu, from which about a thousand of their sailors returned to man the batteries and gunboats.

In the camps along the Beauport shore were about fourteen thousand men, besides Indians. The regulars held the center; the militia of Quebec and Three Rivers were on the right and those of Montreal on the left. In Quebec itself there was a garrison of between one and two thousand men under the Chevalier de Ramesay. Thus the whole number, including Indians, amounted to more than sixteen thousand, and though the Canadians who formed the greater part of it were of little use in the open field, they could be trusted to fight well behind intrenchments.

Against this force, posted behind defensive works on positions almost impregnable by nature, Wolfe brought less than nine thousand men available for operations on land. The steep and lofty heights that lined the river made the cannon of the ships for the most part useless, while the exigencies of the naval service forbade employing the sailors on shore. In two or three instances only, throughout the siege, small squads of them landed to aid in moving and working cannon, and the actual fighting fell to the troops alone.

Days and weeks wore on and at Quebec the first excitement gave way to restless impatience. Why did not the English come? Many of the Canadians thought that Heaven would interpose and wreck the English fleet, as it had wrecked that of Admiral Walker half a century before. There were processions, prayers and vows toward this happy consummation. Food was scarce. Bigot and Cadet lived in luxury; fowls by thousands were fattened with wheat for their tables, while the people were put on rations of two ounces of bread a day.

Durell and his ships were reported to be still at Isle-aux-Coudres. Vaudreuil sent there a party of Canadians and they captured three midshipmen, who, says Montcalm, had gone ashore *pour polissonner,* that is, on a lark. These youths were brought to Quebec, where they increased the general anxiety by grossly exaggerating the English force.

At length it became known that eight English vessels were anchored in the north channel of Orleans, and on the twenty-first of June the masts of three of them could plainly be seen. One of the fire ships was consumed in a vain attempt to burn them and several fire rafts and a sort of infernal machine were tried with no better success; the unwelcome visitors still held their posts.

Meanwhile the whole English fleet had slowly advanced, piloted by Denis de Vitre, a Canadian of good birth, captured at sea some time before and now compelled to serve, under a threat of being hanged if he refused. Nor was he alone, for when Durell reached the place where the river pilots were usually taken on board he raised a French flag to his masthead, causing great rejoicings among the Canadians on shore, who thought that a fleet was come to their rescue and that their country was saved. The pilots launched their canoes and came out to the ships, where they were all made prisoners. Then the French flag was lowered and the red cross displayed in its stead. The spectators on shore turned from joy to despair, and a priest who stood watching the squadron with a telescope is said to have dropped dead with the revulsion of feeling.

Towards the end of June the main fleet was near the mountain of Cape Tourmente. The passage called the Traverse, between the cape and the lower end of the Island of Orleans, was reputed one of the most dangerous parts of the St. Lawrence, and as the ships successively came up the captive pilots were put on board to carry them safely through, on pain of death.

Vaudreuil was blamed for not planting cannon at a certain plateau on the side of the mountain of Cape Tourmente, where the gunners would have been inaccessible, and from which they could have battered every passing ship with a plunging fire. As it was, the whole fleet sailed safely through. On the twenty-sixth they were all anchored off the south shore of the Island of Orleans, a few miles from Quebec.

That night Lieutenant Meech, with forty New England rangers, landed on the Island of Orleans and found a body of armed inhabitants who tried to surround him. He beat them off and took possession of a neighboring farmhouse, where he remained till daylight, then pursued the enemy and found that they had crossed to the north shore. The whole army now landed and were drawn up on the beach.

670

As they were kept there for some time, Knox and several brother officers went to visit the neighboring church of St. Laurent, where they found a letter from the parish priest, directed to "The Worthy Officers of the British Army," praying that they would protect the sacred edifice and also his own adjoining house, and adding, with somewhat needless civility that he wished they had come sooner, that they might have enjoyed the asparagus and radishes of his garden, now unhappily going to seed. The letter concluded with many compliments and good wishes, in which the Britons to whom they were addressed saw only "the frothy politeness so peculiar to the French." The army marched westward and encamped. Wolfe, with his chief engineer Major Mackellar and an escort of light infantry, advanced to the extreme point of the island.

Here he could see, in part, the desperate nature of the task he had undertaken. Before him, three or four miles away, Quebec sat perched upon her rock, a congregation of stone houses, churches, palaces, convents and hospitals; the green trees of the seminary garden and the spires of the cathedral, the Ursulines, the Récollets and the Jesuits. Beyond rose the loftier height of Cape Diamond, edged with palisades and capped with redoubt and parapet. Batteries frowned everywhere: the Château battery, the Clergy battery, the Hospital battery on the rock above and the Royal, Dauphin's and Queen's batteries on the strand, where the dwellings and warehouses of the lower town clustered beneath the cliff.

Full in sight lay the far-extended camp of Montcalm, stretching from the St. Charles beneath the city walls to the chasm and cataract of the Montmorenci. From the cataract to the river of Beauport its front was covered by earthworks along the brink of abrupt and lofty heights; and from the river of Beauport to the St. Charles, by broad flats of mud swept by the fire of redoubts, intrenchments, a floating battery and the city itself. Above the city, Cape Diamond hid the view, but could Wolfe have looked beyond it, he would have beheld a prospect still more disheartening. Here, mile after mile, the St. Lawrence was walled by a range of steeps, often inaccessible, and always so difficult that a few men at the top could hold an army in check, while at Cap-Rouge, about eight miles distant, the high plateau was cleft by the channel of a stream which formed a line of defense as strong as that of the Montmorenci. Quebec was a natural fortress.

Bougainville had long before examined the position and reported that "by the help of intrenchments, easily and quickly made, and defended by three or four thousand men, I think the city would be safe. I do not believe that the English will make any attempt against it; but they may have the madness to do so, and it is well to be prepared against surprise."

Not four thousand men, but four times four thousand, now stood in its defense, and their chiefs wisely resolved not to throw away the advantages of their position. Nothing more was heard of Vaudreuil's bold plan of attacking the invaders at their landing, and Montcalm had declared that he would play the part not of Hannibal but of Fabius. His plan was to avoid a general battle, run no risks and protract the defense till the resources of the enemy were exhausted or till approaching winter forced them to withdraw. Success was almost certain but for one contingency. Amherst, with a force larger than that of Wolfe, was moving against Ticonderoga. If he should capture it and advance into the colony, Montcalm would be forced to weaken his army by sending strong detachments to oppose him. Here was Wolfe's best hope. This failing, his only chance was in audacity. The game was desperate, but intrepid gamester as he was in war, he was a man in the last resort to stake everything on the cast of the dice.

The elements declared for France. On the afternoon of the day when Wolfe's army landed, a violent squall swept over the St. Lawrence, dashed the ships together, drove several ashore and destroyed many of the flatboats from which the troops had just disembarked. "I never saw so much distress among shipping in my whole life," writes an officer to a friend in Boston. Fortunately the storm subsided as quickly as it rose.

Vaudreuil saw that the hoped-for deliverance had failed, and as the tempest had not destroyed the British fleet, he resolved to try the virtue of his fire ships. "I am afraid," says Montcalm, "that they have cost us a million, and will be good for nothing after all." This remained to be seen. Vaudreuil gave the chief command of them to a naval officer named Delouche, and on the evening of the twenty-eighth, after long consultation and much debate among their respective captains, they set sail together at ten o'clock. The night was moonless and dark. In less than an hour they were at the entrance of the north channel. Delouche had been all enthusiasm, but as he neared the danger his nerves failed and he set fire to his ship half an hour too soon, the rest following his example.

There was an English outpost at the Point of Orleans, and about eleven o'clock the sentries descried through the gloom the ghostly outlines of the approaching ships. As they gazed, these mysterious strangers began to dart tongues of flame; fire ran like lightning up their masts and sails, and then they burst out like volcanoes. Filled as they were with pitch, tar and every manner of combustible, mixed with fireworks, bombs, grenades and old cannon, swivels and muskets loaded to the throat, the effect was terrific.

The troops at the Point, amazed at the sudden eruption, the din of the explosions and the showers of grapeshot that rattled among the trees, lost their wits and fled. The blazing dragons hissed and roared, spouted sheets of fire, vomited smoke in black, pitchy volumes and vast illumined clouds, and shed their infernal glare on the distant city, the tents of Montcalm and the long red lines of the British Army, drawn up in array of battle lest the French should cross from their encampments to attack them in the confusion. Knox calls the display "the grandest fireworks that can possibly be conceived."

Yet the fire ships did no other harm than to burn alive one of their own captains and six or seven of his sailors who failed to escape in their boats. Some of them ran ashore before reaching the fleet; the others were seized by the intrepid English sailors, who, approaching in their boats, threw grappling irons upon them and towed them towards land till they swung around and stranded. Here, after venting their fury for a while, they subsided into quiet conflagration, which lasted till morning. Vaudreuil watched the result of his experiment from the steeple of the church at Beauport, then returned dejected to Quebec.

Wolfe longed to fight, but his sagacious enemy would not gratify him. From the heights of Beauport, the rock of Quebec or the summit of Cape Diamond, Montcalm could look down on the river and its shores as on a map and watch each movement of the invaders. He was hopeful, perhaps confident, and for a month or more he wrote almost daily to Bourlamaque at Ticonderoga in a cheerful and often a jocose vein, mingling orders and instructions with pleasantries and bits of news. Yet his vigilance was unceasing. "We pass every night in bivouac, or else sleep in our clothes. Perhaps you are doing as much, my dear Bourlamaque."

Wolfe, held in check at every other point, had one movement in his power. He could seize the heights of Point Levi, opposite the city, and this, along with his occupation of the Island of Orleans, would give him command of the Basin of Quebec. From there also he could fire on the place across the St. Lawrence, which is here less than a mile wide.

The movement was begun on the afternoon of the twenty-ninth, when, shivering in a north wind and a sharp frost, a part of Monckton's brigade was ferried over to Beaumont, on the south shore, and the rest followed in the morning. The rangers had a brush with a party of Canadians, whom they drove off, and the regulars then landed unopposed. Monckton ordered a proclamation, signed by Wolfe, to be posted on the door of the parish church. It called on the Canadians in peremptory terms to stand neutral in the contest, promised them, if they did so, full protection in property and religion, and threatened that if they presumed to resist the invaders, their houses, goods and harvests should be destroyed and their churches despoiled. As soon as the troops were out of sight, the inhabitants took down the placard and carried it to Vaudreuil.

The brigade marched along the river road to Point Levi, drove off a body of French and Indians posted in the church and took possession of the houses and the surrounding heights. In the morning they were intrenching themselves when they were greeted by a brisk fire from the edge of the woods. It came from a party of Indians, whom the rangers presently put to flight and, imitating their own ferocity, scalped nine of them.

Wolfe came over to the camp on the next day, went with an escort to the heights opposite Quebec, examined it with a spyglass and chose a position from which to bombard it. Cannon and mortars were brought ashore, fascines and gabions made, intrenchments thrown up and batteries planted. Wolfe's guns at Point Levi could destroy the city but could not capture it, yet doubtless they would have good moral effect, discourage the French and cheer his own soldiers with the flattering belief that they were achieving something.

The guns of Quebec showered balls and bombs upon his workmen, but they still toiled on and the French saw the fatal batteries fast growing to completion. The citizens, alarmed at the threatened destruction, begged the governor for leave to cross the river and dislodge their assailants. At length he consented. A party of twelve or fifteen hundred was made up of armed burghers, Canadians from the camp, a few Indians, some pupils of the seminary and about a hundred volunteers from the regulars. Dumas, an experienced officer, took command of them, and going up to Sillery, they crossed the river on the night of the twelfth of July.

They had hardly climbed the heights of the south shore when they grew exceedingly nervous, though the enemy was still three miles off. The seminary scholars fired on some of their own party, whom they mistook for English, and the same mishap was repeated a second and third time. A panic seized the whole body and Dumas could not control them. They turned and made for their canoes, rolling over each other as they rushed down the heights, and reappeared at Quebec at six in the morning, overwhelmed with despair and shame.

The presentiment of the unhappy burghers proved too true. The English batteries fell to their work and the families of the town fled to the country for safety. In a single day eighteen houses and the cathedral were burned by exploding shells, and fiercer and fiercer the storm of fire and iron hailed upon Quebec.

Wolfe did not rest content with distressing his enemy. With an ardor and a daring that no difficulties could cool, he sought means to strike an effective blow. It was nothing to lay Quebec in ruins if he could not defeat the army that protected it. To land from boats and attack Montcalm in front, through the mud of the Beauport flats or up the heights along the neighboring shore, was an enterprise too rash even for his temerity. It might, however, be possible to land below the cataract of Montmorenci, cross that stream higher up and strike the French Army in flank or rear, and he had no sooner secured his positions at the points of Levi and Orleans than he addressed himself to this attempt.

On the eighth several frigates and a bomb ketch took their stations before the camp of the Chevalier de Lévis, who, with his division of Canadian militia, occupied the heights along the St. Lawrence just above the cataract. Here they shelled and cannonaded him all day, though, from his elevated position, with very little effect. Towards evening the troops on the Point of Orleans broke up their camp. Major Hardy, with a detachment of marines, was left to hold that post, while the rest embarked at night in the boats of the fleet. They were the brigades of Townshend and Murray, consisting of five battalions, with a body of grenadiers, light infantry and rangers—in all, three thousand men. They landed before daybreak in front of the parish of L'Ange Gardien, a little below the cataract. The only opposition was from a troop of Canadians and Indians, whom they routed after some loss, climbed the heights, gained the plateau above and began to intrench themselves. A company of rangers, supported by detachments of regulars, was sent into the neighboring forest to protect the parties who were cutting fascines, and apparently also to look for a fording place.

Lévis, with his Scotch-Jacobite aide-de-camp Johnstone, had watched the movements of Wolfe from the heights across the cataract. Johnstone says that he asked his commander if he was sure there was no ford higher up on the Montmorenci by which the English could cross. Lévis averred that there was none, and that he himself had examined the stream to its source, on which a Canadian who stood by whispered to the aide-de-camp: "The general is mistaken; there is a ford."

Johnstone told this to Lévis, who would not believe it and so browbeat the Canadian that he dared not repeat what he had said. Johnstone, taking him aside, told him to go and find somebody who had lately crossed the ford and bring him at once to the general's quarters, whereupon he soon reappeared with a man who affirmed that he had crossed it the night before with a sack of wheat on his back. A detachment was immediately sent to the place, with orders to intrench itself, and Repentigny, lieutenant of Lévis, was posted not far off with eleven hundred Canadians.

Four hundred Indians passed the ford under the partisan Langlade, discovered Wolfe's detachment, hid themselves and sent their commander to tell Repentigny that there was a body of English in the forest who might all be destroyed if he would come over at once with his Canadians. Repentigny sent for orders to Lévis, and Lévis sent for orders to Vaudreuil, whose quarters were three or four miles distant. Vaudreuil answered that no risk should be run and that he would come and see to the matter himself.

It was about two hours before he arrived, and meanwhile the Indians grew impatient, rose from their hiding place, fired on the rangers and drove them back with heavy loss upon the regulars, who stood their ground and at last repulsed the assailants. The Indians recrossed the ford with thirty-six scalps.

If Repentigny had advanced and Lévis had followed with his main body, the consequences to the English might have been serious, for as Johnstone remarks, "a Canadian in the woods is worth three disciplined soldiers, as a soldier in a plain is worth three Canadians." Vaudreuil called a council of war. The question was whether an effort should be made to dislodge Wolfe's main force. Montcalm and the governor were this time of one mind and both thought it inexpedient to attack, with militia, a body of regular troops whose numbers and position were imperfectly known. Bigot gave his voice for the attack. He was overruled and Wolfe was left to fortify himself in peace.

The position of the hostile forces was a remarkable one. They were separated by the vast gorge that opens upon the St. Lawrence; an amphitheater of lofty precipices, their brows crested with forests and their steep brown sides scantily feathered with stunted birch and fir. Into this abyss leaps the Montmorenci with one headlong plunge of nearly two hundred and fifty feet, a living column of snowy white, with its spray, its foam, its mists and its rainbows; then spreads itself in broad, thin sheets over a floor of rock and gravel and creeps tamely to the St. Lawrence. It was but a gunshot across the gulf, and the sentinels on each side watched each other over the roar and turmoil of the cataract.

Day after day went by and the invaders made no progress. Flags of truce passed often between the hostile camps. "You will demolish the town, no doubt," said the bearer of one of them, "but you shall never get inside of it." To which Wolfe replied: "I will have Quebec if I stay here till the end of November."

Sometimes the heat was intense and sometimes there were floods of summer rain that inundated the tents. Along the river, from the Montmorenci to Point Levi, there were ceaseless artillery fights between

677

gunboats, frigates and batteries on shore. Bands of Indians infested the outskirts of the camps, killing sentries and patrols. The rangers chased them through the woods; there were brief skirmishes, and scalps lost and won.

A part of the fleet worked up into the basin, beyond the Point of Orleans, and here on the warm summer nights officers and men watched the cannon flashing and thundering from the heights of Montmorenci on one side and those of Point Levi on the other, and the bombs sailing through the air in fiery semicircles. Often the gloom was lighted up by the blaze of the burning houses of Quebec, kindled by incendiary shells.

Both the lower and the upper town were nearly deserted by the inhabitants, some retreating into the country and some into the suburb of St. Roch, while the Ursulines and Hospital nuns abandoned their convents to seek harborage beyond the range of shot. The city was a prey to robbers, who pillaged the empty houses till an order came from headquarters promising the gallows to all who should be caught. News reached the French that Niagara was attacked and that the army of Amherst was moving against Ticonderoga. The Canadians deserted more and more. They were disheartened by the defensive attitude in which both Vaudreuil and Montcalm steadily persisted and, accustomed as they were to rapid raids, sudden strokes and a quick return to their homes, they tired of long weeks of inaction.

On the eighteenth of July the English accomplished a feat which promised important results. The French commanders had thought it impossible for any hostile ship to pass the batteries of Quebec, but about eleven o'clock at night, favored by the wind and covered by a furious cannonade from Point Levi, the ship *Sutherland,* with a frigate and several small vessels, sailed safely by and reached the river above the town. Here they at once attacked and destroyed a fire ship and some small craft that they found there.

Now, for the first time, it became necessary for Montcalm to weaken his army at Beauport by sending six hundred men, under Dumas, to defend the accessible points in the line of precipices between Quebec and Cap-Rouge. Several hundred more were sent on the next day, when it became known that the English had dragged a fleet of boats over Point Levi, launched them above the town and dispatched troops

678

to embark in them. Thus a new feature was introduced into the siege operations and danger had risen on a side where the French thought themselves safe. On the other hand, Wolfe had become more vulnerable than ever. His army was now divided, not into three parts but into four, each so far from the rest that in case of sudden attack it must defend itself alone. That Montcalm did not improve his opportunity was apparently due to want of confidence in his militia.

Vaudreuil now tried again to burn the English fleet. "Late last night," writes Knox, under date of the twenty-eighth, "the enemy sent down a most formidable fire raft, which consisted of a parcel of schooners, shallops and stages chained together. It could not be less than a hundred fathoms in length, and was covered with grenades, old swivels, gun and pistol barrels loaded up to their muzzles, and various other inventions and combustible matters. This seemed to be their last attempt against our fleet, which happily miscarried, as before; for our gallant seamen, with their usual expertness, grappled them before they got down above a third part of the Basin, towed them safe to shore, and left them at anchor, continually repeating, *All's well*. A remarkable expression from some of these intrepid souls to their comrades on this occasion I must not omit, on account of its singular uncouthness; namely: 'Damme, Jack, didst thee ever take hell in tow before?' "

According to a French account, this aquatic infernal machine consisted of seventy rafts, boats and schooners. Its failure was due to no shortcoming on the part of its conductors, who, under a brave Canadian named Courval, acted with coolness and resolution. Nothing saved the fleet but the courage of the sailors, swarming out in their boats to fight the approaching conflagration.

It was now the end of July. More than half the summer was gone and Quebec seemed as far as ever beyond the grasp of Wolfe. Its buildings were in ruins and the neighboring parishes were burned and ravaged, but its living rampart, the army of Montcalm, still lay in patient defiance along the shores of Beauport, while above the city every point where a wildcat could climb the precipices was watched and guarded and Dumas with a thousand men held the impregnable heights of Cap-Rouge. Montcalm persisted in doing nothing that his enemy wished him to do. He would not fight on Wolfe's terms and

Wolfe resolved at last to fight him on his own; that is, to attack his camp in front.

The plan was desperate, for after leaving troops enough to hold Point Levi and the heights of Montmorenci, less than five thousand men would be left to attack a position of commanding strength, where Montcalm at an hour's notice could collect twice as many to oppose them. But Wolfe had a boundless trust in the disciplined valor of his soldiers and an utter scorn of the militia who made the greater part of his enemy's force.

Towards the Montmorenci the borders of the St. Lawrence are extremely high and steep. At a mile from the gorge of the cataract there is, at high tide, a strand about an eighth of a mile wide between the foot of these heights and the river, and beyond this strand the receding tide lays bare a tract of mud nearly half a mile wide. At the edge of the dry ground the French had built a redoubt mounted with cannon, and there were other similar works on the strand a quarter of a mile nearer the cataract. Wolfe could not see from the river that these redoubts were commanded by the musketry of the intrenchments along the brink of the heights above. These intrenchments were so constructed that they swept with cross fires the whole face of the declivity, which was covered with grass and was very steep. Wolfe hoped that if he attacked one of the redoubts the French would come down to defend it, and so bring on a general engagement, or, if they did not, that he should gain an opportunity of reconnoitering the heights to find some point where they could be stormed with a chance of success.

In front of the gorge of the Montmorenci there was a ford during several hours of low tide, so that troops from the adjoining English camp might cross to co-operate with their comrades landing in boats from Point Levi and the Island of Orleans. On the morning of the thirty-first of July, the tide then being at the flood, the French saw the ship *Centurion,* of sixty-four guns, anchor near the Montmorenci and open fire on the redoubts. Then two armed transports, each of fourteen guns, stood in as close as possible to the first redoubt and fired upon it, stranding as the tide went out till in the afternoon they lay bare upon the mud. At the same time a battery of more than forty heavy pieces, planted on the lofty promontory beyond the Montmorenci, began a furious cannonade upon the flank of the French intrenchments. It did no great harm, however, for the works were protected by a great number of traverses, which stopped the shot, and the Canadians who manned this part of the lines held their ground with excellent steadiness.

About eleven o'clock a fleet of boats filled with troops, chiefly from Point Levi, appeared in the river and hovered off the shore west of the parish church of Beauport, as if meaning to land there. Montcalm was perplexed, doubting whether the real attack was to be made here or toward the Montmorenci. Hour after hour the boats moved to and fro, to increase his doubts and hide the real design, but he soon became convinced that the camp of Lévis at the Montmorenci was the true object of his enemy, and about two o'clock he went there, greeted as he rode along the lines by shouts of *Vive notre Général!*

Lévis had already made preparations for defense with his usual skill. His Canadians were reinforced by the battalions of Béarn, Guienne and Royal Roussillon, and as the intentions of Wolfe became certain, the right of the camp was nearly abandoned, the main strength of the army being gathered between the river of Beauport and the Montmorenci, where according to a French writer there were, towards the end of the afternoon, about twelve thousand men.

At half-past five o'clock the tide was out and the crisis came. The batteries across the Montmorenci, the distant batteries of Point Levi, the cannon of the *Centurion* and those of the two stranded ships all opened together with redoubled fury. The French batteries replied, and amid this deafening roar of artillery the English boats set their troops ashore at the edge of the broad tract of sedgy mud that the receding river had left bare. At the same time a column of two thousand men was seen, a mile away, moving in perfect order across the Montmorenci ford.

The first troops that landed from the boats were thirteen companies of grenadiers and a detachment of Royal Americans. They dashed swiftly forward, while at some distance behind came Monckton's brigade, composed of the fifteenth, or Amherst's regiment, and the seventy-eighth, or Fraser's Highlanders. The day had been fair and warm, but the sky was now thick with clouds and large raindrops began to fall, the precursors of a summer storm.

With the utmost precipitation, without orders and without waiting for Monckton's brigade to come up, the grenadiers in front made a rush for the redoubt near the foot of the hill. The French abandoned it, but the assailants had no sooner gained their prize than the thronged heights above blazed with musketry and a tempest of bullets fell among them. Nothing daunted, they dashed forward again, reserving their fire and struggling to climb the steep ascent, while with yells and shouts of *Vive le Roi!* the troops and Canadians at the top poured upon them a hailstorm of musket balls and buckshot and dead and wounded in numbers rolled together down the slope.

At that instant the clouds burst and the rain fell in torrents. "We could not see halfway down the hill," says the Chevalier Johnstone, who was at this part of the line. Ammunition was wet on both sides and the grassy steeps became so slippery that it was impossible to climb them. The English say that the storm saved the French; the French, with as much reason, that it saved the English.

The baffled grenadiers drew back into the redoubt. Wolfe saw the madness of persisting and ordered a retreat. The rain ceased and troops of Indians came down the heights to scalp the fallen. Some of them ran towards Lieutenant Peyton, of the Royal Americans, as he lay disabled by a musket shot. With his double-barreled gun he brought down two of his assailants, when a Highland sergeant snatched him in his arms, dragged him half a mile over the mud flats and placed him in one of the boats. A friend of Peyton, Captain Ochterlony, had received a mortal wound and an Indian would have scalped him but for the generous intrepidity of a soldier of the battalion of Guienne, who, seizing the enraged savage, held him back till several French officers interposed and had the dying man carried to a place of safety.

The English retreated in good order, after setting fire to the two stranded vessels. Those of the grenadiers and Royal Americans who were left alive rowed for the Point of Orleans, the fifteenth regiment rowed for Point Levi, and the Highlanders, led by Wolfe himself, joined the column from beyond the Montmorenci, placing themselves in its rear as it slowly retired along the flats and across the ford, the Indians yelling and the French shouting from the heights, while the British waved their hats, daring them to come down and fight.

The grenadiers and the Royal Americans, who had borne the brunt of the fray, bore also nearly all the loss, which in proportion to their numbers was enormous. Knox reports it at four hundred and forty-three, killed, wounded and missing, including one colonel, eight captains, twenty-one lieutenants and three ensigns.

Vaudreuil, delighted, wrote to Bourlamaque an account of the affair. "I have no more anxiety about Quebec. M. Wolfe, I can assure you, will make no progress. Luckily for him, his prudence saved him from the consequences of his mad enterprise and he contented himself with losing about five hundred of his best soldiers. Deserters say that he will try us again in a few days. That is what we want; he'll find somebody to talk to."

CHAPTER 16

~~~~~~

Amherst's Campaign

PITT HAD DIRECTED THAT, WHILE QUEBEC WAS AT-
tacked, an attempt should be made to penetrate into Canada by
way of Ticonderoga and Crown Point. Thus the two armies might
unite in the heart of the colony, or at least a powerful diversion might
be effected in behalf of Wolfe. At the same time Oswego was to be
re-established and the possession of Fort Duquesne, or Pittsburgh,
secured by reinforcements and supplies, while Amherst, the commander-in-chief, was further directed to pursue any other enterprise
which in his opinion would weaken the enemy without detriment to
the main objects of the campaign. He accordingly resolved to attempt
the capture of Niagara.

Brigadier Prideaux was charged with this stroke; Brigadier Stanwix
was sent to conduct the operations for the relief of Pittsburgh; and
Amherst himself prepared to lead the grand central advance against
Ticonderoga, Crown Point and Montreal.

Towards the end of June he reached that valley by the head of Lake
George which for five years past had been the annual mustering place
of armies. Here were now gathered about eleven thousand men, half
regulars and half provincials, drilling every day, firing by platoons,
firing at marks, practicing maneuvers in the woods, going out on
scouting parties, bathing parties, fishing parties, gathering wild herbs
to serve for greens, cutting brushwood and meadow hay to make hospital beds.

This army embarked on Saturday, the twenty-first of July. The

Reverend Benjamin Pomeroy watched their departure in some concern and wrote on Monday to Abigail his wife: "I could wish for more appearance of dependence on God than was observable among them, yet I hope God will grant deliverance unto Israel by them."

There was another military pageant, another long procession of boats and banners among the mountains and islands of Lake George. Night found them near the outlet and here they lay till morning, tossed unpleasantly on waves ruffled by a summer gale. At daylight they landed, beat back a French detachment and marched by the portage road to the sawmill at the waterfall. There was little resistance. They occupied the heights and then advanced to the famous line of intrenchment against which the army of Abercrombie had hurled itself in vain. These works had been completely reconstructed, partly of earth and partly of logs. Amherst's followers were less numerous than those of his predecessor, while the French commander Bourlamaque had a force nearly equal to that of Montcalm in the summer before, yet he made no attempt to defend the intrenchment, and the English, encamping along its front, found it an excellent shelter from the cannon of the fort beyond.

Amherst brought up his artillery and began approaches in form, when on the night of the twenty-third it was found that Bourlamaque had retired down Lake Champlain, leaving four hundred men under Hebecourt to defend the place as long as possible. This was in obedience to an order from Vaudreuil, requiring him on the approach of the English to abandon both Ticonderoga and Crown Point, retreat to the outlet of Lake Champlain, take post at Isle-aux-Noix and there defend himself to the last extremity—a course unquestionably the best that could have been taken, since obstinacy in holding Ticonderoga might have involved the surrender of Bourlamaque's whole force, while Isle-aux-Noix offered rare advantages for defense.

The fort fired briskly. A cannon shot killed Colonel Townshend and a few soldiers were killed and wounded by grape and bursting shells, when at dusk on the evening of the twenty-sixth an unusual movement was seen among the garrison and about ten o'clock three deserters came in great excitement to the English camp. They reported that Hebecourt and his soldiers were escaping in their boats and that a match was burning in the magazine to blow Ticonderoga to atoms. Amherst offered a hundred guineas to any one of them who would point out the match, that it might be cut, but they shrank from the perilous venture.

All was silent till eleven o'clock, when a broad, fierce glare burst on the night and a roaring explosion shook the promontory. Then came a few breathless moments and then fragments of Fort Ticonderoga fell with clatter and splash on the water and the land. It was but one bastion, however, that had been thus hurled skyward. The rest of the fort was little hurt, though the barracks and other combustible parts were set on fire, and by the light the French flag was seen still waving on the rampart. A sergeant of the light infantry, braving the risk of other explosions, went and brought it off.

Thus did this redoubted stronghold of France fall at last into English hands, as in all likelihood it would have done a year sooner if Amherst had commanded 'in Abercrombie's place, for with the deliberation that marked all his proceedings, he would have sat down before Montcalm's wooden wall and knocked it to splinters with his cannon.

He now set about repairing the damaged works and making ready to advance on Crown Point, when on the first of August his scouts told him that the enemy had abandoned this place also and retreated northward down the lake. Well pleased, he took possession of the deserted fort and, in the animation of success, thought for a moment of keeping the promise he had given to Pitt "to make an irruption into Canada with the utmost vigor and dispatch."

Wolfe, his brother in arms and his friend, was battling with the impossible under the rocks of Quebec, and every motive, public and private, impelled Amherst to push to his relief, not counting costs or balancing risks too nicely. He was ready enough to spur on others, for he wrote to Gage: "We must all be alert and active day and night; if we all do our parts the French must fall," but far from doing his, he set the army to building a new fort at Crown Point, telling them that it would "give plenty, peace, and quiet to His Majesty's subjects for ages to come."

Then he began three small additional forts, as outworks to the first, sent two parties to explore the sources of the Hudson; one party to explore Otter Creek; another to explore South Bay, which was already well known; another to make a road across what is now the state of Vermont, from Crown Point to Charlestown, or "Number Four" on the Connecticut; and another to widen and improve the old French road between Crown Point and Ticonderoga. His industry was untiring. A great deal of useful work was done, but the essential task of making a diversion to aid the army of Wolfe was needlessly postponed.

It is true that some delay was inevitable. The French had four armed vessels on the lake and this made it necessary to provide an equal or superior force to protect the troops on their way to Isle-aux-Noix. Captain Loring, the English naval commander, was therefore ordered to build a brigantine, and this being thought insufficient, he was directed to add a kind of floating battery, moved by sweeps. Three weeks later, in consequence of further information concerning the force of the French vessels, Amherst ordered an armed sloop to be put on the stocks, and this involved a long delay. The sawmill at Ticonderoga was to furnish planks for the intended navy but, being overtaxed in sawing timber for the new works at Crown Point, it was continually breaking down. Hence much time was lost, and autumn was well advanced before Loring could launch his vessels.

Meanwhile news had come from Prideaux and the Niagara expedition. That officer had been ordered to ascend the Mohawk with five thousand regulars and provincials, leave a strong garrison at Fort Stanwix on the Great Carrying Place, establish posts at both ends of Lake Oneida, descend the Onondaga to Oswego, leave nearly half his force there under Colonel Haldimand and proceed with the rest to attack Niagara. These orders he accomplished.

Haldimand remained to reoccupy the spot that Montcalm had made desolate three years before, and while preparing to build a fort, he barricaded his camp with pork and flour barrels lest the enemy should make a dash upon him from their station at the head of the St. Lawrence Rapids. Such an attack was probable, for if the French could seize Oswego, the return of Prideaux from Niagara would be cut off, and when his small stock of provisions had failed he would be reduced to extremity.

Saint-Luc de la Corne left the head of the rapids early in July with a thousand French and Canadians and a body of Indians, who soon made their appearance among the stumps and bushes that surrounded the camp at Oswego. The priest Piquet was of the party, and five deserters declared that he solemnly blessed them and told them to give the English no quarter. Some valuable time was lost in bestowing the benediction, yet Haldimand's men were taken by surprise. Many of them were dispersed in the woods, cutting timber for the intended fort, and it might have gone hard with them had not some of La Corne's Canadians become alarmed and rushed back to their boats, upsetting Father Piquet on the way. These being rallied, the whole party ensconced itself in a tract of felled trees so far from the English that their fire did little harm. They continued it about two hours and resumed it the next morning, when, three cannon being brought to bear on them, they took to their boats and disappeared, having lost about thirty killed and wounded, including two officers and La Corne himself, who was shot in the thigh. The English loss was slight.

Prideaux safely reached Niagara and laid siege to it. It was a strong fort, lately rebuilt in regular form by an excellent officer, Captain Pouchot of the battalion of Béarn, who commanded it. It stood in the angle formed by the junction of the river Niagara with Lake Ontario and was held by about six hundred men, well supplied with provisions and munitions of war.

Higher up the river, a mile and a half above the cataract, there was another fort, called Little Niagara, built of wood and commanded by the half-breed officer, Joncaire-Chabert, who with his brother Joncaire-Clauzonne and a numerous clan of Indian relatives had so long thwarted the efforts of Johnson to engage the Five Nations in the English cause. But recent English successes had had their effect. Joncaire's influence was waning, and Johnson was now in Prideaux's camp with nine hundred Five Nation warriors pledged to fight the French. Joncaire, finding his fort untenable, burned it and came with his garrison and his Indian friends to reinforce Niagara.

Pouchot had another resource, on which he confidently relied. In obedience to an order from Vaudreuil, the French population of the Illinois, Detroit and other distant posts, joined with troops of western Indians, had come down the lakes to recover Pittsburgh, undo the work of Forbes and restore French ascendancy on the Ohio. Pittsburgh had been in imminent danger, nor was it yet safe, though General Stanwix was sparing no effort to succor it. These mixed bands of white men and red, bushrangers and savages, were now gathered, partly at Le Bœuf and Venango but chiefly at Presq'isle, under command of Aubry, Ligneris, Marin and other partisan chiefs, the best in Canada. No sooner did Pouchot learn that the English were coming to attack him than he sent a messenger to summon them all to his aid.

The siege was begun in form, though the English engineers were so incompetent that the trenches, as first laid out, were scoured by the fire of the place and had to be made anew. At last the batteries opened fire. A shell from a coehorn burst prematurely just as it left the mouth of the piece, and a fragment, striking Prideaux on the head, killed him instantly. Johnson took command in his place and made up in energy what he lacked in skill. In two or three weeks the fort was in extremity. The rampart was breached, more than a hundred of the garrison were killed or disabled and the rest were exhausted with want of sleep. Pouchot watched anxiously for the promised succors, and on the morning of the twenty-fourth of July a distant firing told him that they were at hand.

Aubry and Ligneris, with their motley following, had left Presq'isle a few days before, to the number, according to Vaudreuil, of eleven hundred French and two hundred Indians. Among them was a body of colony troops, but the Frenchmen of the party were chiefly traders and bushrangers from the West, connecting links between civilization and savagery. Some of them indeed were mere white Indians, imbued with the ideas and morals of the wigwam, wearing hunting shirts of smoked deerskin embroidered with quills of the Canada porcupine, painting their faces black and red, tying eagle feathers in their long hair or plastering it on their temples with a compound of vermilion and glue. They were excellent woodsmen, skillful hunters and perhaps the best bushfighters in all Canada.

When Pouchot heard the firing he went with a wounded artillery officer to the bastion next the river, and as the forest had been cut away for a great distance, they could see more than a mile and a half along the shore. There, by glimpses among trees and bushes, they descried bodies of men, now advancing and now retreating; Indians in rapid movement and the smoke of guns, the sound of which reached their ears in heavy volleys or a sharp and angry rattle.

Meanwhile the English cannon had ceased their fire and the silent trenches seemed deserted, as if their occupants were gone to meet the advancing foe. There was a call in the fort for volunteers to sally and destroy the works, but no sooner did they show themselves along the covered way than the seemingly abandoned trenches were thronged with men and bayonets and the attempt was given up. The distant firing lasted half an hour, then ceased, and Pouchot remained in suspense till at two in the afternoon a friendly Onondaga, who had passed unnoticed through the English lines, came to him with the announcement that the French and their allies had been routed and cut to pieces. Pouchot would not believe him.

Nevertheless his tale was true. Johnson, besides his Indians, had with him about twenty-three hundred men, whom he was forced to divide into three separate bodies—one to guard the bateaux, one to guard the trenches and one to fight Aubry and his band. This last body consisted of the provincial light infantry and the pickets, two companies of grenadiers and a hundred and fifty men of the forty-sixth regiment, all under command of Colonel Massey.

They took post behind an abatis at a place called La Belle Famille, and the Five Nations warriors placed themselves on their flanks. These savages had shown signs of disaffection, and when the enemy approached they opened a parley with the French Indians, which, however, soon ended and both sides raised the war whoop. The fight was brisk for a while, but at last Aubry's men broke away in a panic. The French officers seem to have made desperate efforts to retrieve the day, for nearly all of them were killed or captured, while their followers, after heavy loss, fled to their canoes and boats above the cataract, hastened back to Lake Erie, burned Presq'isle, Le Bœuf and Venango and, joined by the garrisons of those forts, retreated to Detroit, leaving the whole region of the upper Ohio in undisputed possession of the English.

At four o'clock on the day of the battle, after a furious cannonade on both sides, a trumpet sounded from the trenches and an officer approached the fort with a summons to surrender. He brought also a paper containing the names of the captive French officers, though some of them were spelled in a way that defied recognition. Pouchot, feigning incredulity, sent an officer of his own to the English camp,

690

who soon saw unanswerable proof of the disaster, for here, under a shelter of leaves and boughs near the tent of Johnson, sat Ligneris, severely wounded, with Aubry, Villiers, Montigny, Marin and their companions in misfortune—in all, sixteen officers, four cadets and a surgeon.

Pouchot had now no choice but surrender. By the terms of the capitulation, the garrison were to be sent prisoners to New York, though honors of war were granted them in acknowledgment of their courageous conduct. There was a special stipulation that they should be protected from the Indians, of whom they stood in the greatest terror, lest the massacre of Fort William Henry should be avenged upon them. Johnson restrained his dangerous allies, and though the fort was pillaged, no blood was shed.

The capture of Niagara was an important stroke. Thenceforth Detroit, Michilimackinac, the Illinois and all the other French interior posts were severed from Canada and left in helpless isolation.

Meanwhile, Amherst was working at his fort at Crown Point, while the season crept away and Bourlamaque lay ready to receive him at Isle-aux-Noix. "I wait his coming with impatience," writes the French commander, "though I doubt if he will venture to attack a post where we are intrenched to the teeth and armed with a hundred pieces of cannon." Bourlamaque now had with him thirty-five hundred men, in a position of great strength. Isle-aux-Noix, planted in mid-channel of the Richelieu soon after it issues from Lake Champlain, had been diligently fortified since the spring.

It was the eleventh of October before the miniature navy of Captain Loring—the floating battery, the brig and the sloop that had been begun three weeks too late—was ready for service. They sailed at once to look for the enemy. The four French vessels made no resistance. One of them succeeded in reaching Isle-aux-Noix; one was run aground; and two were sunk by their crews, who escaped to the shore.

Amherst, meanwhile, leaving the provincials to work at the fort, embarked with the regulars in bateaux and proceeded on his northern way till, on the evening of the twelfth, a head wind began to blow and, rising to a storm, drove him for shelter into Ligonier Bay on the west side of the lake. On the thirteenth it blew a gale. The lake raged like an angry sea, and the frail bateaux, fit only for smooth water, could not have lived a moment. Through all the next night the gale continued, with floods of driving rain. "I hope it will soon change," wrote Amherst on the fifteenth, "for I have no time to lose."

He was right. He had waited till the season of autumnal storms, when Nature was more dangerous than man. On the sixteenth there was frost and the wind did not abate. On the next morning it shifted to the south but soon turned back with violence to the north, and the ruffled lake put on a look of winter, "which determined me," says the general, "not to lose time by striving to get to the Isle-aux-Noix, where I should arrive too late to force the enemy from their post, but to return to Crown Point and complete the works there."

This he did, and spent the remnant of the season in the congenial task of finishing the fort.

The Heights of Abraham

WOLFE WAS DEEPLY MOVED BY THE DISASTER AT the heights of Montmorenci, and in a General Order on the next day he rebuked the grenadiers for their precipitation. "Such impetuous, irregular and unsoldierlike proceedings destroy all order, make it impossible for the commanders to form any disposition for an attack, and put it out of the general's power to execute his plans. The grenadiers could not suppose that they could beat the French alone."

The French were elated by their success. "Everybody," says the commissary Berniers, "thought that the campaign was as good as ended, gloriously for us." They had been sufficiently confident even before their victory, and the bearer of a flag of truce told the English officers that he had never imagined they were such fools as to attack Quebec with so small a force.

Wolfe, on the other hand, had every reason to despond. At the outset, before he had seen Quebec and learned the nature of the ground, he had meant to begin the campaign by taking post on the Plains of Abraham and from there laying siege to the town, but he soon discovered that the Plains of Abraham were hardly more within his reach than was Quebec itself. Such hope as was left him lay in the composition of Montcalm's army. He respected the French commander and thought his disciplined soldiers not unworthy of the British steel, but he held his militia in high scorn and could he but face them in the open field, he never doubted the result. But Montcalm also distrusted them and persisted in refusing the coveted battle.

Wolfe now sent rangers, light infantry and Highlanders to waste the settlements far and wide. Wherever resistance was offered, farmhouses and villages were laid in ashes, though churches were generally spared. St. Paul, far below Quebec, was sacked and burned and the settlements of the opposite shore were partially destroyed. The parishes of L'Ange Gardien, Château Richer and St. Joachim were wasted with fire and sword. Night after night the garrison of Quebec could see the light of burning houses as far down as the mountain of Cape Tourmente.

"Women and children," such were the orders of Wolfe, "are to be treated with humanity; if any violence is offered to a woman, the offender shall be punished with death." These orders were generally obeyed. The English, with the single exception of Montgomery, killed none but armed men in the act of resistance or attack. Vaudreuil's war parties spared neither age nor sex.

Montcalm let the parishes burn and still lay fast intrenched in his lines of Beauport. He would not imperil all Canada to save a few hundred farmhouses, and Wolfe was as far as ever from the battle that he coveted.

Hitherto his attacks had been made chiefly below the town, but these having failed, he now changed his plan and renewed on a larger scale the movements begun above it in July. With every fair wind, ships and transports passed the batteries of Quebec, favored by a hot fire from Point Levi, and generally succeeded with more or less damage in gaining the upper river. A fleet of flatboats was also sent there and twelve hundred troops marched overland to embark in them, under Brigadier Murray. Admiral Holmes took command of the little fleet now gathered above the town and operations in that quarter were systematically resumed.

Vaudreuil now saw his mistake in sending the French frigates up the river out of harm's way and withdrawing their crews to serve the batteries of Quebec. Had these ships been there, they might have overpowered those of the English in detail as they passed the town. An attempt was made to retrieve the blunder. The sailors were sent to man the frigates anew and attack the squadron of Holmes. It was too late. Holmes was already too strong for them and they were re-called. Yet the difficulties of the English still seemed insurmountable. Dysentery and fever broke out in their camps, the number of their effective men was greatly reduced, and the advancing season told them that their work must be done quickly or not done at all.

On the other side, the distress of the French grew greater every day. Their army was on short rations. The operations of the English above the town filled the camp of Beauport with dismay, for troops and Canadians alike dreaded the cutting off of their supplies. These were all drawn from the districts of Three Rivers and Montreal, and at best they were in great danger, since when brought down in boats at night they were apt to be intercepted, while the difficulty of bringing them by land was extreme, through the scarcity of cattle and horses. Discipline was relaxed, disorder and pillage were rife, and the Canadians deserted so fast that towards the end of August two hundred of them, it is said, would sometimes go off in one night.

Early in the month the disheartening news came of the loss of Ticonderoga and Crown Point, the retreat of Bourlamaque, the fall of Niagara and the expected advance of Amherst on Montreal. Lévis was dispatched to the scene of danger, and Quebec was deplorably weakened by his absence.

About this time the Lower Town was again set on fire by the English batteries and a hundred and sixty-seven houses were burned in a night. In the front of the Upper Town nearly every building was a ruin. At the General Hospital, which was remote enough to be safe from the bombardment, every barn, shed and garret, and even the chapel itself, were crowded with sick and wounded, with women and children from the town and the nuns of the Ursulines and the Hôtel-Dieu, driven there for refuge. Bishop Pontbriand, though suffering from a mortal disease, came almost daily to visit and console them from his lodging in the house of the curé at Charlesbourg.

Towards the end of August the sky brightened again. It became known that Amherst was not moving on Montreal, and Bourlamaque wrote that his position at Isle-aux-Noix was impregnable. On the twenty-seventh a deserter from Wolfe's army brought the welcome assurance that the invaders despaired of success and would soon sail for home, while there were movements in the English camps and fleet that seemed to confirm what he said. Vaudreuil breathed more freely.

Meanwhile a deep cloud fell on the English. Since the siege began Wolfe had passed with ceaseless energy from camp to camp, animating the troops, observing everything and directing everything, but now the pale face and tall, lean form were seen no more and the rumor spread that the general was dangerously ill. He had in fact been seized by an access of the disease that had tortured him for some time past, and fever had followed. His quarters were at a French farmhouse in the camp at Montmorenci, and here, as he lay in an upper chamber, helpless in bed, his singular and most unmilitary features haggard with disease and drawn with pain, no man could less have looked the hero.

But as the needle, though quivering, points always to the pole, so, through torment and languor and the heats of fever, the mind of Wolfe dwelt on the capture of Quebec. His illness, which began before the twentieth of August, had so far subsided on the twenty-fifth that Knox wrote in his diary of that day: "His Excellency General Wolfe is on the recovery, to the inconceivable joy of the whole army." On the twenty-ninth he was able to write or dictate a letter to the three brigadiers, Monckton, Townshend and Murray: "That the public service may not suffer by the General's indisposition, he begs the brigadiers will meet and consult together for the public utility and advantage, and consider of the best method to attack the enemy."

The letter then proposes three plans, all bold to audacity. The first was to send a part of the army to ford the Montmorenci eight or nine miles above its mouth, march through the forest and fall on the rear of the French at Beauport, while the rest landed and attacked them in front. The second was to cross the ford at the mouth of the Montmorenci and march along the strand, under the French intrenchments, till a place could be found where the troops might climb the heights. The third was to make a general attack from boats at the Beauport flats. Wolfe had before entertained two other plans, one of which was to scale the heights at St. Michel, about a league above Quebec, but this he had abandoned on learning that the French were there in force to receive him. The other was to storm the Lower Town, but this also he had abandoned, because the Upper Town, which commanded it, would still remain inaccessible.

The brigadiers met in consultation, rejected the three plans proposed in the letter and advised that an attempt should be made to gain a footing on the north shore above the town, place the army between Montcalm and his base of supply and so force him to fight or surrender. The scheme was similar to that of the heights of St. Michel. It seemed desperate, but so did all the rest, and if by chance it should succeed, the gain was far greater than could follow any success below the town. Wolfe embraced it at once.

Not that he saw much hope in it. He knew that every chance was against him. Disappointment in the past and gloom in the future, the pain and exhaustion of disease, toils and anxieties "too great," in the words of Burke, "to be supported by a delicate constitution, and a body unequal to the vigorous and enterprising soul that it lodged," threw him at times into deep dejection. By those intimate with him he was heard to say that he would not go back defeated, "to be exposed to the censure and reproach of an ignorant populace." In other moods he felt that he ought not to sacrifice what was left of his diminished army in vain conflict with hopeless obstacles. But his final resolve once taken, he would not swerve from it. His fear was that he might not be able to lead his troops in person.

"I know perfectly well you cannot cure me," he said to his physician, "but pray make me up so that I may be without pain for a few days, and able to do my duty: that is all I want."

Perhaps he was as near despair as his undaunted nature was capable of being. In his present state of body and mind he was a hero without the light and cheer of heroism. He flattered himself with no illusions, but saw the worst and faced it all. He seems to have been entirely without excitement. The languor of disease, the desperation of the chances and the greatness of the stake may have wrought to tranquilize him. His energy was doubly tasked: to bear up his own sinking frame and to achieve an almost hopeless feat of arms.

Wolfe's first move towards executing his plan was the critical one of evacuating the camp at Montmorenci. This was accomplished on the third of September. Montcalm sent a strong force to fall on the rear of the retiring English. Monckton saw the movement from Point Levi, embarked two battalions in the boats of the fleet and made a feint of landing at Beauport. Montcalm recalled his troops to repulse the threatened attack and the English withdrew from Montmorenci unmolested, some to the Point of Orleans, others to Point Levi.

697

On the night of the fourth a fleet of flatboats passed above the town with the baggage and stores. On the fifth, Murray, with four battalions, marched up the river Etechemin and forded it under a hot fire from the French batteries at Sillery. Monckton and Townshend followed with three more battalions, and the united force of about thirty-six hundred men was embarked on board the ships of Holmes, where Wolfe joined them on the same evening.

These movements of the English filled the French commanders with mingled perplexity, anxiety and hope. A deserter told them that Admiral Saunders was impatient to be gone. Vaudreuil grew confident. Yet he was ceaselessly watchful. So was Montcalm, and on the night of the second he snatched a moment to write to Bourlamaque from his headquarters in the stone house by the river of Beauport: "The night is dark; it rains; our troops are in their tents, with clothes on, ready for an alarm; I in my boots; my horses saddled. In fact, this is my usual way. I wish you were here; for I cannot be everywhere, though I multiply myself and have not taken off my clothes since the twenty-third of June."

Meanwhile no precaution was spared. The force under Bougainville above Quebec was raised to three thousand men. He was ordered to watch the shore as far as Jacques-Cartier and follow with his main body every movement of Holmes's squadron. There was little fear for the heights near the town; they were thought inaccessible.

Even Montcalm believed them safe and had expressed himself to that effect some time before. "We need not suppose," he wrote to Vaudreuil, "that the enemy have wings," and again, speaking of the very place where Wolfe afterwards landed, "I swear to you that a hundred men posted there would stop their whole army." He was right. A hundred watchful and determined men could have held the position long enough for reinforcements to come up.

The hundred men were there. Captain de Vergor, of the colony troops, commanded them, and reinforcements were within his call, for the battalion of Guienne had been ordered to encamp close at hand on the Plains of Abraham. Vergor's post, called Anse du Foulon, was a mile and a half from Quebec. A little beyond it, by the brink of the cliffs, was another post called Samos, held by seventy men with four cannon, and beyond this again the heights of Sillery were guarded by a hundred and thirty men, also with cannon. These were outposts of Bougainville, whose headquarters were at Cap-Rouge, six miles above Sillery, and whose troops were in continual movement along the intervening shore.

Thus all was vigilance, for while the French were strong in the hope of speedy delivery, they felt that there was no safety till the tents of the invader had vanished from their shores and his ships from their river. "What we know," says one of them, "of the character of M. Wolfe, that impetuous, bold and intrepid warrior, prepared us for a last attack before he left us."

Wolfe had been very ill on the evening of the fourth. The troops knew it and their spirits sank, but after a night of torment he grew better and was soon among them again, rekindling their ardor and imparting a cheer that he could not share. For himself he had no pity, but when he heard of the illness of two officers in one of the ships he sent them a message of warm sympathy, advised them to return to Point Levi and offered them his own barge and an escort. They thanked him but replied that, come what might, they would see the enterprise to an end.

Another officer remarked in his hearing that one of the invalids had a very delicate constitution. "Don't tell me of constitution," said Wolfe; "he has good spirit, and a good spirit will carry a man through everything." An immense moral force bore up his own frail body and forced it to its work.

Major Robert Stobo, who five years before had been given as a hostage to the French at the capture of Fort Necessity, arrived about this time in a vessel from Halifax. He had long been a prisoner at Quebec, not always in close custody, and had used his opportunities to acquaint himself with the neighborhood. In the spring of this year he and an officer of rangers named Stevens had made their escape with extraordinary skill and daring, and he now returned to give his countrymen the benefit of his local knowledge.

His biographer says that it was he who directed Wolfe in the choice of a landing place. Be this as it may, Wolfe in person examined the river and the shores as far as Pointe-aux-Trembles, till at length, landing on the south side a little above Quebec and looking across the water with a telescope, he descried a path that ran with a long slope up the face of the woody precipice and saw at the top a cluster of tents. They were those of Vergor's guard at the Anse du Foulon, now called Wolfe's Cove. As he could see but ten or twelve of them, he thought that the guard could not be numerous and might be overpowered. His hope would have been stronger if he had known that Vergor had once been tried for misconduct and cowardice in the surrender of Beauséjour and saved from merited disgrace by the friendship of Bigot and the protection of Vaudreuil.

The morning of the seventh was fair and warm, and the vessels of Holmes, their crowded decks gay with scarlet uniforms, sailed up the river to Cap-Rouge. A lively scene awaited them, for here were the headquarters of Bougainville and here lay his principal force, while the rest watched the banks above and below. The cove into which the little river runs was guarded by floating batteries; the surrounding shore was defended by breastworks; and a large body of regulars, militia and mounted Canadians in blue uniforms moved to and fro, with restless activity, on the hills behind.

When the vessels came to anchor, the horsemen dismounted and formed in line with the infantry, then with loud shouts the whole rushed down the heights to man their works at the shore. That true Briton, Captain Knox, looked on with a critical eye from the gangway of his ship and wrote that night in his diary that they had made a ridiculous noise. "How different!" he exclaims, "how nobly awful and expressive of true valor is the customary silence of the British troops!"

In the afternoon the ships opened fire, while the troops entered the boats and rowed up and down as if looking for a landing place. It was but a feint of Wolfe to deceive Bougainville as to his real design. A heavy easterly rain set in on the next morning and lasted two days without respite. All operations were suspended and the men suffered greatly in the crowded transports. Half of them were therefore landed on the south shore, where they made their quarters in the village of St. Nicolas, refreshed themselves and dried their wet clothing, knapsacks and blankets.

For several successive days the squadron of Holmes was allowed to drift up the river with the flood tide and down with the ebb, thus passing and repassing incessantly between the neighborhood of Quebec on one hand and a point high above Cap-Rouge on the other, while

Bougainville, perplexed and always expecting an attack, followed the ships to and fro along the shore, by day and by night, till his men were exhausted with ceaseless forced marches.

At last the time for action came. On Wednesday, the twelfth, the troops at St. Nicolas were embarked again and all were told to hold themselves in readiness. Wolfe, from the flagship *Sutherland,* issued his last general orders. "The enemy's force is now divided, great scarcity of provisions in their camp, and universal discontent among the Canadians. Our troops below are in readiness to join us; all the light artillery and tools are embarked at the Point of Levi; and the troops will land where the French seem least to expect it. The first body that gets on shore is to march directly to the enemy and drive them from any little post they may occupy; the officers must be careful that the succeeding bodies do not by any mistake fire on those who go before them. The battalions must form on the upper ground with expedition, and be ready to charge whatever presents itself. When the artillery and troops are landed, a corps will be left to secure the landing place, while the rest march on and endeavor to bring the Canadians and French to a battle. The officers and men will remember what their country expects from them, and what a determined body of soldiers inured to war is capable of doing against five weak French battalions mingled with a disorderly peasantry."

The spirit of the army answered to that of its chief. The troops loved and admired their general, trusted their officers and were ready for any attempt.

Wolfe had thirty-six hundred men and officers with him on board the vessels of Holmes and he now sent orders to Colonel Burton at Point Levi to bring to his aid all who could be spared from that place and the Point of Orleans. They were to march along the south bank, after nightfall, and wait further orders at a designated spot convenient for embarkation. Their number was about twelve hundred, so that the entire force destined for the enterprise was at the utmost forty-eight hundred. With these, Wolfe meant to climb the heights of Abraham in the teeth of an enemy who, though much reduced, were still twice as numerous as their assailants.

Admiral Saunders lay with the main fleet in the Basin of Quebec. This excellent officer, whatever may have been his views as to the necessity of a speedy departure, aided Wolfe to the last with unfailing energy and zeal. It was agreed between them that while the general made the real attack, the admiral should engage Montcalm's attention by a pretended one. As night approached, the fleet ranged itself along the Beauport shore; the boats were lowered and filled with sailors, marines and the few troops that had been left behind, while ship signaled to ship, cannon flashed and thundered, and shot plowed the beach, as if to clear a way for assailants to land. In the gloom of the evening the effect was imposing.

Montcalm, who thought that the movements of the English above the town were only a feint, that their main force was still below it and that their real attack would be made there, was completely deceived and massed his troops in front of Beauport to repel the expected landing. But while in the fleet of Saunders all was uproar and ostentatious menace, the danger was ten miles away, where the squadron of Holmes lay tranquil and silent at its anchorage off Cap-Rouge.

It was less tranquil than it seemed. All on board knew that a blow would be struck that night, though only a few high officers knew where. Colonel Howe, of the light infantry, called for volunteers to lead the unknown and desperate venture, promising in the words of one of them "that if any of us survived we might depend on being recommended to the general." As many as were wanted—twenty-four in all —soon came forward. Thirty large bateaux and some boats belonging to the squadron lay moored alongside the vessels, and late in the evening the troops were ordered into them, the twenty-four volunteers taking their place in the foremost. They held in all about seventeen hundred men. The rest remained on board.

Bougainville could discern the movement and misjudged it, thinking that he himself was to be attacked. The tide was still flowing, and the better to deceive him, the vessels and boats were allowed to drift upward with it for a little distance, as if to land above Cap-Rouge.

The day had been fortunate for Wolfe. Two deserters came from the camp of Bougainville with intelligence that, at ebb tide on the next night, he was to send down a convoy of provisions to Montcalm. The necessities of the camp at Beauport and the difficulties of transportation by land had before compelled the French to resort to this perilous means of conveying supplies, and their boats, drifting in darkness under the shadows of the northern shore, had commonly passed in safety. Wolfe saw at once that if his own boats went down in advance of the convoy, he could turn the intelligence of the deserters to good account.

He was still on board the *Sutherland*. Every preparation was made and every order given; it only remained to wait the turning of the tide. Seated with him in the cabin was the commander of the sloop of war *Porcupine,* his former schoolfellow, John Jervis, afterwards Earl St. Vincent. Wolfe told him that he expected to die in the battle of the next day, and taking from his bosom a miniature of Miss Lowther, his betrothed, he gave it to him with a request that he would return it to her if the presentiment should prove true.

Towards two o'clock the tide began to ebb and a fresh wind blew down the river. Two lanterns were raised into the maintop shrouds of the *Sutherland*. It was the appointed signal. The boats cast off and fell down with the current, those of the light infantry leading the way. The vessels with the rest of the troops had orders to follow a little later.

For full two hours the procession of boats, borne on the current, steered silently down the St. Lawrence. The stars were visible but the night was moonless and sufficiently dark. The general was in one of the foremost boats, and near him was a young midshipman, John Robison, afterwards professor of natural philosophy in the University of Edinburgh. He used to tell in his later life how Wolfe, with a low voice, repeated Gray's *Elegy Written in a Country Churchyard* to the officers about him. Probably it was to relieve the intense strain of his thoughts.

"Gentlemen," he said as his recital ended, "I would rather have written those lines than take Quebec."

As they neared their destination the tide bore them in towards the shore, and the mighty wall of rock and forest towered in darkness on their left. The dead stillness was suddenly broken by the sharp *"Qui vive!"* of a French sentry, invisible in the thick gloom. *"France!"* answered a Highland officer of Fraser's regiment from one of the boats of the light infantry. He had served in Holland and spoke French fluently.

"What regiment?"

"The Queen's," replied the Highlander. He knew that a part of that corps was with Bougainville. The sentry, expecting the convoy of provisions, was satisfied and did not ask for the password.

Soon after, the foremost boats were passing the heights of Samos when another sentry challenged them, and they could see him through the darkness running down to the edge of the water, within range of a pistol shot. In answer to his questions, the same officer replied in French: "Provision boats. Don't make a noise; the English will hear us." In fact the sloop of war *Hunter* was anchored in the stream not far off. This time, again, the sentry let them pass.

In a few moments they rounded the headland above the Anse du Foulon. There was no sentry there. The strong current swept the boats of the light infantry a little below the intended landing place. They disembarked on a narrow strand at the foot of heights as steep as a hill covered with trees can be. The twenty-four volunteers led the way, climbing with what silence they might, closely followed by a much larger body. When they reached the top they saw in the dim light a cluster of tents at a short distance and immediately made a dash at them. Vergor leaped from bed and tried to run off, but was shot in the heel and captured. His men, taken by surprise, made little resistance. One or two were caught and the rest fled.

The main body of troops waited in their boats by the edge of the strand. The heights near by were cleft by a great ravine choked with forest trees, and in its depths ran a little brook called Ruisseau St. Denis, which, swollen by the late rains, fell plashing in the stillness over a rock. Other than this no sound could reach the strained ear of Wolfe but the gurgle of the tide and the cautious climbing of his advance parties as they mounted the steeps at some little distance from where he sat listening.

At length from the top came a sound of musket shots, followed by loud huzzas, and he knew that his men were masters of the position. The word was given. The troops leaped from the boats and scaled the heights, some here, some there, clutching at trees and bushes, their muskets slung at their backs. Tradition still points out the place, near the mouth of the ravine, where the foremost reached the top.

Wolfe said to an officer near him: "You can try it, but I don't think you'll get up." He himself, however, found strength to drag himself up with the rest. The narrow slanting path on the face of the heights had been made impassable by trenches and abatis, but all obstructions were soon cleared away and then the ascent was easy. In the gray of the morning the long file of red-coated soldiers moved quickly upward and formed in order on the plateau above.

Before many of them had reached the top, cannon were heard close on the left. It was the battery at Samos firing on the boats in the rear and the vessels descending from Cap-Rouge. A party was sent to silence it. This was soon effected, and the most distant battery at Sillery was next attacked and taken. As fast as the boats were emptied they returned for the troops left on board the vessels, and for those waiting on the southern shore under Colonel Burton.

The day broke in clouds and threatening rain. Wolf's battalions were drawn up along the crest of the heights. No enemy was in sight, though a body of Canadians had sallied from the town and moved along the strand towards the landing place, from which they were quickly driven back. He had achieved the most critical part of his enterprise, yet the success that he coveted placed him in imminent danger. On one side was the garrison of Quebec and the army of Beauport, and Bougainville was on the other. Wolfe's alternative was victory or ruin, for if he should be overwhelmed by a combined attack, retreat would be hopeless. His feelings no man can know, but it would be safe to say that hesitation or doubt had no part in them.

He went to reconnoiter the ground and soon came to the Plains of Abraham, so called from Abraham Martin, a pilot known as Maître Abraham, who had owned a piece of land here in the early times of the colony. The plains were a tract of grass, tolerably level in most parts, patched here and there with cornfields, studded with clumps of bushes and forming a part of the high plateau at the eastern end of which Quebec stood. On the south it was bounded by the declivities along the St. Lawrence; on the north, by those along the St. Charles, or rather along the meadows through which that lazy stream crawled like a writhing snake. At the place that Wolfe chose for his battlefield the plateau was less than a mile wide.

There the troops advanced, marched by files till they reached the ground and then wheeled to form their line of battle, which stretched across the plateau and faced the city. It consisted of six battalions and the detached grenadiers from Louisbourg, all drawn up in ranks three deep. Its right wing was near the brink of the heights along the St. Lawrence, but the left could not reach those along the St. Charles. On this side a wide space was perforce left open, and there was danger of being outflanked. To prevent this, Brigadier Townshend was stationed here with two battalions, drawn up at right angles with the rest and fronting the St. Charles. The battalion of Webb's regiment, under Colonel Burton, formed the reserve; the third battalion of Royal Americans was left to guard the landing, and Howe's light infantry occupied a wood far in the rear. Wolfe, with Monckton and Murray, commanded the front line, on which the heavy fighting was to fall, and which, when all the troops had arrived, numbered less than thirty-five hundred men.

Quebec was not a mile distant, but they could not see it, for a ridge of broken ground intervened, called Buttes-à-Neveu, about six hundred paces off. The first division of troops had scarcely come up when, about six o'clock, this ridge was suddenly thronged with white uniforms. It was the battalion of Guienne, arrived at the eleventh hour from its camp by the St. Charles. Some time after, there was hot firing in the rear. It came from a detachment of Bougainville's command attacking a house where some of the light infantry were posted. The assailants were repulsed and the firing ceased. Light showers fell at intervals, besprinkling the troops as they stood patiently waiting the event.

Montcalm had passed a troubled night. Through all the evening the cannon bellowed from the ships of Saunders and the boats of the fleet hovered in the dusk off the Beauport shore, threatening every moment to land. Troops lined the intrenchments till day, while the general walked the field that adjoined his headquarters till one in the morning, accompanied by the Chevàlier Johnstone and Colonel Poulariez. Johnstone says that he was in great agitation and took no rest all night.

At daybreak he heard the sound of cannon above the town. It was the battery at Samos firing on the English ships. He had sent an officer to the quarters of Vaudreuil, which were much nearer Quebec, with orders to bring him word at once should anything unusual happen. But no word came, and about six o'clock he mounted and rode there with Johnstone. As they advanced, the country behind the town opened more and more upon their sight, till at length, when opposite Vaudreuil's house, they saw across the St. Charles, some two miles away, the red ranks of British soldiers on the heights beyond.

"This is a serious business," Montcalm said, and sent off Johnstone at full gallop to bring up the troops from the center and left of the camp. Those of the right were in motion already, doubtless by the governor's order. Vaudreuil came out of the house. Montcalm stopped for a few words with him, then set spurs to his horse and rode over the bridge of the St. Charles to the scene of danger. He rode with a fixed look, uttering not a word.

The army followed in such order as it might, crossed the bridge in hot haste, passed under the northern rampart of Quebec, entered at the Palace Gate and pressed on in headlong march along the quaint narrow streets of the warlike town: troops of Indians in scalp locks and war paint, a savage glitter in their deep-set eyes; bands of Canadians whose all was at stake, faith, country and home; the colony regulars; the battalions of Old France, a torrent of white uniforms and gleaming bayonets, La Sarre, Languedoc, Roussillon, Béarn—victors of Oswego, William Henry and Ticonderoga. So they swept on and poured out upon the plain, some by the gate of St. Louis and some by that of St. John, and hurried breathless to where the banners of Guienne still fluttered on the ridge.

Montcalm was amazed at what he saw. He had expected a detachment and he found an army. Full in sight before him stretched the lines of Wolfe: the close ranks of the English infantry, a silent wall of red, and the wild array of the Highlanders, with their waving tartans and bagpipes screaming defiance. Vaudreuil had not come; but not the less was felt the evil of a divided authority and the jealousy of the rival chiefs. Montcalm waited long for the forces he had ordered to join him from the left wing of the army. He waited in vain. It is said that the governor had detained them, lest the English should attack the Beauport shore. Even if they did so, and succeeded, the French might defy them could they but put Wolfe to rout on the Plains of Abraham. Neither did the garrison of Quebec come to the aid of Montcalm. He sent to Ramesay, its commander, for twenty-five fieldpieces which were on the Palace battery. Ramesay would give him only three, saying that he wanted them for his own defense. There were orders and counterorders; misunderstanding, haste, delay, perplexity.

Montcalm and his chief officers held a council of war. It is said that he and they alike were for immediate attack. His enemies declare that he was afraid lest Vaudreuil should arrive and take command, but the governor was not a man to assume responsibility at such a crisis. Others say that his impetuosity overcame his better judgment, and of this charge it is hard to acquit him. Bougainville was but a few miles distant and some of his troops were much nearer. A messenger sent by way of Old Lorette could have reached him in an hour and a half at most, and a combined attack in front and rear might have been concerted with him. If, moreover, Montcalm could have come to an understanding with Vaudreuil, his own force might have been strengthened by two or three thousand additional men from the town and the camp of Beauport, but he felt that there was no time to lose, for he imagined that Wolfe would soon be reinforced, which was impossible, and he believed that the English were fortifying themselves, which was no less an error.

He has been blamed not only for fighting too soon but for fighting at all. In this he could not choose. Fight he must, for Wolfe was now in a position to cut off all his supplies. His men were full of ardor and he resolved to attack before their ardor cooled. He spoke a few words to them in his keen, vehement way.

"I remember very well how he looked," one of the Canadians, then a boy of eighteen, used to say in his old age. "He rode a black or dark bay horse along the front of our lines, brandishing his sword, as if to excite us to do our duty. He wore a coat with wide sleeves, which fell back as he raised his arm, and showed the white linen of the wristband."

The English waited the result with a composure which, if not quite real, was at least well feigned. The three fieldpieces sent by Ramesay plied them with canister shot and fifteen hundred Canadians and Indians fusilladed them in front and flank. Over all the plain, from behind bushes and knolls and the edge of cornfields, puffs of smoke sprang incessantly from the guns of these hidden marksmen. Skirmishers were thrown out before the lines to hold them in check and the soldiers were ordered to lie on the grass to avoid the shot. The firing was liveliest on the English left, where bands of sharpshooters got under the edge of the declivity, among thickets and behind scattered houses, whence they killed and wounded a considerable number of Townshend's men. The light infantry were called up from the rear. The houses were taken and retaken and one or more of them was burned.

Wolfe was everywhere. How cool he was, and why his followers loved him, is shown by an incident that happened in the course of the morning. One of his captains was shot through the lungs, and on recovering consciousness he saw the general standing at his side. Wolfe pressed his hand, told him not to despair, praised his services, promised him early promotion and sent an aide-de-camp to Monckton to beg that officer to keep the promise if he himself should fall.

It was towards ten o'clock when, from the high ground on the right of the line, Wolfe saw that the crisis was near. The French on the ridge had formed themselves into three bodies, regulars in the center, regulars and Canadians on right and left. Two fieldpieces, which had been dragged up the heights at Anse du Foulon, fired on them with grapeshot, and the troops, rising from the ground, prepared to receive them. In a few moments more they were in motion.

They came on rapidly, uttering loud shouts and firing as soon as they were within range. Their ranks, ill ordered at the best, were further confused by a number of Canadians who had been mixed among the regulars and who, after hastily firing, threw themselves on the ground to reload.

The British advanced a few rods; then halted and stood still. When the French were within forty paces the word of command rang out and a crash of musketry answered all along the line. The volley was delivered with remarkable precision. In the battalions of the center, which had suffered least from the enemy's bullets, the simultaneous explosion was afterwards said by French officers to have sounded like a cannon shot. Another volley followed and then a furious clattering fire that lasted but a minute or two. When the smoke rose, a miserable sight was revealed: the ground cumbered with dead and wounded, the advancing masses stopped short and turned into a frantic mob, shouting, cursing, gesticulating. The order was given to charge.

Then over the field rose the British cheer, mixed with the fierce yell of the Highland slogan. Some of the corps pushed forward with the bayonet; some advanced firing. The clansmen drew their broadswords and dashed on, keen and swift as bloodhounds. At the English right, though the attacking column was broken to pieces, a fire was still kept up, chiefly, it seems, by sharpshooters from the bushes and cornfields, where they had lain for an hour or more.

Here Wolfe himself led the charge, at the head of the Louisbourg grenadiers. A shot shattered his wrist. He wrapped his handkerchief about it and kept on. Another shot struck him and he still advanced, when a third lodged in his breast. He staggered, and sat on the ground. Lieutenant Brown, of the grenadiers, one Henderson, a volunteer in the same company, and a private soldier, aided by an officer of artillery who ran to join them, carried him in their arms to the rear. He begged them to lay him down. They did so, and asked if he would have a surgeon.

"There's no need," he answered, "it's all over with me."

A moment after, one of them cried out: "They run; see how they run!"

"Who run?" Wolfe demanded, like a man roused from sleep.

"The enemy, sir. Egad, they give way everywhere!"

"Go, one of you, to Colonel Burton," returned the dying man. "Tell him to march Webb's regiment down to Charles River, to cut off their retreat from the bridge."

Then, turning on his side, he murmured, "Now, God be praised, I will die in peace!" and in a few moments his gallant soul had fled.

Montcalm, still on horseback, was borne with the tide of fugitives towards the town. As he approached the walls a shot passed through his body. He kept his seat. Two soldiers supported him, one on each side, and led his horse through the St. Louis Gate.

On the open space within, among the excited crowd, were several women, drawn no doubt by eagerness to know the result of the fight. One of them recognized him, saw the streaming blood and shrieked, "O my God! my God! the Marquis has been killed!"

"It's nothing, it's nothing," replied the death-stricken man. "Don't be troubled for me, my good friends."

The rout had just begun when Vaudreuil crossed the bridge from the camp of Beauport. It was four hours since he first heard the alarm, and his quarters were not much more than two miles from the battle-field. He does not explain why he did not come sooner. It is certain that his coming was well timed to throw the blame on Montcalm in case of defeat, or to claim some of the honor for himself in case of victory. When he perceived the situation Vaudreuil lost no time in recrossing the bridge and joining the militia in the redoubt at the farther end, where a crowd of fugitives soon poured in after him.

Montcalm was dying. His second-in-command, the Brigadier Sene-zergues, was mortally wounded. The army, routed and demoralized, was virtually without a head, and the colony, yesterday cheered as on the eve of deliverance, was plunged into sudden despair. "Ah, what a cruel day!" cries Bougainville. "How fatal to all that was dearest to us! My heart is torn in its most tender parts. We shall be fortunate if the approach of winter saves the country from total ruin."

Before midnight the English had made good progress in their re-doubts and intrenchments, had brought cannon up the heights to defend them, planted a battery on the Côte Ste.-Geneviève, descended into the meadows of the St. Charles and taken possession of the Gen-eral Hospital, with its crowds of sick and wounded.

Their victory had cost them six hundred and sixty-four of all ranks, killed, wounded and missing. The French loss is placed by Vaudreuil at about six hundred and forty and by the English official reports at about fifteen hundred. Measured by the numbers engaged, the Battle of Quebec was but a heavy skirmish. Measured by results, it was one of the great battles of the world.

Vaudreuil went from the hornwork to his quarters on the Beauport road and called a council of war. It was a tumultuous scene. A letter was dispatched to Quebec to ask advice of Montcalm. The dying general sent a brief message to the effect that there was a threefold choice—to fight again, retreat to Jacques-Cartier or give up the colony.

There was much in favor of fighting. When Bougainville had gathered all his force from the river above, he would have three thousand men, and these, joined to the garrison of Quebec, the sailors at the batteries and the militia and artillerymen of the Beauport camp, would form a body of fresh soldiers more than equal to the English then on the Plains of Abraham. Add to these the defeated troops and

711

the victors would be greatly outnumbered. Bigot gave his voice for fighting. Vaudreuil expressed himself to the same effect but he says that all the officers were against him.

The governor at least might have taken a night for reflection. He was safe behind the St. Charles. The English, spent by fighting, toil and want of sleep, were in no condition to disturb him. A part of his own men were in deadly need of rest; the night would have brought refreshment and the morning might have brought wise counsel. Vaudreuil would not wait, and orders were given at once for retreat. It began at nine o'clock that evening. Quebec was abandoned to its fate. The cannon were left in the lines of Beauport, the tents in the encampments, and provisions enough in the storehouses to supply the army for a week.

"It was not a retreat," says Johnstone, who was himself a part of it, "but an abominable flight, with such disorder and confusion that, had the English known it, three hundred men sent after us would have been sufficient to cut all our army to pieces. The soldiers were all mixed, scattered, dispersed, and running as hard as they could, as if the English army were at their heels."

They passed Charlesbourg, Lorette and St. Augustin, till on the fifteenth they found rest on the impregnable hill of Jacques-Cartier, by the brink of the St. Lawrence, thirty miles from danger.

In the night of humiliation when Vaudreuil abandoned Quebec, Montcalm was breathing his last within its walls. When he was brought wounded from the field he was placed in the house of the Surgeon Arnoux, who was then with Bourlamaque at Isle-aux-Noix, but whose younger brother, also a surgeon, examined the wound and pronounced it mortal.

"I am glad of it," Montcalm said quietly, and then asked how long he had to live.

"Twelve hours, more or less," was the reply.

"So much the better," he returned. "I am happy that I shall not live to see the surrender of Quebec."

He is reported to have said that since he had lost the battle it consoled him to have been defeated by so brave an enemy, and some of his last words were in praise of his successor, Lévis, for whose talents and fitness for command he expressed high esteem. When Vaudreuil sent to ask his opinion, he gave it, but when Ramesay, commandant of the garrison, came to receive his orders, he replied:

"I will neither give orders nor interfere any further. I have much business that must be attended to, of greater moment than your ruined garrison and this wretched country. My time is very short; therefore pray leave me. I wish you all comfort, and to be happily extricated from your present perplexities."

Nevertheless he thought to the last of those who had been under his command and sent the following note to Brigadier Townshend: "Monsieur, the humanity of the English sets my mind at peace concerning the fate of the French prisoners and the Canadians. Feel towards them as they have caused me to feel. Do not let them perceive that they have changed masters. Be their protector as I have been their father."

Bishop Pontbriand, himself fast sinking with mortal disease, attended his deathbed and administered the last sacraments. He died peacefully at four o'clock on the morning of the fourteenth. He was in his forty-eighth year.

In the confusion of the time no workman could be found to make a coffin, and an old servant of the Ursulines, known as Bonhomme Michel, gathered a few boards and nailed them together so as to form a rough box. In it was laid the body of the dead soldier, and late in the evening of the same day he was carried to his rest. There was no tolling of bells or firing of cannon. The officers of the garrison followed the bier, and some of the populace, including women and children, joined the procession as it moved in dreary silence along the dusky street, shattered with cannon ball and bomb, to the chapel of the Ursuline convent.

Here a shell, bursting under the floor, had made a cavity which had been hollowed into a grave. Three priests of the cathedral, several nuns, Ramesay with his officers, and a throng of townspeople were present at the rite. After the service and the chant the body was lowered into the grave by the light of torches, and then, says the chronicle, "the tears and sobs burst forth. It seemed as if the last hope of the colony were buried with the remains of the General."

In truth, the funeral of Montcalm was the funeral of New France.

Utter confusion reigned in the disheartened garrison of Quebec.

713

Men deserted hourly, some to the country and some to the English camp, while Townshend pushed his trenches nearer and nearer to the walls, in spite of the cannonade with which Fiedmont and his artillerymen tried to check them. On the evening of the seventeenth the English ships of war moved towards the Lower Town and a column of troops was seen approaching over the meadows of the St. Charles, as if to storm the Palace Gate. The drums beat the alarm, but the militia refused to fight. Their officers came to Ramesay in a body, declared that they had no mind to sustain an assault, that they knew he had orders against it, that they would carry their guns back to the arsenal, that they were no longer soldiers but citizens, that if the army had not abandoned them they would fight with as much spirit as ever, but that they would not get themselves killed to no purpose. The town major, Joannès, in a rage, beat two of them with the flat of his sword.

The white flag was raised. Joannès pulled it down, thinking, or pretending to think, that it was raised without authority, but Ramesay presently ordered him to go to the English camp and get what terms he could. He went, through driving rain, to the quarters of Townshend and, in hope of the promised succor, spun out the negotiation to the utmost, pretended that he had no power to yield certain points demanded, and was at last sent back to confer with Ramesay, under a promise from the English commander that if Quebec were not given up before eleven o'clock, he would take it by storm. On this Ramesay signed the articles and Joannès carried them back within the time prescribed.

The conditions granted were favorable, for Townshend knew the danger of his position and was glad to have Quebec on any terms. The troops and sailors of the garrison were to march out of the place with the honors of war and to be carried to France. The inhabitants were to have protection in person and property and free exercise of religion.

In the afternoon a company of artillerymen with a fieldpiece entered the town and marched to the place of arms, followed by a body of infantry. Detachments took post at all the gates. The British flag was raised on the heights near the top of Mountain Street, and the capital of New France passed into the hands of its hereditary foes.

The Fall of Canada

BRIGADIER MURRAY WAS NOW IN COMMAND OF Quebec, since the disabled Monckton, oldest brigadier, and Townshend had both returned to England after the victory. Murray was a gallant soldier, upright, humane, generous, eager for distinction and more daring than prudent. He befriended the Canadians, issued strict orders against harming them in person or property, hanged a soldier who had robbed a citizen of Quebec and severely punished others for slighter offenses of the same sort.

In general the soldiers themselves showed kindness towards the conquered people. During harvest they were seen helping them to reap their fields, without compensation, and sharing with them their tobacco and rations. The inhabitants were disarmed and required to take the oath of allegiance. Murray reported in the spring that the whole country, from Cap-Rouge downward, was in subjection to the British Crown.

December came and brought the Canadian winter, with its fierce light and cold, glaring snow fields and piercing blasts that scorch the cheek like a firebrand. The men were frostbitten as they dug away the dry, powdery drifts that the wind had piled against the rampart. The sentries were relieved every hour, yet feet and fingers were continually frozen. The clothing of the troops was ill suited to the climate, and though stoves had been placed in the guard and barrack room, the supply of fuel constantly fell short.

The cutting and dragging of wood was the chief task of the garrison

715

for many a week. Parties of axmen, strongly guarded, were always at work in the forest of Ste.-Foy, four or five miles from Quebec, and the logs were brought to town on sledges dragged by the soldiers. Eight of them were harnessed in pairs to each sledge, and as there was always danger from Indians and bushrangers, every man carried his musket slung at his back. The labor was prodigious, for frequent snowstorms made it necessary again and again to beat a fresh track through the drifts.

The men bore their hardships with admirable good humor, and once a party of them on their return, dragging their load through the street, met a Canadian, also with a load of wood, which was drawn by a team of dogs harnessed much like themselves. They accosted them as yoke fellows, comrades and brothers, asked them what allowance of pork and rum they got and invited them and their owner to mess at the regimental barracks.

From the time when the English took possession of Quebec, reports had come in through deserters that Lévis meant to attack and recover it. Early in November there was a rumor that he was about to march upon it with fifteen thousand men. In December word came that he was on his way, resolved to storm it on or about the twenty-second and dine within the walls, under the French flag, on Christmas Day.

He failed to appear, but in January a deserter said that he had prepared scaling ladders and was training his men to use them by assaults on mock ramparts of snow. There was more tangible evidence that the enemy was astir. Murray had established two fortified outposts, one at Ste.-Foy and the other farther on at Old Lorette. War parties hovered around both and kept the occupants in alarm. A large body of French grenadiers appeared at the latter place in February and drove off a herd of cattle, when a detachment of rangers, much inferior in number, set upon them, put them to flight and recovered the plunder. At the same time a party of regulars, Canadians and Indians took up a strong position near the church at Point Levi and sent a message to the English officers that a large company of expert hairdressers were ready to wait upon them whenever they required their services. The allusion was, of course, to the scalp-lifting practices of the Indians and bushrangers.

The river being now hard frozen, Murray sent over a detachment of light infantry under Major Dalling. A sharp fight ensued on the snow around the church and in the neighboring forest, where the English soldiers, taught to use snowshoes by the rangers, routed the enemy and killed or captured a considerable number. A third post was then established at the church and the priest's house adjacent. Some days after, the French came back in large numbers, fortified themselves with felled trees and then attacked the English position. The firing being heard at Quebec, the light infantry went over to the scene of action, and Murray himself followed on the ice, with the Highlanders and other troops. Before he came up the French drew off and retreated to their breastwork, where they were attacked and put to flight, the nimble Highlanders capturing a few, while the greater part made their escape.

Fresh reports came in from time to time that the French were gathering all their strength to recover Quebec, and late in February these stories took a definite shape. A deserter from Montreal brought Murray a letter from an officer of rangers, who was a prisoner at that place, warning him that eleven thousand men were on the point of marching to attack him. Three other deserters soon after confirmed the news but added that the scheme had met with a check, for as it was intended to carry the town by storm, a grand rehearsal had taken place with the help of scaling ladders planted against the wall of a church, whereupon the Canadians rushed with such zeal to the assault that numerous broken legs, arms and heads ensued, along with ruptures, sprains, bruises and dislocations; insomuch, said the story, that they became disgusted with the attempt.

All remained quiet till after the middle of April, when the garrison was startled by repeated assurances that at the first breaking up of the ice all Canada would be upon them. Murray accordingly ordered the French inhabitants to leave the town within three days.

The effective strength of the garrison was reduced to less than half, and of those that remained fit for duty hardly a man was entirely free from scurvy. The rank and file had no fresh provisions, and in spite of every precaution, this malignant disease, aided by fever and dysentery, made no less havoc among them than among the crews of Jacques-Cartier at this same place two centuries before. Of about seven thousand men left at Quebec in the autumn, scarcely more than three thousand were fit for duty on the twenty-fourth of April, 1760. About seven hundred had found temporary burial in the snowdrifts, as the frozen ground was impenetrable as a rock.

Meanwhile Vaudreuil was still at Montreal, where he says that he "arrived just in time to take the most judicious measures and prevent General Amherst from penetrating into the colony." During the winter some of the French regulars were kept in garrison at the outposts and the rest quartered on the inhabitants, while the Canadians were dismissed to their homes, subject to be mustered again at the call of the governor. Both he and Lévis were full of the hope of retaking Quebec. He had spies and agents among Murray's soldiers, and though the citizens had sworn allegiance to King George, some of them were exceedingly useful to his enemies.

Vaudreuil had constant information of the state of the garrison. He knew that the scurvy was his active and powerful ally and that the hospitals and houses of Quebec were crowded with the sick. At the end of March he was informed that more than half the British were on the sick list, and it was presently rumored that Murray had only two thousand men able to bear arms. With every allowance for exaggeration in these reports, it was plain that the French could attack their invaders in overwhelming force.

The difficulty was to find means of transporation. The depth of the snow and the want of draft animals made it necessary to wait till the river should become navigable, but preparation was begun at once.

Lévis was the soul of the enterprise. Provisions were gathered from far and near. Cannon, mortars and munitions of war were brought from the frontier posts and butcher knives were fitted to the muzzles of guns to serve the Canadians in place of bayonets. All the workmen about Montreal were busied in making tools and gun carriages. Stores were impressed from the merchants, and certain articles, which could not otherwise be had, were smuggled with extraordinary address out of Quebec itself.

Early in spring the militia received orders to muster for the march. There were doubts and discontent, but, says a contemporary, "sensible people dared not speak, for if they did they were set down as English." Some there were who in secret called the scheme "Lévis's folly," yet it was perfectly rational, well conceived and conducted with vigor and skill.

Two frigates, two sloops of war and a number of smaller craft still remained in the river, under command of Vauquelin, the brave officer who had distinguished himself at the siege of Louisbourg. The stores and cannon were placed on board these vessels, the army embarked in a fleet of bateaux, and on the twentieth of April the whole set out together for the scene of action.

They comprised eight battalions of troops of the line and two of colony troops, with the colonial artillery, three thousand Canadians and four hundred Indians. When they left Montreal their effective strength, besides Indians, is said by Lévis to have been six thousand nine hundred and ten, a number which was increased as he advanced by the garrisons of Jacques-Cartier, Deschambault and Point-aux-Trembles, as well as by the Canadians on both sides of the St. Lawrence below Three Rivers, for Vaudreuil had ordered the militia captains to join his standard with all their followers, armed and equipped, on pain of death. These accessions appear to have raised his force to between eight and nine thousand.

The ice still clung to the riverbanks, the weather was bad and the navigation difficult, but on the twenty-sixth the army landed at St. Augustin, crossed the river of Cap-Rouge on bridges of their own making and moved upon the English outpost at Old Lorette. The English abandoned it and fell back to Ste.-Foy. Lévis followed. Night came on, with a gale from the southeast, a driving rain and violent thunder, unusual at that season. The road, a bad and broken one, led through the marsh called La Suède. Causeways and bridges broke down under the weight of the marching columns and plunged the men into water, mud and half-thawed ice. "It was a frightful night," says Lévis, "so dark that but for the flashes of lightning we should have been forced to stop."

The break of day found the vanguard at the edge of the woods bordering the farther side of the marsh. The storm had abated, and they saw before them, a few hundred yards distant through the misty air, a ridge of rising ground on which stood the parish church of Ste.-Foy, with a row of Canadian houses stretching far to right and left. This ridge was the declivity of the plateau of Quebec.

719

The church and the houses were occupied by British troops, who as the French debouched from the woods opened on them with cannon and compelled them to fall back. Though the ridge at this point is not steep, the position was a strong one, but had Lévis known how few were as yet there to oppose him, he might have carried it by an assault in front. As it was, he resolved to wait till night and then flank the enemy by a march to the right along the border of the wood.

It was the morning of Sunday, the twenty-seventh. Till late in the night before, Murray and the garrison of Quebec were unaware of the immediate danger, and they learned it at last through a singular stroke of fortune.

Sometime after midnight the watch on board the frigate *Racehorse,* which had wintered in the dock at the Lower Town, heard a feeble cry of distress from the midst of the darkness that covered the St. Lawrence. Captain Macartney was at once informed of it, and through an impulse of humanity, he ordered a boat to put out amid the drifting ice that was sweeping up the river with the tide. Guided by the faint cries, the sailors found a man lying on a large cake of ice, drenched and half dead with cold, and taking him with difficulty into their boat, they carried him to the ship.

It was long before he was able to speak intelligibly, but at last, being revived by cordials and other remedies, he found strength to tell his benefactors that he was a sergeant of artillery in the army that had come to retake Quebec; that in trying to land a little above Cap-Rouge, his boat had been overset, his companions drowned and he himself saved by climbing upon the cake of ice where they had discovered him; that he had been borne by the ebb tide down to the Island of Orleans and then brought up to Quebec by the flow; and, finally, that Lévis was marching on the town with twelve thousand men at his back.

He was placed in a hammock and carried up Mountain Street to the quarters of the general, who was roused from sleep at three o'clock in the morning to hear his story. The troops were ordered under arms, and soon after daybreak Murray marched out with ten pieces of cannon and more than half the garrison. His principal object was to withdraw the advanced posts at Ste.-Foy, Cap-Rouge, Sillery and Anse du Foulon.

The storm had turned to a cold, drizzling rain, and the men, as

720

they dragged their cannon through snow and mud, were soon drenched to the skin. On reaching Ste.-Foy, they opened a brisk fire from the heights upon the woods which now covered the whole army of Lévis and, being rejoined by the various outposts, returned to Quebec in the afternoon after blowing up the church, which contained a store of munitions that they had no means of bringing off.

When they entered Quebec a gill of rum was served out to each man, several houses in the suburb of St. Roch were torn down to supply them with firewood for drying their clothes, and they were left to take what rest they could against the morrow. The French, meanwhile, took possession of the abandoned heights, and while some filled the houses, barns and sheds of Ste.-Foy and its neighborhood, others, chiefly Canadians, crossed the plateau to seek shelter in the village of Sillery.

Three courses were open to Murray. He could defend Quebec, fortify himself outside the walls on the Buttes-à-Neveu or fight Lévis at all risks. The walls of Quebec could not withstand a cannonade, and he had long intended to intrench his army on the Buttes as a better position of defense, but the ground, frozen like a rock, had thus far made the plan impracticable. Even now, though the surface was thawed, the soil beneath was still frost-bound, making the task of fortification extremely difficult, if indeed the French would give him time for it.

Murray was young in years and younger still in impulse. He was ardent, fearless, ambitious and emulous of the fame of Wolfe. "The enemy," he soon after wrote to Pitt, "was greatly superior in number, it is true, but when I considered that our little army was in the habit of beating that enemy, and had a very fine train of field artillery; that shutting ourselves at once within the walls was putting all upon the single chance of holding out for a considerable time a wretched fortification, I resolved to give them battle; and half an hour after six in the morning, we marched with all the force I could muster, namely three thousand men." Some of these had left the hospitals of their own accord in their eagerness to take part in the fray.

The rain had ceased, but as the column emerged from St. Louis Gate the scene before them was a dismal one. As yet there was no sign of spring. Each leafless bush and tree was dark with clammy

721

moisture; patches of bare earth lay oozy and black on the southern slopes. But elsewhere the ground was still covered with snow, in some places piled in drifts and everywhere sodden with rain, while each hollow and depression was full of that half-liquid, lead-colored mixture of snow and water which New England schoolboys call "slush," for all drainage was stopped by the frozen subsoil.

The troops had with them two howitzers and twenty fieldpieces, which had been captured when Quebec surrendered and had formed a part of that very battery which Ramesay refused to Montcalm at the battle of the autumn before. As there were no horses, the cannon were dragged by some of the soldiers, while others carried picks and spades, for as yet Murray seems not to have made up his mind whether to fortify or fight. Thus they advanced nearly half a mile, till, reaching the Buttes-à-Neveu, they formed in order of battle along their farther slopes, on the same ground that Montcalm had occupied on the morning of his death.

Murray went forward to reconnoiter. Immediately before him was a rising ground, and beyond it a tract of forest called Sillery Wood, a mile or more distant. Nearer, on the left, he could see two blockhouses built by the English in the last autumn, not far from the brink of the plateau above the Anse du Foulon, where Wolfe climbed the heights. On the right, at the opposite brink of the plateau, was a house and a fortified windmill belonging to one Dumont.

The blockhouses, the mill and the rising ground between them were occupied by the vanguard of Lévis's army, while behind he could descry the main body moving along the road from Ste.-Foy, then turning, battalion after battalion, and rapidly marching across the plateau along the edge of Sillery Wood. The two brigades of the leading column had already reached the blockhouses by the Anse du Foulon and formed themselves as the right wing of the French line of battle, but those behind were not yet in position.

Murray, kindling at the sight, thought that so favorable a moment was not to be lost and ordered an advance. His line consisted of eight battalions, numbering a little above two thousand. In the intervals between them the cannon were dragged through slush and mud by five hundred men, and at a little distance behind, the remaining two battalions followed as a reserve. The right flank was covered by

Dalling's light infantry; the left by Hazen's company of rangers and a hundred volunteers under Major MacDonald. They all moved forward till they were on nearly the same ground where Wolfe's army had been drawn up. Then the cannon unlimbered and opened on the French with such effect that Lévis, who was on horseback in the middle of the field, sent orders to the corps of his left to fall back to the cover of the woods.

The movement caused some disorder. Murray mistook it for retreat and commanded a farther advance. The whole British line, extending itself towards the right, pushed eagerly forward, in doing which it lost the advantage of the favorable position it had occupied, and the battalions of the right soon found themselves on low ground, wading in half-melted snow which in some parts was knee deep. Here the cannon could no longer be worked with effect. Just in front a small brook ran along the hollow through soft mud and saturated snowdrifts, then gurgled down the slope on the right to lose itself in the meadows of the St. Charles. A few rods before this brook stood the house and windmill of Dumont, occupied by five companies of French grenadiers. The light infantry at once attacked them.

A furious struggle ensued, till at length the French gave way and the victors dashed forward to follow up their advantage. Their ardor cost them dear. The corps on the French left, which had fallen back into the woods, now advanced again as the cannon ceased to play, rushing on without order but with the utmost impetuosity, led by a gallant old officer, Colonel Dalquier, of the battalion of Béarn. A bullet in the body could not stop him. The light infantry were overwhelmed, and such of them as were left alive were driven back in confusion upon the battalions behind them, along the front of which they remained dispersed for some minutes, preventing the troops from firing on the advancing French, who thus had time to re-form their ranks.

At length the light infantry got themselves out of the way and retired to the rear, where, having lost nearly all their officers, they remained during the rest of the fight. Another struggle followed for the house and mill of Dumont, of which the French again got possession, to be again driven out, and it remained as if by mutual consent unoccupied for some time by either party. For above an hour more the

723

fight was hot and fierce. "We drove them back as long as we had ammunition for our cannon," says Sergeant John Johnson, of the fifty-
eighth regiment, but now it failed and no more was to be had, because,
in the eccentric phrase of the sergeant, the tumbrils were "bogged in
deep pits of snow."

While this was passing on the English right, it fared still worse with
them on the left. The advance of the line was no less disastrous here
than there. It brought the troops close to the woods which circled
round to this point from the French rear and from which the Canadians, covered by the trees, now poured on them a deadly fire. Here, as
on the right, Lévis had ordered his troops to fall back for a time, but
when the fire of the English cannon ceased they advanced again, and
their artillery, though consisting of only three pieces, played its part
with good effect.

Hazen's rangers and MacDonald's volunteers attacked and took the
two adjacent blockhouses, but could not hold them. Hazen was
wounded, MacDonald killed and their party overpowered. The British
battalions held their ground till the French, whose superior numbers
enabled them to extend themselves on both sides beyond the English
line, made a furious attack on the left wing, in front and flank.

The reserves were ordered up and the troops stood for a time in
sullen desperation under the storm of bullets, but they were dropping
fast in the bloodstained snow and the order came at length to fall back.
They obeyed with curses: "Damn it, what is falling back but retreating?" The right wing, also outflanked, followed the example of the
left. Some of the corps tried to drag off their cannon but, being prevented by the deep mud and snow, they spiked the pieces and abandoned them. The French followed close, hoping to cut off the fugitives
from the gates of Quebec, till Lévis, seeing that the retreat, though
precipitate, was not entirely without order, thought best to stop the
pursuit.

The fight lasted about two hours and did credit to both sides. The
Canadians not only showed their usual address and courage when
under cover of woods but they also fought well in the open field, and
the conduct of the whole French force proved how completely they
had recovered from the panic of the last autumn. From the first they
were greatly superior in number, and at the middle and end of the

affair, when they had all reached the field, they were more than two against one. The English, on the other hand, besides the opportunity of attacking before their enemies had completely formed, had a vastly superior artillery and a favorable position, both of which advantages they lost after their second advance.

The English lost above a thousand, or more than a third of their whole number, killed, wounded and missing. They carried off some of their wounded but left others behind, and the greater part of these were murdered, scalped and mangled by the Indians, all of whom were converts from the mission villages. English writers put the French loss at two thousand and upwards, which is no doubt a gross exaggeration. Lévis declares that the number did not exceed six or eight hundred but afterwards gives a list which makes it eight hundred and thirty-three.

Murray had left three or four hundred men to guard Quebec when the rest marched out, and adding them to those who had returned scathless from the fight, he now had about twenty-four hundred rank and file fit for duty. Yet even the troops that were rated as effective were in so bad a condition that the hyperbolical Sergeant Johnson calls them "half-starved, scorbutic skeletons." That worthy soldier, commonly a model of dutiful respect to those above him, this time so far forgets himself as to criticize his general for the "mad enthusiastic zeal" by which he nearly lost the fruits of Wolfe's victory. In fact, the fate of Quebec trembled in the balance. "We were too few and weak to stand an assault," continues Johnson, "and we were almost in as deep a distress as we could be."

At first there was some drunkenness and some plundering of private houses, but Murray stopped the one by staving the rum barrels of the sutlers and the other by hanging the chief offender. Within three days order, subordination, hope and almost confidence were completely restored.

Not a man was idle. The troops left their barracks and lay in tents close to their respective alarm posts. On the open space by St. Louis Gate a crowd of convalescents were busy in filling sandbags to strengthen the defenses, while the sick and wounded in the hospitals made wadding for the cannon. The ramparts were faced with fascines, of which a large stock had been provided in the autumn; *chevaux-de-frise* were planted in exposed places; an outwork was built to protect

725

St. Louis Gate; embrasures were cut along the whole length of the walls; and the French cannon captured when the town was taken were planted against their late owners. Every man was tasked to the utmost of his strength, and the garrison, gaunt, worn, besmirched with mud, looked less like soldiers than like overworked laborers.

Lévis and his army were no less busy in digging trenches along the stony back of the Buttes-à-Neveu. Every day the English fire grew hotter, till at last nearly a hundred and fifty cannon vomited iron upon them from the walls of Quebec, and May was well advanced before they could plant a single gun to reply. Their vessels had landed artillery at the Anse du Foulon, but their best hope lay in the succors they daily expected from the river below.

In the autumn Lévis, with a view to his intended enterprise, had sent a request to Versailles that a ship laden with munitions and heavy siege guns should be sent from France in time to meet him at Quebec in April, while he looked also for another ship, which had wintered at Gaspé and which therefore might reach him as soon as navigation opened. The arrival of these vessels would have made the position of the English doubly critical, and on the other hand, should an English squadron appear first, Lévis would be forced to raise the siege.

Thus each side watched the river with an anxiety that grew constantly more intense, and the English presently descried signals along the shore which seemed to say that French ships were moving up the St. Lawrence. Meantime, while doing their best to compass each other's destruction, neither side forgot the courtesies of war. Lévis heard that Murray liked spruce beer for his table and sent him a flag of truce with a quantity of spruce boughs and a message of compliment; Murray responded with a Cheshire cheese, and Lévis rejoined with a present of partridges.

Bad and scanty fare, excessive toil and broken sleep were telling ominously on the strength of the garrison when, on the ninth of May, Murray, as he sat pondering over the fire at his quarters in St. Louis Street, was interrupted by an officer who came to tell him that there was a ship of war in the basin beating up towards the town. Murray started from his reverie and directed that British colors should be raised immediately on Cape Diamond.

The halyards being out of order, a sailor climbed the staff and drew up the flag to its place. The news had spread. Men and officers, divided between hope and fear, crowded to the rampart by the Château, where Durham Terrace now overlooks the St. Lawrence, and every eye was strained on the approaching ship, eager to see whether she would show the red flag of England or the white one of France.

Slowly her colors rose to the masthead and unfurled to the wind the red cross of St. George. It was the British frigate *Lowestoffe*. She anchored before the Lower Town and saluted the garrison with twenty-one guns. "The gladness of the troops," says Knox, "is not to be expressed. Both officers and soldiers mounted to the parapet in the face of the enemy and huzzaed with their hats in the air for almost an hour. The garrison, the enemy's camp, the bay, and circumjacent country resounded with our shouts and the thunder of our artillery, for the gunners were so elated that they did nothing but load and fire for a considerable time. In short, the general satisfaction is not to be conceived, except by a person who had suffered the extremities of a siege, and been destined, with his brave friends and countrymen, to the scalping knives of a faithless conqueror and his barbarous allies."

The *Lowestoffe* brought news that a British squadron was at the mouth of the St. Lawrence and would reach Quebec in a few days. Lévis, in ignorance of this, still clung to the hope that French ships would arrive strong enough to overpower the unwelcome stranger. His guns, being at last in position, presently opened fire upon a wall that was not built to bear the brunt of heavy shot, but an artillery better and more numerous than his own almost silenced them and his gunners were harassed by repeated sallies. The besiegers had now no real chance of success unless they could carry the place by storm, to which end they had provided abundant scaling ladders as well as petards to burst in the gates. They made, however, no attempt to use them.

A week passed, when on the evening of the fifteenth the ship of the line *Vanguard* and the frigate *Diana* sailed into the harbor, and on the next morning the *Diana* and the *Lowestoffe* passed the town to attack the French vessels in the river above. These were six in all—two frigates, two smaller armed ships and two schooners, the whole under command of the gallant Vauquelin.

He did not belie his reputation; fought his ship with persistent bravery till his ammunition was spent, refused even then to strike his flag, and, being made prisoner, was treated by his captors with distinguished honor. The other vessels made little or no resistance. One of them threw her guns overboard and escaped; the rest ran ashore and were burned.

The destruction of his vessels was a deathblow to the hopes of Lévis, for they contained his stores of food and ammunition. He had passed the preceding night in great agitation, and when the cannonade on the river ceased he hastened to raise the siege. In the evening deserters from his camp told Murray that the French were in full retreat, on which all the English batteries opened, firing at random through the darkness and sending cannon balls ricocheting, bowling by scores together, over the Plains of Abraham on the heels of the retiring enemy.

Murray marched out at dawn of day to fall upon their rear, but with a hundred and fifty cannon bellowing behind them, they had made such speed that, though he pushed over the marsh to Old Lorette, he could not overtake them. They had already crossed the river of Cap-Rouge. Why, with numbers still superior, they went off in such haste, it is hard to say. They left behind them thirty-four cannon and six mortars, with petards, scaling ladders, tents, ammunition, baggage, intrenching tools, many of their muskets and all their sick and wounded.

The effort to recover Quebec did great honor to the enterprise of the French, but it availed them nothing, served only to waste resources that seemed already at the lowest ebb and gave fresh opportunity of plunder to Cadet and his crew, who failed not to make use of it.

The retreat of Lévis left Canada little hope but in a speedy peace. This hope was strong, for a belief widely prevailed that, even if the colony should be subdued, it would be restored to France by treaty. Its available force did not exceed eight or ten thousand men, as most of the Canadians below the district of Three Rivers had sworn allegiance to King George, and though many of them had disregarded the oath to join the standard of Lévis, they could venture to do so no longer. The French had lost the best of their artillery, their gunpowder was falling short, their provisions would barely carry them to harvest time and no more was to be hoped for, since a convoy of ships which had sailed from France at the end of winter, laden with supplies of all kinds, had been captured by the English. The blockade of the St. Lawrence was complete. The western Indians would not fight and even those of the mission villages were wavering and insolent.

Yet Vaudreuil and Lévis exerted themselves for defense with an energy that does honor to them both. "Far from showing the least timidity," says the ever-modest governor, "I have taken positions such as may hide our weakness from the enemy."

He stationed Rochbeaucourt with three hundred men at Pointe-aux-Trembles; Repentigny with two hundred at Jacques-Cartier; and Dumas with twelve hundred at Deschambault to watch the St. Lawrence and, if possible, prevent Murray from moving up the river. Bougainville was stationed at Isle-aux-Noix to bar the approach from Lake Champlain, and a force under La Corne was held ready to defend the rapids above Montreal, should the English attempt that dangerous passage. Prisoners taken by war parties near Crown Point gave exaggerated reports of hostile preparation and doubled and trebled the forces that were mustering against Canada.

These forces were nevertheless considerable. Amherst had resolved to enter the colony by all its three gates at once and, advancing from east, west and south, unite at Montreal and crush it as in the jaws of a vice. Murray was to ascend the St. Lawrence from Quebec, while Brigadier Haviland forced an entrance by way of Lake Champlain, and Amherst himself led the main army down the St. Lawrence from Lake Ontario.

This last route was long, circuitous, difficult and full of danger from the rapids that obstructed the river. His choice of it for his chief line of operation, instead of the shorter and easier way of Lake Champlain, was meant, no doubt, to prevent the French Army from escaping up the lakes to Detroit and the other wilderness posts, where it might have protracted the war for an indefinite time, while the plan adopted, if successful, would make its capture certain.

The plan was a critical one. Three armies advancing from three different points, hundreds of miles apart, by routes full of difficulty, and with no possibility of intercommunication, were to meet at the same place at the same time, or, failing to do so, run the risk of being destroyed in detail. If the French troops could be kept together, and if the small army of Murray or of Haviland should reach Montreal a few days before the co-operating forces appeared, it might be separately attacked and overpowered. In this lay the hope of Vaudreuil and Lévis.

After the siege of Quebec was raised, Murray had an effective force of about twenty-five hundred rank and file. As the spring opened, the invalids were encamped on the Island of Orleans, where fresh air, fresh provisions and the change from the pestiferous town hospitals wrought such wonders on the scorbutic patients that in a few weeks a considerable number of them were again fit for garrison duty, if not for the field.

Thus it happened that on the second of July twenty-four hundred and fifty men and officers received orders to embark for Montreal, and on the fifteenth they set sail, in thirty-two vessels, with a number of boats and bateaux. They were followed some time after by Lord Rollo, with thirteen hundred additional men just arrived from Louisbourg, the King having ordered that fortress to be abandoned and dismantled.

They advanced slowly, landing from time to time, skirmishing with detachments of the enemy who followed them along the shore, or more frequently trading with the farmers who brought them vegetables, poultry, eggs and fresh meat. They passed the fortified hill of Jacques-Cartier, whence they were saluted with shot and shell, stopped at various parishes, disarmed the inhabitants, administered oaths of neutrality, which were taken without much apparent reluctance, and on the fourth of August came within sight of Three Rivers, then occupied by a body of troops expecting an attack.

Towards seven o'clock they reached the village of Sorel, where they found a large body of troops and militia intrenched along the strand. Bourlamaque was in command here with two or three thousand men, and Dumas with another body was on the northern shore. Both had orders to keep abreast of the fleet as it advanced, and thus French and English alike drew slowly towards Montreal, where lay the main French force under Lévis, ready to unite with Bourlamaque and Dumas and fall upon Murray at the first opportunity.

Montreal was now but a few leagues distant and the situation was becoming delicate. Murray sent five rangers towards Lake Champlain to get news of Haviland and took measures at the same time to cause the desertion of the Canadians, who formed the largest part of the opposing force. He sent a proclamation among the parishes, advising the inhabitants to remain peacefully at home, promising that those who did so should be safe in person and property and threatening to burn every house from which the men of the family were absent.

These were not idle words. A detachment sent for the purpose destroyed a settlement near Sorel, the owners of which were in arms under Bourlamaque. "I was under the cruel necessity of burning the greatest part of these poor unhappy people's houses," wrote Murray. "I pray God this example may suffice, for my nature revolts when this becomes a necessary part of my duty."

On the other hand, he treated with great kindness all who left the army and returned to their families. The effect was soon felt. The Canadians came in by scores and by hundreds to give up their arms and take the oath of neutrality, till before the end of August half Bourlamaque's force had disappeared. Murray encamped on Isle Ste.-Thérèse, just below Montreal, and watched and waited for Haviland and Amherst to appear.

There seemed good hope of stopping the advance of Haviland. To this end Vaudreuil had stationed Bougainville at Isle-aux-Noix with seventeen hundred men, and Roquemaure at St. John, a few miles distant, with twelve or fifteen hundred more, besides all the Indians.

Haviland embarked at Crown Point with thirty-four hundred regulars, provincials and Indians. Four days brought him to Isle-aux-Noix. He landed, planted cannon in the swamp and opened fire. Major Darby with the light infantry, and Rogers with the rangers, dragged three light pieces through the forest and planted them on the riverbank in the rear of Bougainville's position, where lay the French naval force, consisting of three armed vessels and several gunboats. The cannon were turned upon the principal ship. A shot cut her cable and a strong west wind drove her ashore into the hands of her enemies. The other vessels and gunboats made all sail for St. John but stranded in a bend of the river, where the rangers, swimming out with their tomahawks, boarded and took one of them, and the rest soon surrendered.

It was a fatal blow to Bougainville, whose communications with St. John were now cut off. In accordance with instructions from Vaudreuil, he abandoned the island on the night of the twenty-seventh of

August and, making his way with infinite difficulty through the dark forest, joined Roquemaure at St. John, twelve miles below. Haviland followed, the rangers leading the way.

Bougainville and Roquemaure fell back, abandoned St. John and Chambly and joined Bourlamaque on the banks of the St. Lawrence, where the united force at first outnumbered that of Haviland, though fast melted away by discouragement and desertion. Haviland opened communication with Murray and they both looked daily for the arrival of Amherst, whose approach was rumored by prisoners and deserters.

The army of Amherst had gathered at Oswego in July. On the tenth of August it was all afloat on Lake Ontario, to the number of ten thousand one hundred and forty-two men, besides about seven hundred Indians under Sir William Johnson.

Before the fifteenth the whole had reached La Présentation, otherwise called Oswegatchie or La Galette, the seat of Father Piquet's mission. Near by was a French armed brig, the *Ottawa,* with ten cannon and a hundred men, threatening destruction to Amherst's bateaux and whaleboats. Five gunboats attacked and captured her. Then the army advanced again and were presently joined by two armed vessels of their own which had lingered behind, bewildered among the channels of the Thousand Islands.

Near the head of the rapids, a little below La Galette, stood Fort Lévis, built the year before on an islet in mid-channel. Amherst might have passed its batteries with slight loss, continuing his voyage without paying it the honor of a siege, and this was what the French commanders feared that he would do. "We shall be fortunate," Lévis wrote to Bourlamaque, "if the enemy amuse themselves with capturing it. My chief anxiety is lest Amherst should reach Montreal so soon that we may not have time to unite our forces to attack Haviland or Murray."

If he had better known the English commander, Lévis would have seen that he was not the man to leave a post of the enemy in his rear under any circumstances, and Amherst had also another reason for wishing to get the garrison into his hands, for he expected to find among them the pilots whom he needed to guide his boats down the rapids.

He therefore invested the fort, and on the twenty-third cannonaded it from his vessels, the mainland and the neighboring islands. It was commanded by Pouchot, the late commandant of Niagara, made prisoner in the last campaign and since exchanged. As the rocky islet had but little earth, the defenses, though thick and strong, were chiefly of logs, which flew in splinters under the bombardment. The French, however, made a brave resistance. The firing lasted all day, was resumed in the morning and continued two days more when Pouchot, whose works were in ruins, surrendered himself and his garrison. On this, Johnson's Indians prepared to kill the prisoners, and being compelled to desist, three fourths of them went home in a rage.

Now began the critical part of the expedition, the descent of the rapids. The Galops, the Rapide Plat, the Long Saut, the Côteau du Lac, were passed in succession with little loss, till they reached the Cedars, the Buisson and the Cascades, where the reckless surges dashed and bounded in the sun, beautiful and terrible as young tigers at play. Boat after boat, borne on their foaming crests, rushed madly down the torrent. Forty-six were totally wrecked, eighteen were damaged, and eighty-four men were drowned.

La Corne was watching the rapids with a considerable body of Canadians, and it is difficult to see why this bold and enterprising chief allowed the army to descend undisturbed through passes so dangerous. At length the last rapid was left behind, and the flotilla, gliding in peace over the smooth breast of Lake St. Louis, landed at Isle Perrot, a few leagues from Montreal. In the morning, September sixth, the troops embarked again, landed unopposed at La Chine, nine miles from the city, marched on without delay and encamped before its walls.

The Montreal of that time was a long, narrow assemblage of wooden or stone houses one or two stories high, above which rose the peaked towers of the seminary, the spires of three churches, the walls of four convents, with the trees of their adjacent gardens, and, conspicuous at the lower end, a high mound of earth crowned by a redoubt, where a few cannon were mounted. The whole was surrounded by a shallow moat and a bastioned stone wall, made for defense against Indians and incapable of resisting cannon.

On the morning after Amherst encamped above the place, Murray landed to encamp below it, and Vaudreuil, looking across the St. Law-

733

rence, could see the tents of Haviland's little army on the southern shore. Bourlamaque, Bougainville and Roquemaure, abandoned by all their militia, had crossed to Montreal with the few regulars that remained with them.

The town was crowded with noncombatant refugees. Here, too, was nearly all the remaining force of Canada, consisting of twenty-two hundred troops of the line and some two hundred colony troops, for all the Canadians had by this time gone home. Many of the regulars, especially of the colony troops, had also deserted, and the rest were so broken in discipline that their officers were forced to use entreaties instead of commands. The three armies encamped around the city amounted to seventeen thousand men. Amherst was bringing up his cannon from La Chine, and the town wall would have crumbled before them in an hour.

On the night when Amherst arrived, the governor called a council of war. It was resolved that since all the militia and many of the regulars had abandoned the army, and the Indian allies of France had gone over to the enemy, further resistance was impossible. Vaudreuil laid before the assembled officers a long paper that he had drawn up, containing fifty-five articles of capitulation to be proposed to the English, and these were unanimously approved.

In the morning Bougainville carried them to the tent of Amherst. He granted the greater part, modified some and flatly refused others. That which the French officers thought more important than all the rest was the provision that the troops should march out with arms, cannon and the honors of war, to which it was replied: "The whole garrison of Montreal and all other French troops in Canada must lay down their arms, and shall not serve during the present war."

This demand was felt to be intolerable. The governor sent Bougainville back to remonstrate, but Amherst was inflexible. Then Lévis tried to shake his resolution and sent him an officer with the following note: "I send your Excellency M. de la Pause, Assistant Quartermaster-General of the Army, on the subject of the too rigorous article which you dictate to the troops by the capitulation, to which it would not be possible for us to subscribe."

Amherst answered the envoy: "I am fully resolved, for the infamous part the troops of France have acted in exciting the savages to perpetrate the most horrid and unheard of barbarities in the whole progress of the war, and for other open treacheries and flagrant breaches of faith, to manifest to all the world by this capitulation my detestation of such practices." And he dismissed La Pause with a short note, refusing to change the conditions.

On the next morning, September eighth, Vaudreuil yielded and signed the capitulation. By it Canada and all its dependencies passed to the British Crown. French officers, civil and military, with French troops and sailors, were to be sent to France in British ships. Free exercise of religion was assured to the people of the colony and the religious communities were to retain their possessions, rights and privileges. All persons who might wish to retire to France were allowed to do so, and the Canadians were to remain in full enjoyment of feudal and other property, including Negro and Indian slaves.

Half the continent had changed hands at the scratch of a pen. Governor Bernard, of Massachusetts, proclaimed a day of thanksgiving for the great event, and the Boston newspapers recount how the occasion was celebrated with a parade of the cadets and other volunteer corps, a grand dinner in Faneuil Hall, music, bonfires, illuminations, firing of cannon, and above all, by sermons in every church of the province, for the heart of early New England always found voice through her pulpits.

On the American continent the war was ended, and the British colonists breathed for a space as they drifted unwittingly towards a deadlier strife. They had learned hard and useful lessons. Their mutual jealousies and disputes, the quarrels of their governors and assemblies, the want of any general military organization and the absence, in most of them, of military habits, joined to narrow views of their own interest, had unfitted them to the last degree for carrying on offensive war.

Nor were the British troops sent for their support remarkable in the beginning for good discipline or efficient command. When hostilities broke out, the army of Great Britain was so small as to be hardly worth the name. A new one had to be created, and thus the inexperienced Shirley and the incompetent Loudon, with the futile Newcastle behind them, had, besides their own incapacity, the disadvantage of raw troops and half-formed officers, while against them

735

stood an enemy who, though weak in numbers, was strong in a centralized military organization, skillful leaders armed with untrammeled and absolute authority, practiced soldiers and a population not only brave but in good part inured to war.

The nature of the country was another cause that helped to protract the contest. "Geography," says Von Moltke, "is three fourths of military science," and never was the truth of his words more fully exemplified. Canada was fortified with vast outworks of defense in the savage forests, marshes and mountains that encompassed her, where the thoroughfares were streams choked with fallen trees and obstructed by cataracts. Never was the problem of moving troops, encumbered with baggage and artillery, a more difficult one. The question was less how to fight the enemy than how to get at him. If a few practicable roads had crossed this broad tract of wilderness, the war would have been shortened and its character changed.

From these and other reasons, the numerical superiority of the English was to some extent made unavailing. This superiority, though exaggerated by French writers, was nevertheless immense if estimated by the number of men called to arms, but only a part of these could be employed in offensive operations. The rest garrisoned forts and blockhouses and guarded the far reach of frontier from Nova Scotia to South Carolina, where a wily enemy, silent and secret as fate, choosing their own time and place of attack and striking unawares at every unguarded spot, compelled thousands of men, scattered at countless points of defense, to keep unceasing watch against a few hundred savage marauders. Full half the levies of the colonies, and many of the regulars, were used in service of this kind.

In actual encounters the advantage of numbers was often with the French, through the comparative ease with which they could concentrate their forces at a given point. Of the ten considerable sieges or battles of the war, five, besides the great bushfight in which the Indians defeated Braddock, were victories for France, and in four of these—Oswego, Fort William Henry, Montmorenci and Ste.-Foy—the odds were greatly on her side.

Yet in this, the most picturesque and dramatic of American wars, there is nothing more noteworthy than the skill with which the French and Canadian leaders used their advantages; the indomitable spirit with which, slighted and abandoned as they were, they grappled with prodigious difficulties, and the courage with which they were seconded by regulars and militia alike. In spite of occasional lapses, the defense of Canada deserves a tribute of admiration.

CHAPTER 19

~~~~~~

Peace

WHILE FREDERICK OF PRUSSIA WAS FIGHTING FOR
life and crown, an event took place in England that was to
have great influence on the war. Walpole recounts thus, writing to
George Montagu on the twenty-fifth of October, 1760: "My man
Harry tells me all the amusing news. He first told me of the late Prince
of Wales's death, and today of the King's; so I must tell you all I know
of departed majesty. He went to bed well last night, rose at six this
morning as usual, looked, I suppose, if all his money was in his purse,
and called for his chocolate. A little after seven he went into the
closet; the German *valet-de-chambre* heard a noise, listened, heard
something like a groan, ran in, and found the hero of Oudenarde and
Dettingen on the floor with a gash on his right temple by falling against
the corner of a bureau. He tried to speak, could not, and expired. The
great ventricle of the heart had burst. What an enviable death!"

The old King was succeeded by his grandson, George III, a mirror
of domestic virtues, conscientious, obstinate, narrow. His accession
produced political changes that had been preparing for some time. His
grandfather was German at heart, loved his continental kingdom of
Hanover and was eager for all measures that looked to its defense and
preservation. Pitt, too, had of late vigorously supported the continental war, saying that he would conquer America in Germany. Thus
with different views the King and the minister had concurred in the
same measures.

But George III was English by birth, language and inclination. His ruling passion was the establishment and increase of his own authority. He disliked Pitt, the representative of the people. He was at heart averse to war, the continuance of which would make the Great Commoner necessary and therefore powerful, and he wished for a peace that would give free scope to his schemes for strengthening the prerogative. He was not alone in his pacific inclinations. The enemies of the haughty minister, who had ridden roughshod over men far above him in rank, were tired of his ascendancy and saw no hope of ending it but by ending the war. Thus a peace party grew up, and the young King became its real, though not at first its declared, supporter.

Early in 1761 the King, a fanatic for prerogative, set his enginery in motion. The elections for the new Parliament were manipulated in his interest. If he disliked Pitt as the representative of the popular will, he also disliked his colleague, the shuffling and uncertain Newcastle, as the representative of a too powerful nobility. Elements hostile to both were introduced into the Cabinet and the great offices.

The King's favorite, the Earl of Bute, supplanted Holdernesse as Secretary of State for the Northern Department; Charles Townshend, an opponent of Pitt, was made Secretary of War; Legge, Chancellor of the Exchequer, was replaced by Viscount Barrington, who was sure for the King; while a place in the Cabinet was also given to the Duke of Bedford, one of the few men who dared face the formidable minister. It was the policy of the King and his following to abandon Prussia, hitherto supported by British subsidies, make friends with Austria and Russia at her expense and conclude a separate peace with France.

France was in sore need of peace. The infatuation that had turned her from her own true interest to serve the passions of Maria Theresa and the Czarina Elizabeth had brought military humiliation and financial ruin. Abbé de Bernis, Minister of Foreign Affairs, had lost the favor of Madame de Pompadour and had been supplanted by the Duc de Choiseul.

The new minister had gained his place by pleasing the favorite, but he kept it through his own ability and the necessities of the time. Choiseul was vivacious, brilliant, keen, penetrating; believing nothing, fearing nothing; an easy moralist, an uncertain ally, a hater of priests;

light-minded, inconstant; yet a kind of patriot, eager to serve France and retrieve her fortunes.

He flattered himself with no illusions. "Since we do not know how to make war," he said, "we must make peace," and he proposed a congress of all the belligerent powers at Augsburg.

But preliminary negotiations failed, and they were not resumed until 1762, when the financial condition of France was desperate. Her people were crushed with taxation; her debt grew apace; and her yearly expenditure was nearly double her revenue. Choiseul felt the need of immediate peace, and George III and Bute were hardly less eager for it, to avert the danger of Pitt's return to power and give free scope to their schemes for strengthening the prerogative.

Therefore, in September 1762, the parleys began once more. The Duke of Bedford was sent to Paris to settle the preliminaries and the Duc de Nivernois came to London on the same errand. The populace were still for war. Bedford was hissed as he passed through the streets of London and a mob hooted at the puny figure of Nivernois as he landed at Dover.

The great question was, Should Canada be restored? Should France still be permitted to keep a foothold on the North American continent? Ever since the capitulation of Montreal a swarm of pamphlets had discussed the momentous subject. Some maintained that the acquisition of Canada was not an original object of the war; that the colony was of little value and ought to given back to its old masters; that Guadeloupe should be kept instead, the sugar trade of that island being worth far more than the Canadian fur trade; and lastly, that the British colonists, if no longer held in check by France, would spread themselves over the continent, learn to supply all their own wants, grow independent and become dangerous.

Nor were these views confined to Englishmen. There were foreign observers who clearly saw that the adhesion of her colonies to Great Britain would be jeopardized by the extinction of French power in America. Choiseul warned that they "would not fail to shake off their dependence the moment Canada should be ceded," while thirteen years before, the Swedish traveler Kalm declared that the presence of the French in America gave the best assurance to Great Britain that its own colonies would remain in due subjection.

The most noteworthy argument on the other side was that of Franklin, whose words find a strange commentary in the events of the next few years. He affirmed that the colonies were so jealous of each other that they would never unite against England. "If they could not agree to unite against the French and Indians, can it reasonably be supposed that there is any danger of their uniting against their own nation, which it is well known they all love much more than they love one another? I will venture to say union amongst them for such a purpose is not merely improbable, it is impossible," that is, he prudently adds, without "the most grievous tyranny and oppression," like the bloody rule of "Alva in the Netherlands."

If Pitt had been in office he would have demanded terms that must ruin past redemption the maritime and colonial power of France, but Bute was less exacting. In November the plenipotentiaries of England, France and Spain agreed on preliminaries of peace, in which the following were the essential points.

France ceded to Great Britain Canada and all her possessions on the North American continent east of the river Mississippi, except the city of New Orleans and a small adjacent district. She renounced her claims to Acadia and gave up to the conqueror the island of Cape Breton, with all other islands in the Gulf and River of St. Lawrence. Spain received back Havana and paid for it by the cession of Florida, with all her other possessions east of the Mississippi. France, subject to certain restrictions, was left free to fish in the Gulf of St. Lawrence and off a part of the coast of Newfoundland, and the two little islands of St. Pierre and Miquelon were given her as fishing stations on condition that she should not fortify or garrison them.

In the West Indies, England restored the captured islands of Guadeloupe, Marigalante, Désirade and Martinique, and France ceded Grenada and the Grenadines, while it was agreed that of the so-called neutral islands, St. Vincent, Dominica and Tobago should belong to England and St. Lucia to France.

In Europe, each side promised to give no more help to its allies in the German war. France restored Minorca and England restored Belleisle; France gave up such parts of Hanoverian territory as she had occupied and evacuated certain fortresses belonging to Prussia, pledging herself at the same time to demolish, under the inspection of English engineers, her own maritime fortress of Dunkirk.

In Africa, France ceded Senegal and received back the small island of Gorée. In India she lost everything she had gained since the peace of Aix-la-Chapelle, recovered certain trading stations but renounced the right of building forts or maintaining troops in Bengal.

On the day when the preliminaries were signed, France made a secret agreement with Spain by which she divested herself of the last shred of her possessions on the North American continent. As compensation for Florida, which her luckless ally had lost in her quarrel, she made over to the Spanish Crown the city of New Orleans and under the name of Louisiana gave her the vast region spreading westward from the Mississippi towards the Pacific.

These preliminaries were embodied in the definitive treaty concluded at Paris on the tenth of February, 1763. Peace between France and England brought peace between the warring nations of the Continent. Austria, bereft of her allies and exhausted by vain efforts to crush Frederick, gave up the attempt in despair and signed the treaty of Hubertsburg. The Seven Years' War was ended.

"This," said Earl Granville on his deathbed, "has been the most glorious war and the most triumphant peace that England ever knew." Not all were so well pleased, and many held with Pitt that the House of Bourbon should have been forced to drain the cup of humiliation to the dregs. Yet the fact remains that the Peace of Paris marks an epoch than which none in modern history is more fruitful of grand results. With it began a new chapter in the annals of the world.

As the historian Green wrote in his *History of the English People,* "It is no exaggeration to say that three of the many victories of the Seven Years' War determined for ages to come the destinies of mankind. With that of Rossbach began the re-creation of Germany; with that of Plassey the influence of Europe told for the first time since the days of Alexander on the nations of the East; with the triumph of Wolfe on the Heights of Abraham began the history of the United States."

So far, however, as concerns the war in the Germanic countries, it was to outward seeming but a mad debauch of blood and rapine, ending in nothing but the exhaustion of the combatants. The havoc had been frightful. According to the King of Prussia's reckoning, eight hundred and fifty-three thousand soldiers of the various nations had lost their lives, besides hundreds of thousands of noncombatants who had perished from famine, exposure, disease or violence. And with all this waste of life not a boundary line had been changed.

The rage of the two empresses and the vanity and spite of the concubine had been completely foiled. Frederick had defied them all and had come out of the strife intact in his own hereditary dominions and master of all that he had snatched from the Empress-Queen, while Prussia, portioned out by her enemies as their spoil, lay depleted indeed and faint with deadly striving, but crowned with glory and with the career before her which, through tribulation and adversity, was to lead her at last to the headship of a united Germany.

Through centuries of strife and vicissitude the French monarchy had triumphed over nobles, parliaments and people, gathered to itself all the forces of the State, beamed with illusive splendors under Louis the Great and shone with the phosphorescence of decay under his contemptible successor, till now, robbed of prestige, burdened with debt and mined with corruption, it was moving swiftly and more swiftly towards the abyss of ruin.

While the war hastened the inevitable downfall of the French monarchy, it produced still more notable effects. France under Colbert had embarked on a grand course of maritime and colonial enterprise and followed it with an activity and vigor that promised to make her a great and formidable ocean power. It was she who led the way in the East, first trained the natives to fight her battles and began that system of mixed diplomacy and war which, imitated by her rival, enabled a handful of Europeans to master all India. In North America her vast possessions dwarfed those of every other nation. She had built up a powerful navy and created an extensive foreign trade.

All this was now changed. In India she was reduced to helpless inferiority, with total ruin in the future, and of all her boundless territories in North America nothing was left but the two island rocks on the coast of Newfoundland that the victors had given her for drying her codfish. Of her navy scarcely forty ships remained. All the rest were captured or destroyed. She was still great on the continent of

Europe, but as a world power her grand opportunities were gone.

In England as in France the several members of the State had battled together since the national life began, and the result had been, not the unchecked domination of the Crown but a system of balanced and adjusted forces in which King, nobility and Commons all had their recognized places and their share of power. Thus in the war just ended two great conditions of success had been supplied: a people instinct with the energies of ordered freedom, and a masterly leadership to inspire and direct them.

All and more than all that France had lost, England had won. Now, for the first time, she was beyond dispute the greatest of maritime and colonial powers. Portugal and Holland, her precursors in ocean enterprise, had long ago fallen hopelessly behind. Two great rivals remained, and she had humbled the one and swept the other from her path. Spain, with vast American possessions, was sinking into the decay which is one of the phenomena of modern history, while France, of late a most formidable competitor, had abandoned the contest in despair. England was mistress of the seas and the world was thrown open to her merchants, explorers and colonists. A few years after the Peace the navigator Cook began his memorable series of voyages and surveyed the strange and barbarous lands which aftertimes were to transform into other Englands, vigorous children of this great mother of nations.

It is true that a heavy blow was soon to fall upon her. Her own folly was to alienate the eldest and greatest of her offspring. But nothing could rob her of the glory of giving birth to the United States, and though politically severed, this gigantic progeny were to be not the less a source of growth and prosperity to the parent that bore them, joined with her in a triple kinship of laws, language and blood. The war or series of wars that ended with the Peace of Paris secured the opportunities and set in action the forces that planted English homes in every clime and dotted the earth with English garrisons and posts of trade.

With the Peace of Paris ended the checkered story of New France, a story which would have been a history if faults of constitution and the bigotry and folly of rulers had not dwarfed it to an episode. Yet it is a noteworthy one in both its lights and its shadows: in the disinterested zeal of the founder of Quebec, the self-devotion of the early missionary martyrs and the daring enterprise of explorers; in the spiritual and temporary vassalage from which the only escape was to the savagery of the wilderness; and in the swarming corruptions which were the natural result of an attempt to rule, by the absolute hand of a master beyond the Atlantic, a people bereft of every vestige of civil liberty. Civil liberty was given them by the British sword, but the conqueror left their religious system untouched, and through it they imposed upon themselves a weight of ecclesiastical tutelage that found few equals in the most Catholic countries of Europe.

Scarcely were they free from the incubus of France when the British provinces showed symptoms of revolt. The measures on the part of the mother country which roused their resentment, far from being oppressive, were less burdensome than the navigation laws to which they had long submitted, and they resisted taxation by Parliament simply because it was in principle opposed to their rights as freemen. They did not, like the American provinces of Spain at a later day, sunder themselves from a parent fallen into decrepitude, but with astonishing audacity they affronted the wrath of England in the hour of her triumph, forgot their jealousies and quarrels, joined hands in the common cause, fought, endured and won.

The disunited colonies became the United States. The string of discordant communities along the Atlantic coast grew to a mighty people, joined in a union which the earthquake of civil war served only to compact and consolidate. Those who in the weakness of their dissensions needed help from England against the savage on their borders have become a nation that may defy every foe but that most dangerous of all foes, herself, destined to a majestic future if she will shun the excess and perversion of the principles that made her great, prate less about the enemies of the past and strive more against the enemies of the present, resist the mob and the demagogue as she resisted Parliament and King, rally her powers from the race for gold and the delirium of prosperity to make firm the foundations on which that prosperity rests, and turn some fair proportion of her vast mental forces to other objects than material progress and the game of party politics.

She has tamed the savage continent, peopled the solitude, gathered

745

wealth untold, waxed potent, imposing, redoubtable. And now it remains for her to prove, if she can, that the rule of the masses is consistent with the highest growth of the individual; that democracy can give the world a civilization as mature and pregnant, ideas as energetic and vitalizing, and types of manhood as lofty and strong as any of the systems which it boasts to supplant.

Index

Index